World Trade, Child Labour and Transnational C

World Trade Institute Advanced Studies

VOLUME 14

The titles published in this series are listed at *brill.com/wtia*

World Trade, Child Labour and Transnational Constitutionalism

The Case for a New Legal Humanism

By

Franziska Humbert

BRILL | NIJHOFF

LEIDEN | BOSTON

The open access publication of this book has been published with the support of the Swiss National Science Foundation.

The Library of Congress Cataloging-in-Publication Data is available online at https://catalog.loc.gov

LC record available at https://lccn.loc.gov/2023049186
LC ebook record available at https://lccn.loc.gov/2023049187

Typeface for the Latin, Greek, and Cyrillic scripts: "Brill". See and download: brill.com/brill-typeface.

ISSN 2405-9331
ISBN 978-90-04-69089-9 (hardback)
ISBN 978-90-04-69090-5 (e-book)
DOI 10.1163/9789004690905

This book is printed on acid-free paper and produced in a sustainable manner.

Contents

Foreword

The breadth of this work is impressive. It reaches way beyond the complex problem of child labour in international trade regulation, challenging it itself. It builds and projects nothing less than a new regulatory approach, found across theories of multi-level governance and of constitutionalization of international and transnational law, in order to tackle problems identified and at hand. While most theories are framed in the abstract, this book is built bottom-up. In doing so, it shows the need for a broader framework in order to properly address child labour in domestic and international law. Obviously, the approach is of general interest. What is developed for child labour, may also inspire other regulatory problems. The book is of great interest to policy-makers, practising lawyers, scholars and students alike.

The new approach – termed New Legal Humanism – is the result of a detailed analysis of existing trade rules, the policy spaces under GATT, the TBT Agreement and the Agreement on Government Procurement. And it results from discussing the conceptual difficulties encountered in taking into account all pertinent rules of international law, including ILO standards and the basic prohibition of child labour, forming part of *jus cogens*.

Building upon previous work published by the author on the subject of child labour in ILO law, the reader will find a detailed discussion of MFN, national treatment and the exceptions, including national security, in WTO jurisprudence of the GATT, as well as of related agreements, all of which is of general interest and beyond the specific problem addressed. Importantly, the reader will also find that fragmentation in international law does not allow to properly address all of the complex normative interactions at hand in addressing child labour, which, in turn, induced the author to developing her broader framework. In this context, the book offers a unique and amazingly concise discussion of different schools and approaches to multi-level governance in international law scholarship, from global administrative law to different variants of constitutionalization and their critics.

The author succeeds in identifying shared and common grounds upon which she builds her own approach. In this age of regression and increasing nationalism, it is heartening to read a convincing recourse to idealism and the tradition of natural law. The rule of law and human rights are found to pertain to the basic foundations of law in a world of diverging values. They provide the basis for operational proposals on enhanced cooperation between the ILO and the WTO in treaty-making and transnational dispute settlement. In conclusion, the book makes an important contribution to international law scholarship.

Throughout all her research, Franziska Humbert has worked as a legal adviser to Oxfam, preoccupied with a host of issues other than child labour and international law. To complete her habilitation at the University of Bern and a rich and inspiring book next to it are outstanding achievements. The Series is proud to include this impressive work.

Thomas Cottier
Series Editor, Former Managing Director of the World Trade Institute
Berne, August 2023

Preface

Child labour still is a major problem worldwide. Being prevalent in many global value chains, it is at the same time a phenomenon and a challenge of globalization. In my book 'The Challenge of Child Labour in International Law', based upon my PhD admitted by the Faculty of Law, University of Berne, in 2007, I have aimed at highlighting the interlinkage between child labour and trade and suggested devising an ILO-WTO enforcement regime as a possible solution. It was then when under the influence of the 'Zeitgeist' of the early Millennium where the Appellate Body of the WTO had solved with brilliance the 'trade ... and' question in the *US–Shrimp* case, traditional doctrines of international law were questioned and a new constitutionalism claimed by legal scholarship, the idea was born to further analyse the constitutionalist approach to international law, taking the case of trade and child labour. The present study is therefore influenced by this idealistic thinking, attempting to give more adequate answers to pressing questions of enhanced international interdependence and globalization of markets.

The study begins with recapitulating how the issues of child labour and trade are interrelated in global value chains and dealt with in existing social clauses of trade agreements and Generalized Systems of Preferences. A major part of the study then carefully analyses the *status quo* of trade measures on child labour in WTO law and makes proposals how to achieve more coherence between human rights and trade law where needed. Observing a 'modest constitutionalization' of WTO law *de lega lata*, another major part of the study discusses different theories on constitutionalism and other approaches to international law with a view to assessing whether such theories have the potential to promote effective solutions for trade and child labour. I conclude by developing my own approach, a New Legal Humanism as a new cognitive frame promoting integration of the global legal order in general and the adoption of an ILO-WTO implementation mechanism *de lege ferenda* on trade and child labour in particular.

Being well aware that times have changed since the beginning of the 21st century with the Russian War against Ukraine, the US shaken by a serious political crisis and autocratic regimes rising worldwide, I nevertheless wish to make a timely though idealistic contribution to the evolution of international law. The new encyclical 'Fratelli Tutti' by Pope Francis on a new world order putting human dignity at the centre gives me some hope that this wish is not in vain.

Franziska Humbert
Berlin, August 2023

Acknowledgements

This book is based on the postdoctoral thesis and "Habilitationsschrift" "The WTO and Child Labour – The Case for a New Legal Humanism in International Law – A Contribution to the Debate on Transnational Constitutionalism" approved by the Faculty of Law of the University of Berne in November 2021.

I am particularly thankful to Thomas Cottier for his long-term support and useful comments. I have also greatly benefitted from comments by and discussions with Peter van Bossche, Markus Krajewski, Elisabeth Bürgi, Lorand Bartels and Katja Gehne. I am also grateful to my parents for their support.

Franziska Humbert
Berlin, August 2023

Abbreviations

ACP	African Caribbean Pacific
ASEAN	Association of South East Asian Nations
CARIFORUM	Caribbean Forum of African, Caribbean and Pacific States
CESCR	Committee on Economic, Cultural and Social Rights
CETA	EU-Canada Comprehensive Trade Agreement
CRC	Convention on the Rights of the Child
CSR	Corporate Social Responsibility
DSU	Dispute Settlement Understanding
EC	European Community
ECCHR	European Centre on Constitutional and Human Rights
ECHR	European Convention on Human Rights
ECJ	European Court of Justice
ECOSOC	Economic and Social Council
EEC	European Economic Community
EPA	European Partnership Agreement
EU	European Union
FTA	Free Trade Agreement
GATS	General Agreement on Trade in Services
GATT	General Agreement on Tariffs and Trade
GIZ	Gesellschaft für Internationale Zusammenarbeit
GPA	Agreement on Government Procurement
GSP	Generalised System of Preferences
HRC	Human Rights Committee
ICC	International Criminal Court
ICCPR	International Covenant on Civil and Political Rights
ICESCR	International Covenant on Economic, Social and Cultural Rights
ICJ	International Court of Justice
ICSID	International Centre for Settlement of Investment Disputes
IFWEA	International Federation of Workers' Educations Associations
ILC	International Law Commission
ILO	International Labour Organization
IMF	International Monetary Fund
IPEC	International Programme on the Elimination of Child Labour
ISO	International Organization for Standardization
MFN	Most-Favoured-Nation
NAALC	North American Agreement on Labour Cooperation
NAFTA	North American Free Trade Agreement

NGO	Non-governmental Organization
npr-ppm	non-product-related process and production method
OECD	Organization for Economic Cooperation and Development
OHCHR	Office of the High Commissioner for Human Rights
OJ	Official Journal of the European Union
Oxfam	Oxford Committee for Famine Relief
ppm	process and production method
SPS	Sanitary and Phytosanitary
TBP	time-bound programme
TBT	Technical Barriers to Trade
TEU	Treaty on the European Union
TFEU	Treaty on the Functioning of the European Union
TNC	transnational company
TPRM	Trade Policy Review Mechanism
TRIPS	Trade-Related Aspects of Intellectual Property Rights
TTIP	Transatlantic Trade and Investment Partnership
UDHR	Universal Declaration of Human Rights
UFLPA	Uyghur Forced Labor Prevention Act
UN	United Nations
UNCTAD	United Nations Conference for Trade and Development
UNESCO	United Nations Educational, Scientific and Cultural Organization
UNGP	United Nations Guiding Principles on Business and Human Rights
UNICEF	United Nations Children's Fund
UNITA	National Union for the Total Independence of Angola
US	Unites States
VCLT	Vienna Convention on the Law of Treaties
WHO	World Health Organization
WRO	Withhold Release Orders
WTO	World Trade Organization

Introduction

1 Globalization, Child Labour and the International Legal Order

Child labour remains one of the major global problems today. According to the global estimates by the International Labour Organization (ILO) and UNICEF (United Nations Children's Fund) of 2020, there are 160 million child labourers worldwide of which 79 million are in hazardous work.[1] In absolute numbers, child labour increased by over eight million since 2016.[2] This is the first rise of child labour in 20 years. And as a result of the current COVID-19 pandemic, even more children risk being pushed into child labour.[3] Being prevalent in many global value chains such as the textile, cocoa and extractive sector, child labour is also a phenomenon of globalization and has a human rights and trade dimension.[4] In my book, 'The Challenge of Child Labour in International Law', which sets out the status of child labour in public international law, I have shown that the child labour and trade regimes are already linked under international law, and I recommended a common legal framework, an ILO-WTO (World Trade Organization) enforcement regime while leaving many questions open.[5] Among these questions for further research was the main issue of constitutionalization, i.e. the question whether the existing international legal order needed a new constitutional frame for accommodating different legal and policy interests.[6]

Until today, no such joint ILO-WTO enforcement regime has been contemplated, let alone implemented. However, the topic has not gone away. For example, CETA, the EU-Canada Comprehensive Economic Trade Agreement, concluded in 2016, contains chapter 23 on trade and labour, which provides for an enhanced role of civil society and cooperation with the ILO.[7] At the international level however, the linkage between the ILO and WTO has remained weak

1 ILO/UNICEF (Child Labour, Global Estimates of 2020), p. 8.
2 Ibid.
3 Ibid.
4 See for example UNICEF/Fair Labour Association/Mitigating Child Labour Risks in Cotton; UNICEF, Richards/Wilde; Myers.
5 Humbert (The Challenge of Child Labour).
6 Ibid., p. 388; Cottier (Trade and Human Rights), p. 129 et seq.
7 Art. 22.5 and Art. 23.7 of CETA, Council of Europe, Interinstitutional File: 2016/0206(NLE), 14 September 2016, Comprehensive Economic and Trade Agreement between Canada of the one part, and the European Union and its Member States, of the other part; see also European Commission (EU-Canada Comprehensive Economic Trade Agreement).

 | DOI:10.1163/9789004690905_002

apart from joint research[8] or technical exchanges with regard to supporting members' global economies.[9]

What weighs more, the whole multilateral order seems to be currently threatened by the Russian war against Ukraine and the growing US-China rivalry. Current trends point toward a further ramping up of geopolitical competition, increasing economic protectionism and fragmentation, and a loosening of the structures of the international order.[10] The US resistance to appoint new WTO Appellate Body members undermining the review system is just one example.[11] There is of course the Multi-Party Interim Appeal Arbitration Arrangement with currently 26 members, the EU counting as just one member, but the international trade regime nevertheless has been weakened.[12] The global pandemic of COVID-19, which started in winter 2020 in China and has officially ended in May 2023,[13] has increased this trend. Autocratic states have become even more so, and the UN Security Council seems to have disappeared completely since the outbreak.[14] COVID-19, instead of bringing about joint solutions, seems to have increased fragmentation in international law and policy.[15]

On the other hand, the COVID-19 pandemic has dramatically revealed how vulnerable workers at the bottom of the supply chain, and how interdependent economies are. The cut of supplier contracts by European purchasing companies has left thousands of workers in Bangladesh without salary.[16] At the same time, the automobile industry suffered from closure of factories during

8 WTO/ILO, Jansen/Lee; see also ILO (ILO and WTO issue new joint study).
9 See WTO (The WTO and International Labour Organization).
10 Carnegie Europe, Lehne, After Russia's War against Ukraine: What kind of world order?, 28 February 2023, https://carnegieeurope.eu/2023/02/28/after-russia-s-war-against-ukraine-what-kind-of-world-order-pub-89130; see also Hamilton/Ohlberg; Süddeutsche Zeitung, ‚Neue Weltordnung' 13 February 2020.
11 Süddeutsche Zeitung, Björn Finke, ‚Welthandelsorganisation, Retter gesucht', 3 June 2020; WTO, Appellate Members, https://www.wto.org/english/tratop_e/dispu_e/ab_members_descrp_e.htm Van den Bossche/Zdouc, pp. 318 et seqq.
12 For further explanation, see Van den Bossche/Zdoucs, pp. 324–327.
13 WHO, Statement on the fifteenth meeting of the IHR (2005) Emergency Committee on the COVID-19 pandemic, 5 May 2023, https://www.who.int/news/item/05-05-2023-statement-on-the-fifteenth-meeting-of-the-international-health-regulations-(2005)-emergency-committee-regarding-the-coronavirus-disease-(covid-19)-pandemic.
14 Süddeutsche Zeitung, Stefan Kornelius, ‚Viel Schatten, Die Corona-Krise stellt die Leistungsfähigkeit der verschiedenen Regierungsformen und die internationale Ordnung auf die Probe', 11/12/13 April 2020.
15 For an excellent treatise of fragmentation in international law, see Cottier/Delimatsis.
16 ECCHR (Garment supply chains).

the lockdown in China.[17] Put simply, the Corona-crisis has brought to light what should be common sense anyway: Global solutions are needed for global problems.

In an era of globalization, global problems essentially need to be dealt also at an international level, be it climate change or child labour in global trade. The crucial question however is what exactly needs to be regulated at international level, and what exactly at national or regional level, and how these different levels should interact. How should horizontal interaction of different political and legal areas should look like, and how should substantial and institutional coherence work and be framed? The fundamental question underlying these issues, however, is whether the current private law paradigm of international law based on state consent, a law *inter* nations, is still a valid approach or whether a new cognitive frame is needed to solve global problems.

The present study will deal with these questions taking the example of trade and child labour.

2 Contents

Chapter 1 recapitulates the interaction of child labour and trade, presenting the global dimension of child labour, the trade and child labour linkage and the need for global rules beyond domestic regulation.

The second chapter turns to trade regulation and analyses the status quo of child labour in trade law, i.e. it examines whether existing unilateral trade measures are consistent with WTO law, thus to what extent the current trade order is already capable of taking non-economic values such as human rights into account.

The third chapter then asks whether the current legal order based on state consent is still a proper and sufficient framework to promote global regulation in response to global challenges, such as child labour and trade. In the search of answers, it examines various schools of thought theorizing new approaches to bring about greater coherence to a largely fragmented international legal order, in particular global legal pluralism, the global administrative school and various constitutionalist models. The case of child labour puts these theories to a test and examines them from the specific angle of child labour protection and the prospects to address related regulatory problems. It prepares the

17 Spiegel, ‚Chinas Autoindustrie erwartet Erholung bis Herbst', 12 March 2020, https://www.spiegel.de/wirtschaft/chinas-autoindustrie-erwartet-erholung-bis-herbst-a-d8ae91a3-939a-44d1-af27-ed15502eb692.

ground to present my own theory which I present in terms of a New Legal Humanism.

The fourth chapter concludes by presenting the implications of the New Legal Humanism as a new approach to the global legal order, using the trade and child labour example. Specifically, it elaborates an ILO-WTO implementation mechanism on child labour *de lege ferenda,* building upon this new approach.

CHAPTER 1

The Problem of Child Labour and Trade

1 Introduction

This chapter identifies child labour as a major challenge of today's globalization which needs to be addressed by the international community. It highlights the international dimension of child labour, pointing to the limits of purely national solutions in combating child labour. It also refers to the trade dimension of child labour, outlining the structure of the global economy where international value chains closely tie states together. Finally, it points to the *ius cogens* nature of the right of children to be protected from child labour. The chapter concludes by stressing the need for global solutions including trade measures.

The chapter essentially draws on my previous work and analysis provided in the book 'The Challenge of Child Labour in International Law'.[1] It provides the background and sets the stage for subsequently assessing the trade linkage and theorizing the constitutionalization of international law.

2 The International Dimension of Child Labour

2.1 *Child Labour as a Global Problem*

2.1.1 The Concept of Child Labour

Child labour remains a widespread problem around the world. It persists as one of the major global problems today. Yet not all work done by children is intolerable and exploitative.[2] Child work not interfering with schooling and the child's physical, mental and social development can be beneficial. ILO and UNICEF differentiate between three categories of illicit child labour

- labour that is performed under the minimum age for this kind of work and thus likely to impede a child's education and full development;
- hazardous work that jeopardizes the physical, mental or moral well-being of a child, either because of its nature or because of the conditions in which it is carried out;

1 Humbert (The Challenge of Child Labour).

2 For a detailed account on the definition, concept, forms, statistics and causes of child labour, see Humbert (The Challenge of Child Labour), pp. 14–33.

- and the unconditional worst forms of labour such as slavery, trafficking, debt bondage, forced labour forced recruitment of children for use in armed conflict, prostitution and pornography, and illicit action.[3]

Hazardous child work is inter alia found in small-scale mining, carpet, waving, construction-related activities, leather-tanning tourism and agriculture.[4] For the purpose of this work, the term 'exploitative child labour' or 'child labour' shall be employed interchangeably for intolerable forms of child work.

2.1.2 The Limits of Domestic Regulations

There are still 160 million child labourers worldwide.[5] Although there have been cases where countries on their own made considerable progress in eliminating child labour,[6] one of the lessons learnt by the International Programme for the Elimination of Child Labour (IPEC) is that an enabling international environment and international cooperation including organizations such as the International Labour Organization, the World Bank, United Nations Educational, Scientific and Cultural Organization (UNESCO) and the World Health Organization (WHO) is a key strategic goal.[7] Governments often lack the political will and the financial and human resources to effectively combat child labour on their own. Thus, it has been recommended that international action is needed to prompt governments to implement national policies and to generate technical and financial assistance.[8] This line of reasoning has been confirmed by including the target to reach free, equitable and quality primary and secondary education for all boys and girls by 2030 into UN Sustainable Development Goal 4.[9]

2.1.3 Trade and Child Labour

The trade and labour linkage is another reason why child labour cannot be perceived as a purely domestic problem. Already during the Industrial Revolution in Europe in the nineteenth century, the fear existed that trade pressures would

3 UNICEF (The State of the World's Children 1997), p. 24.
4 Cf. Humbert (The Challenge of Child Labour), pp. 19–22.
5 ILO/UNICEF (Child Labour, Global Estimates of 2020), p. 8.
6 See for example the Bolsa Escola programme implemented in Brazil from 2001 to 2003 helping children to attend school by financially supporting their mothers, assessed by de Janvry/Finan/Sadoulet.
7 See ILO (The End of Child Labour: Within Reach), para 162 and ILO/IPEC (IPEC Action against Child Labour: Highlights 2002), p. 18.
8 See references in Humbert, pp. 27–34.
9 UN (The 17 Goals).

hamper the adoption of domestic laws for the elimination of child labour.[10] Most importantly, the Preamble of the ILO Constitution, established by the Treaty of Versailles, states that unfair labour conditions in one country may impact on the welfare of other countries:

> Whereas also the failure of any nation to adopt humane conditions of labour is an obstacle in the way of other nations which desire to improve the conditions in their own countries.[11]

Equally, the Declaration of Philadelphia of 1944 submits that 'poverty anywhere constitutes a danger to prosperity everywhere', and that the ILO will address the social implications of economic and financial policies and fully cooperate with international bodies promoting a high and steady volume of international trade.[12] As regards child labour in developing countries, the ILO has found that when replacing children with adult workers in export industries, slightly higher prices have to be paid by consumers in import countries.[13] To avoid 'beggar-thy-neighbour' policies of developing countries, a global strategy is needed.

The same line of reasoning can also be found in more recent US trade laws such as the US Generalized System of Preferences (GSP) providing for labour rights conditionality[14] and the amended Section 307 of the Tariff Act of 1930 prohibiting *inter alia* imports made with forced child labour.[15] Both measures were – at least originally – based on the rationale that unfair working conditions abroad have a bad impact on US commerce and should be tackled by trade measures.[16] For example, initially, Section 307 of the Tariff Act of 1930 allowed the admission of products of forced labour if it could be shown that no

---

10 Leary (Workers' Rights and International Trade), p. 183.

11 ILO, Part XIII (Labour) of the Treaty of Versailles of 28 June 1919, Section I (Geneva: International Labour Office).

12 ILO, Declaration adopted by the Conference. Appendix XIII, Record of Proceedings, International Labour Conference, twenty-sixth session, Philadelphia, Montreal, 1944, p. 621 et seq.

13 ILO (Child Labour: Targeting the Intolerable 1998), p. 19 et seq.

14 US Code Title 19 – Customs Duties, Chapter 12, Trade Act of 1974, Subchapter V – Generalized System of Preferences. In 2021, the GSP expired, pending congressional renewal; see https://www.cbp.gov/trade/priority-issues/trade-agreements/special-trade-legislation/generalized-system-preferences.

15 US Code Title 19 – Customs Duties, Chapter 4, Tariff Act of 1930, Subtitle II – Special Provisions, Part I, Section 1307, June 17, 1930, ch. 497, title III, § 307, 46 Stat. 689; Pub. L. 106–200, title IV, § 411(a), May 18, 2000, 114 Stat. 298, Pub. L. 114–125, title IX, &910 (a) (1), Feb. 24, 2016, 130 Stat. 239; https://www.law.cornell.edu/uscode/text/19/.

16 See Humbert (The Challenge of Child Labour), pp. 284 et seqq. with further references.

comparable product was made in the US or the level of domestic production did not meet domestic demand ("consumptive demand" clause).[17] Protecting domestic producers was therefore the central legislative concern. In 2015, the US Congress removed the 'consumptive demand' clause, giving more weight to human rights concerns.[18]

So do other existing trade measures on child labour. Various EU and Members States' trade policies aim at establishing respect for human and labour rights,[19] eradicating poverty[20] or promoting socially responsible production.[21] Hence, as is the case with the ILO Constitution,[22] human dignity is another rationale on which trade measures on child labour are based.

Whatever the objective of such trade measures may be, it is important to note that the trade and labour linkage exists and that there is today a magnitude of all sorts of international trade measures on child labour, including social clauses in regional and bilateral trade agreements,[23] GSPs, unilateral trade measures and private initiatives.[24] Thus, child labour is already dealt with as a global problem.

The question, however, is whether the *status quo* of international law is satisfactory since on the one hand, it is questionable whether such measures are compatible with WTO law, and on the other hand, whether a multilateral solution including a joint, global strategy may be more appropriate and effective in combating child labour. Both questions will be subsequently dealt with in the study.

2.1.4 Child Labour in International Value Chains

Another related reason why child labour needs to be perceived as a global problem is the well-known phenomenon of internationalization of corporate

17 Cf. Humbert (The Challenge of Child Labour), p. 320–321.

18 114th Congress, Public Law 114–125, 130 Stat. 239, February 24, 2016, Trade Facilitation and Trade Enforcement Act of 2015, 19 USC 4301 note.

19 European Commission (Generalized System of Preferences).

20 European Commission (EU Trade policy and ACP Countries).

21 Cf. Loi du 27 février 2002 visant à promouvoir la production socialement responsible, Moniteur Belge du 26-03-2002, entrée en vigueur 01-09-2002, modifié 28-12-2017, Affaires économiques, Publication 26-03-2002, numéro 2002011065, p. 12428, dossier numéro: 2002-02-27/32, Justel, législation consolée, http://www.ejustice.just.fgov.be/cgi_loi/change_lg.pl?language=fr&la=F&cn=2002022732&table_name=loi; see also Peeters.

22 Cottier/Caplazi, p. 474; Lee (Globalization and labour standards), p. 174.

23 For the purpose of this work, the term 'social clause' refers to any linkage of trade and labour or human rights rules in one agreement, see also Humbert (The Challenge of Child Labour), p. 4.

24 For an overview see Humbert (The Challenge of Child Labour), pp. 195–375.

value chains that has come along with trade liberalization over the past twenty years. Transnational companies (TNCs) have increasingly based their business model on outsourcing production through global supply chains that demand low-cost and 'flexible' labour.[25] The book 'The Challenge of Child Labour in International Law' provides numerous examples for systematic use of child labour in global supply chains of TNCs.[26] More recent examples are the cocoa industry that still relies on widespread child labour in the Ivory Coast, and the garment and mining industry.[27] In response to ongoing public criticism of unfair labour conditions in foreign supplier plants of TNCs, companies together with other stake-holders including non-governmental organizations (NGOs), consumer groups, governments and trade unions have developed numerous private and public initiatives which can be summarized under the label Corporate Social Responsibility (CSR).[28] A noteworthy instrument at the international level are the UN Guiding Principles on Business and Human Rights (UNGPs) adopted by the Human Rights Council in 2011.[29] Thus, different stakeholders such as consumers, companies, governments, international organizations or NGOs care about child labour abroad and not only feel responsible but also have already adopted various measures to address the problem.[30]

In recent years, there has been a proliferation of domestic legislation implementing the UNGP and holding transnationally operating companies accountable for human rights abuses in their value chain.[31] Prominent examples include the US California Transparency in Supply Chains Act of 2010 on slavery and human trafficking,[32] the French loi de vigilance,[33] the EU Directive on Non-Financial Reporting 2014/95/EU,[34] the Dutch *Wet Zorgplicht*

25 Oxfam International (Trading Away Our Rights, Women Working in Global Supply Chains), p. 17.

26 Humbert (The Challenge of Child Labour), pp. 332–375.

27 See p. 1.

28 For the concept of CSR and the various initiatives developed under the name of CSR, see Humbert (The Challenge of Child Labour), pp. 332–374.

29 UN/Human Rights Council (UNGP).

30 It should however be noted that while many companies are truly committed to behave socially responsible, still a lot of them consider this as a public relations exercise, see for example Oxfam Germany (Sweet Fruit).

31 See for an excellent overview Grabosch.

32 California Code, Civil Code, CIV Sec. 1714.43, https://codes.findlaw.com/ca/civil-code/civ-sect-1714-43.html.

33 Loi relative au devoir de vigilance des societés mères et des entreprises donneuses d'ordre, n° 2017–399 du 27 mars 2017, www.legifrance.gouv.fr/eli/loi/2017/3/27/2017-399/jo/texte.

34 Directive 2014/95/EU of the European Parliament and of the Council of 22 October 2014 amending Directive 2013/34/EU as regards disclosure of non-financial and diversity

Kinderarbeid,[35] the German Act on Corporate Due Diligence in Supply Chains,[36] the proposed EU Corporate Sustainability Due Diligence Directive[37] and the proposed EU Forced Labour Regulation.[38] The question is whether international law can support and promote such private law approaches.

2.2 *The Protection from Exploitative Child Labour as* Ius Cogens

As the analysis in the book 'The Challenge of Child Labour in International Law' reveals, the prohibition of child labour is contained in numerous United Nations (UN) and ILO conventions and declarations. The almost universal ratification of the Convention on the Rights of Child (CRC)[39] suggests that there is a global consensus among states that child labour is intolerable and must be eliminated. Art. 32 of the CRC and the ILO Core Conventions No. 138 and 182 – i.e. the Minimum Age Convention and the Worst Forms of Child Labour Convention – are the central legal provisions and instruments prohibiting child labour. They reflect the distinction between tolerable child work and exploitative child labour made in ILO and UNICEF reports on child labour.[40] While the ILO Minimum Age Convention No. 138 aims at preventing exploitation of children by setting minimum ages for admission to employment and referring to all three categories of child labour mentioned above including child labour performed under a minimum age and thus likely to interfere with basic education, the ILO Worst Forms of Child Labour Convention No. 182 focusses on hazardous work and the unconditional worst forms of child labour and does not include child labour under a certain minimum age and the lack of basic education in its definition of the worst forms of child labour.[41]

The prohibition of child labour as defined by these international instruments has been qualified as a general principle of law and even as an *ius cogens*

information by certain large undertakings and groups L330/1; For a critical assessment, see Humbert (CSR Directive and Its German Implementation).

35 *Wet Zorgplicht Kinderarbeid*, 7 February 2017, Kamerstukken 34506, nr. 1–3.

36 Gesetz über die unternehmerischen Sorgfaltspflichten in Lieferketten, 16 July 2022, BGBL 2021 I Nr. 46, 22.07.2021, p. 2959.

37 COM(2022) 71 final.

38 Regulation of the European Parliament and of the Council on prohibiting products made with forced labour on the Union market COM(2022) 453 final.

39 See the status of ratification at the Office of the High Commissioner for Human Rights, https://indicators.ohchr.org/, as of July 2020, 196 states have ratified the CRC.

40 See above, p. 5.

41 Cf. Humbert (The Challenge of Child Labour), p. 102; On the relationship between ILO Convention No. 138 and 182, see Humbert in Schall/Theusinger/Pour Rafsendjani, § 2, para. 64.

norm.[42] As such, it forms part of those obligations that the ICJ considered to be 'obligations of a state towards the international community as a whole', which are 'the concern of all states' and for whose protection all states have a 'legal interest', i.e. they apply *erga omnes*.[43] This suggests that all states are responsible for combating child labour. Whilst it will be elaborated later in this book what exactly such state responsibility entails, it suffices for the moment to state that the right to be protected from child labour is an issue of global concern of all states, for whose protection all states are responsible.

While classifying the prohibition of child labour as a norm of *ius cogens* should be uncontroversial in cases of worst forms of child labour prohibited by ILO Convention No. 182, it might be questionable with regard to the first category of intolerable child labour performed at too young an age and interfering with basic education.[44] Since education is still often considered as a trade-off of lesser importance than cheap labour, it is argued that only the most severe forms of child labour form part of *ius cogens*.[45] While this sounds convincing, it should be recalled that the first category differs from 'light work' after school at the age of twelve or thirteen, and that child labour under the age of ten and interfering with basic education has been qualified as exploitative by UNICEF and the ILO and as a slavery-like practice by the Working Group on Contemporary Forms of Slavery in its Programme of Action for the Elimination of Exploitation of Child Labour for the UN Commission on Human Rights.[46] Also, until today, 176 states have ratified the Minimum Age Convention, which is a further indication for a global consensus on a broad definition of intolerable child labour. Most importantly, household work and work in family undertakings and work as part of education is excluded from minimum age legislation.[47] Thus, small-holders in the cacao sector in Ghana and the Ivory

---

42 Humbert (The Challenge of Child Labour), pp. 110–121.

43 The ICJ stated in the case Barcelona Traction, Light and Power Company, Ltd. (*Belgium v. Spain*), Judgement, Second Phase, ICJ Reports 1970, pp. 3–358, para. 33: 'In particular, an essential distinction should be drawn between the obligations of a state towards the community as a whole and those of a state vis-à-vis another state in the field of diplomatic protection. By their very nature, the former are the concern of all states. In view of the importance of the rights involved, all states can be held to have a legal interest in their protection; they are obligations *erga omnes*.'

44 Cf. Humbert (The Challenge of Child Labour), p. 118–119.

45 Cottier (The Principle of Common Concern of Humankind), p. 53; Cottier (Improving Compliance: Jus cogens and International Economic Law), pp. 339–340.

46 See above, p. 5; van Bueren, p. 264: UN Commission on Human Rights (Programme pf Action for the Elimination of the Exploitation of Child Labour); Humbert (The Challenge of Child Labour), p. 43.

47 Humbert (The Challenge of Child Labour), p. 119.

Coast, where child labour is prevalent, would not violate ILO Convention No. 138 when letting their children work in the cocoa harvest.[48] Given that also this first category of child labour severely impedes a child's development, the qualification as *ius cogens* seems appropriate.

3 The Need for Global Solutions Including Trade Measures

Having established that child labour is a global problem, it is only logical to look for global solutions, since global problems need global solutions. As suggested in 'The Challenge of Child Labour in International Law', an ideal solution would comprise trade measures complementing the rather weak ILO and UN implementation systems for the prohibition of child labour, the main reason being the effectiveness of trade measures (if designed and applied in the right way including the use of complementary measures).[49] For example, it has been found that trade measures can serve as a deterrent for companies as regards the use of child labour or be an incentive for governments to improve labour standards.[50] This conclusion seems to be confirmed by recent action against forced labour under Sec. 307 of the US Tariff Act banning forced child labour and the proposed EU Regulation on Forced Labour.[51] The book recommended a multilateral solution at the global level *de lege ferenda* instead of a variety of regional and unilateral trade measures on child labour arguing that by creating the same conditions for all countries, the problem of the 'race to the bottom' could be addressed.[52] Domestic legislation holding transnational operating companies accountable and corporate social responsibility for international value chains (CSR) should complement such multilateral solutions.

Before discussing such proposals, the legal situation under the *status quo* for trade measures on child labour will be examined. It will be analysed what solutions for the problem of child labour and trade measures *de lege lata* exist and if so, whether they are adequate.

---

48 For permissible child work and non-permissible child labour in Ghana and the Ivory-Coast, see International Cocoa Initiative, Vigneri, Serra, Cadenas. *Researching the Impact of Increased Cocoa Yields on the Labour Market and Child Labour Risk in Ghana and Côte d'Ivoire*. Retrieved 13 January 2023, from https://www.cocoainitiative.org/

49 Humbert (The Challenge of Child Labour), pp. 373–375.

50 Ibid., pp. 248–253 and pp. 368–369.

51 See below, pp. 15–16.

52 Humbert (The Challenge of Child Labour), p. 374.

CHAPTER 2

The Status Quo of Trade Measures on Child Labour in WTO Law

1 Introduction

Building on the assumption that trade measures should supplement the existing ILO and UN implementation mechanisms for the prohibition of child labour,[1] this chapter will examine the *status quo* of existing trade measures on child labour in WTO law. This analysis will help to clarify the current relationship between the international trade order and domestic law. The fundamental tension between the liberal devotion to trade liberalization and member states' right to tax, legislate and regulate according to domestic policy will be at the core of this analysis. To what extent should WTO rules impact on domestic policies of Member states?[2] From a broader perspective, the following analysis seeks to assess the current legal order asking whether the current trade order is able to take non-trade concerns such as child labour adequately into account or new solutions are needed.

The WTO is the principal institution for multilateral trade regulation and the successor of the General Agreement on Tariffs and Trade (GATT) of 1947.[3] The WTO Charter contains in its Annex 1 the multilateral agreements consisting of agreements in goods, that is GATT 1994 and its related agreements, and agreements in services, that is the General Agreement on Trade in Services (GATS) and its annexes, and the Agreement on Trade-Related Aspects of Intellectual Property Rights (TRIPS).[4] Annex 2 to the WTO Charter contains the Dispute Settlement Understanding (DSU) and Annex 3 the Trade Policy Review Mechanism (TPRM), which are both obligatory to WTO members.

1 For an elaboration of this thesis, see Humbert (The Challenge of Child Labour), pp. 195–375.

2 Note that the WTO dispute settlement system has been weakened by the US blockage regarding the Appellate Body and an Multi-Party Interim Appeal Arbitration Arrangement has been introduced (Van den Bossche/Zdouc, pp. 324–326). Nevertheless, conclusions as to the substantive WTO-obligations remain valid.

3 Jackson (The World Trading System), p. 31.

4 The WTO legal texts are embodied in the Final Act Embodying the Results of the Uruguay Round of Multilateral Trade Negotiations, signed by ministers in Marrakesh in April 1995, available at www.wto.org/english/docs_e/legal_e/ursum_e.htm.

1.1 *Unilateral Trade Measures*

Unilateral trade measures relating to child labour whose WTO-compatibility could be questioned are for example the US[5] and EU Generalized Systems of Preferences (GSPs) with regard to their labour rights conditionalities,[6] the US import ban on goods produced with forced or indentured child labour (Section 307 of the Tariff Act of 1930 (19 United States C. 1307)),[7] the US Uyghur Forced Labor Prevention Act (UFLPA) banning goods presumably made with forced (child) labour from Xinjiang, China,[8] the Belgian Social Label Law[9] and the Kimberley Process Certification Scheme.[10] [11] The proposed EU Regulation on Forced Labour including forced child labour modelled on Section 307 of the Tariff Act of 1930 also potentially violates the WTO/GATT non-discrimination rules.[12]

What do these measures regulate specifically? The US and the EU GSPs include a set of labour rights conditionalities, requiring certain developing countries to respect certain labour rights including the prohibition of child labour in order to be eligible or, as in the case of the EU, to get further tariff preferences.[13] The EU GSP will be renewed in 2024 to better reflect the EU's policy priorities especially in the area of climate change and sustainability.[14]

---

5 US Code Title 19 – Customs Duties, Chapter 12, Trade Act of 1974, Subchapter V – Generalized System of Preferences. In 2018, the GSP expired pending congressional renewal, see https://www.cbp.gov/trade/priority-issues/trade-agreements/special-trade-legislation/generalized-system-preferences.

6 Regulation (EU) No 978/2012 of the European Parliament and of the Council of 25 October 2012 applying a scheme of generalised tariff preferences and repealing Council Regulation (EC) No 732/2008, OJ 2012 L 303, 31.10.2012.

7 US Code Title 19 – Customs Duties, Chapter 4, Tariff Act of 1930, Subtitle II – Special Provisions, Part I, Section 1307, June 17, 1930, ch. 497, title III, § 307, 46 Stat. 689; Pub. L. 106–200, title IV, § 411(a), May 18, 2000, 114 Stat. 298, Pub. L. 114–125, title IX, &910 (a) (1), Feb. 24, 2016, 130 Stat. 239; https://www.law.cornell.edu/uscode/text/19/.

8 19 U.S.C. 1307 and 4681, 22 U.S.C. 2656, 6901, 7101 and 7107, Public Law Public Law 117–78, H.R. 6256, December 2021, https://www.govinfo.gov/app/details/PLAW-117publ78.

9 Loi relative au devoir de vigilance des societés mères et des entreprises donneuses d'ordre, n° 2017–399 du 27 mars 2017, www.legifrance.gouv.fr/eli/loi/2017/3/27/2017-399/jo/texte.

10 https://www.kimberleyprocess.com/documents/10540/11192/KPCS%20Core%20Document?version=1.0&t=1331826363000.

11 For an analysis of existing trade measures on child labour see Humbert (The Challenge of Child Labour), pp. 195–375.

12 COM(2022) 453 final.

13 For more details see Humbert (The Challenge of Child Labour) pp. 284–318. Although Humbert examined the earlier Council Regulation (EC) No. 2501/2001, her analysis is still valid since the main provisions for the general as well as the special incentive arrangement for sustainable governance and development have not changed.

14 See for example GSPhub, A new GSP, https://gsphub.eu/about-gsp.

The US import ban on goods made with forced or indentured child labour is a trade restriction for foreign goods produced by child labour.[15] Since its 'consumptive demand clause' was removed in 2015,[16] civil society and the responsible US authority, US Customs Border Protection (CBP), have increasingly used Section 307. In accordance with 19 C.F.R. §12.42, NGOs have reported various instances of forced labour used in goods such as carpets from Nepal, palm oil from Malaysia and seafood from Thailand.[17] In turn, CBP has initiated investigations and issued 'Withhold Release Orders (WRO)' in accordance with 19 CFR § 12.42 (e) or 'Findings' in accordance with 19 CFR § 12.42 (f) for relevant goods in case they could conclude that such goods were the product of forced labour.[18] Such enforcement actions (or the threat of those) prompted for example palm oil industries in Malaysia to repay recruitment fees of over 115.4 million US $ to nearly 82,000 migrant workers and the Thai Government to commit to end the manufacture of fishing nets using prison labour but did not led to improvements of working conditions in the carpet industry in Nepal.[19] CBP also started to modify or revoke WROs and Findings where the situation had partially improved and some of the ILO indicators of forced labour[20] been removed, mostly through corporate due diligence measures such as audits or payment of recruitment fees.[21] While such system of trade incentives to stop forced labour can be deemed to have functioned well in a number of cases, civil society strongly criticizes the lack of real remediation measures for workers.[22]

The UFLPA aims at ensuring that goods made with forced labour in the Xinjiang Uyghur Autonomous Region of the People's Republic of China do not enter the US market. Media and other reports have alleged that in recent years millions of Uyghurs have been detained in re-education camps and forced to work in factories in Xinjiang, under a government-led labour transfer scheme.[23] The OHCHR has stated that this could be assessed as a crime against

15 For more details see Humbert (The Challenge of Child Labour), pp. 318–322.

16 See above, p. 8 and Humbert (The Challenge of Child Labour), pp. 320–321.

17 For an overview and analysis of case studies, see The Remedy Project, 'Putting things right: Remediation of forced labour under Tariff Act 1930', 28 April 2023.

18 Casey.

19 The Remedy Project, 'Putting things right: Remediation of forced labour under Tariff Act 1930', 28 April 2023, pp. 16 et seqq.

20 ILO indicators of forced labour, https://www.ilo.org/global/topics/forced-labour/publications/WCMS_203832/lang--en/index.htm.

21 The Remedy Project, 'Putting things right: Remediation of forced labour under Tariff Act 1930', 28 April 2023, pp. 11, 16, 22 with further references.

22 Ibid., pp. 24–33.

23 Business and Human Rights Resource Centre, Major brands implicated in report on forced labour beyond Xinjiang, March 2020, https://www.business-humanrights.org/en/latest-news/investors-human-rights-groups-call-on-us-to-enact-a-regional-ban-on-cotton-imports-from-xinjiang-based-on-evidence-of-forced-labour/.

humanity.[24] Evidence has indicated that Uyghurs and other ethnic minorities are being employed under conditions of forced labour in factories supplying major global companies. The law creates a rebuttable presumption that goods produced or manufactured in Xinjiang or by certain entities with ties to the region are made with forced labour, unless CBP determines otherwise. CBP began enforcing the rebuttable presumption on June 21, 2022.[25] The Forced Labor Enforcement Task Force under the Secretary of Homeland Security specified the list of entities whose merchandise is subject to the rebuttable presumption.

The Belgian Social Label Law provides for the granting of a public social label to products produced in conformity with the ILO Core Conventions.[26] [27]

The proposed EU Forced Labour Regulation differs from Section 307 of the Tariff Act of 1930 to the extent it explicitly addresses economic operators and already prohibits the placing and making available of any product made with forced labour on the Union market, thus including domestic companies and products in its scope.[28] It has a direct impact on trade since in case of forced (child) labour, the customs authorities will not release products for free circulation in the EU market nor for export, Art. 19 of the Regulation. Where economic operators can demonstrate that they conducted corporate due diligence in relation to forced labour, the competent authorities will not initiate an investigation of products, Art. 4 (7) of the Regulation. This provision mirrors the practice by the CBP of modifying WRO or Findings in case of removal of due diligence measures by companies.[29]

A slightly different kind of unilateral trade measures on child labour are measures that were taken by ILO members following the recommendation of the Governing Body to the International Labour Conference under Art. 33 of the ILO Constitution to review their relations with Myanmar such as the

24 OHCHR, Assessment of human rights concerns in the Xinijang Uyghur Autonomous Region, People's Republic of China, https://www.ohchr.org/en/documents/country-reports/ohchr-assessment-human-rights-concerns-xinjiang-uyghur-autonomous-region.

25 Casey.

26 The ILO Core Conventions encompass the prohibition of forced labour and child labour, freedom of association and the right to organize and bargain collectively, equal remuneration for men and women for work of equal value and non-discrimination in employment, see Humbert (The Challenge of Child Labour), pp. 103–107.

27 For more details see Humbert (The Challenge of Child Labour), pp. 323–329.

28 Art. 3 of the EU Forced Labour Regulation, COM (2022), 453 final.

29 See above, p. 15.

2003 US Burmese Freedom and Democracy Act.[30] The US Act provides for a general ban on any article from Myanmar until the country's government had made substantial progress to end violations of workers' rights including child labour.[31]

A measure supporting the implementation of US trade measures on child labour is the list of goods probably produced by child labour and their source countries maintained by the Bureau of International Labour Affairs, required under the Trafficking Victims Protection Reauthorization Act (TVPRA) of 2005 and subsequent reauthorizations.[32] The aim of the list is primarily to raise public awareness about forced labour and child labour around the world and to promote efforts to combat them by engaging with foreign governments to combat forced and child labour.

The Kimberley Process Certification Scheme is a response to the wars in West Africa involving child soldiers and financed by 'conflict diamonds'. It requires participants to ensure that a Kimberly Process Certificate accompanies each shipment of rough diamonds. They also have to ensure that no shipment is imported from non-participants.[33]

Finally, private sector action on child labour also may be trade distorting and has to be analysed with a view to its compatibility with WTO law.[34]

1.2 *Defining PPMs and Rules of Interpretation*

All these measures can be divided into product-specific and country-specific measures. Measures such as the US import ban on goods produced with forced or indentured child labour are product-specific measures regulating process and production methods. Measures regulating process and production methods are commonly referred to as ppm-measures.[35] The OECD draws a distinction between measures regulating non-product-related process and production methods and measures regulating product-related process and production methods as for example regulations concerning the materials

30 US Burmese Freedom and Democracy Act of 2003, Public 108–61, 108th Congress, 28 July 2003, H. R. 2330, https://www.congress.gov/bill/108th-congress/house-bill/2330, For details see Humbert (The Challenge of Child Labour), pp. 188–190.

31 Section 3 (a) of the US Burmese Freedom and Democracy Act of 2003.

32 Public Laws 109–164, https://www.dol.gov/agencies/ilab/about/laws.

33 For more details see Humbert (The Challenge of Child Labour), pp. 329–331.

34 For an analysis of existing private section action on child labour see Humbert (The Challenge of Child Labour), pp. 332–373.

35 OECD (PPMS).

allowed to be contained in a product.[36] In the latter case, the measure has some impact on the physical characteristics of the product. Under this terminology, child labour is a non-product-related ppm (npr-ppm). Npr-ppms are among the most controversial issues in the trade and environment debate and also hotly debated in the field of climate change.[37] A prominent example for npr-ppms in the area of climate change and environment are methods causing emissions during production or transportation.[38] Relevant trade measures are climate border adjustments in the form of a charge or a tax on goods that compensate for the competitive disadvantage caused by unilateral climate protection measures.[39] Since such measures typically adjust taxes, the term 'border tax adjustments' is commonly referred to when discussing border adjustments.[40] When applied to imports, border adjustments typically raise the price of a product.[41] Concrete examples include proposals for extending the EU Emissions Trading System to imports or calculating the EU Emissions Trading System on the basis of the carbon footprint[42] as well as the EU carbon border adjustment mechanism proposed by the EU Green Deal.[43] The distinction between ppms and npr-ppms and their product-relatedness will become relevant when discussing the WTO-compatibility of such measures.[44]

Country-specific measures such as the US Burmese Freedom and Democracy Act of 2003 providing for a general ban on any good from Burma have to be qualified as general sanctions or countermeasures. Whilst most product-specific measures on child labour target child labour in the export industry, country-specific measures also address child labour in the domestic industry of the targeted country. The OECD has defined trade sanctions as bans or restrictions placed on products other than the particular product that does not comply with the ppm-requirement specified by the importing country.[45]

---

36 The OECD (OECD (PPMS), p. 7) distinguishes between ppm-measures that affect the characteristics of a product that has a negative impact on the environment at the consumption stage (product-related ppms), and ppm-measures where the process and productions method has a negative impact on the environment at the production stage (non-product-related ppms).

37 Cf. for example Will, p. 143; Quick and Lau; Kaufmann/Weber, pp. 508–510.

38 Cf. Vranes, p. 191.

39 Will, p. 5 et seqq.

40 See for example Vranes with further references; Border tax adjustments will also be discussed when analysing the compatibility of npr-ppms, see pp. 64 et seqq.

41 Will, p. 5.

42 For a thorough discussion of this topic see Will.

43 EU Communication, The Green Deal, COM(2019) 640 final; See also Van den Bossche, p. 29.

44 See pp. 66 et seqq.

45 OECD (PPMS), p. 6.

While the OECD-terminology will not be strictly adhered to, the country-product distinction is an important distinction that has to be borne in mind when analysing WTO law.

A measure that also lies somewhere in between these categories is the Kimberley Process Certification Scheme. On the one hand, it refers to products by requiring certificates for diamonds. On the other hand, it is origin-related because participants in the scheme may reject diamonds from the territory of non-participants.[46] Applying the terms from above, it is however not a ppm-measure in its original sense since child labour is not used to produce the diamonds but linked to the use of diamonds. Such measures have been termed 'semi-tailored' sanctions.[47]

The following sections will discuss the compatibility of the specific trade measures with the relevant provisions of WTO law referring to panel and Appellate Body decisions and existing literature.[48] The analysis will only include trade in goods. The discussion of substantive law will focus on the questions whether WTO law applies to npr-ppm-measures, what 'like products' are and how to resolve the problem of extraterritoriality.

The question of whether ILO or UN human rights law or other public international law constitutes a valuable defence under WTO law concerns issues of jurisdiction and applicable laws. These issues are closely linked to the central question of coherence of international law and will be dealt with after having reviewed the relevant provisions of WTO law.

As regards rules of interpretation, Art. 3 (2) of the DSU[49] stipulates that the WTO legal texts must be interpreted in accordance with customary rules of interpretation of public international law. Such interpretation rules are contained in Art. 31 of the Vienna Convention on the Law of Treaties (VCLT), which forms part of customary law.[50] The main obligation contained in Art. 31 (1) of VCLT is that terms shall be interpreted in good faith in accordance with the ordinary meaning to be given to the terms of the treaty in their context and the light of the object and purpose of the treaty. Art. 31 (2) of the VCLT further provides that the context includes the full text, the Preamble, the Annexes and

46 Cf. Kimberley Process, https://www.kimberleyprocess.com/en/what-kp.

47 Cleveland, pp. 138 et seqq; see also Nadakavukaren Schefer, pp. 391–450.

48 The chapter will not examine whether regional and bilateral social clauses are compatible with WTO law since this question has to be solved under GATT Article XXIV, which provides exceptions for customs unions and free trade areas, and is therefore beyond the scope of this work.

49 The DSU applies to the central WTO agreements.

50 Jackson (The World Trading System), p. 121.

any mutually agreed interpretive language. Art. 31 (3) of the VCLT provides that account shall be taken of any subsequent practice or interpretations as well as relevant rules of international law applicable in the relations between the parties. Thus, before addressing the specific provisions, the object and purpose of the WTO will be shortly described. Moreover, the underlying economic rationale for the GATT will be explained.

When construing the different provisions of WTO law, the relevant WTO jurisprudence will be considered. It should be noted that adopted panel reports under the GATT CONTRACTING PARTIES and the WTO Dispute Settlement Body do not constitute a definitive interpretation, but create legitimate expectations among WTO members and should therefore be taken into account.[51] According to Art. XVI of the WTO Agreement and Art. 3.1 of the DSU, GATT practice has to be considered in dispute resolution.

In May 2003, the General Council of the WTO adopted a waiver with respect to those WTO obligations that are relevant for the WTO law compatibility of the Kimberley Process Certification Scheme.[52] In July 2018, the General Council approved the request for extending the waiver by another six years until December 2024.[53] However, due to its unique nature and its potential model character for future schemes, the WTO law compatibility of the Scheme will be examined, assuming there was no waiver.

As a final remark, it should be noted that goods made with child labour shall be all those parts, inputs or substances of which have been produced by children. Thus, the whole supply chain will be covered. Such an extensive definition can be justified using the principle of effective treaty interpretation in relation to international conventions prohibiting child labour.

2 The Rationale of the WTO and the GATT 1994

The international economic system is based on the theory of comparative advantage of David Ricardo.[54] This theory stipulates that a country has a comparative advantage in the production of a good if its opportunity costs are lower than those of others. These costs represent the optimal use of the resources of that country. Even if one country A can produce all goods in a model with less

51 *Japan–Alcoholic Beverages*, report of the Appellate Body, p. 14.

52 Decision of 15 May 2003, WT/L/518 (27 May 2003).

53 WTO General Council, Extension of Waiver Concerning Kimberley Process Certification Scheme for rough Diamonds, Waiver Decision, WT/L/1039.

54 *Japan–Alcoholic Beverages*, report of the Appellate Body, p. 17.

production costs than another country B, there is still a trade advantage for the two countries if the ratio of production costs of the two products compared differs.[55] In that case, country A will produce and trade the product where the difference in the production costs are higher, that is where its cost advantage is comparatively higher.[56] Hence, instead of producing all goods by themselves, countries should specialize in the production of the good in which it has a comparative advantage. As a result, economic efficiency and welfare is achieved if there is liberal trade with minimal governmental interference with trade flows. The theory of comparative advantage serves consumers as they have a greater choice in products at better prices.[57]

Accordingly, the primary goal of the GATT is the removal of trade barriers to the free movement of goods such as tariffs.[58] The Preamble of the GATT reads in part:

> Being desirous of contributing to these objectives by entering into reciprocal and mutually advantageous arrangements directed to the substantial reduction of tariffs and other barriers to trade and to the elimination of discriminatory treatment in international commerce.

Thus, the GATT essentially seeks to reduce trade barriers and avoid non-discriminatory treatment. As will be discussed below, besides tariff bindings, the two main obligations of the GATT are the non-discriminatory treatment obligations requiring equal treatment of foreign nations and prohibiting worse treatment of foreign goods than domestic goods. They both also serve the aim of liberal trade and economic efficiency. If governments apply trade barriers uniformly without regard for the origin of goods, the market system of goods allocation and production will have maximum effect.[59] The national treatment obligation pursues trade liberalization by seeking to reduce restrictions to imports.[60]

---

55 Ibid., p. 16.

56 That is if the United Kingdom can produce cars at 2 units production costs and radios at 5 whereas Portugal produces cars at 3 units of production costs and radios at 10, there will be trade benefits for both countries if Portugal trades cars where its disadvantage is comparatively less. Conversely, the United Kingdom will trade in radios where its trade advantage is comparatively high.

57 Jackson (The World Trading System), p. 17.

58 Ibid., p. 16.

59 Ibid., p. 159.

60 Ibid., p. 213.

It is however of most importance that trade liberalization is not the objective *per se* of the international economic system but a means to achieve general social and economic welfare taking into account non-economic goals. Accordingly, the Preamble to the Agreement Establishing the WTO reads in part:

> *Recognizing* that their relations in the field of trade and economic endeavour should be conducted with a view to raising standards of living, ensuring full employment and a large and steadily growing volume of real income and effective demand, and expanding the production of and trade in goods and services while allowing for the optimal use of the world's resources in accordance with the objective of sustainable development, seeking both to protect and preserve the environment and to enhance the means for doing so in a manner consistent with their respective needs and concerns at different levels of economic development,
>
> [...]
>
> *Being desirous* of contributing to these objectives by entering into reciprocal and mutually advantageous arrangements directed to the substantial reduction of tariffs and other barriers to trade and to the elimination of discriminatory treatment in international trade relations,
>
> *Resolved* therefore, to develop an integrated, more viable and durable multilateral trading system encompassing the General Agreement on Tariffs and Trade, the results of past trade liberalization efforts and all of the results of the Uruguay Round of Multilateral Trade Negotiations,
>
> *Determined* to preserve the basic principles and to further the objectives underlying this multilateral trading system.

Thus, trade liberalization has the objective of raising standards of living and allowing for the optimal use of the world's resources in accordance with the objective of sustainable development.

3 Trade Measures concerning Child Labour under the Most-Favoured-Nation Clause of GATT Article I

3.1 *Most-Favoured-Nation Obligations*

MFN obligations have been the central pillar of trade policy for centuries.[61] Such an obligation in a treaty between two states typically requires each of them to accord to the other state any advantage covered by the treaty that the

61 Jackson (The World Trading System), p. 157.

state accords to a third state. There are conditional and unconditional MFN obligations. In case of an unconditional clause, when state A grants a privilege to state C and has an MFN obligation to state B, it has to grant the same privilege to state B. In case of a conditional MFN, state A only has to grant the same privilege to B after B has accorded to A some reciprocal advantage. It has been found that unconditional MFN treatment is the most desirable policy for the world as a whole.[62] The GATT MFN clause is unconditional.

3.2 *The Relationship with the TBT Agreement*

The question arises how the MFN clause relates to the Agreement on Technical Barriers to Trade (TBT Agreement), which also regulates MFN and national treatment of products. According to the Appellate Body in *EC–Asbestos*, obligations under the Agreement on Technical Barriers to Trade (TBT Agreement)[63] and the national treatment obligation of GATT Art. III are cumulative.[64] In *EC–Asbestos*, the Appellate Body examined first the TBT Agreement before turning to GATT Art. III.[65] In *EC–Sardines*, the Appellate Body held that having found that the measure at issue was inconsistent with the TBT Agreement, GATT Art. III:4 did not need to be examined.[66] Accordingly, it is now well established in WTO jurisprudence that panels will scrutinize the measure at issue firstly under the TBT Agreement before examining their compliance with GATT provisions.[67] In some cases, they may exercise judicial economy when it comes to the GATT review. However, since one purpose of this study is to thoroughly assess the current interpretation of WTO rules, for reasons of clarity, the GATT provisions will be analysed firstly given that the WTO adjudicating bodies and legal literature very much draw on central findings and legal thinking made in relation to GATT provisions when interpreting the TBT Agreement.[68]

3.3 *The Scope of GATT Article I:1*

The basic MFN obligation is contained in GATT Art. I:1 and reads:

62 Davey/Pauwelyn, p. 16.

63 Agreement on Technical Barriers to Trade, 15 April 1994, WTO Agreement, Annex 1A, Results of the Uruguay Round of Multilateral Trade Negotiations: The Legal Texts, p. 138.

64 *EC–Asbestos*, report of the Appellate Body, para. 80.

65 Ibid., paras. 59 et seqq.

66 *EC–Sardines*, report of the Appellate Body, para. 313.

67 Cf. for example *US–COOL*, report of the Appellate Body; *US–Tuna II (Mexico)*, report of the Appellate Body; *EC–Seal Products*, report of the Appellate Body.

68 Cf. for example *US–Clove Cigarettes*, report of the Appellate Body.

General Most-Favoured-Nation Treatment

1. With respect to customs duties and charges of any kind imposed on or in connection with importation or exportation or imposed on the international transfer of payments for imports or exports, and with respect to the method of levying such duties and charges, and with respect to all rules and formalities in connection with importation and exportation, and with respect to all matters referred to in paragraph 2 and 4 of Article III, any advantage, favour, privilege or immunity granted by any Member to any product originating in or destined for any other country shall be accorded immediately and unconditionally to the like product originating in or destined for the territories of all other Members.

The Appellate Body in its report *Canada–Automotives* defined the object and purpose of GATT Art. I:1 to prohibit discrimination among like products originating in or destined for different countries.[69] Apart from supporting economic efficiency through the uniform application of trade barriers, it serves trade liberalization because trade concessions have to be generalized.[70] It also reduces transaction costs because it reduces the need for negotiation. GATT Art. I:1 requires equal treatment of any country with respect to imports and exports. It covers duties and charges, all rules and formalities related to importation and exportation and internal taxation and internal regulations of the type covered by GATT Art. III:4.

In *Canada–Automotives*, the Appellate Body stated that the prohibition of discrimination under GATT Art. I:1 included both *de iure* and *de facto* discrimination.[71] Thus, it also applies to measures that on their face, are origin-neutral.

Existing unilateral measures concerning child labour that may violate GATT Art. I:1. are for example the EU and US GSPs. The preferences granted depend *inter alia* on whether certain beneficial countries implement prohibitions of child labour. This could be *de iure* discriminatory treatment contrary to GATT Art. I:1 since tariff preferences are not granted to all countries alike. The EU and US GSPs are however supposed to be justified by the Enabling Clause. This issue will be dealt with below.

Another example for a measure that may involve a *de iure* violation of GATT Art. I:1 is the 2003 US Burmese Freedom and Democracy Act, which prohibits imports from Myanmar.[72] The UFLPA directly addressing the Uyghur region

69 *Canada–Automotives*, report of the Appellate Body, para. 84; WTO Analytical Index, p. 138.

70 Jackson (The World Trading System), p. 161.

71 WTO Analytical Index, p. 138; *Canada–Automotives*, report of the Appellate Body, para. 78.

72 Burmese Freedom and Democracy Act, Public 108–61, 108th Congress, 28 July 2003, H. R. 2330.

in China could also be a *de iure* discrimination. The US ban on goods made with forced or indentured child labour and the proposed EU Forced Labour Regulation could be a *de facto* violation of GATT Art. I:1 since forced child labour occurs only in some exporting states, which could therefore be discriminated against. The same holds true for the Belgian Social Label Law since companies supplying from countries where child labour prevails may be disadvantaged. Finally, the Kimberley Process Certification Scheme may violate the MFN clause since diamonds from participant countries are treated more favourably than diamonds from non-participant countries.[73]

Considering that the Scheme provides for a total ban, the question arises however whether GATT Art. I or GATT Art. XI, prohibiting quantitative restrictions, applies. Likewise, it is questionable whether the US Burmese Freedom and Democracy Act of 2003 imposing a general ban on products coming from Myanmar constitutes a violation of GATT Art. I:1.

However, where a ban is the corollary of internal measures applying to the like domestic products, it can be argued that by applying Note *Ad* Article III, the ban can be regarded as an internal measure within the meaning of GATT Art. III:4.[74] Applying to internal measures as defined by GATT Art. III:4, GATT Art. I:1 would be applicable. The relationship between GATT Art. III and XI and the meaning of the Note *Ad* to GATT Art. III have been subject of lengthy debate among scholars and been analysed by several GATT and WTO panels.[75]

The ban provided for by the US Burmese Freedom and Democracy Act can be qualified as a political sanction or countermeasure directed at imports from Myanmar rather than the corollary of an internal measure. Hence, GATT Art. XI applies. The same holds true for the UFLPAagainst Xinjiang, China. By contrast, the bans provided for under the Kimberley Process Certification Scheme are intended to make the certification scheme effective. They can therefore be regarded as internal measures within the meaning of GATT Art. I read in conjunction with GATT Art. III:4.

The US ban on products made with forced or indentured child labour can be regarded as a corollary of the domestic prohibition of forced child labour and thus comes within the scope of GATT Art. I:1. The US measure could therefore

73 According to Section III (c) of the Kimberley Process Certificate, participants shall import no shipment from non-participants.

74 *EC–Asbestos*, report of the panel, para. 8.90 et seq.; For an extensive discussion of the problem see below p. 61.

75 See for example *EC–Asbestos*, report of the panel, para. 8.90 et seq.; *US–Tuna I*, report of the panel, paras. 5.8–5.19.

be a *de facto* violation of GATT Art. III:4 in conjunction with GATT Art. I:1. The same holds true for the proposed EU Forced Labour Regulation.

3.4 *Like Products*

GATT Art. I:1 requires equal treatment of foreign products that are 'like'. Thus, if carpets made with child labour are unlike carpets not made with child labour, a ban on goods made with child labour such as the US ban on goods made with forced or indentured child labour will not discriminate *de facto* against goods from countries where the occurrence of child labour is high, e.g. India. The same holds true for the Belgian Social Label Law. If products made with child labour and products made not with child labour are not 'like products', a label 'child labour free' cannot be said to distinguish between 'like products'. The central question for most trade measures on child labour is therefore what the meaning of the word 'like' is. In case of national bans under the Kimberley Process Certification Scheme however, such question is not central since the distinction between diamonds is made on the country of origin, i.e. whether or not they participate in the Scheme. In the other cases, one differentiates between products made with child labour and products not made with child labour and thus draws a distinction between products on the basis of their process and production method not related to the physical qualities of a product. This issue is commonly referred to as 'ppm-distinction'[76] or 'process-product' doctrine whereby (npr)ppm-measures are regarded as *prima facie* GATT-illegal.[77] Since most cases on the 'process-product' doctrine have arisen under the national treatment clause of GATT Art. III, this issue will be dealt with when examining GATT Art. III. In this section, the concept of 'like products' as applied under GATT Art. I:1 will be examined with a view to determine possible differences to the like product concept in GATT Art. III. The case law on GATT Art. III with regard to concept of 'like products' and the ppm-debate will inform GATT Art. I.[78]

The Appellate Body in *Japan–Alcoholic Beverages* stated that the concept of likeness was a relative one that evoked the image of an accordion:

76 Jackson (Comments on Shrimp/Turtle), pp. 303–307.

77 Hudec (The Product-Process Distinction), p. 187 uses this term for describing a doctrine the effect of which was to make it *prima facie* GATT-illegal for governments to impose tax or regulatory disadvantages on imported products because of the way they were produced. The term will be used in the same sense in this work; For the definition and differentiation between ppms and npr-ppms, see also above, p. 17.

78 Cf. Van den Bossche/Zdouc, p. 351, who also deal with this issue under GATT Art. III.

> The accordion of likeness stretches and squeezes in different places as different provisions of the WTO Agreement are applied. The width of the accordion in any one of those places must be determined by the particular provision in which the term "like" is encountered as well as by the content and circumstances that prevail in any given case to which that provisions may apply.[79]

Hence, different readings of the word 'like' under GATT Art. I:1 and III are possible. Moreover, the meaning of the word 'like' may be determined on a case-by-case basis. What are the criteria then that have been used to identify products as like under GATT Art. I:1, and are they completely different from those applied under GATT Art. III? Most GATT and WTO legal rulings start with citing the report of the Working Party of 1970, which reads:

> Some criteria were suggested for determining, on a case-by-case basis, whether a product is "similar": the product's end uses in a given market; consumers' tastes and habits, which change from country to country, the product's properties, nature, and quality.[80]

These criteria refer both to competitive arguments as well as to physical characteristics. However, they are merely 'suggestions' and not an authoritative interpretation.

Regarding tariffs, panels have used different tariff classifications to determine whether products are unlike. In the panel report *Germany–Sardines*, the panel held that Germany was allowed to lower its tariffs on sardines without lowering its tariffs on sprats and herrings, which were in different tariff classifications.[81] By contrast, in another case, Spain was not allowed to differentiate between different types of coffee beans for tariff purposes.[82] The panel held that unroasted coffee was unroasted coffee.[83] In another case, the panel held that so-called dimension lumber was not necessarily like dimension lumber from another country, and that Japan was allowed to impose different tariffs on different species of lumber.[84] In the panel's view, GATT Art. I:1 allowed for

79 *Japan–Alcoholic Beverages*, report of the Appellate Body, p. 21.

80 Working Party Report on *Border Tax Adjustments*, adopted on 2 December 1970, BISD 18 S/97 (1971), para. 18.

81 *Germany–Sardines*, report of the panel.

82 *Spain–Unroasted Coffee*, report of the panel, para. 4.3.

83 Ibid.

84 *Japan–Lumber*, report of the panel, paras. 5.14–5.16.

rather fine tariff classifications. Specifically, it stated that tariff differentiation was a legitimate tool for a party to pursue its interest, 'comprising both its protection needs and its requirements for the purposes of tariff-and trade-negotiations'.[85] While not explicitly relying on arguments related to the different physical characteristics of different species of lumber, the panel seemed to be in favour of them.

Except for the case *Spain–Unroasted Coffee*, these rulings seem to suggest that under GATT Art. I, countries may legitimately draw rather fine distinctions between products related to physical characteristics to protect their national interests. The policy goal of GATT Art. I:1 with regard to tariffs supports this view. While pursuing a non-discrimination policy, GATT Art. I:1 does not aim at a complete elimination of tariffs.[86] Instead, it allows governments to maintain tariffs, that is a certain degree of market distortion.[87]

MFN-treatment under GATT Art. I:1 needs to be reconciled with the goal of promoting trade liberalization on the basis of the political principle of reciprocity – that is that governments only lower their tariffs when other governments also lower their tariffs.[88] If MFN-treatment was extended to 'free-riders' that do not pay for the advantages granted to them, they would receive unreciprocated benefits. Thus, there is a common understanding between governments that fine product distinctions are allowed to discriminate against 'free-riders'.[89] However, countries are not allowed to discriminate against other countries by name.[90] In *Spain–Unroasted Coffee*, it was held that the Spanish tariff classification had an origin-based discriminatory purpose that was contrary to reciprocity demands.[91]

However, in *EEC–Beef*, the panel concluded that consideration concerning the balance of concessions could not change the finding that GATT Art. II:1 concerning bound tariffs had been violated by the EEC treating beef from Canada less favourably than beef from the US.[92] Although in this case, Canada was a free-rider benefiting from the tariff concession made by the EEC to the US, the panel did not allow for the discrimination against Canada. Thus, although it seems justifiable that governments discriminate against countries that are

85 Ibid., para. 5.10.
86 Hudec (Like Product), p. 108.
87 Ibid.
88 Ibid., p. 109.
89 Ibid.; Jackson (The World Trading System), p. 160.
90 Hudec (Like Product), p. 109.
91 Ibid.
92 *EEC–Beef*, report of the panel, para. 4.6.

free-riders on the basis of fine product distinctions in case of tariffs, the case-law is not coherent with regard to the application of the principle of reciprocity. In this case however, a possible reason why the panel did not consider the question of balance of payments could be that the measure in question was so specific that only meat from the US could meet the requirements.

The *EEC–Beef* case at least seems to suggest that differences in method of manufacture are a possible basis for defining tariff classifications of products. The measure in question allowed for a tariff quota for meat from cattle at a certain age and fed in a certain way, for which a certain certificate had been issued.[93] The panel did not question the possibility to rely on production methods as a basis for tariff differentiations but the fact that only a specific US agency could issue the required certificate.

Regarding internal measures as defined in GATT Art. I:1 in conjunction with GATT Art. III:4, two cases deal explicitly with the definition of 'like products'; i.e. *Australia–Ammonium Sulphate*[94] and *EC–Animal Fee Proteins*.[95] They both rely on physical characteristics as well as tariff classifications in other countries. The underlying idea apparently was that as long as other countries have the same tariff classification, protective and discriminatory purposes are less likely.[96]

Some authors have been suggested that the definition of 'like products' should be given a broader interpretation, i.e. not referring to such detailed production methods as in the case of cattle in *EC–Animal Fee Proteins* described above, when applied to internal measures – that is taxes and internal regulations – than when applied to tariffs.[97] The policy behind GATT Art. III:2 referring to taxes and GATT Art. III:4 referring to internal regulations is the elimination of discrimination between foreign and domestic products. In contrast to tariffs, there is no reason to allow for a certain degree of market distortion.[98] The principle of reciprocity inherent in tariff negotiations, which could justify a certain degree of market distortion such as in the case of *EC–Animal Fee Proteins*, has no relevance in relation to internal measures under the national treatment clause of GATT Art. III. The same holds true for internal measures with regard to MFN treatment.[99] Thus, in relation to internal

93 *EEC–Beef*, report of the panel, paras. 2.4 and 2.5.

94 *Australia–Ammonium Sulphate*, report of the Working Party.

95 *EC–Animal Fee Proteins*, report of the panel.

96 Hudec (Like Product), p. 118.

97 Ibid., p. 112; Hanoitis, p. 417.

98 Hudec (Like Product), p. 108.

99 Ibid.

measures coming under GATT Art. I:1 and GATT Art. III,[100] the narrow interpretation of 'like products' used in case of tariffs, as for example in the case of *EC–Animal Fee Proteins,* does not apply. However, this does not mean that the term 'like products' with regard to internal regulations necessarily needs to be interpreted in exactly the same way under GATT Art. I:1 and GATT Art. III. GATT Art. III:2 concerning fiscal measures differentiates between the term 'like products' and 'directly competitive or substitutable products'. Therefore, one has to decide whether the term 'like products' of GATT Art. I:1 only refers to 'like products' in a possibly rather narrow sense or also includes 'directly competitive or substitutable products'. Since the main reason for interpreting 'like products' under GATT Art. III:2 in a rather narrow sense is the existence of the term 'directly competitive or substitutable products',[101] there is no reason for excluding this type of products from the scope of GATT Art. I:1.

In sum, the definition of 'like products' with regard to tariffs contained in GATT Art. I:1 may differ from the one used in GATT Art. III. Although the case law is not coherent, most cases allow for a rather narrow interpretation. However, this conclusion does not seem to have a bearing on the question whether in general, npr-ppm-distinctions are allowed under GATT Art. I. If the outcome of the analysis under GATT Art. III is that npr-ppm-distinctions are not allowed, it does not seem likely that product distinctions related to child labour may be legitimate under GATT Art. I:1 with regard to tariffs. The principle of reciprocity – even if accepted as a justification for otherwise illegitimate product distinctions such as production methods with regard to cattle – is not an appropriate basis on which to allow for npr-ppm-distinctions.

3.5 *Any Advantage*

The Appellate Body in the report *EC–Bananas III* gives a broad meaning to the term 'advantage'.[102] In *Canada–Automotives*, it is made clear that GATT Art. I:1 referred to 'any advantage given to any product'.[103]

However, the question is whether an advantage is only accorded where most – not only some – imported products from one WTO member are better treated than products from another WTO member. Some authors argue that some proof is needed that a disadvantaged product is imported far more

100 Davey/Pauwelyn, p. 35.

101 This issue will be extensively dealt with under GATT Art. III, pp. 55 et seqq; see also Davey/Pauwelyn, p. 35.

102 *EC–Bananas III*, report of the Appellate Body, para. 206, cited in WTO Analytical Index, p. 139.

103 *Canada–Automotives*, report of the Appellate Body, para. 79; WTO Analytical Index, p. 139.

frequently from the complaining WTO member than from another WTO member, which thus *de facto* receives an advantage.[104] These arguments relate to the discussion of a necessary 'asymmetric impact' of origin-neutral measures under the equal treatment obligation of GATT Art. III and will be further discussed there.[105] Therefore, the question what exactly the term 'advantage' means will also be postponed.

The remaining question here is whether an 'asymmetric impact' is required also in case of *de iure* distinctions. In relation to GATT Art. III, it has been stated by the WTO adjudicating bodies that a formal separation, in and of itself, does not necessarily compel the conclusion that the treatment to the foreign product is less favourable than the treatment accorded to the domestic product and thus in violation of GATT Art. III.[106] Since there is no reason why cases under GATT Art. I should be resolved differently, this reasoning most likely also applies to GATT Art. I.

Most of the relevant trade measures on child labour involving a *de iure* distinction and falling under GATT Art. I will have a discriminatory effect. For example, national bans on products stemming from non-participants under the Kimberley Process Certification Scheme put products from non-participants at a disadvantage since they may not be imported. The withdrawal of trade advantages accorded to Myanmar by the EC also placed Myanmar at a disadvantage.

3.6 *Immediately and Unconditionally*

GATT Art. I:1 stipulates that advantages have to be granted 'immediately and unconditionally' to like products from all other WTO members. The question is what exactly the term 'conditionally' means and whether any condition attached to an advantage is *per se* in violation of GATT Art. I:1. The answer to this question should provide an indication of whether npr-ppm-distinctions are allowed under GATT Art. I:1 and potentially under GATT Art. III. If this term is understood as meaning that conditions related to the process and production methods cannot be attached to an advantage conferred upon WTO members, no such distinction should be allowed to make between otherwise 'like products'. And *vice versa*, if conditions not directly related to products characteristics may be attached to advantages conferred to one country, it should be permitted to distinguish between products on the basis of their process and

104 Davey/Pauwelyn, p. 40.

105 See below p. 167.

106 *Korea–Beef*, report of the Appellate Body, para. 144.

production methods under GATT Art. I and III. A closer look at GATT and WTO jurisprudence will help to answer this question.

3.6.1 GATT and WTO Jurisprudence

The panel and Appellate Body have dealt in several cases with conditions not directly related to the product.

The *Belgian Family Allowances* case involved a tax on imported goods, which granted exemptions to goods from countries with a similar system of family allowances to the Belgian system.[107] The background of the law was that in Belgium, the system of family allowances was financed by a tax on Belgian employers. The panel found that the Belgian legislation introduced discrimination between countries that have a similar system of family allowances and those having a different system or no system at all, thereby making the granting of the tax exemption dependent on certain conditions. Accordingly, it found a violation of GATT Art. I and possibly GATT Art. III:2.[108] Being one of the earliest cases, it is a weak legal ruling, not defining what conditions are GATT-inconsistent. However, since the tax clearly discriminated on the basis of origin referring to the legal system in different countries, the panel might not have considered this as necessary.[109]

As mentioned above, the panel in *EEC–Beef*, had to deal with a tariff quota adopted by the EEC for meat from cattle at a certain age and raised under certain conditions, which also had to be accompanied by a certain certificate issued by an agency listed in an annex. The panel found that since the only authorized agency to issue the certificate was the USDA (US Department of Agriculture), the EEC measure in fact violated GATT Art. I:1.[110] The EEC regulation also stated that beef graded USDA 'choice' or 'prime' automatically met the requirements of the tariff quota.[111] The panel found that the latter provision could constitute an advantage accorded to the US, but that only the practical application could make the provision inconsistent with GATT Art. I:1.[112] It concluded that the EEC measure and its annex violated GATT Art. I:1.[113] It is noteworthy that the panel did not automatically qualify the detailed conditions

107 *Belgian Family Allowances*, report of the panel.

108 Ibid., para. 8.

109 For a detailed discussion of the case see Hudec (Essays on the Nature of International Trade Law), pp. 41 et seqq.

110 *EEC–Beef*, report of the panel, para. 4.2 (a).

111 *EEC–Beef*, report of the panel, paras. 2.4 and 2.5.

112 Ibid., para. 4.2 (b).

113 Ibid., paras. 4.2 and 4.3.

for the application of the tariff quota to imported beef provided for in the EEC measure as being inconsistent with GATT Art. I:1. Instead, in reaching its conclusion, it referred to the fact that overall, the application of these conditions would in effect deny like products of other origin than the US access to the EEC market. Thus, according to this case, to impose conditions is not *per se* contrary to GATT Art. I:1.

In *Indonesia–Automobile Industry*, advantages depended on whether an Indonesian company had made a deal with Korean companies to produce a National Car, or on the level of local content of motor vehicles, or on whether a motor vehicle was a National Car (under the Indonesian National Car Programme) and had complied with certain local content requirements or had incorporated a certain percentage of 'counter-purchased' parts and components exported from Indonesia.[114] After having found that National Cars and the parts and components thereof imported to Indonesia from Korea are to be considered 'like' other similar motor vehicles and parts and components imported from other members,[115] the panel stated explicitly:

> The existence of these conditions is inconsistent with the provisions of GATT Art. I:1 which provides that tax and customs duty advantages accorded to products of one Member (here on Korean products) be accorded to imported like products from other Members "immediately and unconditionally". For the reasons discussed above, we consider that the June 1996 car programme which introduced discrimination between imports in the allocation of tax and customs duty benefits based on various conditions and other criteria not related to the imports themselves and the February car programme which also introduce discrimination between imports in the allocation of customs duty benefits based on various conditions and other criteria not related to the imports themselves, are inconsistent with Art. I of GATT.[116]

In *Canada–Automotives*, the panel had to rule on advantages accorded to motor vehicles if imported by importers who met certain conditions.[117] Specifically, the manufacturer's local production of motor vehicles had to achieve a minimum amount of Canadian value added, and its local production had to maintain a minimum ratio ('production-to-sales' ration) with respect to its sales

114 *Indonesia–Automobile Industry*, report of the panel.
115 Ibid., para. 14.142.
116 *Indonesia–Automobile Industry*, report of the panel, paras. 14.146–14.147.
117 *Canada–Automotive Industry*, report of the panel, paras. 2.1–2.35.

of motor vehicles in Canada.[118] In 1989, the list of eligible manufacturers was closed. The European Communities and Japan argued that the limitation of the eligibility for the advantage to certain manufacturers constituted *de facto* discrimination inconsistent with GATT Art. I:1.[119] Japan argued that, by making the import duty exemption conditional upon criteria that were unrelated to the imported product itself, Canada failed to accord the import duty exemption immediately and unconditionally to like products originating in all WTO members.[120] Canada argued that GATT Art. I:1 only prohibited conditions related to the national origin of the imported product. Thus, she was entitled to treat products differently so long as the distinction in treatment was based on criteria other than national origin.[121] To rule otherwise would be contrary to GATT Art. II, which provides for tariff bindings subject to conditions or qualifications.[122] GATT Art. I would contain no prohibition of origin-neutral measures.[123]

The panel stated that there was a difference between the situation where an advantage, which has been granted to country A, was extended to all other WTO members 'unconditionally', and the situation where an advantage was accorded to other WTO members subject to conditions.[124] It held that whether an advantage was accorded 'unconditionally' could not be determined independently of an examination of whether it involved discrimination between like products of different countries.[125] Specifically, this means that subjecting an advantage to conditions not related to the product is not *per se* inconsistent with GATT Art. I:1.[126] Rather, whether the conditions attached to the advantage cause a violation of GATT Art. I:1 depends upon whether or not such conditions discriminate with respect to the origin of products.[127] Specifically, the obligation to accord 'unconditionally' to third countries, which are WTO members, an advantage that has been granted to any other country means that the extension of that advantage may not be made subject to conditions with respect to the situation or conduct of those countries.[128] Regarding the

118 Ibid., para. 2.2.
119 Ibid., para. 10.17.
120 Ibid., para. 10.18.
121 Ibid., para. 10.20.
122 Ibid.
123 Ibid., para. 10.24.
124 Ibid.
125 Ibid., para. 10.22; this passage was not reviewed by the Appellate Body Report.
126 Ibid., para. 10.29.
127 Ibid., para. 10.20.
128 Ibid., para. 10.23.

report of the panel in *Indonesia–Automobile Industry*, the panel held that the statement on conditions not related to products themselves had to be seen in the context of the specific conditions in that case, which entailed different treatment of like products depending upon their origin.[129] As to the Canadian measures, the panel noted that the advantages were confined to certain manufacturers that were present in Canada in a certain base year and met certain performance requirements.[130] Because of the existing intra-firm trade, benefiting imports would tend to originate from countries where benefiting importers have links of ownerships or control with producing companies.[131] Thus, the panel found that the import duty exemption on motor vehicles entailed a distinction between exporting countries depending upon whether or not producers in such countries were related to eligible manufacturers.[132] It concluded that in the context of intra-firm trade, the limitation of the availability of the import duty exemption to certain manufacturers discriminated regarding the origin of products.[133] Contrary to the argument of Canada, that discrimination did not result from the commercial decisions of importers but from the limitation of the number of eligible importers in the context of intra-firm trade.[134] Accordingly, GATT Art. I:1 was violated.

The Appellate Body followed the panel holding that the Canadian measure did not accord the same duty exemption 'immediately' and 'unconditionally' to like motor vehicles of *all* other members, as required by GATT Art. I:1.[135] It did not specifically comment on the statement of the panel that taxes that were conditioned upon criteria not related to the product itself would not be *per se* inconsistent with GATT Art. I. Rather it underlined that the object and purpose was to prohibit discrimination among like products originating in or destined for different countries.[136]

In *US–Certain EC Products*, the US increased the bonding requirements on imports from the European Communities in order to ensure payment of additional import duties.[137] The panel in this case found that the regulatory distinction did not depend on any characteristics of the product but exclusively

---

129 Ibid., para. 10.28.

130 Ibid., para. 10.41.

131 Ibid., para. 10.45.

132 Ibid., para. 10.46.

133 Ibid.

134 Ibid.

135 *Canada–Automotive Industry*, report of the Appellate Body, para. 85.

136 Ibid., para. 84.

137 *US–Certain EC Products*, report of the panel, cited in WTO Analytical Index, p. 144.

on the origin of the product and targeted exclusively some imports from the European Communities.[138]

Finally, in *EC–Tariff Preferences*, the panel held that the term 'unconditionally' had a broader meaning than simply that of not requiring compensation for the advantage granted to another WTO member.[139] Instead, it found that the term should be understood in its ordinary meaning, i.e. 'not limited by or subject to any conditions'.[140] It concluded that the Drug Arrangements of the EU GSP according privileges to beneficiary developing countries with a certain drug problem were contrary to GATT Art. I:1. This case does not give a definite answer on how to understand the term 'unconditionally'. On the one hand, it suggests that any conditioning of advantages should be prohibited but on the other hand, one should note that the conditions in question referred to the situation of certain countries, namely those with a drug problem. That is, the conditions referred to discriminated with respect to origin (disadvantaging products from countries not having a drug problem). Hence, one could conclude that conditions that do not necessarily relate to the situation of certain countries might have been allowed.

Moreover, the panels in *Colombia–Ports of Entry* and in *US–Poultry* (*China*) again referred to *Canada–Automotives* stating that conditions attached to an advantage granted will only violate GATT Art. I:1 if they discriminate with respect to the origin of products.[141]

In sum, GATT and WTO jurisprudence on conditionality in MFN clauses seems to suggest that conditions not related to the products themselves are allowed as long as they do not refer to the situation or conduct of countries and discriminate with respect to the origin of products. Hence, npr-ppm-measures are not *prima facie* illegal under the term 'unconditionally' within the meaning of GATT Art. I:1 because they may or may not discriminate with respect to origin. The same could hold true in relation to the concept of 'like product'.

3.6.2 Trade Measures on Child Labour

In the light of the foregoing, the question is whether trade measures concerning child labour discriminate with respect to the origin of products.

138 *US–Certain EC Products*, report of the panel, para. 6.54 cited in WTO Analytical Index, p. 144.

139 *EC–Tariff Preferences*, report of the panel, para. 7.59.

140 Ibid.

141 *Colombia–Ports of Entry*, report of the panel, paras. 7.362–7.366; *US–Poultry* (*China*), report of the panel, paras. 7.437–7.440.

US and EU GSPs grant tariff reductions to certain developing countries. They accord 'advantages' that are not given to other WTO members not being classified as a beneficiary developing country. Since these advantages are simply not available for developed countries, GSPs violate GATT Art. I:1 on their face. However, as will be discussed later, such schemes have been allowed under the so-called Enabling Clause.

The special incentive arrangement for sustainable development and good governance of the EU GSP, the so-called EU GSP + scheme, providing further preferences for countries that have ratified and implemented core human rights and labour rights conventions as well as other sustainable development conventions, could also be said to infringe GATT Art. I:1 because it attaches certain non-trade-conditions to the granting of trade preferences.

In a similar vein, the US GSP law stipulates that developing countries that have not implemented their commitments to eliminate worst forms of child labour are not eligible.[142] Thus, the US scheme also attaches non-trade conditions referring to national law and policy to trade preferences, thereby possibly violating GATT Art. I:1.

Applying the rationale contained in the panel reports above, especially in *Belgian Family Allowances*, *Canada–Automotives* and *EC–Tariff Preferences*, the question is whether the application of such conditions amount to discrimination with respect to the origin of products. Since the conditions in question refer to the situation or conduct of countries, namely to national labour laws and policies, both schemes constitute a *de facto* discrimination based on the origin of products and thus a violation of GATT Art. I:1.

Bans under the Kimberley Process Certification Scheme relate to the legal situation of a country, namely whether it is a participant or not of the certification scheme. Such national measures are therefore contrary to GATT Art. I:1.

The question is whether the proposed EU Forced Labour Regulation or the US ban on products made with forced or indentured child labour or other tariff reductions on products not made with child labour are granted 'unconditionally' within the meaning of GATT Art. I:1. Such measures are origin-neutral and relate to the producer or the production method, a characteristic not related to the product itself. They do not on their face relate to the situation or conduct of countries. Thus, one could conclude that the condition of not using child labour does not involve discrimination based on the origin of products. However, the question whether the criterion of child labour *de facto* relates to the origin of products. For example, in Asia, 6.0 per cent of all children are

142 19 Unites StatesC. sec. 2462 (b) (2) (H).

caught in child labour whereas in other regions such as Europe, no child labour has been found.[143] Thus, the US ban would treat products from India worse than for example products from the EU and is therefore likely to be contrary to GATT Art. I.

However, as described above, in some sectors child labour has diminished greatly, for example in the export textile sector in Cambodia due to ILO and other programmes.[144] Thus, some producers might nowadays be able to change from child labourers to adult workers. How this factor should be taken into account and how to evaluate reasons for detrimental trade effects will be explored under the equal treatment obligation of GATT Art. III:4. The result of this analysis will then be applied to GATT Art. I. For the moment it suffices to state that trade measures on child labour such the US ban on goods made with child labour are likely to impose GATT Art. I:1-inconsistent conditions on MFN clauses. The same holds true for the Belgian Social Label Law and the proposed EU Forced Labour Regulation.

3.7 *Exceptions under the Enabling Clause*

As mentioned above, the EU and US GSP would in theory violate GATT Art. I:1 because they grant tariff preferences to certain developing countries that they do not extend to other WTO members. In order to remedy this situation, the so-called 'Enabling Clause' was adopted at the end of the Tokyo Round allowing developed countries to grant tariff preferences to developing countries.[145] It replaced a waiver of 1971.[146] As mentioned above, under the US GSP, a beneficiary country is ineligible if such country has not implemented its commitments to eliminate the worst forms of child labour. Under the EU GSP, in addition to preferential tariff treatment, beneficiary developing countries may be granted further preferences if they have implemented, *inter alia*, the ILO Conventions relating to child labour. Both sets of conditionalities have been said to be contrary to GATT Art. I:1.

To what extend the Enabling Clause allows GSP granting countries to attach non-trade conditions to the granting of tariff preferences has been decided by the Appellate Body report *EC–Tariff Preferences*.[147] In this case, India had brought a claim before the panel that the Drug Arrangements under the

---

143 ILO/UNICEF (Child Labour, Global Estimates of 2020), p. 12.

144 See Humbert (The Challenge of Child Labour), p. 252.

145 Davey/Pauwelyn, p. 24.

146 GATT CONTRACRING PARTIES, Generalized System of Preferences, Decision of 25 June 1971, BISD 18S/24 (1972).

147 *EC–Tariff Preferences*, report of the Appellate Body.

corresponding EU GSP were contrary to GATT Art. I:1 and paragraphs 2(a), 3(a) and 3(c) of the Enabling Clause.[148] The following sections will focus on two controversial issues discussed in the Appellate Body report: the relationship between the Enabling Clause and GATT Art. I:1 and the term 'non-discrimination' in the Enabling Clause.

3.7.1 The Relationship between the Enabling Clause and GATT Art. I:1

The Enabling Clause reads in part:[149]

> Differential and More Favourable Treatment, Reciprocity and Fuller Participation of Developing Countries
>
> [...]
>
> 1. Notwithstanding the provisions of Article I of the General Agreement, Contracting Partiesmay accord differential and more favourable treatment to developing countries without according such treatment to other Contracting Parties [footnote omitted].
> 2. The provisions of paragraph 1 apply to the following [footnote omitted]:
>   a) Preferential tariff treatment accorded by developed Contracting Partiesto products originating in developing countries in accordance with the Generalized System of Preferences[3].
>
>   [...]
>
>   d) Special treatment of the least developed among the developing countries in the context of any general or specific measures in favour of developing countries.
> 3. Any differential and more favourable treatment provided under this clause:
>   a) shall be designed to facilitate and promote the trade of developing countries and not to raise barriers to or create undue difficulties for the trade of any other contracting parties.
>   b) [...]
>   c) Any differential and more favourable treatment provided under this clause shall be designed and, if necessary modified,

148 *EC–Tariff Preferences*, Request for Consultations by India, WT/DS246/1/G/L/521, 12 March 2002.

149 GATT CONTRACTING PARTIES, Decision of 28 November 1979, 'Differential and More Favourable Treatment, Reciprocity and Fuller Participation of Developing Countries', BISD, 26/203 (1980).

> to respond positively to the development, financial and trade needs of developing countries.
>
> 3 (footnote original) As described in the Decision of the CONTRACTING PARTIES of June 25 1971, relating to the establishment of 'generalised, non-reciprocal and non-discriminatory preferences beneficial to the developing countries' (BISD 18/S/24).

The Enabling Clause is an integral part of the GATT 1994.[150] The first main interpretational question with regard to the Enabling Clause is whether it constitutes an exception to the GATT or whether it applies independently, which would have consequences for the allocation of burden of proof. In *EC–Tariff Preferences*, the panel found that the Drug Arrangements of the EU GSP violated GATT Art. I:1 and were not justified by either the Enabling Clause or GATT Art. XX (b). Specifically, it held that the Enabling Clause had to be qualified as an exception, which required that identical tariff preferences had to be provided to all developing countries.[151]

On appeal, the EU was of the view that the Enabling Clause was part of 'a special regime for developing countries' that 'encourages' the granting of tariff preferences by developed countries to developing countries.[152] In its opinion, it existed on an equal footing with GATT Art. I:1, excluding the application thereof. Similarly, the dissenting panel member referred to the Latin origins of the word 'notwithstanding', which means 'despite the law', not an exception to the law.[153] Bartels equally held that a good case could be made that the Enabling Clause rather should be seen as an 'autonomous right' entitling a WTO member to provide preferential tariff treatment to developing countries.[154] In the same vein, Howse maintains that 'GSP operates "notwithstanding" Article I entirely'.[155]

The Appellate Body upheld the panel's view that the Enabling Clause was to be considered an exception. It argued that while the Clause had a critical role in encouraging the granting of special and differential treatment to developing WTO members, this would not on its own contradict the classification of the Enabling Clause as an exception.[156] It also held that the term 'notwithstanding'

150 *EC–Tariff Preferences*, report of the Appellate Body, para. 90.
151 *EC–Tariff Preferences*, report of the panel, para. 7.177.
152 *EC–Tariff Preferences*, report of the Appellate Body, para. 85.
153 *EC–Tariff Preferences*, report of the panel, para. 9.13.
154 Bartels (The WTO Enabling Clause), p. 518.
155 Howse (India's WTO Challenge), p. 390.
156 *EC–Tariff Preferences*, report of the Appellate Body, para. 98.

meant 'in spite of' and could be understood as referring to an exception.[157] It finally stated that the Enabling Clause did not exclude the applicability of GATT Art. I:1 but applied concurrently and took precedence to the extent of a conflict between the two provisions.[158]

In the light of the resulting allocation of burden of proof obliging the EU to submit sufficient evidence to prove that its own Drug Arrangements comply with the Enabling Clause, the view taken by the Appellate Body is acceptable.

3.7.2 The Term 'Non-discrimination' in the Enabling Clause

The second major issue regarding the application of the Clause concerns the term 'non-discrimination' in footnote 3 to paragraph 2 a) of the Enabling Clause.

In *EC–Tariff Preferences*, the Appellate Body did not consider the question whether the rules on the eligibility as a beneficiary were consistent with the Enabling Clause.[159] Instead, it limited its analysis to the question whether they were allowed to impose non-trade conditions on beneficiary countries.[160] Since the focus of this chapter is the compatibility of trade measures on child labour with WTO law, the issues of graduation and differentiation between developing countries according to their level of development will not be discussed here.[161] However, it will be touched upon later in this work when assessing whether the traditional view on international economic law is still adequate.

While the EU did not appeal the panel's view that under the Enabling Clause, a GSP must be generalized, non-discriminatory and non-reciprocal, other commentators are of the view that in contrast to creating binding legal obligations, the Enabling Clause is of an aspirational nature.[162] The US pointed to the language of footnote 3 to the Clause and stated that the words 'as described' simply are a cross reference rather than imposing obligations.[163] This argument is not convincing. The fact that the footnote is a cross reference to the GSP Decision of 1971 does not reveal anything about the legal nature of the Enabling Clause. In this sense, it has been argued that the aspiration

157 Ibid., para. 90.

158 Ibid., para. 102.

159 Ibid., paras. 128 and 129.

160 *EC–Tariff Preferences*, report of the Appellate Body, para. 129.

161 For a critique of unilaterally applied graduation rules, see Cottier (From Progressive Liberalization to Progressive Regulation in WTO Law), p. 782.

162 Third Party Submission of the US, *EC–Tariff Preferences*, report of the Appellate Body, para. 75; Howse (India's WTO Challenge), p. 394 et seq.

163 Third Party Submission of the US, *EC–Tariff Preferences*, report of the Appellate Body, para. 75.

contained in the 1971 Waiver that developed GATT CONTRACTING PARTIES will extend on a more general basis preferential tariff treatment contained in the Waiver, indicated that the Enabling Clause had the effect of converting what before was merely aspirational language into a binding condition.[164] Howse, by contrast, argues that preferential tariff treatment under GSP was never meant to be based on legal obligations referring to the relevant UNCTAD instruments and the Doha Decision on Implementation in 2001.[165] However, WTO member practice suggests the contrary. The EU as well as the US in several statements confirmed the view that they considered the criteria referred to in the Enabling Clause as obligatory.[166] The Appellate Body equally qualified the Enabling Clause as imposing legal obligations referring to the French and Spanish texts of the Enabling Clause, which use the words 'as defined' rather than 'as described'.[167] In the light of the foregoing and with a view to the conformity and predictability of all existing and future GSP, the view that the Enabling Clause imposes legal obligations is preferable.

Regarding the meaning of non-discriminatory, the panel followed India's view holding that the term 'non-discriminatory' required that identical tariff preferences under GSP schemes should be provided to all developing countries without differentiation, except for the implementation of *a priori* limitations.[168] India relied on the fact that in the New Shorter Oxford English Dictionary, to discriminate meant to make or constitute a difference in or between; distinguish and to make a distinction in the treatment of different categories of people or things.[169] In its view, all developing countries are similarly situated and, therefore, cannot be treated differently including different treatment depending on certain conditions that are the same for all developing countries.[170] Furthermore, the panel held that paragraph 3 c) of the Enabling Clause referred to the 'needs' of *all* developing countries, thereby prohibiting tariff preferences to be granted only to a sub-category of developing countries.[171] It stated that the objective of 'elimination of discriminatory

164 Bartels (The WTO Enabling Clause), p. 520.

165 Doha Decision on Implementation in 2001, WTO Ministerial Conference and UNCTAD, Midrand Declaration and a Partnership for Growth and Development, both documents cited in Howse (Back to Court After Shrimp/Turtle?), pp. 1352 and 1353.

166 Statements of the EU and the US quoted in Bartels (The WTO Enabling Clause), pp. 521 and 522.

167 *EC–Tariff Preferences*, report of the Appellate Body, para. 147.

168 *EC–Tariff Preferences*, report of the panel, para. 7.161.

169 *EC–Tariff Preferences*, report of the Appellate Body, para. 151.

170 Ibid., para. 153.

171 Ibid., para. 64.

treatment in international commerce', contained in the Preamble to the GATT 1994, guided the interpretation of the term 'non-discriminatory'.[172] Finally, it argued that paragraph 2 d) of the Enabling Clause, allowing differentiation between developing and least developed countries, would be rendered redundant if paragraph 2 a) allowed for differentiation between developing countries subject to certain condition.[173]

By contrast, the EU asserted that the term 'non-discrimination' did not refer to formally equal treatment but treating different situations differently.[174] It also referred to a definition contained in the New Shorter Oxford English Dictionary.[175] It based its view *inter alia* on paragraph 3 c) of the Enabling Clause, which, in its view, required that tariff treatment under the Enabling Clause should respond to the development, financial and trade needs of individual developing countries.[176] This view is shared by some legal scholars who hold that the Enabling Clause permits variable treatment that allows a developed country to treat developing countries differently if the distinction is aimed at furthering the development, financial and trade needs of (individual) developing countries.[177] However, they point to the difficulty in responding in non-discriminatory terms to the development needs of developing countries.[178] For example, a GSP programme may discriminate on a *de facto basis* if certain countries are unable to comply with certain development standards.[179] This point will be discussed later.

The Appellate Body correctly took the view of the EU. It started its analysis stating that both parties to the dispute agreed that similarly situated countries should not be treated differently.[180] However, it did not conclude that GSP granting countries had to provide for identical tariff treatment of all developing countries.[181] Instead, it held that there was no textual basis in paragraph 3 c) of the Enabling Clause for the conclusion that preferential treatment should respond to development needs of *all* developing countries.[182] It rightly maintained that it would be 'simply unrealistic to assume that such

172 Ibid., para. 170.
173 Ibid., para. 172.
174 Ibid., para. 149.
175 Ibid., para. 151.
176 Ibid., para. 149.
177 Harrison, p. 165; Bartels (The WTO Enabling Clause), p. 524 et seqq.
178 Harrison, p. 165 et seq.; Bartels (The WTO Enabling Clause), p. 524 et seq.
179 Bartels (The WTO Enabling Clause), p. 525.
180 *EC–Tariff Preferences*, report of the Appellate Body, para. 153.
181 Ibid., para. 156.
182 Ibid., para. 159.

development will be in lockstep for all developing countries at once, now and for the future'.[183] In addition, the Appellate Body pointed to the Preamble to the WTO Agreement, which recognizes 'the need for positive efforts designed to ensure that developing countries, and especially the least developed among them, secure a share in the growth in international trade commensurate with the needs of their economic development'.[184] It convincingly argued that the word 'commensurate' supported the view that indeed developing countries might have different needs according to their levels of development.[185] Finally, it stated that paragraph 2 d) of the Enabling Clause referring to special treatment of least developed countries is not rendered redundant if differentiation between developing countries is allowed under paragraph 2 a).[186] That is, if paragraph 2 d) did not exist, GSP regarding least developed countries would have to prove that they complied with the criteria contained in paragraph 2 a). In conclusion, one should adopt the view of the Appellate Body that the term 'non-discriminatory' does not require formally equal treatment of all developing countries but equal treatment of all similarly-situated GSP beneficiaries that have the same development, financial and trade needs.[187] Referring to paragraph 3 a) of the Enabling Clause, the Appellate Body added that GSP should not impose unjustifiable burdens on other WTO members.[188]

Hence, conditionality regimes setting forth objective criteria for the granting of tariff preferences to beneficiary countries, and determining prerequisites for the withdrawal of such preferences, and being available to all similarly situated countries with the same development needs, are non-discriminatory as defined in paragraph 2 a) read in conjunction with paragraph 3 c) of the Enabling Clause. To be consistent with the Enabling Clause, such regimes would also have to be generalized and non-reciprocal and would have to comply with the other requirements of the Clause.

3.7.3 The Compatibility of the Drug Arrangements with the Enabling Clause

With regard to the Drug Arrangements the Appellate Body started its analysis stating that the preferences under the Drug Arrangements were not available to all countries that were similarly situated.[189] They did not set forth objective

183 Ibid., para. 161.
184 Ibid.
185 Ibid.
186 Ibid., para. 172.
187 Ibid., para. 173.
188 Ibid., para. 167.
189 Ibid., para. 180.

criteria to be met in order to become a beneficiary.[190] In addition, they did not determine criteria for the removal of benefits under the Drug Arrangements.[191] Instead, there was a closed list of beneficiaries suffering from illicit drug production and trafficking. The Appellate Body correctly concluded that the Drug Arrangements were not 'non-discriminatory' as required by footnote 3 of the Enabling Clause.[192]

The Appellate Body did not examine whether the Drug Arrangements *per se* responded positively to the development needs of developing countries in accordance with paragraph 3 c) of the Enabling Clause but whether identical tariff was available to all countries with the same drug problem.[193] The former analysis would relate to the problem raised by some legal authors regarding the *de facto* discrimination of special incentive regimes.[194] These authors are concerned about cases where unequal effects may flow from a facially non-discriminatory measure.[195] Since the term 'development' is enormously flexible, it is relatively easy to conceive of a scheme where formally equal treatment results in *de facto* discrimination because not similarly situated countries have to comply with the same standards although some countries are not able to comply with them. This point will be discussed in turn.

3.7.4 The Compatibility of the Special Incentive Arrangement for Sustainable Development and Good Governance of the EU GSP with the Enabling Clause

According to Art. 9 (1) paras. a – f of Regulation (EU) 978/2012, the special incentive arrangement for sustainable development and good governance may be granted to vulnerable countries within the meaning of Annex VII that have ratified and undertook to ensure an effective implementation of all the human rights conventions and conventions regarding the environment and good governance listed in Annex VIII, *inter alia* the CRC and ILO Conventions No. 138 and 182. They also have to accept the reporting obligations of the relevant conventions and have to subject themselves to a regular monitoring and review of the Commission. Tariff preferences may be withdrawn temporarily if serious and systematic human or labour rights violations occur, Art. 19 (1) para. a of Regulation (EU) 978/2012, or where undertakings regarding ratification,

190 Ibid., paras. 182 and 183.
191 Ibid., para. 183.
192 Ibid., para. 189.
193 Ibid., paras. 179 and 180.
194 Bartels (The WTO Enabling Clause), p. 525; Harrison, p. 164 et seq.
195 Bartels (The WTO Enabling Clause), p. 524.

implementation or monitoring processes are not complied with, Art. 15 (1) of Regulation (EU) 978/2012.

As analyzed above, paragraph 2 a) read in conjunction with paragraph 3 a) of the Enabling Clause requires preferential tariff treatment to be 'non-discriminatory', i.e. to provide equal treatment to all similarly situated GSP beneficiaries that have the same development, financial and trade needs. Specifically, conditionality regimes need to set out objective criteria for the granting of tariff preferences to beneficiary countries, and to determine prerequisites for the withdrawal of such preferences, and have to be available to all similarly situated countries.

The special incentive arrangement for sustainable development and good governance provides for objective criteria, namely to ratify and implement the listed conventions in Annex VIII. Withdrawal may also only take place if serious labour or human rights violations occur or if the conventions ratified are no longer incorporated or if the relevant national legislation is not implemented or monitoring processes not complied with, thus only according to objective criteria. Consequently, the decisive question is whether the regime is available to similarly situated countries having the same development needs.

As its name suggests, the special incentive arrangement for sustainable development and good governance should in theory be considered to target the need of all development countries for sustainable development and good governance, comprising the need to ratify and effectively implement relevant human rights and environmental conventions. The crucial question is whether all developing countries are similarly situated since countries may not be in a similar position to e.g. reduce the incidence of child labour because of their different technical and financial resources. However, in case of child labour, it can be argued that given that the prohibition of child labour is almost universally accepted and has the status of *ius cogens*, and that the corresponding state duty to protect is absolute and immediate, developing countries should be *treated* as being similarly situated vis-à-vis the condition to implement the prohibition of child labour.

The situation is however different with regard to most of the other human rights and environmental conventions contained in Annex VIII. Since they are neither ratified nor accepted by all developing countries, these countries should not be deemed to be in similar situation. Thus, to a large extent, the EU GSP could in principle be considered to be *de facto* discriminatory because it treats countries with a different development need similarly.

However, according to the 11th recital of the Preamble to Regulation (EU) No 978/2012, additional preferences should be granted only to those developing countries that due to a lack of diversification and insufficient integration within the international trading system are vulnerable and need help to assume the special burdens and responsibilities resulting from the ratification and implementation. Being nevertheless in a better position than least-developed countries, they are considered to be able to dedicate resources to sustainable development. In this context, 'vulnerable' means that the country is not classified as a high-income country by the World Bank, whose GSP exports are concentrated in very few products (the seven largest sections of GSP covered imports into the EU represent more than 75 per cent in value of its total GSP covered imports) and with a low level of exports – under 6.5 per cent – to the EU.[196] Thus, restricting the availability of the special incentive arrangement only to a special category of developing countries with defined financial needs, the EU at least attempts to respond adequately to the different development needs of different countries. However, given the broad scope of the criteria and the variety of countries that could be classified as being 'vulnerable', the risk of *de facto* discrimination still exists. Yet, according to Art. 9 (b), (d) and (e) of Regulation (EU) No 978/2012, the emphasis of the conditions imposed is on the ratification and undertakings to ensure implementation and to accept the reporting requirements by the relevant conventions rather than costly implementation steps. Hence, the resulting discrimination will be negligible.

Finally, the point could be made that by giving the EU implementation bodies a degree of discretion when granting or withdrawing preferential tariff treatment under the special incentive arrangements, the special incentive arrangements amount to *de facto* discrimination.[197] This may lead – as it was the case – to politically biased decisions.[198]

However, first and foremost, it should be mentioned that the EU institutions have much less discretion under the current GSP than before. For example, as regards the initiation of the withdrawal procedure, Art. 17 (2) of the former Council Regulation (EC) No 732/2008 read: 'Where [...] the Commission may decide'[...]', whereas now, Art. 15 of Regulation (EU) 978/2012 reads: 'Where [...] the Commission has reasonable doubt' [...], it shall [...]'. Secondly, even if a measure permits a high degree of discretion, it should not automatically be qualified as being discriminatory. If the resulting administrative measures are discriminatory, they have to be challenged separately. Indeed, it has been long-established GATT doctrine that where a legislation merely grants a discretion

196 GSPhub, GSP +, https://gsphub.eu/about-gsp/gsp-plus.

197 For example, Art.15 (9) Regulation (EU) 978/2012 provides that 'Where the Commission considers [...], it shall', the Commission has some discretion when withdrawing preferences.

198 For the EU GSP case on Pakistan see Humbert (The Challenge of Child Labour), pp. 310–311.

that may or may not be used in such manner to violate WTO rules, a complainant must base its case on an actual instance where the application of the law – i.e. the exercise of discretion – violates WTO rules.[199] If e.g. another beneficiary country wanted to challenge the non-withdrawal of preferential treatment to Pakistan, it would have to challenge this administrative act and not the special incentive arrangement *per se*. The WTO adjudicating bodies would then examine whether the decision in itself violates the criteria of the Enabling Clause. Such an examination would analyse whether the decision was based on non-discriminatory criteria.

One panel decision indicates however that the legislation itself and not the administrative decision should be scrutinized where the discretionary nature of the legislation is such as to deprive a WTO member of the normal enjoyment of those rights.[200] This is not the case with the current EU GSP.

As regards the criterion that preferential treatment has to be 'generalized', there was a consensus that the term referred to the original objective of the 1971 Waiver to replace the fragmented system of preferences that were based on historical and political ties between developed countries and former colonies by a generalized system applicable to all developing countries.[201] Considering that preferential treatment has to be 'non-discriminatory', the term may be deemed to be legally redundant.[202]

Another question is whether the special incentive arrangement was 'non-reciprocal' as defined in footnote 3 of the Enabling Clause. One could argue that the scheme is not 'non-reciprocal' since it attaches condition to trade preferences. However, having found that footnote 3 to the Enabling Clause allows for special incentive arrangements providing for non-trade conditions that are available to all developing countries with the same development needs, one is precluded from arguing that these schemes have to be 'non-reciprocal' in the sense of not imposing non-trade conditions. Such an interpretation would nullify the former finding since it would prohibit any type of special incentive arrangement providing for non-trade conditions.

In conclusion, the EU GSP should be considered to be compatible with the Enabling Clause.

---

199 *US–Superfund*, report of the panel, para. 5.2.9; Howse (Back to Court After Shrimp/Turtle?), pp. 1352, 1366.

200 *US–Section 301 Trade Act*, report of the panel, paras. 7.87–7.92.

201 *EC–Tariff Preferences*, report of the Appellate Body, para. 155.

202 Bartels (The WTO Enabling Clause), p. 523.

3.7.5 The Compatibility of the Labour Rights Clause of the US GSP with the Enabling Clause

According to 19 United StatesC. sec. 2462 (b) (2) (H), countries are not eligible for GSP treatment if they have not implemented their commitments to eliminate the worst forms of child labour as defined in ILO Convention No. 182. In addition, under 19 United StatesC. sec. 2462 (b) (2) (G), countries are not eligible if they have not taken or are not taking steps to afford to workers in that country internationally recognized worker rights including provision for a minimum age for employment. These provisions do not apply if the President determines that it is in the national economic interest of the US to designate a country as beneficiary country.[203]

19 United StatesC. sec. 2462 (d) (2) grants the President the power to withdraw duty-free treatment with respect to any beneficiary country if the President determines that as a result of changed circumstances such country would be barred from designation as a beneficiary developing country under subsection (b) (2) referring to mandatory criteria including the requirement to implement a country's commitment to eliminate the worst forms of child labour and to take steps to provide for a minimum age for employment. These provisions are also subject to the national interest clause mentioned above.

As mentioned above, to be 'non-discriminatory' under paragraph 2 a) read in conjunction with paragraph 3 c) of the Enabling Clause, conditionality regimes need to set out objective criteria for the granting of tariff preferences to beneficiary countries, and to determine prerequisites for the withdrawal of such preferences, and have to be available to all similarly situated countries that have the same development needs.

As regards the case of child labour, the provisions granting duty-free treatment to beneficiary countries contain objective conditions relating to the elimination of the worst forms of child labour as well as to the provision of a minimum age for employment. So do the withdrawal provisions.

The need to be addressed by the preferential tariff treatment is the protection from child labour. As argued above, given that the prohibition of child labour is universally recognized and has the status of *ius cogens*, potential beneficiary countries should be treated as having the same development needs and being similarly situated with respect to the requirement to implement commitments to eliminate the worst forms of child labour. Those WTO members that have ratified ILO Convention No. 138 concerning a minimum age or are ILO members and by virtue of their membership under an obligation to

203 19 United StatesC. section 2462 (b) (2).

respect this Convention can also be regarded as being similarly situated with a view to the requirement to provide for a minimum age for employment.[204] The remaining WTO members are indirectly bound by the ILO Core Conventions through the Singapore Ministerial Declaration, which affirms the commitment to internationally recognized labour standards as stated in the ILO Declaration on Fundamental Rights at Work.[205]

In sum, to the extent the US GSP attaches the granting of tariff preferences to conditions with regard to child labour, it appears to be non-discriminatory within the meaning of the Enabling Clause.

However, the implementation provisions grant much discretion to the US implementation bodies.[206] In the granting as well as in the withdrawal procedure, the national economic interest of the US may take precedence over the labour rights performance of a beneficiary country. Also, the wording of 'taking steps' is a grey legal concept. The GSP Subcommittee has a lot of discretion when accepting or rejecting petitions since there are no guidelines when a petition should be rejected. In contrast to the EU GSP, neither is cooperation required with the beneficiary country nor are ILO decisions referred to. As described by Humbert, the US GSP indeed often has been used in a discriminatory manner.[207]

The question therefore arises whether the discretionary nature of this legislation is such as to deprive a WTO member of the normal enjoyment of its rights under GSP labour conditionality. However, with regard to child labour, the conditionality regime of the US GSP does not leave much room for discriminatory treatment of eligible countries because firstly, the relevant criteria are mandatory and secondly, while the wording at some points may be vague and grey legal concepts are used, the discretionary nature of this legislation is not such as to deprive beneficiary countries of their rights. The bulk of the criticism rather seems to lie in the application of the national interest clause, which apparently had been used in the interest of US companies.[208] The national economic interest clause permits the President to designate country A where the incidence of child labour is high as a beneficiary country only because it is

---

204 According to the ILO Declaration on Fundamental Principles and Rights at Work, all ILO members, by virtue of their membership have an obligation to respect, promote and realize the principles of the fundamental rights including the Minimum Age Convention No. 138, see Humbert (The Challenge of Child Labour), p. 103.

205 WTO, Singapore Ministerial Declaration, 13 December 1996, WT/MIN(96)/DEC/W, para.4.

206 For a detailed description of the US GSP, see Humbert (The Challenge of Child Labour), pp. 285–300.

207 Ibid., pp. 293–297.

208 Ibid, p. 294.

in the national interest of the US. In contrast, country B, using child labour but not being of national economic interest to the US, could be denied duty-free tariff treatment. Thus, under the national interest clause, similarly situated countries can be treated differently. Country B does not have any possibility of influencing the decision of the President. The President is not only free to apply this provision or not, the term 'national economic interest' also is a vague and non-predictable criterion, and a grey legal concept. In contrast to the vague wording such as 'taking steps', which, if applied in a reasonable way, leads to non-discriminatory treatment, the term 'national economic interest', even if applied in a reasonable way, may nevertheless cause discriminatory treatment. Thus, this term is of such a discretionary nature as to potentially deprive WTO members of their rights under the conditionality regime.

However, one could argue that similar to the security exception under GATT Art. XXI (b), GSP granting countries should have the right to protect their national economic interest. This could be all the more the case given that the preferential tariff treatment is voluntary. Under GATT Art. XXI (b) WTO members have a very broad discretion to take national security measures that they consider necessary and that would otherwise violate the GATT. However, a difference should be made between issues of national security potentially threatening the life and physical integrity of the population and the national *economic* interest. What is more, there are good reasons to argue that the national economic interest of the US is sufficiently protected by other provisions of the US GSP, e.g. through the exclusion of 'import-sensitive' products from GSP-eligible articles.[209] In addition, countries graduate from GSP treatment if they have become high income countries.[210] There is thus no need to have a general clause for the national economic interest. Instead, one could think of introducing a special safeguard clause similar to the one under the EU GSP that may be applied if imports from a beneficiary country impose 'serious difficulties' for an EU producer. Finally, it should be taken into account that the original intent of GSP regimes was to replace fragmented ties with certain developing countries.[211] But special ties would be built with certain developing countries if WTO law allowed for special tariff treatment provided to countries that are of special economic interest to the US. The national interest clause

209 The President may qualify products that are problematic for the US economy as 'import-sensitive', 19 United StatesC. sec. 2463 (b) (1) (A) and sec. 2463 (b) (3) of Title V of the Trade Act of 1974.

210 19 United StatesC. sec. 2462 (e) of Title V of the Trade Act of 1974.

211 This objective originally referred to the term 'generalized'. It should however also be pursued under the more specific term 'non-discriminatory'.

bears the risk of rendering the condition of non-discrimination under the Enabling Clause void. In conclusion, because of its national interest clause, the US GSP in its current form should be considered inconsistent with the Enabling Clause.

Being discriminatory, the US GSP neither can be regarded to be general. However, not asking for trade concessions, it is nevertheless non-reciprocal in accordance with the Enabling Clause.

3.8 *Conclusion*

The MFN treatment clause contained in GATT Art. I:1 is one of the central pillars of the WTO. It prohibits discrimination between WTO members with regard to imports and exports. The MFN clause prohibits *de iure* and *de facto* violations.

Measures taken in response to the recommendations of the ILO Governing Body under Art. 33 of the ILO Constitution in relation to child labour possibly violate GATT Art. I:1 in case they withdraw MFN treatment with regard to Myanmar. Other measures that may violate GATT Art. I:1 are bans implemented under the Kimberley Process Certification Scheme regarding non-participants and the UFPLA. Such measures constitute *de iure* violations of GATT Art. I:1.

Since child labour is a process and production method, the question arises whether national measures may differentiate between products on the basis of their process and production methods. Such a measure is for example the proposed EU Forced Labour Regulation, the US ban on goods made with forced or indentured child labour or the Belgian Social Label Law, possibly constituting a *de facto* violation.

The definition of 'like products' contained in GATT Art. I:1 with regard to tariffs allows for a rather narrow interpretation including differentiations based on the method of manufacture. This narrow interpretation is attributable to the principle of reciprocity, which applies to tariff negotiations. Differentiations between products on the basis of their product and production method are generally allowed where the principle of reciprocity demands it, as argued by prominent scholars.[212] This is different from the question whether generally, different tariffs can be applied to products made with and without child labour. This discussion will be postponed until after this discussion has been conducted in relation to GATT Art. III:4.

With regard to internal measures as defined in GATT Art. I:1 in conjunction with GATT Art. III:2 and III:4, the term 'like products' has a broader meaning

212 See Hudec (Like Product).

and should be interpreted in the same way as in GATT Art. III. It should also be interpreted as to include 'directly competitive and substitutable products'. Whether this broader meaning allows for 'npr-ppm-distinctions' will be discussed when examining GATT Art. III.

According to the panel in *Canada–Automotives*, not all conditions that do not relate to the products themselves are GATT Art. I:1-inconsistent, only those conditions that entail discrimination based on the origin of products. Does this mean that higher tariff on products made with child labour are possible under GATT Art. I? As just stated, the WTO-compatibility of npr-ppms will be revisited under GATT Art. III.[213] For the moment, it suffices to state that GATT-jurisprudence offers some space for npr-ppms.

The question is also what an advantage is and whether it is required that more products from the complaining WTO member than from the defending member have to be disadvantaged. This discussion will also be postponed after the question has been answered in relation to GATT Art. III.

The Enabling Clause is an exception to GATT Art. I:1 and allows for preferential tariff treatment of developing countries if it is 'generalized, non-reciprocal and non-discriminatory'. To what extend GSP granting countries are allowed to attach non-trade conditions to the granting of tariff preferences recently has been decided by the Appellate Body report *EC–Tariff Preferences*.[214] The term 'non-discriminatory' does not require formally equal treatment of all developing countries but equal treatment of all similarly situated GSP beneficiaries that have the same development needs. Specifically, conditionality regimes need to set forth objective criteria for the granting and withdrawal of preferential tariff treatment to beneficiary countries.

The special incentive arrangement for sustainable development and good governance under the EU GSP are 'non-discriminatory' in the meaning of the Enabling Clause. However, it suffers from several shortcomings.[215] It has for example been suggested to introduce a multilateral review mechanism for such regimes. These ideas will be revisited when discussing proposals for the improvement of the current state of WTO law *de lege ferenda*.

The labour clause of the US GSP provides for objective criteria for the granting and withdrawing of duty-free tariff treatment to beneficiary developing countries. However, since it contains a national economic interest clause, it is not 'non-discriminatory' in the meaning of the Enabling Clause.

---

213 See the discussion on p. 90 et seq.

214 *EC–Tariff Preferences*, report of the Appellate Body.

215 For an analysis and evaluation of the EU GSP see Humbert (The Challenge of Child Labour), pp. 300 et seqq.

4 Compatibility of Trade Measures on Child Labour with GATT Art. II

Whilst GATT Art. I generally prohibits discrimination between imports through tariffs and internal measures, GATT Art. II concerns bound tariffs in the schedules of concessions. Trade measures on child labour that could violate this provision are punitive tariffs on products made with child labour.

GATT Art. II reads:

> 1. a) Each contracting party shall accord to the commerce of the other Contracting Partiestreatment no less favourable than that provided for in the appropriate Part of the appropriate Schedule annexed to this Agreement.
>   b) The products described in Part I of the Schedule relating to any contracting party, which are the products of territories of other contracting parties, shall, on their importation into the territory to which the Schedule relates, and subject to the terms, conditions or qualifications set forth in that Schedule, be exempt from ordinary customs duties in excess of those set forth and provided therein.

Accordingly, a WTO member may not charge taxes that are in excess of those set forth in its schedules. GATT Art. II:1 implements the MFN treatment in the field of applied tariff rates. Punitive tariffs on products made with child labour that are listed in the members' schedules would be in excess of bound tariffs as provided in WTO members' schedules. Thus, GATT Art. II:1 (a) would be violated. Another question is of course whether WTO members can negotiate tariff levels conditioned on members' compliance with child labour standards. GATT Art. II:1 (b) refers to 'terms, conditions or qualifications'. The question is whether such conditions this can be read to refer to human rights obligations regarding child labour?[216] The answer depends on whether one allows for npr-ppm-measures with regard to child labour and how one reads the term 'treatment no less favourable'. Since GATT and WTO jurisprudence have extensively dealt with these questions under GATT Art. III, the answer the question will be postponed until after the analysis of GATT Art. III.

216 Cf. Marceau (Trade and Labour), p. 548.

5 Trade Measures concerning Child Labour under GATT Art. III

5.1 *Overview over the Structure and Scope of GATT Art. III*

5.1.1 The Structure

The second major obligation of non-discriminatory treatment after the MFN obligation is the national treatment obligation contained in GATT Art. III. It requires the treatment of imported goods, once they have cleared customs and border procedures, to be no worse than that of domestic goods.

The text of the relevant provisions reads as follows:

> 1. The Contracting Parties recognize that internal taxes and other internal charges, and laws, regulations and requirements, affecting the internal sale, offering for sale, purchase, transportation, distribution or use of products, and internal quantitative regulations requiring the mixture, processing or use of products in specified amounts or proportions, should not be applied to imported or domestic products so as to afford protection to domestic production*.
> 2. The products of the territory of any contracting party imported into the territory of any other contracting party shall not be subject, directly or indirectly, to internal taxes or other charges of any kind in excess of those applied, directly or indirectly, to like domestic products. Moreover, no contracting party shall otherwise apply internal taxes or other internal charges to imported or domestic products in a manner contrary to the principles set forth in paragraph 1*.
> 4. The products of the territory of any contracting party imported into the territory of any other contracting party shall be accorded treatment no less favourable than that accorded to like products of national origin in respect of all laws, regulations and requirements affecting their internal sale, offering for sale, purchase, transportation, distribution or use. The provisions of this paragraph shall not prevent the application of differential internal transportation charges which are based exclusively on the economic operation of the means of transport and not on the nationality of the product.

The asterisks refer to the *Ad* Note to GATT Art. III which reads:

> Any internal tax or other internal charge, or any law, regulation or requirement of the kind referred to in paragraph 1 which applies to an imported product and to the like domestic product, and is collected or enforced in the case of the imported product at the time or point of importation, is

> nevertheless to be regarded as an internal tax or other internal charge, or a law, regulation or requirement of the kind referred to in paragraph 1, and is accordingly subjected to the provisions of Article III.
>
> *Paragraph* 2
>
> A tax conforming to the requirements of the first sentence of paragraph 2 would be considered to be inconsistent with the provisions of the second sentence only in cases where competition was involved between, on the one hand, the taxed product and, on the other hand, a directly competitive or substitutable product which was not similarly taxed'.

Unilateral measures on child labour that might contravene the national treatment obligation contained in GATT Art. III are, for example, the proposed EU Forced Labour Regulation, US import ban on goods made by forced or indentured children and restrictions imposed under the Belgian Social Label Law. These measures could violate the national treatment obligation if they treated imported products such as textiles or toys worse than domestic toys or textiles not produced by children. Measures under the Kimberley Process Certification Scheme possibly violate the national treatment clause because bans against non-participants discriminate against foreign products. Since the certification requirements of the Kimberley Process Certification Scheme place the same burden on all participants regardless of production methods, they are not likely to violate the national treatment obligation and will not be examined under GATT Art. III.

The national treatment obligation refers to internal fiscal measures as well as internal regulations. One obvious aim is to protect the tariff bindings under GATT Art. II, which could be defeated easily by e.g. discriminatory value added taxes (VAT).[217] However, since not all tariffs are bound and GATT Art. III extends to products not bound under GATT Art. II, its general goal is to reduce restrictions on imports.[218]

Specifically, GATT Art. III lays out the following obligations:

In *Japan–Alcoholic Beverages*, the Appellate Body agreed with the panel that the first paragraph of GATT Art. III contained the general principle that internal measures should not be applied 'so as to afford protection' to domestic

217 Jackson (The World Trading System), p. 213; For example, if country A binds its tariffs for bananas at three per cent in exchange for a tariff concession of country B, this concession could be defeated if country A imposes a value added tax of 70 per cent on bananas and zero per cent on apples. This example is based on the assumption that the importing country produces apples, but does not produce bananas.

218 *Japan – Alcoholic Beverages*, report of the Appellate Body, p. 17; John H. Jackson (The World Trading System), p. 213.

production, and that this principle informed the rest of GATT Art. III.[219] GATT Art. III:2, on the other hand, contained specific obligations regarding internal taxes and other charges.[220] Nonetheless, the Appellate Body found that due to the different wording in the two sentences of GATT Art. III:2, the first paragraph informed the sentences of paragraph 2 in different ways.[221]

GATT Art. III:2, first sentence, prohibits imposing taxes in excess of those applied to like domestic products. The second sentence, read together with Note *Ad* to GATT Art. III, prohibits tax differentiation between directly competitive or substitutable products. In contrast to the first sentence, the second sentence specifically refers to the principle of GATT Art. III:1, i.e. to avoid protection of domestic production. Thus, the test for the first sentence seems to be whether a) the products are like and b) foreign goods are taxed in excess of the former. The test for the second sentence seems to be whether a) the products are competitive or substitutable, b) domestic and foreign goods are not similarly taxed and c) the dissimilar taxation works so as to afford protection.

GATT Art. III:4 does not differentiate between like products and directly competitive or substitutable products. It holds that foreign goods that are like domestic goods shall not be treated less favourably. Therefore, the question is whether the term 'like' has the same meaning in GATT Art. III:2 and GATT Art. III:4. If this were the case, the scope of GATT Art. III:4 would not cover regulatory measures that discriminate against directly competitive and substitutable foreign products, thereby potentially defeating the prohibition of discriminatory fiscal measures covered by Art. III:2, second sentence. In *EC–Asbestos*, the Appellate Body reconciled GATT Art. III:2 and III:4, holding:

> we need not rule, and do not rule, on the precise product scope of Article III:4, we do conclude that the product scope of Article III:4, although broader than the *first* sentence of Article III:2, is certainly *not* broader than the *combined* product scope of the two sentences of Article III:2 of the GATT 1994.[222]

The product scope of GATT Art. III:2 and III:4 therefore seems to be almost congruent although it is still possible that Art. III:2 is a bit broader. The reading that the scope of GATT Art. III:4 corresponds more or less with the combined scope of GATT Art. III:2 and 4 is supported by the wording of GATS Art. XVII.

219 *Japan–Alcoholic Beverages*, report of the Appellate Body, p. 17–18.
220 Ibid.
221 Ibid.
222 *EC–Asbestos*, report of the Appellate Body, para. 99.

GATS Art. XVII neither differentiates between 'like services' and 'directly competitive or substitutable services', nor does it distinguish between fiscal and regulatory measures. Since it is rather unlikely that the drafters of the GATS wanted to exclude the group of directly competitive or substitutable products, GATS Art. XVII should be read to include this group. The same should hold true for GATT Art. III:4.

The summary records of the Third Committee at the Havana Conference give an idea of what the drafters of the GATT had in mind when introducing 'directly competitive or substitutable products' in GATT Art. III:2:

> the second sentence of [GATT Art. III:2], far from being a departure from the principle of national treatment, was intended to strengthen that principle and prevent its abuse. Illustrating the case of tung oil and linseed oil, which could be considered be competitive and substitutable, he stated that the United States, under the first sentence of paragraph 1 of the Article, would be required to apply the same taxation policy to a domestic product as to a like imported product. The first sentence was, however, qualified by the second sentence if no substantial domestic production existed, a tax could not be placed on tung oil in order to protect linseed oil which was not similarly taxed.[223]

This example indicates that 'like' in the first sentence has a rather narrow scope requiring products to have essentially the same physical properties whereas 'directly competitive or substitutable products' e.g. only have the same common end-use. However, the reason why the drafters introduced this group of products only in paragraph 2 and not in 4 could be that the group of 'directly competitive or substitutable products' under GATT Art. III:2 has an even broader scope. Indeed, Hudec argues that to reconcile paragraph 2 and 4, one should interpret 'directly competitive or substitutable products' to have a broader scope than 'like products' under GATT Art. III:4.[224] This could be justified by arguing that differences in tax rates are inherently arbitrary, and thus harder to justify than regulatory distinctions.[225]

In short, to be consistent with GATT Art. III, measures must not differentiate between like products (or, in case of GATT Art. III:2, second sentence, directly competitive or substitutable products) and not discriminate against

223 E/CONF.2/C.3/SR.11 p. 1 and Corr.2, cited in GATT Guide, I, pp. 159–160.

224 Hudec (Like Product), p. 107.

225 Ibid.

foreign goods. Thus, GATT Art. III:2 and III:4 both provide an obligation of similarity and of equal treatment.[226]

5.1.2 Origin-Neutral Measures

Most measures on (forced) child labour such as the proposed EU Forced Labour Regulation, the US ban on goods made with forced child labour or labelling laws such as the Belgian Social Label Law are origin-neutral, i.e. they accord facially similar treatment to domestic and foreign goods. This is because child labour is prohibited in almost all countries worldwide. Bans against non-participant countries under the Kimberley Process Certification Scheme directly discriminate against foreign products, clearly violating the national treatment obligation. The legal analysis under GATT Art. III will therefore focus on the three measures mentioned above.

Origin-neutral measures may put a heavier burden on imported goods if only imported goods are made with child labour. A hypothetical case would be toys made in China in comparison with toys made in the EU. The question therefore is whether GATT Art. III prohibits both *de iure* and *de facto*, or 'implicit' discrimination.[227] In *Japan–Imported Wines and Alcoholic Beverages* the panel held that an origin-neutral tax on alcoholic beverages constituted a violation of GATT Art. III:2.[228] In *EC–Asbestos*, the Appellate Body found that an origin-neutral measure prohibiting the sale of products containing asbestos was covered by GATT Art. III:4.[229] Other rulings applying GATT Art. III to origin-neutral measures include *US–Malt Beverages*, *Japan–Alcoholic Beverages* and *Chile–Alcoholic Beverages*.[230] Thus, according to GATT and WTO jurisprudence, GATT Art. III applies to *de facto* discrimination. In addition, the language of GATT Art. III:1 'so as to afford protection' strongly suggests that a measure that is facially non-discriminatory but has the effect of affording protection needs to be examined under GATT Art. III.[231]

---

226 Fauchald, p. 445; It should be noted that equal treatment does not mean identical treatment.

227 *De facto* discrimination refers to rules that although being origin-neutral on their face, yet have the effect of discriminating against foreign products. By contrast, *de iure* discrimination relates to rules that discriminate on the basis of the origin of foreign goods.

228 *Japan–Imported Wines and Alcoholic Beverages*, report of the panel.

229 *EC –Asbestos*, report of Appellate Body.

230 *US–Malt Beverages*, report of the panel; *Japan–Alcoholic Beverages*, report of the panel and Appellate Body, *Chile–Alcoholic Beverages*, report of the panel and Appellate Body.

231 Jackson (The World Trading System), p. 217.

5.1.3 Voluntary Action

The Belgian Social Label Law grants a social label to products from a company that has *voluntarily* accepted and complied with the implementation procedure provided by the law. The question therefore is whether voluntary measures come within the scope of GATT Art. III. In relation to the TBT Agreement, opinions diverge on this issue.[232]

Regarding GATT Art. III, the panel in *Canada–Automotives* held that a measure can be subject to GATT Art. III:4 even if its compliance is not mandatory. It explicitly stated:

> We note that it has not been contested in this dispute that, as stated by previous GATT and WTO panel and appellate body reports, Article III:4 applies not only to mandatory measures but also to conditions that an enterprise accepts in order to receive an advantage, including in cases where the advantage is in the form of a benefit with respect to the conditions of importation of a product.[233]

This reasoning has also been applied in *EC–Parts and Components*.[234] Conversely, it has been held that the term 'requirement' in GATT Art. III:1 does not necessarily refer to legally enforceable measures, but that there are many forms of government action that can be effective in influencing the conduct of private parties.[235] Thus, a law providing for a voluntary label that is likely to accord market benefits to the applicant falls under the scope of GATT Art. III:4. There is no reason to treat fiscal measures differently. The reasoning of the panel should therefore apply to the whole of GATT Art. III.

The question then arises whether other private sector action such as private social labelling initiatives like RUGMARK or codes of conduct of multi-stakeholder initiatives are also subject to GATT disciplines. It follows from the cited jurisprudence that only such action that is partly controlled by governments may come under the GATT disciplines. This view finds some support in literature that holds that government-sponsored labelling plans of a voluntary nature do fall under GATT rules, provided that the governmental involvement is instrumental to the operation of such plans and offers either incentives for compliance or disincentives for deviation.[236] Such a finding is in accordance

232 Committee on Technical Barriers to Trade, G/TBT/M/23 and 24.

233 *Canada–Automotives*, report of the panel, para. 10.73.

234 *EC –Parts and Components*, report of the panel, para. 5.21.

235 *Canada–Automotives*, report of the panel, paras. 10.106–10.107; *EC –Parts and Components*, report of the panel, para. 5.21.

236 Zedalis, p. 337.

with the rationale of the GATT/WTO being an intergovernmental agreement. Although some of the described initiatives may be sponsored by governments,[237] they are not controlled by them and thus do not fall under GATT disciplines.

5.1.4 The *Note Ad* to GATT Art. III

In case import bans can be regarded as internal measures, the US import ban on goods produced with forced or indentured child labour could be examined not only under the prohibition of import restrictions contained in GATT Art. XI but also under GATT Art. III:4. This problem relates to the relationship between GATT Art. III, XI and the Note *Ad* to GATT Art. III. Although GATT Art. XI is primarily concerned with import restrictions and quotas, according to the Note *Ad*, measures that apply to both imported and domestic products are to be regarded as internal measures. The US import prohibition applies only to imported products. However, under US law, forced child labour is prohibited.[238] One could therefore argue that since forced child labour is prohibited domestically, domestic products are subject to the same requirement as imported products, i.e. both must not be made with child labour. Thus, the import ban only makes the internal measure effective for imported products and could therefore be regarded as an internal measure in the meaning of the Note *Ad* to GATT Art. III. Then again, one could argue that the explicit ban only applies to imported products and that the domestic prohibition of child labour is of a fairly different nature. The question therefore is whether the measure applying to the foreign product must be identical with the one applying to the domestic product, and if not, to what extend they have to be similar.

In *US–Tuna I*, the panel ruled on an import prohibition relating to process and production methods.[239] The US Marine Mammal Protection Act of 1972 (MMPA) prohibits tuna fishing in the Eastern Tropical Pacific Ocean where commercial fishing particularly endangers dolphins. The MMPA also prohibits the importation of tuna caught with commercial fishing technology resulting in the incidental killing of dolphins. The MMPA does not contain a provision relating to the internal sale, offer for sale, purchase etc., as required by GATT Art. III:1.

The panel held that the Note *Ad* covered only measures applied to imported products, which were of the same nature as those applied to the domestic

237 For example, the RUGMARK initiative had been sponsored at the time by the GTZ, see Humbert (The Challenge of Child Labour), pp. 362–363.

238 Cf. 18 United StatesC. § 1589, ch. 77.

239 *US–Tuna I*, report of the panel.

products, such as a prohibition on imports that implemented an internal sales prohibition applied to both imported and domestic products and is enforced at the border.[240] However, the underlying argument seemed to be that GATT Art. III and its Note *Ad* only referred to measures 'affecting products *as such*', thereby excluding measures relating to the process or production method.[241] The panel explicitly stated that even if the internal measures in question could be regarded as an internal sales regulation corresponding with the import ban (regulating tuna harvesting but not the sale of tuna), the import prohibition would not meet the requirements of GATT Art. III because this article requires a comparison of the measures affecting products as a product.[242] Thus, the panel primarily relied on the 'product-process' doctrine[243] when defining the scope of the Note *Ad*.

However, the question whether GATT Art. III and its Note *Ad* cover also process-based measures does not have to be resolved at this point. What has to be resolved under Note *Ad* to GATT Art. III is the relationship of the measure applying to domestic products with the respective border measure. According to the panel, an import ban on tuna harvested in a dolphin-unfriendly manner implemented jointly with an internal prohibition of e.g. the sale of tuna harvested in a dolphin-unfriendly manner would clearly be covered by the Note *Ad*, although it could be termed a ppm-measure. Whilst the scope of GATT Art. III obviously determines the scope of the Note *Ad*, the prior interpretative issue is the relationship between the measures in question.[244]

In *Argentina–Bovine Hides*, the panel held that the different taxation methods for imported and domestic products where not so significant as to fall outside the scope of the Note *Ad* to GATT Art. III.[245] In *EC–Bananas III*, the Appellate Body found that import licence requirements qualified as internal measures because they included operator category rules that were intended to ensure that EC banana ripeners obtained a share of the quota rents, and thereby affected the sale of products.[246] In *EC–Asbestos*, the panel pointed out

240 Ibid, para. 5.11.

241 Ibid. paras. 5.11 and 5.14; Hudec (Product-Process Distinction), p. 194.

242 *US–Tuna I*, report of the panel, paras. 5.15.

243 Hudec uses this term to describe a doctrine that has the effect of making it *prima facie* GATT-illegal for governments to impose tax or regulatory disadvantages on imported products because of the way they were produced, see Hudec (Product-Process Distinction), p. 187. This term will be used in the same sense in this work.

244 Cf. Hudec (Product-Process Distinction), p. 194.

245 *Argentina–Bovine Hides*, report of the panel, paras. 11.150 and 11.154.

246 WTO Analytical Index, Vol. I, para. 96, *EC –Bananas III*, report of the Appellate Body, para. 211.

that the French word used in the Note *Ad* '*comme*' could not be interpreted as requiring an identical measure to be applied to imported products and domestic products.[247] Further, the panel relied on GATT jurisprudence citing *US–Section 337*.[248] In this case, the domestic measure was substantive and procedural patent law whereas the foreign measure, i.e. Section 337, prohibited the import of goods suspected of violating a US patent law. Under US patent law, remedies operate *in personam* whereas Section 337 is an *in rem* exclusion order.[249] The panel held that although of a different nature, Section 337 could be seen as a means of enforcement of US patent law, including its procedural provisions.[250] In *EC–Asbestos*, the panel pointed out that the foreign measures in question in *US–Section 337* were not the same as the equivalent measures applicable to domestic products.[251] It follows that the foreign and the respective domestic measure do not have to be of the same nature. Rather, the foreign measure can be regarded as an internal measure within the meaning of GATT Art. III:4 if it makes the domestic measure effective or, using the words of the EC, if the import ban in question is the 'logical corollary' of the domestic measure.[252] This interpretation is in accordance with the historic interpretation of the Note *Ad* according to which a regulation enforced at the border is valid if it meets the national treatment standard of GATT Art. III.[253]

Since the US import ban on goods produced by forced child labour is the logical corollary of the internal prohibition of forced child labour, it could be covered by GATT Art. III through its Note *Ad*.

Having said that, the main problem in relation to measures concerning child labour is whether npr-ppm-measures that do not have any impact on the characteristics of the product are covered by GATT Art. III. If they are covered, the next question is whether such measures violate GATT Art. III or not. With regards to the obligation of similarity of products contained in GATT Art. III, domestic measures concerning child labour could be GATT-consistent if products made with child labour were not like products that were not made with child labour within the meaning of GATT Art. III:2 or 4. In relation to the obligation of equal treatment, one possibility to make these measures GATT Art.

247 *EC–Asbestos*, report of the panel, para. 8.94.
248 *US–Section 337*, report of the panel.
249 *US–Section 337*, report of the panel, para. 2.8 (k) (1).
250 *US–Section 337*, report of the panel, paras. 3.6, 5.10.
251 *EC–Asbestos*, report of the panel, para. 8.95.
252 Ibid. para. 8.90.
253 Protocol Modifying Part II and Art. XXVI of the GATT, signed at Geneva, 14 Sept. 1948, 62 U.N.T.S. 104, cited in Vázquez, p. 811, fn. 48.

III-consistent would comprise an interpretation that allows for certain flexibility for *bona fide* measures, for example, measures concerning child labour. These issues will be dealt with in the next sections.

5.2 *The Coverage of GATT Art. III in Relation to PPM-Measures*

As mentioned above, the first question is whether GATT Art. III covers npr-ppm-measures. The *US–Tuna I* panel mentioned above explicitly held that examining the wording of GATT Art. III:4, this provision only applied to measures affecting tuna *as a product*, thereby excluding from the scope of GATT Art. III regulations governing the harvesting of tuna.[254] The panel based its argumentation on the Working Party Report on Border Tax Adjustments, adopted by the Contracting Partiesin 1970, which stated that only taxes levied directly on the product were eligible for border tax adjustments.[255]

Other rulings seem to contradict this finding. In *Italian Discrimination*, the panel held that GATT Art. III applied not only to measures directly regulating the sale or purchase of products, but also to laws and regulations that might adversely modify the conditions of competition between domestic and foreign products.[256] As mentioned above, the panel in *US–Section 337* applied GATT Art. III to procedural aspects of infringements of proceedings under US patent law.[257]

Moreover, the words 'directly or indirectly' in GATT Art. III:2 suggest that at least as regards fiscal measures, taxes not directly imposed on the product should be included in the examination of GATT Art. III. As stated in discussions in Commission A at the London session of the Preparatory Committee, the word 'indirectly' would cover even a tax not on the product itself, but on the processing of the product.[258]

Many authors rightly argue that the exclusion of npr-ppm-measures from the scope of GATT Art. III is simply wrong.[259] Looking at the ordinary meaning given to the terms of a treaty in accordance with Art. 31 (1) of the VCLT, the question is whether the measures 'affect[ing] the sale, offer[ing] for sale, purchase, transportation [...] of products'.[260] Measures that prohibit the import of tuna

254 *US–Tuna I*, report of the panel, para. 5.15.

255 Ibid. para. 5.13.

256 *Italian Discrimination*, report of the panel, para. 12.

257 *US–Section 337*, report of the panel, paras. 3.6, 5.10.

258 EPCT/A/PV/9 p. 19; EPCT/W/181, pp. 3 cited in GATT Guide, p. 141.

259 Hudec (Product-Process Distinction), pp. 197 et seqq.; Howse/Regan, pp. 253 et seqq.; Bronckers/McNelis; Thaggert, pp. 75 et seqq.

260 GATT Art. III:1.

harvested by certain methods definitely affect the sale of the tuna harvested under those methods, at least in terms of quantity and price.[261] Further, if npr-ppm-measures were excluded from the scope of GATT Art. III, taxes or internal regulations on npr-ppms would be treated *a priori* better than product-related taxes, which is a result that the drafters of the GATT would certainly not have wanted.[262] The latter argument is based on the assumption that GATT Art. III does not create a general right of access but rather a negative right that access shall not be restricted by discriminatory measures of various sorts.[263] This is apparent from the text that is phrased in a negative way by utilizing words such as ‚should not', 'shall not' and 'shall be ... no',[264] as well as from the context that groups GATT Art. III with Art. XI. This article provides for the elimination of quantitative restrictions. Thus, both rules can be qualified as limits to trade liberalizations whereas Art. XX provides general exceptions.

The panel in *US–Tuna I* also cited the Working Party Report on Border Tax Adjustments as a basis for limiting the application of the Note *Ad* to taxes or regulations borne by products.[265] According to this Report, only taxes directly levied on products are eligible for border tax adjustment.[266] Under the tax adjustment, taxes like sales or excise taxes on imported products can be refunded by export subsidies and do not qualify as internal taxes under the Note *Ad* to GATT Art. III. In contrast, taxes on producers, for example, corporate or income taxes, do qualify as internal taxes under the Note *Ad* to GATT Art. III. The rationale for this is that in contrast to taxes on production, taxes on products are reflected in consumer prices and may cause trade distortion. Therefore, they have to be equalized.[267]

Several arguments can be made against applying the rationale of the Working Party Report to limit the scope of GATT Art. III. Firstly, the analogy between taxes and regulations is not always valid because they might have different effects.[268] Secondly, the distinction between taxes borne by the product and those borne by producers is not always true anymore.[269] There is no

261 The whole point of the dispute of the *US–Tuna I* case was that the ban on tuna might reduce the sale of foreign tuna. See also Howse/Regan, p. 254.

262 Howse/Regan, p. 257.

263 Ibid.

264 GATT Art. III:1, 2, 4.

265 Thaggert, p. 79; Hudec (Product-Process Distinction), p. 195.

266 Working Party Report on Border Tax Adjustment, adopted on 2 December 1970, GATT BISD, 18S/97, paras. 4, 14.

267 Hudec (The Product-Process Distinction), p. 195; Hudec (Essays on the Nature of International Trade Law), p. 43.

268 Thaggert, p. 76.

269 Demaret/Stewardson, pp. 7, 14.

basis to the view that taxes on production wholly burden the producer,[270] as some production costs may be transferred to consumers.[271] For example, under the VAT system, GATT permits rebates on the entire stage of value added to exported goods, including those inputs that are not embodied in the product.[272] These taxes are thus treated as if they are borne by the product no matter the physical connection and the policy purpose such as the environment, as stated by the panel in *US–Superfund*.[273] This is also the case with carbon taxes that are shifted to the consumer and increase the price of the products. What matters is the price signal that reflects the cost of the product and establish a close connection to the product.[274] Consequently, there is no reason to treat npr-ppm-measures any differently. In conclusion, GATT Art. III applies to npr-ppm-measures.

5.3 *Like Products*

As mentioned above, the first obligation that GATT Art. III imposes is the obligation of similarity, namely that products are 'like' or, in case of Art. III:2, second sentence, 'directly competitive or substitutable'. One possibility for trade measures concerning child labour to be GATT Art. III-consistent is to allow for product distinctions based on their process and production methods not reflected in the final product. This would be against the 'product-process' doctrine, whereby npr-ppm-measures are *prima facie* GATT illegal, and which several GATT/WTO panels have applied, as will be seen below.[275] The validity of the 'product-process' doctrine obviously relates to the general question of how to define 'like products'. Except for the Antidumping Agreement,[276] the term 'like products' is nowhere defined in the GATT. However, early GATT practice already found that the narrow definition contained in the Antidumping

270 Thaggert, p. 79.

271 Demaret/Stewardson, p. 15.

272 Thaggert, p. 78.

273 *US–Superfund*, report of the panel, para. 5.2.4.

274 Cf. Vranes, p. 193; Will, p. 134.

275 For an overview of the debate on npr-ppms in the field of climate change and the environment and their GATT-III-compatibility, see Van den Bossche (WTO law as a constraint on domestic environmental policy), pp. 31–36.

276 Art. 2.6 of the Agreement on Implementation of Art. VI of GATT 1994 (hereinafter Antidumping Agreement) reads: 'Throughout this Agreement the term "like product" ("produit similaire") shall be interpreted to mean a product which is identical, i.e. alike in all respects to the product under consideration, or in the absence of such a product, another product which, although not alike in all respects, has characteristics closely resembling those of the product under consideration.'

Agreement of 1979 was not suitable for the different purpose of GATT Art. III.[277]

As mentioned above, most cases interpreting the term 'like products' start with citing the Working Party Report on Border Tax Adjustments:

> Some criteria were suggested for determining, on a case-by-case basis, whether a product is "similar": the product's end uses in a given market; consumers' tastes and habits, which change from country to country, the product's properties, nature, and quality.[278]

While the Working Party Report was adopted by the CONTRACTING PARTIES and relied upon by the Appellate Body, its criteria are referred to as 'suggestions'. The list is not exhaustive. Thus, the question arises whether governments may use process and production methods not reflected in the final product as a criterion for distinguishing between products. That would mean rejecting the 'product-process' doctrine mentioned above. In this case, one would have to decide whether different npr-ppms would be sufficient to distinguish between two otherwise like products. The next section will analyse the GATT/WTO jurisprudence and legal literature with a view to finding out whether such an interpretation would be valid under current WTO law.

Before entering into the analysis, a last point should be mentioned. The question arises whether the term 'like' has different meanings under the different provisions in GATT Art. III. As mentioned above, the Appellate Body introduced the idea of an accordion in relation to likeness, which would allow for different meanings of 'like' in the different provisions.[279] In addition, it has been established that although broader than the product scope under GATT Art. III:2, first sentence, the product scope of GATT Art. III:4 is not broader than the combined product scope of GATT Art. III:2, first and second sentence. Therefore, if products are allowed to be distinguished on the basis of their process and productions methods that are not reflected in the final product under GATT Art. III:4, they certainly are under GATT Art. III:2, first sentence. Thus, for the moment, the provisions will be examined together. The next question is whether like products made and not made with child labour although being dissimilar, are nonetheless directly competitive or substitutable.

---

277 *Japan–Imported Wines and Alcoholic Beverages*, report of the panel, para. 5.6.

278 Working Party Report on Border Tax Adjustments, adopted on 2 December 1970, BISD 18S/97, para. 18.

279 See above p. 26.

5.3.1 Npr-ppms: A Valid Criterion to Distinguish between Products?

5.3.1.1 *The Legal Rulings*

5.3.1.1.1 Belgian Family Allowances

The first legal case that could be regarded as dealing with npr-ppm-measures is the *Belgian Family Allowances* case[280] even though it does not mention the 'product-process' doctrine. The case involved a special tax on imported goods to finance a system of family allowances, which goods from countries with a similar system of family allowances were exempted from. In Belgium, the system of family allowances was financed by a tax on Belgian employers. The panel found that the Belgian legislation discriminated between countries that also have such a family allowances system and those that have a different system or no system of this kind at all, thereby making the granting of a tax exemption dependent on certain conditions. Accordingly, it found a violation of GATT Art. I, and possibly GATT Art. III:2.[281] This case does not explicitly rule out npr-ppm-measures, but rules out different treatment not based on products but on the varying national laws of exporting countries.[282] As mentioned above, such measures are contrary to GATT Art. I because they relate to the situation or conduct of a country and therefore constitute *de facto* discrimination.[283] This case can be taken as evidence that country-based measures are generally not permitted under GATT Art. I and III. Yet, some authors rely on this case to defend the 'product-process' doctrine.[284]

5.3.1.1.2 US–Tuna I and II

The second legal case on npr-ppm-measures is the *US–Tuna I* case mentioned above.[285] Having established that the Note *Ad*, cannot be applied to npr-ppm-measures, the panel concluded that GATT Art. III:4 called for 'a comparison of the treatment of imported tuna *as a product* with that of domestic tuna *as a product*', and that different regulations as to the harvesting methods did not affect tuna as a product.[286] However, since the panel does not offer any explanation for this finding, and since at first sight, there is no compelling reason why non-product-related process and production methods should not be

280 *Belgian Family Allowances*, report of the panel, see also above, p. 32.
281 *Belgian Family Allowances*, report of the panel, para. 8.
282 Similarly, Neumann, p. 132.
283 One could equally qualify this discrimination as *de iure* discrimination since the measure is not origin-neutral.
284 Jackson (Comments on Shrimp/Turtle), p. 304.
285 *US–Tuna I*, report of the panel.
286 *US–Tuna I*, report of the panel, paras. 5.11–5.15.

taken into account, this ruling cannot be taken as a sufficient basis for establishing the above-mentioned 'product-process' doctrine whereby npr-ppm-measures are *prima facie* GATT-inconsistent.

The second *US–Tuna* panel followed the approach taken by the first.[287] It did not take into consideration that the US did not prohibit the sale of tuna harvested by a dolphin-hostile method, but concentrated on the 'product concept' of GATT Art. III. The panel held that GATT Art. III required a comparison between treatment of foreign and national products, not between policies or practices of foreign countries and the importing country.[288] Accordingly, the Note *Ad* would also only cover those measures that applied to products *as products*.[289] The panel stressed that the Note *Ad* did not apply to measures that accorded less favourable treatment to products that were not produced in conformity with domestic policies.[290] Accordingly, the panel held that the US measures did not affect the inherent character of tuna as a product and that the Note *Ad* to GATT Art. III was not applicable.[291]

Again, this approach is not very convincing, as it neither explains what is meant by 'product as a product', nor gives a legal rationale. Although not explicitly, the panel seems to rely on extraterritoriality when holding that foreign products should not have to comply with domestic policies. This argument will be dealt with later in this work.

5.3.1.1.3 US–Malt Beverages

The next case where the panel ruled on npr-ppm-measures was the *US–Malt Beverages* case.[292] The panel examined several US measures such as tax rates, sales requirements, licensing fees and tax exemptions. One claim by the Government of Canada was that tax credits on beer from small domestic breweries whose annual production of beer fell below a certain limit violated GATT Art. III:1 and III:2 as they were not applicable to imported beer.[293] The panel held that beer from large breweries was like beer from small breweries.[294] Since the US had not made the case that the size of breweries affected the nature of the beer produced, or otherwise affected beer as a product, the panel

287 *US–Tuna II*, report of the panel.
288 Ibid., para. 5.8.
289 Ibid.
290 Ibid.
291 Ibid., para. 5.9.
292 *US–Malt Beverages*, report of the panel.
293 Ibid., para. 5.18.
294 Ibid.

concluded that even if tax credits were available to foreign small breweries, imported beer from large breweries would be taxed in excess of domestic beer from small breweries, and therefore the measure would still be inconsistent with GATT Art. III:2, first sentence.

The panel relied on the product concept of the *US–Tuna I and II* cases, but created some space for future measures through the formulation 'otherwise affected beer as a product'. Indicating that measures may affect products in other ways than having a direct impact on their nature points to the possibility that products might be affected by e.g. their process and productions methods not reflected in the final product, and thereby having an effect on the price of the product. In addition, the fact that the panel explicitly mentioned the failure of the US to assert that the size of breweries affected the nature of the products, or otherwise affected beer as a product, also might be interpreted as suggesting that if the US had made the argument, they might have been successful.

5.3.1.1.4 US–Automobiles

The following panel report *US–Automobiles*, which was not adopted, was a clearer statement in favour of the 'product-process' doctrine.[295] The panel ruled on three different kinds on domestic measures imposed by the US: a luxury tax imposed on the first retail sale of vehicles for over US $ 30,000, which applied to domestic and imported vehicles alike; the so-called gas guzzler tax imposed on the sale of automobiles within 'model types' whose fuel economy failed to meet certain fuel economy requirements; and finally the CAFE requirements that required an average fuel economy value to be calculated for each manufacturer's and importer's entire fleet of vehicles, known as 'corporate average fuel economy'.[296] Failure to provide this figure was unlawful and resulted in a civil penalty.

The panel examined the CAFE standards under GATT Art. III:4. The panel held that although the regulation did not regulate products as such, but was imposed on producers, it was nevertheless covered by GATT Art. III:4 since it affected the conditions of competition.[297] It cited a former panel that had found that the word 'affecting' implied that GATT Art. III:4 referred not only to laws that directly governed the sale of products, but to all measures that might adversely modify the conditions of competition.[298] The EC argued that

295 *US–Automobiles*, report of the panel, see also references in the footnotes below.
296 *US–Automobiles*, report of the panel, paras. 2.2 et seqq.
297 Ibid., paras. 5.45 and 5.46.
298 Ibid., para. 5.45 citing *Italian Discrimination*, report of the panel, para. 12.

because the CAFE regulation advantaged full-line manufacturers by letting them average out the fuel economy of their fleet by combining large and small cars in their calculations in order to attain the required standard, EC limited-line car manufacturers were prejudiced within the meaning of GATT Art. III:4. Applying GATT Art. III:4, the panel noted that depending on the importer/manufacturer, 'like' large cars with a low fuel economy could be combined with small cars with a high fuel economy. Thus, an imported large car that could not be combined with a small car would be treated less favourably than a like domestic large car that could be combined with smaller ones.[299] The panel then noted that the difference in treatment under the CAFE standards depended on several factors not directly related to the product as a product, including the ownership and control of the manufacturer/importer.[300] It therefore raised the question whether such measures were permitted by GATT Art. III:4. It proceeded to analyse the language of GATT Art. III, holding that GATT Art. III:1 referred to measures 'affecting the sale, offering for sale, purchase, transportation, distribution or use of products', and that these activities related to the product as a product, not to the producer.[301] As in the first *US–Tuna* case, it pointed to the Working Party Report on Border Tax Adjustments that limited border tax adjustments to taxes borne by the product. It held that this limitation on the choice of domestic policy measures that might be applied to imported products mirrored one of the central purposes of GATT Art. III, namely to ensure the security of tariff bindings.[302] In addition, the obligation of unconditional MFN treatment in the application of GATT Art. III:4 through GATT Art. I could be undermined.[303] It concluded that GATT Art. III:4 did not permit an imported product to be treated less favourably than a like domestic product based on factors not directly relating to the product as such.[304] Accordingly, the CAFE regulations, relating to the control or ownership of producers/importers and also according less favourable treatment to imported products, violated GATT Art. III:4. The panel therefore did not find it necessary to examine the words 'so as to afford protection'.

This case for the first time elaborated on the 'product-process' doctrine. Before analysing the arguments, some doubts should be raised as to whether the measure in question was correctly qualified as a non-product-related

299 Ibid., para. 5.50.
300 Ibid.
301 *US–Automobiles*, report of the panel, para. 5.52.
302 Ibid., para. 5.53.
303 Ibid.
304 Ibid., para. 5.54.

measure.[305] One could legitimately assert that the corporate fleet average of fuel economy was the total of the fuel economy levels of each vehicle, and that therefore the penalty to be paid by the manufacturer would be no different than a tax that is based on individual taxes dependent on the actual fuel economy of each vehicle sold that year.[306] The fact that the payment of the penalty depended on the corporate average of fuel economy does not change the character of fuel economy as a product characteristic.[307] However, the panel rightly pointed to the fact that the civil liability largely depended on the law's definitions of 'manufacturer' and 'importer' in relation to control and ownership.[308] Viewed from this perspective, the penalty might be characterized as not being directly related to the product. However, this example demonstrates that it can be difficult to distinguish between measures directly related to the product and those that are not directly related to the product.

As to the explanation of the 'product-process' doctrine, the panel began with citing the product language used in the *US–Tuna* cases. Although stating that npr-ppm-measures were covered by GATT Art. III:4 because the word 'affect' also related to measures that adversely modify the conditions of competition,[309] it found that the provision nevertheless only permitted measures that are directly related to the product because GATT Art. III:4 only related to measures 'affecting the internal sale, offering for sale, purchase, transportation, distribution or use of products', i.e. activities relating to the product *as a product*.[310] This reasoning raises some doubts because the word 'affect' seems to have two meanings: On the one hand, it includes measures not directly related to the product as such, for example, measures that modify the conditions of competition, when interpreting the scope of GATT Art. III:4 in general; and on the other hand, it excludes measures not directly related to the product as a product when determining the scope of the prohibition contained in GATT Art. III:4.

The panel then gave a legal rationale for the 'product-process' doctrine. It pointed to the 'product concept' of the Working Party Report on Border Tax Adjustments and linked it to the purpose of GATT Art. III, i.e. to secure tariff

305 Demaret/Stewardson, p. 39.
306 Hudec (Product-Process Distinction), p. 203.
307 Ibid. p. 203.
308 For example, the treatment of vehicles imported under CAFE by more than one importer depends on whether the importers are under common control. If the importers are not under common control, their fleets would be treated differently, *US–Taxes on Automobiles*, para. 2.17.
309 *US–Automobiles*, para. 5.45.
310 Ibid., para. 5.52.

bindings. It held that the CONTRACTING PARTIES could not be expected to negotiate tariff commitments if these could be frustrated through the application of measures affecting imported products subject to tariff commitments, and triggered by factors unrelated to the products as such.[311] Whilst this is correct, one could argue that this purpose could also be achieved by examining those measures under the requirements of GATT Art. III:4 and not prohibiting them *per se*. Specifically, one would first ask whether the measures distinguish between like products, taking into account tariff classifications and if they do, whether they accord foreign like products less favourable treatment. This issue will be elaborated on later in this work. Finally, the panel pointed to the MFN clause stating that it also applied unconditionally when applied in conjunction with GATT Art. III:4. To allow for conditions not related to the product as such would therefore be in contradiction to GATT Art. I applied in conjunction with GATT Art. III:4. This argument appears to be convincing and will be analyzed in more detail below.

5.3.1.1.5 US–Gasoline

The WTO case *US–Gasoline* concerned the US Clean Air Act under which refiners were required to sell gasoline with a certain degree of cleanliness depending on specific baseline figures.[312] Domestic refiners could use individual baselines determined by data on the quality of the gasoline that they produced in 1990. Foreign refiners had to use the statutory baseline reflecting average US gasoline quality in 1990. In addition, if actual 1990 data was not available, importers and blenders were assigned the statutory baseline. For many foreign producers, the quality of gasoline under the statutory baseline was higher than the quality of the gasoline they had produced in 1990.[313] The application of two different baselines for foreign and domestic products thus caused *de iure* and *de facto* discrimination.

Although not mentioned in the panel report, the Clean Air Act could be regarded as a npr-ppm-measure violating the 'product-process' doctrine.[314] Whilst the US Act aimed at raising the quality of gasoline and could therefore be qualified as a measure directly related to the product, the different treatment under the different baseline figures depended on factors not directly related to the product as a product, but on the origin of the refiner. This would even be the case if foreign refiners had been accorded individual baselines

311 Ibid., para. 5.53.

312 *US–Gasoline*, report of the panel and the Appellate Body.

313 Hudec (Product-Process Distinction), p. 208.

314 Ibid.

because in that case, the baseline standard still depended on the producer. That is, the quality of the gasoline depended on how the producer in question produced gasoline in the year 1990 instead of depending on product characteristics set forth in the law. However, the panel did not qualify the baseline system as a npr-ppm-measure prohibited by GATT Art. III:4. It held that imported and domestic gasoline were 'like products' within the meaning of GATT Art. III:4. It further stated that because domestic gasoline was generally subject to an individual baseline whilst imported gasoline was not, and imported gasoline generally did not meet the statutory standard, imported products were less favourably treated within the meaning of GATT Art. III:4.[315] It then held that the baseline regulations could not be justified either under GATT Art. XX (b) relating to the protection of human, animal or plant life or health, or under GATT Art. XX (g) relating to the conservation of exhaustible natural resources.[316] Venezuela, Brazil and the US only appealed the findings under GATT Art. XX, not GATT Art. III.[317] Accordingly, the Appellate Body reversed the finding of the panel and held that the baseline requirements were covered by GATT Art. XX (g), but not justified.[318]

The rulings were understood as meaning that if the US made available the individual baseline to foreign refiners, they would be GATT-consistent.[319] Since the individual baseline requirements could be qualified as measures not directly related to the product, but rather to the producer, the cases could be taken as evidence against the 'product-process' doctrine.[320] However, as mentioned above, neither the panel nor the Appellate Body made such statements.

To the contrary, the panel followed the panel in *US–Malt Beverages*. When deciding on the part of the measure that prohibited importers to use their individual baseline in case they could not provide sufficient data, it explicitly stated that GATT Art. III:4 did not allow less favourable treatment based on the characteristics of the producer and the nature of the data held by it.[321] It further explained that such an interpretation would expose imported products to a highly subjective and variable treatment depending on extraneous factors.[322] This would result in great instability and uncertainty in the conditions

315 *US–Gasoline*, report of the panel, para. 6.10.
316 Ibid., paras. 6.25, 6.39–6.40.
317 *US–Gasoline*, report of the Appellate Body, p. 11.
318 Ibid., pp. 19–21.
319 Hudec, (Product-Process Distinction), p. 208.
320 Ibid.
321 *US–Gasoline*, report of the panel, para. 6.11.
322 Ibid., para. 6.12.

of competition.[323] These considerations strongly support the 'product-process' doctrine of the GATT rulings. However, when applying the necessity test under GATT Art. XX (b),[324] the panel stated that a less GATT-inconsistent measure would have been individual baselines made up of data from current foreign refiners.[325] This again could be taken as meaning that a measure relating to the producer could be GATT-consistent.[326] This, however, is not the case. The alternative GATT measure recommended under GATT Art. XX does not have to be GATT-consistent.[327] The defendant would have to challenge it in another case.

The Appellate Body followed the approach of the panel. In conclusion, although offering some support for a rejection of the 'product-process' doctrine, the rulings cannot be used as evidence for the GATT-legality of npr-ppm-measures.

5.3.1.1.6 Canada–Periodicals

The case *Canada–Periodicals* involved an 80 per cent excise tax on all advertisements published in a split-run edition of a periodical.[328] According to the Excise Tax Act, a split-run edition is an edition of an issue of a periodical distributed in Canada, in which more than 20 per cent of the editorial material is the same or substantially the same as the editorial material that appears in one or more excluded editions of one or more issues and contains an advertisement that does not appear in identical form in all of the excluded editions.[329] The US, the complainant in the case, argued that the tax depended on the characteristics of the producer – on the fact that the publisher runs a split-run edition and that a similar magazine is sold outside the Canadian market.[330] A split-run magazine could not be differentiated from a non-split-run magazine simply upon an examination of its physical form or editorial content.[331] In the view of the US, the tax violated the 'product-process' doctrine.[332] As in the *US–Malt Beverages* case, the tax therefore had to be found to violate GATT

323 Ibid.

324 Under the necessity test of GATT Art. XX (b), one has to examine whether an alternative measure is available that is less inconsistent with other GATT provisions, *US–Gasoline*, report of the panel, para. 6.25.

325 Ibid.

326 Hudec, (Product-Process Distinction), p. 210.

327 Ibid., p. 211.

328 *Canada–Periodicals*, report of the panel and the Appellate Body.

329 *Canada–Periodicals*, report of the panel, paras. 2.1–2.19.

330 Ibid., paras. 3.60, 3.64.

331 *Canada–Periodicals*, report of the panel, para. 3.60.

332 Ibid., para. 3.74.

Art. III:2,[333] A tax that favoured one type of production method would be obviously protectionist and should be GATT-inconsistent.[334] Canada argued that the tax depended on a producer-based characteristic that did affect the product in question.[335] That is, the criterion to have a split-run edition in fact targeted periodicals with non-Canadian content and thus a product characteristic.[336] Furthermore, Canada argued that the product characteristic was indeed the central objective of the tax.[337] Canada concluded that since the editorial content was the most important characteristic of a periodical, split-run periodicals and non-split-run periodicals could be considered as having different product characteristics, and therefore as non-like products within the meaning of GATT Art. III:2.[338] The US replied that even if the tax was directed at the editorial content, it actually drew the distinction between magazines whose content was sold in another country and magazines whose content was only sold in Canada.[339] Both parties of the dispute in fact supported the 'product-process' doctrine.

The panel did not rule on the 'product-process' doctrine, but held that the criterion of split-run periodicals related to factors outside of the Canadian market – whether the same editorial content was included in a foreign edition and whether the periodical contained different advertisements in foreign editions.[340] It then used the example of Harrowsmith Country Life, which had previously published a US and a Canadian edition, to demonstrate that these two editions were like because they had common end-uses, similar physical properties and had been designed for the same readership with the same tastes and habits.[341] The Appellate Body reversed that finding but did not rule on the 'product-process' doctrine either. The Appellate Body stated that the panel had compared the wrong pair of products since they were both editions of the same magazine as well as imported products.[342] It should have applied the criteria of the product's end-uses in a given market, consumers' tastes and habits, and the product's properties, nature and quality to other evidence provided by

333 Ibid., para. 3.64.
334 Ibid., para. 3.80.
335 Ibid., paras. 3.61, 3.64.
336 Ibid., paras. 3.62, 3.66.
337 Ibid., paras. 3.69, 3.88.
338 Ibid., paras. 3.66–3.71.
339 Ibid., para. 3.81.
340 Ibid., para. 5.24.
341 Ibid., para. 5.26.
342 *Canada–Periodicals*, report of the Appellate Body, p. 23.

the parties.[343] It then decided that it could not rule on the matter for lack of sufficient findings of fact and decided the case under GATT Art. III:2, second sentence.[344]

Again, in this case, the measure contained both non-product-related factors such as the producer's requirement to publish a split-run periodical as well as product-related factors such as editorial content. The panel did not openly address the question of these factors' relationship and which factor pre-dominated in their decision. Although it first stated that the measure essentially relied on factors external to the Canadian market,[345] in the next sentence, it noted that 'putting these external factors aside' split-run periodicals could be quite similar,[346] thereby relying on the editorial content that apparently in its view was independent of whether the periodical was split-run or not. The underlying rationale of the panel's reasoning might have been that the tax did not directly address the criterion of editorial content, which was an argument put forward by the US. By contrast, the Appellate Body seemed to treat the split-run criterion as a product-related criterion, criticizing that the panel had not focussed more on the actual product.[347] This could be taken to signify a rejection of the 'product-process' doctrine or simply that the Appellate Body followed Canada's argument to treat the split-run criteria as product-related criteria.[348] In any case, the Appellate Body did not give recognition to the 'product-process' doctrine.[349] In conclusion, neither the panel nor the Appellate Body report of the *Canada–Periodicals* clarified the 'product-process' doctrine.

5.3.1.1.7 Indonesia–Automobile Industry

In *Indonesia–Automobile Industry*, the panel applied the 'product-process' doctrine citing *US–Malt Beverages* and *US–Gasoline*.[350] As mentioned above, the case concerned internal taxes and regulations, and national car programmes that depended on either the products' country of manufacture; on their level of local content; on whether a motor vehicle was a National Car (under the

343 *Canada–Periodicals*, report of the Appellate Body pp. 22, 23; For a profound critique of this reasoning see Cone.

344 *Canada–Periodicals*, report of the Appellate Body, p. 24.

345 *Canada–Periodicals*, report of the panel, para. 5.24.

346 *Canada–Periodicals*, report of the panel, para. 5.25.

347 *Canada–Periodicals*, report of the Appellate Body, p. 23; Hudec (The Product-Process Distinction), p. 214.

348 Hudec, p. 214.

349 Cone.

350 *Indonesia–Automobile Industry*, report of the panel, para. 14.113.

Indonesian National Car Programme) and had complied with certain local content requirements; had incorporated a certain percentage of 'counter-purchased' parts and components exported from Indonesia; or on the characteristics of the car manufacturers.[351] Applying GATT Art. III:2, first sentence, the panel first referred to the criteria of the Working Party Report on Border Tax Adjustments stating that the National Cars and the imported cars had the same end-uses and the same basic properties, nature and quality, and that there were no differences as to consumers' tastes and habits.[352] When looking for comparable imported cars, it stated that any imported car would be taxed in excess of 'like' domestic cars. Since the distinction made by the Indonesian measure was not based on the product *per se*, but rather on factors such as the nationality of the producer or the origin of the parts and components contained in the product, even a product identical in all respects to a domestic product, except for its origin or other factors not related to the product as such, would be subject to a different level of taxation.[353] It then cited the Appellate Body report of *Canada–Periodicals* to state that this case was different,[354] thereby suggesting that this case involved a measure based on product characteristics. The panel continued that an imported motor vehicle alike in all aspects relevant to a likeness determination would be taxed at a higher rate simply because of its origin or lack of sufficient local content.[355] It then held that such an origin-based distinction would be enough to find a violation of GATT Art. III:2, first sentence, recalling in a footnote that former panels such as *US–Malt Beverages* and *US–Gasoline* had found that differences in producers' characteristics could not justify a different tax treatment of the product.[356]

This case refers to the 'product-process' distinction, but without delivering further legal arguments. It should be noted however that the measure in question constituted *de iure* discrimination directly related to the origin of products. From the wording of the case, it can be concluded that the fact that process-based measures were involved weighed less than the discrimination with respect to the origin of products. In addition, the statement of the panel concerning the Appellate Body report of *Canada–Periodicals* is interesting, as it supports the suggestion that the measures in this case related to product characteristics.

351 *Indonesia–Automobile Industry*, report of the panel.

352 *Indonesia-Automobile Industry*, report of the panel, para. 14.110.

353 *Indonesia–Automobile Industry*, para. 14.112.

354 *Indonesia–Automobile Industry*, para. 14.113.

355 Ibid.

356 Ibid., fn. 708.

5.3.1.1.8 US–Shrimp

The next case involving a npr-ppm-measure was the *US–Shrimp* case.[357] Under the US Endangered Species Act, all US shrimp trawlers were required to use turtle excluder devices in specified areas with high turtle mortality rates. Later, the US introduced a measure that prohibited the import of shrimps harvested by a method that may endanger sea turtles, subject to certain conditions. The measure was subsequently accompanied by several guidelines that allowed for the import of shrimps under certain conditions. The facts of the case mirrored those of the *US–Tuna* cases, where the US Marine Mammal Protection Act regulating tuna harvesting to protect dolphins also provided for an import prohibition of tuna that was harvested in dolphin-unfriendly ways. However, all parties agreed that the measure under examination in the present case was an import prohibition that had to be examined under GATT Art. XI.[358] Especially the US in the *US–Tuna* cases had argued that because the enforcement of the US requirements in the case of the imported product took place at the border, the Note *Ad* Article III explicitly recognized it.[359] Therefore, the measure – a ppm – had to be analyzed under GATT Art. III:4, which does not distinguish between the laws, regulations and requirements that had an impact on the physical characteristics of a product and those that otherwise affected the internal sale.[360] The US in *US–Shrimp* therefore seems to have accepted the 'product-process' doctrine. The panel accordingly decided the case under GATT Art. XI, citing the *US–Tuna* cases.[361] Since the issue was not appealed, the Appellate Body did not consider the issue.[362]

The *Shrimp/Turtle* case seems to confirm that the 'product-process' doctrine is accepted by the WTO adjudicating bodies as well as by most of the WTO members.

5.3.1.1.9 EC–Asbestos

This case concerned a French Government Decree declaring a ban on asbestos including the import and sale of asbestos fibres and all materials containing asbestos fibres.[363] There were certain exceptions to the ban in case there was no substitute available that posed a lesser risk to human health. Canada had

357 *US–Shrimp*, report of the panel and Appellate Body.
358 *US–Shrimp*, report of the panel, paras. 7.13–15.
359 *US–Tuna I*, para. 3.19.
360 *US–Tuna I*, paras. 3.18, 3.20.
361 *US–Shrimps*, report of the panel, para. 7.16.
362 *US–Shrimps*, report of the Appellate Body.
363 *EC–Asbestos*, report of the panel, paras. 2.1–7.

complained that the ban resulted in the 'less favourable treatment' of imported asbestos fibres and products containing asbestos compared to that of like domestic products, thus constituting a violation of GATT Art. III. Comparing asbestos fibres to certain substitutes, the panel held that the health risk caused by asbestos fibres was not an appropriate criterion to define 'likeness'.[364] Relying mainly on the similar end-uses of both types of fibres, it concluded that imported and domestic products were 'like products'.[365] The same held true for products containing asbestos.[366] The Appellate reversed these findings and stated inter alia that the criteria of the Working Party Report on Border Tax Adjustments referring to end-uses and consumers' tastes and habits were key criteria since they related to the competitive relationship between products, which is the core of GATT Art. III.[367] With regard to the relationship between GATT Art. III and GATT Art. XX, it stated that

> We do not agree with the Panel that considering evidence relating to the health risks associated with a product, under Article III:4, nullifies the effect of Article XX(b) of the GATT 1994. Article XX(b) allows a Member to "adopt and enforce" a measure, *inter alia*, necessary to protect human life or health, even though that measure is inconsistent with another provision of the GATT 1994. Article III:4 and Article XX(b) are distinct and independent provisions of the GATT 1994 each to be interpreted on its own.[368]

While this case does not deal with a npr-ppm, its findings seem to suggest that for the determination of the likeness of products neither the qualification of the measure as a npr-ppm-measure nor its policy objective as being one included in the list of GATT Art. XX is decisive. What matters is whether products are in a competitive relationship. Thus, consumers' tastes and habits have a decisive role in the analysis, not so much the characterization of the measure as a npr-ppm.[369]

364 *EC–Asbestos*, report of the panel, paras. 8.129–132.
365 Ibid., para. 8.144.
366 Ibid., paras. 8.145–150.
367 Ibid., para. 117, see below, p. 111.
368 Ibid., para 115.
369 For a more thorough analysis, see below, p. 111.

5.3.1.1.10 US–Tuna II (Mexico)

The third case on tuna concerned the US labelling scheme applying a label to tuna caught either in a dolphin friendly way or outside the Eastern Tropical Pacific region.[370] This time, the Appellate Body found that the TBT Agreement covered npr-ppms, holding that the labelling scheme was a technical regulation within the meaning of the TBT Agreement. While it may decide differently in case of measures other than labelling requirements falling under GATT Art. III, the decision may open some way for the inclusion of npr-ppm-measures under the GATT.

5.3.1.1.11 US–Clove Cigarettes

In *US–Clove Cigarettes*, the Appellate Body, having to rule on the 'likeness' of menthol and clove cigarettes, held with regard to GATT Art. III:4:

> In the light of this context and of the object and purpose of the *TBT Agreement*, as expressed in its preamble, we consider that the determination of likeness under Article 2.1 of the *TBT Agreement*, as well as under Article III:4 of the GATT 1994, is a determination about the nature and extent of a competitive relationship between and among the products at issue. To the extent that they are relevant to the examination of certain "likeness" criteria and are reflected in the products' competitive relationship, regulatory concerns underlying technical regulations may play a role in the determination of likeness.[371]

Thus, here again, it seems that it is not the nature or type of the measure and its relation to the product or production process what matters but the competitive relationship between the products in question.

5.3.1.1.12 EC–Seal Products

The case *EC–Seal Products* dealt with a npr-ppm-measure.[372] The measure at issue was a ban on the import of seals except when the seals products were hunted by Inuit or other indigenous communities, or were imported by travellers for their personal use or were by-products of hunting for the purpose of the sustainable management of marine resources. The Appellate Body held that the main feature of the measure were the exceptions relating to the identity of the hunter, or the type or purpose of the hunt. Hence, the measure could

370 *US–Tuna II* (Mexico), report of the Appellate Body.

371 *US–Clove Cigarettes*, report of the Appellate Body, para. 120; see also below, p. 114.

372 *EC–Seals*, report of the Appellate Body.

not be considered as laying down product characteristics as required by the definition of a technical regulation according to the TBT Agreement. Instead, it had to be examined under the GATT.[373] Considering that the EC Seal regime may potentially qualify as a related process and production method according to the definition of a technical regulation, the Appellate Body nevertheless refrained from completing the legal analysis because in his view, the question had not been explored sufficiently by the panel.[374] This cautious approach does however not rule out npr-ppms and may be taken as an indication that npr-ppms at least are not *per se* contrary to WTO law.

5.3.1.1.13 Conclusion

It can be concluded that the GATT and WTO jurisprudence has not finally ruled on the 'product-process' doctrine. Of the five cases that explicitly referred to the 'product-process' doctrine,[375] three were not adopted[376] and one involved direct discrimination,[377] i.e. the measure would have been invalidated anyway. Only the *US–Malt Beverages* case was adopted and involved an origin-neutral measure. The panel on *US–Malt Beverages* did not explicitly declare npr-ppm-measures as *prima facie* GATT-illegal but stated that products could not be differentiated according to their production methods. Whilst some of the cases delivered a legal rationale for the doctrine, none of the cases examined could establish a textual basis of the doctrine. Holding that GATT Art. III:4 required a comparison between products as products, they did neither explain why npr-ppm-measures could not affect the sale of products, nor why products could not be differentiated on the basis of their process and production method. The legal arguments refer to the Working Party Report on Border Tax Adjustments, which limits eligible taxes to taxes directly borne by the product. However, as explained above, the application of the rationale of the Report to all fiscal measures and regulations of GATT Art. III:4 does not always work. Other arguments refer to the purpose of GATT Art. III to secure tariff bindings, to the issue of extraterritoriality, the relationship between unconditional MFN treatment required by GATT Art. I, and the product concept contained in GATT Art. III. Since these arguments have been commented on by many legal authors, they will be discussed in the next sections.

---

373 Ibid., para. 5.1.3.3.4.

374 Ibid., para. 5.69.

375 *US–Tuna I* and *II*, *US–Automobiles*, *US–Malt Beverages*, *Indonesia–Automobile Industry*.

376 *US–Tuna I* and *II*, *US–Automobiles*.

377 *Indonesia–Automobile Industry*.

The case *US–Shrimp* reflects the consensus among WTO members on the validity of the 'product-process' doctrine.

The remaining cases involve measures that contain factors related to product characteristics as well as factors related to the producer, i.e. not directly related to the product. The fact that only the panel in *US–Gasoline* referred to the 'product-process' doctrine, and only in relation to one part of the measure, could be proof of the fact that the doctrine is sometimes difficult to apply and that the WTO adjudicating bodies tend to resolve cases without taking recourse to the 'product-process' doctrine. In *Canada–Periodicals*, although the measure clearly related to producer characteristics, both the panel and the Appellate Body were reluctant to apply the 'product-process' doctrine. In the cases *EC–Asbestos* and *US–Clove Cigarettes*, while not dealing with npr-ppms, the Appellate Body emphasized that the list contained in the Working Party's report is not a closed one and that it is the competitive relationship between products what matters, leaving room for npr-ppms as a criterion to distinguish between products.[378] In its rulings *US–Tuna II (Mexico)* and *EC–Seal Products*, the Appellate Body has shown some openness to npr-ppms in relation to the TBT Agreement.

Upcoming panel decisions will hopefully contribute to clarify the WTO-compatibility of npr-ppms. In both cases *EU and Certain Member States–Palm Oil (Malaysia)* and *EU–Palm Oil (Indonesia)* on the EU's Renewable Energy Directive II, 2018/2001/EU, (RED II), a panel decision is expected in 2023.[379] RED II allows for trade measures based on sustainability criteria for the production of and incorporates a decision to progressively phase out usage and imports of biofuels made partially or wholly from unsustainable production by 2030.[380] Indonesia and Malaysia argue that such policy measures discriminate against their export-oriented palm oil industry.

5.3.1.2 *Contesting the 'Product-Process' Doctrine*

Several legal authors dispute the 'product-process' doctrine.[381] They hold the view that npr-ppms are not *prima facie* GATT-illegal. Their first argument is

---

378 For a thorough discussion of the term likeness, see below, pp. 103 et seqq.

379 See WTO Dispute Settlement, *EU—Palm Oil (Indonesia)*, https://www.wto.org/english/tratop_e/dispu_e/cases_e/ds593_e.htm and *EU and Certain Member States—Palm Oil (Malaysia)*, https://www.wto.org/english/tratop_e/dispu_e/cases_e/ds600_e.htm.

380 Cf. Oeschger/Bürgi Bonanomi.

381 Howse/Regan; Regan (Regulatory Purpose); Fauchald, p. 454; Thaggert, p. 78; Bronckers/McNelis, pp. 376 et seqq.; Whilst not arguing in favour of process-based measures, Hudec (The Product-Process Distinction) critically reviews the GATT/WTO case law, revealing some contradictions in the application of the 'product-process' doctrine. He takes the

that nothing in the text of GATT Art. III indicates that process-based distinctions are GATT-illegal. In relation to the repeated use of the word 'product' in GATT Art. III, they state that this would only indicate that GATT Art. III is about trade in goods.[382] When it comes to 'likeness', they hold that physical similarity is not necessarily the decisive criterion.[383] Admitting that physically similar is the ordinary meaning of 'like', they hold that, despite the rule of treaty interpretation of Art. 31 (1) of the VCLT, there is no such thing as 'ordinary meaning'. Instead, the context informs the meaning of the term from the start. Since the real issue is whether regulatory distinctions have a rational relation to some non-protectionist regulatory purpose, 'like' means 'not differing in any respect relevant to an actual non-protectionist policy'. Thus, physical similarity is not decisive and npr-ppm-measures are not *per se* rendered GATT-inconsistent. They reject the argument that physical similarity entails likeness stating that the fact that physical similar products are more likely to be like is too general to solve the question on the meaning of likeness.

In relation to the contextual argument that to allow for npr-ppm-measures under considerations of the regulatory purpose would render GATT Art. XX redundant, they state that these exceptions still apply to facially discriminatory measures.

Analysing the GATT/WTO jurisprudence, they state that the only cases establishing the 'product-process' doctrine are *US–Malt Beverages* and *US–Automobiles*, neither of which were convincing. After close examination of the *Japan–Alcoholic Beverages* case they conclude that a consideration of the regulatory purpose of the measure is still possible.

Regarding labelling, they hold the opinion that a government may legitimately prohibit the sale of goods made entirely by the disfavoured process rather than having recourse to less trade-restrictive measure such as labelling.[384] Governments should have the right to effectively prevent that externalities such as environmentally unfriendly practices are imposed on national consumers.

On the issue of extraterritoriality – i.e. that process-based measures are inherently extraterritorial and should therefore be prohibited as they infringe on the sovereignty of foreign countries –, they maintain that to the contrary, to prevent a country from prohibiting the import of goods it does not want

view that the 'like product' concept is an open-ended standard the interpretation of which depends on the will of governments.

382 Howse/Regan, p. 254.

383 For an overview on the arguments see Howse/Regan, p. 260 et seqq.

384 Ibid. p. 274.

would infringe on the sovereignty of the importing country.[385] Since the GATT does not provide a general right of market access, there is no reason to use the sovereignty argument only in favour of the exporting country.[386] Moreover, process-based measures are not necessarily extraterritorial in the sense that the importing country would not have any interest in their regulation since most of these measures concern matters of global interest such as the ozone layer.[387]

As to arguments of protectionism, they hold that eliminating a competitive advantage to foreign products is necessary for reasons of economic efficiency.[388] That is, to be economically efficient, externalities also need to be internalized in foreign countries. Regarding the question of who determines what externalities have to be internalized, they hold that any matter that a country considers as referring to universally binding norms on moral grounds can legitimately be internalized.[389] In addition, where process-based measures concern regulations such as laws against child labour, the competitive advantage of the foreign country relies on legal facts and is not a true comparative advantage that achieves economic efficiency.[390] As to the problem which country should pay for the internalization, the authors hold that this problem is not only inherent to process-based measures but also common to product-related measures.[391] In the context of distributive justice, they hold that although it can be true that poor producers from poor countries who have to meet higher production standards may be worse off, this does not hold true in all cases, and that again, this is not a problem unique to process-based measures.[392] Most importantly, with a view to the climate crisis and the need for sustainable development, other authors argue that a narrow interpretation of 'likeness' allowing for npr-ppm-measures that enables countries to differentiate products based on how they are produced follows from 'systemic' interpretative approaches, whereby WTO rules should be interpreted and applied in relation and by reference to a broader normative environment informed by sustainability concerns.[393]

385 Ibid. p. 275; Neumann, p. 131.
386 Ibid.
387 Ibid. p. 278.
388 Ibid. p. 280.
389 Ibid. pp. 280, 282–284.
390 Ibid. p. 281.
391 Ibid.
392 Ibid. pp. 287, 288.
393 Musselli/Solar/Tribaldos/Bürgi Bonanomi, p. 28.

Finally, it is argued that the *per se* GATT-illegality of ppm-measures might lead to the invalidation of relatively harmless regulations.[394]

5.3.1.3 *Defending the 'Product-Process' Doctrine*

The majority of authors seems to be in favour of the 'product-process' doctrine.[395] In addition to the legal arguments put forward by the jurisprudence, the main arguments are as follows.

In contrast to what has been asserted, they hold that there is 'justifiable text'.[396] The very word 'product' instead of 'process' indicates that one has to focus on the characteristics of a product, not on its process or production method.[397]

Another argument arises out of the context: GATT Art. XX (e) provides an exception for measures aimed at the prohibition of goods made with prison labour.[398] This is proof of the fact that the treaty drafters wanted to rather examine labour standards – if eligible – under GATT Art. XX, and that consequently, npr-ppm-measures related to labour standards have to be regarded as GATT Art. III-inconsistent.[399] Moreover, if measures related to prison labour are justified under GATT Art. III, the GATT Art. XX exception is rendered redundant.[400]

The other argument put forward by advocates of the 'process-product' doctrine is that their opponents have interesting ideas, but miss trade policy's real issue: The real problem is how to develop substantive criteria to prevent the potential abuse of process-oriented trade barriers.[401] In the context of trade policy, a bright-line rule is needed that can be easily administered by trade officials. If one does not rely on objective criteria, the danger exists that panels decide for themselves what criteria are appropriate to distinguish between products.[402]

In addition, process-based measures are inherently extraterritorial because they relate to policies of other WTO members.[403] By contrast, product-related

394 Hudec (The Product-Process Distinction), p. 192 refers to objections within the trade community.

395 Jackson (Comments on Shrimp/Turtle); Quick/Lau; Zedalis; Davey/Pauwelyn; Mavroidis (Like Products).

396 Jackson (Comments on Shrimp/Turtle), p. 302.

397 Ibid., p. 303.

398 Quick/Lau, p. 453.

399 Ibid., p. 455.

400 Ibid., p. 453.

401 Jackson (Comments on Shrimp/Turtle), p. 304.

402 Davey/Pauwelyn, p. 38.

403 Marceau/Trachtmann, p. 858.

measures regulate products coming under the jurisdiction of the importing member. Thus, the 'product-process' distinction is a clear rule to avoid extra-territorial measures. As regards the internalization of externalities, the question is to what extent one country can coerce another country to internalize 'externalities' that other WTO members do not regard as an externality.[404] In terms of procedure, the question arises whether it should really be the WTO's adjudicating bodies that decide which process-based measures are GATT-legal, rather than governments deciding in negotiation processes.[405]

5.3.1.4 *Evaluation*

Both sides rely on intellectually appealing arguments. The aim of this section is to analyse these arguments in view of the international trade context as well as legal certainty and predictability.

5.3.1.4.1 The Term 'Products'

Regarding the textual basis, at first glance, one has to concede that indeed, all relevant provisions of GATT Art. III:1, 2 and 4, employ the word 'like *products*'. However, since the focus is not on the products *per se*, but on the question by which criteria a measure should differentiate between them, there is nothing in the text to conclude that one should only focus on the product characteristics. As Howse rightly argues, the word 'product' is just an indication that national treatment is required in relation to trade in goods.

5.3.1.4.2 Physical Similarities

With regard to the term 'likeness', it has been argued that physical similarities should not be the decisive criterion since an ordinary meaning of the word within the meaning of Art. 31 (1) of the VCLT does not exist. Indeed, in relation to the term 'like', even the Appellate Body submitted in *EC–Asbestos* that the dictionary meaning 'Having the same characteristics or qualities as some other ... thing; of approximately identical shape, size, etc., with something else; similar', leaves much room for interpretation.[406] After all, most products at issue will have many physical characteristics in common. The dictionary meaning does not reveal the extent to which products have to share the same characteristics. Also, the definition does not say from whose perspective 'likeness' has to

---

404 Jackson (Comments on Shrimp/Turtle), p. 307.

405 Jackson (Comments on Shrimp/Turtle), p. 307; Mavroidis (Like Products) argues that any change to the current law on 'like products' should occur through a legislative amendment of GATT Art. XX; Quick/Lau, pp. 455, 456.

406 *EC–Asbestos*, report of the Appellate Body, paras. 90–92.

be determined. Consumers have different views than producers or the government. Most importantly, some consumers may qualify physically similar products as dissimilar, for example sustainability-oriented consumers may regard e.g. Fair-Trade coffee not as substitutable with conventional coffee, thus classify the products according to their production method instead of their physical similarity. In *Philippines–Distilled Spirits*, the Appellate Body confirmed the panel's finding that the consumer perception is also relevant when determining the physical similarity of products.[407] These considerations indeed support the conclusion that the meaning of 'like' depends on the context and does not *a priori* exclude factors such as process and production methods. Whether the relevant context will be the regulatory purpose of the measure, as argued by opponents of the 'product-process' doctrine, will be discussed in the next section.

Yet, one final consideration on 'physical similarity' should be made. The opponents of the 'product-process' doctrine hold that the fact that most physically similar products are likely to be like is too general to solve the question of likeness. However, it can be assumed that products with a high degree of similarity in most cases tend to be in a competitive relationship.[408] Since the purpose of GATT Art. III is to avoid discrimination between foreign and domestic goods, which can only occur if products are in a competitive relationship, competitiveness matters when defining the likeness of products. Thus, although physical similarity might not be the decisive criterion, it is certainly an important criterion when determining likeness. As the Appellate Body states in *EC–Asbestos*, it will be difficult to find 'like' products that have a high degree of physical dissimilarity.[409]

5.3.1.4.3 The Context

The contextual argument that the prison labour exception under GATT Art. XX (e) provides evidence that npr-ppm-measures, especially labour standards, should be dealt with under that provision at first sight seems to be convincing. If they were examined under GATT Art. III, GATT Art. XX could be rendered redundant, at least in relation to prison labour. In this context, it is argued that the short list of policy objectives contained in GATT Art. XX makes clear that origin-neutral measures were not intended to be examined under GATT Art. XX.[410] While seven of the objectives contained in GATT Art. XX are normally

407 *Philippines–Distilled Spirits*, report of the Appellate Body, paras. 130–133.

408 Hudec (Like Product), p. 103.

409 *EC–Asbestos*, report of the Appellate Body, para. 118.

410 Roessler (Beyond the Ostensible), p. 778.

not invoked in this context because they deal with the import and export of products, the remaining three are not enough to cover all origin-neutral ppm-measures.[411] As is the case with measures concerning child labour, most npr-ppm-measures are origin-neutral.[412] They could therefore be dealt with perfectly under GATT Art. III whilst GATT Art. XX retains its role for facially discriminatory measures. However, whether origin-neutral npr-ppm-measures should be exclusively dealt with under GATT Art. III is doubtful. At this point, it suffices to state that npr-ppm-measures do not need to be prohibited *per se* by GATT Art. III, only those that do not fulfil the 'like product' criteria. Whether these criteria only refer to the regulatory purpose of a measure or include other criteria as well will be discussed below. Thus, while the contextual argument is a strong, it is not compelling. Further, relevant context is also the preamble to the WTO Agreement, which states that the prohibition of non-discrimination should contribute to the objective of sustainable development and thus gives some leeway to npr-ppm-measures with this policy goal. This argument will be dealt with when discussing the relevance of regulatory purposes.[413]

5.3.1.4.4 GATS Art. XVII

The national treatment clause contained in GATS Art. XVII relating to services may be used as evidence that distinctions not related to the product itself are allowed under GATT Art. III. GATS Art. XVII holds that national treatment extends to suppliers of services. Thus, measures that are primarily aimed at suppliers of services in contrast to the services themselves are not *per se* GATS-illegal. Since the GATS was only adopted at the Uruguay Round, it can be assumed that its clauses are based on former GATT practice and experience. Hence, GATT Art. III must be interpreted as not prohibiting *per se* measures that are not directly related to products.

5.3.1.4.5 Circumvention of Tariff Bindings?

With regard to the various arguments put forward by the jurisprudence, the one referring to the function of GATT Art. III to secure tariff bindings appears to be convincing. If governments were free to distinguish between products on the basis of production methods used, they could easily circumvent their tariff concessions. However, as the Appellate Body stated in *Japan–Alcoholic Beverages*, the purpose of GATT Art. III was not limited to protect tariff

---

411 Ibid.

412 Since they concern process or production methods, they do not (facially) relate to the origin of products.

413 See below, pp. 147 et seqq.

concessions under GATT Art. II, but to generally prohibit the use of internal measures so as to afford protection to domestic production.[414] Moreover, as argued above, product distinctions could be made taking tariff concessions into account. Indeed, in a case that will be discussed below, the Appellate Body included tariff classifications among the criteria upon which it defined 'likeness'.[415]

5.3.1.4.6 The Unconditionality of the MFN Clause

One argument with respect to GATT Art. I refers to the relationship between the prohibition of a condition under the MFN clause and the 'like products' concept under GATT Art. III. If GATT Art. III allowed for conditions not related to products that were prohibited under GATT Art. I:1, tariff concessions made under GATT Art. II – and multilaterally applied through GATT Art. I – could be defeated. In addition, the right to unconditional MFN treatment in the application of Art. III:4, which is specifically mentioned in GATT Art. I:1, would not be assured.[416] The question therefore is whether GATT Art. I:1 prohibits conditions not directly related to the product. As mentioned above, this question has been answered in *Canada–Automotive Industry*.[417] The panel held that whether an advantage was accorded 'unconditionally' could not be determined independently of an examination of whether it involved discrimination between like products from different countries.[418] Specifically, the panel stated that this meant that making an advantage subject to conditions not related to the product was not *per se* inconsistent with GATT Art. I:1.[419] Rather, the obligation to accord 'unconditionally' to third countries an advantage that has been granted to any other country means that the extension of that advantage may not be made subject to conditions with respect to the situation or conduct of those countries.[420] It follows that the illegality of conditions attached to an advantage cannot be concluded from the fact that they are conditions not directly related to the product, but only from the fact that they discriminate between countries.

---

414 *Japan–Alcoholic Beverages*, report of the Appellate Body, pp. 16–17.

415 *EC–Asbestos*, report of the Appellate Body, para. 101; *Philippines–Distilled Spirits*, report of the Appellate Body, paras. 158–165.

416 Cf. *US–Taxes on Automobiles*, para. 5.54.

417 *Canada–Automotive Industry*, report of the panel, para. 10.22; this passage was not reviewed by the Appellate Body Report.

418 Ibid.

419 Ibid., para. 10.29.

420 Ibid, para. 10.23.

The same should hold true for GATT Art. III: Distinctions based on process or production methods not reflected in the final product are not *per se* prohibited, only if they discriminate against foreign products, i.e. if they specifically refer to the situation or conduct of foreign countries. However, before arriving at this conclusion, one has to ask whether conditionality under GATT Art. I:1 means the same thing as conditionality under GATT Art. III. It might be the case that only GATT Art. I permits conditions not directly related to the product. Yet, at this point this consideration is irrelevant since the question was whether the unconditionality in GATT Art. I:1 would prevent GATT Art. III from imposing conditions not related to the product, not the other way around. However, since the conclusion just mentioned is important for the validity of the 'process-product' doctrine, it shall be stated that at first glance, there is no reason to assume that the two non-discrimination clauses should be treated differently. The only difference mentioned earlier in this work referred to more government flexibility to discriminate under GATT Art. I with respect to the principle of reciprocity. Still, this does not mean that governments generally have more flexibility under the MFN clause to discriminate on the basis of process and production methods such as child labour, than under the national treatment clause. Thus, the term 'conditionality' has to be interpreted in the same way as under GATT Art. I and III. It can therefore be concluded that GATT Art. III does not *per se* prohibit countries from imposing conditions under their fiscal and regulatory measures, provided that they do not relate to the situation or conduct of a country.

5.3.1.4.7 Labelling

The argument by advocates of the 'product-process' doctrine that governments have to take recourse to labelling when they want to prohibit a certain production method does not add on the debate. This is because labelling itself is a npr-ppm-measure that distinguishes between products on the basis of their process and production methods, e.g. between products made with or without child labour.

5.3.1.4.8 The Issue of Extraterritoriality

With a view to the arguments examined so far, it seems that npr-ppm-measures do not have to be considered to be *prima facie* GATT-illegal. However, one of the main arguments in favour of the 'process-product' doctrine is that npr-ppm-measures are inherently extraterritorial and infringe on the sovereignty of other WTO members. This argument, together with those related to protectionism, is at the core of the debate and shall now be examined carefully.[421]

As stated above, npr-ppm-measures such as those related to child labour or environmental issues (e.g. the protection of dolphins or turtles) are policy-based measures and necessarily refer to the policy of other WTO members, whether they have the same policy or not. Admittedly, product-based measures concerning what individual materials products are allowed to be made of equally touch upon the policy of other WTO members. But since the products are imported into the country prohibiting certain materials, they are in the territory and under the jurisdiction of the importing country. The country may therefore legitimately legislate that certain materials may not to be contained in (imported) products. By contrast, as the process and production method prohibited by the importing country does not occur in its territory, it falls primarily under the jurisdiction of the exporting country.

Even if one accepted the argument that the sovereignty of the importing state is violated if the state is prevented from prohibiting products made in a manner it opposes, this would not solve the conflict. The question is which states' sovereignty prevails, and this should be the state whose sovereignty is more infringed upon. Thus, one could argue that the sovereignty of the exporting state should prevail because here, material interests are involved whereas the importing state only relies on moral grounds – it just does not want products made with child labour. However, since it is difficult to weigh material interests against morality, this line of reasoning does not provide a fully satisfactory answer.

5.3.1.4.9 The Concept of Sovereignty and Extraterritorial Jurisdiction

Instead, it should be asked what the concept of sovereignty or extraterritorial jurisdiction really means, and how the conflict can be solved in accordance with international law. In this context, one should recall the Appellate Body report on *US–Gasoline*, which held that the WTO agreements should not be read 'in clinical isolation from public international law'.[422] According to Art.

421 Other authors such as Bartels (Extraterritorial Jurisdiction), Blüthner, p. 359 et seqq. and Feddersen, p. 262 deal with this problem under GATT Art. XX. However, other authors raise the issue also in relation to GATT Art. III, see for example Howse/Regan, p. 274 et seqq. and Marceau/Trachtmann, p. 858. Since the argument is made that GATT Art. III prohibits ppm-measures because of their extraterritoriality, the issue will also be discussed here. The discussion is without prejudice as to whether extraterritorial measures are compatible with GATT Art. XX.

422 *US–Gasoline*, report of the Appellate Body, p. 18.

3 (2) of the DSU, the WTO agreements have to be interpreted in line with customary rules of international law. As stated above, Art. 31 (3) lit. c of the VCLT is such a rule, and states that any relevant rule of international law applicable in the relations between the parties can be referred to in the interpretation. Thus, international law on sovereignty and extraterritorial effects of state acts can be applied. One can of course argue that the GATT *per se* prohibits infringements upon the sovereignty of member states. However, being members of the GATT, countries have already transferred part of their sovereignty to GATT. Thus, the question is how much sovereignty they have transferred. The text of GATT Art. III is silent on this.

The principle of sovereignty is a principle of international law and stipulates that whilst a state is supreme internally, it must not intervene in the domestic jurisdiction of other states.[423] The exclusivity of jurisdiction of states over their respective territories is thus a central attribute of sovereignty.[424] However, it is questionable whether states are prevented from attaching legal consequences within its territory to a situation or occurrence outside its territory. This is exactly the case with ppm-measures: In case foreign producers want to export the goods they produced into the territory of the legislating state, in contrast to safety regulations targeting consumers of the regulating state, npr-ppm-measures force foreign nationals to produce in accordance with their prescriptions even without any measurable physical effect of the production method on consumers. It is held that this kind of legislation, where foreign nationals abroad cannot reasonably afford to disregard the prescriptions without suffering considerable hardship, is a case of territorial jurisdiction with extraterritorial effects.[425] General rules of public international law allow this kind of legislation if a 'meaningful connection'[426] or an 'adequate minimum contact'[427] to the situation abroad can be established. It depends on the area of law however whether extraterritorial effects are justified in the individual case.[428]

For example, in competition law, the US has established the 'effects' doctrine.[429] According to this doctrine, in case of substantial intentional effects within its domestic jurisdiction, a state may regulate economic matters outside its territory.[430] For example, in *Hartford Fire Insurance Co. v. California,*

423 Shaw, p. 454.
424 Steinberger, p. 516.
425 Meng, p. 338.
426 Bartels (Extraterritorial Jurisdiction), p. 370.
427 Meng, p. 340.
428 Ibid.
429 Shaw, p. 484.
430 Ibid.

substantial effects in antitrust matters were considered enough.[431] The doctrine was heavily disputed by other states. Accordingly, attempts were made to introduce a rule of reason test that ended up being rejected.[432] In a recent case, the EC seems to have applied the 'effects' doctrine.[433]

Applying this doctrine to the present case where the process and production method used by the exporting state only has a moral effect within the domestic jurisdiction of the regulating state,[434] i.e. not an intended and substantial one, one has to conclude that the importing country must be denied extra-territorial jurisdiction. However, it has to be noted that npr-ppm-measures, in contrast to the case of antitrust matters, are a case of territorial jurisdiction with extraterritorial effects and not extraterritorial jurisdiction in its proper sense. Hence, the threshold for a sufficient domestic effect should not be as high as in antitrust matters. Thus, in principle, npr-ppm-measures with extra-territorial effects should be allowed under general international law and not be *per se* GATT-illegal.

Moreover, the concept of territorial sovereignty has been changed by transnational concerns such as human rights. As Kaufmann rightly holds, globalisation has altered the meaning of sovereignty by changing the state's sphere of influence.[435] It is widely accepted that human rights are not purely internal affairs anymore.[436] Some provisions of the UDHR have become part of customary law that is binding upon all states.[437] The Maastricht Principles from 2011 explicitly state in principle 24 that every state has the obligation separately, and jointly through international cooperation, to protect economic, social and cultural rights of persons within their territories and extraterritorially.[438] Principle 25 sets forth the obligation to protect human rights abroad where there is a reasonable link between the State concerned and the conduct it

---

431 Direct, substantial and foreseeable effect coupled with intent is the basis for jurisdiction in the US, Lowenfeld, p. 47.

432 Shaw, p. 484.

433 Ibid., p. 490; Cottier (Anti-Trust Rules in Domestic Jurisdiction), p. 483.

434 The moral effect is that products made with child labour would be imported contrary to the morals of the importing state. However, if it could be established that child labour abroad had detrimental trade effects for the importing country, there would be a substantial effect.

435 Kaufmann (Globalization and Labour Rights), p. 285.

436 Shaw, p. 202.

437 Humbert (The Challenge of Child Labour), pp. 47–53.

438 The Maastricht Principles by the ETO consortium constitute an international expert consortium on extraterritorial obligations on human rights, see https://www.etoconsortium.org/nc/en/main-navigation/library/maastricht-principles/?tx_drblob_pi1%5BdownloadUid%5D=23.

seeks to regulate, including where relevant aspects of a non-State actor's activities are carried out in that State's territory. In legal literature it is held that in the area of business and human rights, there is a green light for extraterritorial jurisdiction if regulation is concerned with an issue about which there is international concern.[439] In any event, it is part of the concept of sovereignty to enter into international treaties.[440] For example, under the almost universally ratified CRC, states have the international obligation to prohibit child labour. Hence, they have restricted their sovereignty on that matter. It follows that a country that has ratified the CRC cannot use the concept of sovereignty to argue against a law that regulates child labour. On the contrary, in the area of child labour, one should in principle assume a 'meaningful connection' to the jurisdiction of another state. Along the same lines, the opponents of the 'process-product' doctrine argue that most npr-ppm-measures are not extraterritorial but of common global interest. In its General Comment No. 16 on state obligations, the Committee on the Rights of the Child submitted that states were obligated to protect children's rights in the context of businesses' extraterritorial activities and operations, provided that there is a reasonable link between the State and the conduct concerned.[441]

One could argue however that states parties to human rights treaties have only ceded their sovereignty to the extent that they are now under reporting obligations regarding their own territory and other enforcement procedures contained in these treaties. According to the ICJ, the '*erga omnes* character of a norm and the rule of consent to jurisdiction are two different things'.[442] Ruffert defends a so-called 'prohibition of interference'[443] between different international organizations that have different enforcement systems, which should particularly apply between the ILO and the WTO.[444] Accordingly, ILO norms may not be relied on if this contradicts with the enforcement procedures provided for by the ILO. Human rights treaties usually do also not provide for trade measures. Thus, states that do not fulfil their state obligations under human rights treaties normally do not have to fear trade embargoes or labelling obligations.

---

439 Zerk, p. 213.

440 Malanczuk, p. 18.

441 Committee on the Rights of the Child, 'General Comment No. 16 (2013) on State obligations regarding the impact of the business sector on children's rights', para. 43, CRC/C/GC/16, 27 April 2013.

442 ICJ, East Timor, Rep. 1995, p. 102, cited in Neumann, p. 393.

443 Translation: by the author, original German text: Störungsverbot.

444 Ruffert, pp. 147, 162, 167.

However, the obligation that WTO agreements should not be read 'in clinical isolation from public international law',[445] should be taken seriously. If one argued that because of different enforcement obligations under human rights treaties than under trade agreements, the concept of sovereignty could be relied upon to defeat trade measures aimed at human rights enforcement, human rights obligations would not be adequately taken into account under the concept of sovereignty. The obligation to take other rules of international law into account when interpreting the agreements would risk losing all meaning. Accordingly, regardless of the actual enforcement obligation, rules of sovereignty should in principle not prevent one WTO member from inducing another WTO member to implement its substantive international obligation to eliminate child labour instead of employing children in its export industry. However, it still depends upon individual case and the applicable law whether considerations of human rights law will prevail over WTO law. It should only be noted here, that the concept of sovereignty does not stand in the way of taking npr-ppms. Thus, in human rights matters, the concept of sovereignty should in principle be interpreted to mean that rules on extraterritorial jurisdiction should permit domestic acts having an extraterritorial effect.

In a similar vein, Bartels argues that a state needs a legitimate interest to exercise extraterritorial jurisdiction.[446] He holds that Art. XX is to be read consistently with the rules governing a WTO members' right to exercise legislative jurisdiction over activities and things located outside of its territory, and that this provision should apply to save various trade measures designed to promote and protect human rights outside of the territory of the regulating member; in particular, measures targeted at the process and production method of a particular product.[447]

5.3.1.4.10 The Concept of Ius Cogens and Erga Omnes

Given the nature of the international prohibition of child labour as a peremptory norm,[448] one may also refer to the concept of *ius cogens* and *erga omnes* for justifying the legality of measures having an extraterritorial effect. In relation to the *erga omnes* concept, the ICJ has stated that some obligations

445 *US–Gasoline*, report of the Appellate Body, p. 18.

446 Bartels (Extraterritorial Jurisdiction), p. 374 et seq.

447 Bartels, (Extraterritorial Jurisdiction), p. 402; However, in his view, lawful countermeasures under the rules of state responsibility, which enforce other WTO members' human rights obligations, do not fall under that exception because the WTO is a self-contained regime, p. 394.

448 See above, p. 197.

of states are 'obligations of a state towards the international community as a whole' which are 'the concern of all states' and in whose protection all states have a 'legal interest'.[449] *Ius cogens* norms can be said to apply *erga omnes*, since all states have an interest in implementing peremptory norms.[450] Thus, one might conclude that all states are entitled to take measures to ensure compliance with peremptory norms, wherever violations occur. In principle, such measures may include economic countermeasures and *argumentum a maiore ad minus* unilateral origin-neutral trade measures with extraterritorial effects. In accordance with the Articles on Responsibility of States for Internationally Wrongful Acts (hereinafter Articles on State Responsibility),[451] countermeasures shall be understood as measures that would otherwise be contrary to the international obligations of an injured state vis-à-vis the responsible state. They are measures by which injured states may seek to vindicate their rights and to restore the legal relationship with the responsible state that has been ruptured by the internationally wrongful act.[452] However, the ICJ was not explicit on *what* measures third states may take to induce fulfil *erga omnes* obligations.[453]

Before elaborating on this issue, one has to examine whether states may be held responsible for violations committed by private parties since most often private employers use child labour. According to Art. 2 of the Articles on State Responsibility, states are responsible in case the act is attributable to the state and constitutes a breach of an international obligation of the state. In principle, states are only responsible for the acts of their agents, not private parties.[454] According to Art. 12 of the Articles on State Responsibility, a breach occurs when state conduct is 'not in conformity with what is required of it by that obligation'. Conduct proscribed by an international obligation may involve an act or an omission or a combination of acts and omissions; it may

449 ICJ, *Barcelona Traction, Light & Power Company, Ltd. (Belgium v Spain)*, Judgement, Second Phase, ICJ Reports (1970), pp. 3–358, para. 33.

450 Frowein (Obligations Erga Omnes), p. 757; Frowein (Reactions), pp. 405 and 406.

451 A/RES/56/83 of 12 December 2001, A/56/49(Vol. I)/Corr.4; *Yearbook of the International Law Commission,* 2001, vol. II (Part Two).

452 See UN (Materials on the Responsibility of States for Internationally Wrongful Acts), p. 497; For the purpose of this work, countermeasures and reprisals have the same meaning.

453 See however Meron (Human Rights and Humanitarian Norms), p. 194 et seq. who maintains that there is a growing acceptance in contemporary international law of the principle that on the basis of human rights provisions of the UN Charter, states not directly affected by a breach of human rights have the right both to make representations directly to the state accused of such violations, and to complain before the organs of the UN.

454 Verdross/Simma II, p. 855; UN (Materials on the Responsibility of States for Internationally Wrongful Acts), p. 57.

involve the passage of legislation, or specific administrative or other action in a given case.[455] In relation to *ius cogens*, it has been stated that non-fulfilment of a treaty obligation classified as *ius cogens* may entail state responsibility.[456]

State obligations in cases of child labour have been analysed in detail by Humbert.[457] They include the adoption of legislative, administrative, social and educational measures including provisions for penal sanctions, minimum age legislation, other preventive measures, labour inspections of private parties, removal of children from the worst forms of child labour, and recovery, rehabilitation and reintegration of exploited children. It follows that states not only have the obligation to refrain from exploiting children, but also to protect them from violations committed by third parties. This obligation includes removing children from situations of economic exploitation and fulfilling certain obligations like providing free basic education, and other recovery, rehabilitation and social reintegration measures. Failure to comply with such obligations can be qualified as an omission and as such a breach of an international obligation according to Art. 12 of the Articles on State Responsibility. Thus, while it is often private employers who use child labour, states can be held responsible under international law for their failure to take the necessary action to prevent child labour.

To find out *what* measures third states might take to induce states to comply with their obligations, one should look at Art. 48 and 54 of the Articles on State Responsibility. According to Art. 48 (1) lit. (b), any state other than the injured state is entitled to invoke the responsibility of another state if the obligation breached is owed to the international community as a whole. Art. 54 of the Articles on State Responsibility provides that these Articles do not prejudice the right of any state other than the injured state to take lawful measures against that state to ensure cessation of the breach and reparation in the interest of the beneficiaries of the obligation breached. Such wording suggests that state might be entitled to impose economic measures against another state to ensure the cessation of the occurrence of child labour, provided that such measures are lawful. Considering the strong opposition to third-party countermeasures,[458] Art. 54 however does not give specific guidance as to what measures are lawful, serving as a saving clause and leaving the resolution of the matter to the further development of international law.[459] The UN Materials on the

455 UN (Materials on the Responsibility of States for Internationally Wrongful Acts), p. 22, 180.

456 Verdross/Simma, p. 333.

457 Humbert (The Challenge of Child Labour), pp. 35–121. See also Alston (The Right to Protection from Economic Exploitation), pp. 1241–1272.

458 See references in Tams, p. 790.

459 UN (Materials on the Responsibility of States for Internationally Wrongful Acts), p. 530.

Responsibility of States for Internationally Wrongful Acts do however refer to economic measures and cite the trade embargo adopted by the EC against Argentina when it invaded the Falkland Islands.[460] Such trade embargo was held to be contrary to GATT Art. III and XI and disputed whether it was justifiable under the security exception of GATT Art. XXI (b) (iii).[461]

In a similar vein, another author, referring to state practice, maintains that non-forcible proportionate countermeasures of states against violations of obligations of *erga omnes* are allowed where no institutional system exists or functions properly.[462] In contrast to reprisals, economic measures are mere retorsions where no specific international legal obligation has to be disregarded.[463]

Finally, the resolution of the *Institut de droit international* also maintains that states, acting individually or collectively, are entitled to take diplomatic, economic and other measures towards any other state that has violated human rights, provided that such measures are permitted under international law and do not involve the use of armed force in violation of the UN Charter.[464]

It thus seems important to distinguish between forcible and economic countermeasures. While forcible countermeasures are prohibited by Art. 2 (4) of the UN Charter, economic countermeasures are in principle not prohibited in international law.[465]

It follows that in principle, economic countermeasures taken by third parties in the collective interest are allowed in cases of human rights violations of *ius cogens* character. This conclusion however is subject to important conditions: The requirements of Art. 49 et seq. of the Articles on State Responsibility pertaining to the application of countermeasures should be observed. In accordance with the proportionality requirement contained in Art. 51, countermeasures should only be used in cases of serious breaches of human rights norms where violations are taking place on a larger scale.[466] Most importantly, according to Art. 55 of the Articles on State Responsibility, no special rules

460 UN (Materials on the Responsibility of States for Internationally Wrongful Acts), p. 528.

461 GATT L.5319/Rev. 1 and GATT C/M/157, pp. 5–6.

462 Frowein (Obligations Erga Omnes), p. 758; See also Verdross/Simma II, p. 909.

463 Frowein (Reactions), p. 425; International law distinguishes between reprisals and retorsions. Reprisals are considered a response to an international wrongful act, as the response itself would be otherwise illegal, Partsch, p. 204, Frowein (Reactions), p. 425.

464 Resolution adopted by the *Institut de droit international* at its session in Santiago de Compostela on 13 September 1989, Annuaire de l'Institut de droit international, 63 II (1990), pp. 338, 340, cited in Frowein (Reactions), p. 409 et seq.

465 Schröder, p. 588.

466 This is in accordance with the literature cited, see Frowein (Reactions), p. 400.

of international law must exist. The same has been stated above when maintaining that countermeasures are only allowed where 'no institutional system exists or functions properly'. Trade measures are clearly regulated by WTO law. Bartels considers the WTO as a 'self-contained regime' that excludes any recourse to countermeasures.[467] The issue of whether the GATT/WTO is a 'self-contained regime' or a *lex specialis* system according to Art. 55 of the Articles on State Responsibility has been discussed by Marceau.[468] Without solving the matter conclusively, she convincingly argues that given that the 'WTO is not to be read in clinical isolation from public international law', it is more fruitful to read the WTO as a system of *lex specialis*. This line of reasoning seems to have also been followed by the Arbitrators in *EC–Bananas*, paras. 6.12–6.16, when applying the principle of proportionality as contained in the Articles on State Responsibility under the DSU.[469]

At this point, it must be recalled that the original question was not whether countermeasures were legal under general international law, but whether unilateral trade measures on child labour with extraterritorial effects were consistent with GATT norms. The starting point was that if economic countermeasures could legally be taken under general international law in response to human rights violations, unilateral origin-neutral trade measures on child labour should be held consistent with GATT Art. III, *argumentum a maiore ad minus*. Consequently, the *lex specialis* problem regarding the WTO/GATT does not arise anymore since this only applies to countermeasures taken outside the GATT/WTO system.

As regards the remaining legal requirements for countermeasures, one must recall the difference between npr-ppm-measures on child labour and countermeasures. Npr-ppm-measures on child labour are unilateral origin-neutral trade measures that also apply domestically whereas, as stated above, countermeasures are taken in response to an international wrongful act committed by another state. Countermeasures are thus country-based measures since they relate to another state, and as such, facially discriminatory and contrary to GATT Art. III. Bearing in mind the differences and focussing on the extraterritoriality of npr-ppm-measures, one may conclude that the specific conditions pertaining to countermeasures do not have to be met by npr-ppm-measures to be GATT-consistent. Moreover, the GATT itself provides for special conditions to be met. The general legality of non-forcible countermeasures in case of

467 Bartels, (Extraterritorial Jurisdiction), p. 394.

468 Marceau (WTO and Human Rights I), p. 766 et seq.

469 See Desmedt, p. 450.

fundamental human rights violations may be thus relied upon to justify states applying npr-ppm-measures with extraterritorial effect.

In conclusion, in relation to child labour, the argument relating to unlawful extraterritorial effects and infringement of sovereignty can be disposed of.

5.3.1.4.11 Protectionism

The other main argument by advocates of the 'product-process' doctrine is that npr-ppm-measures are inherently protectionist in that they want to protect goods produced by the domestic industry. Indeed, as has been seen in the case of the US GSP, considerations of domestic job protection are in some cases part of the rationale of the law.[470] Even the ILO Constitution recognizes in its Preamble:

> Whereas also the failure of any nation to adopt humane conditions of labour is an obstacle in the way of other nations which desire to improve the conditions in their own countries.

This can be taken as a recognition of the fact that most countries that introduce higher labour standards, i.e. certain npr-ppm-measures, have an interest in other countries also introducing higher labour standards because they fear competition from countries with lower labour standards. Thus, they tend to protect their domestic industry against goods made through lower labour standards. It follows that disguised protectionism is indeed a great danger.

The opponents of the 'product-process' doctrine argue that in order to be economically efficient, a country has the right to force other countries to internalize externalities that it considers appropriate. However, to coerce another country to internalize an externality that it does not consider as important is not in accordance with the concept of sovereignty as contained in international law.[471] Apart from where it has given up its sovereignty, a country has exclusive domestic jurisdiction. However, as mentioned above, in case of child labour, most countries have taken on international human rights obligations and ceded part of their sovereignty.

In addition, as argued above, a competitive advantage based on legal facts such as missing laws on child labour or missing enforcement is not a true comparative advantage, but a market failure.[472] Thus, in these cases, protectionist

---

470 See Humbert (The Challenge of Child Labour), p. 284.

471 Jackson (Comments on Shrimp/Turtle), p. 304 rightly points out that some of the arguments draw upon conclusions from US law that are not applicable in the WTO law context.

472 Cf. Hepple, p. 18.

side effects could be justified. Instead of rejecting npr-ppm-measures on grounds of protectionism *per se*, the question which trade measures aimed at abolishing child labour should be dismissed as protectionist, and which measures should be retained as pursuing a true *bona fide* aim, should therefore be resolved by applying the legal criteria of GATT Art. III and XX.

5.3.1.4.12 Evolutionary Interpretation

In accordance with the principle of evolutionary interpretation used by the Appellate Body in *US–Shrimp*,[473] one could argue that with the proliferation of child labour standards and trade measures on child labour, an evolutionary interpretation of GATT Art. III should allow for 'like product' distinctions based on processes and production methods that are not reflected in the final product.[474]

5.3.1.4.13 Conclusion

It follows that the 'product-process' doctrine should not be maintained under current WTO law. Npr-ppm-measures should not be held *prima facie* GATT Art. III-inconsistent.

However, as indicated above, it does not follow that products that are produced differently are *ipso facto* not 'like products'. The discussion on protectionism has shown that some justification is needed in case of npr-ppm-measures. Thus, a second interpretational step is required when assessing the legality of npr-ppm-measures. This is in accordance with the argument by advocates of the 'product-process' doctrine that the real problem is to develop substantive criteria to prevent the potential misuse of process-oriented trade barriers. Otherwise, governments could use any process-based measure to protect their domestic goods. The legal certainty and predictability of the world trade system would be at risk.

Substantive criteria are contained in the definition of 'like products', in the obligation of equal treatment contained in GATT Art. III, and under the general exceptions contained in GATT Art. XX. As stated above, some of the opponents of the 'process-product' doctrine argue that the regulatory purpose of the measure should be decisive when deciding whether the npr-ppm-measure is GATT-consistent, and that this criterion should be examined under the term of 'like products'. In the aftermath of the *EC–Asbestos* case, it could be possible to allow for npr-ppm-measures under the criterion of consumers' tastes and

473 Appellate Body Report, *US–Shrimps*, para. 130.
474 Appleton, p. 482 mentions that argument without supporting it.

habits contained in the Working Party Report. The question is whether this is an adequate criterion in terms of a bright-line rule and easy to be administered by trade officials. If additional criteria have to be developed, the question is whether this should be done by the WTO adjudicating bodies or member governments in a negotiating process. In addition, the criteria should take account of the arguments related to the costs of internalization and distributive justice. These issues will be further examined during the course of this work.

5.3.2 Regulatory Purpose or Market-Oriented Approach?

The main obstacle for measures relating to child labour to be considered GATT Art. III-consistent is obviously that products made with child labour usually do not display physical dissimilarities. They are thus considered to be 'like' products not made with child labour. By contrast, measures related to child labour could be GATT Art. III-consistent if 'likeness' was defined as 'not differing with respect to a non-protectionist regulatory purpose'[475] since measures related to child labour are related to a non-protectionist policy purpose.

Various scholars have argued for the consideration of the regulatory purpose[476] under the 'like product' definition to defend origin-neutral product distinctions including origin-neutral npr-ppm-measures. Other scholars are in favour of a definition of likeness based on commercial criteria. Before discussing both positions, the relevant legal rulings will be examined.

5.3.2.1 *The Legal Rulings*

5.3.2.1.1 US–Malt Beverages

The first case that considered the regulatory purpose of a measure under the definition of 'like products' was the *US–Malt Beverages* case.[477] One measure under scrutiny was a lower tax accorded to wines made of a certain type of grape.[478] Whilst Canada argued that this was discriminatory, the US held the view that the measure was origin-neutral and non-discriminatory. The panel held that with a view to the purpose of GATT Art. III contained in paragraph 1, i.e. to avoid protectionism, apart from the criteria used in the Working Party Report, the regulatory purpose had to be taken into account. Specifically, different categories of products might be differentiated for policy purposes not related to the protection of domestic production.[479] The US tax accorded

475 Howse/Regan, p. 260.

476 The term 'regulatory purpose' refers to the policy purposes of both fiscal and non-fiscal measures.

477 *US–Malt Beverages*, report of the panel.

478 *US–Malt Beverages*, report of the panel, para. 5.23.

479 Ibid., para. 5.25.

preferential treatment to a certain type of grape that grew only in some geographical areas. The panel therefore found that the geographical distinction afforded protection to domestic production.[480] Since the US had not put forward any public policy purpose, and the lower tax rate in fact was not available to Canadian wines, the panel found a violation of GATT Art. III:2.[481]

The second measure involving a consideration of the regulatory purpose was a regulation relating to the sale, distribution and sale of products that distinguished between beer with an alcohol content above 3.2 per cent by weight and above 5 per cent by volume.[482] Canada argued that all beer was like beer regardless of the alcohol content, and that the measure discriminated against imported beer because of restrictions as to the point of sale and different labelling requirements for beer of high alcohol content.[483] The US argued that the measure was an origin-neutral measure, that beer with low alcohol content was different from beer with high alcohol content, and that the measure could be justified on grounds of human life and health, and public morals under GATT Art. XX.[484]

The panel stated that product distinctions should not only be made with respect to product characteristics, but also in the light of the purpose of GATT Art. III.[485] The purpose would be to avoid protectionism of domestic production, not the harmonization of internal measures.[486] Accordingly, when defining likeness, the regulatory autonomy should be taken into account, i.e. non-protectionist measures with environmental purposes should not be prohibited.[487] The panel held that with respect to their physical characteristics, beer with high and beer with low alcohol content was similar. However, there was a certain market specialization, i.e. consumers and manufacturers differentiated between beer with low and beer with high alcoholic content in their purchasing, advertising and marketing.[488] In addition, the law applied equally to imported and domestic products, without imposing a heavier burden on imported products.[489] With respect to the legislative objective, the panel noted that it could be related to health, public morals or tax revenue reasons,

480 Ibid., para. 5.26.
481 Ibid.
482 Ibid., para. 5.70.
483 Ibid.
484 Ibid.
485 Ibid., para. 5.71.
486 Ibid., para. 5.72.
487 Ibid.
488 Ibid., para. 5.73.
489 Ibid.

none of which would work to favour domestic producers over foreign producers.[490] Accordingly, the two types of beer were not 'like products' under GATT Art. III:4.[491]

This case obviously established a new definition of 'like', referring to both the regulatory purpose of a measure and the effect of a measure, i.e. whether domestic products are afforded better treatment than imported products. It should be noted that regarding the two measures examined above, the panel analysed both aim and effect of the measure and found them both to be either protectionist or not. This leaves open the question what happens in case a protectionist effect exists, but not a protectionist aim.

5.3.2.1.2 US–Automobiles

The next case that considered the regulatory purpose was *US–Automobiles*.[492] As mentioned above, the panel ruled on a luxury tax imposed by the US on the first retail sale of vehicles over US Dollar 30,000, which applied to domestic and imported vehicles alike. Following the panel in *US–Malt Beverages*, the panel held that the purpose of GATT Art. III to avoid protectionism had to be taken into account when interpreting GATT Art. III:2.[493] The term 'so as to afford protection' suggested both 'aim and effect'. Hence, when defining 'likeness' the 'aim and effect' of a measure were relevant.[494] A measure could be said to have the aim of affording protection if that was the declared goal, not merely an incidental effect.[495] The effect of affording protection would be achieved by giving greater competitive opportunities to domestic products.[496] Applying these considerations to the luxury tax, the panel stated that the protective aim had to be determined not only on legislative statements but also on the legislative structure and wording.[497] The panel concluded that the aim was to raise tax revenue, taking note of the fact that conditions of competition did not vary greatly above or under the threshold of US Dollar 30,000.[498] As to the discriminatory effect, the panel stated that there was not enough evidence to conclude that the conditions of competition were in favour of US cars.[499]

490 Ibid., para. 5.74.
491 Ibid. para. 5.75.
492 *US–Automobiles*, report of the panel.
493 Ibid., para. 5.7.
494 Ibid., para. 5.10.
495 Ibid.
496 Ibid.
497 Ibid., para. 5.12.
498 Ibid.
499 Ibid., para. 5.13.

Specifically, apart from trade flows, there was no evidence that EC manufacturers neither had the capacity, nor produced cars that could be sold below the threshold.[500] The panel concluded that the measure did not create conditions of competition that inherently divided the products into two classes.[501] Therefore, GATT Art. III:2 was not violated.[502]

The panel in this case elaborated on the approach taken by the panel in *US–Malt Beverages*, establishing the so-called 'aim and effect' test. It should be stressed that according to the panel, when discerning the aim, not the statements of the legislators, but the overall structure and the wording of the law mattered to them. Further, the panel reconciled the 'effects' test with the conventional approach taken in *Japan–Imported Wines and Alcoholic Beverages*,[503] i.e. to rely on the conditions of competition rather than on the actual trade flows. Specifically, it stated that an 'inherent effect' of the measure was needed. In contrast to actual trade flows, the panel relied on the fact that manufacturers generally had both the capacity to meet the requirements of the favourable tax treatment and in fact did produce cars that met these requirements.

The 'inherence' requirement had the advantage of separating mere incidental effects from more deliberate trade effects.[504] However, this 'inherence' requirement has been disputed by several authors.[505] It is argued that this criterion is too permissive of regulatory autonomy stating that to require foreign producers to change their products in order to profit from the lower tax was *ipso facto* an adverse treatment, and that such a requirement denied them their competitive advantage, the economic premise of the world trading system.[506] However, if one reads the text carefully, one will notice that in fact, the

500 Ibid., para. 5.14.

501 Ibid.

502 In a similar vein, deciding on the Gas Guzzler Tax, the panel held that the technology to manufacture high fuel economy automobiles – above the 22.5 mpg threshold – was not inherent to the US, nor were low fuel economy automobiles inherently of foreign origin, as the panel noted from fuel economy figures submitted by the parties. Equally, the panel was not convinced that the existence of many versions of a given automobile model type was an inherent characteristic of domestic automobiles, or that the existence of only a few or no versions was an inherent characteristic of automobiles of foreign origin. Finally, it held that it had not been shown that light trucks as defined in the gas guzzler measure were inherently of domestic origin. The panel noted that such products were in fact common within the model range of foreign products. *US–Automobiles*, report of the panel, paras. 5.25, 5.31 and 5.34.

503 *Japan–Imported Wines and Alcoholic Beverages*, report of the panel, para. 5.5.

504 Hudec (Requiem for an Aim and Effects Test), p. 629, fn. 21.

505 Verhoosel, p. 53; Mattoo/Subramanian, pp. 311 and 312.

506 Verhoosel, p. 53; Ehring, p. 968.

panel also relied on the fact that EC automobile manufacturers produced a wide range of automobiles that could meet the lower tax. Thus, it did not rely solely on the fact that producers could easily change their production line, but that they already had the opportunity to sell their cars below the threshold. The report can therefore be read as meaning that the test was whether the adverse effect of the measure was typically borne by EC cars. That is, the test asked whether in general, foreign products were capable of benefiting from receiving the same treatment as domestic products and whether they in fact benefited from such treatment given the way foreign are produced, including product characteristics and production methods. Accordingly, under that test, any measure related to the situation or conduct of foreign countries would be prohibited as discriminatory. That test is neither too permissive of regulatory trade barriers, nor does it rely solely on actual trade flows since it takes into account potential trade flows as well. It also does not prohibit measures that have mere incidental trade effects. This test also corresponds to the test developed under GATT Art. I:1 under the term 'unconditionally'.[507] The obligation to accord an advantage that has been granted to any other country 'unconditionally' to third countries that are WTO members means that the extension of that advantage may not be made subject to conditions with respect to the situation or conduct of those countries.[508] The test developed by the panel thus seems to be convincing and should be elaborated on. However, it is questionable whether the test should be conducted under the term 'like products' since it refers to trade effects. It seems to be more appropriate to conduct this test under the equality of treatment obligation. This issue will be dealt with in more detail below.

5.3.2.1.3 Japan–Alcoholic Beverages

The next case involving 'like products' was *Japan–Alcoholic Beverages*.[509] This case concerned the Japanese Liquor Tax Law, which applied different tax rates to different types of beverages. For each category, the tax rate was different, depending on the alcohol content per litre. Shochu fell into a different category than Western spirits such as whisky and other spirits and liquors. The complainants claimed that this system violated GATT Art. III:2, first sentence and GATT Art. III:2, second sentence because shochu was taxed at a lower rate than the other products. The panel observed that whilst the second sentence of GATT Art. III:2 referred to the general principles contained in paragraph 1,

507 *Canada-Automotives*, report of the panel, para. 10.23.

508 Ibid., para. 10.23.

509 *Japan–Alcoholic Beverages*, report of the panel and Appellate Body.

the first sentence did not contain such a reference. Analysing the first sentence, it rejected the 'aim and effect' test put forward by Japan and the US.[510] It recalled that only the second sentence referred to the general principle of 'so as to afford protection'. Further, the aim was difficult to discern since there were often several aims behind a measure. If such a test was applied under GATT Art. III, GATT Art. XX would be rendered redundant. In addition, such a test was without a textual basis. Consequently, under the first sentence, the test was whether the products concerned were 'like'; the measure was an internal tax or charge; and whether the tax imposed on foreign products was 'in excess of' the tax imposed on like domestic products.[511] Regarding the term 'like', the panel cited the criteria of the Working Party Report of Border Tax Adjustments, adding the criterion of 'tariff classification', and stated that 'like' was to be interpreted on a 'case-by-case' basis.[512] Under the first sentence, it should be construed narrowly. Applying this rationale to the facts of the case, the panel held that vodka and shochu were 'like products' since they largely shared the same physical characteristics and were classified under the same tariff heading.[513] Since vodka was taxed in excess of shochu, GATT Art. III:2, first sentence was violated. The panel then examined other products such as whisky in comparison with shochu under GATT Art. III:2, second sentence. In its view, the compared products had different physical characteristics and were consequently not 'like products' within GATT Art. III:2, first sentence.

The Appellate Body confirmed these findings. It began by stating that the aim of GATT Art. III was to avoid protectionism and that therefore this article was not confined to the protection of tariff concessions.[514] It emphasized that GATT Art. III:1 informed the two sentences of GATT Art. III:2 in two different ways: Whilst the first sentence was an 'expression' of the general principle, the special reference to the first paragraph contained in the second sentence made clear that 'protective application' needed to be established separately. Accordingly, the test under the first sentence only required two steps, i.e. to determine whether products were 'like', and whether a higher tax was imposed on imported products. In addition, it elaborated on the narrow interpretation of the word 'like' in the first sentence. It held that 'likeness' was an 'accordion' that 'stretches' and 'squeezes' under the different norms of the WTO Agreement, and that under the first sentence, it 'is meant to be narrowly

510 *Japan–Alcoholic Beverages*, report of the panel, para 6.18.
511 Ibid., para 6.19.
512 Ibid., paras. 6.2–22.
513 Ibid., para 6.23.
514 *Japan–Alcoholic Beverages*, report of the Appellate Body, p. 16.

squeezed'.[515] Referring to the relevance of tariff classifications, it confirmed that vodka and shochu were 'like'.[516]

These rulings are a clear rejection of an 'aim and effect' test under the word 'like'. The findings are based on a very textual interpretation of GATT Art. III, relying heavily on the structure of the provision. The main argument was that the first sentence of paragraph 1 did not refer to the general aim of avoiding protection. This cautious approach might have been due to the fact that at the time of the ruling, the WTO was a very young institution and the adjudicating bodies wanted to stick to the text – although they interfered more with governments regulatory autonomy than under an 'aim and effect' test. As mentioned above, the argument in relation to GATT Art. XX can be repudiated on the ground that it can still retain its function in relation to facially discriminatory measures that cannot by rescued by an 'aim and effect' test. However, the argument underlining the difficulty of discerning the aim of a measure seems to be convincing at first sight. It will be further examined below. As stated above, existing laws on child labour do indeed have several aims including protectionist ones.[517] Finally, strictly speaking, the panel and Appellate Body only rejected the 'aim and effect' test in relation to fiscal measures. Whilst the different structure of GATT Art. III:4 offers the possibility to come to another conclusion in the case of internal regulations, later rulings decided otherwise.[518]

5.3.2.1.4 EC–Bananas III

The *EC–Bananas III* case firmly rejects an 'aim and effect' test under GATT Art. III and GATS Art. II or XVII.[519] The case concerned the EC's import regime for bananas. The services regulation was origin-neutral, but shifted advantages to wholesalers who dealt in EC and ACP bananas.[520] The Appellate Body explicitly stated that it did not see any authority in either GATS Art. II or XVII to introduce an 'aim and effect' test.[521] In contrast to GATT Art. III:1, there was no provision of 'so as to afford protection'.[522] It confirmed the reasoning of *Japan–Alcoholic Beverages* regarding an 'aim and effect' test.[523]

515 Ibid., p. 21.

516 Ibid., p. 23.

517 See Humbert (The Challenge of Child Labour), pp. 284 et seqq.

518 See *EC–Asbestos*, report of the Appellate Body, which will be discussed below, pp. 111 et seqq.

519 *EC–Bananas III*, report of the Appellate Body, para. 241.

520 Hudec (Requiem for an Aim and Effects Test), p. 640.

521 *EC–Bananas III*, report of the Appellate Body, para. 241.

522 Ibid., paras. 215 and 216.

523 Ibid., para. 241.

5.3.2.1.5 Korea–Alcoholic Beverages

The next case on 'like products' was *Korea–Alcoholic Beverages.*[524] Under the Korean tax regime for alcoholic beverages, different tax rates are imposed on various categories of spirits including soju, a Korean spirit, and 'Western-style' spirits such as whisky and brandy. The complainants argued that the tax rates were inconsistent with GATT Art. III:2, second sentence. The panel stated that both sentences of GATT required a comparison of two pairs of products; but only 'directly competitive or substitutable products' involved an inquiry into the extent of the difference in taxation and whether the taxation differences were applied 'so as to afford protection' to the domestic industry.[525] It then found that the category of 'like products' was a subset of 'directly competitive or substitutable products', and that all 'like products' were, by definition, 'directly competitive or substitutable products'.[526] Accordingly, it began its analysis with GATT Art. III:2, second sentence. It stated that a direct competitive relationship between products required evidence that consumers considered the products to be alternative ways of satisfying one particular need or taste.[527] Then, it established the criteria to be used to establish a direct competitive relationship, i.e. the physical characteristics of a product, its end-uses, channels of distribution and price.[528] In addition, it found quantitative studies of cross-price elasticity relevant but not decisive, and referred to evidence of competitive relationships in other markets and potential competition including future competition as relevant criteria.[529] The panel then applied the criteria to the facts of the case and found that on balance, the evidence supported that there was a present direct competition, and a strong potentially direct competitive relationship between imported and domestic products.[530]

The Appellate Body upheld the panel's findings stating that latent consumer demand was relevant in an examination of 'directly competitive' products.[531] Equally, future competition had to be taken into account since the object and purpose of GATT Art. III was the maintenance of equality of competitive conditions for imported and domestic products.[532] The Appellate Body confirmed the panel's finding that the focus should not be on the quantitative extent of

524 *Korea–Alcoholic Beverages*, report of the panel and the Appellate Body.
525 *Korea–Alcoholic Beverages*, report of the panel, para. 10.35.
526 Ibid., para. 10.36.
527 Ibid., paras. 10.40.
528 Ibid., para. 10.43.
529 Ibid., paras. 10.44–50.
530 Ibid., paras. 10.95–98.
531 *Korea–Alcoholic Beverages*, report of the Appellate Body, paras. 112–124.
532 Ibid., paras. 125–127.

competition since that would result in a 'trade effects' test.[533] Instead, the focus should be on the nature of competition, i.e. the quality of competition.[534] To rule otherwise would make cross-price elasticity the decisive criterion.[535] The Appellate Body also confirmed the finding that evidence from other markets was relevant to establish a competitive relationship between domestic and imported products.[536]

These rulings also reject an 'aim and effect' test in that they rely on the competitive relationship between the group of imported and domestic products. Stating that 'like products' are a 'subset' of 'directly competitive and substitutable products', they implicitly make the competitive relationship the decisive criterion for 'like products' as well. Both rulings place special emphasis on the question whether consumers consider or could consider the two products or groups of products as alternative ways of satisfying one particular need or taste. Thus, it is not the aim or regulatory purpose of a measure that matters, but the consumers' point of view. The rulings then elaborate on the question of which consumers' view was relevant. These issues will be examined in detail below, for the moment it suffices to state that according to *Korea–Alcoholic Beverages*, 'like products' have to be defined in the market place.

5.3.2.1.6 EC–Asbestos

The Appellate Body Report on *EC–Asbestos*[537] confirmed the findings of the Appellate Body report in *Korea–Alcoholic Beverages*, elaborating on the market-oriented definition of 'like products'.[538] Noting that the ordinary meaning of 'like' as 'physically similar' did not reveal much, the Appellate Body evoked the general principle contained in GATT Art. III:1 to avoid protectionism, i.e. to provide for equality of competitive conditions.[539] Accordingly, the term 'like' had to apply to products that are in a competitive relationship.[540] Next, the Appellate Body cited the criteria of the Working Party Report on Border Tax Adjustments – physical properties, end-uses, consumers' tastes and habits – plus tariff classifications, stressing that they provided a framework for the term 'likeness', and that each criterion should be given weight.[541] In relation

533 Ibid., paras. 128–131.
534 Ibid., para. 133.
535 Ibid., para. 134.
536 Ibid., paras. 135–138.
537 *EC–Asbestos*, report of the Appellate Body.
538 See above, pp. 79 et seqq.
539 *EC–Asbestos*, report of the Appellate Body, para. 97.
540 Ibid., para. 99.
541 Ibid., paras. 101, 102, 109.

to physical properties, it stated that those properties likely to influence the competitive relationship between products in the market place were the relevant ones.[542] Evidence related to health risks might be relevant in assessing the competitive relationship.[543] In contrast to the opinion of the panel, the Appellate Body held that considering health risks under GATT Art. III would not make GATT Art. XX inutile[544] for under GATT Art. III, the question was whether products were in a competitive relationship, whereas under GATT Art. XX the question was whether the measure served a legitimate goal. Reflecting the competitive relationship between products and thus relating to the core of GATT Art. III, the criteria referring to end-uses and consumers' tastes and habits were key criteria.[545] At the same time, the Appellate Body held that if two products were physically different, there was a strong burden on the complaining party to demonstrate that products were in such a competitive relationship to be considered as 'like' within the meaning of GATT Art. III.[546] In any event, if products were physically different, a panel could not conclude without examining consumers' tastes and habits that products were 'like'.[547] In response to the argument that the government measure in place might have suppressed consumer demand, and that therefore that criterion was invalid, the Appellate Body argued that there might be 'latent demand' or evidence from other markets, as already stated in *Korea–Alcoholic Beverages*.[548] Applying these statements to the facts of the case, it held that the products were physically dissimilar due to the health risk.

The Appellate Body concluded that in the absence of evidence of consumers' tastes and habits to prove their competitiveness, the products in question had to be regarded as unlike.[549]

One member of the Appellate Body wrote in a divergent opinion that the lethal health risk in the present case should make the products *a priori* 'unlike', and that the 'fundamentally' economic interpretation of 'likeness' raised some substantial doubts.[550] Such view is also discussed in literature with regard to climate-related risks of products.[551]

---

542 Ibid., para. 114.
543 Ibid., para. 115.
544 Ibid.
545 Ibid., para. 117, see above, pp. 79 et seqq.
546 Ibid., para. 118.
547 Ibid., para. 121.
548 Ibid., para. 123.
549 Ibid., para. 126.
550 Ibid., paras. 153, 154.
551 Will, p. 151.

As stated above, this case clearly rejects the definition of 'likeness' solely based on the regulatory purpose of the measure. At the same time, the Appellate Body made clear that the that policy objectives can be referred to also under GATT Art. III, not only under GATT Art. XX. With a view to the purpose of GATT Art. III to avoid protectionism, the main and sufficient criterion was the competitive relationship of the groups of products to be compared. However, in the future, under the criterion of competitiveness, the regulatory purposes of a measure might be taken into account: In the present case, the regulatory purpose obviously was the health risk that was taken into account under the criterion of physical similarity. The Appellate Body stated however that whilst physical dissimilarity was a strong indication that two products were not in a competitive relationship, this finding can be reversed if e.g. strong evidence of consumers' tastes and habits prove the contrary. Conversely, otherwise 'like products' can be found 'unlike' within the meaning of GATT Art. III if consumers do not regard them as 'like'. Thus, if consumer preferences confirm that a certain measure with a certain regulatory purpose does not unjustifiably differentiate between a certain pair of products, such a measure can be regarded as not differentiating between 'like products'. It should be highlighted that evidence of consumers' tastes and habits might be found in third markets or established on latent demand. In contrast to the main findings, the concurrent opinion seems to oppose this market-oriented approach to likeness and to favour an approach whereby the regulatory purpose of a measure is an independent factor when establishing likeness.

5.3.2.1.7 Philippines–Distilled Spirits

The Appellate Body in the rather recent case *Philippines–Distilled Spirits* dealing with different taxes on domestic spirits made from designated raw materials and imported spirits made from non-designated raw materials under GATT Art. III: 2, first and second sentence followed the market-oriented approach of *EC–Asbestos*.[552] It held that none of the criteria that a panel considers when determining 'likeness' had an overarching role in the determination of 'likeness'. Rather, a panel examines these criteria in order to make a determination about the nature and extent of a competitive relationship between and among the products.[553] Accordingly, it found that a difference in raw materials does not prevent a finding of 'likeness' as long as such a difference leaves fundamentally unchanged the competitive relationship among the products at issue.[554]

552 *Philippines–Distilled Spirits*, report of the Appellate Body.

553 Ibid., para. 119.

554 Ibid., para. 125.

5.3.2.1.8 US–Clove Cigarettes

Interestingly, the panel in *US–Clove Cigarettes,* dealing with the difference between menthol and clove cigarettes under the national treatment obligation contained in Art. 2.1 of the TBT Agreement, held that the declared legitimate public health objective of the measure, namely the reduction of youth smoking, must permeate and inform the likeness analysis, especially given the mention of the protection of health in the preamble to the WTO Agreement.[555] This could be taken as a revival of the 'aim and effect' test.[556] However, drawing on the jurisprudence of GATT Art. III, the Appellate Body reversed this finding and found that the term 'likeness' was about the nature and extent of a competitive relationship between and among products.[557] Like in *EC–Asbestos*, it found that regulatory concerns may play a role in the determination of likeness if such concerns are relevant when examining the 'likeness' criteria and bear on the competitive relationship of the products at issue.[558] The Appellate Body considered the regulatory purpose when examining the equal treatment obligation under Art. 2.1 TBT Agreement.[559]

5.3.2.1.9 Conclusion

In conclusion, it can be maintained that the current WTO jurisprudence favours a market-oriented approach to the term 'likeness'. Whilst two GATT cases held that 'likeness' should be determined on an 'aim and effect' tests, this approach was explicitly rejected by later WTO rulings at least with regard to GATT Art. III:2, first sentence. However, regulatory purposes may be considered when they affect the competitive relationship between products.

5.3.2.2 *Consideration of the Regulatory Purpose*

Several legal authors argue for a consideration of the regulatory purpose of the measure when defining 'like products'.[560] Their arguments overlap with those made under the 'process-products' debate. They argue that the ordinary meaning of 'likeness', i.e. 'physically similar', does not help to explain

555 *US–Clove Cigarettes*, report of the panel, para. 7.116.

556 Howse (Cigarettes and Public Health at the WTO), p. 1.

557 *US–Clove Cigarettes*, report of the Appellate Body, para. 111 et seqq.

558 Ibid., para. 120; see also above p. 81.

559 Ibid., paras. 167–182.

560 Howse/Regan; Regan (Regulatory Purpose); Roessler (Beyond the Ostensible); Roessler (The Scope of Regulatory Autonomy); Hudec (Requiem for an Aim and Effects Test) does not confine the 'aim and effect' test to the issue of like products but argues for a consideration of aims and effects also under other non-discrimination provisions.; Mattoo/Subramanian.

'likeness' within the meaning of GATT.[561] Listing the factors of the Working Party Report does not give guidance as to which degree of competitiveness is required and why.[562] The criterion of 'competitive relationship', relied on in *EC–Asbestos* does not really help to define 'likeness'.[563] Thus, 'likeness' has to be interpreted in view of the purpose of GATT Art. III:1, i.e. to avoid protectionism.[564] Protectionist measures are only those with a protectionist purpose.[565] 'Like' has to be interpreted as 'not differing in any respect relevant to an actual non-protectionist policy'.[566] The first reason for this is that 'so as to afford protection to domestic production' has a purposive connotation.[567] Second, a disproportionate impact does not matter.[568] The disparate impact of measures does not matter because measures that relate to a non-protectionist goal are globally efficient and non-objectionable.[569] Accordingly, not only consumers' perspectives of 'like products' – i.e. the competitive relationship – but also the regulatory purpose of a measure has to be taken into account when defining 'likeness'.[570]

GATT Art. XX is not rendered inutile because it retains its role in case of facially discriminatory measures.[571] The policy objectives contained in GATT Art. XX that do not refer to the many policy objectives that may be provided by origin-neutral measures prove that non-protectionist origin-neutral measures were not intended to be examined under GATT Art. XX.[572] To hold otherwise would mean to inappropriately shift the burden of proof for origin-neutral measures.[573] Along the same lines, Hudec points to the fact that EC law also provides for two justification standards, depending on whether *de iure* or *de facto* discrimination was involved.[574]

Other arguments relate to the difficulty of discerning the protectionist aim: In this context, the defendants of the 'regulatory purpose' theory argue that various panel and Appellate Body reports such as Appellate Body Reports on

561 Howse/Türk, p. 302; Howse/Regan, pp. 260 and 261.
562 Hudec (Requiem for an Aim and Effects Test), p. 626.
563 Regan (Regulatory Purpose), p. 445.
564 Ibid., p. 446 et seq.
565 Regan (Regulatory Purpose) p. 450; Howse/Türk, p. 302.
566 Howse/Regan, p. 260.
567 Regan (Regulatory Purpose), p. 450.
568 Ibid., pp. 452–454.
569 Ibid.
570 Ibid., p. 454.
571 Ibid., pp. 454–458; Roessler, p. 777 et seq.
572 Roessler (Beyond the Ostensible), p. 778; Roessler (The Scope of Regulatory Autonomy), p. 2.
573 Roessler (Beyond the Ostensible), p. 778.
574 Hudec (Requiem for an Aim and Effects Test), p. 621.

Australia–Salmon,[575] *Chile–Alcoholic Beverages*[576] and *Canada–Periodicals*[577] have shown that the WTO dispute settlement bodies are able to deal with the regulatory purpose.[578]

Referring to the jurisprudence, the argument is that rather than relying on consumers' tastes and habits, the WTO adjudicating bodies should rely on the regulatory purpose.[579] Relying on a 'rational' consumer would really be an appeal to the Appellate Body's own regulatory purpose.[580] In addition, if consumers consider two categories of products as unlike, there is no need to introduce a regulatory distinction.[581] Conversely, consumers may rarely consider products as unlike if a governmental measure says the contrary. In the same vein, Roessler holds that 'regulations that distinguish between different types of products and accord one of them less favourable treatment are typically adopted precisely because the market does not make the distinction that the regulator considers necessary'.[582] Regan argues that in *EC–Asbestos*, the Appellate Body considered physical properties as an independent criterion that required consideration of the regulatory purpose.[583] The proper reading of the report suggests that not consumer preferences, but the regulatory purpose matters when determining the relevant physical characteristics.[584] Referring to *Japan–Alcoholic Beverages*[585] the argument is that the Appellate Body, without openly admitting so, in fact reached its conclusion on 'likeness' by examining whether the measure it had a protectionist purpose.[586] Despite the different wording of the two sentences contained in GATT Art. III:2, the purpose of avoiding protectionism must be taken into account.[587]

575 *Australia–Salmon*, report of the Appellate Body.
576 *Chile–Alcoholic Beverages*, report of the Appellate Body.
577 *Canada–Periodicals*, report of the Appellate Body.
578 Regan (Regulatory Purpose), pp. 458–464.
579 Ibid., p. 466.
580 Ibid.
581 Ibid.
582 Roessler (The Scope of Regulatory Autonomy), p. 1.
583 Ibid., p. 467 et seq.
584 Ibid.
585 *Japan–Alcoholic Beverages*, report of the Appellate Body.
586 Regan (Regulatory Purpose), p. 473; Howse/Regan, pp. 264 and 265.
587 Regan (Regulatory Purpose), pp. 454–458 and p. 476 et seq.; Roessler (Beyond the Ostensible), p. 775.

5.3.2.3 *Non-consideration of the Regulatory Purpose or Market-Oriented Approach*

Many legal authors argue against the consideration of the regulatory purpose of a measure under GATT Art. III.[588] They cite the WTO cases *Japan–Alcoholic Beverages* and *EC–Asbestos*, stating that these cases have rightly defined 'likeness' on purely commercial criteria relating to the competitive relationship between products.[589] Former WTO adjudicators hold that the 'regulatory intent' or 'aim-and-effect' approach to determining 'likeness' has been abandoned by the Appellate Body.[590] The 'aim and effects' theory is criticized for its lack of textual basis and the considerable risk that the rule of reason test in GATT Art. XX is circumvented.[591] As stated in *Japan–Alcoholic Beverages*, GATT Art. III:2, first sentence and GATT Art. III:4 do not refer to GATT Art. III:1.[592] In addition, the words in GATT Art. III:1 'should not be applied so as to afford protection' relate to the effect of a measure, not to the purpose.[593] In the context of GATT Art. XX, any rule of reason test should be prohibited under GATT Art. III.[594] To do otherwise would mean to amend the treaty without the treaty-maker.[595] If panels could determine what legitimate policy objectives are, apart from the lack of legitimacy, there would be a violation of the GATT being a negative integration scheme.[596] To put away with extraneous factors such as regulatory purpose would have the merit to make panels concentrate on the likeness or substitutability test itself.[597] This would enhance predictability.

5.3.2.4 *Evaluation*

Similar to the 'process-product' debate, both sides make appealing arguments. Whilst it is true that the ordinary meaning of 'like' as 'physically similar' does not offer much guidance as to the degree of 'likeness', it is not true that the economic criteria relating to the competitive relationship provided by WTO jurisprudence are incapable of determining what 'like products' are. Both rulings

---

588 Quick/Lau, pp. 426–431; Blüthner, fn. 98; Choi, pp. 81–83; Davey/Pauwelyn, p. 38; Mavroidis (Like Products), p. 130 et seqq.; Slotboom, p. 576; Fauchald, pp. 464 argues against a consideration of 'aim and effects' under the 'like products' issue.; Horn/Mavroidis, pp. 60.

589 Quick/Lau, p. 428 et seq., p. 455; Fauchald, p. 464; Bronckers/McNelis, pp. 370 et seqq.

590 Van den Bossche/Zdouc, p. 426.

591 Choi, pp. 81–84.

592 Ibid.

593 Blüthner, p. 299.

594 Quick/Lau, p. 455; Davey/Pauwelyn, p. 38.

595 Quick/Lau, p. 456.

596 Horn/Mavroidis, p. 60.

597 Choi, p. 83.

on *Korea–Alcoholic Beverages* and EC*–Asbestos* offer instructive guidance on how to establish that products are 'like' in the context of the competitive relationship. These rulings are based on the assumption that if consumers do not regard products as substitutable, these products are not in a competitive relationship. As a result, there is no risk of protectionism. Since the aim of GATT Art. III is to avoid protection of the domestic industry, this reasoning is convincing and in accordance with Art. 31 (1) of the VCLT. The opponents wrongly argue that although the competitive relationship might be relevant, the regulatory purpose of a measure is needed as an additional criterion. In order to reach a satisfying result when assessing consumer preferences, panels should increasingly take recourse to more or less objective criteria such as improved economic or econometric criteria based on market analysis. Thus, so far, the market-oriented approach of the WTO jurisprudence relating to the competitive relationship seems to be convincing. Most importantly, it does not exclude the regulatory purpose entirely. As the Appellate Body pointed out in EC*–Asbestos,* it is possible to take account of the regulatory purpose if it affects the competitive relationship between imported and domestic products.

Even if one admits that the words 'should not be applied so as to afford protection to domestic production', contained in GATT Art. III:1, have a purposive connotation through the use of the words 'so as to', the word 'applied' indicates that the effect of a measure is equally important. In addition, the French version 'ne devront pas être appliqués aux produits importés ou nationaux *de maniére à* protéger la production nationale' and the Spanish version 'no deberían aplicarse a los productos importados o nacionales *de manera que* se proteja la producción nacional', both use the formulation 'in a way that [...]'. It follows that the emphasis is on *how* measures are used and not on their purpose. Measures should not be used in such a way that they protect domestic industry. That is not to say that GATT Art. III relies on trade effects. This means only that a measure that does not have the potential to actually afford protection to the domestic industry is not prohibited under GATT Art. III. In addition, as stated above, the economic rationale of the WTO/GATT Agreement is liberal trade and economic efficiency by reducing government intervention. Consequently, in accordance with Art. 31 (1) of the VCLT, in the light of its object and purpose as reflected in the preamble to the WTO, GATT Art. III should be interpreted as prohibiting measures that have the potential to distort liberal trade. If a measure does not have the potential to have any detrimental trade effects, it cannot distort liberal trade and should not be prohibited. Hence, the aim of GATT Art. III is not to only prohibit measures that have a protectionist aim, but also those measures that cause a (potential) protectionist trade effect.[598] To only prohibit domestic measures on the basis of their protectionist purpose would therefore be contrary to the aim of GATT Art. III.

This reading should be valid despite the rulings of *US–Malt Beverages* and *US–Automobiles* that explicitly refer to an 'aim and effect' test. However, to argue that 'like products' have to be determined with reference to the aim and effect of a measure is contrary to the text and structure of GATT Art. III:2 and 4, which contain an obligation of similarity *and* equal treatment. The obligation of equal treatment is expressed in the formulations 'in excess of', 'not similarly taxed', 'so as to afford protection' regarding fiscal measures under GATT Art. III:2, and 'less favourable treatment' regarding non-fiscal measures under GATT Art. III:4. If the aim and effect of a measure were examined under the term 'like products', the text of the provisions referring to the equal treatment obligation would be rendered inutile. Moreover, to interpret the term 'like' on the basis of an 'aim and effect' test would render the word 'like' superfluous.

In this context, it should however be noted that the textual argument based on the different wording of the first and second sentence of GATT Art. III:2 and GATT Art. III:4, which does not refer to GATT Art. III:1, is not compelling. As Roessler rightly argues, the lack of reference to GATT Art. III:1 in the provisions mentioned cannot be relied upon as an argument that when interpreting these provisions, the aim and effect of a measure must not be taken into account. Paragraph 1 clearly contains the purpose of the entire article and has to be taken into account when interpreting the different provisions.[599] As will be argued below, the aim and effect of a measure shall be taken into account under the obligation of equal treatment. Regarding the different wording of GATT Art. III:2, first and second sentence, there are better ways to take into account the difference in the wording of the provisions of GATT Art. III, than refusing to interpret the first sentence in the light of GATT Art. III:1.

As argued by the panel in *Japan–Alcoholic Beverages*, it might indeed be difficult to determine the non-protectionist aim of a measure: Under the US GSP and the Omnibus Trade and Competitiveness Act of 1998, considerations of protection of domestic jobs are part of the rationale of the law.[600] Equally, the ILO states in its preamble that low labour standards can be a hindrance to the introduction of high labour standards in other countries. These considerations lead to the conclusion that it is highly probable that trade laws that pursue

598 In a similar vein, Horn/Mavroidis, p. 60 argue that it should not suffice that a measure is intended to serve some legitimate purpose to make it GATT Art. III-legal.

599 Roessler (Beyond the Ostensible), p. 775; Verhoosel, p. 75.

600 Humbert (The Challenge of Child Labour), pp. 284 et seqq.

better labour standards also pursue the protection of domestic industry. Since in these cases trade effects have to be relied upon in order to find out which purpose prevailed, the regulatory goal of a measure cannot be the sole criterion under GATT Art. III. Thus, the (potential) protectionist effect of a measure is equally important. However, the protectionist effect of a measure has to be analysed under the obligation of equal treatment. Without a difference in treatment of foreign and domestic products, there cannot be a protectionist effect. Hence, this obligation would be meaningless if the protectionist effect was analysed under the term 'like products'. Moreover, if there is some good aim and some protectionist effect, a balancing test might be required. Since GATT Art. XX provides for a detailed balancing test,[601] the question is whether aims and effects should be considered at all under GATT Art. III. Finally, it should be noted in this regard that it might generally be difficult to decide that an aim is non-protectionist since this decision involves a reflection of legitimate policy objectives, which should be left to governments and treaty-making bodies. These questions will be answered below.

Regarding the role of GATT Art. XX, as stated above, it might well be that the drafters thought of this provision as a justification for only facially discriminatory measures: Between 1948 and 1990, only a very small number of cases concerned origin-neutral measures.[602] The list of policy purposes is indeed very limited under GATT Art. XX. It does not take account of all the various non-protectionist policy purposes origin-neutral measures might encompass. It is thus possible that GATT Art. III is meant to provide more flexibility for origin-neutral measures than commonly supposed. However, the text and structure of GATT Art. III do not allow for an 'aim and effect' test under the term 'like products'. Whether GATT Art. XX is only aimed at discriminatory measures or prohibits any rule of reason test under GATT Art. III will be examined under the equal treatment obligation.

It is rightly argued that in the light of legal certainty and predictability, the 'likeness' of products shall be determined on the basis of economic factors that trade officials can deal with. Even though previous panels may have unconsciously taken recourse to an 'aim and effect' test, this does not lead *ipso facto* to the conclusion that they should do so in the future.

In conclusion, instead of referring to the regulatory purpose of a measure, the term 'like products' should be defined by economic or econometric

601 It will be examined in detail below, pp. 214et seqq., what kind of balancing test GATT Art. XX provides for.

602 Hudec, (Requiem for an Aim and Effects Test), p. 622, fn. 8.

criteria that establish a competitive relationship between foreign and domestic products.

5.3.3 Defining Like Products under a Market-Based Approach: Are Consumer Preferences Decisive?

Having established that the term 'like products' needs to be defined in the market place, the question arises whether products can be distinguished on the basis of their production method relating to child labour under market-based criteria. Hence, the following section will present firstly the criteria applied by the jurisprudence with a special focus on consumer preferences. Secondly, their appropriateness in defining 'like products' will be discussed in order to be able to determine whether those products made with child labour and those not made with child labour would be considered 'like products' under WTO law.

5.3.3.1 *The Legal Rulings*

5.3.3.1.1 Japan–Imported Wines and Alcoholic Beverages

The first main case on 'like products' taking market-based criteria into account was the GATT case *Japan–Imported Wines and Alcoholic Beverages.*[603] The case concerned the Japan Liquor Tax that classified alcoholic beverages into nine categories and applied different tax rates to each category of alcoholic beverages. The EC complained that the Japanese system of taxation was discriminatory and in contravention of GATT Art. III:1 and 2.[604] Specifically, the tax assessment basis was characterized by establishing product categories that amounted to penalizing imports. In addition, the application of different rates for similar products resulted in a heavier burden on imported products.[605] In order to determine 'like products', the panel cited the criteria of the Working Party Report on Border Tax Adjustments as well as tariff classifications and held that imported and Japanese gin, liquor, brandy etc. was 'each in its end-use … a well defined and single product intended for drinking'.[606] It stated that minor differences in taste, colour and other properties did not prevent products from qualifying as 'like products'.[607] With a view to other products such as vodka and Japanese shochu, it looked at consumers' preferences, asserting that the term 'likeness' included not only objective factors such as composition and manufacturing processes, but also more subjective factors such as

603 *Japan–Imported Wines and Alcoholic Beverages,* report of the panel.

604 Ibid., para. 3.1.

605 Ibid.

606 Ibid., para. 5.6.

607 Ibid.

consumption and use by consumers.[608] It noted that vodka and shochu were both made with similar raw materials and could thus be considered as 'like products'.[609] It then rejected the argument that traditional Japanese drinking habits regarding shochu led to a different conclusion.[610] Since consumer habits were variable in time and space, considering shochu and vodka as 'unlike products' held the risk of using different taxes to crystallize consumer preference for traditional domestic products.[611] The panel decided the issue under GATT Art. III:2, second sentence, stating that vodka and shochu were directly competitive or substitutable products.[612] With regard to *ad valorem* taxes, it held that 'like products' did not become unlike because of differences in local consumer traditions, or differences in prices that were often influenced by other market conditions.[613] Such a tax policy would solidify consumer preferences for traditional products.[614] In conclusion, it found that the Japanese taxation system with regard to alcoholic beverages violated GATT Art. III:2.

Whilst mainly relying on objective factors such as composition, general end-use and other product qualities such as taste, the panel also examined market-based criteria such as consumer preferences. However, in contrast to the Appellate Body in *EC–Asbestos* or *Korea–Alcoholic Beverages*, it did not refer to actual consumers' tastes and habits based on market analysis, but on general local consumer traditions. It rightly stated that these traditions may change. However, this is not to say that consumer preferences identified by profound market analysis and surveys that take into account changing retail prices may not be used to distinguish products. The underlying assumption of the panel was that a direct tax on products necessarily determined consumer preferences due to the resulting higher retail price.

However, if market-based analysis shows that consumer preferences change despite the higher retail price of the imported product, there is no reason why consumer preferences should not be a decisive criterion. As will be seen, in later cases panels rightly based their decisions on consumers' views as reflected by market analysis. In a similar vein, Choi argues that the panel should have examined whether or not the tax on shochu and vodka would have been *likely* to crystallize consumer habits in Japan.[615]

608 Ibid., para. 5.7.
609 Ibid.
610 Ibid.
611 Ibid.
612 Ibid.
613 Ibid., para. 5.9.
614 Ibid.
615 Choi, p. 25.

5.3.3.1.2 Japan–Alcoholic Beverages

The next case involving 'like products' was *Japan–Alcoholic Beverages*, which was already presented above.[616] When defining 'like products' under GATT Art. III, first sentence, the panel relied on physical characteristics and tariff classifications.[617] However, it stated that 'like products' were a subset of 'directly competitive or substitutable products'.[618] Examining the term 'directly and substitutable products' according to GATT Art. III:2, second sentence, it held that the decisive criterion was whether they had common end-uses as shown, *inter alia*, by the elasticity of substitution.[619] Yet, in order to determine 'like products', it was necessary that they essentially possessed the same characteristics.[620] Only 'directly competitive or substitutable products' required a more flexible approach.[621] In order to determine the elasticity of substitution, the panel noted that marketing strategies could be relevant, but that consumer preference surveys should be conducted according to some appropriate statistical methodologies.[622] It used a time-series analysis that demonstrated that as a result of the new Japanese tax law the market share of whisky compared to shochu had fallen.[623] Thus, it concluded that there was an elasticity of substitution between shochu and whisky.[624] In addition, it relied on a Japanese consumer survey that stated that in case shochu was unavailable ten per cent of consumers would switch to other spirits and whisky.[625] The panel also stated that econometric principles such as cross-price elasticity of demand, i.e. the responsiveness of the demand for one product to the change in the demand for the other product, should be considered.[626] The more sensitive the demand for one product is to changes in the price of the other product, all other things being equal, the more directly competitive they are.[627] The Appellate Body largely confirmed these findings stating that elasticity of substitution was relevant.[628]

616 *Japan–Alcoholic Beverages*, report of the panel and Appellate Body.
617 *Japan–Alcoholic Beverages*, report of the panel, para 6.23.
618 Ibid., paras. 6.21–6.22.
619 Ibid., para 6.22.
620 Ibid.
621 Ibid.
622 Ibid., para. 6.31.
623 Ibid., para. 6.30.
624 Ibid.
625 Ibid., para. 6.31.
626 Ibid., paras. 6.22, 6.31.
627 Ibid.
628 *Japan–Alcoholic Beverages*, report of the Appellate Body, p. 26.

It also agreed that cross-price elasticity was not the decisive criterion.[629]

While the panel and the Appellate Body both relied on more objective criteria such as physical similarities, they nevertheless demonstrated some openness to market-based criteria. Stating that 'like products' were a subset of 'directly and substitutable products', they noted that in the definition of 'like products', market-based criteria were relevant. This is correct since according to Art. 31 (1) of the VCLT, when determining 'like products', one has to take account of the purpose of GATT Art. III, i.e. to avoid protectionism. Thus, 'like products' should be competitive products since only competitive products may benefit from protectionist measures. The panel and the Appellate Body gave detailed instruction as to what market-based criteria could be used. However, as one author rightly pointed out, the sort of 'non-availability' test used should be replaced since in the case of non-availability of a product, even the most faithful consumer to a particular product would switch to another product.[630]

5.3.3.1.3 Canada–Periodicals

The case *Canada–Periodicals* was already presented above.[631] It concerned a tax on advertisements in split-run editions directed at the Canadian market. The US had claimed that the tax violated GATT Art. III:2, first sentence. When determining like products, the Appellate Body agreed with the use of hypothetical examples in case the protective measure has suppressed competition and imports.[632] As mentioned above, it then referred to criteria of the Report of the Working Party.[633] Having reversed the findings of the panel report, the Appellate Body examined the tax under the second sentence and followed the US arguments that the very existence of the tax itself was proof of competition between split-run periodicals and non-split-run periodicals.[634] This is an interesting argument and relates to the question discussed below whether consumers' tastes and habits can exist independently of governmental measures. It is however noteworthy that the Appellate Body approved of the use of hypothetical examples, which could be regarded as a first attempt to refer to potential demand. This question touches upon issues that were raised in later cases, i.e. that one should take into account not only the quantity of competition, but also the quality thereof. Both points will be discussed below.

629 Ibid.
630 Choi, p. 29.
631 *Canada–Periodicals*, report of the panel and Appellate Body.
632 Ibid.
633 *Canada–Periodicals*, report of the Appellate Body, p. 22.
634 Ibid., p. 27.

5.3.3.1.4 Korea–Alcoholic Beverages

The case *Korea–Alcoholic Beverages* elaborated on the econometric criteria to be used.[635] As stated above, it recalled that 'like products' were a subset of 'directly and substitutable products' and began its analysis under GATT Art. III, second sentence. The decisive criterion was whether consumers considered the products to be alternative ways of satisfying a particular need or taste.[636] The criteria to be used included the physical characteristics of a product; its end-uses based on consumer surveys and marketing strategies of companies; channels of distribution; and price.[637] However, the criterion of end-uses based on marketing campaigns was not sufficient since marketing campaigns and consumption patterns may change over time.[638] By the same token, absolute prices were less significant than relative price movements.[639] Therefore, quantitative studies of cross-price elasticity were relevant, but not decisive; evidence of competitive relationships in other markets relevant; and potential competition including future competition to be taken into account.[640] Regarding consumable products like the Korean alcoholic beverage soju, the willingness to occasionally substitute one product for another should be sufficient to demonstrate a certain degree of cross-price elasticity.[641] The panel then weighed the criteria. As the panel did in *Japan–Alcoholic Beverages*, the panel in this case also based its findings on a cross-price elasticity of demand analysis, referring to the Dodwell Study.[642] According to that study, if the price of soju increased by 20 per cent and the price of imported brown spirits decreased, 28.4 per cent of consumers would switch to imported spirits.[643] Regarding white spirits, 23.8 per cent of consumers would switch to imported products if the price of soju increased by 20 per cent.[644] Referring to the nature of competition, the panel stated that the market conditions, i.e. whether it was a closed market with substantial tax differentials, would have to be looked at.[645] Therefore, evidence from other markets was needed. In this regard, the panel stated that end-uses in other markets are a relevant criterion.[646] In addition, marketing strategies

635 *Korea–Alcoholic Beverages*, report of the panel and the Appellate Body.
636 *Korea–Alcoholic Beverages*, report of the panel, paras. 10.37–10.40.
637 Ibid., para. 10.43.
638 Ibid., 10.76.
639 Ibid., para. 10.94.
640 Ibid., 10.44–50.
641 Ibid., para. 10.91.
642 Ibid., paras. 10.56–11.20.
643 Ibid., para. 10.88.
644 Ibid.
645 Ibid., para. 10.78.
646 Ibid.

of Korean producers in response to changes in markets, and strategies aimed at other markets provided significant evidence.[647] Finally, the panel noted that while criteria under competition law defining the market should be utilized, the interpretation of the market in WTO law should be broader.[648] Whereas antitrust law addressed firms that threatened competition, GATT Art. III focused on the promotion of economic opportunities for importers through the elimination of discriminatory governmental measures that impair international trade.

As stated above, the Appellate Body confirmed the panel's findings elaborating on criteria as latent (potential) and future consumer demand.[649] In its view, apart from the objective of GATT Art. III to maintain equality of competition, the word 'substitutable' clearly indicated that the competitive relationship of products did not have to be analysed exclusively by reference to current consumer preferences.[650] As the panel in *Japan–Imported Wines and Alcoholic Beverages* found,[651] the Appellate Body stressed that exclusive reliance on current consumer preferences could lead to protective taxation since consumer behaviour might be influenced by taxation.[652] Thus, evidence of latent or potential demand was needed.[653] Since the object and purpose of GATT Art. III was to maintain the equality of competition, it was legitimate to consider whether products would become directly competitive or substitutable in the near future.[654] Cross-price elasticity studies involved an assessment of latent demand since they endeavoured to predict the change in demand that would result from a change in the price of a product following, *inter alia*, a change in the relative tax burdens on domestic and imported products.[655] However, the Appellate Body confirmed the panel's finding that relying exclusively on the quantitative nature of competition could result in a trade effects test, which is not adequate under GATT Art. III.[656] Instead, one should focus on the quality of competition, i.e. *why* there has been competition or not.[657] Therefore, cross-price elasticity was not the decisive criterion.[658] The Appellate Body

647 Ibid., para. 10.79.
648 Ibid., para. 10.81.
649 *Korea–Alcoholic Beverages*, report of the Appellate Body, paras. 112–124, 125–127.
650 Ibid., paras. 114–127.
651 *Japan–Imported Wines and Alcoholic Beverages*, report of the panel, paras. 5.7 and 5.9.
652 *Korea–Alcoholic Beverages*, report of the Appellate Body, para. 120.
653 Ibid.
654 Ibid., paras. 125–127.
655 Ibid., para. 121.
656 Ibid., paras. 128–131.
657 Ibid., paras. 132–134.
658 Ibid., para. 134.

emphasized that evidence from other markets was relevant where trade or competition barriers had influenced demand in the domestic market.[659]

The panel and Appellate Body Report elaborated on the market-based approach taken in the Japanese cases. The main improvement was to include latent (potential) and future demand based *inter alia* on evidence taken from other markets when considering 'directly competitive or substitutable products'. However, as one author has rightly pointed out, when considering evidence from other markets, empirical evidence is needed to show that the other markets looked at are comparable to the market under review.[660]

5.3.3.1.5 Chile–Alcoholic Beverages

The case *Chile–Alcoholic Beverages* followed the approach taken in *Korea–Alcoholic Beverages.*[661] In this case, the EC claimed that the Chilean tax system on alcoholic beverages violated GATT Art. III, second sentence.[662] The panel considered end-uses as shown by the elasticity of substitution based on market studies as a key criterion.[663] The overlap of end-uses could also be demonstrated by marketing strategies used in advertising.[664] Physical similarities and cross-price elasticity were also relevant.[665] It referred to the Gemines Study that provided a cross-price elasticity of 0.26 in relation to whisky and Chilean pisco.[666] The elasticity of 0.26 meant that a 10 per cent rise in the price of whisky would lead to an increase of 2.6 per cent in the demand for Chilean pisco.[667] The panel found that this was a relatively low cross-price elasticity, though that could be due to other factors such as the protective measure itself.[668] It also held that consideration should be given as to whether the products could reasonably be expected to become directly competitive or substitutable in the near future.[669] In conclusion, it stressed that due consideration should be given to marketing strategies identifying the market segment that products belong to, as well as to the properties or characteristics from which their utility is derived.[670]

659 Ibid., para. 137.
660 Choi, p. 30.
661 *Chile–Alcoholic Beverages*, report of the panel and Appellate Body.
662 *Chile–Alcoholic Beverages*, report of the panel, para. 7.1.
663 Ibid., paras. 7.31–44.
664 Ibid., paras. 7.45–47.
665 Ibid., paras. 7.48–54 and paras. 7.60–79.
666 Ibid., para. 7.71.
667 Choi, fn. 282.
668 Ibid., paras. 7.71–79.
669 Ibid., para. 7.24.
670 Ibid., paras. 7.81–82.

The panel in this case paid special attention to marketing strategies of companies, and consumer theory where one should examine the utility that consumers derive from a product. It also relied on cross-price elasticity, but considered that this was not the relevant criterion because of potential influential effects of protective government measures. In this regard, it should be noted that if cross-price elasticity studies take into account the potential effect of the protective measure they could be a reliable criterion.

5.3.3.1.6 EC–Asbestos

As stated above, in *EC–Asbestos*, the Appellate Body confirmed the market-oriented approach to 'like products'.[671] It held that the determination of 'likeness' under GATT Art. III:4 was a determination of the nature and extent of a competitive relationship between products.[672] It stated that each of the criteria of the Working Party Report on Border Tax Adjustments – physical properties, end-uses, consumers' tastes and habits – plus tariff classifications should be given weight.[673] In relation to physical properties, it stated that those properties that were likely to influence the competitive relationship between products in the market place were relevant.[674] The Appellate Body then emphasized that the criteria referring to end-uses and consumers' tastes and habits were key criteria.[675] However, if two products were physically different, there was a heavy burden on the complaining party to demonstrate that products were in such a competitive relationship to be considered as 'like' within the meaning of GATT Art. III.[676] With regard to consumers' tastes and habits, it emphasized – without making a definite statement – that these were very likely to be shaped by the health risks associated by a product that is known to be highly carcinogenic.[677] It also referred to latent demand that had been suppressed by the regulatory measure based on evidence from third markets, as already stated in *Korea–Alcoholic Beverages*.[678]

This case explicitly confirmed the market-oriented approach taken by previous panels on the term 'like products' in GATT Art. III. It highlighted the

671 *EC–Asbestos*, report of the Appellate Body.
672 Ibid., para. 37.
673 Ibid., paras. 101, 102, 109.
674 Ibid., para. 114.
675 Ibid., para. 117.
676 Ibid., para. 118.
677 Ibid., para. 122.
678 Ibid., para. 123.

importance of consumers' views, i.e. demand-side criteria, which however are likely to be informed by physical properties such as health risks.

5.3.3.1.7 Philippines–Distilled Spirits

The Appellate Body in *Philippines–Distilled Spirits* followed the market-based approach of the previous WTO case law and relied on criteria such as physical characteristics, end-uses, tariff classification, regulatory regimes and consumers' tastes and habits discussing *inter alia* substitutability studies, price competition, marketing strategies and market segmentation.[679] It stressed that products that are close to being perfectly substitutable can be 'like products' according to GATT Art. III:2, first sentence, whilst products that compete to a lesser degree would fall within the scope of the second sentence.[680] The Appellate Body rejected the argument put forward by the Philippines that the two sets of imported and domestic products were not 'directly competitive or substitutable' under GATT Art. III:2, second sentence because high-priced and non-sugar-based imported spirits and domestic low-priced and sugar-based spirits were sold in two different market segments, imported high-priced spirits being only available to a narrow segment of the Filipino population.[681] It found that the panel had correctly held that GATT Art. III protected not only some but all instances of direct competition and that it was sufficient that there was some overlap in the prices of imported and domestic distilled spirits for both high-priced and low-priced products, and that many consumers were able to buy high-priced imported spirits 'at least on special occasions'.[682] With regard to the latter argument, the Appellate Body stressed that no identity in the nature and frequency of the consumer's purchasing behaviour was required and that latent demand of the population as well as other factors such as marketing strategies had to be taken into account.[683]

Whilst it is convincing to refer not only to actual demand but also to latent demand and other factors such as marketing strategies because the measure at issue may have suppressed consumer demand – which indeed might have been the case with the Filipino excise tax, it is nevertheless questionable to rely on some overlap in prices and the fact that a 'narrow segment' of consumers is able to buy high-priced imported spirit 'at least on special occasions'. It is of course correct that not only the quantity but also the quality of competition

679 *Philippines–Distilled Spirits*, report of the Appellate Body, paras. 109–241.

680 Ibid., para. 149.

681 Ibid., paras. 209–221.

682 Ibid., paras. 215–216, 221.

683 Ibid., paras. 216–218.

should be considered, but in fact, the Appellate Body has set the bar very low for determining products as 'like'. With regard to a fictitious tax on toys made with child labour, it would not be desirable to qualify high-priced domestic toys made without child labour as being directly substitutable to low-priced imported toys made with child labour just because there are also some high-priced imported toys that a narrow segment of consumers is able to buy.

5.3.3.1.8 US–Clove Cigarettes

As indicated above, the Appellate Body in *US–Clove Cigarettes* followed the approach in *EC–Asbestos* and held that the determination of 'likeness' in Art. 2.1 of the TBT Agreement was a determination about the nature and extent of a competitive relationship between the products at issue.[684] When comparing imported clove cigarettes with domestic menthol cigarettes under the criterion of consumers' tastes and habits, it referred to *Philippines–Distilled Spirits* and held that actual competition may be limited to a segment of the market, i.e. in this case young smokers who 'perceive that clove and menthol cigarettes as sufficiently substitutable'.[685]

Here again, it is questionable whether reliance only on a segment of the market is desirable, especially with regard to products made with child labour since one may very easily qualify products made with child labour and not made with child labour as like and the measure at issue in violation of WTO law.[686]

5.3.3.1.9 Conclusion

To summarize, the following criteria are applied by the jurisprudence to define 'like products':[687] Objective factors include physical similarity and common end-uses, while subjective factors include end-uses as shown by elasticity of substitution. The degree of elasticity of substitution can be demonstrated by referring to different marketing strategies utilized by producers in e.g. advertising, consumer preferences based on statistical data, time-series analysis of the products' market share, cross-price elasticity of demand, channels of

684 *US–Clove Cigarettes*, report of the Appellate Body, para. 120.

685 Ibid., paras. 143 and 144.

686 Cf. Pauwelyn (Questions on Impact of Cloves on GATT National Treatment).

687 It has to be recalled that most of the cases analysed were decided under 'directly competitive and substitutable products'. However, since 'like products' are by definition 'directly competitive and substitutable products', the same criteria may be used for 'like products'. Yet, as indicated by the panel in *Japan–Alcoholic Beverages* and the Appellate Body in *EC–Asbestos*, with regard to 'like products', physical similarities are more important.

distribution, and absolute prices. In addition, the measure itself may indicate that products are directly competitive. When analysing consumer preferences, potential and future demand need to be taken into account in order to analyse consumer demand without a measure's market-distorting effect. This might be done either by cross-price elasticity studies that take into account price changes following a higher tax; by relying on data on consumption patterns in other markets; or by analysing marketing strategies of domestic producers in response to imports. Tariff classifications were also relevant, but less significant. Since physical similarities are a strong indication of a competitive relationship between products, and therefore also of them being 'like products'. However, the 'likeness' of dissimilar products can still be shown by relying on consumers' views. In any event, each criterion of the Working Party Report on Border Tax Adjustment has to be taken into account. There is a strong tendency among the dispute settlement bodies to rely on cross-price elasticity whilst underlining that it is not the decisive criterion. They argue that results of studies on cross-price elasticity might be influenced by protective government measures. Hence, one should rather take account of the nature of the competition, i.e. whether the relevant market was a closed market. If so, potential demand and evidence from other markets need to be taken into account. In more recent case law, the Appellate Body has relied on a segment of the market in order to prove the competitive relationship. Especially in case of child labour, such an approach may be too permissive for the determination of 'likeness'.

Finally, the difference between the terms 'like' and 'directly competitive and substitutable' is the degree of competitiveness; the same holds true for the various meanings of 'like' in the different provisions, as indicated by the Appellate Body in *Japan–Alcoholic Beverages*, evoking the image of an accordion.[688]

5.3.3.2 *Relevant Criteria to Determine Likeness*

Agreeing with the market-based approach to the term 'likeness' in GATT Art. III, the criteria offered by the jurisprudence have to be discussed in detail to be able to determine whether physically identical products might be considered 'unlike'.[689] Accordingly, the meaning and relevance of each factor will now be examined and evaluated.

688 *Japan–Alcoholic Beverages*, report of the Appellate Body, p. 21.

689 For the parallel discussion of emissions as a basis to differentiate between products and the ensuing WTO compatibility of climate border adjustments, see Will, pp. 131–164.

5.3.3.2.1 Physical Similarities

As indicated by the Appellate Body in EC–*Asbestos*, physical similarities play an important role since physically similar products are more likely to be in a competitive relationship than physically dissimilar products. However, the complainants may prove the contrary if enough evidence exists that consumers regard physically dissimilar products to be in very high degree of competitiveness.[690] Thus, physical similarity is not decisive. Rather, it is used to establish the competitive relationship in the first place. Only those physical properties that affect the competitive relationship matter. This is to be welcomed since the ultimate aim of GATT Art. III is to avoid protectionism and protectionism can only exist if there is a competitive relationship between products. It follows that in theory, products made with child labour and products not made with child labour may be regarded as not 'like' or 'directly competitive or substitutable products'.

5.3.3.2.2 Common End-Uses versus End-Uses as Shown by Elasticity of Substitution

The same reasoning should hold true for end-uses since similar end-uses may also be determined based on consumer surveys and marketing strategies. Thus, products should not be looked at primarily on the basis of whether they have a general common end-use given certain physical properties, but whether they satisfy the same particular need of the consumer. This aspect was stressed in *Chile–Alcoholic Beverages* as the panel pointed to companies' marketing strategies that highlighted product distinctions as tools for analysis.[691] It also pointed to a consumer theory that paid special attention to the properties or characteristics of a product from which the consumer derives utility.[692] The Appellate Body in EC–*Asbestos* underlined that one had to distinguish between the extent to which products are capable of performing the same or similar functions (end-uses), and the extent to which consumers are willing to use the products to perform these functions (consumers' tastes and habits).[693] Thus, one has to differentiate between common end-uses based on the physical properties of products, and end-uses as shown by elasticity of substitution.

---

690 Cf. EC–*Asbestos*, report of the Appellate Body, para. 118.

691 *Chile–Alcoholic Beverages*, report of the panel, paras. 7.45–47.

692 Ibid., paras. 7.81–82.

693 EC–*Asbestos*, report of the Appellate Body, para. 117. Although this was a case decided under GATT Art. III:4, the same shall hold true for taxes.

5.3.3.2.3 Common End-Uses

As regards common end-uses, identical products that only differ as to whether they were made by children are *ipso facto* capable of performing the same functions and therefore have a common end-use. Based on this factor, they are 'like products'.

5.3.3.2.4 End-Uses as Shown by Elasticity of Substitution / Consumers' Tastes and Habits

Since it is possible to argue that consumers caring about children do not derive the same utility from a product made with child labour, the criterion of consumers' tastes and habits may qualify products made and not made with child labour as different products.

5.3.3.2.5 Companies' Marketing Strategies

As shown by Humbert,[694] companies have started to recognize consumers' awareness of labour conditions, and adopted codes of conduct and other strategies to demonstrate their corporate social responsibility. Former examples include labels for carpets 'not made with child labour'[695] as well as for footballs 'Guarantee: Manufactured without child labour'.[696] Leading international food and clothing retailers such as the German company Lidl and H&M increasingly use their sustainability strategy for attracting consumers.[697]

It is thus imaginable that corporations increasingly base their advertising and other marketing strategies on their corporate behaviour regarding the (non-)use of child labour. As in the case of Fairtrade coffee,[698] which is regarded as an individual market segment, companies could create a separate market segment for products made without child labour. Such marketing strategies have been defined as strategies related to 'ethical consumerism' or 'ethical management dimensions'.[699] 'Ethical consumerism' relates to matters of conscience such as human rights, labour standards, animal rights and environmental protection. It is defined as 'the conscious and deliberate choice to

694 Humbert (The Challenge of Child Labour), pp. 335–373.

695 See for example the former RUGMARK label described on Humbert (The Challenge of Child Labour) pp. 362–363.

696 Label programme of Reebok International Limited and the ILO, referred to in Ratnam, p. 470 and Auger/Burke/Devinney/Louviere, p. 282.

697 See for example https://info.lidl/en/responsibility or https://www2.hm.com/en_us/sustainability-at-hm.html.

698 See for example https://www.fairtrade-deutschland.de/produkte/kaffee.

699 Auger/Burke/Devinney/Louviere, p. 282.

make certain consumption choices due to personal and moral beliefs'.[700] Thus, it may be possible in the future to rely on marketing strategies to determine a different market segment for products made with child labour.

5.3.3.2.6 Direct Consumers' Views

In addition, several studies exist that demonstrate that consumers increasingly take ethical factors including child labour into account in their choices. For example, a survey by Corporate Edge has shown that 57 per cent of consumers said that they would stop buying a product if they knew that children were being employed to make it.[701] A study by Market & Opinion Research International (MORI) found that over one third of consumers in the UK were seriously concerned with ethical issues, which could result in a relatively large market share for ethical products.[702] However, later studies found that moral judgements do not automatically translate into corresponding behaviour, and that people are strongly influenced by personal costs.[703] Accordingly, consumers might not actually do what that say. Thus, these studies might provide some additional evidence, but are not sufficient to prove that products are 'unlike'. In the area of climate change-related measures, Will convincingly concludes that consumer views need to be independent of the price effect of the measure, otherwise, any price-based measure would be compatible with GATT Art. III.[704]

5.3.3.2.7 Cross-Price Elasticity of Demand

The WTO jurisprudence has also relied on cross-price elasticity of demand to determine demand substitutability. The cross-price elasticity of demand of one product with respect to another product is equal to the percentage change in the quantity demanded of the former divided by the percentage change in the price of the latter.[705] The more willing consumers are to substitute one product with a different product, if the price of the former product is raised by a slight percentage, the higher the elasticity of demand is. If for example 80 per cent of consumers switch to the other product if the price of the original product is

700 See Auger, Devinney, p. 3.

701 Ibid., p. 1.

702 Ibid., p. 4.

703 See Auger/Burke/Devinney/Louviere, p. 284, see also Welt am Sonntag / Gesellschaft für Konsumforschung, 4 October 2015, https://www.welt.de/finanzen/verbraucher/article147168433/Deutsche-wollen-faire-Produkte-aber-bitte-billig.html.

704 Will, p. 133.

705 Heertje/Wenzel, pp. 138–141; Goco, p. 331.

raised by 20 per cent, the quotient is 4. If only 10 per cent of consumers switch as a result of a percentage change of price by 20 per cent, the quotient is 0.5. This means, if the quotient is large and positive, then the products are substitutes, however if the quotient is close to zero, then they are not related.[706]

Whilst various panels utilized this criterion, they all stressed that it was not the decisive criterion. In *Chile–Alcoholic Beverages*, the panel found the products directly competitive despite the low elasticity coefficient.[707] The criterion of cross-price elasticity is used in both European and US antitrust and competition law to define the relevant market. In European competition law, using cross-price elasticity the question is whether consumers would switch to readily available substitutes in case of a relative price increase of e.g. five to ten per cent.[708] If the availability of immediate substitutes made the price increase unprofitable due to the resulting loss of sales, additional possible substitutes would be included in the market calculation until the price increase would be profitable. Accordingly, the smallest set of products within which the small price increase would be profitable is the relevant market.[709]

As stated above, the panel on *Korea–Alcoholic Beverages* noted that whilst criteria under competition law defining the market should be utilized, the interpretation of the market in WTO law should be broader.[710]

Choi suggests that the market definition of antitrust law should be used in WTO law.[711] He opines that the threshold switching rate, i.e. the rate of consumers that switch to another product in response to a price increase of the former product, should be the same as in antitrust law.[712] He points to the fact that the threshold used in antitrust law is a benefit-loss turning point for producers. The threshold used in antitrust law is the point where price change rates equalize substitution rates. For example, if a price is raised by five per cent and five per cent of consumers switch to the other product, the producer will not suffer a loss of sales.[713] Whilst Choi recognizes the different aims of competition law and WTO law, he points out that the market definition should be the same because the common purpose is to determine available substitutes.[714]

---

706 Goco, p. 331.

707 *Chile–Alcoholic Beverages*, report of the panel, paras. 7.60–79.

708 'Commission Notice on the Definition of the Relevant Market for the Purpose of Community Competition Law', OJ 1997 C 372/5.

709 Ibid.

710 *Korea–Alcoholic Beverages*, report of the panel, para. 10.81.

711 Choi, pp. 57 et seqq.

712 Ibid., p. 57.

713 Ibid.

714 Ibid., p. 58.

However, the market definition should be adapted to the context of trade law. The purpose of antitrust or competition law is to secure competition in a given market from the point of view of the producer. Thus, it is correct to ask how much a producer can increase the price without suffering a loss. WTO law, or more specifically GATT Art. III merely aims at securing equal conditions for foreign and domestic goods by prohibiting protective governmental measures. In *Korea–Alcoholic Beverages*, the panel rightly stated that trade law addressed the potential of products to compete when entering a foreign market while antitrust law addresses the actual mechanisms.[715] Thus, a market definition should be assumed to take into account potential competition. The question under trade law is at what relative price movements a government is likely to introduce protective measures. Thus, the market definition includes all products – if sold in the importing state – that may cause a price decrease of domestic products. Goco has convincingly argued that in WTO law, the relevant market should be defined as the 'reference' good or service and all other goods or services that, if sold or made available in a member state at the world price, will lead to a decrease in the price of the 'reference' good by a certain percentage.[716] This is a potentially broader set of products than the smallest set of products where a price increase would be profitable.

Such a price decrease is likely to occur following trade liberalization, if the number of people that buys the cheaper imported product is at least the same as the number of people that buys the domestic product, i.e. if the quantity in demand of each product is the same. In order to remain competitive, the domestic producer would have to lower its price to at least the price of the imported product. Two products thus can be said to be in the same market if their change in quantity of demand by a certain percentage in relation to the change in price by a certain percentage is at least equal. That is, all products can be said to be in the same market for which the cross-price elasticity of demand is at least equal or greater than that of the product in question.[717] In such a situation, it is likely that a government will protect its domestic producers.[718]

One would thus have to determine the cross-price elasticity of both the imported product made with child labour and the domestic product not made with child labour, and compare them. Having established the cross-price

715 *Korea–Alcoholic Beverages*, report of the panel, para. 10.81.

716 Goco, p. 333.

717 See for an illustrative description of the problem Goco, p. 334.

718 Such a scenario occurred in the textile industry when the EU (re-)introduced import quotas in response to cheap imports from China to protect the textile industry in Southern Europe (Süddeutsche Zeitung 17 August 2005).

elasticity of the imported product following trade liberalization, i.e. assuming the protective measure was eliminated, one would have to ask consumers of the domestic product in question whether they would buy the cheaper product if they knew that it was made with child labour. This could be the case if for example toys made with child labour from China were made available. If the same percentage of consumers would then buy the imported cheaper product as currently buy the domestic product, i.e. the same change in quantity of demand by percentage occurred, domestic producers would be forced to lower their prices to at least the price of the foreign product and both products would have the same cross-price elasticity.

Indeed, some studies exist on hypothetical price movements of products (not) made with child labour. They indicate that the concept of cross-price elasticity can be used for products (not) made with child labour.

Existing research focussed on the question whether people were willing to pay more for products made with acceptable ethical features. One study indicated that 75 per cent of consumers said that they would pay US Dollar 5 more on a US Dollar 20 item if they knew it was not fabricated in a sweatshop.[719] However, this means that 25 per cent of consumers would still buy the other product made with child labour that costs 20 per cent less. This means that in case the price of an item is raised by 20 per cent, 25 per cent of consumers would switch to the other product. The switching rate of consumers is thus higher than the price rise. Hence, under antitrust law, the products would be in the same market and the respective products in question 'like products'. Under the proposed market definition for WTO law, one would have to look at the cross-price elasticity of the cheaper product made with child labour and compare it with the percentage changes in demand and price of the product made without child labour. Since this is potentially a broader market, it is likely that the respective products are also in the same market.

Another study found that consumers were willing to pay 28 per cent more for US Dollar 10 items, but only 15 per cent more for US Dollar 100 items.[720] Thus, the higher the price is, the lower the willingness is to spend money on ethical features of a product. Cross-price elasticity studies should take this into account.

Also, these studies precondition that consumers know about labour conditions. Only in case there was a label saying 'made with child labour', consumers can make a choice. In this case, it is likely that a separate market exists for

719 See Auger/Burke/Devinney/Louviere, p. 284.

720 Ibid.

products not made with child labour. However, the label needed could also be regarded as protective and contrary to GATT Art. III. Yet before discussing this issue, the reliability of these studies will be explored.

The studies mentioned so far contain some shortcomings and methodological flaws. It has been suggested that it is unknown how important ethical factors are in fact, and that even studies related to the dollar value of those features are unreliable since the response variability is lower than in reality and ethical features are overestimated.[721] If one has to choose between functionally identical products,[722] it is easier to choose the product not made with child labour than in the case where there are a variety of other functional and ethical features. In addition, the wording and the structure of surveys often allows consumers to conceal their real attitude, and which in fact they often do on sensitive matters such as child labour.[723] This phenomenon is called incentive compatibility. For that reason, recent research has used more complex survey methods including ethical disposition surveys and a choice experiment offering various ethical features including child labour, as well as various functional features.[724] The products chosen were bath soap and athletic shoes. The respondents were made up of a diverse group of consumers including undergraduate students from Hong Kong, Australian MBA students, and Amnesty International supporters, and consisted of men, women, singles, married persons etc.[725]

The results of the study were the following: Ethical features may have an effect on purchasing decisions of up to 20.4 per cent;[726] child labour is clearly the most important ethical feature;[727] and most consumers do not know about the ethical features of a product.[728] Consumers' demand for ethical products is thus a latent one. Information on ethical features can significantly affect purchase decisions, i.e. by up to 28.5 per cent in case of athletic shoes, which is the product for which the ethical feature of child labour was examined.[729] The product value of the ethical feature of child labour extends from 31 per cent to 94 per cent,[730] i.e. people would pay between 31 and 94 per cent more if the

721 Ibid, p. 285.
722 The price may of course vary since that is taken into account in the survey.
723 Auger/Devinney, p. 6.
724 Auger/Burke/Devinney/Louviere, p. 285.
725 Ibid., p. 288.
726 Ibid., p. 291.
727 Ibid.
728 Ibid., p. 296.
729 Ibid., p. 291.
730 Ibid., p. 295.

product were not made with child labour.[731] Contrary to the results of previous studies, the total value of the product does not seem to matter a lot.[732] However, consumers would not sacrifice product performance for ethical considerations.[733]

Another recent study on this subject that used a different methodology, i.e. hour-long in-depth interviews, found that consumers are not generally very concerned with ethical issues.[734] Only if they are made alert by media reports, they are likely to consider ethical features in their choices.[735] Cultural influences generally do not matter.[736] This study relates to the previous study in that it highlights the importance of adequate information on ethical issues.

In the context of cross-price elasticity and demand substitutability, the results of these studies have the following implications:

The fact whether products are made with child labour significantly matters to consumers. They would be likely to switch to another product not made with child labour even if they had to pay, in some cases, 94 per cent more. Thus, a distinct market segment of ethically produced products might exist. However, this consumption pattern depends on whether consumers are informed about the ethical feature of child labour since most consumers are ignorant of products' ethical features. Thus, the results of the study represent the latent demand rather than actual demand. Most importantly, it is not known how many consumers would buy the more expensive product not made with child labour. Thus, one cannot establish cross-price elasticity. Only the previous studies that contain some methodological flaws indicate that products made with child labour and products not made with child labour are relatively cross-price elastic. The question therefore is which studies can be used in the trade context. In this regard, one has to recall that in the trade context, the initial question was whether physically (and presumably offering identical functions) identical products can be distinguished by their production methods. If consumers make their product choice on functional features instead of ethical factors such as child labour, this means that products made with child labour are not in a distinct market and therefore 'like products'. Therefore, only studies focussing on one ethical feature and referring to cross-price elasticity should be used in the first place. However, due to methodological flaws such

731 Ibid., p. 298.
732 Ibid., p. 295.
733 Ibid., p. 300.
734 Belk/Devinney/Eckhardt, p. 282.
735 Ibid., p. 283.
736 Ibid., p. 282.

as consumers' incentive compatibility, the results of these studies should be tested against the choice experiment. In conclusion, the questionnaire should first ask whether consumers of the domestic product in question would switch to a cheaper product knowing that it was made with child labour. As done in the choice experiment, one should ask different consumer segments including those consumers who care about child labour and those who do not. To prove the results of the questionnaire, the same consumers should participate in a choice experiment.

In conclusion, the concept of cross-price elasticity should be used under WTO law. However, the relevant market is broader than under competition law. It includes all imports that may cause a price decrease of domestic products. This group of products includes those whose cross-price elasticity is at least equal or greater than that of the product that is considered to be 'like'. Recent studies have indicated that ethical features, in particular child labour, matter to consumers, but that currently products made and not made with child labour would be in the same market under antitrust law, and potentially under WTO law. Nevertheless, consumers are increasingly aware of ethical features. Hence, in the future, products made with and made without child labour may not be in the same market. So, according to the criterion of cross-price elasticity, these two product categories may in the future be considered not to be 'directly competitive' and thus not 'like' products within the meaning of GATT Art. III:2 and 4, despite their physical similarities.

5.3.3.2.8 Potential Demand

It is argued that consumers' tastes and habits, and the concept of cross-price elasticity should not be the decisive criteria since consumers' views could be influenced by protective measures.[737] Along the same lines, the Appellate Body in *Canada–Periodicals*, argued that the very existence of the tax was proof of competition between split-run periodicals and non-split-run periodicals.[738] The Appellate Body in *Korea–Alcoholic Beverages* rightly stated that in this case evidence of latent or potential demand was needed.[739] It convincingly argued that the word 'substitutable' indicated that the requisite relationship might exist between products that are not, at a given moment, considered by consumers to be substitutes, but which were, nonetheless, capable of being substituted for one another.[740] As mentioned above, cross-price

737 Quick/Lau, p. 431 et seq.; *Chile–Alcoholic Beverages*, report of the panel, paras. 7.60–79.

738 *Canada–Periodicals*, report of the Appellate Body, p. 27.

739 *Korea–Alcoholic Beverages*, report of the Appellate Body, para. 120.

740 Ibid., para. 114.

elasticity studies are based on hypothetical price changes, so they are capable of taking the price-distorting effect of protective governmental measures into account. Therefore, they relate to potential demand. This is also shown by the market studies in relation to child labour presented above, which signify latent demand. Admittedly, consumers could be influenced to the extent that their tastes and habits are 'frozen' so that they cannot answer the questionnaire ignoring the protective effect of the measure. In this case, as suggested by the Appellate Body on *Korea–Alcoholic Beverages*, evidence could be taken from other markets.[741] As stated by the panel on *Korea–Alcoholic Beverages*, direct consumer views based on surveys, or as shown by marketing strategies of domestic companies and studies of cross-price elasticity can be used as evidence from other markets. However, panels should be careful when choosing the comparable market, otherwise they risk changing the concept of end-uses in a given market into generalized end-uses.[742] It follows that potential demand based on evidence from other markets should be referred to in order to remedy shortcomings of cross-price elasticity studies.

Nevertheless, some argue that the concept of latent demand raises some doubts, asserting that there will hardly be any cases in which it can be proven that consumer preferences were developed without governmental protective measures.[743] In case of child labour, consumers are generally aware of the issue of child labour as the surveys mentioned above and companies' marketing strategies indicate.[744] However, to change their purchasing decisions in favour of ethically acceptable products, consumers have to be confronted with information on ethical factors. In addition, they are not able to distinguish between products made with and products made without child labour if this is not labelled. Thus, one could argue that consumer preferences cannot exist without the introduction of a government measure such as a mandatory label. Yet, in the case of child labour, consumer preferences exist independent of governmental measures to label products made without child labour due to extensive coverage by the media. The fact that consumers forget about the issue and need to be reminded by a governmental measure or media reports does not make these preferences disappear. Put differently, in the case of child labour, the governmental measure would not influence consumers, but reflect their latent preferences. Contrary to the example used by Quick and Lau,[745] it

741 Ibid., para. 137.

742 Choi, p. 79.

743 Quick/Lau, p. 433; Verhoosel, p. 57.

744 See above pp. 133 et seqq.

745 Quick/Lau, p. 432 et seq.

is the media and not a government campaign that influence consumers in the first place. Moreover, at least in the textile sector, consumers have the possibility to and do indeed make purchasing decisions in favour of brands that are associated with good behaviour. Consumers may also grow suspicious in cases of unusually low prices. In conclusion, the case of child labour is one where consumer preferences may develop without the influence of governmental measures.

Finally, the Appellate Body in *Korea–Alcoholic Beverages* rightly argues that to rely too much on the quantity of competition would be akin to a 'trade effects' test, which is not adequate under GATT Art. III.[746] One should therefore look at the nature of the competition and assess whether the market was non-competitive. If so, evidence from other markets is needed. Hence, one could use quantitative data such as cross-price elasticity as *prima facie* evidence that can only be rebutted by submitting other evidence based e.g. on marketing strategies or evidence from other markets. In a similar vein, another author argues that not only the degree of competitiveness, but also the degree of rivalry, i.e. the degree of competition, is important.[747] It is asserted that in case competition is intense, domestic products will not benefit from the measure favouring domestic products.[748] In this case the measure should not be found to be protective.[749]

5.3.3.2.9 Future Demand

The Appellate Body in *Korea–Alcoholic Beverages* also rightly relied on the concept of future demand.[750] Although this concept overlaps with the concept of latent demand, it differs to the extent that it does not refer to current consumers' tastes and habits that are hidden, but to those evolving in the near future. As the Appellate Body stated, this concept is required by the word 'substitutable' and the aim of GATT Art. III to protect expectations of equal conditions of competition between imported and domestic products. GATT Art. III would be of no practical value for the industry if future dimensions of the conditions of competition between imported and domestic products were not included in the term 'like or directly competitive or substitutable products'.[751] Especially in the case of child labour, due to the increasing amount of new initiatives in

---

746 *Korea–Alcoholic Beverages*, report of the Appellate Body, para. 130.
747 Neven.
748 Ibid., p. 423.
749 Ibid.
750 *Korea–Alcoholic Beverages*, report of the Appellate Body, paras. 125–127.
751 Choi, p. 77.

the area of corporate social responsibility and growing awareness among consumers, it is highly probable that over the next years, there will be widespread demand for products not made by child labour. Similarly, with regard to emissions and climate-friendly products, Will argues that time matters with regard to consumer preferences.[752] Considerations relating to future demand should therefore be taken into account when interpreting 'like' or 'directly competitive or substitutable products'.

5.3.3.2.10 Differences in (Absolute) Prices

Differences in (absolute) prices can also play a role. The panel in *Indonesia–Automobile Industry* convincingly argued that the huge price differences between the Indonesian National Car 'Timor' and a Rolls Royce could be taken as a manifestation of the physical and non-physical differences between the products, and therefore of the low degree of substitutability between these groups of products.[753] However, the panel also rightly stated in *Korea–Alcoholic Beverages* that absolute prices are less important than behavioural changes that occur due to relative price movements.[754] Caution must be exercised when referring to absolute price ratio differences because prices can be influenced by exchange rates, and high business or distribution costs caused by government policies.[755]

5.3.3.2.11 Time-Series Analysis

In addition, one could utilize time-series analysis of the market share of products, if available. If for example the market share of products not made with child labour fell by a certain percentage, whereas the market share of products made with child labour rose by a certain percentage over a certain period of time, one could conclude that this pair of products is directly competitive. Since it is assumed that the products in question are physically identical and therefore few other reasons exist to explain this trend, this would be a strong indication that they are indeed directly competitive.

5.3.3.2.12 Tariff Classifications and Channels of Distribution

The remaining criteria such as tariff classifications and channels of distribution will generally not be very relevant since the presumption is that the products are physically identical. The relevant products are thus likely to be

752 Will, p. 133.
753 *Indonesia–Automobile Industry*, report of the panel, para. 14.175.
754 *Korea–Alcoholic Beverages*, report of the panel, para. 10.94.
755 Ibid.

classified under the same tariff heading and distributed through the same channels. However, it is imaginable that in the future, there might be different channels of distribution for e.g. fairly traded T-shirts not made with child labour in special shops as is currently the case with Fair Trade coffee. In this case, different channels of distribution would become relevant.

5.3.3.2.13 Supply Substitutability

Finally, it has been suggested that from the perspective of welfare economics and the objective of the GATT to protect competitive relationships between products and therefore producers, a supply substitutability test should be included in the 'likeness' or 'substitutability' determination.[756] It is argued that high supply substitutability mitigates distortion generated by discriminatory measures in competitive relationships between foreign and domestic producers.[757] The underlying reasoning of this is highly convincing: For example, a higher tax on product A could put foreign producers at a disadvantage from the beginning, but if they are capable of switching easily to product B (on which there is a lower tax) they do not suffer a loss. In this case, the discriminatory effect of the higher tax is mitigated. Consequently, in this case, the objective of GATT Art. III to avoid protectionism is achieved and the provision not violated. In a similar vein, in *US–Automobiles,*[758] the panel, when denying a discriminatory effect, relied on the fact that manufacturers generally had both the capacity to meet the requirements of the favourable tax treatment and in fact did produce cars that met the requirements. Other authors argue that especially in cases of low demand substitutability, supply-side factors should be considered.[759]

However, it is questionable whether these considerations should be included in the determination of 'like or directly or substitutable products'. The panel in *US–Automobiles* referred to producer-related considerations when analysing the 'inherent trade effect' of the measure.[760] Indeed, the advocate of the supply substitutability test himself admits that the test could be applied under the equal treatment obligation.[761] However, he argues in favour of a two-fold consideration under the first and second prong of non-discrimination clauses. Yet, there is no reason why considerations relating to the trade effect of a measure

756 Choi, p. 35.
757 Ibid., p. 40.
758 *US–Automobiles*, report of the panel, para. 5.14.
759 Horn/Mavroidis, p. 61.
760 *US–Automobiles*, report of the panel, para. 5.14.
761 Choi, p. 44.

should be included in the determination of 'like products'. By contrast, this would overload the test under 'like products' and would risk being rather confusing for the trade community. The more competitive products are from the consumers' point of view, the more likely it is that they are 'like products' in the meaning of GATT Art. III. However, the more substitutable they are from the producers' point of view, the more likely it would be under the supply substitutability test that they are not 'like products'. In addition, it is more appropriate to first examine the market share of the respective products in question under the equal treatment obligation and then analyse the resulting trade effect, taking into account the capacity of producers to deal with that effect. If a measure proves to have no protective effect at all, or does not have the potential to have a trade-distorting effect, it does not matter whether producers have the ability to switch to another product. Whether and what detrimental trade effect is needed for a measure to violate GATT Art. III represents another problem that has to be solved. It is therefore preferable to examine these issues together under the second prong of the non-discrimination clauses, i.e. under the equality of treatment obligation of GATT Art. III.

5.3.3.3 *Conclusion*

It follows that market-based criteria are appropriate to define 'like' or 'directly competitive or substitutable products'. The main question is whether consumers regard two groups of products as directly competitive or substitutable, i.e. whether demand substitutability exists. To establish demand substitutability, one has to examine the physical similarity of the products, their common end-uses and their end-uses as shown by elasticity of substitution. To determine elasticity of substitution, marketing strategies of companies, direct consumers' views, and cross-price elasticity of demand have to be examined. However, in contrast to antitrust law, the market definition under WTO law includes all products – if made available in a member state at the world price – that may cause a price decrease of domestic products. Since consumers' views might be influenced by the protective measure in question and GATT Art. III aims at maintaining equal conditions of competition, considerations of potential and future demand have to be included. This may be done by looking at evidence from other markets. In addition, the nature of the competition has to be examined, comparing competition in the domestic market with competition in other markets. Finally, differences in absolute prices, time-series analysis of the market share of the product, as well as tariff classifications and channels of distributions might be useful criteria. Supply substitutability will be analysed under the obligation of equal treatment.

When applied to products made with and made without child labour, these criteria have the following result: Since both product groups have the same physical properties, they are physically similar and have the same common end-use. However, an increasing amount of companies' marketing strategies and studies offering direct consumers' views exist that indicate that products made without child labour could make up a different market segment. Whilst to date no study relating to cross-price elasticity exists that states that products made with child labour are in-elastic vis-à-vis products not made with child labour, existing studies do prove that the concept of cross-price elasticity may be used in relation to products made with child labour. To be in the same market, products have to possess a cross-price elasticity that is at least equal to or greater than that of the product that is considered to be 'like'. Recent studies have indicated that ethical features, in particular child labour, matter to consumers, but that currently products made and not made with child labour would still be in the same market under antitrust law and potentially under WTO law. However, consumers have become aware of ethical features, so in the future products made with and without child labour might no longer be in the same market. To confirm the results of the studies conducted on cross-price elasticity, one should use a choice experiment that asks different groups of consumers and uses a variety of products made up of various functional and ethical factors. Moreover, to remedy shortcomings inherent to the criteria mentioned, recourse has to be taken to potential and future demand, price differences, time-series analysis, tariff classifications and channels of distribution. Based on these criteria, it is possible that products made with and without child labour might be considered as not being 'like' or 'directly competitive or substitutable products'.

5.3.4 Conclusion

In conclusion, the term 'like products' under GATT Art. III has to be read in the following way: npr-ppm-measures are not *prima facie* GATT Art. III-inconsistent. Whether products can be differentiated according to the way they are produced depends on the interpretation of the term 'likeness'. 'Likeness' does not mean 'not differing with respect to a non-protectionist regulatory purpose'. Neither should one take recourse to the 'aim and effects' of a measure. Instead, 'like' has to be determined on market-based criteria establishing demand substitutability of the two product groups in question. In future cases, products made with child labour might be found to be a different product group than products made without child labour.

What follows for the proposed EU Forced Labour Regulation and the US ban on goods made with forced or indentured child labour is that depending on whether in the EU or US market, products made with child labour are in the same market segment as products made without child labour, the respective measure would distinguish between like products, and thereby either violate the obligation of similarity or not. As to the Belgian Social Label Law, the same analysis would have to be made of the Belgian market.

According to the studies cited above, at present all three measures are likely to violate the obligation of similarity.

5.4 *Equality of Treatment*

Having concluded that current studies do not define different markets for products made with child labour and products made without child labour, the question arises whether measures distinguishing between those groups of products violate the obligation of equal treatment contained in GATT Art. III. As mentioned above, the obligation of equal treatment is expressed in the formulations 'in excess of', 'not similarly taxed' and 'so as to afford protection' regarding fiscal measures under GATT Art. III:2, and 'less favourable treatment' regarding non-fiscal measures under GATT Art. III:4. As mentioned above, measures regarding child labour are origin-neutral. They only violate GATT Art. III if they *de facto* discriminate against foreign goods. Thus, the question is whether the obligation of equal treatment requires a measurable discriminatory impact. Another question is whether *de minimis* exceptions exist for negligible differences in treatment.

Different legal views exist on the content of this obligation. They reach from requiring a discriminatory purpose and/or effect of the measure to a type of necessity test. The following section will explore the content of the obligation and examine whether trade measures concerning child labour such as the US ban on goods made with forced or indentured child labour violate the obligation of equal treatment.

5.4.1 The Legal Rulings

The following section will analyse the relevant legal rulings to the extent they discuss the purpose and/or trade effects of a measure under the equal treatment obligation.

5.4.1.1 *The Relevance of the Purpose of Measures*

5.4.1.1.1 Japan–Alcoholic Beverages

In *Japan–Alcoholic Beverages* the panel held that for a measure to be 'so as to afford protection' in accordance with GATT Art. III:2, second sentence, the purpose or aim of the measure did not need to be established.[762] Rather, it was sufficient that the dissimilarity in taxation was not *de minimis.*[763] The Appellate Body argued that it was not necessary to look at the many reasons legislators and regulators had for their actions.[764] However, it did not totally dismiss the regulatory purpose, making the rather mysterious statement:[765]

> although it is true that the aim of a measure may not be easily ascertained, nevertheless its protective application can most often be discerned from the design, the architecture, and the revealing structure of measure.[766]

As Hudec rightly noted, this statement would make much more sense if the word 'application' were replaced by the word 'purpose'.[767] This is because only the purpose or aim of a measure can be discerned from the design of a measure, whereas the application of a measure will be discerned from individual cases where the measure is applied, as the term suggests. Equally in terms of grammar, it makes more sense to read the second part of the sentence as containing the word 'purpose'. For having read 'although ... the aim', the reader expects another, somehow contradictory statement on the aim of the relevant measure. Thus, it could be appropriate to rely on the aim of a measure as manifested in its structure.

The Appellate Body confirmed that a protective application only had to be established under GATT Art. III:2, second sentence.[768] Since the first sentence did not specifically refer to paragraph 1, i.e. to the words 'so as to afford protection', the presence of a protective application did not need to be established separately.[769] Instead, there was *ipso facto* protective application if foreign goods were taxed in excess of the 'like' domestic goods.

5.4.1.1.2 Canada–Periodicals

Another case ruling on the words 'so as to afford protection' was *Canada–Periodicals.*[770] The Appellate Body started its analysis by reiterating the

---

762 Ibid., para 6.33.
763 Ibid.
764 *Japan–Alcoholic Beverages*, report of the Appellate Body, p. 27.
765 Horn/Mavroidis, p. 58 do not understand either what exactly the Appellate Body had in mind.
766 *Japan–Alcoholic Beverages*, report of the Appellate Body, p. 29.
767 Hudec (Requiem for an Aim and Effects Test), p. 631.
768 *Japan–Alcoholic Beverages*, report of the Appellate Body, pp. 18–19.
769 Ibid.
770 *Canada–Periodicals*, report of the Appellate Body.

statement of the Appellate Body in *Japan–Alcoholic Beverages* concerning the aim of a measure.[771] However, when establishing the protective application, the Appellate Body heavily relied on statements from government officials referring to the policy objective of the internal measure under scrutiny.[772] Having found on the basis of these statements that the policy objective was to protect the Canadian periodical industry, it concluded that the measure was 'clearly to afford protection'.[773] This case supports the argument that the regulatory aim of a measure is important under the obligation of equal treatment. In contrast to the case of *Japan–Alcoholic Beverages*, it does not refer to the structure of the law, but to statements of legislators.

5.4.1.1.3 EC–Bananas III

As mentioned above, the *EC–Bananas III* case firmly rejects any sort of 'aim and effect' test under GATT Art. III and GATS Art. II or XVII.[774] The Appellate Body held that since GATT Art. III:4 did not refer to GATT Art. III:1, there was no examination of whether the measure was 'so as to afford protection'.[775]

5.4.1.1.4 Chile–Alcoholic Beverages

By contrast, the case *Chile–Alcoholic Beverages* took recourse to the regulatory aim of a measure when interpreting 'so as to afford protection'.[776] It explicitly stated that the statutory purposes or objectives of a member's legislature and government as a whole are pertinent to the extent that they are given objective expression in the statute itself.[777] The Appellate Body proceeded to analyse the structure and application of the tax law and concluded that 75 per cent of domestic production was located in the fiscal category with the lowest rate, whereas approximately 95 per cent of the directly competitive or substitutable imports were found in the fiscal category with the highest tax rate.[778] It also analysed the non-progressive nature of the structure of the law.[779] It then compared the aims of the tax law put forward by Chile with the structure of the law and found that there was no relationship between the aim and the architecture

771 Ibid., p. 32.
772 Ibid., p. 33.
773 Ibid., p. 34.
774 *EC–Bananas III*, report of the Appellate Body, para. 241.
775 Ibid., para. 216.
776 *Chile–Alcoholic Beverages*, report of the Appellate Body, para. 62.
777 Ibid.
778 Ibid., para. 67.
779 Ibid., para. 65.

of the tax law.[780] This was regarded as proof of the fact that the structure of the tax law was discriminatory.[781] In response to the Chilean argument that it was wrong to refer to the aim of the measure, the Appellate Body stressed that the measure's purposes as manifested in the design of the measure were extremely pertinent.[782] It pointed out however that the tax measure did not have to be necessary to achieve the stated policy goal.[783]

Such reasoning is in line with the comment by Hudec on the Appellate Body's statement in *Japan–Alcoholic Beverages*,[784] namely that it is not the protective application, but the protectionist purpose that should be revealed by analysing the structure and design of a measure. The Appellate Body rightly did not rely on the statement of legislators – as was the case in *Canada–Periodicals* – but the structure of the measure in question.

5.4.1.1.5 EC–Asbestos

There is no consensus among legal authors whether the case *EC–Asbestos*[785] confirms or rejects an 'aim and effect' test.[786] The controversial *obiter dictum* reads as follows:

> We recognize that, by interpreting the term "like products" in Article III:4 in this way, we give the provision a relatively broad product scope – although no broader than the product scope of Article III:2. In so doing, we observe that there is a second element that must be established before a measure can be held to be inconsistent with Article III:4. Thus, even if two products are "like", that does not mean that a measure can be held to be inconsistent with Article III:4. A complaining Member must still establish that the measure accords to the group of "like" *imported* products "less favourable treatment" than it accords to the group of "like" *domestic* products. The term "less favourable treatment" expresses the general principle, in Article III:1, that internal regulations "should not be applied … so as to afford protection to domestic production". If there is "less favourable treatment" of the group of "like" imported products,

780 Ibid., para. 69.
781 Ibid.
782 Ibid., para. 71.
783 Ibid., para. 72.
784 Hudec (Requiem for an Aim and Effects Test), p. 631.
785 *EC–Asbestos*, report of the Appellate Body.
786 While Howse/Türk argue in favour of an 'aim and effect' test, Quick/Lau argue contra an 'aim and effect' test.

> there is, conversely, "protection" of the group of "like" domestic products. However, a Member may draw distinctions between products which have been found to be "like", without, for this reason alone, according to the group of "like" *imported* products "less favourable treatment" than that accorded to the group of "like" *domestic* products. In this case, we do not examine further the interpretation of the term 'treatment no less favourable' in Article III:4, as the Panel's findings on this issue have not been appealed or, indeed, argued before us.[787]

Some authors argue that this *obiter dictum* simply means that 'like products' might be regulated differently but equivalently.[788] It is however not probable that the Appellate Body used an *obiter dictum* to restate what had already been established in the case of *US–Section 337*.[789] The panel in *US–Section 337* dealt with *de iure* discrimination and held that the 'less favourable treatment' had to refer to each case of the imported products, rejecting any notion of balancing more favourable treatment of some imported products against less favourable treatment of other imported products, thereby calling for an effective equality of opportunities.[790] Most importantly, it is rightly argued that because of the required comparison of the whole group of imported and domestic like products in contrast to a comparison of just *some* products, such a reading would constitute a departure from *US–Section 337*.[791] Put differently, the *obiter dictum* cannot be understood as meaning that in case of facially discriminatory treatment the whole group of imported and like domestic products should be compared. Consequently, it is argued, the *obiter dictum* refers to something else.

Howse and Türk argue that the Appellate Body reintroduced an 'aim and effect' test.[792] Ehring opines that paragraph 100 provides evidence of an 'asymmetric impact' test.[793]

5.4.1.1.6 Dominican Republic–Cigarettes

In *Dominican Republic–Cigarettes*, the Appellate Body stated that a detrimental effect explained by factors unrelated to the foreign origin of the product, such as the market share of the importer, does not necessarily constitute 'less

787 *EC–Asbestos*, report of the Appellate Body, para. 100.
788 Quick/Lau, p. 434.
789 *US–Section 337*, report of the panel, para. 5.11.
790 *US–Section 337*, report of the panel, para. 5.14.
791 Ibid., para. 5.14; This argument has been made by Howse/Türk, p. 297.
792 Howse/Türk, p. 299.
793 Ehring, p. 946.

favourable treatment'.[794] In this specific case, the detrimental effect was a difference in per-unit costs of the bond requirement for cigarettes. The per-unit costs of the bond requirement were higher for imported than for domestic products. The difference between the per-unit costs of the bond requirement for Dominican and Honduran cigarettes could however be explained by the fact that the importer of Honduran cigarettes had a smaller market share than domestic producers (the per-unit cost of the bond requirement being the result of dividing the cost of the bond by the number of cigarettes sold in the Dominican market).[795]

This case could be taken as an indication that an inquiry into the reason of the detrimental effect was necessary in order to find out whether the adverse effect was based on the origin of products or not. Put differently, this could be taken as a cautious hint that the regulatory purpose of the measure could help to reveal protection of domestic products.

5.4.1.1.7 Mexico–Soft Drinks and Other Beverages

The panel in *Mexico–Soft Drinks and Other Beverages* held that under the term 'so as to afford protection' in GATT Art. III:2, second sentence, the declared intention of legislators and regulators of the member adopting the measure should not be totally disregarded, particularly when the explicit objective of the measure was that of affording protection to domestic production.[796] Accordingly, it referred to Mexican legislative sources and found that the tax in question was applied so as to afford protection to the domestic sugar industry.[797]

5.4.1.1.8 EC–Biotech Products

The case *EC–Biotech Products* concerned EC measures regarding the approval of biotech products and safeguard measures of Member States prohibiting the import and marketing of specific biotech products.[798] Argentina maintained that the failure to consider product applications constituted 'less favourable treatment' to the biotech products concerned than to like non-biotech products.[799] Taking up the approach of the Appellate Body in *Dominican Republic–Cigarettes,* the panel held that given that Argentina had not argued

794 *Dominican Republic–Cigarettes*, report of the Appellate Body, para. 96.

795 Ibid.

796 *Mexico–Soft Drinks and Other Beverages,* report of the panel, paras. 8.91–8.94.

797 Ibid., para. 8.95.

798 *EC–Approval and Marketing of Biotech Products*, report of the panel.

799 Ibid., para. 7.2512.

that the treatment of products differed depending on their origin, it was 'not self-evident that the alleged less favourable treatment of imported biotech products is explained by the foreign origin of these products rather than, for instance, a perceived difference between biotech products and non-biotech products in terms of their safety, etc.'.[800] Thus, the panel relied on missing evidence for a discriminatory purpose of the measure when deciding that there was no 'less favourable treatment'.

5.4.1.1.9 Thailand–Cigarettes (Philippines)

In the case *Thailand–Cigarettes* (Philippines), the Appellate Body had to decide whether by subjecting only imported cigarettes to certain administrative requirements related to VAT liabilities including sanctions, Thailand treated imported cigarettes less favourably than domestic cigarettes.[801] It concluded that such an examination had to include 'consideration of the design, structure, and expected operation of the measure at issue'.[802] It stressed that 'in any event, there must be in every case a genuine relationship between the measure at issue and its adverse impact on competitive opportunities for imported versus like domestic products to support a finding that imported products are treated less favourably'.[803]

One legal author opines that it is possible to interpret the statement on the genuine relationship between the measure and its adverse impact as meaning that if the measure genuinely serves a non-discriminatory policy objective, it does not accord less favourable treatment.[804] Indeed, the Appellate Body does not only utilize the word 'genuine' but also looks at the design and structure of the law, which is according to *Chile–Alcoholic Beverages* an expression of the measure's purpose.[805] Thus, this case could be taken as referring cautiously to the aim of a measure.

5.4.1.1.10 Philippines–Distilled Spirits

Following the decision of *Japan–Alcoholic Beverages*, the Appellate Body in the case *Philippines–Distilled Spirits* clearly rejected any consideration of aim or effect holding that that the question under the term 'so as to afford protection' is none of intent but rather of the protective application of the measure,

800 Ibid., para. 7.2514.
801 *Thailand–Cigarettes* (Philippines), report of the Appellate Body.
802 Ibid., para. 134.
803 Ibid.
804 Zhou, p. 1091.
805 See above, p. 149 and *Chile–Alcoholic Beverages*, report of the Appellate Body, para. 71.

which can be revealed from its design, architecture and structure.[806] It also recalled that the dissimilar taxation had to be more than *de minimis* and might be evidence of the protective application.[807] Referring to the panel's findings that all domestic spirits enjoy the flat tax rate whereas imported spirits are subject to a tax between 10 to 40 times higher, it upheld the panel's findings that the tax at issue was 'so as to afford protection'.[808] Interestingly, in the latter statement, it used the words 'protective nature' rather than 'protective application', which in principle includes aim and effect of a measure. This is another indication that it makes much more sense to argue with Hudec that it is rather the purpose and effect of the measure that is revealed by the design in contrast to its application, which would normally be shown through practice.

5.4.1.1.11 US–Clove Cigarettes

Analysing the term 'less favourable treatment' in Art. 2.1 TBT Agreement, the Appellate Body in the case *US–Clove Cigarettes* also extensively dealt with the equal treatment obligation of GATT Art. III:4.[809] Specifically, it stated that the 'non-discrimination obligation of Art. 2.1 of the TBT Agreement is expressed in the same terms as that of Article III:4 of the GATT 1994'.[810] It referred to the jurisprudence on GATT Art. III:4 including *Korea–Various Measures on Beef* and *EC–Asbestos* with its important paragraph 100 stating that 'less favourable treatment' occurs when regulatory distinctions modify the conditions of competition in the marketplace to the detriment of the group of imported products vis-à-vis the group of domestic like products.[811] Most importantly, it stated in footnote 372:

> We disagree with the United States to the extent that it suggests that *Dominican Republic – Import and Sale of Cigarettes* stands for the proposition that, under Article III:4, panels should inquire further whether "the detrimental effect is unrelated to the foreign origin of the product". [...] Although the statement referred to by the United States, when read in isolation, could be viewed as suggesting that further inquiry into the rationale for the detrimental impact is necessary, in that dispute the Appellate Body rejected Honduras' claim under Article III: 4 because:

806 *Philippines–Distilled Spirits*, report of the Appellate Body, paras. 250.
807 Ibid.
808 Ibid., para. 257.
809 US–Clove Cigarettes, report of the Appellate Body, paras. 161–236.
810 Ibid., para. 176.
811 Ibid., paras. 177–179.

> the difference between the per-unit costs of the bond requirement alleged by Honduras is explained by the fact that the importer of Honduran cigarettes has a smaller market share than two domestic producers.
>
> In *Thailand–Cigarettes (Philippines)*, the Appellate Body further clarified that for a finding of less favourable treatment under Art. III:4 "there must be in every case a genuine relationship between the measure at issue and its adverse impact on competitive opportunities for imported versus like domestic products to support a finding that imported products are treated less favourably". [...] The Appellate Body eschewed an additional inquiry as to whether such detrimental impact was related to the foreign origin of the products or explained by other factors or circumstances.

Thus, this case seems to be a clear rejection of a consideration of the regulatory purpose of the measure under the equal treatment obligation, calling merely for a comparison of the treatment of the group of imported and domestic products and denying an additional inquiry into the reason for the detrimental effect.[812] Clarifying that neither the finding made in *Thailand–Cigarettes (Philippines)* nor the one in *Dominican Republic–Cigarettes* should be read as leaving some room for the consideration of regulatory purposes, the Appellate Body apparently intends to reject any form of 'aim and effect' test. However, Howse argues that footnote 372 should not be taken as evidence that no further inquiry into the detrimental impact should be made.[813] He holds that footnote 372 merely states that in *Dominican Republic–Cigarettes*, no further inquiry was necessary because the detrimental impact was due to market considerations. This issue will be revisited when assessing the jurisprudence and legal literature.

In contrast to its analysis of GATT Art. III:4, the Appellate Body explicitly called for an 'aim and effect' test with regard to Art. 2.1 of the TBT Agreement, given the context and the object and the purpose of the TBT Agreement.[814] As will be discussed in detail under the TBT Agreement, it held that Art. 2.1 did not prohibit 'detrimental impact on imports that stems exclusively from a legitimate regulatory distinction'.[815] In case of *de facto* discrimination, the existence of a detrimental impact on the group of imported products was not

812 Cf. Pauwelyn (Questions on Impact of Cloves on GATT National Treatment).

813 Howse in Pauwelyn (Questions on Impact of Cloves on GATT National Treatment).

814 *US–Clove Cigarettes*, report of the Appellate Body, para. 181; see also Roessler (The Scope of Regulatory Autonomy), p. 4.

815 *US–Clove Cigarettes*, report of the Appellate Body, para. 181.

sufficient, instead, a panel had to further examine whether the detrimental impact stemmed from a legitimate regulatory distinction rather than reflecting discrimination. In particular, a panel had to examine the design, architecture, revealing structure, operation and application of the measure and specifically whether the measure was even-handed in order to determine whether it was discriminatory.[816]

Some legal authors argue that given the extensive reliance by the Appellate Body on the interpretation of GATT Art. III:4 and the reference to the common purpose of the TBT Agreement and GATT Art. III:4 to strike a balance between, on the one hand, the objective of trade liberalization and, on the other hand, members' right to regulate,[817] the consideration of regulatory purposes under GATT Art. III:4 should be possible.[818] This point will be taken up below.

5.4.1.1.12 US–Tuna II (Mexico)

The case *US–Tuna II* (Mexico) closely follows the approach of *US–Clove Cigarettes* and refers to GATT Art. III:4 as relevant context for interpreting Art. 2.1 of the TBT Agreement.[819] Thus, when examining 'less favourable treatment' under the latter provision, a panel should analyse whether the measure at issue modifies the conditions of competition in the relevant market to the detriment of the group of imported products vis-à-vis the group of like domestic products.[820] However, the Appellate Body goes on stating that under Art. 2.1 of the TBT Agreement, the analysis must continue as to whether the potential adverse effect stems from a legitimate regulatory distinction. He is silent on the question whether such as an analysis is appropriate under GATT Art. III:4. Thus, this case seems to be another rejection of an 'aim and effect' test.

5.4.1.1.13 EC–Seal Products

In *EC–Seal Products*, the Appellate Body extensively dealt with the argument put forward by the EU that the interpretation of 'less favourable treatment' of GATT Art. III:4 should follow the interpretation of the national treatment standard in Art. 2.1 of the TBT Agreement and included an inquiry into whether the detrimental impact on competitive opportunities for like products stems exclusively from a legitimate regulatory distinction.[821] Firstly, it

816 Ibid.
817 Ibid., paras. 96 and 174.
818 Zhou, pp. 1111–1115; Howse and Pauwelyn in Pauwelyn (Questions on Impact of Cloves on GATT National Treatment).
819 *US–Tuna II* (Mexico), report of the Appellate Body, para. 214.
820 Ibid., para. 215.
821 *EC–Seals*, report of the Appellate Body, paras. 5.100–5.130.

reiterated its findings made in *US–Clove Cigarettes*, *US–Tuna II* (*Mexico*) and *Thailand–Cigarettes* (*Philippines*) and held that under GATT Art. III:4, for a measure to be found to modify the conditions of competition in the relevant market to the detriment of imported products, there must be a 'genuine' relationship between the measure at issue and the adverse impact on competitive opportunities for imported products.[822] It emphasized that the analysis into whether the detrimental effect had a genuine relationship to, or was attributable to the specific measure at issue, did not involve an assessment of whether such detrimental impact stemmed exclusively from a legitimate regulatory distinction.[823] Secondly, referring to its findings in *Thailand–Cigarettes* (*Philippines*), it rejected the EU's argument that para. 100 of *EC–Asbestos* left some room for an additional inquiry beyond the search for a detrimental impact on competitive opportunities.[824] Thirdly, relying on *Japan–Alcoholic Beverages* and *EC–Asbestos*, it held that contrary to the view of the EU, the general principle in GATT Art. III:I 'so as to afford protection' was inherent in the 'less favourable treatment standard' GATT Art. III:4 and did not mean that a panel should examine the regulatory purpose of the measure.[825] Finally, it dealt with the argument that by applying different legal standards under Art. 2.1 of the TBT Agreement and GATT Art. III:4 could leave to asymmetrical outcomes under the respective agreements, especially given that the list of possible legitimate objectives that could rescue the measure was open under Art. 2.1 of the TBT Agreement in contrast to the exclusive list GATT. Art. XX.[826] The Appellate argued that both provisions provided relevant context for each other and recalled its finding from *US–Clove Cigarettes* that the balance between the desire to avoid unnecessary obstacles to international trade and the Members' right to regulate stated in the preamble of the TBT Agreement was not, in principle, different from the balance between the non-discrimination and the general exceptions clause of the GATT.[827] It noted that the covered agreements had to be interpreted in a coherent manner, but not in an identical way.[828] In its view, the contextual interpretation of Art. 2.1 of the TBT Agreement is due to the fact that the TBT Agreement does not contain an exception clause.[829] By

822 Ibid., para. 5.101.
823 Ibid., para. 5.105.
824 Ibid., para. 5.106–5.110. For para. 100 of *EC–Asbestos*, see above, p. 150 et seq.
825 Ibid., para. 5.111–5.117.
826 Ibid., para. 5.118.
827 Ibid., para. 5.123.
828 Ibid.
829 Ibid., 5.124.

contrast, GATT Art. XX constitutes such a clause. According to the Appellate Body, the structure of the latter provision weighs heavily against the consideration of the regulatory purpose under GATT Art. III:4.[830] Most importantly, it held that in this case, no imbalance between the provisions could arise because the measure was not a technical regulation, and that the EU had not mentioned any concrete example where asymmetrical outcomes could arise. It stressed its role as the judiciary to interpret the WTO agreements in the light of their object and purpose in contrast to the legislative role of Members who have the authority to address any imbalance between the WTO agreements.[831]

Thus, this case seems to firmly reject any consideration of purpose under GATT Art. III:4. However, Howse argues that given the logical implication of making 'a large universe of laws and regulations' *prima facie* illegal under WTO law, the decision still leaves some policy space for 'innocent regulation to pass muster under Articles I:1 and III:4'.[832]

5.4.1.1.14 Argentina–Financial Services

The Appellate Body in *Argentina–Financial Services* held that under the 'treatment no less favourable' standard in Art. XVII:1 of GATS, regulatory aspects should be taken into account to the extent they have a bearing on the 'analysis of whether *the measure at issue* modifies the conditions of competition'.[833] However, if regulatory aspects are considered in order to justify a measure, they should be addressed under the relevant exception clauses.[834]

5.4.1.2 *The Relevance of Trade Effects of Measures*

As stated above, the main question regarding trade effects is whether adverse trade affects are needed to violate GATT Art. III, and how they can be measured. For example, it could be that only *some* imported products have to be treated worse than like domestic products or *most* imported products. A different question is whether the adjudicating bodies have to rely on existing commercial data or whether they can rely on potential trade effects. Whilst the majority of cases explicitly state that GATT Art. III protects equal conditions of competition and not actual trade flows, they all rely on commercial data. Thus, it will now be analysed how they made use of this data.

830 Ibid., 5.125.

831 Ibid. See Roessler (The Scope of Regulatory Autonomy), p. 6 for a thorough critique of that statement.

832 Howse (Sealing the Deal: The WTO's Appellate Body Report in EC–Seal Products), p. 1.

833 *Argentina–Financial Services*, report of the Appellate Body, para. 6.127.

834 Ibid., para. 6115.

5.4.1.2.1 US–Superfund

The first main case elaborating on the relevance of a measure's trade effects was *US–Superfund*.[835] This case concerned, *inter alia*, an excise tax on petroleum that was imposed at a higher rate on imported products than on the like domestic product, and therefore was inconsistent with GATT Art. III:2, first sentence.[836] The US made the argument that the tax differential was so small that its commercial effects were insignificant.[837] The panel concluded that to rely on trade effects would mean to interpret GATT Art. III as aiming at protecting expectations on export volumes.[838] This was however not the case. It explained this reasoning by stating that a high non-discriminatory tax could have more adverse trade effects on imports than a low discriminatory tax.[839] It then noted that the US could make the tax GATT-consistent by raising the tax on domestic products, by lowering the tax on imported products, or by fixing a new common tax rate for both imported and domestic products.[840] It concluded that because each of the measures would have a different trade impact, the trade impact of the discriminatory measure could not be determined.[841] Thus, the rationale of GATT Art. III was to protect expectations on the competitive relationship between imported and domestic products.[842]

Whilst it is questionable to simply rely on the difficulty of determining the precise adverse trade effects,[843] it is correct that the main objective of GATT Art. III is to protect expectations on competitive conditions. Merely relying on actual trade effects would hinder countries from challenging legislation that currently does not apply to their trade. This would also endanger the predictability needed to plan future trade. It is however questionable whether measures that do not have any potential trade effect should be regarded as contrary to GATT Art. III. Finally, the argument that the tax differential is too small to have a significant trade effect rather refers to a possible *de minimis* rule than to the question how many imported products are concerned. Since GATT Art. III:2, first sentence, is not a *de minimis* rule the panel was right to ignore the argument made by the US.

835 *US–Superfund*, report of the panel.
836 Ibid., para. 5.1.12.
837 Ibid., para. 3.1.2.
838 Ibid., para. 5.1.9.
839 Ibid.
840 Ibid.
841 *US–Superfund*, report of the panel, para. 5.1.9.
842 Ibid.
843 Neven, p. 426 argues that this reasoning is hard to understand because if trade effects are not relevant, one must wonder how to assess the competitive relationship at all.

5.4.1.2.2 Japan–Imported Wines and Alcoholic Beverages

In the case of *Japan–Imported Wines and Alcoholic Beverages*, when analyzing the obligation of equal treatment under the first sentence of paragraph 2 of GATT Art. III, the panel both relied on the fact that *most* imported products were subject to higher internal tax rates,[844] as well as on the fact that *some* imported products were subject to higher internal tax rates.[845] It is therefore not conclusive on the matter.

5.4.1.2.3 US–Malt Beverages

As stated above, the case *US–Malt Beverages* relied on trade effects using an 'aim and effect' test under the term 'like products'.[846] Stating that the regulatory geographical distinction between certain types of grapes afforded protection, the panel relied on the fact that *most* imported products were discriminated against.[847] Equally, when assessing the regulatory distinction between beer with low and high alcohol content, it pointed to the fact that the burden resulting from these regulations did not fall more heavily on imports.[848] When ruling on the tax differentiation between small beer producers and large beer producers, the panel implicitly relied on the fact that small producers are mainly domestic producers and large producers foreign.[849] Thus, in all three cases, the panel seems to have used a test that requires that *most* imported products are discriminated against.

5.4.1.2.4 US–Automobiles

The case *US–Automobiles* equally referred to trade effects under term 'like products'.[850] As stated above, it even specified the trade effects test stating that the adverse trade effects on imports had to be 'inherent' to the measure.[851] It was concluded that this 'inherence' test should be understood as asking whether in general, foreign products were capable of benefiting from the same treatment, and in fact benefited from the same treatment.[852] Accordingly, any measure whose effects related to a situation or conduct of a country would be regarded as discriminatory. Mere incidental trade effects were thereby

844 *Japan–Imported Wines and Alcoholic Beverages*, report of the panel, para. 5.9 lit. a).
845 Ibid., para. 5.9 lit. d).
846 *US–Malt Beverages*, report of the panel.
847 Ibid., para. 5.26.
848 Ibid., para. 5.73.
849 Ehring, p. 941.
850 *US–Automobiles*, report of the panel, para. 5.14.
851 Ibid.
852 See above p. 106 et seq.

excluded. Consequently, not only *most* imported products had to be discriminated against, but the discriminatory effect also had to be related to the situation of foreign products, i.e. foreign producers. This case thus introduced a rather high threshold for trade effects.[853]

5.4.1.2.5 US–Gasoline

The Appellate Body in *US–Gasoline* restated its finding from *US–Section 337*, which rejected any form of balancing less favourable treatment to some imported products to more favourable treatment to other imported product calling for an effective equality of opportunities, and applied this to GATT Art. III:2 and 4.[854]

5.4.1.2.6 Canada–Periodicals

In *Canada–Periodicals*, the Appellate Body stated that GATT Art. III:2, second sentence is also violated, when only some of the directly competitive or substitutable imported products are not similarly taxed.[855]

5.4.1.2.7 Japan–Alcoholic Beverages

In *Japan–Alcoholic Beverages*, when assessing whether the tax discriminated against foreign products, the panel simply stated that vodka was taxed in excess of shochu.[856] It did not refer to the fact that most vodka was imported and most shochu domestically produced. However, since most vodka was imported, it could be that the panel implicitly relied on that fact.[857] Equally, when analysing the dissimilar taxation under the second sentence of GATT Art. III:2, the Appellate Body confined itself to upholding the panel's conclusion that higher taxes on imported alcoholic products distorted the competitive relationship between imports and domestic products.[858] It then stressed that in contrast to the first sentence, the dissimilar taxation had to be more than *de minimis* and that the words 'so as to afford protection' had to be examined separately.[859] This case is therefore not conclusive on trade effects.

853 Ehring, p. 940.
854 *US–Gasoline*, report of the Appellate Body.
855 *Canada–Periodicals*, report of the Appellate Body, para. 474.
856 *Japan–Alcoholic Beverages*, report of the panel, para. 6.24.
857 WorldTradeLaw.net, Commentary on Appellate Body Report, *Japan–Alcoholic Beverages*, p. 11.
858 *Japan–Alcoholic Beverages*, report of the Appellate Body, p. 26–27.
859 Ibid., p. 31.

5.4.1.2.8 Korea–Alcoholic Beverages

In *Korea–Alcoholic Beverages*, the Appellate Body followed the approach of the panel.[860] It relied on the fact that the tax structure operated in a way that the higher taxes were almost exclusively imposed on imported products, while domestic products fell in the lower categories.[861] It made the enlightening remark that,

> [t]here was virtually no imported soju so the beneficiaries of this structure are almost exclusively domestic producers.[862]

This is a clear example of a discriminatory effect that the Appellate Body could not disregard.

5.4.1.2.9 Chile–Alcoholic Beverages

The Appellate Body based its argumentation in *Chile–Alcoholic Beverages* on the fact that 75 per cent of all domestic production at issue was in the category with the lowest tax rates, whereas about 95 per cent of the directly competitive or substitutable products were located in the category with the highest tax rate.[863] In response to the Chilean argument that domestic products comprised the major part in the higher tax bracket, the Appellate Body rightly argued that it was not appropriate to compare the relative proportion of domestic versus imported products within a particular fiscal category,[864] as this could be due to the protective measure itself, which constituted a trade barrier to imports. Apart from that, it is inappropriate to follow the dividing line of the tax law when comparing the groups of domestic and imported products because that would almost never result in an origin-neutral measure violating GATT Art. III.[865]

5.4.1.2.10 Korea–Various Measures on Beef

This case concerned a dual retail distribution system for the sale of beef under which imported beef was to be sold only at special locations such as specialised stores selling only imported beef or in separate sections of supermarkets.[866]

---

860 *Korea–Alcoholic Beverages*, report of the Appellate Body, para. 150.
861 Ibid.
862 Ibid.
863 *Chile–Alcoholic Beverages*, report of the Appellate Body, paras. 49–55.
864 Ibid., para. 52.
865 Ehring, p. 927.
866 *Korea–Various Measures on Beef*, report of the Appellate Body.

Dealing with a facially discriminatory measure, the Appellate Body found that 'a formal difference in treatment between domestic and imported products is neither necessary nor sufficient for a violation of Article III:4'.[867] Emphasizing that there needs to be a modification of the conditions of competition to the detriment of imported products, it noted that as an effect of the measure imported beef was sold in 5,000 shops in contrast to domestic beef, which was sold in 45,000 shops, and found 'less favourable treatment'.[868]

5.4.1.2.11 EC–Asbestos

As mentioned above, calling for a comparison of the group of domestic and imported products, it is argued that in *EC–Asbestos*, the Appellate Body introduced some sort of 'discriminatory effect' test, which will be dealt with below.[869]

5.4.1.2.12 Dominican Republic–Cigarettes

As stated above, in *Dominican Republic–Cigarettes*, the Appellate Body stated that a detrimental effect on a given imported product explained by factors unrelated to the foreign origin of the product, such as the market share of the importer, does not necessarily imply that the measure accords less favourable treatment.[870]

This statement could be understood as meaning that the Appellate Body called for a connection between the detrimental effect and the origin of the product. Hence, this case could be a confirmation of an 'inherence' or 'supply substitutability' test.[871] Both tests justify detrimental effects if such effects do not refer to the specific factual or legal situation of producers in foreign countries. Put differently, foreign producers are only discriminated against in case they are not capable to switching to other products.

5.4.1.2.13 Canada–Wheat Exports and Grain Imports

In *Canada–Wheat Exports and Grain Imports*, the panel had to rule on additional administrative requirements and limitations on imported grain.[872] As regards Canada's arguments that the requirements were not very onerous it

867 Ibid., para. 137.

868 Ibid., 143–145.

869 *EC–Asbestos*, report of the Appellate Body, para. 100; Ehring, p. 946.

870 *Dominican Republic–Cigarettes*, report of the Appellate Body, para. 96.

871 See above, p. 106et seq. and p. 144et seq; cf. also Zhou, p. 1088 discussing an 'impossibility test'; Bartels (Trade and Human Rights), p. 587.

872 *Canada–Wheat Exports and Grain Imports*, report of the panel.

found that there was nevertheless 'less favourable treatment' because GATT Art. III:4 was not a *de minimis* rule.[873]

5.4.1.2.14 Mexico–Soft Drinks and Other Beverages

Finally, in *Mexico–Soft Drinks and Other Beverages*, the panel stated in relation to GATT Art. III:2, first sentence, that Mexico produces cane sugar whereas the United States produces beet sugar. It concluded that the situation in which beet sugar is liable to higher taxes than those applied to cane sugar is *in effect* (emphasis original) one where imported products are subject to taxes in excess of those applied to the like domestic products.[874] In relation to GATT Art. III:4, it held that almost all imported products are accorded less favourable treatment as a result of the application of the challenged measures, since almost all imported products are comprised of non-cane sugar sweeteners, and the only sweetener exempted from the measures (cane sugar) is almost exclusively a domestic product.[875] It added however that it did not rule that such a finding was necessary.[876] Thus, while the panel seems to favour an approach where most imported products are treated worse, it is cautious to rule on it.

5.4.1.2.15 Thailand–Cigarettes (Philippines)

As stated above, the Appellate Body stressed that the analysis of the term 'less favourable treatment' included 'consideration of the design, structure, and expected operation of the measure at issue'.[877] Furthermore, it found that 'such scrutiny may well involve – but does not require – an assessment of the contested measure in the light of evidence regarding the actual effects of that measure in the market'.

This finding read together with the finding on the genuine relationship between the measure and its adverse impact confirms that while a violation of GATT Art. III does not require evidence of actual trade effects, there must be a structural relationship between the measure and its adverse trade effects, that is some evidence is needed to prove potential adverse effects of the measure at issue that are not just incidental. In a similar vein, another legal author argues that this finding may be taken as advancing a 'causation' test, i.e. some proof that the measures actually caused the disparate impact.[878]

873 Ibid., para. 6.190.
874 *Mexico–Soft Drinks and Other Beverages*, report of the panel, paras. 8.54–8.58.
875 Ibid., paras. 8.114–115.
876 Ibid.
877 Ibid., para. 134.
878 Zhou, p. 1091.

5.4.1.2.16 Philippines–Distilled Spirits

As mentioned above, in the case, the Appellate Body relied on the findings of panel regarding the fact that all imported spirits are subject to a much higher tax, i.e. on a visible discriminatory effect.[879]

5.4.1.2.17 US–Clove Cigarettes

Referring to GATT Art. III jurisprudence when interpreting GATT Art. III:4, the Appellate Body confirmed previous findings in prior disputes that the term 'less favourable treatment' required a comparison between the group of imported products to the group of domestic products.[880] It added that such a comparison could include 'like products' from other Members than the complainant.[881]

5.4.1.2.18 EC–Seal Products

Clarifying that the statement in *Dominican Republic–Cigarettes* with regard to the origin-neutral explanatory factors for the trade effect simply meant that the measure had to be attributable to an adverse effect, the Appellate Body in *EC–Seal Products* does not seem to call for an 'inherence' or 'supply substitutability test'.[882] The decision confirms previous findings that the term 'less favourable treatment' requires a comparison between the group of imported products to the group of domestic products.[883]

5.4.1.3 *Summary*

To sum up, according to recent WTO jurisprudence, *purposes of measures* should not be considered under GATT Art. III. While the case *Chile–Alcoholic Beverages* seemed to open some space for the consideration at least of the objective aim as expressed in the structure and design of a measure in relation to fiscal measures covered by GATT Art. III:2, second sentence, the decision of *Philippines–Distilled Spirits* seems to have closed the door by merely relying on economic considerations such as the difference in taxation. However, this might change again in future given that what is actually revealed by a dissimilar taxation disfavouring foreign products is the protective nature of a measure including aim and effect and not the protective application. With respect to GATT Art. III:4, the decision of *EC–Seal Products* seems to have refuted almost

879 *Philippines – Cigarettes*, report of the Appellate Body, para. 255.
880 *US–Clove Cigarettes*, para. 179.
881 Ibid., para. 194.
882 *EC–Seals*, report of the Appellate Body, para. 5.103.
883 Ibid., para. 5.117.

any argument in favour of a consideration of the policy purpose of the measure. The question as to whether this rather radical approach is useful will be discussed below.

Regarding *trade effects*, it seems to be clear that a violation of the obligation of equality of treatment does not depend on actual trade affects, and that a formal difference in treatment is neither necessary nor sufficient. In a similar vein, in case of facially discriminatory treatment, balancing of more favourable treatment to less favourable treatment to imported products vis-à-vis domestic products is prohibited. While in earlier cases, panels and the Appellate Body sometimes relied on the fact that *some* imported products were treated worse than like domestic products in contrast to more recent cases that *most* imported products were treated worse, it now seems to be well-established that especially GATT Art. III:4 calls for a comparison of the group of imported products vis-à-vis the group of domestic products, where most imported products have to be treated worse. Two cases provided some room for the introduction of an 'inherency' or 'supply substitutability test', which does not seem to be the approach of the Appellate Body in *EC–Seal Products*.

Finally, while neither GATT Art. III:2, first sentence nor GATT Art. III:4 constitute a *de minimis* rule, GATT Art. III:2, second sentence does.

5.4.2 Consideration of Purposes

As indicated above, Howse and Türk have argued that the Appellate Body in paragraph 100 of the Appellate Body Report *EC–Asbestos* reintroduced an 'aim and effect' test under the equal treatment obligation manifested in the words 'less favourable treatment'.[884] They justify their reasoning with the Appellate Body's suggestion of the interchangeability or equivalence of the notion of 'less favourable treatment' with the general notion in GATT Art. III:1 that measures should not be applied 'so as to afford protection to domestic production'.[885] They conclude that under the term 'less favourable treatment', the same test as under the term 'so as to afford protection' has to be applied. That is, generally the design and structure of a measure have to be examined in order to find out whether it is protective, whilst evidence of legislative intent may sometimes be highly relevant.[886] They differentiate between an objective purpose, i.e. the best understanding of what a measure is about considering its provisions, structure, and political and historical context; and evidence of the subjective

884 Howse/Türk, p. 299.
885 Ibid., p. 299, fn. 56.
886 Ibid.

purpose in the form of ministerial or legislative statements.[887] Stating that such an analysis of the second stage of GATT Art. III:4 would be a safeguard against the possibility that the non-protective regulatory purpose under the term 'like products' had not been taken into account, they suggest that regulations with a non-protectionist aim should not be qualified as according 'less favourable treatment' to foreign products.[888]

With respect to the new developments in recent case law such as *EC–Seal Products*, Howse has stated that the non-consideration of regulatory purposes would lead to extreme outcomes and would be hard to reconcile with the intent and text of GATT.[889]

In a similar vein, other legal authors proposed that 'so as to afford protection' should be interpreted as referring to the protection of expectations concerning the intent behind domestic regulations.[890] This protective intent should be revealed by the structure and design of a measure.[891] Equally, DiMascio and Pauwelyn have argued that in two cases, the Appellate Body seems to have re-introduced the 'aim and effect' test under the 'so as to afford protection' requirement.[892] They applaud that the Appellate Body in cases such as *Chile–Taxes on Alcoholic Beverages* or *Dominican Republic–Cigarettes* examined the policy basis of the measures at issue and argue for a future consideration of the relation between the policy basis of the measure and the measure itself.[893] In particular, they submit that the measure should be, depending on the importance of the policy goal, 'related to', 'substantially related to' or, in some cases, 'necessary to achieve' the policy objective.

5.4.3 The 'Asymmetric Impact' Test

Whilst disagreeing on the relevance of the legislative purpose of a measure, Ehring interprets paragraph 100 of the *EC–Asbestos* Appellate Body report in a similar way regarding trade effects.[894] He also refers to the group comparison between foreign and domestic products together with the statement of the Appellate Body that measures distinguishing between foreign and domestic like products do not necessarily accord 'less favourable treatment' to the

887 Howse/Regan, p. 265.
888 Howse/Türk, p. 298.
889 Howse (Sealing the Deal: The WTO's Appellate Body Report in *EC–Seal Products*), p. 1.
890 Horn/Mavroidis, pp. 39 and 58.
891 Horn/Mavroidis, p. 58.
892 DiMascio/Pauwelyn (Non-Discrimination in Trade and Investment-Treaties), p. 65.
893 Ibid., p. 83–84.
894 Ehring, p. 944; Fauchald, p. 468.

former group. In his view, these statements make perfect sense if they are read as meaning that it does not suffice that only some imported products receive worse treatment.[895] This reading would be confirmed by the statement that 'less favourable treatment' is equivalent to protection.[896] He stresses that the *obiter dictum* should not be read as meaning that a difference in treatment is not necessarily a disadvantage.[897] Firstly, such a reading would be too trivial for an *obiter dictum*. Secondly, this has already been stated in *Korea–Beef*.[898] Relying on EC–*Asbestos* as well as on some of the other cases cited above, Ehring argues for an 'asymmetric impact' test in contrast to a 'diagonal' test to be applied under the equal treatment obligation in relation to origin-neutral measures.[899] Under the 'diagonal' test, some imported products have to be treated 'less favourable' than like domestic products, whereas under the 'asymmetric impact' test, most imported products have to be treated worse than like domestic products.[900] Hence, there must be an asymmetric distribution of imports and domestic goods.[901]

Ehring defends his asymmetric impact approach with a vast array of well-reasoned arguments and finds some support in WTO legal literature.[902] Arguments refer to EC law and practice, which generally favour the 'asymmetric impact' approach.[903] Most importantly, in his view, the approach is reflected in the language of GATT Art. III:2 and 4, which uses the terms 'products' and 'domestic production' instead of 'a product' or 'some domestic production', indicating that more than some foreign products need to be discriminated against.[904] Moreover, the term 'national treatment' already

895 Ehring, p. 944.
896 Ibid.
897 Ibid., p. 945.
898 *Korea–Beef*, report of the Appellate Body, paras. 135–137.
899 Ehring extends his considerations to GATT Art. I:1.
900 Ehring, p. 924.
901 Ibid., p. 925.
902 Davey/Pauwelyn, p. 39 et seq.; Howse/Türk, p. 298; Hudec (Requiem for an Aims and Effects Test), pp. 639, 641; Hudec (Like Product), p. 118; Verhoosel, p. 89; Howse and Türk, p. 298 argue in a very similar way to Ehring, pointing to the *obiter dictum* of the Appellate Body in EC–*Asbestos* where it requires a comparison between the whole group of imported products and domestic like products when interpreting 'less favourable treatment'. They interpret this *obiter dictum* as a clear reference to a necessary discriminatory impact on foreign producers, noting that it was not enough that e.g. just one particular foreign producer faced a heavier burden; Fauchald, p. 467 et seqq. however takes a slightly different approach arguing for a case-by-case approach where it is also possible to rely on the 'diagonal approach'.
903 Ehring, p. 949.
904 Fauchald, pp. 468, 469.

suggests that in case members treat foreign products in exactly the same way as domestic products, only a disproportionate burden on imported products may violate the national treatment obligation.[905] It is argued that the diagonal approach amounts to a market access right, which is contrary to the purpose of GATT Art. III.[906] The 'asymmetric impact' approach does not contradict the object and purpose of GATT Art. III, i.e. to protect equal conditions of competition.[907] This is because the approach does not rely on actual trade effects but on existing commercial data only to explore the overall competitive relationship between (potential) imports and like domestic imports.[908]

Ehring also argues that the 'asymmetric impact' approach is in accordance with the rationale of WTO law, i.e. the theory of comparative advantage.[909] In contrast to the diagonal approach favouring only the competitive advantage of some imported products of a sub-sector, the asymmetric impact approach focuses on the advantage of the entire group of foreign products by WTO members.[910] Most importantly, in his view, the 'asymmetric impact' approach enhances the regulatory autonomy of WTO members in a world with increasing product differentiation and direct competitiveness between products.[911] Referring to the history of GATT, he states that Article 18 was not meant to prohibit measures assisting a particular domestic product if they were directed against the production of another domestic product and against imports.[912] In response to the argument that an 'asymmetric impact' approach is unclear as to the exact number of imports that have to be discriminated against, it is pointed out that the degree of competition between products and the level of differentiation, i.e. the vertical trade effects, could also be taken into account.[913] The greater the degree of competition, the smaller the level of differentiation and asymmetric impact has to be. As to the heavier burden of proof allocated to the complainant, it is suggested that it should be sufficient to present some commercial data to make a *prima facie* case.[914] Taking into account the protective effect of the measure itself, advocates of the 'asymmetric impact' approach

905 Ehring, pp. 959 and 960.
906 Ehring, p. 957; Howse/Regan, p. 257.
907 Ibid., p. 961.
908 Ibid.
909 Ibid.
910 Ibid., p. 962.
911 Ehring, p. 954.
912 Ibid., p. 963, citing Reports of Committees and Principal Sub-Committees, United Nations Conference on Trade and Development, ICITO 1/8, p. 61, para. 36 (1948).
913 Ehring, p. 966; Fauchald, p. 475.
914 Ehring, p. 967.

point to the possibility of referring to historical data or to evidence from other markets.[915] Finally, the problem is raised which imports to rely on, only those from the complainant or from all exporting countries?[916] One author has suggested taking both kinds of evidence into account.[917] This question seems to be decided by *US–Clove Cigarettes* favouring an inclusion of 'like products' also from other Members than the complainant.[918]

5.4.4 Supply Substitutability

It has been indicated above that it might be appropriate to conduct an 'inherence effects' or a 'supply substitutability' test under the equal treatment obligation.[919] While the *Dominican Republic–Cigarettes* case could be read so as to confirm the approach of *US–Automobiles*, the *EC–Seal Products* decision does not seem to follow this approach.

According to legal literature, the factors determining high or low supply substitutability could be direct views of producers; the cross-price elasticity of supply between the two products in question; and dynamic time-series analysis.[920] A cross-price elasticity analysis would evaluate the reactions of producers in response to changes in relative prices.[921] In contrast to demand substitutability, the switching rate could be assessed against an 'Industry Average Substitution Rate'.[922] This means that the rate would be evaluated based on the average costs of switching of one industry sector and the resulting ability of producers to change to another product.[923] How both tests relate to each other and whether and how they should be applied will be discussed in the evaluation below.

5.4.5 Necessity Test

Another author suggests conducting an integrated necessity test under the national treatment obligation.[924] In an attempt to create a more rule-oriented

915 Ehring, pp. 969 and 970; Fauchald, pp. 476 and 477 stresses that historical data can be used in a case where domestic producers choose to adjust to a measure while foreign firms do not.

916 Ehring, pp. 969 and 970.

917 Fauchald, pp. 474, 475.

918 Ibid., para. 194.

919 See the presentation of the 'supply substitutability' test above pp. 144et seqq.

920 Choi, p. 67.

921 Ibid.

922 Ibid., pp. 68 and 69.

923 Ibid., p. 69.

924 Verhoosel, pp. 51 et seqq.

test, he argues that no discrimination analysis in WTO law can be performed without carrying out a necessity test.[925] To merely rely on adverse effects caused by regulatory heterogeneity would mean to equate non-discrimination with deregulation, which is not the objective of the WTO Agreement.[926] He further argues that in the case *Chile–Alcoholic Beverages*, the Appellate Body and the panel *de facto* applied a necessity test.[927] Hence, instead of a likeness test, the legitimate regulatory objective should be examined and a 'least trade-restrictive means' test conducted.[928] In contrast to the regulatory purpose approach, the merit of a necessity test would be that it avoids the difficulty of revealing the protective intent and the need to determine a legitimate purpose as such.[929] The third judicial assessment should be the finding of adverse effects.[930] Quoting the Appellate Body Report *Chile–Alcoholic Beverages*, the author supports the thesis that most imported products need to be adversely affected.[931]

In response to the argument that GATT Art. XX would be rendered redundant if such a test were introduced under GATT Art. III, the author refers to the argument from above, i.e. that GATT Art. XX would retain its role regarding *de iure* discrimination.[932] In his view, the merit of a necessity test under GATT Art. III lies in the fact that GATT Art. III does not provide an exhaustive list of legitimate policy purposes.[933]

5.4.6 Evaluation

5.4.6.1 *The Relevance of Regulatory Purposes*

As stated above, the Appellate Body in several decisions seems to have closed the door for a consideration of regulatory purposes under GATT Art. III. This is to be deplored given that, as Howse rightly argues, in the future, a large number of measures with non-protective aims such as health, safety or public morals will risk being qualified as *prima facie* GATT-inconsistent. Consequently, regulatory autonomy could be severely constrained.

Most importantly, when looking at the text and structure of GATT Art. III, i.e. the words 'so as to afford protection' in GATT Art. III:1 and 2 with their

925 Ibid., pp. 51 et seqq, p. 76.
926 Ibid., pp. 76 and 78.
927 Ibid., pp. 30 and 93.
928 Ibid., p. 89.
929 Cf. Ibid., pp. 55, 93, 111.
930 Ibid., p. 89.
931 Ibid.
932 Ibid., p. 94.
933 Ibid., pp. 93 and 108.

purposive connotation, it only seems logical to take the regulatory aim into account, at least as objectively manifested in the structure of the measure, as did the Appellate Body in the *Chile–Alcoholic Beverages* case. To hold with Hudec, it makes much more sense to reveal the aim and effect of a measure rather than its protective application, which the Appellate Body maintained to have done in the *Japan–Alcoholic Beverages* and *Philippines–Distilled Spirits* decisions – since the application is usually shown through practice. Since the principle of GATT Art. III:1 informs the whole article, consideration of purposes should be possible not only under GATT Art. III:2, second sentence, but also under GATT Art. III:2, first sentence and GATT Art. III:4.[934]

As regards the interpretation of prior case law, it is difficult to understand why the statement by the Appellate Body in *Dominican Republic–Cigarettes* 'explained by factors or circumstances unrelated to the foreign origin', should not be understood as meaning that rationales of the measure that have no connection to the origin of products help the measure to qualify as not according 'less favourable treatment'. If the Appellate Body had merely meant that the adverse impact was not attributable to the measure, why would it have referred to factors unrelated to the origin of a measure instead of calling for a connection between the measure and its effect? In a similar vein, the requirement of 'a genuine relationship between the measure at issue and its adverse impact' postulated by the decision *Thailand–Cigarettes (Philippines)* makes more sense if read so as to refer to relationship between the aim as expressed in the structure of the measure and its adverse impact rather than simply saying that the measure should be attributable to the adverse impact. This is because firstly, as Zhou rightly argues, the word 'genuine' has a purposive connotation.[935] And secondly, if the design of the measure, i.e. its objective aim, is so as to systematically disadvantage foreign products and there is an adverse trade effect, the measure can be safely assumed to be protectionist. Most importantly, in the same decision, the Appellate Body calls for consideration of the design and structure of the measure at issue – i.e. exactly those elements that in *Chile–Alcoholic Beverages* it had qualified as an expression of the purpose of the measure.[936]

In *EC–Seal Products*, the Appellate Body remains rather vague when discussing the meaning of paragraph 100 of *EC–Asbestos*, merely referring to 'a point at which the differential treatment of imported and like domestic products

934 Cf. Roessler (Beyond the Ostensible).

935 Zhou, p. 1091.

936 Cf. *Chile–Alcoholic Beverages*, report of the Appellate Body, para. 71 and *Thailand–Cigarettes (Philippines)*, report of the Appellate Body, para. 134.

amounts to "treatment no less favourable".[937] It makes much more sense to argue with Howse and Türk that the Appellate Body in the *EC–Asbestos* decision through the words 'without, for this reason alone' alluded to an additional inquiry into the purpose, or, according to Ehring, to an 'asymmetric impact test'.

Concerning the argument put forward by the Appellate Body in *EC–Seal Products* relating to the structure of GATT Art. XX that weighs heavily against a consideration of policy purposes under GATT Art. III,[938] it is of course true that full account of the regulatory purpose including its balancing against a potential discriminatory impact should be taken under GATT Art. XX. As will be elaborated below, to conduct a sort of necessity or rule reason test under GATT Art. III would contravene the rules of interpretation since such a reading has no basis in the text.[939] However, there is no reason why the regulatory purpose as expressed in the design of a measure should not be taken into account as an additional factor beyond examining detrimental impacts on conditions of competition when revealing the protective nature of the measure. The *bona fide* aim should be considered when the trade impact of a measure is not measurable or otherwise unclear, complementing the analysis of the conditions of competition. Hence, it would not be enough that a measure has a *bona fide* aim to make it GATT Art. III-consistent. As the panel in *Chile–Alcoholic Beverages* rightly stated, good objectives should not be able to rescue an otherwise inconsistent measure.[940] Whilst this statement merely referred to the subjective aim as manifested in legislative statements, it should be extended to the objective aim of a measure. A measure such as the Belgian Social Label Law can have a good subjective purpose that is objectively reflected in its structure, but still amount to discrimination. In such a case, the aim should be balanced against the asymmetric impact of the measure taking into account all relevant factors. But this should be done under GATT Art. XX as will be elaborated below.

It is also noteworthy that, despite its rather economic reading of GATT Art. III, the Appellate Body in the *EC–Seal Products* decision makes a cautious suggestion that it might be appropriate to take account of legitimate policy objectives under the non-discrimination obligation of the GATT in order to avoid potential imbalances with Art. 2.1 of the TBT Agreement.[941] It defends its rather narrow reading of GATT Art. III by referring to its limited mandate and

---

937 *EC–Seal Products*, report of the Appellate Body, para. 5.109.
938 Ibid., *EC–Seal Products*, report of the Appellate Body, para. 5.112.
939 See below, p. 179 et seq.
940 *Chile–Alcoholic Beverages*, report of the panel, para. 7.159.
941 See *EC–Seal Products*, report of the Appellate Body, paras. 5.128–5.129.

to the fact that the EU had not presented any examples of such imbalances.[942] Whilst it is true that a more flexible reading of the exception clauses contained in GATT Art. XX may cover more measures protecting health, safety or human rights than commonly assumed, and few imbalances exist, it is also true that the text of GATT Art. III allows for a broader reading in favour of a consideration of the policy purpose.

Finally, it should be emphasized that, as argued by Howse and Türk and stated in *Chile–Alcoholic Beverages*, it is the 'objective' aim, i.e. the provisions, structure, design and historical and political context, what has to be considered. To complement the analysis, it should be allowed to rely on ministerial and legislative statements. As stated in *Chile–Alcoholic Beverages,* legislative statements should be rationally related to the provisions of the law.[943] The analysis should reveal whether the law is suited to attain its declared aim. It should be stressed that the analysis is different from a necessity or rule of reason test, which include a least restrictive means test.[944] If the analysis shows that the aim cannot be attained by the measure, there is a heavy burden on the defendant to demonstrate that the measure was not protectionist.

In the *Chile–Alcoholic Beverages,* Appellate Body examined trade flows and the non-progressive nature of the law, i.e. anomalies in the law.[945] The examination of trade flows should however be separate from the examination of the aim of a measure since they refer to the *trade effect* of a measure.

It follows from the evaluation that trade measures concerning child labour should firstly be analysed with a view to revealing their aim. The Belgian Social Label Law affixes a social label to products that are made *inter alia* in accordance with its conformity criteria implementing ILO Conventions No. 138 and No. 182 on child labour. It has a coherent structure addressing both domestic and foreign products. No anomaly seems to exist. In addition, its stated aim is to promote socially responsible production.[946] The declared aim rationally relates to the content of the law. Thus, based on the analysis of its subjective and objective purpose, the measure seems to be a *bona fide* regulation.

---

942 For a thorough critique of this statement, see Roessler (The Scope of Regulatory Autonomy), p. 6.

943 Ibid., para. 69.

944 What is required under GATT Art. III is to prove what in German is called the 'Geeignetheit' of the measure. This means that the measure hypothetically is able to implement the desired aim, see Pieroth/Schlink, p. 322. For example, speed limits hypothetically may reduce the death of forests.

945 *Chile–Alcoholic Beverages*, report of the Appellate Body, paras. 63–76.

946 See Humbert (The Challenge of Child Labour), pp. 323–329 and fn. 38.

The US ban on goods made with forced or indentured child labour – if regarded as the logical corollary of the national prohibition of domestic forced or indentured child labour – also has a coherent structure addressing both domestic and imported products. The purpose of the reduction of child labour can be understood from the structure of the law. Hence, the ban may also be qualified as a *bona fide* regulation.

The proposed EU Forced Labour Regulation seeks to prevent the placing and making available on the Union market of products made with forced labour, i.e. it includes also both domestic and imported products. Its enforcement regime involving competent authorities from Member States and customs authorities and giving companies the possibility to prove that they engage in preventing forced labour, thereby avoiding sanctions seems to be suited to reach its aim. It can also be regarded as a *bona fide* regulation.

5.4.6.2 *The Relevance of Trade Effects*

Examining the divergent approaches to trade effects in case law, the statement of the Appellate Body in paragraph 100 of *EC–Asbestos* seems to be crucial. As some authors rightly point out, it makes sense to interpret this passage so as to refer to a discriminatory effect in the sense of an 'asymmetric impact'. The measure at issue was an origin-neutral measure so the statement clearly concerned *de facto* discrimination. Hence, the question was whether only some products should be compared, or the whole group of imported and domestic products. The Appellate Body determined that a government might treat some imported products worse 'without, for this reason alone, according to the group of 'like' *imported* products less favourable treatment than that accorded to the group of 'like' *domestic* products'.[947] It is hardly conceivable that the Appellate Body intended to refer to the fact that a facially discriminatory measure did not necessarily discriminate against imported products.

As mentioned above, the Appellate Body in subsequent cases confirmed that in relation to GATT Art. III:4, rather than single products, the whole groups of domestic and imported products have to be compared.[948]

This is a welcome development since there are much better arguments in favour of an asymmetric impact than for a 'diagonal test'. Indeed, only where most imported products are treated worse, the comparative advantage of a WTO member is endangered. If a member was forced to repeal a ban on foreign products in cases where only some imported products were treated worse,

---

947 *EC–Asbestos*, para. 100.

948 See for example above p.164, *Mexico–Soft Drinks and other Beverages*, report of the Appellate Body.

GATT Art. III would function as a market access right. The main advantage of an 'asymmetric impact' approach is the enhancement of the regulatory autonomy of members.

The approach is in accordance with the aim of GATT Art. III to protect conditions of competition rather than actual trade flows. As has been stated above, the approach uses the *ratio* between imported and domestic products to predict the expectations of WTO members. Similar to the examination of the degree of competitiveness, evidence from other markets and potential trade flows have to be taken into account in order avoid that a protective measure crystallizes historical trade flows.

However, a potential shortcoming might be the difficulty of determining the precise asymmetric impact. What does 'most imported products' mean? It has been suggested balancing the level of differentiation between the groups of products and the degree of competitiveness with the number of foreign products that are disfavoured.[949] That is, the more competitive products are and the higher the level of differentiation is between the two groups of products, the less imported products have to be disfavoured. However, in case of regulatory measures other than taxes, the level of differentiation is difficult to determine. As the above analysis has shown, the degree of competitiveness between products is not a clear-cut concept either, and depends on a range of factors.

Hence, in a situation where the extent of the discriminatory impact is unclear, the regulatory purpose should come in. This could be the case where the distribution of disfavoured products between imports and domestic products is more or less the same. Moreover, where data are lacking and the precise impact is difficult to measure, the *bona fide* aim of a measure could determine whether the measure should be regarded as non-discriminatory. In a similar vein, Fauchald suggests that the regulatory purpose may play a role when the geographic distribution of discriminatory effects is unclear.[950]

The 'asymmetric impact' approach should also apply to GATT Art. III:2. There is no reason why the arguments raised in favour of such an approach should not be valid in the field of taxation. As regards the first sentence of GATT Art. III:2, it should be noted that the asymmetric impact requirement should not be equated with a *de minimis* rule. That is the fact that the first sentence is not a *de minimis* rule – like GATT Art. III:4 – does not contradict the application of an asymmetric impact test.

---

949 Ehring, p. 966.
950 Fauchald, p. 477.

5.4.6.3 *'Supply Substitutability' and 'Inherence' Test*

Notwithstanding the *EC–Seal Products* decision, it will now be considered whether it is recommendable to complement the 'asymmetric impact' approach with an 'inherence' test or 'supply substitutability' test, as did the judiciary in the *US–Automobiles* case and perhaps had in mind in the *Dominican Republic–Cigarettes* decision.[951]

As will be recalled, the 'inherence' test should be understood as asking whether in general, foreign products are capable of benefiting from the same treatment accorded to domestic products and in fact benefited from the same treatment. Thus, this test dismisses all measures as discriminatory that relate to a legal or factual situation in, or the conduct of foreign countries. By contrast, measures will not be dismissed if their detrimental impact is due to different market shares as was the case in *Dominican Republic–Cigarettes.* An obvious example of an inherently discriminatory measure is a measure that prohibits the sale of products made in contravention of minimum age regulations because it discriminates against products coming from countries where the minimum age of employment is lower.[952] Another example referring to the legal situation is that of a country putting a higher tax on all products from countries that have not implemented ILO Conventions No. 138 and 182. Such a tax would be *prima facie* GATT Art. III-inconsistent. Obviously, such a measure would primarily be examined under GATT Art. I.[953]

The situation is more difficult when the measure refers to the factual situation of foreign countries and the question is whether foreign producers are capable of switching to the favoured product. This is where the supply substitutability test comes in. This test elaborates on the 'inherence' test, exploring the factual situation and suggesting specific criteria to determine the ability of foreign producers to change to another product. For example, where a measure just prohibits the sale and import of products made with child labour, one should ask – applying the specific criteria of the supply substitutability test – whether foreign producers are capable of producing products without child labour. If the protective effect of such a measure is mitigated by high supply substitutability, the measure should not be dismissed as discriminatory.

The merit of this approach is that it enhances the regulatory autonomy of members and takes due account of the trade reality. It is a well-elaborated approach where *bona fide* measures that in principle disfavour foreign

951 *US–Automobiles*, report of the panel, para. 5.14, *Dominican Republic–Cigarettes*, report of the Appellate Body, para. 96.

952 This would be a situation similar to the one in *US–Shrimps.*

953 Such a measure was the subject of the *Belgian Family Allowances* case, see above p. 32.

products but do not damage foreign producers would not be dismissed easily. In addition, in case of low demand substitutability and high supply substitutability, such a test could provide evidence that the low demand substitutability was due to a crystallization of consumer preferences and thus reveal the trade distorting effect of the measure at issue. In any event, it is only logical to not merely consider consumer views but also producers' view when assessing trade impacts. Finally, although the Appellate Body in the EC–*Seal Products* decision does not seem to read the *Dominican Republic–Cigarettes* as requiring an 'inherence' test, it does not openly contradict such a reading. What it clearly rejects is an interpretation of the statement in *Dominican Republic–Cigarettes* as calling for an inquiry into rationale of the measure.[954]

It follows that both the 'inherence' and 'supply substitutability' test should complement the 'asymmetric impact' test. It should be added that the supply substitutability test should only be applied where foreign producers already produce and export the favoured product. This would be a safeguard against the potential misuse of this rather high threshold. Otherwise, as has been argued, this test risks forcing producers to switch to another product, thereby undermining their comparative advantage. By contrast, if a large share of foreign producers already exports the favoured product, the assumed comparative advantage of the complainant only exists in a sub-sector.

Now, as regards the Belgian Social Label Law, it is likely that there will be an asymmetric detrimental impact on the majority of products from foreign countries as compared to domestic products since child labour prevails in developing countries. More foreign products are likely to be made with child labour than domestic products and therefore cannot be accorded the label. The potential detrimental impact is not due to coincidences such as greater market shares of domestic products but relates to the factual situation in other countries, i.e. it is inherently discriminatory. The next question is whether producers are able to switch to products made without child labour in situations where some producers already export the relevant products made without child labour. The fact that in recent years child labour has greatly diminished in many of the garment industry's supplier factories in developing countries is an indication that supply substitutability could be rather high in some countries.[955] However, since in most cases where child labour exists the average switching costs of producers in the short term is probably too high to easily

954 EC–*Seals*, report of the Appellate Body, para. 5.117.

955 See for example the success of the US-Cambodia TA and ILO 'Better Factories' programme in Cambodia 286 or of the Bangladeshi Exporters' Initiative in Humbert (The Challenge of Child Labour) pp. 252–253 and pp. 368–369.

switch to products made without child labour, it is questionable whether supply substitutability could be established in a lot of cases. It is thus likely that in most cases, there will be an asymmetric discriminatory impact on foreign products made with child labour that is not mitigated by supply substitutability.

The same holds true for the US ban on goods made by forced or indentured children and the EU Forced Labour Regulation.

If the asymmetric discriminatory impact of both measures is measurable and clear, it cannot be remedied by the *bona fide* aim of the measures. Hence, the measures at issue would probably be found to violate GATT Art. III:4. This could be different if a balancing or necessity test were allowed under GATT Art. III:4.

5.4.6.4 *Necessity Test*

As mentioned above, Verhoosel has suggested conducting a necessity test under GATT Art. III.[956] His main argument is appealing. It states that every non-discrimination analysis has to include a necessity test since the WTO Agreement does not pursue deregulation.

However, there is no textual basis for introducing a necessity test under GATT Art. III. GATT Art. III merely contains an obligation of similarity and equal treatment. To equate non-discrimination in GATT Art. III with a necessity test contravenes the rules of interpretation contained in Art. 31 of the VCLT. Under this provision, an interpretation may not go beyond the clear meaning of the terms of the treaty. This would however be the case if a necessity test were conducted under GATT Art. III.

Only where the judiciary has the legitimacy to adopt a dynamic interpretation, the limits set by the literal meaning of the words are wider. For example, the ECJ had this legitimacy when inventing the mandatory requirements as an expression of rule of reason test in its *Cassis de Dijon* ruling.[957] The EU practice is however not comparable because the ECJ practice relating to free movement of goods is a system of negative harmonization. That is to say, the ultimate objective is uniformity between member states achieved through judicial decisions on national measures related to the free movement of goods.[958] Such an objective may justify introducing a necessity test into a non-discrimination provision. By contrast, the aim of the GATT is merely non-discrimination, and

956 See above p. 170 et seq.

957 Cf. Mavroidis (Like Products), p. 130; ECJ, Case 170/78, *Cassis de Dijon, Rewe v. Bundesmonopolverwaltung*, [1979] ECR 649.

958 Weatherill/Beaumont, p. 524.

the WTO adjudicating bodies do not have the legitimacy to adopt a dynamic interpretation.

Most importantly, the wording of GATT Art. XX providing for a sophisticated necessity test suggests that the drafters intended to conduct such a test under GATT Art. XX. Although it is not inconceivable that GATT Art. XX was designed only for cases of *de iure* discrimination, this interpretation is ultimately not convincing. Already the requirement contained in the *chapeau* of GATT Art. XX that a measure should not be 'a means of disguised discrimination' suggests that *de facto* discriminatory measures are covered by GATT Art. XX. It is not probable that the trade community at that time did not think of the whole range of *de facto* discrimination. The statement in the travaux préparatoires regarding the aim of the second sentence of GATT Art. III to prevent taxes on products that are not domestically produced demonstrates that the drafters thought of the inventive spirit of governments when adopting measures in order to circumvent the non-discrimination clause.[959] Moreover, an origin-neutral quantitative measure not coming under GATT Art. III would be incapable of justification. The Appellate Body Report *US–Shrimp* decided the origin-neutral measure under GATT Art. XX.[960]

Verhoosel bases his necessity approach on the panel and Appellate Body ruling in *Chile–Alcoholic Beverages*. However, the Appellate Body rightly stated that the panel merely related the structure of the law to its declared policy purposes. The panel used the lack of any relation between the structure of the law and the policy purpose to *confirm* the discriminatory design.[961]

To illustrate the difference between a rational relationship and a necessity test, one should examine the Belgian Social Label Law. The Belgian Social Label Law affixes a label to both foreign and domestic products if they are *inter alia* made without child labour, which is in accordance with its declared aim to promote social production. Its content and structure relate to its declared goal. However, it is questionable whether the law is necessary in terms of a less trade-restrictive means test to achieve this goal.

Finally, since the consideration of both the regulatory purpose and the 'asymmetric impact' test take due account of regulatory autonomy, there is no need to conduct a necessity test under GATT Art. III instead of Art. XX.

---

959 For the statement see above p. 58.

960 *US–Shrimp*, report of the Appellate Body.

961 *Chile–Alcoholic Beverages*, report of the Appellate Body, para. 69, emphasis original.

5.5 *Contextual Approach*

Addressing the shortcomings of the strict necessity test contained in GATT Art. XX and the need for a wider set of legitimate policy objectives recognized as legitimate, other authors have suggested a contextual approach combining GATT Art. III and XX.[962] In their view, it is not enough to take account of the regulatory purpose of GATT Art. III, but that one should also subject the measures to a scrutiny similar to a necessity test in order to avoid inefficient policy choices.[963] Accordingly, a country is allowed to adopt measures other than the economically superior ones if it can demonstrate their non-feasibility.[964]

Whilst agreeing with the demonstrated need to remedy the shortcomings of the present textual approach to GATT Art. III and XX, and its often-unsatisfactory results, this approach unfortunately has to be dismissed as contravening the rules of interpretation. To transfer a weakened necessity test from GATT Art. XX to GATT Art. III clearly goes beyond what is meant by giving meaning to the ordinary meaning of the terms of the treaty. In the light of the suggested approach to GATT Art. III that promotes more sophisticated market-based criteria for the definition of 'like products', takes account of the regulatory objective as manifested in the structure of the law, favours a discriminatory 'asymmetric impact' approach, and includes a 'supply substitutability' test, there is no need to introduce a contextual approach to enhance regulatory autonomy.

However, the considerations referring to the efficiency principle to be introduced into a necessity test clearly merit closer consideration. The Appellate Body itself has begun to relax the necessity test to a certain extent, stating that necessary refers to a continuum where 'indispensable' lies at one end and 'making a contribution to' at the other end.[965] This issue will be elaborated on below, also with regard to a constitutionalization of WTO law.[966] Further, the contextual approach is supported by a constitutional reading of WTO law.[967]

5.6 *Ius Cogens*

5.6.1 Does Child Labour Law supersede GATT Law?

Having concluded that the international prohibition of child labour as defined in ILO and UN Conventions is a peremptory norm of international law, i.e. *ius*

962 Mattoo/Subramanian.
963 Ibid., p. 313 et seq.
964 Ibid., pp. 318 and 319.
965 *Korea–Beef*, report of the Appellate Body, para. 161.
966 See below, p.219.
967 See below, p.396.

cogens, one might argue that the prohibition of child labour supersedes the respective GATT provision and makes trade measures on child labour GATT-consistent. It has to be recalled that norms of *ius cogens* automatically annul or modify any inconsistent provision. The GATT Art. III-inconsistency of trade measures enforcing international child labour law would therefore not matter anymore. However, according to Art. 53 of the VCLT, in order to make a treaty void, there has to be a conflict between the peremptory norm and the treaty norm. Art. 64 states:

> If a new peremptory norm of general international law emerges, any existing treaty which is in conflict with that norm becomes void and terminates.

Since ILO Convention No. 182 only entered into force in 1999, one could argue that the *ius cogens* norm on child labour only emerged after the WTO Agreement and its Annexes entered into force. In this case, Art. 64 of the VCLT would apply. In any event, both Art. 53 and 64 of the VCLT require the existence of a conflict. Therefore, the question is how a conflict is defined, and whether GATT provisions prohibiting trade-related measures concerning child labour are in conflict with international child labour law as part of *ius cogens*.

Many legal authors argue in favour of a narrow interpretation of a conflict.[968] They hold with Jenks that

> [A] conflict of law-making treaties arises only where simultaneous compliance with the obligations of different instruments is impossible. There is no conflict if the obligations of one instrument are stricter than, but not incompatible with, those of another, or if it is possible to comply with the obligations of one instrument by refraining from exercising a privilege or discretion accorded by another. The presumption against conflict is especially reinforced in cases where separate agreements are concluded between the same parties, since it can be presumed that they are meant to be consistent with themselves, failing any evidence to the contrary.[969]

Thus, it is suggested that before acknowledging a conflict, one should attempt to resolve the issue through interpretation. In case of WTO law, it is suggested

968 Marceau (WTO Dispute Settlement and Human Rights), p. 792; Karl, p. 468; Jenks, p. 425; Jennings/Watts, p. 1280, Fitzmaurice, p. 237.

969 Jenks, p. 425.

that only where compliance with a WTO provision necessitates a violation of a human rights treaty, rules of conflict should apply.[970]

Other authors argue in favour of a wider definition of conflict. Pauwelyn defines a conflict as: if one norm constitutes, has led to, or may lead to, a breach of the other.[971] More specifically, he determines four possible situations of conflict. Situation 1 refers to mutually exclusive obligations, situation 2 to a command and a prohibition of a conduct in the same circumstances, situation 3 to a command and a right as exemption from that command, and situation 4 to a prohibition and a right.[972] Only the last situation goes beyond the definition proposed by the other authors. It refers for example to a situation where the WTO provision prohibits trade restrictions and an environmental agreement provides for the right to use such trade restrictions.[973]

However, both proposed definitions do not include the situation of origin-neutral trade measures concerning child labour, which have an asymmetric discriminatory impact and arguably contravene GATT Art. III. The contradicting norms would be the relevant ILO and UN Conventions, especially No. 138 and 182, and the CRC, having evolved into *ius cogens*. Since none of them include the right to adopt trade restrictions, none of the legal authors would acknowledge a conflict in this situation.

In conclusion, international child labour norms, despite of a *ius cogens* nature, do not render void the relevant WTO provision, i.e. GATT Art. III.

However, the wider definition of conflict includes the case of the 2003 US Burmese Freedom and Democracy Act that was adopted following an ILO recommendation under Art. 33. Since this measure is origin-related and primarily a GATT Art. XI case, it will be dealt with under GATT Art. XI. In case countries withdraw trade privileges such as tariffs in relation to Myanmar following the ILO recommendation, GATT Art. I would apply. Whether GATT Art. I would be superseded by *ius cogens* in this case will be examined when applying the results to GATT Art. I.

5.6.2 Taking Account of the Ius Cogens Character in the Interpretation?

One might argue however that norms of *ius cogens* have to be given special weight in the interpretation due to the very nature of *ius cogens*. Indeed, it has been asserted that in the light of the drastic consequences of a conflict with *ius cogens*, a strong presumption of conformity of other law with *ius cogens*

970 Marceau (WTO Dispute Settlement and Human Rights), p. 792.

971 Pauwelyn (Conflict of Norms), p. 176.

972 Ibid., pp. 180–188.

973 Ibid., p. 187.

exists.[974] The ILC has also stated that in practice, peremptory norms of general international law generate strong interpretative principles that will resolve all or most conflicts.[975] This statement could be extended to mean that wherever a divergence or tension between obligations imposed by *ius cogens* norms (i.e. international child labour norms), and prohibitions contained in other norms (i.e. GATT non-discrimination clauses and quantitative restrictions) appears, there is a strong presumption that the divergence will be resolved. Thus, in the interpretation of trade measures concerning child labour, the fact that the law implements an international norm that has the character of *ius cogens* could be given priority. One could therefore argue that where measures aim at implementing child labour norms that have an asymmetric discriminatory impact, the *ius cogens* aim prevails over the discriminatory impact. This is obviously the only case where the *ius cogens* nature can become relevant. If there is no asymmetric discriminatory impact, the measure does not violate GATT Art. III in the first place.

The merit of this interpretation is that in cases of *ius cogens*, governments would not have to fear that their trade measures contravene the basic WTO obligations on non-discrimination. It has been rightly argued that governments consider it as very different whether their measures are GATT Art. III-consistent or whether they violate GATT Art. III, but are justified under GATT Art. XX.[976] This is understandable since in the first case, there is no breach of the law at all, whereas in the second case, there is a breach of the law that has been justified. In addition, the WTO adjudicating bodies would not need to apply the cumbersome necessity test and the requirements of the *chapeau* of GATT Art. XX. The *ius cogens* solution offers a clear-cut criterion that could potentially increase legal certainty and predictability.

However, this interpretation is questionable if one looks at the nature and scope of GATT Art. III and XX, their legal relationship, the legal consequences of *ius cogens*, and the factual result of such an interpretation.

If one took account of the *ius cogens* aim under GATT Art. III, this would potentially narrow the scope of this non-discrimination provision and have a bearing on GATT Art. XX, the general exception clause for policy measures. Early GATT-cases have adopted a different reading and put forward a narrow interpretation of GATT Art. XX suggesting that while the substantive provisions

974 Marceau (WTO Dispute Settlement and Human Rights), p. 799.

975 UN (Materials on States Responsibility in International Wrongful Acts), p. 295.

976 Regan (Further Thoughts), p. 749; Hudec (Requiem for an Aim and Effects), p. 39.

of GATT are to be construed broadly, the exceptions are limited and have to be construed narrowly.[977] However, in *US–Shrimp*, the Appellate Body held:

> The relationship between the affirmative commitments set out in, e.g. Articles I, III and XI, and the policies and interests embodied in the 'General Exceptions' listed in Article XX, can be given meaning within the framework of the General Agreement and its object and purpose by a treaty interpreter only on a case-to-case basis, by careful scrutiny of the factual and legal context in a given dispute, without disregarding the words actually used by the WTO Members themselves to express their intent and purpose.[978]

This has been interpreted as qualifying GATT Art. XX as a balancing provision striking a balance between, on the one hand, trade liberalisation, market access and non-discrimination rules and, on the other hand, other societal values and interests.[979] Thus, instead of being an exception that has to be construed narrowly, it is a balancing provision the scope of which is to be determined on a case-by case basis. This reading has been confirmed by subsequent cases such as *EC–Asbestos* where the Appellate Body held explicitly that Art. III:4 and Art. XX (b) are distinct and independent provisions of the GATT 1994 and have to each be interpreted on their own. The scope and meaning of GATT Art. III:4 should not be broadened or restricted beyond what is required by the normal customary rules of treaty interpretation.[980] The Appellate Body in *Thailand–Cigarettes* (*Philippines*) also found that the analysis under GATT Art. III:4 and XX (d) were distinct and separate.[981]

Thus, according to WTO jurisprudence, the relationship between GATT Art. III and XX in principle does not necessarily imply that GATT Art. III must be construed so broadly as not to allow for consideration of the *ius cogens* aim of a measure. However, according to WTO jurisprudence, the aim of a measure is to be considered and weighed against its trade-restrictiveness under GATT Art. XX. Thus, only if one would allow the *ius cogens* aim to immediately rescue the measure notwithstanding its discriminatory trade effect, the *ius cogens* aim could be considered under GATT Art. III.

---

977 *US–Malt Beverages*, report of the panel, para. 5.41; but cf. Neumann, p. 134 who argues for a wide interpretation of 'likeness' as well as for a wide interpretation of GATT Art. XX.

978 *US–Shrimp*, report of the Appellate Body.

979 Van den Bossche/Zdouc, p. 595.

980 *EC–Asbestos*, report of the Appellate Body, para. 115.

981 *Thailand–Cigarettes* (*Philippines*), report of the Appellate Body, para 173.

Such an interpretation is however not in accordance with the general international law on *ius cogens*. Even though violations of *ius cogens* norms may in specific cases entitle states to take countermeasures against other states, these measures still must be proportionate in accordance with Art. 51 of the Articles on State Responsibility. This implies that *ius cogens* measures should not be allowed without conducting any type of proportionality or necessity test as required by GATT Art. XX.

Most importantly, as will be seen below, the Appellate Body held that under the necessity test of GATT Art. XX, the interpretation of 'necessary' involved a process of weighing and balancing factors such as the contribution made by the measure to the enforcement of the law at issue, the importance of the common interests or values protected, and the accompanying impact of the law or regulation on imports or exports.[982] Hence, the *ius cogens* aim of trade measures on child labour can be given due account under GATT Art. XX.

As regards trade measures, it is important that all aspects of the measure are thoroughly examined. As has been demonstrated above, trade measures on child labour can have negative effects for the children concerned. For example, immediately after the announcement of a US ban prohibiting goods made with child labour, many children in Bangladesh were dismissed and faced destitution and prostitution.[983] The positive effect came only later when the Bangladeshi Exporters' Initiative or the RUGMARK initiative, which both also provided for rehabilitation measures, were introduced. Thus, from a developmental perspective, the effectiveness of a measure should be evaluated under the GATT. This can perfectly be done under the necessity or proportionality test of GATT Art. XX as did the Appellate Body in *US–Shrimp*.[984] Hence, an interpretation that gives the *ius cogens* aim priority without balancing it against the discriminatory effect of a measure should be avoided.

It follows from above that the Belgian Social Label Law probably has to be interpreted as being GATT Art. III-inconsistent because of its potential asymmetric discriminatory impact, despite the law having a *bona fide* aim that can be considered as part of *ius cogens*. The same holds true for the US ban on goods made with indentured or forced child labour or the proposed EU Forced Labour Regulation.

982 *Korea–Beef*, report of the Appellate Body, para. 164.

983 See Humbert (The Challenge of Child Labour), pp. 368–369.

984 *US–Shrimp*, report of the Appellate Body, para. 141.

5.7 *Conclusion*

In conclusion, while most recent WTO jurisprudence seems to close the door for the consideration of regulatory purposes or an 'inherence' or 'supply substitutability' test of GATT Art. III, such an interpretation is recommendable and possible according to earlier cases. The merit of such an interpretation is that it allows more regulatory autonomy for WTO members.

It can be assumed that the market-based approach to the 'like product' definition offers some help to measures concerning child labour under GATT Art. III. Whilst not excluding npr-ppm-measures *per se*, it however does not provide a general solution. Only in rare cases market analysis will demonstrate that products made with child labour are not like products made without child labour. In the case of the Belgian Social Label Law, the proposed EU Forced Labour Regulation and the US ban on goods made with forced or indentured child labour, it basically depends on the demand substitutability in the US, EU and Belgian market whether these measures may legally distinguish between products made with child labour and those made without child labour.

In a similar vein, it depends on the individual circumstances whether unilateral measures aiming at the abolition of child labour, such as the US ban on goods made with forced or indentured child labour, the proposed EU Forced Labour Regulation or the Belgian Social Label Law, violate the equal treatment obligation. The outcome of the analysis made above is that under the equal treatment obligation, the regulatory purpose and the asymmetric discriminatory impact of the measure should be considered. A *bona fide* aim should complement the trade effects test if it cannot clearly be established that most foreign products are treated worse than domestic products. In this case, the measure concerned would not be dismissed as protectionist.

The 'asymmetric impact' test should be complemented by an 'inherence' and 'supply substitutability' test. This test takes due account of supply factors such as the legal and factual situation of producers. The merit of this test is that it complements the demand substitutability factors and provides a more complete picture of the trade situation.

Most measures on child labour will have a *bona fide* aim, but an asymmetric discriminatory impact in that they treat most imported products worse than domestic products. This is probably the case for the Belgian Social Label Law, the proposed EU Forced Labour Regulation and the US ban on goods made with forced or indentured child labour. Since most producers will not be able to substitute children workers with adult workers without increasing the price, the majority of measures on child labour at present will probably violate GATT Art. III.

While it is appealing to take due account of the nature of *ius cogens* and interpret GATT Art. III in a way that gives the *ius cogens* aim of a measure *ipso facto* priority over its discriminatory trade effect, such a solution raises some concerns. Taking account of the nature and purpose of GATT Art. III and XX in accordance with Art. 31 of the VCLT, their legal relationship as established by the WTO jurisprudence, the legal consequences of *ius cogens*, and the developmental aspects of such an interpretation, it follows that the *ius cogens* aim should not prevail *per se*, but be duly considered under GATT Art. XX.

In conclusion, for the time being, most trade measures concerning child labour are not likely to be in accordance with GATT Art. III because of their potential asymmetric discriminatory impact.

6 Application of the Results Found under GATT Art. III to GATT Art. I

6.1 *Introduction*

As announced above, the discussion of 'like products' under GATT Art. I will be revisited. In particular, it will now be examined whether the results found under GATT Art. III can be applied to GATT Art. I.

Further, it will be analysed whether regulatory purposes or/and an asymmetric discriminatory impact of the measure in question have to be taken into account in the analysis under GATT Art. I. In the context of the regulatory purpose, the *ius cogens* character of international child labour law will be considered. The 'inherence' test and 'supply substitutability test' applied under GATT Art. III will also be discussed in relation to GATT Art. I.

The analysis of the WTO compatibility of the proposed EU Forced Labour Regulation, the US ban on goods made with forced or indentured child labour and the Belgian Social Label Law will then be completed.

6.2 *Like Products*

It has to be recalled that generally, the term 'like products' as applied under GATT Art. I should be read in the same way as under GATT Art. III. More narrow interpretations only apply where the principle of reciprocity demands it. As established above and in accordance with GATT Art. III, the term 'like' in GATT Art. I should be read to include 'directly competitive and substitutable' products.

Regarding npr-ppm-measures, it follows that npr-ppm-measures such as trade measures concerning child labour are not *per se* GATT Art. I-inconsistent. Instead, the market-based criteria elaborated under GATT Art. III should be applied to GATT Art. I. Thus, demand substitutability between two groups of products is the main criterion. Factors establishing demand substitutability are physical similarities, common end-uses, marketing strategies of companies, direct consumer views, absolute prices, and cross-price elasticity. Potential and future demand and evidence from other markets should be considered. Tariff classifications used by other WTO members are also highly relevant.

As under GATT Art. III, the concept of cross-price elasticity would have to be used. One would thus have to determine the cross-price elasticity of both the imported products made with child labour and the imported product not made with child labour and compare them. Having established the cross-price elasticity of the imported product following trade liberalization, i.e. assuming the protective measure was eliminated, one would have to ask consumers of the other imported product in question whether they would buy the cheaper product if they knew that it was made with child labour. If the cross-price elasticity is at least equal, the measure is likely to be protectionist.

However, as stated above, it might be that in some markets, products not made with child labour are likely to constitute a distinct market segment soon. Higher tariffs on products made with child labour that are not listed may therefore not be prohibited by GATT Art. I.

So far, there are not many examples where the 'like product' issue has become relevant. GSPs are country-specific measures. The same goes for bans under the Kimberley Process Certification Scheme because they are enforced against non-participants and therefore not based on product characteristics. The same holds true for withdrawal of MFN treatment following the ILO recommendation in the Myanmar case.

Cases where the 'like product' issue could become relevant are the proposed EU Forced Labour Regulatio and the US ban on products made with forced or indentured child labour. Depending on whether in the EU or US market, products made with child labour are in the same market segment as products not made with child labour, the respective measures would violate the obligation of similarity or not.

6.3 *Regulatory Purposes and Ius Cogens*

6.3.1 Regulatory Purpose

As seen above, there is a strong argument to be made that under GATT Art. III, the regulatory purpose of the measure in question should be considered when determining whether the measure violates GATT Art. III. Whereas the purpose of a measure shall not be considered under the term 'like products', it shall be looked at under the equal treatment obligation to complement the discriminatory impact analysis. The textual basis for this interpretation is GATT Art. III:1 that states that measures 'should not be applied so as to afford protection'. The purposive connotation of these words induced the GATT/WTO jurisprudence and many legal scholars to interpret the GATT Art. III:2 and 4 as taking account of the legal purpose of the measure, i.e. whether it aims at protecting domestic production.

By contrast, GATT Art. I does not provide for such a textual basis. The reference to GATT Art. III is limited to the different nature of GATT Art. III measures. That means that internal measures such as those contained in the different provisions of GATT Art. III are included under the scope of GATT Art. III. Thus, an interpretation that considered the regulatory purpose of a measure under GATT Art. I would go beyond the ordinary meaning of the terms of the treaty and contravene the rules of interpretation.

As a final remark, it should be noted that in relation to discrimination between imports, there is less danger of disguised protection of products. Thus, the aim of a measure may be less important when determining discrimination.

6.3.2 Ius Cogens

6.3.2.1 *Does Child Labour Law Supersede GATT Art. I?*

The question arises whether in case of a conflict, the international prohibition of child labour, having the character of *ius cogens*, supersedes GATT Art. I.

The question is whether a conflict exists between the ILO recommendation adopted in the Myanmar case and GATT Art. I.[985] According to the ILO recommendation, ILO constituents are asked to review their relations with Mynanmar and possibly to withdraw trade privileges or other trade benefits in order to combat cases of, *inter alia*, forced child labour[986] while GATT Art. I provides for MFN treatment. The same question can be raised regarding the Kimberley Process Certification Scheme providing for national bans to stop the trade in conflict diamonds, which is *inter alia* targeted at child soldiers. The ILO recommendation as well as the Kimberley Process Certification Scheme can thus be said to aim at implementing *ius cogens*. If these situations constituted a conflict between an *ius cogens* norms and GATT Art. I, Article 53 and 64 of the VCLT would render the prohibition of discrimination against imports from Myanmar or non-participants of the Kimberley Process Certification Scheme under GATT Art. I void.

Following the view of Pauwelyn, one could assume a conflict since one provision, i.e. the ILO recommendation or the Kimberley Process Certification Scheme, provides for the right to use trade measures whereas the other

985 See the discussion on *ius cogens* superseding GATT law above p. 182.

986 See Humbert (The Challenge of Child Labour), pp. 185–186.

provision, i.e. the GATT provision, prohibits such measures.[987] It is however questionable whether this conflict involves *ius cogens* that renders the WTO provision void, as provided for by Article 53 and 64 of the Vienna Convention. For the *ius cogens* rule is the prohibition of child labour. The prohibition does however not provide for the right to take trade measures. The question therefore is whether the ILO recommendation or the Kimberley Process Certification Scheme providing for the right to take trade measures is also part of *ius cogens*. This is however not the case. Instead, the right to take trade measures can be a legal consequence of *ius cogens*, as examined above.[988] It is another question whether an *ius cogens* rule to protect nationals of other states from genocide may evolve in the future. The Resolution adopted by the General Assembly in the 2005 World Summit provides for a responsibility to protect populations from genocide, war crimes, ethnic cleansing and crimes against humanity through collective action in accordance with the UN Charter.[989] However, at present, there is no such rule. Thus, even though there might be a conflict between the ILO recommendation or the Kimberley Process Certification Scheme and GATT Art. I, there is no conflict involving *ius cogens* that leads to the nullification of the WTO provision.

In the same sense, Pauwelyn distinguishes between an inherent normative conflict where one norm constitutes the breach of another, and other conflicts. Such an inherent conflict arises when a norm conflicts with another norm of *ius cogens*.[990] By contrast, if the exercise of rights under one treaty constitutes breach under the other norm, there is a conflict in applicable law.[991] Thus, the wider definition of conflicts does not refer to the situation of a conflict in Art. 53 or 64 of the VCLT where the *ius cogens* norms renders the other norm void.

In conclusion, the ILO recommendation to withdraw trade privileges does not supersede GATT Art. I. Unilateral action following the ILO recommendation would be contrary to GATT Art. I, in case it violates the remaining obligations imposed by GATT Art. I.

---

987 See the wider definition of a conflict by Pauwelyn above p. 183.

988 In the same sense, Vázquez, p. 821 argues that the GATT would only be in conflict with an *ius cogens* norm if the *ius cogens* norm required countries to ban the importation of goods made with child labour.

989 Resolution adopted by the General Assembly, 2005 World Summit Outcome, A/Res/60/1, 24 October 2005, para. 138 et seq.

990 Pauwelyn (Conflict of Norms), p. 276.

991 Ibid., p. 275.

6.3.2.2 *The Role of Ius Cogens in the Interpretation*

Another question is whether the *ius cogens* nature of the prohibition of child labour plays a special role in the interpretation. Under GATT Art. III, the question was whether the *ius cogens* nature might be given special weight when determining the aim of a measure. Since under GATT Art. I, the aim of a measure is irrelevant, the *ius cogens* aim of a measure neither matters in the interpretation.

Thus, the *bona fide* aim of the proposed EU Forced Labour Regulation, the US ban on goods made with forced or indentured child labour or of the Belgian Social Label Law does not matter in relation to GATT Art. I:1.

6.4 *'Asymmetric Impact'*

Having concluded that under GATT Art. III, a measure needs to have an asymmetric impact, the question is whether this applies also to GATT Art. I.

Several authors argue in favour of an asymmetric discriminatory impact to be considered under GATT Art. I.[992] They argue that the discriminatory impact finds some basis in the word 'advantage' etc., i.e. proof is needed that a particular product that receives an advantage is imported far more frequently from the complaining WTO member than from the defendant WTO member.[993] Only in that case, the favoured WTO member would receive a *de facto* advantage. Ehring states that border measures should come under scrutiny imposed by the discriminatory impact test wherever they cross the boundaries of likeness.[994]

Indeed, there is no reason why the 'asymmetric impact' test should not be applied to GATT Art. I. Ehring rightly states that the danger to turn GATT Art. I into a market access right exists as well.[995] He holds that if a WTO member withdraws special treatment granted to some country and has to do that by equalizing treatment within the overall group of products, at whatever level, including a level that is less advantageous than the best treatment available, there no longer exists any advantage that is not accorded to like products.[996] Furthermore, if a tariff binding under GATT Art. II prohibits the withdrawal of the advantage granted to a part of like products, the member in question has no other choice but to extend the best available treatment existing for imports to all like products originating in other WTO members.

992 Davey/Pauwelyn, pp. 40 and 41; Ehring, p. 954 et seqq.
993 Davey/Pauwelyn, p. 40.
994 Ehring, p. 954.
995 Ibid., p. 956.
996 Ibid.

These considerations apply *a fortiori* in the light of what has been established by the jurisprudence under the term 'unconditionally'. The jurisprudence on conditionality in MFN clauses has established that conditions not related to the products themselves are allowed as long as they do not refer to the situation or conduct of countries and discriminate with respect to the origin of countries.[997] In relation to npr-ppm-measures, this test should be understood to refer to the production method of the imported products and asks whether producers from that country predominantly and necessarily use the favoured production method. It is like the 'inherence' or 'supply substitutability' test applied under GATT Art. III. Since these tests establish a much a higher threshold for measures to be GATT-illegal, it should be *a fortiori* allowed to require an asymmetric discriminatory impact of the border measure in question.

The US ban on goods made with forced or indentured child labour is likely to have an asymmetric discriminatory impact on for example textiles from India as opposed to textiles from the US. The same holds true for the Belgian Social Label Law and the proposed EU Forced Labour Regulation.

6.5 *'Supply Substitutability' and 'Inherence' Test*

As examined above, the prohibition of conditionality in GATT Art. I seems to suggest that conditions not related to the products themselves are allowed as long as they do not refer to the situation or conduct of countries and discriminate with respect to the origin of products. The question is what exactly is meant by 'the situation and conduct of countries' and whether the 'supply substitutability' and 'inherence effects' test applied under GATT Art. III should also be used here. While the 'inherence' test should be understood to generally refer to the legal and factual situation of a country, the 'supply substitutability' test elaborates on the 'inherence' test, exploring the factual situation and suggesting specific criteria to determine the ability of foreign producers to change to another product.[998] Specifically, a switching rate of producers is evaluated on the average costs of switching of one industry sector and the resulting ability of producers to change to another product established accordingly.[999]

There is no reason why these tests should not be applied under GATT Art. I in relation to the obligation of granting advantages 'unconditionally'. It has to be recalled that the merit of these tests is that they enhance the regulatory autonomy of members and take due account of the real-world situation of

997 See the discussion of the terms 'immediately and unconditionally' above p. 31.

998 See above pp. 106 et seqq. and pp. 144 et seqq.

999 Choi, p. 69.

trade. Measures that only have incidental trade effects would not be dismissed easily.

Thus, in the above-mentioned case of tariff reductions on products not made with child labour or the US ban on products made with forced or indentured child labour, the ability of producers to quickly change from child labourers to adult workers may be evaluated on the switching rate of the industry sector as well as the other criteria employed by the substitutability test. Depending on that switching rate, some producers in developing countries may be able to change quickly to a production process not employing children. Considering the improvements made in the textile and clothing sector in Asia, it seems to be likely that some textile and clothing producers in e.g., Cambodia might be able to replace children by adult workers while Indian cotton farmers or cocoa farmers in the Ivory Coast would face more difficulties because of probable price increases. Thus, in some cases the mentioned trade measures on child labour may pass the 'supply substitutability' test and be GATT Art. I:1 consistent. The same holds true for the Belgian Social Label Law.

6.6 *Conclusion*

In conclusion, the general approach under GATT Art. I and III is similar. In relation to the term 'like products', the same market-based criteria should be used. Whether the proposed EU Forced Labour Regulation, the US ban on goods made with forced or indentured child labour or the Belgian Social Label Law may legally distinguish between products made with forced or indentured child labour depends on whether these two groups belong to the same market segment.

Since there is no textual basis, the regulatory purpose of the measure should not be considered in the analysis under GATT Art. I:1. Neither should its *ius cogens* aim.

The ILO recommendation aiming at eliminating child labour and providing for withdrawal of MFN-treatment does not supersede GATT Art. I. Thus, unilateral action taken in accordance with the ILO recommendation violates GATT Art. I. So do national import bans under the Kimberley Process Certification Scheme regarding non-participants.

To be inconsistent with GATT Art. I, an origin-neutral measure needs to have an asymmetric discriminatory impact. A textual basis can be found in the word 'advantage' etc. Moreover, having established that only measures providing for conditions that relate to the situation or conduct of specific countries are prohibited under the unconditional MFN clause, an 'asymmetric impact' test, *a fortiori*, should be allowed. Under the term 'immediately' and 'unconditionally', the 'supply substitutability' and 'inherence' test conducted under GATT Art. III should be applied.

The proposed EU Forced Labour Regulation, the US ban on goods made with forced or indentured child labour and the Belgian Social Label Law may have an asymmetric discriminatory impact on some WTO members. However, in some cases the supply substitutability test may apply and make the measures GATT Art. I:1-consistent.

7 Application of the Results Found under GATT Art. III to GATT Art. II

The results of the analysis of GATT Art. III should basically also be applicable to GATT Art. II. This means that like products are those that are in the same market using econometric criteria. There is no reason why npr-ppms should be prohibited *per se* given that conditions may be included in the tariff schedules. Thus, a higher tariff on products made with child labour is possible but would of course be contrary to the requirement of a 'treatment no less favourable'. As is the case with GATT Art. I, there is no textual basis for considering the regulatory purpose. The legality of such tariffs would therefore depend on their compatibility with GATT Art. XX or XXI.

8 Compatibility of Trade Measures on Child Labour with Quantitative Restrictions of GATT Art. XI and XIII

Another mainstay of classical regulation of trade in goods is the prohibition of quantitative restrictions according to GATT Art. XI. GATT Art. XIII calls for non-discriminatory administration of quantitative restrictions. However, if GATT Art. XI is violated – as might be the case with quantitative restrictions on child labour – GATT Art. XIII has no independent meaning.[1000] GATT Art. XI reads:

> *General Elimination of Quantitative Restrictions*
>
> 1. No prohibitions or restrictions other than duties, taxes or other charges, whether made effective through quotas, import or export licences or other measures, shall be instituted or maintained by any

1000 *US–Shrimp*, report of the panel, para. 34.

contracting party on the importation of any product of the territory of any other contracting party or on the exportation or sale for export of any other contracting party.

8.1 *Trade Measures on Child Labour as Quantitative Restrictions*

The provision prohibits any trade restriction imposed at the border upon the importation of a product.[1001] Import bans such as the US ban on goods made with child labour, the 2003 US Burmese Freedom and Democracy Act and the UFLPA restrict trade at the border.[1002] Measures implemented under the Kimberley Process Certification Scheme that ban diamonds coming from non-participants and the proposed EU Forced Labour Regulation, providing for suspension of release of free circulation of products entering the EU in case of evidence of forced labour,[1003] also constitute an import restriction prohibited by GATT Art. XI. Except for the 2003 US Burmese Freedom and Democracy Act and the UFLPA, all these measures were already found to possibly violate GATT Art. I and GATT Art. III:4.

The relationship between GATT Art. XI:1 and III:4 is clarified by the Note *Ad* to GATT Art. III and the relating GATT/WTO jurisprudence.[1004] Accordingly, GATT Art. III:4 applies if the measure is applicable to both the imported product and the domestic product. The measure applying to the foreign product does however not have to be identical to the measure applying to the domestic product. Rather, it must make the domestic measure effective, being a logical corollary of this measure. By contrast, a ban applying only to foreign products falls under GATT Art. XI.

If a measure has already been found as violating GATT Art. III:4, a panel will refrain from examining the measure under GATT Art. XI for reasons of judicial economy.[1005] In accordance with Art. 7 (2) of the DSU however, if the parties to the dispute do not invoke GATT Art. III:4 but GATT Art. XI, the WTO adjudicating bodies will solve the case under GATT Art. XI.[1006] Art. 7 of the DSU clearly states that the jurisdiction of a panel is established by its terms of reference, which contain the legal claims the panel may consider.[1007]

1001 Kennedy, p. 127.
1002 *US–Shrimp*, report of the panel, para. 7.16.
1003 Art. 15–21 of the EU Regulation.
1004 See above p. 61.
1005 Cf. *EC–Asbestos*, report of the panel, para. 8.99.
1006 Cf. *US–Shrimp*, report of the panel.
1007 *India – Patents (US)*, report of the Appellate Body, paras. 92–93 cited in WTO Analytical Index, p. 1327.

Thus, if a WTO member invokes GATT Art. XI, the mentioned trade measures will possibly be found to violate GATT Art. XI but may be justified under GATT Art. XX.

8.2 *The Ius Cogens Nature of the Prohibition of Child Labour*

With regard to the *ius cogens* nature of the protection of children from economic exploitation, it should be stated that international norms on the prohibition of child labour do not prevail *per se* over GATT Art. XI.[1008] This is because there is no conflict between the *ius cogens* norm on child labour and GATT norms. A conflict might arise between the ILO recommendation to review trade relations in the Myanmar case and GATT Art. XI, but such recommendation – whilst aiming at enforcing *ius cogens* – is not a peremptory norm in and of itself. The US Burmese Freedom and Democracy Act therefore possibly violate GATT Art. XI.

9 Trade Measures on Child Labour under the GATT Art. XIX

GATT Art. XIX has been called the 'Escape Clause' and provides for the most significant safeguard mechanism of the international trading system.[1009]

It reads:

> 1. (a) If, as a result of unforeseen developments and of the effect of the obligation incurred by a contracting party under this Agreement, including tariff concessions, any product is being imported into the territory of that contracting party in such increased quantities and under such conditions as to cause or threaten serious injury to domestic producers in that territory of like or directly competitive products, the contracting party shall be free, in respect of such product, and to the extent and for such time as may be necessary to prevent or remedy such injury, to suspend the obligation in whole or in part or to withdraw or modify the concession.

GATT Art. XIX provides for the temporary suspension of GATT/WTO obligations in situations where increased importation of a product causes or threatens serious injury to domestic producers because of unforeseen developments. According to Art. 5:1 of the Agreement on Safeguards containing provisions on

1008 See above, pp. 181 et seqq.

1009 Jackson (The World Trading System), p. 181.

the application of safeguard measures according to GATT Art. XIX, the rationale of the such safeguard mechanism is the protection of the domestic industry.[1010]

For example, in 2005, when the quotas on textiles under the WTO Agreement on Textiles and Clothing were lifted, European producers feared that the surge in Chinese textiles imports could be highly damaging to the domestic textiles industry.[1011] The EU however did not invoke the Escape Clause but requested the use of urgency procedure written into the Commission Guidelines under the Textile Specific Safeguard Clause written into China's protocol of accession to the WTO.[1012] The following consultations with China led to adoption of a Memorandum of Understanding (MoU) between the European Commission and the Chinese Ministry of Commerce from June 2005 on import rates for textiles.[1013] The MoU provided for agreed growth rates on imports over a period of three years.[1014]

The question is whether GATT Art. XIX can be used to sanction increasing imports of products made with child labour.

A WTO member could suspend its tariff concessions or impose quantitative restrictions on products made with child labour if these were imported as a result of unforeseen developments in such quantities to cause a serious injury to domestic producers.

'Increased quantities' within the meaning of GATT Art. XIX:1 includes the relative increase of imports, Art. 2.1 of the Agreement on Safeguards. The 'increased imports' must be a causal result of 'unforeseen developments.' The Appellate Body insisted that the term 'unforeseen developments' has to be considered although it is not mentioned in the Agreement on Safeguards.[1015] It is however questionable whether increasing imports may be considered as a result of child labour. Low labour standards are probably not the only reason for increased imports. Increasing imports might also be attributable to better production facilities. Most importantly, low labour standards, especially child labour, are the result of several factors including poverty, customs and societal attitudes and the educational system, i.e. rather long-term factors.[1016]

1010 Cf. Blüthner, p. 323.

1011 European Commission, Textile sector, EU-China textile agreement 10 June 2005, Memo – Brussels, 12 June 2005, https://ec.europa.eu/commission/presscorner/detail/en/MEMO_05_201.

1012 Ibid.

1013 Ibid.

1014 Ibid., p. 2.

1015 *Argentina–Footwear*, report of the Appellate Body, para. 88 et seqq.; see also Van den Bossche/Zdouc, pp. 691–692.

1016 Cf. Humbert (The Challenge of Child Labour), pp. 25–30.

The protection of the domestic industry should however not be the underlying rationale when using trade measures to combat child labour.

In conclusion, GATT Art. XIX is not an appropriate basis for trade measures to combat child labour.

10 Trade Measures concerning Child Labour under GATT Art. XX

10.1 *Overview over the Scope and Structure of GATT Art. XX*

GATT Art. XX contains a list of exceptions to GATT obligations. It includes governmental measures undertaken to effectively implement certain national policies.[1017]

The relevant text of GATT Art. XX is as follows:

> General exceptions
>
> Subject to the requirement that such measures are not applied in a manner which would constitute a means of arbitrary or unjustifiable discrimination between countries where the same conditions prevail, or a disguised restriction on international trade, nothing in this Agreement shall be construed to prevent the adoption or enforcement by any contracting party of measures:
>
> a) necessary to protect public morals;
> b) necessary to protect human, animal or plant life or health;
> e) relating to the products of prison labour;

According to WTO jurisprudence, GATT Art. XX can justify measures that condition market access on the policies adopted by exporting WTO members.[1018] Those measures might be recognized as exceptions to substantive obligations established in GATT 1994 because domestic policies embodied in those measures have been recognized as important and legitimate in character.[1019] Relevant GATT obligations are for example GATT Art. I, III or XI.[1020] Most importantly, in *US–Gasoline*, the Appellate held that the relationship between the obligations and the policies embodied in GATT Art. XX should

1017 Jackson (The World Trading System), p. 232.

1018 *US–Shrimp*, report of the Appellate Body, para. 121.

1019 Ibid.

1020 Ibid., paras. 156 and 159.

be given meaning on a case-to-case basis.[1021] Thus, rather than having to be construed narrowly as is normally the case with exceptions, GATT Art. XX is in essence a balancing provision reconciling trade liberalisation with other societal values.[1022]

Thus, GATT-inconsistent unilateral trade measures on child labour could potentially be justified under GATT Art. XX. To recall, concrete examples are the US ban on goods produced by forced or indentured child labour, the Belgian Social Label Law, the UFLPA, the proposed EU Forced Labour Regulation, the 2003 US Burmese Freedom and Democracy Act and bans under the Kimberley Process Certification Scheme. Other examples could be higher taxes on goods made with child labour.

In relation to the preamble, i.e. the *chapeau* of GATT Art. XX, it has been held that it embodies the recognition of the part of WTO members of the need to maintain a balance of rights and obligations between the right of a member to invoke one or another of the exceptions of GATT Art. XX on the one hand, and the substantive rights of the other members on the other hand.[1023] The *chapeau* is considered as an expression of good faith.[1024] In the jurisprudence of the Appellate Body to date, the main question under the *chapeau* has been whether the *application* of the domestic measure constitutes a means of arbitrary or unjustifiable discrimination between countries where the same conditions prevail.[1025]

The structure of GATT Art. XX has been interpreted as follows. GATT Art. XX provides for a two-tiered test: Firstly, the measure at issue must come under one or another of the particular exceptions listed in paragraphs lit. a to j. Secondly, the measure must comply with the requirements of the *chapeau*.[1026]

With regard to the different wording of the various paragraphs, for example the formulation 'necessary' *versus* the formulation 'relating to' etc., it has been stated that the degree of connection required between the measure under appraisal and the state interest or policy interest varies under the different exceptions.[1027]

1021 *US–Gasoline*, report of the Appellate Body, p. 18.
1022 Van den Bossche/Zdouc, p. 595.
1023 *US–Shrimp*, report of the Appellate Body, para. 156.
1024 Ibid., paras. 158–159.
1025 Ibid., para. 160.
1026 *US–Gasoline*, report of the Appellate Body, p. 22.
1027 Ibid., p. 17.

From the various exceptions contained in GATT Art. XX, lit. a, b and e seem to have the greatest potential to cover trade measures on child labour and will be analysed in turn.

10.2 *The Public Morals Exception*

GATT Art. XX (a) permits trade measures that are necessary to protect public morals. That is, they must be designed to protect public morals meaning that the policy objective pursued by the measure is the protection of public morals and they must be necessary to fulfil that policy objective.[1028] Defining human dignity, measures aiming at implementing human rights may fall within the purview of this exception.[1029] Since the protection from child labour is a fundamental human right with *ius cogens* character, measures aiming at the abolition of child labour may potentially be considered to protect public morals. Indeed, in the view of Marceau, WTO members may want to justify human rights measures invoking the exception for public morals.[1030] In legal literature, similar to the ppm-issue discussed above, GATT Art. XX (a) is seen as an important portal for taking human rights into account when interpreting WTO law.[1031] As such, it is argued, it might serve as an important bridge between trade and human rights law, allowing and encouraging WTO members to respect their human rights obligations.[1032] Before discussing such wider implications of the proposed interpretation of relevant WTO provisions for the relationship of trade and human rights law and the potential need for reforms, this study will examine the public morals exception in detail, taking into account relevant GATT/WTO jurisprudence and arguments found in legal literature. The following sections will focus on the meaning of the term 'public morals', the issue of extraterritoriality and the 'necessary' requirement in GATT Art. XX (a).

10.2.1 The Term 'Public Morals'

The term 'public morals' has for the first time been defined by the panel in *US–Gambling* in relation to GATS Art. XIV (a).[1033] The definition was upheld by the Appellate Body[1034] and adopted by the panel in *China–Publications and*

1028 Cf. Van den Bossche/Zdouc, p. 629.
1029 Cf. the Preamble of the Universal Declaration of Human Rights, 1948.
1030 Marceau (WTO Dispute Settlement and Human Rights II), p. 206.
1031 See for example Cottier/Pauwelyn/Bürgi, p. 12.
1032 Marceau (WTO Dispute Settlement and Human Rights I), p. 786.
1033 *US–Gambling*, report of the panel.
1034 *US–Gambling*, report of the Appellate Body.

Audiovisual Products, the first case where GATT Art. XX (a) was invoked.[1035] Specifically, the panel in *US–Gambling* held the term 'public morals' denoted

> Standards of right or wrong conduct maintained by or on behalf of a community or nation.[1036]

Furthermore, the panel held that the term 'public morals' was an evolutionary concept that varied in time and space and was determined by factors such as social, ethical and religious values.[1037] It said that members should be given some scope to define and apply for themselves the concepts of 'public morals' and 'public order' in their respective territories, according to their systems and values.[1038] Thus, the panel showed deference and flexibility for members' policy decisions.[1039]

The panel also referred to the term 'public order', stating that the term 'public order' suggested that 'public order' referred to the preservation of the fundamental interests of a society, as reflected in public policy and law. These fundamental interests can relate, *inter alia*, to standards of law, security and morality.[1040] Although the terms 'public order' and 'public morals' are obviously not identical, it is argued here that the meaning of the term 'public morals' used in GATT Art. XX (a) and the term 'public morals and public order' used in GATS Art. XIV (a) should be read so as to have the same reach. There is no reason why a measure should be exempted under GATS and condemned under GATT.[1041] This is all the more the case since both concepts overlap, as rightly argued by the panel.[1042] Admittedly, the Appellate Body in *US–Gambling* pointed to the different wording of GATS Art. XIV and GATT Art. XX, thereby indicating that the scope of the former provision could potentially be broader.[1043] However, this observation should not be read so as to mean that the term 'public morals' does not encompass core elements of the term 'public order'. Hence, GATT Art. XX (a) also refers to fundamental interests of society reflected in standards of law.

1035 *China–Publications and Audiovisual Products*, report of the panel, see also Van den Bossche/Zdouc, p. 629.

1036 *US–Gambling*, report of the panel, para. 6.462.

1037 Ibid. para. 6.461.

1038 Ibid.

1039 See also Delimatsis, p. 278.

1040 *US–Gambling*, report of the panel, para. 6.467.

1041 Cf. Marceau (WTO Dispute Settlement and Human Rights II), p. 202.

1042 *US–Gambling*, report of the panel, para. 6.462.

1043 *US–Gambling*, report of the Appellate Body, para. 291, fn 349.

The Appellate Body report *EC–Seal Products* has confirmed the findings of the panel in *US–Gambling*, stressing that members have the right to determine their own level of protection and may set different levels of protection when responding to similar interests of moral concern.[1044]

Whilst it is convincing to give members some policy space, it is also persuasive to hold with some legal authors that because of the purpose of GATT Art. XX to reconcile diverging interests of different WTO members, the term 'public morals' cannot be determined from a purely domestic point of view.[1045] The standard applied by *EC–Seal Products* does give WTO-members almost too much policy space that bears the risk of abuse of this provision and eventually discrimination. However, the panel in *Brazil–Taxation* held that it was within the scope of the term 'public morals' to bridge the digital divide and promote social inclusion. It emphasized that the particular objective must be a public moral objective for that member.[1046]

In light of these findings, human rights including the prohibition of child labour may well be found standards that determine conduct as right or wrong on behalf of a community or nation. Also, human rights including the prohibition of child labour may well be said to constitute a fundamental interest of a society reflected in public policy and a standard of law. Trade measures that pursue the protection of children from labour may thus be deemed to be designed to protect public morals.[1047]

Such a reading of the term 'public morals' is in accordance with the rules of interpretation of public international law. As mentioned above, the GATT 'is not to be read in clinical isolation from public international law'.[1048] While it might not seem to be necessary to refer to general international law given the broad scope the Appellate Body in *EC–Seal Products* has accorded to GATT Art. XX (a), it is nevertheless a useful exercise because this method of interpretation has the merit to also include the international perspective and to provide for more legal predictability and possibly more coherence of international law. According to Art. 31 (3) lit. c of the VCLT, any relevant rule of international law applicable in the relations between the parties may be taken into account. In *US–Shrimp*, the Appellate Body held that the words of GATT Art. XX should be read in the light of contemporary concerns of nations.[1049] Without explicitly

1044 *EC–Seal Products*, report of the Appellate Body, para. 5.200; Van den Bossche/Zdouc, p. 634.

1045 Feddersen, p. 252; Blüthner, p. 344 et seq.; Charnovitz (The Moral Exception), p. 701.

1046 Brazil – Taxation, report of the panel, para. 7.567.

1047 See also Cottier (The Implications of EC–Seal Products), p. 86.

1048 *US–Gasoline*, report of the Appellate Body, p. 18.

1049 *US–Shrimp*, report of the Appellate Body, para. 129.

referring to Art. 31 (3) lit. c of the VCLT, it took for example recourse to the 1982 United Nations Convention on the Law of the Sea and the Convention on Biological Diversity,[1050] stating that the term 'natural resources' in Art. XX (g) was not static but 'evolutionary' and thus to be read as including living resources.[1051]

It is however subject to question whether all WTO members must have ratified the human rights treaty referred to or at least the parties to the conflict. Referring to Art. 38 (1) ICJ Statute, Foltea holds that the treaty referred must be binding on the parties to conflict.[1052] Marceau has convincingly argued that it is sufficient under Art. 31 (3) lit. c of the VCLT that a majority of states parties of the treaty to be interpreted has accepted the treaty referred to.[1053] Specifically, she contends that the usage of the word 'parties' throughout Art. 31 of the VCLT reaching from 'all the parties' over 'one or more parties' to the 'other parties' suggests that the more general term 'the parties' refers to an uncertain number of parties. The Appellate Body in *US–Shrimp* took recourse to the Convention on Biological Diversity even though not all parties to the dispute were party to the Convention, relying also on the acknowledgement by the international community to protect living natural resources.[1054]

The same should hold true for the term 'public morals', given that human behaviour changes rapidly. Thus, human right norms that are applicable among WTO members may be in principle taken into account. Some legal scholars however argue that ILO norms should not be used to interpret GATT Art. XX (a) because of the different enforcement system of the ILO.[1055] Rather, ILO norms should be treated as evidence of national public morals. In the same vein, Foltea has read the *US–Shrimp* report as referring to Art. 31 (1) of the VCLT and the 'ordinary meaning' of the terms of the treaty.[1056] She held that the Appellate Body regarded all the documents referred to rather as evidentiary material than as normative rules.[1057] However, the Appellate Body, when referring to the Convention on Biological Diversity and UNCLOS, explicitly noted that Thailand and the US had not ratified but signed the Convention.[1058] This

1050 Ibid., para. 130.
1051 Ibid.
1052 Foltea, p. 114.
1053 Marceau (WTO Dispute Settlement and Human Rights I), p. 415. For a more detailed discussion of this issue see also Neumann, p. 368 et seqq.
1054 *US–Shrimp*, report of the Appellate Body, paras. 130–132.
1055 Ruffert, p. 164; Neumann, p. 403.
1056 Foltea, pp. 98–99.
1057 Ibid., p. 99.
1058 *US–Shrimp*, report of the Appellate Body, fn. 111.

reference to the status of ratification of the treaties with regard to the parties to the dispute indicates that Art. 31 (3) lit. c of the VCLT is applied here. The difference between the two paragraphs is, as Foltea rightly holds, that Art. 31 (3) lit. c of the VCLT pursues a more formal and systematic integration and is better suited to ensure coherence of international law.[1059] It makes of course a difference whether the WTO adjudicator refers to norms of other international treaties as facts or whether it uses them as authoritative legal norms when interpreting GATT norms. Thus, Art. 31 (3) lit. c of the VCLT should be applied when referring to UN and ILO norms.

The problem of different enforcement measures under different international enforcement mechanisms under the ILO and the WTO will be discussed below under the scope of application.

In addition, it has been argued that it would not be in accordance with the current interdependent public legal order not to take treaties into account that are ratified or accepted by the majority of states parties and that protect fundamental interests of states and human rights.[1060] The same reasoning should apply if one party to the conflict has not ratified the treaty referred to.[1061]

The panel in the *EC–Biotech Products* decision did not refer to Art. 31 (3) lit. c of the VCLT but to Art. 31 (1) of the VCLT according to which the terms of a treaty must be interpreted in accordance with the 'ordinary meaning' to be given to its terms in their context and in the light of its object and purpose.[1062] Specifically, it held that Art. 31 (3) lit. c of the VCLT only referred to such treaties that are applicable to all the parties of the dispute because otherwise, a sovereign state would be bound by a treaty it did not ratify. It argued that international conventions may also provide evidence of the ordinary meaning of the terms in the same way that dictionaries do.[1063] As discussed above, it is however preferable to apply Art. 31 (3) lit. c of the VCLT if possible.

The prohibition of child labour is contained in numerous human rights treaties that are ratified by a high number of states including the almost universally ratified CRC[1064] and the Worst Forms of Child Labour Convention.[1065] In addition, according to the ILO Declaration on Fundamental Principles and

1059 Foltea, p. 99.

1060 Neumann, p. 385.

1061 Ibid.

1062 *EC–Biotech Products*, report of the panel, paras. 7.70–7.72.

1063 Ibid., paras. 7.90–7.94.

1064 The CRC is ratified by 196 states except for the US that has only signed the Convention, https://indicators.ohchr.org/.

1065 ILO Convention No. 182 is ratified by 187 states, https://www.ilo.org/dyn/normlex/en/f?p=NORMLEXPUB:11300:0::NO:11300:P11300_INSTRUMENT_ID:312327:NO.

Rights at Work, ILO members have to respect, promote and realize the principles contained in the ILO Conventions No. 138 and 182.[1066] Thus, in case of child labour a majority of WTO members has ratified the relevant ILO and UN Conventions. In most cases, at least the parties to the disputes will be parties to the treaty referred to. It should therefore be possible to apply Art. 31 (3) lit. c of the VCLT and refer to ILO and UN Conventions on child labour when construing the term 'public morals'. The easiest way to construe 'public morals' as including the prohibition of child labour is of course to rely on its '*ius cogens*' nature as argued above, because *ius cogens* norms apply *erga omnes*, i.e. vis-à-vis all states.[1067]

The proposed reading of the public morals clause finds further support in the preparatory work to GATT Art. XX and prior trade treaties with a moral exception. The travaux préparatoires and prior trade treaties can be regarded as a means of supplementary interpretation within the meaning of Art. 32 of the VCLT.[1068] While the legislative history of GATT Art. XX (a) only reveals that this provision may be applicable to alcohol and thus suggests a broad scope,[1069] the travaux préparatoires of earlier trade treaties are more helpful. For example, the negotiating history of the 1927 International Convention for the Abolition of Import and Export Prohibitions and Restrictions[1070] reveals that the 'exception for prohibitions or restrictions imposed for moral or humanitarian reasons, provided that the manufacture of and trade in goods to which the prohibition relate are also prohibited or restricted in the interior of the country', was partly considered to permit export bans on goods made under forced or compulsory labour.[1071] Numerous other bilateral and multilateral treaties prohibit trade on moral grounds prohibiting slave trade,[1072] the

1066 See Humbert (The Challenge of Child Labour), p. 104 et seq.

1067 See above, p. 96 et seq.

1068 Charnovitz (The Moral Exception), p. 705 held that such prior trade treaties constituted preparatory work according to Art. 32 of the VCLT.

1069 Statement of a Norwegian delegate in the Report of the Drafting Committee of the United Nations Conference on Trade and Employment, UN ESCOR, UN Doc. E/PC/T/34, Mar.5, 1947 cited in Charnovitz (The Moral Exception), p. 704.

1070 International Convention For the Abolition of Import and Export Prohibitions and Restrictions, Nov. 8, 1927, 36 Stat. 2461, 97 L.N.T.S. 393, cited in Charnovitz (The Moral Exception), p. 706; The Convention did not entered into force.

1071 Statement of Senator Arthur Vandenberg in 71 CONG. Rec 3744 (1929), cited in Charnovitz (The Moral Exception), p. 707.

1072 e.g. Additional Convention between Great Britain and Portugal for the Prevention of the Slave Trade, July 28, 1817, Art. III, 67 Consol. T. S. 373, 398 cited in Charnovitz (The Moral Exception), p. 711.

importation of opium,[1073] traffic in liquor[1074] and obscene publications,[1075] or the importation of fish caught by the use of explosives.[1076] Noteworthy is an informal moral embargo of 1940 prohibiting the export of gasoline for any country engaged in the bombing of civilians.[1077]

In sum, the term 'public morals' can be read to encompass the prohibition of child labour.

10.2.2 Scope of Application – Extraterritoriality

10.2.2.1 *The Ius Cogens Nature of the Prohibition of Child Labour*

Having established that the term 'public morals' may be read to refer to international rules prohibiting child labour, the question arises whether GATT Art. XX (a) allows for domestic measures that aim at eliminating child labour abroad, i.e. extraterritorial measures.[1078] Regarding the substance of the term child labour, there is in principle no territorial limitation included. By contrast, it is the very rationale of *ius cogens* to establish an *ordre public* for the international community.[1079] *Ius cogens* norms apply *erga omnes*. Thus, one could argue that the public morals of the international community are concerned and that there is no problem of extraterritoriality. In a similar vein, Feddersen

1073 International Opium Convention, Jan. 1912, Art. 7, 38 Stat. 1912, 1931 cited Charnovitz (The Moral Exception), p. 711.

1074 Convention for the Suppression of the Contraband Traffic in Alcoholic Liquors, Aug. 9, 1925, 42 L.N.T.S. 73 cited in Charnovitz (The Moral Exception), p. 712.

1075 International Convention for the Suppression of the Circulation of and Traffic in Obscene Publications, opened for signature Sept. 12, 1923, art. 1, 27 L.N.T.S. 215, 223 cited in Charnovitz (The Moral Exception), p. 712.

1076 Agreement Concluded between the Delegates of the Kingdom of Italy and the Kingdom of the Serbs, Croats and Slovenes, Regarding a Draft Convention for the Regulation of Fishing in the Adriatic, Sept. 14, 1921, art. 28, 19 L.N.T.S. 29, 45 cited in Charnovitz (The Moral Exception), p. 712.

1077 11 Dig. Of Int'L Law 423 (Marjorie M. Whiteman ed., 1968) cited in Charnovitz (The Moral Exception), p. 715.

1078 The Appellate Body in *US–Shrimp*, para. 133 deals with extraterritoriality when discussing the policy goal of the measure. Other authors, e.g. Blüthner, p. 359, deal with it under the *chapeau* of GATT Art. XX. In view of the author of this study, as will be explained below, the issue of extraterritoriality under GATT Art. XX lit. a concerns the question whether domestic measures – even if they also protect the public morals of the nationals of the regulating state – may aim at protecting children abroad. Only when knowing whether children abroad may be targeted as a policy goal, one can ask whether a measure is necessary to protect these children. By contrast, the test under the *chapeau* reveals whether the regulating state acted in good faith when adopting an extraterritorial measure.

1079 Verdross/Simma, p. 328; Marceau (WTO Dispute Settlement and Human Rights II), p. 213; Hailbronner, p. 5 et seq.

concludes from the universally applicable prohibition of child labour that there is no problem of extraterritorial jurisdiction.[1080]

However, as rightly pointed out by Howse, the question of whether there are territorial limitations to the term 'public morals' in GATT Art. XX (a) is sometimes confused with whether a country could use a provision, such as Art. XX (a), to justify measures that might violate general norms of public international law concerning extraterritorial jurisdiction.[1081] As has been found above, unilateral trade measures on child labour usually pursue several objectives including protecting national interests of commerce and/or morals, and the abolition of child labour abroad.[1082] And according to WTO case law, all the evidence relating to purposes is relevant as long as it has found expression in the design of the statute.[1083] Thus, the issue of extraterritoriality is not resolved by simply referring to the *ius cogens* aim of possible trade measures. Guidance on the issue of extraterritorial applicability of trade measures may be found in the structure of GATT Art. XX itself as well as in applicable rules of general international law on extraterritorial effects of state acts and in the examination of the legal consequences of *ius cogens.*

10.2.2.2 *GATT and WTO Jurisprudence*

The panel in the two cases *US–Tuna I and II* determined that US embargoes on tuna caught in a dolphin-unfriendly way violated GATT Art. XX (b) and (g).[1084]

In particular, the panel in *US–Tuna I* held that neither Art. XX (b) nor (g) permitted an extra-jurisdictional application because this would lead to other CONTRACTING PARTIESjeopardizing their rights.[1085]

Adopting a different approach, the panel in *US–Tuna II* held that the GATT in principle did not prohibit measures regulating things located or actions occurring outside the territorial jurisdiction.[1086] However, it then continued that measures taken so as to force other countries to change their policies

---

1080 Feddersen, pp. 261 and 262; Similarly Neumann, p. 142 who infers from the public indignation in the US or EU about child labour in Asia that domestic public morals of these WTO members are concerned.

1081 Howse (Shrimp/Turtle), p. 1369. In a similar vein, Ruffert, p. 164 and Neumann, p. 403 argue that ILO norms should not be relied upon to interpret GATT Art. XX (a) because such an interpretation interferes with the different enforcement system under the ILO. They call this rule 'Störungsverbot'.

1082 See Humbert (The Challenge of Child Labour in International Law), pp. 284 et seqq.

1083 See above, p. 149.

1084 *US–Tuna I*, report of the panel, para. 7.1; *US–Tuna II*, report of the panel, para. 6.1.

1085 *US–Tuna I*, report of the panel, para. 5.32.

1086 *US–Tuna II*, report of the panel, para. 5.32.

could neither be considered to be related to the conservation of an exhaustible resource nor necessary within the meaning of GATT Art. XX (g) and (b).[1087] If countries were permitted to impose trade embargoes to force other countries to change their policies within their jurisdiction, the objectives of the GATT would be seriously impaired.[1088]

These findings are not of much help regarding the issue of extraterritoriality. They only concern npr-ppm-measures that are able to force other countries to change their policies and leave open the issue of extraterritoriality itself. The panel in both cases failed to set forth criteria for determining the legality of measures with extraterritorial effects in relation to the GATT.

The panel in *EC–Tariff Preferences* found that the Drug Arrangements are not justified under GATT Art. XX (b) because they do not aim at protecting human health in the European Communities.[1089] It thus applied a territorial limitation to GATT Art. XX (b).

In *US–Shrimp*,[1090] the Appellate Body stated:

> The sea turtle species here at stake, i.e., covered by Section 609, are all known to occur in waters over which the US exercises jurisdiction. [...] We do not pass upon the question of whether there is an applied jurisdictional limitation in Article XX (g), and if so, the nature or extent of that limitation. We note only that in the specific circumstances of the case before us, there is a sufficient nexus between the migratory and endangered marine population involved and the United States for purposes of Article XX (g).[1091]

The Appellate Body in this case neither resolved the issue of extraterritoriality in relation to the GATT. Instead, it held that there was a sufficient nexus in case of a physical connection between the public good to be protected and the territory of the regulating state. Put differently, the issue of extraterritoriality and sovereignty cannot be utilized to defeat a measure if there is a sufficient nexus. It is questionable whether this test can and should be applied to child labour or labour standards.

It has rightly been held that when applying the sufficient nexus test to the area of labour rights, one has to take account of the particularities of labour

1087 *US–Tuna II*, report of the panel, paras. 5.27 and 5.39.

1088 Ibid., para. 5.38.

1089 *EC–Tariff Preferences*, report of the panel, para. 7.210.

1090 *US–Shrimp*, report of the Appellate Body, para. 133.

1091 Ibid.

rights.[1092] In the view of Blüthner, the sufficient nexus is established if one can prove that the violation of labour rights in the exporting state causes trade deficits in the importing state.[1093] As demonstrated by US case law, this link is however difficult to establish.[1094] This might be due to the fact that the loss of commercial benefits may be caused by a variety of factors including the general economic situation of the importing country. Whilst an increasing trade deficit in the whole country might be attributable to lower labour standards in exporting countries, it is difficult to establish a causal link in the individual case. However, one could imagine that in a few cases, low-cost imported clothes or carpets made by children in India, China or Bangladesh may cause a loss of market share and therefore job losses in the EU or the US. In these cases, the required link could be established.

Thus, only in a minority of cases, a similar nexus to the one in *US–Shrimp* could be established.

The recent *EC–Seal Products* decision is not of much help either. The Appellate Body upheld the panel's finding that in this case, the measure addressed seal welfare concerns of EU citizens and consumers and, since the participants did not address the issue in their appeals, concluded that

> Accordingly, while recognizing the systemic importance of the question of whether there is an implied jurisdictional limitation in Article XX (a), and, if so, the nature and extent of that limitation, we have decided in this case not to examine this question further.[1095]

It should be noted that it referred to the panel's observation that concerns regarding seal welfare had two aspects, namely the incidence of inhumane killing and the EU citizens' individual and collective participation as consumers in, and exposure to ("abetting"), the economic activity which sustains the market for seal products derived from inhumane hunts.[1096] Thus, the concerns relate on the one hand to seals within and outside the EU and on the other hand to the behaviour of EU consumers and citizens. Therefore, the regulation has some extraterritorial effects. The *EC–Seal Products* decision indicates

1092 Blüthner, p. 371.

1093 Ibid.

1094 A complaint under Section 307 of the Trade Act of 1974 was rejected because a direct link between China's repression of workers' rights and US job losses could not be established, see Humbert. (The Challenge of Child Labour), p. 284 et seq.

1095 *EC–Seal Products*, report of the Appellate Body, para. 5.173.

1096 Ibid., para. 5.139.

that under GATT Art. XX (a), domestic measures that deploy effects abroad can probably be adopted.[1097] Similarly, it has been pointed out[1098] that the Appellate Body in *EC–Seal Products* held that GATT Art. XX justifies exactly those aspects of a measure that were the reason of the GATT-inconsistency in the first place. Given that that such reasons were animal welfare abroad and EU consumers' concerns, such statement also is a strong hint that measures with extraterritorial effects are within the scope.

In sum however, it is still an open question whether GATT Art. XX (a) has a limited territorial jurisdiction.[1099] This will in turn be answered according to the rules of treaty interpretation contained in Art. 31 and 32 of the VCLT, taking recourse to the general international law on extraterritorial jurisdiction and the concept of *ius cogens*.

10.2.2.3 *Interpreting GATT Art. XX (a) in Its Context*

As rightly held by some legal authors, the contextual approach to GATT Art. XX does not solve the problem.[1100] Although GATT Art. XX (e) clearly refers to products made by prison labour and allows for measures with extraterritorial effects, it does not follow that the other exceptions also permit this kind of measures. For one could conclude that either *argumentum e contrario* or *expressio unius est exclusion alterius* the other exception under the remaining paragraphs do not allow for this kind of measures, or that by way of analogy, measures with extraterritorial effects are allowed.[1101] Yet, one can conclude that GATT Art. XX is not inherently hostile to extraterritorial measures.

10.2.2.4 *The General International Law on Extraterritorial Jurisdiction and the Concept of Ius Cogens*

In accordance with Art. 31 (3) lit. c of the VCLT, recourse will be taken to general international law on extraterritorial jurisdiction and general public international law regarding *ius cogens*.

It has been established that indistinctly applicable trade-related npr-ppm-measures relating to child labour with extraterritorial effects are not *per se* contrary to GATT Art. III.[1102] The main legal arguments were that these measures

1097 Cottier (The implications of EC–Seal Products), p. 88.

1098 Cf. Van den Bossche/Zdouc, pp. 600–601 referring to EC – Seal Products, report of the Appellate Body, para. 5.185.

1099 Cf. Van den Bossche/Zdouc, p. 600.

1100 Bartels (Extraterritorial Jurisdiction), pp. 358 and 359; Feddersen, pp. 244 and 245.

1101 Bartels (Extraterritorial Jurisdiction), pp. 358 and 359.

1102 See the discussion above pp. 66 et seqq.

aimed at implementing international human rights norms, thereby relating to international concerns for which states ceded part of their sovereignty. Hence, they established a meaningful connection to foreign state interests in accordance with the general international law on extraterritorial effects of state acts. The same should hold true for GATT Art. XX (a).

As the analysis of GATT Art. III has shown, another legal argument relates to the concept of *ius cogens* and *erga omnes.*[1103] Since violations of peremptory human rights norms may entitle third states to respond to these violations through adopting trade measures, indistinctly applicable npr-ppm-measures on child labour can be argued to be, *argumentum a maiore ad minus*, GATT Art. III-consistent as regards the aspect of extraterritoriality. Thus, indistinctly applicable ppm-measures, which are different from country-based measures, should not be *per se* GATT-inconsistent in case they aim at implementing *ius cogens* norms and apply *erga omnes*. The same should hold true in case of GATT Art. XX (a). Hence, the proposed EU Forced Labour Regulation, US ban on goods made with forced or indentured child labour or the Belgian Social Label Law should not be held contrary to GATT Art. XX (a) because of their extraterritorial effects.

10.2.2.5 *Extraterritoriality and Country-Specific Measures*

The issue of extraterritoriality might be resolved differently in case of country-based measures such as the UFLPA, 2003 US Burmese Freedom and Democracy Act or national bans under the Kimberley Process Certification Scheme. The law on extraterritorial effects does not serve as an interpretational tool since such measures are clearly extraterritorial. It seems more appropriate to draw on general public international law, which allows for countermeasures in response to *ius cogens* violations. It should be recalled that the WTO is a *lex specialis* regime for economic countermeasures.[1104] On this basis, it seems to be appropriate to apply GATT Art. XX (a) to economic countermeasures.

Hahn concluded from the wording, context and drafting history that GATT Art. XXI, rather than GATT Art. XX, conclusively regulates countermeasures taken in response to violations of non-GATT law.[1105] However, he did not examine GATT Art. XX in detail but sought to determine the relationship between GATT Art. XXI and general public international law. In any event, his view that

---

1103 See the discussion of the concept of *ius cogens* and *erga omnes* above p. 96.

1104 See the discussion of countermeasures in response to *ius cogens* and of the *lex specialis* regime above pp. 96 et seqq.

1105 Hahn, p. 365.

GATT law regulates economic countermeasures supports the finding that GATT Art. XX is not hostile to countermeasures.

Having said this, the ruling of the panel and Appellate Body *Mexico–Soft Drinks and Other Beverages* could be interpreted as meaning that GATT Art. XX does not apply to international countermeasures.[1106] In this case, Mexico had argued that its taxes were 'necessary' in accordance with GATT Art. XX (d)[1107] to secure compliance by the US with the US obligations under the NAFTA, an international agreement that is not inconsistent with the provisions of the GATT.[1108] The panel and the Appellate Body both held that the measure in question imposed by Mexico was not 'necessary' to secure compliance with laws or regulations consistent with WTO law stating that GATT Art. XX (d) do not encompass countermeasures in accordance with international obligations.[1109]

Yet, in its analysis, the Appellate Body explicitly relied on the wording and structure of GATT Art. XX (d). It is thus doubtful whether these findings also apply to GATT Art. XX lit. a. Specifically, the Appellate Body examined the term 'laws or regulations' and held that these terms referred only to domestic laws or regulations of the regulating WTO member and did not include obligations of another WTO member under an international agreement (which would give rise to countermeasures).[1110] It argued that the matters listed in GATT Art. XX (d) referred to the domestic legal system and that where international agreements were referred to in GATT, the text would say so.[1111] Thus, this ruling does not exclude countermeasures from the entire scope of GATT Art. XX.

It should however be noted that the Appellate Body in *Mexico–Soft Drinks and Other Beverages* stated that it was not the function of WTO adjudicating bodies to assess whether another international agreement had been violated.[1112] It referred to the drafting history of GATT Art. XX where India rejected

1106 *Mexico–Soft Drinks and Other Beverages*, report of the panel and the Appellate Body Report.

1107 GATT Art. XX (d) reads: '[...] necessary to secure compliance with laws or regulations which are not inconsistent with the provisions of this Agreement, including those relating to customs enforcement, the enforcement of monopolies operated under paragraph 4 of Article II and Article XVII, the protection of patents, trademarks and copyrights, and the prevention of deceptive practices; [...]'.

1108 *Mexico–Soft Drinks and Other Beverages*, report of the panel, para. 8.162.

1109 Ibid., para. 8.170–8.181; *Mexico–Soft Drinks and Other Beverages*, report of the Appellate Body, para. 79.

1110 *Mexico–Soft Drinks and Other Beverages*, report of the Appellate Body, para. 69.

1111 Ibid., paras. 70 and 71.

1112 *Mexico–Soft Drinks and Other Beverages*, report of the Appellate Body, para. 78.

a proposal that GATT Art. XX would allow for retaliatory measures. Hence, the Appellate Body is generally reluctant to assess the legality of trade measures imposed under a different legal regime under GATT Art. XX.

In case of the Burmese Freedom and Democracy Act the question would not be whether the violation of ILO Conventions entitled the ILO Governing Body to recommend trade measures but whether the trade measures recommended are in accordance with the GATT.[1113] The same holds true for national measures imposed under the Kimberley Process Certification Scheme. Thus, both measures may be examined under GATT Art. XX (a). In conclusion, GATT Art. XX (a) should be read so as to apply to countermeasures in case of human rights violations.

10.2.3 The Necessity Test

GATT Art. XX (a) further requires that trade measures have to be necessary to protect public morals.

10.2.3.1 *GATT and WTO Jurisprudence*

In *Colombia–Textiles*, the Appellate Body held that in order to be justified under Art. XX (a), 'first, a measure must be "designed" to protect public morals. Second, the measure must be 'necessary' to protect such public morals'.[1114] 'Designed' to protect public morals requires a relationship between the measure and the protection of public morals, i.e. the measure must not be incapable of protecting public morals.[1115] Specifically, the Appellate Body held that the tariff in question was not incapable of combating money laundering and found a relationship between the measure and the protection of public morals.[1116] Thus, it is a rather broad range of measures that can be found to be designed to protect public morals.

When examining whether a measure is designed at protecting public morals, a panel must not only look at a member's characterization of the objective of the measure but at all evidence put before it.[1117]

The measures at issue, i.e. the US ban on goods made with forced or indentured child labour, the Belgian Social Label Law, the proposed EU Forced Labour Regulation, the UFPLA, the US Burmese Freedom and Democracy Act

1113 See also Marceau (Trade and Labour), p. 553 who holds that countermeasures could find application under the exceptions of GATT Art. XX.

1114 *Colombia–Textiles*, report of the Appellate Body, paras. 5.67–5.68.

1115 Ibid., para. 5.68.

1116 Ibid., para. 5.89; Van den Bossche/Zdouc, p. 635.

1117 *EC–Seal Products*, report of the panel, para. 5.144; cf. Van den Bossche/Zdouc, p. 630.

and national bans under the Kimberley Certification Scheme, can be considered to be not incapable of contributing to protecting children from exploitative labour.

The second element of 'necessity' requires a 'more in-depth, holistic analysis'.[1118]

The first important GATT case on necessity was the *Thailand–Cigarettes* case.[1119] The panel held that the term 'necessary' was the same under paragraphs (b) and (d) and referred to the case *US–Section 337*.[1120] In this case, the panel had stated that a measure was necessary within the meaning of GATT Art. XX (d) if an alternative measure was not reasonably expected to be employed or available.[1121] The panel in *Thailand–Cigarettes* concluded that import restrictions could be considered necessary in terms of GATT Art. XX (b) only if there was no alternative measure consistent with the GATT, or less inconsistent with it, which Thailand could reasonably be expected to employ to achieve its health policies.[1122] Hence, the test was whether the GATT-inconsistency was necessary to achieve the stated goal of the measure.

In *Korea–Beef*, the Appellate Body held that the term 'necessary' referred to a range of degrees of necessity.[1123] At one end of the continuum was necessary as indispensable, at the other end, necessary meant making a contribution to.[1124] In relation to GATT Art. XX (d), it considered a necessary measure to be closer to the pole of indispensable.[1125] Furthermore, it held that the relative importance of the common interests or values that the law to be enforced was intended to protect, should be taken into account.[1126] The more vital or important those interests or values were, the easier it would be to accept as necessary a measure designed as an enforcement instrument.[1127] Another factor was the extent to which the measure contributed to the realization of the aim pursued.[1128] It concluded by stating that a measure that was not indispensable might nevertheless be necessary, and that the interpretation of necessary involved a process of weighing and balancing of factors such as the

1118 Ibid., para. 5.70.
1119 *Thailand–Cigarettes.*
1120 *US–Section 337*, report of the panel.
1121 *US–Section 337*, report of the panel para. 5.26.
1122 *Thailand–Cigarettes*, report of the panel, para. 75.
1123 *Korea–Beef*, report of the Appellate Body, para. 161.
1124 Ibid.
1125 Ibid.
1126 Ibid., para. 162.
1127 Ibid., para. 162.
1128 Ibid., para. 163.

contribution made by the measure to the enforcement of the law at issue, the importance of the common interests or values protected and the accompanying impact of the law or regulation on imports or exports.[1129] It reconciled its findings with the case *US–Section 337* stating that the weighing and balancing process was part of the determination whether an alternative measure was reasonably be expected to be employed or reasonably available.[1130]

The Appellate Body in *EC–Asbestos*[1131] and *Dominican Republic–Cigarettes*[1132] confirmed this sort of necessity test that included a weighing and balancing, taking into account the various interests at stake. In particular, in *EC–Asbestos*, it held that the more important the societal value pursued by the measure at issue and the more this measure contributes to the protection or promotion of this value, the more easily the measure at issue may be considered 'necessary'.[1133] Moreover, the Appellate Body in *Dominican Republic–Cigarettes* has held that an alternative measure must not be merely theoretical in nature, i.e. the member has to be capable of taking it, and the measure must not impose an undue burden on that member, such as prohibitive costs or substantial technical difficulties.[1134] In addition, the alternative measure must ensure the members' right to achieve its desired level of protection with respect to the objective pursued.[1135] Noteworthy, especially with regard to import bans, is the statement of the Appellate Body in *EC–Seal Products* that a responding member cannot be reasonably expected to employ an alternative measure that involves a continuation of the very risk that the challenged measure seeks to halt.[1136] In this case, the EU could not be expected to adopt a certification scheme that risked increasing market access of seals products and exposure of the EU public to more inhumanely killed seals.

In relation to GATS Art. XIV, the Appellate Body confirmed that a necessity test involved a weighing and balancing of the relative importance of the interests or values furthered by the challenged measure along with other factors such as the restrictive impact of the measure on international commerce.[1137] This approach has been reiterated in *China–Publications and Audiovisual Products* and extended to 'those wishing to engage in importing, in particular

1129 Ibid., para. 164.
1130 Ibid., para. 165.
1131 *EC–Asbestos*, report of the Appellate Body, paras. 171–172.
1132 *Dominican Republic–Cigarettes*, report of the Appellate Body, paras. 65–70.
1133 *EC–Asbestos*, report of the Appellate Body, para. 172.
1134 *Dominican Republic–Cigarettes*, report of the Appellate Body, paras. 65–70.
1135 Ibid.
1136 *EC–Seal Products*, report of the Appellate Body, para. 5.273.
1137 *US–Gambling*, report of the Appellate Body, paras. 306 and 307.

on their right to trade'.[1138] It remains to be seen whether such a reading constitutes the first step towards more recognition of individuals and their economic human rights under WTO law.[1139]

The most important case in recent case law is *Brazil–Retreaded Tyres*.[1140] It elaborated on the weighing and balancing test, holding that a panel must firstly

> consider the relevant factors, particularly the importance of the interests at stake, the extent of the contribution to the achievement of the measure's objective, and its trade restrictiveness. If this analysis yields a preliminary conclusion that the measure is necessary, this result must be confirmed by comparing the measure with possible alternatives, which may be less trade restrictive while providing an equivalent contribution to the achievement of the objective. This comparison should be carried out in the light of the importance of the interests or values at stake.[1141]

Further, it held that the

> weighing and balancing is a holistic operation that involves putting all variables of the equation together and evaluating them in relation to each other after having examined them individually, in order to reach an overall judgement.[1142]

As regards the contribution of the measure to achieve its objective, the Appellate Body stated that the measure must either be deemed to already bring about a material contribution to the achievement of its objective shown by evidence and data from past or presence, or be considered to be apt to produce a material contribution referring to either quantitative projections or qualitative reasoning supported by sufficient evidence.[1143] With respect to import bans, it found that a marginal or insignificant contribution was not sufficient.[1144] A sufficient 'contribution exists when there is a genuine relationship of ends and means between the objective pursued and the measure

1138 *China–Publications and Audiovisual Products*, report of the panel, para. 300.
1139 Cf. Delimatsis, p. 285.
1140 *Brazil–Retreaded Tyres*, report of the Appellate Body.
1141 Ibid., para. 178.
1142 Ibid., para. 182.
1143 Ibid., para. 151.
1144 Ibid., para. 150.

at issue'.[1145] In *Colombia–Textiles*, the Appellate Body held that a panel shall assess the quantitative and qualitative contribution of the measure to the end pursued.[1146]

It follows from the above analysis that the necessity test as established by GATT/WTO jurisprudence has evolved from a mere necessity test in a sense of a less trade-restrictive means test to a proportionality test requiring a thorough weighing and balancing of different values.

10.2.3.2 *Questioning the Weighing and Balancing Test under* GATT *Art.* XX

Questioning the weighing and balancing test, some authors have argued in the past that the Appellate Body cannot balance national policy interests with trade interests underlying the WTO agreements as a result of any proportionality requirement.[1147] In their view, the Appellate Body Report in *Korea–Beef*, in contrast to its explicit statements, cannot be read as establishing a balancing test. Instead, the test is whether a measure is sufficiently linked to a stated policy goal.[1148] Moreover, a balancing of constitutional values needs strong democratic legitimacy, also in respect to the application of rules in the dispute settlement process.[1149] In contrast to the EU, where the ECJ conducts a proportionality test, the WTO is not ready for classical proportionality from an institutional perspective.[1150]

As the different tests may lead to very different results, it is important to decide the issue. For example, applying the necessity test as developed in *Thailand–Cigarettes*[1151] to import bans on goods made with child labour, one can easily think of less trade-restrictive measures such as labelling. If one however conducted a weighing and balancing test, one could argue that given the status of the prohibition of child labour as a norm of *ius cogens*, public policy goals of the importing member would prevail over trade interests of other WTO members and make the measure GATT-consistent.[1152]

1145 Ibid., para. 145.
1146 *Colombia–Textiles*, report of the Appellate Body, para. 5.72.
1147 Desmedt, p. 469 et seq.; Blüthner, p. 128 et seq.; Neumann/Türk, p. 214 et seq.
1148 Desmedt, p. 469 et seq.
1149 Neumann/Türk, p. 214 et seq.
1150 Ibid.
1151 *Thailand–Cigarettes*, report of the panel, paras. 74 and 75.
1152 See the discussion under GATT Art. III, pp. 181 et seqq.

10.2.3.3 *Towards Constitutionalization*

Admittedly, the Appellate Body in its case law has not always conducted a proper balancing test in which it weighed public policy interests against the trade impact of a measure. Indeed, for instance in *Korea–Beef*, in essence, it has assessed whether Korea could achieve its desired level of enforcement by more WTO-consistent measures, taking into account the distribution of enforcement costs between imported and domestic products.[1153] In *EC–Asbestos* however, paying due respect to the right of a member to determine its level of health protection, the Appellate Body indirectly gave more weight to the public policy pursued than to the negative impact on trade of the measure.[1154] Equally, in *Brazil–Retreaded Tyres*, the Appellate Body duly considered the trade restrictiveness of the import ban and weighed this against the environmental concerns that the measures sought to protect.[1155] It upheld the panel's finding that the importance of the interests protected by the import ban outweighed its trade restrictiveness.[1156] Also in *EC–Seal Products*, the Appellate Body thoroughly discussed the societal value and objective of the measure, the level of protection sought by the EU, the trade impact and the contribution of the measure to the objective pursued and compared this to alternative measures. It found that the EU did not have to employ a certification scheme that bore the risk of not adequately protecting the welfare concerns of its citizens. However, the Appellate Body in *China–Publications and Audiovisual Products* appears to prove the contrary, holding that a genuine alternative measure was a governmental content review mechanism, i.e. a measure that obviously curtails freedom of expression.[1157] Yet, the decision should not be used as an argument *contra* the application of a weighing and balancing test because the decision may well be the result of the frustration of the members of the Appellate Body by the lack of transparency and evidence caused by China[1158] and as such constitutes an exception to the rule. Also, whilst the human right of freedom of expression was not taken into account, the panel nevertheless weighed and balanced the importance of the objective of Chinese public morals, the contribution of the measures to this aim and their trade restrictiveness.[1159]

1153 *Korea–Beef*, report of the Appellate Body, paras. 178–182.

1154 *EC–Asbestos*, report of the Appellate Body, para. 174.

1155 *Brazil–Retreaded Tyres*, report of the Appellate Body.

1156 Ibid., para. 179.

1157 *China–Publications and Audiovisual Products*, report of the Appellate Body, paras. 322–332.

1158 Cf. Delimatsis, p. 286.

1159 *China–Publications and Audiovisual Products*, report of the panel, paras. 7.848, 7.868, 7.828, 7.836.

Given the number of cases confirming the weighing and balancing test, the WTO adjudicating bodies obviously consider themselves as mature to apply such a test. In addition to the cases cited above, panels and the Appellate Body in for example *US–Shrimp*, the *EC–Biotech Products* and *US–Tuna II* (*Mexico*) already have demonstrated that they are able to take non-economic values protected by public international law into account. In this context, it has been admitted that the relaxation of the necessity test may enhance the coordination of WTO law with other treaties and improve the acceptance of the WTO adjudicating bodies.[1160] Also, if non-economic values are based on international conventions ratified by a majority of WTO members, there is less a risk of a democratic deficit and legitimacy. Equally, in the other cases cited above, the dispute settlement bodies have demonstrated that they are able to strike a reasonable balance between non-economic values such as public morals, human health and trade liberalization. It follows that instead of refraining from weighing and balancing tests that require considering human rights as suggested by some authors,[1161] the Appellate Body should continue to engage in such balancing exercise.

Such view is warranted in light of the fact that the principle of proportionality is enshrined in Art. 51 of the Articles on State Responsibility and has been recognized by the Appellate Body as an authoritative statement of customary international law to be taken into account.[1162] Even though WTO law has been found to be *lex specialis* regime and its necessity test does not mention the word 'proportional', it should nevertheless be construed in line with general international law asking for a proportionality test. As analysed above, WTO law should not be read 'in clinical isolation from international law' and take into account rules of general international law.[1163] According to Art. 51, countermeasures must be commensurate with the injury suffered, taking into account the gravity of the internationally wrongful act and the rights in question. It is widely agreed that the proportionality of countermeasures should be assessed on both quantitative and qualitative grounds, it is not only must the means chosen be appropriate to the aim but the aim itself of the countermeasures must be reasonable and appropriate.[1164] Thus, the importance of the issue of

1160 Neumann/Türk, p. 217.

1161 Delimatsis, p. 287.

1162 *US–Line Pipe*, report of the Appellate Body, para. 259; Materials on the Responsibility of States for Internationally Wrongful Acts, p. 520.

1163 See above, p. 96 and *US–Gasoline*, report of the Appellate Body, p. 18.

1164 See Gabckovo – Nagymaros, ICJ Reports 1997, p. 7, 56; Crawford (State Responsibility), p. 699.

principle involved must be considered. Such analysis shall be partly independent of the question of whether the countermeasure was necessary to achieve the result of ensuring compliance.[1165] Given that already general international law obliges the adjudicator to make a value judgement, there is no obvious reason why the WTO adjudicating bodies should refrain from making value judgements.

In the light of the fact that a reasonable balancing and weighing process is at the heart of constitutionalism, it has convincingly been argued that this recent trend of the WTO jurisprudence towards proportionality can be called a 'constitutionalization in a modest sense'.[1166] And, building on this assumption, the pressing question is whether the functionalist approach of the GATT should move to a constitutionalist framework of analysis? These broader issues will be taken up later in this work when making conclusions from this analysis of the status quo of child labour in WTO law.[1167] For the moment it suffices to state that it is appropriate for the WTO judiciary to conduct a weighing and balancing test. This is all more the case regarding the prohibition of child labour, which is contained in international conventions and even part of *ius cogens*.

10.2.3.4 *Applying the Proportionality Test to Trade Measures on Child Labour*

10.2.3.4.1 US Import Ban on Goods Made with Forced or Indentured Child Labour and the Proposed EU Forced Labour Regulation

In case of the US import ban, the factors to be considered are the *ius cogens* aim of the ban, the implementation of the prohibition of child labour by the CBP,[1168] the contribution of the ban to the reduction of child labour and the adverse trade effect on imports of goods made with child labour into the US.

Alternative measures that could be reasonably available may be labelling requirements. The question is whether these are equally effective. Other less trade-restrictive measures may be the provision of aid to child labourers or import bans accompanied by flanking measures such as financial aid and education.

At first sight, it seems to be appealing to infer from the *ius cogens* nature of the prohibition of child labour that the importance of the reduction of child labour outweighs its trade restrictiveness and makes it 'necessary' within the meaning of GATT Art. XX (a).

1165 UN (Materials on the Responsibility of States for Internationally Wrongful Acts), p. 519.

1166 Cottier (Limits to International Trade), p. 221.

1167 See below Chapter 4, also p. 386.

1168 See above, p. 15.

However, when applying the weighing and balancing test, one has to ask whether a trade ban or other economic measure contributes substantially to the end pursued, i.e. to the protection of children from economic exploitation.

Furthermore, even in case of countermeasures in response to *ius cogens* violations, a proportionality test has to be conducted in accordance with Art. 51 of the Articles on State Responsibility. The *ius cogens* aim thus does not *ipso facto* make a measure 'necessary'. Rather, it is a strong argument in favour of the measure.

When examining to which extend trade measures on child labour contribute to the reduction of child labour, it should be recalled that the announcement of the adoption of the Child Labour Deterrence Act in the US (the 'Harkin Bill') prohibiting imports of goods produced by children made many children in Bangladesh lose their jobs and drove them into prostitution.[1169] Thus, instead of contributing to the reduction of child labour, a blanket ban on imports on goods made with child labour may even make the situation worse.

However, at the same time, it has been found that trade measures can be useful tools for *initiating* action against child labour. For example, in reaction to the announcement of the Child Labour Deterrence Act, the Bangladesh Garment Manufacturers and Exporters Association started an initiative together with the ILO and UNICEF to reduce child labour by enrolling them in schools and paying compensation to families of former child labourers.[1170] This initiative has eventually proven to be successful. The same has been the case with the US ban on goods made with forced and indentured child labour since CBP started modifying WRO in response to removal of ILO forced labour indicators.[1171] Hence, import bans on goods made with child labour may be considered as being 'apt to make a material contribution' to the elimination of child labour. Given the vital interest of society in the reduction of child labour and the universal acceptance of the prohibition of child labour, import bans could be provisionally deemed to be 'necessary'.

Thus, the question is whether there are less trade-restrictive alternative measures. At first sight, the provision of aid to child labourers and their families, or an international complaint with the ILO according to Art. 26 of the ILO Constitution would appear to be less trade restrictive and equally effective. Such a measure would also correspond to the multi-pronged strategy for combating child labour embraced by the ILO or IPEC.[1172]

1169 See Humbert (The Challenge of Child Labour in International Law), pp. 368–369.

1170 Ibid.

1171 See above, p. 15.

1172 Humbert (The Challenge of Child Labour in International Law), pp. 180 et seqq.

However, the provision of aid puts substantial financial and administrative burdens on the regulating member. To reach all potential child labourers worldwide – as does a trade ban at least as regards the export industry – the importing member would have to provide international aid to all countries where child labourers are reported to be, or lodge complaints against all these states. According to the international law on child labour, the primary obligation to take legislative, administrative and educational measures against child labour lies however with the state where the child labour occurs.[1173] The importing state would also have to find out – with the help of the ILO – where to exactly deliver the aid. As regards the lodging of complaint, it should be noted that the ILO complaints procedure does not have a time frame and – as demonstrated by the case of Myanmar – can be very lengthy and cumbersome.[1174] Moreover, the provision of aid or a complaint would not ban immediately goods made with child labour and could therefore be considered to be insufficient to protect the public morals of the importing state. The required level of protection would not be reached. Thus, the provision of aid or an ILO complaint are not equally effective measures.

As regards labelling requirements, they are of course less trade-restrictive than import bans and do not necessarily make children lose their jobs as suppliers may still export to the regulating country. However, in case the label is accorded on a voluntary basis, labelling laws are not equally effective since exporters may still export goods made with child labour to the importing state and consumers even do not know whether or not the goods they purchase are made by children. In case the labelling measures are mandatory, they may have the same adverse effect on children abroad as import bans if not accompanied by additional measures protecting children. Also, effective labelling schemes such as RUGMARK – now called GoodWeave label[1175] – depend on many factors such as a good monitoring system, flanking educational policies, higher salaries for parents and last but not least consumers in the importing state who are willing to pay a higher price.[1176] In addition, since the products with child labour may still access the import market, the level of protection as regards the public morals of the US citizens and consumers is not the same; on the

1173 Ibid., pp. 119–121.

1174 In the case of Myanmar, it took four years before the ILO Governing Body made the recommendation to the International Labour Conference to recommend its member states to review its relations with Myanmar, see Humbert (The Challenge of Child Labour), pp. 183 et seqq.

1175 https://goodweave.org/uk/about/.

1176 Humbert (The Challenge of Child Labour), pp. 362–365.

contrary, the risk continues.[1177] In conclusion, labelling requirements are not equivalent measures that a member should be required to employ.

An alternative measure that is equally effective may be an import ban that is accompanied by rehabilitation measures for former child labourers and their families and supported by financial assistance for foreign exporters provided by the regulating state. Such a measure would also be less trade restrictive than a blanket import ban since it helps exporters to produce their goods without children so that they may export their goods to the regulating state. As shown in the case of the Harkin Bill and the RUGMARK scheme, such a 'cooperative ban' is apt to make a material contribution to the reduction of child labour. The US-Cambodia Free Trade Agreement that linked preferential tariffs and quotas to the implementation of 'internationally recognized labour standards' is another positive example where trade measures were applied in conjunction with labour standards.[1178] It was implemented together with an ILO-IPEC implementation programme that was sponsored by the US.

Yet, one could argue that additional accompanying measures providing for financial and technical assistance constitute an undue financial burden on the regulating state. This is however not the case given that international human rights obligations binding on a majority of states contained in Art. 2 (1) of the ICESCR, Art. 4 of the CRC and ILO Convention No. 182 call for international cooperation and assistance for the implementation of the protection from economic exploitation of children. Moreover, in the light of the fact that in case of the US-Cambodia Free Trade Agreement, the US government did sponsor the ILO-IPEC programme, it does not appear to be inappropriate to require some financial contribution to cooperative efforts to implement the universally accepted prohibition of child labour. The RUGMARK initiative was also sponsored by the predecessor of the German 'Gesellschaft für internationale Zusammenarbeit' (GIZ).

Hence, in case import bans are not accompanied by flanking measures mitigating their trade restrictiveness and improving their effectiveness in reaching their aim, they should not be considered to be necessary.

The question is whether the rather recent practice by CBP to modify or revoke WRO or Findings in response to the (partial) removal of ILO forced labour indicators through e.g. the payment of recruitment fees by companies should be regarded as such flanking measures mitigating the trade restrictiveness of the ban and improving effectiveness.[1179] Several arguments contra such

1177 Cf. EC–Seal Products, report of the Appellate Body, para. 5.273.

1178 Ibid., p. 248 et seqq.

1179 See above, p. 15.

reasoning can be raised. Firstly, as of now, it is only the practice of the enforcement authorities CBP applying the ILO forced labour indicators as a basis for a removal. There are no related provisions in the law. Thus, there is a lack of transparency and the risk of arbitrary decisions, reducing the potential of mitigating the trade restrictiveness of the ban. Secondly, there is no remedy or rehabilitation provision for forced (child) labourers.[1180] And thirdly, although not reported to date, there might be nevertheless job losses or other adverse impacts for former forced (child) workers that also should be compensated for.[1181]

The US import ban in its current form would therefore not be justifiable under the public morals exemption of GATT Art. XX (a).

Such analysis will most probably apply to the proposed EU Forced Labour Regulation. While a less restrictive means may not be available, the question is, whether in its current form, it is suited to make a material contribution to the abolition of forced labour.

Reflecting the enforcement practice by CBP under the US ban on goods made with indentured child labour, the proposed EU Forced Labour Regulation[1182] prohibiting the placement of goods on the EU market provides that where economic operators can demonstrate that they conducted corporate due diligence in relation to forced labour, the Competent authorities will not initiate an investigation of products, Art. 4 (7) of the Regulation. However, as of now, there is no provision for remediation for forced (child) labourers. Thus, as under the US ban, there is some recognition of companies' efforts to reduce child labour but no real rehabilitation or other flanking measures for (forced) child labourers. Accordingly, the proposed EU Forced Labour Regulation should not be considered to be 'necessary' under the public morals exemption of GATT Art. XX (a).

In contrast, the proposed 'Model Law'[1183] for a future EU Regulation on Forced Labour would most likely pass the necessity test: Advancing the EU Regulation, it suggests a complaint procedure for affected people or other stakeholders and makes taking preventive, rehabilitation and remediation measures beyond information provided by social audits by companies a condition for lifting the market prohibition of goods made with forced labour. It can and should serve as a model for future trade measures on child labour consistent with WTO law.

1180 The Remedy Project, p. 21.

1181 Ibid., p. 19.

1182 See above, p.16.

1183 Anti-Slavery/ECCHR/The Greens/EFA.

10.2.3.4.2 Belgian Social Label Law

According to the Belgian Social Label Law, a label may be affixed on products if companies can prove that they have complied with the fundamental ILO Core Conventions including those on child labour. Also, companies from developing countries may be granted aid to be able to implement measures to comply with the ILO Core Conventions.

Thus, it seems to be easy for the Belgian measure to pass the necessity test: While the trade impact is very low given the label is accorded on a voluntary basis and exporters may even get financial support, the societal value is high and ethical consumption capable of making a material contribution to the reduction of child labour.

In conclusion, the Belgian Social Label Law can be regarded as a necessary measure.

10.2.3.4.3 Country-Specific Measures

It will now be examined whether the US ban on *any* good coming from Myanmar and measures implemented under the Kimberley Process Certification Scheme banning diamonds from non-participants can be considered to be 'necessary'. The UFLPA will also be analysed.

With regard to the first two measures, it should be noted that these measures were adopted following multilateral processes in accordance with public international law where other means have been tried before. In one case, the measure followed an ILO recommendation and in the other case, bans are implemented under the Kimberley Process Certification Scheme. The Burmese Freedom and Democracy Act was adopted in response to a complaint under Art. 26 of the ILO.[1184] A less trade-restrictive measure had thus been tried before. Equally, in case of the Kimberley Scheme, there had been earlier calls for restraint in diamond trade by the UN General Assembly and the Security Council.[1185] Given the difficulty in controlling the movement of diamonds, there might be no other equally effective means than trade bans for non-participants to achieve the goal of reducing trade in conflict diamonds.[1186] In addition, its aim to prevent *inter alia* the existence of child soldiers is of highest societal importance.

Still, in the Myanmar case, one could ask whether the US should first have adopted labelling requirements before introducing a complete ban or linked its ban to financial assistance or other flanking measures. However, in the light

1184 See Humbert (The Challenge of Child Labour), pp. 183–192.
1185 Nadakavukaren Schefer, p. 432.
1186 Cf. Ibid.

of the fact that the case had been subject to the ILO special procedures for years without success, where the government has been unwilling to cooperate and the International Labour Conference had finally recommended to the ILO constituents *to review their relations* with Myanmar,[1187] the adoption of the ban should be considered to be necessary.

Moreover, in accordance with the call for coherence in international law,[1188] it is appropriate to regard trade measures on human rights that have been recommended by human rights bodies or other multi-stakeholder initiatives such as the Kimberley Process as necessary within the meaning of GATT Art. XX (a).[1189] It has rightly been argued that the Kimberley Process' goal of completely stopping the trade in conflict diamonds is not reviewable by the WTO.[1190] There is no particular reason for rejecting such an interpretation. Human rights institutions generally provide for the necessary expertise to assess the appropriateness of trade measures in response to human rights violations. This is demonstrated by the fact that most human rights institutions, in particular the ILO, are generally very hesitant to impose trade measures. The case of Myanmar was the first case where trade measures were recommended under Art. 33 of the ILO Constitution. Thus, the risk of abuse of such measures for disguised protectionism is minor. It follows that the US Burmese Freedom and Democracy Act and national measures implemented under the Kimberley Process Certification Scheme should be considered to be necessary within the meaning of GATT Art. XX (a).

The question arises whether economic countermeasures such as the UFPLA[1191] that are not adopted following a multilateral process are necessary within the meaning of GATT Art. XX (a). Several arguments in contra can be raised: First, economic countermeasures in response to human rights violations are seldom effective.[1192] Second, state practice cited in the UN Materials on the Responsibility of States for Internationally Wrongful Acts on Art. 54 concerns massive human rights violations as in the case of *USA–Uganda* (1978) where the crime of genocide was alleged, of *USA–South Africa* (1986) where a state of emergency has been declared and of *Netherlands–Surinam*

1187 See Humbert (The Challenge of Child Labour), pp. 183–192.

1188 See generally Marceau (WTO Dispute Settlement and Human Rights I); Marceau (WTO Dispute Settlement and Human Rights II).

1189 Neumann, p. 448 with further references.

1190 Nadakavukaren Schefer, p. 432.

1191 See above, p. 15.

1192 Graf Vitzhum, p. 588; Rudolf; Vázquez, p. 837.

(1982) where a military government committed very severe human rights violations.[1193] Thus, only massive and widespread violations of fundamental human rights may entitle third states to take countermeasures.

The UFLPA is however likely to meet such a high threshold. It targets a region where evidence of systematic and widespread state-induced forced labour has been found, which has been qualified to be likely to be a crime against humanity.[1194] The necessity test construed in line with the proportionality principle of Art. 51 of the Articles on State Responsibility is also met given the importance and scale of forced labour. Also, less trade restrictive measures and/or the adoption of flanking measures are hardly conceivable since the use forced labour is intended by the government.

10.3 *Human Life and Health*

GATT Art. XX (b) justifies measures necessary to protect human, animal or plant life or health. The relevant case law requires the measure to pass the same two-tier test as under lit. a): The measure must be designed to protect the life or health of humans, animals, or plants; and the measure must be necessary to protect the life or health of humans, animals, or plants.[1195] While the public morals exception appears to be more relevant in case of a human right such as the prohibition of child labour, the exception in GATT Art. XX (b) is often invoked in WTO dispute settlement by the responding party and more than 50 per cent of all quantitative restrictions notified to the WTO up to May 2019 rely on this provision.[1196] Thus, it should also be considered as a possible defence of trade measures on child labour.

10.3.1 Protection of Human Health

Under GATT Art. XX (b), the measure in question has to address a risk to human, animal or plant life or health.[1197] The international prohibition of child labour of the CRC encompasses all work that is likely to interfere with the child's education, and/or to be harmful to the child's health or physical, mental, spiritual,

1193 Frowein (Reactions), p. 420; UN Materials on the Responsibility of States for Internationally Wrongful Acts, pp. 527–530.

1194 See above, p. 15.

1195 Colombia–Textiles, report of the Appellate Body, paras. 5.67–5.68 quoted in Brazil–Taxation, report of the panel, para. 7.869; US–Gasoline, report of the panel, para. 6.20; Brazil–Retreaded Tyres, paras. 7.40–7.41; Van den Bossche/Zdouc, p. 605.

1196 Van den Bossche/Zdouc, p. 601.

1197 Van den Bossche/Zdouc, pp. 605–606 referring to Brazil–Retreaded Tyres, report of the panel, para. 7.102.

moral and/or social development, thus addressing a health risk.[1198] Specifically, Art. 3 (1) of ILO Convention No. 138 and Art. 4 of ILO Convention No. 182 prohibit hazardous labour that is inter alia likely to jeopardize the health of children.[1199] Thus, trade measures referring to these international conventions such as the Belgian Social Label Law certainly can be said to address a health risk. The US ban on goods made with forced indentured or forced child labour, the proposed EU Regulation on Forced Labour including forced child labour, the UFLPA and the US Burmese Freedom and Democracy Act all address forced (children) labour as one of the worst forms of child labour that certainly has an impact on the physical and mental health of children. Reported cases of forced child labour in the cocoa sector in Ghana and the Ivory Coast or in the extractive sector in Peru all seriously jeopardize the health of children.[1200] The wide range of measures considered in the past by the WTO adjudicating bodies to pursue health objectives including measures to protect dolphins[1201] confirm such analysis.

10.3.2 The Issue of Extraterritoriality

Since trade measures aimed at protecting the health of children abroad do not have a link to the regulating state – as in the case of the public morals exception where a link can be established to the public morals of the US citizens who want to buy child labour free products – it might be more difficult to defend trade measures on child labour under GATT Art. XX (b).

The relevant the case law – the same as under GATT Art. XX (a) – does not give a concluding answer as to whether there is a territorial jurisdictional limitation included in the list of exceptions of GATT Art. XX.[1202]

The contextual interpretation does not help either. As analysed above, the fact that Art. XX (e) on prison labour clearly has an extraterritorial element referring to prisoners abroad can be used in both ways; either defending an extraterritorial application by way of analogy or rejecting such an interpretation using the argument of *expressio unius est exclusion alterius*.[1203]

However, as in case of GATT Art. XX (a), the recourse to the law to general international law on extraterritorial jurisdiction and general public international law regarding *ius cogens* will offer a solution.

1198 See Humbert (The Challenge of Child Labour), pp. 67–75.

1199 See Humbert ibid., pp. 90 and 99.

1200 Humbert in Schall/Theusinger/Pour Rafsendjani, § 2, para. 71.

1201 US–Tuna II (Mexico) (Article 21.5), report of the Appellate Body.

1202 See above, pp. 208 et seqq.

1203 See above, p. 211 et seq.

To recall, it has been established that indistinctly applicable trade-related npr-ppm-measures relating to child labour with extraterritorial effects are not *per se* contrary to GATT Art. III.[1204] Aiming at implementing international human rights norms, they establish a meaningful connection to foreign state interests in accordance with the general international law on extraterritorial effects of state acts. The same holds true for GATT Art. XX (a) and also (b) because the health objective is part of the relevant child labour, i.e. human rights norms.

As the analysis of GATT Art. III has shown, recourse to the concept of *ius cogens* and the *erga omnes* principle also support a reading of GATT Art. XX (b) that allows for measures with extraterritorial effect.[1205]

Specifically in case of country-measures such as the UFPLA, the US Burmese Freedom and Democracy Act and national bans under the Kimberley Certification Scheme, it seems appropriate to draw on general public international law allowing for countermeasures in response to *ius cogens* violations.[1206] Thus, the extraterritorial element of trade measures on child labour is not a hindrance in applying GATT Art. XX (b).

10.3.3 The Necessity Test

As under GATT Art. XX (a), the measures in question have to be 'necessary' to protect their policy goal. That is, he measures have to be 'designed' to protect human, animal, or plant life or health.[1207] This is the case

> [I]f the measure is not incapable of protecting [the objective], this indicates the existence of a relationship between the measure and the protection of the [objective].[1208]

The panel in *Brazil–Taxation* concluded that protection of the INOVAR-AUTO programme was not incapable of protecting life and health objectives by contributing ultimately to vehicle safety and reducing CO² emissions.[1209] Since all of the mentioned trade measures on child labour have the potential to initiate action on stopping child labour, they can all be considered to be not incapable of protecting the health of children.

1204 See the discussion above pp. 66 et seqq.
1205 See the discussion of the concept of *ius cogens* and *erga omnes* above p.96.
1206 See the analysis of GATT Art. XX (a) with further references, p. 212 et seq.
1207 See above, p. 201.
1208 Colombia – Textiles, report of the Appellate Body, para. 5.68.
1209 Brazil–Taxation, report of the panel, para. 7.904.

Next, the measures have to be necessary. Because of the identical wording, the same test as under GATT Art. XX (a) should be applied. As the discussion above has concluded, the interpretation of 'necessary' inter alia involves a process of weighing and balancing of factors such as the contribution made by the measure to reach its policy goal, the importance of the common interests or values protected and the accompanying impact of the law or regulation on imports or exports, i.e. the trade-restrictiveness of the measure.[1210]

As already concluded above, under this test, the Belgian Social Label Law should be considered to be necessary. By contrast, the US ban on goods made with forced or indentured child labour and the proposed EU Regulation on Forced Labour should not be considered to be necessary because of their lack of accompanying remedial and preventive measures.[1211] As stated above, in case of trade bans, the contribution to the end pursued should not be marginal.[1212]

Country measures such as the UFPLA, the US Burmese Freedom and Democracy Act and national bans under the Kimberly Certification Scheme should be found to be necessary for the same reasons as under GATT Art. XX (a).[1213]

10.4 *Prison Labour*

GATT Art. XX (e) justifies measures that relate to the products of prison labour.

The exception clearly encompasses all measures that impose trade restrictions on goods made with prison labour including done by children. The question is whether trade measures aiming at the reduction on child labour other than in prison may be justified under this provision. This could be the case if the term 'prison labour' can be construed as meaning forced labour and child labour found to come within the definition of forced labour.

In legal literature, child labour has been found to be a contemporary form of slavery.[1214] As such, it falls under the definition of forced labour since slavery-like practices comprise the necessary elements constituting forced labour.[1215]

Prison labour is addressed in Art. 8 (3) lit. b and lit. c (i) of the ICCPR and Art. 2 (2) lit. c of the ILO Forced Labour Convention. According to Art. 2 of the Forced Labour Convention, forced labour is work that is exacted from any person under the menace of any penalty and for which the said person has not

---

1210 See above, pp. 2015 et seqq.; Cf. *Korea–Beef*, report of the Appellate Body, para. 164.

1211 See above, pp. 221 et seqq.

1212 See above, p. 217.

1213 See above, pp. 226 et seqq.

1214 Humbert (The Callenge of Child Labour), pp. 39–45.

1215 Ibid., p. 59.

offered himself voluntarily. Art. 8 (3) lit. b of the ICCPR considers hard labour imposed as a punishment for a crime and the performance of hard labour in pursuance of a sentence to such punishment by a competent court in countries where such punishment is forced labour but exempts it from the international prohibition of forced labour contained in Art. 8 (3) lit. a of the ICCPR.[1216] Thus, in these cases, prison labour can be equated with forced labour.

However, ordinary work that persons under detention might be required to do in accordance with Art. 8 (3) lit. c (i) of the ICCPR, are not included in the scope of the term 'forced labour'. The same holds true for Art. 2 (c) of the ILO Forced Labour Convention No. 29 that does not consider any work exacted by a person as a consequence of a conviction in a court of law as forced or compulsory labour. Thus, it seems that not all cases of prison labour come within the definition of forced labour. The question is of course to which cases of prison of labour GATT Art. XX (e) refers; it may well be that it only relates to cases of prison labour that fall within the definition of forced labour. On the one hand the concept of prison labour seems to be broader than forced labour and on the other hand, the term 'forced labour' includes more types of work than prison labour. The same holds true as regards the relationship between the terms 'child labour' and 'forced labour'.

So the question arises whether in accordance with the Appellate Body in *US–Shrimp* an 'evolutionary' interpretation of the term 'prison labour' is possible.[1217] Since most of the WTO members are ILO members and most of those are parties to the ICCPR, the ILO Forced Labour Convention and the Worst Forms of Child Labour Convention, which explicitly addresses forced child labour,[1218] forced labour and child labour as prohibited by these Conventions could be argued to be read into the term 'prison labour' in GATT Art. XX (e).

Blüthner objects to such a reading on the ground that, for example, the Forced Labour Convention already existed at the time of the conclusion of the GATT.[1219] If the drafters had wanted to include forced labour, they could have done this by referring to the ILO Convention. Whilst this is a convincing argument, one should also take the following facts into account: Firstly, most of the parties to the ILO Convention No. 29 have ratified the treaty after

1216 Nowak (1993), p. 152.

1217 *US–Shrimps*, report of the Appellate Body, para. 130.

1218 For the required number of parties to be party to the subsequent multilateral treaty see the discussion above p. 204 et seq.

1219 Blüthner, p. 338.

1960.[1220] Secondly, the ICCPR only entered into force in 1976, the Worst Forms of Child Labour Convention in 2000 and the CRC in 1989. Thus, there is a broad consensus today as regards the prohibition of forced labour and child labour. Marceau argues in favour of an evolutionary interpretation of the concept of prison labour, which should look at ILO standards and its supervisory mechanism regarding forced labour.[1221] Whilst pointing out that the ILO Convention No. 29 exempts prison labour from the prohibition of forced labour, she nevertheless emphasizes that privatized prison labour seems to come within the definition. Pointing also to the economic rationale of fair competition of GATT Art. XX (e), she seems to refrain from a reading that equates the concepts of prison labour with forced and child labour.

In accordance with the rules of interpretation as set forth in Art. 38 (1) of the VCLT one should read the exception in its context. Such a reading will show that there are even more aspects to be taken into account. In contrast to GATT Art. XX (a), under which measures have to be 'necessary', GATT Art. XX (e) requires that measures merely have to 'relate' to products of prison labour. The Appellate Body in *US–Gasoline* construed the notion 'relating to' as meaning whether the measure was primarily aimed at the policy goal in the sense that there was a substantial relationship.[1222] Applying this definition to trade measures on child labour, one might find that most such measures including the US ban on goods made with forced or indentured child labour are aimed at their stated objective, i.e. the reduction of child labour abroad, although other objectives such as the protection of domestic jobs may also play a role. The threshold for such trade measures to come within the exceptions of GATT Art. XX (e) is thus lower than under GATT Art. XX (a). Consequently, there is the danger that an evolutionary interpretation of GATT Art. XX (e) would circumvent the conditions set forth by GATT Art. XX (a). Indeed, too broad a reading does not serve the cause of children. For example, the US ban on goods made with forced or indentured child labour does not pass the necessity test because blanket import bans without accompanying measures may make children lose their jobs and drive them into poverty and hardship. Especially in the case of trade measures on child labour, an advanced weighing and balancing test as developed by the WTO jurisprudence is preferable to the easier test under the term 'relating to'.

1220 As of July 2020, 178 states have ratified Convention No. 29, See Normlex, the database of the ILO, https://www.ilo.org/dyn/normlex/en/f?p=NORMLEXPUB:11300:0::NO:11300:P11300_INSTRUMENT_ID:312174:NO.

1221 Marceau (Trade and Labour), p. 552.

1222 *US–Gasoline*, report of the Appellate Body, p. 19.

The drafting history seems to reject a broad interpretation of GATT Art. XX (e) since a proposal by the US to include goods made under degrading or inhumane working conditions such as forced labour was rejected in the negotiations,[1223] the purpose of the provision being purely economic.[1224] While the exception regarding prison labour was to be included in Chapter 4 of the Havana Charter, i.e. trade policy, the exception concerning fair labour conditions was to be included in Chapter 2, Employment and Economic Activity.[1225]

In conclusion, the term 'prison labour' may not be read to refer to child labour other than done in prison. Thus, trade measures on goods made with child labour cannot be justified under GATT Art. XX (e).

10.5 *The Chapeau of GATT Art. XX*

10.5.1 The Traditional Approach to the Chapeau

As stated above, the *chapeau* is considered to be an expression of good faith.[1226] Its purpose is the prevention of abuse of exceptions embodying the doctrine of *abus de droit*.[1227] In particular, the Appellate Body has stated the task of applying the *chapeau* is essentially a delicate one of marking an equilibrium between the right of a member to invoke an exception and the rights of the other members under varying substantive provisions.[1228]

Under the *chapeau* of GATT Art. XX, the traditional view was that one has to examine whether the *application* of a measure constitutes 'a means of arbitrary or unjustifiable discrimination between countries where the same conditions prevail or a disguised restriction on international trade'.

10.5.1.1 *Arbitrary or Unjustifiable Discrimination*

With regard to the question whether there was 'arbitrary and unjustifiable discrimination between countries where the same conditions prevail', the Appellate Body in *US–Shrimp* stated:

1223 Rapports des Commissions et des principales Sous-commissions, Conférence des Nations Unies sur le Commerce et l'emploi tenue à La Havane, Cuba du 21 novembre 1947 au 24 mars 1948, cited in Burda, p. 39.

1224 See also Marceau (Trade and Labour), p. 552.

1225 Blüthner, p. 339; See Article 7, Fair Labour Standards, Havana Charter, Final Act and Related Documents, UNCTAD, Interim Commission for the International Trade Organization, Havana, 1948, E/Conf.2/78, Art. 7.

1226 *US–Shrimp*, report of the Appellate Body, paras. 158–159.

1227 Ibid., para. 158; *US–Gasoline*, report of the Appellate Body, p. 22.

1228 *US–Shrimp*, report of the Appellate Body, para. 159.

> Perhaps the most conspicuous flaw in this measure's application related to its intended and coercive effect on the specific policy decisions made by foreign governments, Members of the WTO. Section 609, in its application, is, in effect, an economic embargo which requires *all other exporting Members* [emphasis original], if they wish to exercise their GATT rights, to adopt *essentially the same* [emphasis original] policy (together with an approved enforcement programme) as that applied to, and enforced on, United States domestic shrimp trawlers. [...] However, any flexibility that may have been intended by Congress when it enacted the statutory provision has been effectively eliminated in the implementation of that policy through the 1996 Guidelines promulgated by the Department of State and through the practice of the administrators in making certification determination.[1229]

According to this view, the application of a measure through administrative acts or guidelines must not be coercive on foreign policies but leave them enough flexibility. The Appellate Body further noted that WTO members using a trade embargo have to take into consideration the different conditions that may occur in the different territories of those other members.[1230] Most importantly, it stated that discrimination does not only occur when countries in which the same conditions prevail are differently treated, but also when the application of the measure at issue does not allow for any inquiry into the appropriateness of the regulatory programme for the conditions prevailing in those exporting countries.[1231] Also, the regulatory state should not only consider the costs for domestic producers to apply a certain standards but also the costs for foreign producers.[1232] The Appellate Body found that the rigidity and inflexibility of the implementation scheme of the trade embargo also constituted 'arbitrary discrimination'.[1233]

In *US–Shrimp Article 21.5*, the Appellate Body recognized that the revised US measure allowed for regulatory programmes that were comparable in effectiveness and was therefore sufficiently flexible to meet the requirements of the chapeau.[1234] Some authors have interpreted this statement as an 'embryonic'

1229 Ibid., para. 161.
1230 Ibid., para. 164.
1231 Ibid., para. 165.
1232 *US–Gasoline*, report of the Appellate Body, p. 28.
1233 *US–Shrimp*, report of the Appellate Body, para. 177.
1234 *US–Shrimp Article 21.5*, report of the Appellate Body, para. 144.

and 'soft' requirement on members to recognize the equivalence of foreign measures comparable in effectiveness.[1235]

As regards measures on child labour, the US ban on goods coming from Myanmar does not constitute 'arbitrary and unjustifiable discrimination' because it is based on the ILO recommendation to adopt trade measures and does not impose US' policies on other countries. The US ban on goods coming from Myanmar as a country-specific measure is an illustrative example for justifiable discrimination between countries where conditions are different. According to the ILO recommendation, there has been massive and widespread occurrence of forced labour including child labour in Myanmar. Thus, there are different conditions in comparison with other countries that justify a different treatment.

In case of the UFPLA, the gravity and scale of forced (child) labour and its systemic and government-led nature make it superfluous to enter inter negotiations with China. The issue of massive human rights violations in Xinjiang have been addressed in political dialogue between the US and China with no result.

The Kimberley Process Certification Scheme has been adopted by a multilateral process. Thus, national bans implemented under this scheme do not impose one country's policies on other countries.[1236]

In the case of the Belgian Social Label Law, first of all, it should be noted that it is a voluntary scheme that applies to companies.[1237] Thus, countries are not forced to apply a certain implementation scheme. Furthermore, corrective action plans, a narrow interpretation of penal provisions and financial aid available for companies from developing countries for compliance costs ensure flexibility in the application of the measure. Notably, costs for foreign producers are taken into account. The measure also does not seem to violate the *chapeau* requirement of 'arbitrary and unjustifiable discrimination'.

However, in relation to the term 'unjustifiable discrimination', the Appellate Body in *US–Shrimp* also referred to the failure of the US to engage in across-the-board negotiations with the objective of concluding bilateral or multilateral agreements for the protection and conservation of sea turtles before enforcing the import prohibition.[1238]

This statement has been interpreted by some authors as meaning that before adopting unilateral trade measures on child labour, a WTO member

1235 Van den Bossche/Zdouc, p. 650 with further references.
1236 Nadakavukaren Schefer, p. 435.
1237 See above p. 16 with further references.
1238 *US–Shrimp*, report of the Appellate Body, para. 166.

has to make serious efforts to implement the ILO Conventions 138 and 182 in foreign countries, including through using the ILO complaints system.[1239] In particular, a WTO member does not only have to try to conclude international agreements on e.g. child labour but also to enter into negotiations on agreements that provide for trade measures.[1240]

The proposed interpretation is very far-reaching.[1241] As has been stated above, the purpose of GATT Art. XX is to allow for certain unilateral trade measures that relate to domestic policies. To oblige WTO members to always enter into negotiations on multilateral or bilateral agreements before adopting unilateral measures would be contrary to this purpose. For if there were a multilateral agreement providing for trade-related measures on child labour, there would be no need for a GATT exception allowing for such measures. While such negotiations may of course fail, it is questionable whether members in each end every case have indeed the obligation to enter into often costly negotiations.

Moreover, if one reads the Appellate Body report carefully, one may draw yet another conclusion. First of all, according to the Appellate Body, the whole *chapeau* relates to the *application* of a measure. Therefore, if at all, it seems to be more appropriate to require negotiations on implementation measures, not on the measure *per se*. Such a reading is confirmed by the Appellate Body that holds that the policies on the TEDs in various maritime areas, and the operating details of these policies, are all shaped by the Department of State, without participation of exporting members.[1242] This statement clearly refers to the application of the measure, not the statutory provision. Also, in *US–Gasoline*, the Appellate Body criticized that the US did not pursue cooperative arrangements on enforcement measures with foreign governments or foreign refiners.[1243]

In addition, in *US–Gambling*, the Appellate Body held that the US was not under an obligation to consult with the complainant before imposing a unilateral measure under GATS Art. XIV.[1244] While this statement was made under the necessity test, it can be taken as an indication that WTO members do not have a general obligation to consult or enter into negotiations on trade

1239 Blüthner, p. 328, fn. 315; Neumann, p. 490 et seq.

1240 Blüthner, p. 328.

1241 In the same vein, McRae, p. 234 argues that to require that only measures that result from negotiations with other members fall within the scope of Art. XX goes too far.

1242 *US–Shrimp*, report of the Appellate Body, para. 172.

1243 *US–Gasoline*, report of the Appellate Body, p. 26–27.

1244 *US–Gambling*, report of the Appellate Body, paras. 315–317.

measures before imposing a measure. Rather, they do have an obligation not to discriminate *if* they enter into negotiations. In *US–Shrimp*, the crucial point was that the US had negotiated with some, but not with other members. This was plainly discriminatory in the view of the Appellate Body, and unjustifiable.[1245]

In *US–Shrimp–Article 21.5*, the Appellate Body confirmed that the measure at issue had been qualified as 'unjustifiable discrimination' because, as applied, the United States treated WTO members differently.[1246] Thus, the emphasis was on the discriminatory element, not on the failure to negotiate.

Most importantly, as has been stated above, the *chapeau* is considered to be an expression of good faith. Thus, instead of a general negotiation requirement, WTO members must enter into negotiations if a failure to do so would constitute a failure to act in good faith, i.e. an *abus de droit*. Hence, it depends on the individual case whether WTO members have to enter into negotiations.[1247] In *US –Shrimps–Article* 21.5, the Appellate Body found that the panel rightly used the conclusion of the Inter-American Convention as an example for serious good faith efforts.[1248]

As regards measures on child labour, as stated above, the ban on goods from Myanmar was indeed adopted following a recommendation as the result of an ILO complaint. The Kimberly Process Certification Scheme was adopted in a multi-stakeholder process. Thus, trade bans adopted under this scheme also fulfil the negotiation requirement. As stated above, since negotiations between the US and China on how to reduce forced labour in Xinjiang are no feasible option, the UFLPAwould probably meet the chapeau requirements without such negotiations.

With regard to the Belgium Social Label Law, one could argue that the EU in earlier trade negotiations in Seattle, Cancun and Doha tried to incorporate labour standards into the WTO agreements and therefore fulfilled the negotiation requirement.

In the more recent *Brazil–Retreaded Tyres* case, the Appellate Body has put the emphasis on yet another requirement. It held that the legal test under the arbitrary or unjustifiable discrimination standard involved an analysis that relates primarily to the cause or the rationale of the discrimination.[1249] Especially, it held that there was an abuse of the exceptions contained in

---

1245 *US–Shrimp*, report of the Appellate Body, para. 172.

1246 *US–Shrimp–Article 21.5*, report of the Appellate Body, para. 119.

1247 Tietje/Wolf, p. 41 equally place the negotiation requirement in the special context of the *Shrimp* case.

1248 *US–Shrimp–Article 21.5*, report of the Appellate Body, para. 133.

1249 *Brazil–Retreaded Tyres*, report of the Appellate Body, para. 225.

GATT – i.e. an *abus de droit* in the sense of the *chapeau* – if 'the reasons given for the discrimination bear no rational connection to the objective falling within the purview of a paragraph of Article XX, or would go against this objective'.[1250] It reversed the panel's finding, which in its view relied on the effects of the discrimination.[1251] In *EC–Seal Products*, the Appellate Body confirmed that 'one of the most important factors in the assessment of arbitrary or unjustifiable discrimination is the question of whether the discrimination can be reconciled with, or is rationally related to, the policy objective with respect to which the measure has been provisionally justified under one of the subparagraphs of Article XX'.[1252] It found that the EU had failed to reconcile discrimination between seal hunts by indigenous communities (IC) and commercial hunts with the object of protecting the public morals regarding seal welfare because IC hunts could be equally cruel and the EU has not done anything to address this issue.[1253] Because the EU seal regime also had some additional ambiguities in the definition of an IC hunt and because the authorities applying these criteria enjoyed a broad discretion bearing the risk that also commercial hunts could enter the market, the Appellate Body found that the seal regime constituted a means of arbitrary or unjustifiable discrimination.[1254] While the final result is convincing given that the EU merely has to slightly improve the implementation scheme of the seal regime, it is not quite comprehensible why the EU should ensure that seal welfare is addressed in IC hunts. It is entirely convincing to accommodate the economic and social interests of indigenous communities in an exception to a trade measure that endangers their existence without attempting to change their way of hunting in light of the fact that the socio-economic conditions of the life of the Inuit have deteriorated dramatically since the seal market was destroyed by *inter alia* the Greenpeace campaign and the EU trade embargo.[1255] Hence, it would have been enough to ask the EU to remove the ambiguities in the implementation mechanism of the exception so that one can clearly distinguish between commercial hunts and IC hunts.

Finally, the Appellate Body in *EC–Seal Products* stated that the respondent can also argue that the conditions between the countries at issue are not the same and therefore arbitrary and unjustifiable discrimination exist.[1256]

1250 Ibid., para. 227.
1251 Ibid., para. 229.
1252 *EC–Seal Products*, report of the Appellate Body, para. 5.318.
1253 Ibid., para. 5.320.
1254 Ibid., para. 5.338.
1255 See Süddeutsche Zeitung, Lutz, ‚Fell über die Ohren', 13th of January 2015.
1256 *EC–Seal Products*, report of the Appellate Body, para. 5.301.

In *US–Shrimp,* in relation to the term 'arbitrary discrimination', the Appellate Body also referred to due process requirements of the implementation system such as transparency, predictability and a right to appeal.[1257]

Since Belgium Social Label Law does not have any ambiguities in its implementation scheme that go against the objective of protecting children from child labour, it can be deemed to genuinely pursue this policy goal. Providing for appeals against enforcement decisions and being transparent and predictable,[1258] the Law fulfils the requirements of the *chapeau.*

Not having any ambiguities and not lacking due process requirements, the same holds true for the US ban on goods from Myanmar, measures under the Kimberley Process Certification Scheme and the UFPLA.

10.5.1.2 *Disguised Restriction in International Trade*

The Appellate Body in *US–Shrimp* did not consider it necessary to examine whether the measure constituted a 'disguised restriction in international trade' if there was 'unjustifiable' and 'arbitrary discrimination'.[1259] In *EC-Asbestos,* the Appellate Body held that 'a disguised restriction' can be found when the requirements of the GATT Art. XX (b) are met, but the measure can be said to disguise the pursuit of trade-restrictive objectives.[1260] Since in such cases, there will also be 'arbitrary and unjustifiable discrimination', it is hardly conceivable where a disguised restriction has a meaning on its own. Since the trade measures in question have not been fount to be arbitrary and unjustifiable discrimination, they also do not constitute disguised restrictions on international trade.

10.5.2 Reconstructing the Chapeau

The Appellate Body's approach to the chapeau has been challenged by Bartels who contends that it is incorrect to distinguish between the contents and the application of a measure.[1261] Instead, in his view, the chapeau comprises a set of conditions that on the one hand prohibit measures that arbitrarily or unjustifiably discriminate between countries where the same conditions prevail, and on the other hand measures that are a 'disguised restriction' in international trade, i.e. adopted for explicit protectionist reasons but with an 'ostensible legitimate objective'.[1262] In his view, the discriminatory elements of a measure

1257 *US–Shrimp,* report of the Appellate Body, paras. 178–183.
1258 See Humbert (The Challenge of Child Labour), pp. 323–329.
1259 *US–Shrimp,* report of the Appellate Body, para. 184.
1260 *EC–Asbestos,* report of the Appellate Body, para. 8.236.
1261 Bartels (The Chapeau), p. 98.
1262 Ibid., p. 97.

should exclusively be assessed under the chapeau and be similar to the one under the non-discrimination obligations of GATT Art. III and I. They could then be justified if either the conditions are different in different countries, or on another ground that is not related to the objective.[1263] Bartels suggests that the discrimination could be justified if necessary to achieve the stated goal not related to the measure. For example, in *EC–Seal Products*, the question would have been whether it was possible for the EU to protect the interests of the indigenous people in a less discriminatory manner, for example by facilitating market access for seal products from Canadian Inuits.[1264] The test for the 'disguised restriction on international trade' would be whether the rationale was merely a 'disguise' for an improper purpose.[1265] Under the general exceptions, one would assess the trade restrictiveness of a measure.

10.5.3 Evaluation

This interpretation appears to be especially appealing in cases where it is difficult to distinguish between the content and the application of a measure. In case of labelling schemes such as the Belgian Social Label Law the specific requirements could be classified as both 'content' or 'implementation measures'. Furthermore, it is very convincing to take due account of the conditions prevailing countries, in particular in case of environmental and social regulation that bears on the financial resources of countries. For example, possible discrimination of Indian goods could be justified because the conditions in Belgium and India are quite different. Bartels explains well that the 'conditions' prevailing in different countries should be understood to be the risks that the measure attempts to address, for example prison labour.[1266] Also, the critique of Bartels regarding the required relationship of the discrimination and the objective of a measure is entirely convincing.[1267] It is difficult to understand to demand that the rationale for the discrimination is related to the objective of the measure especially in the case of an exception as in *EC–Seal Products* because in most cases, the discrimination by its nature will not relate to the objective of the rule.[1268]

1263 Ibid., p. 124.

1264 Ibid., p. 119.

1265 Ibid., p. 123.

1266 Ibid., p. 113.

1267 In *Brazil–Retreaded Tyres*, para. 5.321, the Appellate Body put very much emphasis on the necessary relationship between the discrimination and the objective of a measure.

1268 Cf. the findings of the WTO Appellate Body in *EC–Seal Products* presented above, p. 239.

However, there are many open questions as to for example the possible grounds for justifications of discriminatory measures other than having different conditions. Bartels himself acknowledges that this is an open question and suggests following the approach of *EC–Tariff Preferences*, where the Appellate Body construed 'needs' of developing countries with the help of the text of the WTO Agreement or that of other international organizations.[1269] Also, it is questionable whether the scope of application of the subparagraphs of GATT Art. XX would not be unduly restricted if the discriminatory elements of the measure are exclusively assessed under the chapeau. For to violate the non-discrimination obligations of GATT Art. I and III, a measure has to be discriminatory and would therefore not need to be assessed under the subparagraphs. Only in cases where the discrimination is justified, the subparagraphs would apply. This leads to the question whether the GATT also prohibits trade restrictions, not just discriminatory measures. This is open to debate. Bartels himself submits that almost all GATT obligations are directed expressly or by implication at discriminatory measures.[1270] However, he then holds that GATT 1994 prohibits measures that are both discriminatory and trade restrictive; arguably interpreting these conditions to be cumulative.

With regard to measures on child labour, results would probably be the same under both readings, the traditional one and the new one suggested by Bartels. As indicated above, both measures would probably discriminate against countries with high levels of child labour but could be justified because 'conditions' of the complaining country and the responding country would not be the same. Since they are both measures that obviously pursue a *bona fide* regulatory aim and do not contain protectionist elements, they are also not a 'disguised restriction in international trade' in the way how Bartels reads it. Thus, they would be found consistent with GATT Art. XX.

In conclusion, the suggested interpretation of the chapeau by Bartels merits a closer look by the WTO adjudicating bodies. What makes the new approach appealing, is that it makes use of the whole text of the chapeau, in particular of the sentence 'where the same conditions prevail', which was sometimes neglected by the Appellate Body.

10.6 *Burden of Proof*

As has been stated above, the burden of proof that a measure is justified under the individual paragraphs of GATT Art. XX and the *chapeau* is on the party

1269 Bartels (The Chapeau), p. 118.

1270 Ibid., p. 106.

invoking the exception.[1271] The party invoking the exception as a defence must establish a *prima facie* case showing that the measure is justified.[1272] The burden on the defending party varies according to what has to be proved, in the sense that the burden may be heavier under the *chapeau* than under the individual paragraphs.

In *US–Gambling*, the Appellate Body pointed out that it was not for the responding party to show that there was no reasonably available measure to achieve its objective.[1273] Instead, the responding party had to make a *prima facie* case that the measure was 'necessary' by putting forward evidence and arguments that enabled the panel to conduct the weighing and balancing test.[1274] Only where the complaining party raised a WTO-consistent alternative measure, then the defending party had to demonstrate why its measure remained necessary.[1275] The *EC–Seal Products* decision has confirmed these findings.[1276]

Considering that measures on child labour aim at implementing fundamental human rights, this relaxation of the burden of proof is to be welcomed.

10.7 *Conclusion*

Existing trade measures regarding child labour such as the US import ban on goods made with forced and indentured child labour, the US Burmese Freedom and Democracy Act, the proposed EU Forced Labour Regulation, measures implemented under the Kimberley Process Certification Scheme and Belgian Social Label Law can be said to protect the public morals of the regulating state and the international community in accordance with GATT Art. XX (a). This is all the more convincing in the light of the fact that the international prohibition of child labour is part of *ius cogens* that applies *erga omnes* establishing a public order. However, in order to justify measures with an extraterritorial application under GATT Art. XX (a), public international law on extraterritorial effects of state acts as well the legal consequences of *ius cogens* with regard to possible countermeasures have to be referred to. GATT Art. XX is not inherently hostile to country-based trade measures. Unilaterally adopted economic countermeasures in response to massive and widespread human rights violations

1271 *US–Gasoline*, report of the Appellate Body, p. 22.
1272 *EC–Asbestos*, report of the panel, para. 8.177–8.178.
1273 *US–Gambling*, report if the Appellate Body, para. 309.
1274 Ibid., para. 310.
1275 Ibid.
1276 *EC–Seal Products* report of the Appellate Body, para. 5.261 (referring to Appellate Body report *Brazil–Retreaded Tyres*, para. 156 and *US–Gambling*, para. 311).

may be justified under GATT Art. XX. The trade measures at issue also come within the scope of GATT Art. XX (b) that justifies measures protection human, animal and plant life and health. The term 'prison labour' may not be read to include child labour.

In accordance with WTO jurisprudence, the necessity test under GATT Art. XX (a) and (b) has evolved into a proportionality test that allows for an inquiry into the effectiveness of a measure as well as a weighing and balancing of protected values and the effect of the measure. Under such a test, blanket import bans on goods made with child labour such as the US ban on goods made with forced or indentured child labour and the proposed EU Forced Labour Regulation missing preventive and remedial measures are likely to be contrary to GATT Art. XX (a) whereas Belgian Social Label Law may be justified. In accordance with the call for coherence in international law, measures duly implemented under multilateral human rights schemes should be deemed to be 'necessary' within the meaning of GATT Art. XX.

In WTO jurisprudence the *chapeau* has so far been treated as an expression of good faith. The main question was whether the application of a measure amounts to an *abus de droit*. The WTO adjudicating bodies asked for example whether the measure allowed for enough flexibility for exporting states to implement the measure and contained due process requirements such as transparency, the right to be heard and the right to appeal. While this approach has been endorsed also by legal literature, Bartels has now proposed a new approach. The merit of this approach is that it makes use of the full text of GATT Art. XX and that the – in some cases – artificial distinction between the content and the implementation of a measure will not be necessary.

The analysed measures of child labour will probably be found consistent with the chapeau of GATT Art. XX under both readings.

11 Trade Measures concerning Child Labour under GATT Art. XXI

11.1 *Introduction*

The text of GATT Art. XXI reads as follows:

> Nothing in this Agreement shall be construed
>
> (a) to require any contracting party to furnish any information the disclosure of which it considers contrary to its essential security interests; or

(b) to prevent any contracting party from taking any action which it considers necessary for the protection of its essential security interests;
   i) relating to the fissionable materials or the materials from which they are derived;
   ii) relating to the traffic in arms, ammunition and implements of war and to such traffic in other goods and other materials as is carried on directly for the purpose of supplying a military establishment;
   iii) taken in time of war or other emergency in international relations; or

(c) to prevent any contracting party from taking any action in pursuance of its obligations under the United Nations Charter for the maintenance of international peace and security.

GATT Art. XXI gives WTO members the right to take action to defend their security interests.[1277] In particular, GATT Art. XXI lit. b (iii) seems to be a catch-all clause allowing WTO members to take measures in time of emergency in international relations. Country-measures contrary to GATT Art. XI such as the US 2003 Burmese Freedom and Democracy Act, the UFLPA and bans adopted under the Kimberley Process Certification Scheme that aim at solving African conflicts through stopping trade in conflict diamonds could therefore be justified under GATT Art. XXI (b) (iii). The latter bans could also be justified by GATT Art. XXI (c) because there have been Security Council resolutions calling for a ban of rough diamonds.[1278]

11.2 *GATT Art. XXI (b) (iii)*

11.2.1 Justiciability

The terms of the chapeau of lit. b 'which it considers necessary for the protection of its essential security interests' accords WTO members very wide discretion. For about seventy years, the central question has been whether this provision is justiciable, i.e. whether it is subject to review.

GATT panels have been cautious to define the scope of this provision.[1279] In the case *US–Nicaragua*, the question was whether the US could invoke GATT Art. XXI in order to justify its trade embargo against Nicaragua.[1280] According

1277 Hahn, p. 287.
1278 Nadakavukaren Schefer, p. 439.
1279 *US–Nicaragua*, report of the panel, (not adopted), paras. 5.1–5.3; Hahn, p. 388 et seq.
1280 *US–Nicaragua*, report of the panel.

to the US, GATT Art. XXI left it to each CONTRACTING PARTY to judge what action it considered necessary for the protection of its essential security interests.[1281] Interestingly, the mandate of the panel even precluded it from examining the validity of the US' invocation.[1282] The panel report was never adopted. In another case, where the EEC applied trade restrictions for non-economic reasons against imports from Argentina in 1982, the representative noted that GATT Art. XXI was a general exception but that every CONTRACTING PARTY was the judge of its exercise of these rights.[1283] In the same vein, in 1961, Ghana had stated that its boycott of Portuguese goods was justified under GATT Art. XXI (b) (iii) because the situation Angola was a threat to the whole of Africa that required pressure on Portugal.[1284]

During the discussions in the Geneva session of the Preparatory Committee, it was stated that there was a danger of having too wide an exception 'because that would permit anything under the sun'.[1285] It was concluded that exceptions were needed and that it was a question of balance neither to make them too tight nor too broad.[1286] In the same vein, legal authors have argued that although GATT Art. XXI (b) has a very broad scope, it is an exception clause that is subject to review.[1287]

In 2019, the panel in *Russia–Traffic in Transit*, followed by the panel in *Saudi Arabia– Protection of Intellectual Property Rights*, for the first time has ruled on GATT Art. XX (b) (iii).[1288] While Russia argued that the panel lacked jurisdiction and the US relied on the 'non-justiciable' and 'self-judging' nature of this provision,[1289] the panel concluded that it had jurisdiction.[1290] In Russia's view,

> both the determination of a Member's essential security interests and whether any action is necessary for the protection of a Member's national security interest are at the sole discretion of the Member invoking the provision.[1291]

1281 See GATT Guide, p. 601, 603 and 604.
1282 *US–Nicaragua*, paras. 5.1–5.3.
1283 GATT Guide, p. 600.
1284 Ibid.
1285 Ibid.
1286 Ibid.
1287 Blüthner, p. 327; Hahn, p. 388 ; cf. also Emerson, p. 153; Schloemann/Ohloff, p. 451.
1288 *Russia–Transit in Traffic*, report of the panel; *Saudi Arabia– Protection of Intellectual Property Rights*, report of the panel.
1289 *Russia–Transit in Traffic*, report of the panel, para. 7.52.
1290 Ibid., paras. 7.101–103.
1291 Ibid., para. 7.27.

It also opined that members could determine

> what constitutes an emergency in international relations, and whether such emergency exists in a particular case.[1292]

The panel analysed the adverbial introductory clause 'which it considers' in its context and rightly concluded with regard to the clauses contained in (i) to (iii) that given their limitative function, they should indeed limit the discretion of Members, otherwise reducing their *effet-utile*.[1293] It held that

> as the existence of an emergency in international relations is an objective state of affairs, the determination of whether the action was "taken in time of" an "emergency in international relations" under subparagraph (iii) of Article XXI(b) is that of an objective fact, subject to objective determination [by the panel].[1294]

It then applied a two-tiered test to examine whether the conditions of lit. b (iii) were met, which will be analysed below.

11.2.2 Emergency in International Relations

To be compatible with GATT Art. XXI lit. b (iii), measures have to be 'taken in time of war or other emergency in international relations'. The panel in *Russia–Traffic in Transit* construed the term rather narrowly holding that

> An emergency in international relations would, therefore, appear to refer generally to a situation of armed conflict, or of latent armed conflict, or of heightened tension or crisis, or of general instability engulfing or surrounding a state. Such situations give rise to particular types of interests for the Member in question, i.e. defence or military interests, or maintenance of law and public order interests.

Thus, 'political or economic conflicts with other Members or states' do not fall under this definition.[1295]

In legal literature, it had been argued that in accordance with general rules on state responsibility, an emergency included situations of upcoming armed

1292 Ibid., para. 7.28.

1293 Ibid., paras. 7.63–7.65.

1294 Ibid., para. 7.77.

1295 Cf. Ibid., para. 7.75 and Van den Bossche/Zdouc, p. 677.

conflicts or the commission of an internationally wrongful act of a state.[1296] GATT Art. XXI could be deemed to be *lex specialis* to general rules on state responsibility.[1297] According to Art. 2 of the Articles on State Responsibility, an internationally wrongful act exists if there is a breach of an international obligation attributable to a state. Since according to Art. 48 (1) (b) of the Articles on State Responsibility, countermeasures by others than the injured State are possible if the obligation breached relates to an international obligation owed to the international community as a whole, the violation of *ius cogens* norms such as the prohibition of child labour applying *erga omnes*[1298] could be argued to constitute such an emergency in international relations. In this sense, some authors argue that the most severe sorts of human rights abuses should be regarded as 'emergencies in international relations'.[1299] They stress the historic interpretation according to which the GATT was never intended to deny states the power they otherwise possessed under international law to employ countermeasures in response to violation of international human rights norms by other states.[1300]

All the measures at issue concern widespread, gross and systematic human rights violations with a *ius cogens* nature. That is, they could even be considered to constitute a serious breach of a state obligation according to Art. 40 of the Articles on State Responsibility. To recall, the US Burmese Freedom and Democracy Act was taken in response to abundant evidence of forced child labour found by ILO bodies and their recommendation ILO members to review their relations with Myanmar,[1301] the UFLPA in response to the systematic use of forced (child) labour[1302] and the Kimberley Process Certification Scheme in reaction to African conflicts using inter alia child soldiers.[1303] Thus, using the broader definition of an 'emergency in international relations' proposed by literature, the measures at issue could be said to be taken in time of such an 'emergency in international relations'.

Following the panel reports of both *Russia–Traffic in Transit* and *Saudi-Arabia– Protection of Intellectual Property Rights* that require an armed conflict or heightened crisis that relate to military or public order interests to assume

1296 Hahn, p. 391.
1297 Ibid.
1298 See above p. 96.
1299 Vázquez, p. 825.
1300 Ibid., p. 826 with further references.
1301 Humbert (The Challenge of Child Labour), pp. 184–185.
1302 See above, p. 15.
1303 Nadakavukaren Schefer, p. 411.

an 'emergency in international relations', such conclusion is however questionable. No armed conflict or heightened crisis related to security interests between either the US and Myanmar, the US and China, nor between participants and non-participants in the Kimberley Process Certification Scheme currently exists. In the case of *Saudi-Arabia–Protection of Intellectual Property Rights,* where also no armed conflict existed, the panel found that

> when a group of States repeatedly accuses another of supporting terrorism and extremism, as described in greater detail earlier, that in and of itself reflects and contributes to a "situation ... of heightened tension or crisis" between them that relates to their security interests.[1304]

Not mentioning cases of terrorism or extremism, security interests are however not involved in the case of the measures at issue, at least not at first sight. Thus, under the stricter definition of the two panel reports, an 'emergency in international' can hardly be assumed.

Having however established that GATT Art. XXI (b) (iii) is a *lex specialis* to general international law, it is more convincing to use a broader definition of the term 'emergency in international relations' including a breach of state obligations owed to the international community as a whole in accordance with the law of countermeasures as stated Art. 2 and 48 of the Articles on State Responsibility. The necessary limitation of the scope of GATT Art. XXI (b) (iii) can still be done with regard to the second element, i.e. 'necessary essential security interests'.

11.2.3 Essential Security Interests

The panel in *Russia–Transit in Traffic,* held that

> "Essential security interests", which is evidently a narrower concept than "security interests", may generally be understood to refer to those interests relating to the quintessential functions of the state, namely, the protection of its territory and its population from external threats, and the maintenance of law and public order internally.[1305]

Further, it stated that

1304 *Saudi Arabia– Protection of Intellectual Property Rights,* report of the panel, para. 7.263.
1305 *Russia–Transit in Traffic,* report of the panel, paras. 7.130.

> The obligation of good faith, referred to in paragraphs 7.132 and 7.133 above, applies not only to the Member's definition of the essential security interests said to arise from the particular emergency in international relations, but also, and most importantly, to their connection with the measures at issue. Thus, as concerns the application of Article XXI(b)(iii), this obligation is crystallized in demanding that the measures at issue meet a minimum requirement of plausibility in relation to the proffered essential security interests, i.e. that they are not implausible as measures protective of these interests.[1306]

Thus, while leaving some discretion to the member relying on GATT Art. XXI (b) (iii) to determine its essential security interests, the panel insisted that the measures had to be found to be not implausible to protect the stated security interests. The member invoking the provision has however to determine the necessity in the first place.[1307]

The question therefore is whether the US Burmese Freedom and Democracy Act, the UFLPA and bans under the Kimberley Process Certification Scheme can be considered to be not implausible to protect the essential security interests of the US or participant countries of the Kimberley Process Certification Scheme. While it is of course in general conceivable that widespread (forced) child labour in Myanmar or Xinjiang or child soldiers in African countries causes unrest and might adversely impact US' or other countries' security interests, further explanation would be needed to articulate how the measure at issue is connected to the US' or other countries' essential security interest in the sense of protecting their territory and population from external threats, and maintaining of law and public order internally, as required by the panel.[1308] Since to date, no such explanation has been invoked by the US or participants of the Kimberley Process Certification Scheme, following the panel in *Russia–Traffic in Transit*, a defence under GATT Art. XX (b) (iii) is rather improbable.

In the past however, some authors have argued that national security interests are affected if the defaulting state is responsible for violations of labour rights that have an *ius cogens* character with *erga omnes* obligations.[1309] Marceau had suggested expanding the concept of security to include human rights violations.[1310] She points to the changing concept of a 'threat to

1306 Ibid, para. 7.138.
1307 Ibid., para. 7.131.
1308 Ibid. para. 7.130.
1309 Hahn, p. 369.
1310 Marceau, (WTO Dispute Settlement and Human Rights II), p. 224.

international peace and security' under Chapter VII of the UN Charter, which is now widely regarded as including massive human rights violations.[1311] Hence, she concludes that the concept of security should do the same under GATT Art. XXI where a lesser degree of violation might satisfy the requirements.

While it is convincing to expand the concept of national security to include massive human and labour rights violations, *a fortiori* in case of *ius cogens*, the panel rightly asks for a connection of the measure at issue to the specific essential security interest of the state invoking GATT Art. XXI. It convincingly held that that

> the further an "emergency in international relations" is removed from armed conflict or a breakdown of law and order, the greater the specificity required in the articulation of the 'essential security interests' at issue.[1312]

As stated above, in case of the trade measures on child labour dealt with, such specific explanation would still have to be made to rely on GATT Art. XIII (b) (iii).

11.3 *GATT Art. XXI (c)*

GATT Art. XXI (c) justifies measures taken in pursuance of WTO members' obligations under the UN Charter for the maintenance of international peace and security.

As already mentioned above, there seems to appear a new rule in public international law whereby the concept of threat to international peace and security moves forward and includes certain large scale human rights violations.[1313] It has been argued that under this new rule, certain large scale human rights violations creating a threat to peace may trigger authorization of unilateral action of states.[1314] Hence large scale occurrence of child labour such as in the case of Myanmar or massive occurrence of child soldiers in armed conflicts could be regarded as a threat to international peace and security and entitle to the adoption of unilateral measures.

However, as rightly pointed out by another author, even if large scale human rights violations *entitle* states to act under Chapter VII, they do not *oblige* states to adopt unilateral measures.[1315] This is only the case where the Security

1311 Ibid.
1312 *Russia–Traffic in Transit*, para. 7.135.
1313 Marceau, (WTO Dispute Settlement and Human Rights II), p. 224.
1314 Ibid.
1315 Blüthner, p. 329.

Council adopts a resolution that obliges states to take action in accordance with Art. 41 and 42 of the UN Charter. Thus, GATT Art. XXI(c) only applies where the Security Council has adopted a binding decision requiring members to honour their commitments under the UN Charter.[1316]

The suggested reading is confirmed when examining the corresponding rules of the Havana Charter that referred to measures under Chapter VII of the UN Charter that are taken in accordance with Security Council Resolutions.[1317]

In contrast to the case of Myanmar, in the Kimberly Process, there have been Security Council resolutions.[1318] For example, in 1998, the Security Council adopted a resolution providing for a ban on the trade of rough diamonds originating from UNITA-controlled territories of Angola, holding that the role of the diamond trade threatened international peace and stability.[1319] Likewise, the Security Council adopted resolutions to ban trade with diamonds from Liberia and the Democratic Republic of Congo.[1320] However, as has been rightly argued by one legal author, these resolutions do not extend to the whole territory of the participants of the Kimberly Process Certification Scheme and therefore make GATT Art. XXI (c) only applicable to trade measures directed at diamonds stemming from these territories.[1321] Thus, not all measures implemented under the Kimberly Process Certification Scheme may be justified under GATT Art. XXI (c).

11.4 *Conclusion*

While states have wide discretion under GATT Art. XXI (b) (iii), the provision is justiciable and subject to review.

The term 'emergency in international relations' may be read not only to include armed conflicts and heightened crisis but also wrongful acts of states relating to massive human rights violations with a *ius cogens* nature. The trade measures in question all were taken in response to widespread occurrence of (forced) child labour and child soldiers so that this first element the two-tier test of GATT Art. XXI (b) (iii) would be met.

While it seems convincing to expand the concept of national security to include massive human rights violations with a *ius cogens* nature, members

1316 Van den Bossche/Zdouc, p. 681.

1317 Art. 86:3 cited in Blüthner, p. 329.

1318 Nadakavukaren Schefer, p. 439.

1319 S/Res/1173 (adopted 12 June 1998), quoted in Nadakavukaren Schefer, p. 432.

1320 S/Res/1344 (adopted March 2001) and S/Res/1501 (2003) quoted in Nadakavukaren Schefer, p. 432.

1321 Nadakavukaren Schefer, p. 439.

invoking the security exception would still have to specifically articulate why the measure in question is necessary to protect its essential security interests. Since such explanation has not been made in case of the trade measures on child labour at issue, recourse to GATT Art. XXI (b) (iii) is currently not possible.

GATT Art. XXI (c) can only be invoked where the Security Council has adopted a resolution that obliges states to act under Chapter VII of the UN Charter.

12 Compatibility of Trade Measures on Child Labour with the Agreement on Technical Barriers to Trade

12.1 *Introduction*

The TBT Agreement replaced the former Standards Code introduced in the Tokyo Round, which covered mandatory and voluntary technical specifications, mandatory technical regulations and voluntary standards for industrial and agricultural goods. It was developed with a view to strengthening the disciplines of GATT Art. I, III, XI and XX.[1322] Accordingly, it seeks to reconcile the need to reduce trade barriers through technical regulations with the ability of governments to pursue legitimate policy goals such as consumer protection and human life and health.[1323] Pursuant to Art. II (2) of the Agreement Establishing the WTO in conjunction with its Annex 1, it is part of WTO law. The TBT Agreement, besides providing for the principle of non-discrimination and reduction of trade barriers, contains notification, harmonization and mutual recognition requirements.[1324] It also provides for transparency and participation requirements.[1325]

Trade measures on child labour that could fall within the scope of the TBT Agreement are the Belgian Social Label Law, the proposed EU Forced Labour Regulation, the US ban on goods made with forced or indentured child labour and national measures under the Kimberley Process Certification Scheme since they set forth conditions for products to enter the market of the regulating state. Although not laying down specific product requirements, it could be argued that the US ban on goods coming from Myanmar nevertheless is a product regulation and as such comes within the scope of the TBT Agreement. The same could be done in case of the UFLPA.

1322 Marceau/Trachtmann, p. 816; Cottier/Oesch, p. 750.

1323 Cottier/Oesch, p. 751.

1324 See for example Art. 2.4, 2.7, 2.9 and Art. 5 of the TBT Agreement.

1325 See for example Art. 2.9 of the TBT Agreement.

12.2 *Scope of Application*

12.2.1 Technical Regulation

The TBT Agreement applies to technical regulations as defined in Annex 1.1. It reads:

> 1. Technical regulation
> Document which lays down product characteristics or their related processes and production methods, including the applicable administrative provisions, with which compliance is mandatory. It may also include or deal exclusively with terminology, symbols, packaging, marking or labelling requirements as they apply to a product, process or production method'.

In EC–*Asbestos,* the Appellate Body interpreted this definition and set forth three conditions for a measure to come within this definition. Firstly, the measure must apply to an identifiable product or group of products.[1326] The identifiable products need not be expressly identified in the measure. Secondly, the document must lay down one or more product characteristics of the product.[1327] These characteristics may be intrinsic or related to the product. They may be regulated in either a positive or a negative form.[1328] Thirdly, compliance with the product characteristics must be mandatory.[1329]

The US ban on goods made with forced or indentured child labour applies to products that were produced by children, so does the proposed EU Forced Labour Regulation including forced child labour. They thus apply to an identifiable group of products. National measures under the Kimberley Process Certification Scheme apply to rough diamonds. The Belgian Social Label Law regulates, *inter alia,* that companies that do not employ children may affix a label on their products. It thus applies to products not made with child labour. The US ban on goods coming from Myanmar does however not apply to an identifiable group of products but to any product originating in Myanmar. So does the UFLPAthat applies to all products from Xinjiang, also using a rebuttable presumption. Hence, all measures except the last two fulfil the first criterion.

Before applying the second criterion, which is the heart of the definition and requires a detailed analysis, it will be examined whether the existing measures on child labour are mandatory. In EC–*Sardines* and *US–Tuna II*, the

1326 EC–*Asbestos*, report of the Appellate Body, para. 70.
1327 Ibid., para. 67.
1328 Ibid., para. 69.
1329 Ibid., para. 68.

Appellate Body characterized the measures at issue as technical regulations on the basis that they prescribed the use of a certain label, i.e. 'preserved sardines' and 'dolphin-safe', in an exhaustive way.[1330] This means that these labels set forth a legally mandated definition for certain products and disallow the use of other labels for such products. This is not the case with the Belgian Social Label Law. This law accords a label to products of companies that applied voluntarily[1331] and can prove that their products are produced in accordance with the ILO Core Conventions. The label does not regulate social production in an exclusive way. Companies may still use other labels such as the Fairtrade label in case they want to inform consumers that their products have been produced in conformity with the ILO Core Conventions. Thus, compliance with the law is not mandatory and the law not a technical regulation. The US ban and the proposed EU Forced Labour Regulation are mandatory and fulfil the third condition. Measures implementing the Kimberley Process Certification Scheme are also mandatory measures regulating trade in diamonds.[1332]

The crucial question in relation to trade measures on child labour is whether they can be regarded as laying down product characteristics that 'relate' to the product given child labour does not have a physical impact on the product. It has to be recalled that the OECD draws a distinction between measures regulating npr-ppms, the production method of which does not have a physical impact on the product, and measures regulating product-related ppms, the production method of which is reflected in the specific characteristics of a product.[1333] However, it is not clear whether the same distinction should be drawn with respect to technical regulations. One could also differentiate between product-specific measures such as the US ban on goods made with forced or indentured child labour and country-specific measures such as the US ban on any good coming from Myanmar, which does not lay down specific product or production requirements.

The Appellate Body in *EC–Asbestos*, referring to the examples from the definition such as packaging or labelling requirements, found that product characteristics included not only features and qualities intrinsic to the product itself,

---

1330 *EC–Sardines*, report of the Appellate Body, para. 313; *US–Tuna II*, report of the Appellate Body, para. 198. For a thorough critique of the *US–Tuna II* decision in this regard see also Howse (Consumer Labelling), pp. 593–607.

1331 Cf. on the issue of voluntariness Committee on Technical Barriers to Trade, G/TBT/M/23 and 24.

1332 See the wording of the Kimberley Process Certification Scheme, www.kimberleyprocess.com/documents/10540/11192/KPCS%20Core%20Document?version=1.0&t=1331826363000.

1333 See above text accompanying p. 18, fn. 36.

but also related 'characteristics' such as means of identification, the presentation and the appearance of the product.[1334] This finding has explicitly been confirmed by *EC–Sardines*.[1335]

One could argue that production methods also are related characteristics and as such included in the definition. Given that the second sentence omits the words 'their related', at least labelling requirements that call for information on the production method in the definition seem to be covered by the definition.

The Appellate Body in its recent decision *EC–Seal Products* dealing with an import ban on seal products seems to draw on the reasoning of the Appellate Body in *EC–Asbestos* holding that 'related [PPMs]' may mean something else than product characteristics.[1336] However, it then focussed on the ordinary meaning of the word 'related' meaning *inter alia* 'connected' and the position of the word 'their' before the term 'process and production methods', and concluded that ppms have to be related to product characteristics.[1337] It held that a ppm-measure within the meaning of Annex 1.1 has to have a sufficient nexus to the characteristics of a product. Referring to the second sentence which deals with labelling requirements and omits the word 'their related' in relation to ppms, it argued that the words 'also include' at the beginning of the second sentence prove that this sentence refers to different measures than the first sentence.[1338] Thus, it seems to suggest that while the second sentence refers to ppms not related to product characteristics, the first sentence does not.

Applying its conclusion to the facts of the case, the Appellate Body found that particular emphasis should be put on 'integral and essential' aspects of the measure and focussed its analysis of the EU import ban of seal products on its three exceptions allowing for the import of seal products resulting from hunts traditionally conducted by Inuit, seal products derived from hunts conducted for marine resource management reasons and seal products imported for the personal use of travellers or their families.[1339] It held that the relevant exceptions referring to the identity of the hunter, the type of the hunt and the purpose of the hunt were not product characteristics and therefore the whole measure not a technical regulation.[1340] It did not follow the argumentation

1334 *EC–Asbestos*, report of the Appellate Body, paras. 66–70.
1335 *EC–Sardines*, report of the Appellate Body, paras. 189–191.
1336 *EC–Seal Products*, report of the Appellate Body Report, para. 5.12.
1337 Ibid.
1338 Ibid., para. 5.14.
1339 Ibid, paras. 5.19 and 5.41.
1340 Ibid., para. 5.45.

of the panel which had classified the measure at issue as a whole as a technical regulation laying down product characteristics in a negative form since it prohibited the import of products containing seal.[1341] It also reversed the panel's finding that the criteria contained in the exceptions constitute 'objectively definable features' of the seal products allowed to be placed on the EU market and as such lay down product characteristics.[1342] The Appellate Body explicitly rejected to make a finding on whether the exceptions to the import ban of seal products amounted to related ppms within the meaning of Annex 1.1. It stated however that 'a panel may find it helpful to seek further contextual guidance in other provisions of the TBT Agreement, for example, those pertaining to standards, international standards, and conformity assessment procedures, in delimiting the contours of the term "technical regulation"'.[1343]

Thus, while the Appellate Body appears to be rather reluctant to include npr-ppms into the definition of technical regulations, the matter has not yet been decided. Therefore, the arguments put forward in legal literature will now be considered.

Many legal authors are in line with the Appellate Body in *EC–Seal Products* and rely on the wording 'product characteristics or their related processes and production methods'. They hold that the words 'their related' prove that only production methods reflected in the product itself are covered by the definition.[1344] Whilst they admit that the second sentence omits the words 'their related', leaving room for a broader interpretation at least as regards labelling requirements, they argue that this omission was due to editorial neglect.[1345] Some authors point to the jurisprudence under GATT Art. III that apparently does not allow for distinctions based on measures regulating ppms that are not reflected in the final product under the term 'like products'.[1346] Another author relies on the drafting history stating that most of the delegates were opposed to an extension to measures regulating ppms that are not reflected in the final product.[1347]

1341 *EC–Seal Products*, report of the panel, para. 7.106.

1342 *EC–Seal Products*, report of the Appellate Body Report, para. 5.45.

1343 Ibid., para. 5.60.

1344 Tietje/Wolf, p. 48; Blüthner, p. 280 et seq.; Schlagenhof, pp. 131 and 132; OECD, OCDÉ/GD(97)137, p. 17; Tietje (Voluntary Eco-Labelling), p. 134; Pauwelyn (Human Rights in WTO Dispute Settlement), p. 226. Pauwelyn is however not explicit on whether he rejects a broader interpretation of the term 'technical regulation'.

1345 Tietje/Wolf, p. 48.

1346 Schlagenhof, p. 132. In this work, GATT/WTO jurisprudence will however be interpreted differently.

1347 See Bluethner, pp. 283 and 184 referencing WTO, Negotiating History of the Coverage of the Agreement on Technical Barriers to Trade with Regard to Labelling Requirements,

Referring to the second sentence and the omission of 'their related', other authors suggest that at least measures having the same character as those enumerated in the second sentence, i.e. labelling requirements, should come within the definition of a technical regulation.[1348] Holding that Art. 2.9 of the Agreement obliges members to notify all mandatory labelling requirements, i.e. including those on npr-ppms, Marceau argues that it would only make sense if the substantive rules of the TBT Agreement also apply.[1349]

Other authors do not preclude the possibility of subsuming measures regulating npr-ppms under the definition of a technical regulation.[1350] They hold that it is hardly understandable why measures regulating npr-ppms should not being subjected to the disciplines of the TBT such as the principle of proportionality[1351] or notification, harmonization and mutual recognition.[1352] The definition could be understood as referring to ppm-measures relating to the production of the product as opposed to country-specific measures based on policy considerations.[1353]

In principle, it is indeed hardly understandable why measures regulating npr-ppms should not constitute technical regulations. The wording of Annex 1.1 is not clear as to whether only ppm-measures having a physical impact on the product itself or also npr-ppm-measures should be regarded as relating to the product. As already indicated above, it is also possible to draw the distinction between country-based and product-based measures. Process and production methods such as the use of child labour are related to the product because children make the product. In addition, in case of child labour, there is even a closer nexus because child labour often has an impact on the price of the product. This is similar to the case of environmental taxes that are transmitted to the consumer and reflected in the price of a product.[1354] Thus, a broader reading of 'their related process and production methods' is in theory possible.

Voluntary Standards, and Processes and Production Methods Unrelated to Product Characteristics, WTO Document WT/CTE/W/10, GB/TBT/W/11, 29 August 1995, p. 7 et seqq.

1348 McDonald, p. 256 et seq.; Marceau/Trachtmann, p. 861.

1349 Marceau (Trade and Labour), p. 556.

1350 Marceau/Trachtmann, pp. 861 and 862; Burda, p. 22; Cottier/Oesch, p. 762.

1351 Cottier/Oesch, p. 762; Lopez-Hurtado, p. 738 however does not express a clear view but points to the difficulty of totally excluding social labelling regulations from coverage under WTO agreements.

1352 Marceau/Trachtmann, p. 861.

1353 Ibid., p. 862.

1354 Vranes, p. 193.

However, the ordinary meaning and the order of the words seem to suggest a different reading. According to the Concise Oxford English Dictionary, the term 'technical' means either 'relating to a particular subject, art or craft, or its techniques' or 'requiring special knowledge to be understood' or 'involving or concerned with applied and industrial sciences' or 'relating to the operation of machines' or 'according to a strict application or interpretation of the law or rules'.[1355] In light of the objective of the TBT Agreement to improve efficiency of production as stated in its Preamble it is plausible to assume that the drafters of the TBT Agreement referred to the word 'technical' as meaning 'involving or concerned with applied and industrial sciences'. Here, it is noteworthy that the Appellate Body in *EC–Seal Products* argued that the EC Seals regime regulating the identity of the hunter and the purpose of the hunt seemed to lack 'technical content' as mentioned in Art. 2.9 of the TBT Agreement.[1356] Along the same lines, it is possible to argue that labour standards regulate human behaviour and are part of human policies rather than being concerned with industrial sciences. Admittedly, the drafters also could have thought of 'technical' meaning relating to a particular subject' since for example ILO experts on labour rights are sometimes called 'technical experts', and 'technical cooperation assistance' is an essential means provided by the ILO.

Thus, in accordance with Art. 31 (1) of the VCLT, the term 'technical regulation' will now be interpreted in the light of the object and purpose of the TBT Agreement. As mentioned above, the TBT Agreement was introduced with a view to strengthening GATT disciplines. Hence, at first sight, it seems to be convincing to argue that it does not make sense to exclude measures regulating npr-ppms from review, given that they might be justified anyway under the GATT. The Preamble underlines the important contribution that international standards and conformity assessment systems can make to achieve the objective of the GATT by improving efficiency of production and facilitating the conduct of international trade. Thus, it seems that the object and purpose as expressed in the Preamble rather supports a broad scope of the TBT Agreement. If measures regulating npr-ppms were not covered, they would escape all procedural requirements of the TBT such as Art. 2.9 of the TBT Agreement providing for a notification requirement.

At a closer look however, it seems to be more convincing to restrict the application of the TBT Agreement to ppm-measures that are labelling requirements or other means of identification as stated in Annex 1.1, second sentence. Firstly,

1355 Concise Oxford English Dictionary, 12th edition 2011 (Oxford University Press).
1356 *EC–Seal Products*, report of the Appellate Body, fn. 942.

the omission of the words 'their related' in the second sentence, is a clear indication that npr-ppm-measures are included under the second sentence. Secondly, the case *US–Tuna II (Mexico)* has made clear that labelling requirements regarding production methods not related to the product are included in the definition of a technical regulation. Thirdly, the provisions of the TBT Agreement make more sense in case of regulations that have a strong product nexus. In case of npr-ppms other than labelling requirements, they often seem difficult to apply. For example, it appears to be strange to require mutual recognition and harmonization efforts in accordance with Art. 2.6 and 2.7 of the TBT Agreement for sales prohibitions or trade bans regarding child labour given that the prohibition of child labour is a universally recognized human right and has been developed under the well-established procedures of the ILO. The crucial question regarding trade bans on child labour rather is whether they are necessary in the light of their adverse trade impact, an issue that can perfectly be dealt with under GATT Art. XX. By contrast, mutual recognition and harmonization requirements of the TBT Agreement make completely sense for labelling regulations. In a similar vein, it appears to be strange to require members in accordance with Art. 2.9.4 of the TBT Agreement to allow for comments of other members on a trade ban on child labour given that the prohibition of child labour has been agreed in the ILO and the crucial issue is not the 'technical content' but the trade impact. Also, conformity assessment procedures such as testing sampling or inspection in accordance with Art. 5, 6, 7 8 and 9 of the TBT Agreement seem to be difficult to apply to products made with child labour given the difficulty to verify whether products are indeed not produced by children. This is different in case of labelling requirements on child labour since the conformity assessment will only review whether the products bear the label in accordance with the labelling requirements. The same holds true for other means of identification. Admittedly, labelling schemes such as the 'dolphin-safe' label in the *US–Tuna II* case confront the same difficulties as regards their verification system, but this is different from the conformity assessments as provided for in the TBT Agreement. Finally, according to Art. 11 of the TBT Agreement, members shall advise or provide technical assistance. This includes assisting members to establish national standardizing bodies and participation in international standardization bodies. However, labour standards are normally not subject of such standardization processes but subject to legislative processes. Thus, this provision also does not seem to target non-product-related ppm-measures such as labour standards.

Admittedly, the definition of standards contained in Annex 1.2 of the TBT Agreement relates to 'rules, guidelines or characteristics for products or related processes and productions methods'. The omission of the word 'their' suggests that the definition covers a wide range of ppms that do not necessarily have a strong product nexus. At the same time, the definition still refers to 'related production methods' and thus requires a certain product nexus. Hence, it can be read so as not to include npr-ppms on child labour.

Moreover, according to Art. 2.12 of the TBT Agreement, members have to allow a reasonable interval between the publication of a technical regulation and their entry into force in order to allow time for producers in exporting members to adapt their products or methods of production to the requirement of the importing member. Here again, the text generally refers to 'methods of production'. This could be taken as further evidence that measures regulating npr-ppms are covered by the TBT Agreement. On the other hand, the object and purpose of the obligation makes more sense if applied to regulations with a strong product nexus. National labour law should be adopted in accordance with international labour and human rights conventions and not during a period set by other members. Admittedly, also in case of labelling, other Member States have to adopt their production methods, i.e. working conditions. Yet the difference is that they still may export their products to the regulating state, which would not be the case for a trade ban.

Another argument relates to Art. 2.4 of the TBT Agreement that asks members to base their technical regulations on international standards. As will be discussed below, international standards are voluntary rules developed by an international body. As regards npr-ppms on child labour, relevant international standards could be binding ILO and UN conventions. It is however questionable whether such instruments containing state obligations rather than production requirements for the industry should pass as international standards. As Pauwelyn rightly argues, there is the danger that WTO members that have not ratified the relevant human rights convention have to apply the convention.[1357] While this might be acceptable from a human rights perspective, it is worth noting that members merely have to base their technical regulations on international standards, i.e. they do not have to fully comply with them, which may undermine the proper implementation of UN and ILO conventions.[1358] This problem could be resolved through a better cooperation between the ILO and the WTO in the future but for the moment it appears to be more appropriate to interpret technical regulations and standards so as not to refer to labour and human rights standards including ILO and UN Conventions.

1357 Pauwelyn (Human Rights in WTO Dispute Settlement), p. 227.

1358 Cf. Marceau (Trade and Labour), p. 555.

Arguably, the obligation to refrain from creating unnecessary obstacles to international trade contained in Art. 2.2 of the TBT Agreement could be an argument in favour of including npr-ppms. The obligation relates to trade restrictions, i.e. rules that limit trade but are not necessarily discriminatory. Thus, the scope is potentially broader than GATT Art. III and with a view to promoting trade liberalization, one could argue that the broader the coverage the better. However, it is questionable whether it is useful to subject npr-ppms in the field of labour and environmental standards always to the test of trade restrictiveness. Given that the traditional basis of international law is still state consent rather than constitutional principles a prudent interpretation of the TBT Agreement may be preferable from a labour and human rights perspective. As long as it is not well-established that WTO law has to be interpreted in conformity with human rights, one should limit the choice of measures that fall under the TBT Agreement.

Finally, the drafting history also supports a narrow reading of the term 'technical regulation'.[1359] Thus, with the exception of labelling requirements and other means of identification, the term 'technical regulation' should be construed so as to encompass only those ppms that have a physical impact on the product.

Hence, the US ban on products made with forced or indentured child labour and the proposed EU Labour Regulation, being a measure regulating a npr-ppm, do not qualify as a technical regulation. National measures to be implemented under the Kimberley Process Certification Scheme require certification of rough diamonds and as such constitute labelling requirements coming within the definition of a technical regulation. The required bans on all diamonds originating from non-participants do however not constitute labelling requirements. Such bans are country-specific trade restrictions and do not qualify as a technical regulation.

12.2.2 Standard

Since the Belgian Social Label Law does not provide for a mandatory labelling scheme, it could fall under Annex 1.2 of the TBT Agreement and be subject to the Code of Good Practice contained in Annex 3. The text reads as follows:

1359 WTO, Negotiating History of the Coverage of the Agreement on Technical Barriers to Trade with Regard to Labelling Requirements, Voluntary Standards, and Processes and Production Methods Unrelated to Product Characteristics, WTO Document WT/CTE/W/10, GB/TBT/W/11, 29 August 1995, Section III.

> 1. Standard
>
> Document approved by a recognized body, that provides, for common and repeated use, rules, guidelines or characteristics for products or related processes and production methods, with which compliance is not mandatory. It may also include or deal exclusively with terminology, symbols, packaging, marking or labelling requirements as they apply to a product, process or production method.
>
> Explanatory Note:
>
> The terms as defined in ISO/IEC Guide 2 cover products, processes and services. This Agreement deals only with technical regulations, standards and conformity assessments procedures related to products or processes and production methods. Standards as defined by ISO/IEC Guide 2 may be mandatory or voluntary. For the purpose of this Agreement standards are defined as voluntary and technical regulations as mandatory documents. Standards prepared by the international standardization community are based on consensus. This Agreement covers also documents that are not based on consensus.

As stated above, the definition of the term 'standard' refers to 'products or related processes and production methods' and omits the word 'their'. At the same time, in contrast to the respective second sentence of Annex 1.1 and 1.2, it refers to 'related' production methods, i.e. methods with a certain product nexus. Thus, since there is no reason to differentiate between standards and technical regulations when it comes to ppm-measures, the term 'standards' should also be read so as not to include npr-ppm-measures. As the Belgian Social Label Law regulates labour standards that are not reflected in the final product, it is not covered by the definition contained in the first sentence of Annex 1.2.

However, the Belgian Social Label Law setting forth labelling requirements comes within the definition of the second sentence of Annex 1.2 that omits the word 'related' and therefore can be read to subject labelling requirements on npr-ppms to the scope of the Code of Good Practice, which contains rules for standards in contrast to technical regulations.

The question is whether the increasing amount of private sector standards such as codes of conducts, labelling and multi-stakeholder initiatives fall within the definition of a standard. Such ethical standards are for example the GlobalGAP[1360] label for agricultural products or the label of the Fair Wear Foundation[1361] for textiles. While such standards have the potential to

1360 See www.globalgap.org/de/.

1361 See www.fairwear.org.

improve respect for human rights in production countries, they also put financial burdens on suppliers and can be a barrier for trade.[1362] Therefore, it has been subject to much debate in the SPS Committee, whether members should take responsibility for the WTO-consistency such standards.[1363]

The definition of a standards refers to a document that has to be approved by a recognized body with delegated authority including a private body. Private standards are usually developed by non-profit organizations being a foundation or a charity, i.e. private bodies. However, according to Annex 1.8 of the TBT Agreement, a non-governmental body must have the legal power to enforce a technical regulation. Thus, there must be a link with governmental authorities. Hence, most of the private sector initiatives such as corporate codes of conduct or labelling initiatives, even if they are in some cases sponsored or otherwise supported by governments, are not documents approved by a recognized body and as such not subject to the TBT Agreement. Of course, in case a government officially recognizes and commits to control such standards as in the case of the German recently introduced 'Green Button', the TBT Agreement probably applies.[1364] By contrast, the Belgian Social Label Law is a national law laying down conditions for the granting of a voluntary governmental label. As such, it comes within the purview of the TBT Agreement.

12.3 *Substantive Provisions of the TBT Agreement*

12.3.1 Art. 2.4 of the TBT Agreement

In *EC–Sardines,* the Appellate Body held that after an examination of Art. 2.4 of the TBT Agreement, Art. 2.1 and 2.2 did not need to be addressed anymore.[1365] In *US–Tuna II* however, the Appellate Body started with the examination of Art. 2.1 and 2.2 of the TBT Agreement.[1366] Since the analysis of Art. 2.4 may be relevant for the interpretation of Art. 2.5 and Art. 2.2, this study will begin the analysis with Art. 2.4 of the TBT Agreement.

Art. 2.4 of the TBT Agreement provides:

1362 See for example the discussion in Humbert (The Challenge of Child Labour), pp. 364–266; Civil society asks therefore for a fair distribution of costs between all actors of the supply chain through considering sourcing policies of buying companies; see CorA-Netzwerk (Anforderungen an Multi-Stakeholder-Initiativen), p. 12.

1363 Van den Bossche/Zdouc, p. 1027 with further references.

1364 See www.gruener-knopf.de; translation by the author, German original: Der 'Grüne Knopf'.

1365 *EC–Sardines*, report of the Appellate Body, para. 313.

1366 *US–Tuna II*, report of the Appellate Body.

> Where technical regulations are required and relevant international standards exist or their completion is imminent Members shall use them, or the relevant parts of them, as a basis for their technical regulations except when such international standards or relevant parts would be an ineffective or inappropriate means for the fulfilment of the legitimate objectives pursued, for instance because of fundamental climatic or geographical factors or fundamental technological problems.

The first condition under this provision seems to be that technical regulations must be 'required'. In *EC–Sardines,* the point of controversy between the parties was whether the provision applies to existing technical regulations and whether the measure was based on an international standard.[1367] Both parties accepted that the technical regulation was 'required', or that the member in question had decided that the technical regulation was 'required'.[1368] The measure at issue was an EC-Regulation falling in the scope of application of the Codex Stan 94 developed by the Codex Alimentarius Commission of the United Nations Food and Agriculture Organization and the World Health Organization. It can thus be argued that where the technical regulation at issue comes within the scope of application of an international standard, the technical regulation can be assumed to be 'required'. The question therefore is whether in the area of child labour, international standards exist that are covered by Art. 2.4 of the TBT Agreement.

As stated above, the numerous UN and ILO Conventions prohibiting child labour could potentially qualify as international standards.[1369] The same holds true for the ILO Declaration on Fundamental Principles and Rights at Work,[1370] ILO Tripartite Declaration of Principles concerning Multinational Enterprises[1371] and the OECD Guidelines for Multinational Enterprises.[1372] It

---

1367 Ibid., para. 196 et seq.

1368 *EC–Sardines*, report of the panel, paras. 4.17 and 4.22.

1369 For an overview of UN and ILO conventions and declarations on child labour see Humbert, pp. 35–121; cf. Marceau (Trade and Labour) pp. 555, who seems to argue that ILO standards are relevant standards in this context.

1370 ILO, ILO Declaration on Fundamental Principles and rights at Work, International Labour Conference, eighty-sixth session (Geneva, International Labour Office, 1998). For more information see Humbert, pp. 103–107.

1371 ILO, Tripartite Declaration of Principles concerning Multinational Enterprises and Social Policy, adopted by the Governing Body of the International Labour, Office at its 204th Session (Geneva, November 1977) as amended at its 279th (November 2000) and 295th Session, March 2006 (Geneva: International Labour Office, 2006).

1372 OECD, OECD Guidelines for Multinational Enterprises (OECD Publishing, 2011).

could also be argued that a standard such as ISO 26000 referring to UN and ILO instruments on child labour[1373] and developed by the ISO, an international semi-private body including national governments, or other public sector codes such as the UN Global Compact[1374] come within the definition of 'international standard'.[1375] In *EC–Sardines,* the panel found:

> International standards are standards that are developed by international bodies.[1376]

An international body is defined in Annex 1.4:

> *4. International body or system*
> Body or system whose membership is open to the relevant bodies of at least all Members.

As analysed above, standards in accordance with Annex 1.2 of the TBT Agreement refer to non-binding documents that lay down product characteristics and production methods that are reflected in the final product, thereby excluding npr-ppm-measures on child labour. However, labelling and other identification requirements such as the Belgian Social Label Law are encompassed by the definition of standards.

Since UN and ILO Conventions on child labour contain binding human rights obligations for states instead of labelling rules or other means of identification standards for the private sector, they do not qualify as standards as defined by Annex 1.2. Despite of its non-binding character, the same holds true for the ILO Declaration on Fundamental Principles and Rights at Work.

The question is whether public sector codes addressing the industry but involving governments such as the UN Global Compact, the ILO Tripartite Declaration, the OECD Guidelines and ISO 26 000 qualify as international standards. Such standards are distinct from UN Conventions because they address the private sector. However, they also do not set forth product characteristics or labelling requirements or other means of identification with

1373 DIN ISO 26 000 on file with the author. For the drafting history and further information, see www.iso.org/iso/home/standards/iso26000.htm.

1374 UN Global Compact, www.unglobalcompact.org/.

1375 For an overview of private sector initiatives on child labour see Humbert (The Challenge of Child Labour), pp. 332–375.

1376 *EC–Sardines*, report of the panel, para. 7.63.

a strong product nexus that come within the definition of a standard. Thus, there is no need to ask whether they are 'international standards'.

It is worth noting that the drafters of the ISO 26 000 explicitly rejected the view that the norm would be a standard within the meaning of Art. 2.4 of the TBT Agreement, arguing convincingly that private standards negotiated by the ISO would become binding on WTO members through the back door.[1377] Moreover, the concern has been raised that in case of an overly broad definition of 'international standards', some WTO members in cooperation with business could enforce their standards by creating a standardizing body open to relevant bodies of all WTO members.[1378] Whilst this concern seems to be a justified, it does not apply in case of the ISO 26000 since this norm does not lay down product standards or labelling requirements.

Finally, one could ask whether private labelling schemes on child labour such as the former RUGMARK initiative, which has become the GoodWeave label,[1379] classify as 'international standards' in case they have been developed with the support of governmental organizations such as the GIZ. However, in contrast to public sector codes and the ISO 26 000, such labelling initiatives have not been developed by international bodies that are open to relevant bodies from WTO members as required by Annex 1.4.

Thus, as of now, there are no international standards on child labour within the meaning of Art. 2.4 of the TBT Agreement.

12.3.2 Art. 2.1 of the TBT

Art. 2.1 of the TBT Agreement reads:

> Members shall ensure that in respect of technical regulations, products imported from the territory of any member shall be accorded treatment no less favourable than that accorded to like products of national origin and to like products originating in any other country.

Following GATT Art. I and III, the provision requires MFN treatment and national treatment of products. Since pursuant to Annex 3.D these obligations also apply to standards, relevant standards and technical regulations will be examined together.

1377 The author of this study was part of the negotiation process.

1378 Pauwelyn (Human Rights in WTO Dispute Settlement), p. 227.

1379 Cf. Humbert (The Challenge of Child Labour), p. 362 et seqq. and About Goodweave, https://goodweave.org/uk/about/.

Certification requirements for diamonds traded under the Kimberley Process Certification qualify as technical regulations but are not likely to violate neither the MFN clause nor the national treatment clause because all participants have to provide for the same certification measures.[1380] Trade bans on non-certified diamonds are likely to violate both obligations but do not qualify as technical regulations. By contrast, the Belgian Social Label Law is a standard and could potentially discriminate against countries with a high incidence of child labour and thus violate both the MFN and national treatment obligation.

Like under the GATT, Art. 2.1 of the TBT Agreement requires that the products at issue are 'like products' and that, in case of national treatment, imported and domestic products are treated no less favourably. In case of MFN treatment, products imported from one WTO member must be accorded 'treatment no less favourable' than like products originating in any other country.

In the past, some authors rightly pointed out that an overly broad reading – i.e. to apply Art. 2.1 to discriminatory measures and to origin-neutral measures – would render many technical regulations void since the TBT Agreement does not contain a general exceptions clause such as GATT Art. XX.[1381] As a solution, it had been proposed to either apply GATT Art. XX under the TBT Agreement,[1382] to stretch the definition of 'like products' to allow for distinctions based on ppms that are not reflected in the final product[1383] or to apply Art. 2.1 of the TBT Agreement only to *de iure discrimination* and in case of *de facto* discrimination, to read Art. 2.1 in the light of Art. 2.2 of the TBT Agreement.[1384]

The Appellate Body has now attempted to clarify the scope and meaning of Art. 2.1 in three recent cases, i.e. *US–Clove Cigarettes, US–Tuna II* (*Mexico*) and *US–COOL*.[1385]

12.3.2.1 *'Like Products'*

As regards the concept of 'like products', as stated above, the Appellate Body in *US–Clove Cigarettes* reversed the panel's finding regarding the consideration of

1380 As stated above, although the Kimberley Process Certification Scheme operates under a Waiver, its WTO law compatibility will be examined in order to decide whether the scheme could be used as a model for future schemes.

1381 Marceau/Trachtmann, p. 874; Tietje/Wolf, p. 53.

1382 Marceau/Trachtmann, p. 874.

1383 Ibid.

1384 Tietje/Wolf, p. 55.

1385 *US–Clove Cigarettes*, report of the Appellate Body; *US–Tuna II* (*Mexico*), report of the Appellate Body, *US–COOL*, report of the Appellate Body.

regulatory purposes.[1386] Drawing on the analysis of likeness in *EC–Asbestos* in relation to GATT Art. III:4 it held that

> the determination of likeness under Art. 2.1 of the TBT Agreement, as well as under Article III:4 of the GATT 1994, is a determination about the nature and extent of a competitive relationship between and among the products at issue. To the extent that they are relevant to the examination of certain "likeness" criteria and are reflected in the products' competitive relationship, regulatory concerns underlying technical regulations may play a role in the determination of likeness.[1387]

It pointed to the difficulty in determining the relevant policy goal of a measure in case of several goals and reasoned that considerations regarding the purpose or effect of a measure are better suited under the 'less favourable treatment' concept.[1388] This view is convincing since otherwise, as argued above, the trade effect of the measure as opposed to its aim would not be adequately taken into account.[1389] When determining 'likeness', the Appellate Body uses the same criteria as under GATT Art. III.[1390]

As regards trade measures on child labour, the products at issue in most cases will qualify as 'like products' since they are physically similar and for the time being, most consumers will not make a difference between products made and not made by children.

12.3.2.2 *'Treatment No Less Favourable'*

Drawing on the jurisprudence in relation to GATT Art. III as well as on the context and the object and purpose of the TBT Agreement the Appellate Body in *US–Clove Cigarettes* held:

> Accordingly, where a technical regulation at issue does not *de jure* discriminate against imports, the existence of a detrimental impact on competitive opportunities for the group of domestic like products is not dispositive of less favourable treatment under Art. 2.1. Instead, a panel must further analyze whether the detrimental impact on imports stems

1386 *US–Clove Cigarettes*, report of the Appellate Body, paras. 108–120.
1387 Ibid., para. 120.
1388 Ibid., paras. 113–115 and paras. 111 and 116–117.
1389 Cf. the discussion under GATT Art. III, pp. 175 et seqq.
1390 Cf. for example US Clove–Cigarettes, report of the Appellate Body, paras. 122–155 and the discussion of 'likeness' under GATT Art. III.

> exclusively from a legitimate regulatory distinction rather than reflecting discrimination against the group of imports.[1391]

Thus, in contrast to its findings under GATT Art. III, the Appellate Body in *US–Clove Cigarettes* deemed the consideration of regulatory purposes worth considering.[1392] In reaching its conclusion, it referred to the sixth recital of the Preamble of the TBT Agreement that explicitly acknowledges that members may take measures for particular policy goals such as the protection of human life or health unless they are not applied in a manner that would constitute a means of arbitrary or unjustifiable discrimination.[1393] Also, it emphasized that 'the object and purpose of the TBT Agreement is to strike a balance between, on the one hand, the objective of trade liberalization and, on the other hand, Members' right to regulate'.[1394] Finally, it is worth noting that the Appellate Body observed that the balance set out in the Preamble of the TBT Agreement is not, in principle, different from the balance between GATT Art. III and GATT Art. XX, except that the TBT Agreement does not contain a general exception clause such as GATT Art. XX.[1395] Whilst the consideration of regulatory purposes under the national treatment clause in Art. 2.1 is most welcome, there are still open questions as how to apply this legal test.

In *US–Clove Cigarettes*, the Appellate Body further explained:

> In making this determination, a panel must carefully scrutinize the particular circumstances of the case, that is the design, architecture, revealing structure, operation and application of the technical regulation at issue, an, in particular, whether the measure is even-handed, in order to determine whether it discriminates against the group of imported products.[1396]

Thus, it seems that in relation to Art. 2.1, the Appellate Body deems it useful to consider *inter alia* the design and architecture of a measure in order to reveal the objective aim of a measure, i.e. what it has done earlier in *Chile–Alcoholic Beverages* in relation to GATT Art. III:2. Further, the manner in which the measure is applied will be relevant, in particular its even-handedness in this

1391 *US–Clove Cigarettes*, report of the Appellate Body, para. 182.
1392 For the discussion of regulatory purposes under GATT Art. III, see above, pp. 103 et seqq.
1393 *US–Clove Cigarettes*, report of the Appellate Body, para. 173.
1394 Ibid., para. 174.
1395 Ibid., paras. 96 and 101.
1396 Ibid., para. 182.

regard. This test corresponds to the test under the *chapeau* of GATT Art. XX, where the question is whether the implementation of the measure is not so as to constitute unjustifiable discrimination.

Indeed, what the Appellate Body in its three recent decisions seems to do when applying its new legal test, is to somehow apply the legal standards of the *chapeau*. In *US–Clove Cigarettes*, it found that the policy goal of minimizing costs for the US health care system and the risk of a development of a black market would not be reached by exempting menthol cigarettes from its trade ban, thereby analysing whether the discrimination can be reconciled with, or is rationally related to, the policy objective, i.e. the legal test in relation to the chapeau developed by the Appellate Body in *EC–Seal Products*.[1397] In *US–Tuna II (Mexico)*, the Appellate Body found that the

> difference in labelling conditions for tuna products containing tuna caught by setting on dolphins in the ETP [Eastern Tropical Pacific] on the one hand, and for tuna products containing tuna caught by other fishing methods outside the ETP, on the other hand, is "calibrated" to the risks to dolphins arising from different fishing methods in different areas of the ocean.[1398]

Thus, here also, the legal test seems to be whether there is unjustifiable discrimination in the application of the measure. Finally, in *US–COOL*, the Appellate Body found that the recordkeeping and verification requirements put higher costs on producers using imported livestock and cannot be explained by the need to provide origin information to consumers, thereby constituting unjustifiable discrimination in violation of Art. 2.1 of the TBT Agreement.[1399]

The question is why the Appellate Body does not conduct a proper proportionality test similar to the one developed in the GATT Art. XX jurisprudence. This would be in line with Tietje and Wolf, who argue that Art. 2.1 should be read in light of Art. 2.2 of the TBT Agreement.[1400] This would ensure more balanced results because the level of protection sought by the measure, its contribution to reach its goal and a comparison to an alternative measure would be part of the analysis. For example, in *US–COOL*, the Appellate Body argued that some of the labels in question do not identify which production step

1397 *US–Clove Cigarettes*, report of the Appellate Body, para. 225; *EC–Seal Products*, report of the Appellate Body, para. 5.318.

1398 *US–Tuna II*, report of the Appellate Body, para. 297.

1399 *US–COOL*, report of the Appellate Body, para. 349.

1400 See p. 268.

regarding meat production took place in which country and therefore were not commensurate with the origin information requirements.[1401] As Howse rightly argues, this is a questionable argument since it is far from clear whether more information regarding the production steps is actually wanted by consumers.[1402] Thus, if the panel and Appellate Body had properly considered the level of protection sought by the label, its contribution to the desired objective and possible alternative measures, it might have reached a different conclusion. It is worth noting that in *EC–Seal Products*, the Appellate Body held that there were significant differences between the analyses under Art. 2.1 of the TBT Agreement and the chapeau of GATT Art. XX.[1403] In particular, it stated that a measure could be applied in a manner that would constitute a means of unjustifiable discrimination on grounds that are not necessarily the same as the discrimination in contravention to GATT Art. III.[1404] This statement indicates that under Art. 2.1 of the TBT Agreement, a more comprehensive analysis with regard to discrimination should be conducted. Hence, it should be possible to conduct a sort of proportionality test similar to the one under GATT Art. XX in case the measure is origin-neutral. In light of the Preamble, the test of the chapeau should also apply.

Since the MFN obligation under Art. 2.1 of the TBT Agreement also requires a 'treatment no less favourable' with regard to products originating in any other country, *mutatis mutandis* the findings made above should also apply in this case.

As regards trade measures on child labour, as stated above, there is no equally effective alternative measure to the Belgian Social Label Law and it does not have any features that would make it a means of unjustifiable discrimination.[1405] Put differently, its potential discriminatory effect can be reconciled with its policy goal. Hence, the Belgian Law would comply with the MFN as well as with the national treatment obligation of Art. 2.1 of the TBT Agreement even if the complete proportionality test of GATT Art. XX is applied.

12.3.3 Art. 2.2 of the TBT Agreement

12.3.3.1 *The Scope of Art. 2.2 of the TBT Agreement*

Art. 2.2 of the TBT Agreement reads:

1401 *US–COOL*, report of the Appellate Body, para. 343.
1402 Howse (Consumer Labelling), p. 599.
1403 *EC–Seal Products*, report of the Appellate Body, para. 5.311.
1404 Ibid., para.5.313.
1405 See the discussion under GATT Art. XX, p.226.

> Members shall ensure that technical regulations are not prepared, adopted or applied with a view to or with the effect of creating unnecessary obstacles to international trade. For this purpose, technical regulations shall not be more trade-restrictive than necessary to fulfil a legitimate objective, taking into account the risks non-fulfilment would create. Such legitimate objectives are, inter alia: national security requirements; the prevention of deceptive practices; protection of human health or safety, animal or plant life or health, or the environment. In assessing such risks, relevant elements of consideration are, inter alia: available scientific and technical information, related processing technology or intended end-uses of products.

Since Annex 3.E to the TBT Agreement contains the same obligations for standards, both types of measures will be examined together.

The first sentence of this provision takes further the non-discrimination clauses of the GATT contained in Art. I and III and applies to all measures that may unnecessarily restrict international trade. Thus, not only measures with an unintended discriminatory effect but also measures merely restrict trade are caught by Art. 2.2. In *US–Tuna II (Mexico)*, the Appellate Body stated that trade restrictive meant 'having a limiting effect on trade'.[1406]

National certification requirements of the Kimberley Process Certification Scheme put the same burden on all participants but nevertheless have a trade effect. Thus, they fall within the scope of Art. 2.2 of the TBT Agreement. So does the Belgian Social Label Law.

In contrast to GATT Art. III, the provision only condemns 'unnecessary obstacles'. Art. 2.2, second sentence, explains what 'unnecessary obstacles' means, namely obstacles that are not more trade-restrictive than necessary to fulfil a legitimate objective.

In contrast to GATT Art. XX, the list of legitimate objectives is open. Whilst it has been established that legitimate objectives reflected in the WTO Agreements will be considered to be legitimate, it is still subject to debate whether other objectives such as labour standards or human rights are 'legitimate objectives'. However, taking into the account the purpose of the TBT Agreement as stated in its Preamble to refine the GATT and to strike a balance between trade liberalization and members' policy space, there is no reason why to read Art. 2.2. of the TBT Agreement differently from GATT Art. XX as regards possible policy goals, given that the list is even longer. Since it has been

1406 *US–Tuna II (Mexico)*, report of the Appellate Body, para. 319.

concluded that human rights and labour rights are possible policy goals under GATT Art. XX (a), the same should hold true for Art. 2.2 of the TBT Agreement. Thus, measures under the Kimberley Scheme and the Belgian Social Label Law aiming *inter alia* at eliminating child labour pursue a legitimate objective.

In *US–Tuna II (Mexico)*, the Appellate Body held that the question whether a measure 'fulfils' an objective is concerned with the degree of contribution to the achievement of the objective.[1407] This can be inferred from design, structure and operation of the measure as well as its application.[1408] Most importantly, as under GATT Art. XX, members are in principle free to determine their level of contribution if they comply with the remaining requirements of Art. 2.2 of the TBT Agreement.[1409] However, what counts is the actual contribution, not the intended contribution.[1410] Further, it held that the assessment of 'necessity' involved a relational analysis of the trade-restrictiveness of the measure, the degree of contribution to its objective and the risks non-fulfilment would create.[1411]

In addition to the relational analysis, according to the Appellate Body, the words' more trade-restrictive than necessary' in most cases

> would involve a comparison of the trade-restrictiveness and the degree of achievement of the objective by the measure at issue with that of possible alternative measures that may be reasonably available and less trade restrictive than the challenged measure, taking account of the risks non-fulfilment would create.[1412]

When assessing the risks of non-fulfilment in the comparison with the alternative measure, the nature of the risks and the gravity of the consequences arising from the non-fulfilment have to be taken into account.[1413] As under GATT Art. XX, the comparison with the alternative measure requires a weighing and balancing in the determination whether an alternative measure, which is less trade restrictive, would make an equivalent contribution to the

1407 *US–Tuna II (Mexico)*, report of the Appellate Body, para. 315.
1408 Ibid., para 317.
1409 Ibid., para 316.
1410 Ibid., para 317.
1411 Ibid., para 318.
1412 Ibid., para. 320.
1413 Ibid., para. 321.

relevant objective.[1414] The Appellate Body in *US–Tuna II (Mexico)* stated that this balancing test was similar to proportionality test developed for GATT Art. XX in *Korea–Beef*.[1415] In this context, it has rightly been argued that Art. 2.2 of the TBT Agreement contains the most far-reaching application of the proportionality principle.[1416] However, some argue that by comparison with Art. 5.6 of the SPS Agreement, the necessity test under Art. 2.2 of the TBT Agreement is less stringent than under GATT Art. XX, calling less for an enquiry into the effectiveness of the challenged measure.[1417] This is convincing given that the negative consequences of the non-adoption of the measure also have to be taken into account. Also, an important difference is that under GATT Art. XX, one examines whether the measure is necessary whereas under Art. 2.2 of the TBT Agreement whether the trade-restrictiveness is necessary.[1418]

Another major difference refers to the burden of proof. Whilst under GATT Art. XX, the burden of proof is more or less on the respondent invoking the exception, in case of Art. 2.2 of the TBT Agreement, the complainant must prove that the challenged measure creates an unnecessary obstacle to international trade including identifying alternative measures.[1419]

Finally, it has convincingly been argued that Art. 2.2 of the TBT Agreement has to be read in conjunction with the sixth recital of the Preamble.[1420] It has rightly been concluded that this wording taken from the *chapeau* of GATT Art. XX indicates that the proportionality test under the *chapeau* of GATT Art. XX and Art. 2.2 of the TBT Agreement should be the same, both striking an appropriate balance between the interests of the regulating and exporting WTO members.[1421] In *US–Tuna II (Mexico)*, the Appellate Body has confirmed that the sixth recital of the Preamble is relevant context also for Art. 2.2 of the TBT Agreement. However, in most cases, discriminatory measures that could be caught by the sixth recital will most probably already have been found to violate Art. 2.1 of the TBT Agreement.

Before turning to the examination of trade measures of child labour, Art. 2.5 of the TBT Agreement will briefly be considered. Art. 2.5 of the TBT Agreement

---

1414 Ibid.; A Note from the WTO-Secretariat considered the reference to the risk of non-fulfilment also as a sort of proportionality test, Note of the Secretariat, cited in Marceau/Trachtmann, p. 832.

1415 *US–Tuna II (Mexico)*, report of the Appellate Body, fn 645.

1416 Desmedt, p. 460.

1417 Marceau/Trachtmann, p. 874.

1418 *US–Tuna II (Mexico)*, report of the Appellate Body, para. 319.

1419 Ibid., para. 323.

1420 Tietje/Wolf, p. 56.

1421 Ibid.

provides for the rebuttable presumption of necessity of a technical regulation within the meaning of Art. 2.2 of the TBT Agreement if the measure at issue is adopted for one of the legitimate objectives explicitly mentioned and in accordance with relevant international standards. As discussed above, since for the time being, no standards on child labour in conformity with the TBT Agreement seem to exist, Art. 2.5 will not be examined further.

As regards the consistency of the Belgian Social Label Law with Art. 2.2 of the TBT Agreement, it has been stated above that its trade impact is very low given the label is accorded on a voluntary basis and exporters may even be financially supported. Thus, its trade-restrictiveness is limited. However, the degree of contribution is hard to assess because of a lack of evidence from its application. However, as stated above, regarding its design and structure, it appears to be apt to make a material contribution to the reduction of child labour. Also, since the only conceivable less trade-restrictive measure is the provision of aid to child labourers, which is not equally effective and puts too much a burden on the regulating state, the Belgian Social Label Law does not seem to be more trade-restrictive than necessary. Since there is no reasonably available alternative measure, it is not necessary to consider the risk of non-fulfilment.

As regards certification measures under the Kimberley Scheme, its trade-restrictiveness appears to be limited given that the certification requirement regards all participants equally. The degree of contribution however is questionable since there are increasing reports that the lack of monitoring and traceability conceals human rights violations in the jewellery industry.[1422] At the same, there have been reports, that the scheme has actually reduced the share of blood diamonds in the world to less than 1 per cent.[1423] However, since there is currently no reasonably available alternative measure other than private standards[1424] and it is not sure what would happen if one abolished the Scheme, in the light of its low impact on trade, the Scheme should not be qualified as being 'more trade-restrictive than necessary'.

In conclusion, both the Belgian Social Label Law and national measures under the Kimberley Process Certification Scheme comply with Art. 2.2 of the TBT Agreement.

1422 Rhode, David, The Guardian, The Kimberley Process is a 'perfect cover story' for blood diamonds, 24 March 2014.

1423 Frankfurter Allgemeine Zeitung, T. Scheen, ‚Kein Diamant ist unverfänglich', 12 Dezember 2006.

1424 See for example the Fair-Trade Gold Standard Fairever, see https://www.fairever.gold/de/ueber-uns

12.4 *Conclusion*

The TBT Agreement provides for disciplines for technical regulations that are mandatory and standards that are voluntary. Standards are subject to the Code of Good Practice. With some minor distinctions, the substantive provisions of both regimes are the same.

The analysis suggests that there are still unresolved questions as to how the TBT Agreement should be interpreted. Bearing in mind that one major objective is to refine the GATT and to improve the efficiency of production, as regards the issue of npr-ppms such as child labour, it is proposed here to construe the term 'technical regulation' in a narrow way covering primarily technical rules involving or concerned with applied and industrial sciences with a rather strong product nexus. It has been found that the provisions of the TBT Agreement are better suited to deal with such technical rules and that trade measures on child labour with a looser product nexus – except for labelling measures – are better placed under GATT Art. III and XX.

The main substantive obligations relate to the principle of non-discrimination and the prohibition of trade restrictions that are unnecessary obstacles to international trade. Thus, besides containing MFN and equal treatment obligation, it also covers measures that are non-discriminatory. In contrast to GATT Art. III, a measure will only be discriminatory if it modifies the conditions of competition to the detriment of imported products *and* if the detrimental impact does not stem from a legitimate regulatory distinction rather than reflecting discrimination. While the jurisprudence has drawn on the legal tests of the *chapeau* of GATT Art. XX, it is suggested here to apply the complete proportionality test of GATT Art. XX in order to achieve more balanced results.

The prohibition of trade restrictions that are unnecessary obstacles to international trade contains a proportionality test similar to the one under GATT Art. XX. There are however some differences for example with regard to the burden of proof. With a view to the sixth recital of the Preamble, it is suggested here to also examine whether the measure constitutes arbitrary or unjustifiable discrimination.

Trade measures on child labour that fall within the scope of the TBT Agreement are the Belgian Social Label Law and the Kimberley Process Certification Scheme. They have both been found to be consistent with the principle of non-discrimination as well as not to violate the obligation to refrain from creating unnecessary obstacle to international trade.

13 Compatibility of Trade Measures on Child Labour with the Agreement on Government Procurement

13.1 *Introduction*

The Revised Agreement on Government Procurement (GPA 2012) replaced the Agreement on Government Procurement from 1994.[1425] It is a plurilateral agreement, i.e. cross-retaliation under the DSU procedure is excluded. No dispute may result in suspensions of trade concessions or other obligations under the GPA (2012), and no dispute under the GPA (2012) may result in suspension of concessions or other obligations under any other WTO agreement.[1426] Government procurement means the acquisition by governments and their subsidiary agencies of the goods and services that they need to carry out their functions.[1427]

Since traditionally, governments tended to discriminate in their purchasing policies in favour of their own industry, the GPA (2012) seeks to reduce such discrimination. The primary obligations under the GPA are the MFN obligation, national treatment and obligations regarding transparency. The GPA can be considered as a response to the exceptions for government procurement under Art. III (8) and XVII (2) of the GATT, which are deemed to cover the MFN obligation under GATT Art. I.[1428] The GPA (2012) sets minimum standards for government procurement but does not seek to argue in favour of certain economic concepts such as the 'purity principle'.[1429] On the contrary, the revised GPA opens space to promote the objective of sustainable development by mentioning for example explicitly the environment when talking about the scope of application for technical specifications.[1430]

The much-discussed Massachusetts Burma Law from 1996 is an example for a possible measure on child labour falling under the scope of the GPA.[1431] It prohibits government purchases from persons doing business with Myanmar. It is a government purchasing law targeting, *inter alia*, forced child labour in

1425 Agreement on Government Procurement from 6 April 2014, GPA, www.wto.org/english/docs_e/legal_e/rev-gpr-94_01_e.htm and Agreement on Government Procurement from 1994, www.wto.org/english/docs_e/legal_e/gpr-94_01_e.htm.

1426 Art. XX of the GPA.

1427 Dischendorfer, p. 2.

1428 Ibid., p. 14 et seq.

1429 Steiner (Nachhaltige öffentliche Beschaffung), p.151; Cf. Also Davies, p. 435 with further references.

1430 Art. X of the GPA (2012).

1431 An Act Regulating State Contracts with Companies Doing Business with or in Burma (Myanmar), 1996 Mass. Acts ch. 130 (codified at MASS. GEN. LAWS ch. 7, §§ 22G-M (2000)).

Myanmar. Since the law illustrates very well how measures on child labour may be in conflict with WTO law, its compatibility with the obligations under the GPA (2012) will be discussed even though the constitutionality of the law was successfully challenged before the Supreme Court.[1432]

The new EU Directive 2014/24/EU on government procurement stipulates in its general rules that member states shall ensure compliance with international labour law including the ILO Core Conventions by economic operators.[1433] Art. 57 (4) lit. (a) of the EU Directive 2014/24/EU provides for the opportunity for authorities to exclude operators that demonstrably violated international labour law including the ILO Conventions on child labour. In addition, a conviction for the use of child labour is an explicitly mentioned exclusion ground, Art. 57 (1) lit. (f) of the EU Directive 2014/24/EU. The Directive also allows for award criteria based on social considerations, provided that such criteria are linked to the subject matter of the contract and do not refer to the general corporate policy.[1434] Performance conditions may also include social considerations such as integration of disadvantaged persons amongst the persons assigned to the contract, Recital (99) and Art. 70 of the EU Directive 2014/24/EU. According to Recital (75) and Art. 43 of the EU Directive 2014/24/EU, contracting authorities can refer to social labels in the technical specifications, the award criteria or the contract performance conditions. Annex VII to the EU Directive 2014/24/EU defines technical specifications.[1435] Recital (99) stipulates that technical specifications may refer to social considerations that directly characterise the product such as accessibility for persons with disabilities. Whether technical specifications may also refer to social considerations such as the use of child labour and whether the EU Directive 2014/24/EU is consistent with the GPA (2012) will be examined in turn.

13.2 *Art. IV – General Principles*

Art. IV of the GPA (2012) reads:

> *Non-discrimination*
>
> 1. With respect to any measure regarding government procurement, each Party including its procuring entities, shall accord immediately and unconditionally to the goods and services of any other Party and

1432 Crosby v. National Foreign Trade Council 120 S.Ct. 2288 (2000).

1433 Art. 18 (2) EU Directive 2014/24/EU, OJ L 94/65 (28 March 2014) in conjunction with Annex X.

1434 Art. 67 (2) and (3) and recital (92) and (97) of the preamble to the EU Directive 2014/24/EU.

1435 Annex VII to the EU Directive 2014/24/EU.

to the suppliers of any other Party offering the goods or services of any Party, treatment no less favourable than the treatment the Party, including its procuring entities, accords to:

(a) domestic products, services and suppliers; and

(b) goods, services and suppliers of any other Party.

2. With respect to any measure regarding covered procurement, a Party, including its procuring entities, shall not:

(a) treat a locally established supplier less favourably than another locally established supplier on the basis of the degree of foreign affiliation or ownership; or

(b) discriminate against a locally established supplier on the basis that the goods or services offered by that supplier for a particular procurement are goods or services of any other Party.

Art. IV of the GPA contains the MFN and national treatment clauses. In contrast to GATT Art. I and III, it does not only refer to goods but also to services and suppliers.

13.2.1 MFN Treatment

Like GATT Art. I, the MFN clause stipulates that each party shall provide immediately and unconditionally to the products or services and suppliers of the parties 'treatment no less favourable than that accorded to products or suppliers of other parties'. Products, services and suppliers from importing countries shall be treated equally, irrespective of origin.

In 1998, the EC requested the establishment of a panel under the WTO DSU, contending that the Massachusetts Burma Law by not providing to suppliers of other parties offering products or services immediate and unconditional treatment no less favourable than that accorded to domestic suppliers and that accorded to services and suppliers of any other party, violated Art. III:1 of the GPA (1994).[1436] With a view to the pending case under the US Supreme Court,[1437] the EC and Japan requested the panel to suspend its work in 1999, which was then the case.[1438]

According to Section 22G (a) of the Massachusetts Burma Law, the term 'people doing business with Myanmar' includes persons having a principal place of business in Burma. The Massachusetts Burma Law, by prohibiting the

1436 *United States – Measures Affecting Government Procurement*, Request for establishment of a panel by the EC, 9 September 1998, WT/DS88/3.

1437 See p. 279.

1438 Note of the Secretariat, 14 February 2000, WT/DS95/6.

Massachusetts State authorities to purchase goods from persons doing business with Myanmar, applying an automatic price penalty of 10 per cent on bids from those companies, does not accord suppliers from Myanmar immediate and unconditional treatment no less favourable than that accorded to suppliers from other parties. Also, goods from Myanmar are treated worse than goods from other parties. In relation to Myanmar, it is a country-based and facially discriminatory measure and violates Art. IV:1 (b) of the GPA.[1439]

13.2.2 National Treatment

Art. IV:1 (a) of the GPA (2012) follows GATT Art. III, regulating that products or suppliers offering products of other parties shall be immediately and unconditionally accorded treatment no less favourable than that accorded to domestic products and suppliers.

The Massachusetts Burma Law does not accord suppliers from Myanmar treatment no less favourable than that accorded to domestic suppliers not doing business with Myanmar by applying an automatic price penalty of 10 per cent on bids from companies from Myanmar. The same holds true for goods coming from Myanmar. In relation to Myanmar, the law is facially discriminatory and violates the national treatment obligation.

In relation to parties such as the EU, the question is whether Art. IV:1 (a) of the GPA also covers *de facto* discrimination because the law does not facially discriminate against suppliers from the EU. Following the approach of GATT Art. III Art. IV:1 (a) should also apply in cases of *de facto* discrimination. Accordingly, if the law proves to have an asymmetrical impact on the EU by blacklisting more EU firms than US firms, Art. IV:1 (a) of the GPA will be violated. Indeed, according to the EU, 281 foreign companies and 44 US companies were blacklisted, while four of the US companies and 53 of the foreign companies had subsidiaries in Myanmar.[1440] Thus, the Massachusetts law also violates Art. IV:1 (a) of the GPA (2012) in relation to the EU.

The question is whether one should allow for the consideration of the regulatory purpose in attempt to justify the law, as argues Davies,[1441] following the approach under GATT Art. III. One could hold that the good intention to ban bids from suppliers with links to a regime that at the time relied on forced child labour could rescue the measure. Indeed, there is no reason why choosing a different approach under the GPA than under the GATT. However,

1439 It should however be noted that Myanmar is not a member to the GPA and therefore may not bring a claim either under the DSU or under the GPA.

1440 Cf. Fitzgerald, p. 6.

1441 Davies, p. 436 et seqq.

taking due account of the General Exceptions clause contained in Art. III of the GPA (2012), the regulatory purpose should only be considered to complement the analysis of trade effects, e.g. when the detrimental effect is unclear. If, in contrast, there is a clear detrimental impact, a weighing and balancing of the detrimental impact against the good objective is needed, and this should be done under the exceptions clause as its wording suggests. As held above, such a balancing should take place in any event even though the prohibition of child labour forms part of *ius cogens*.[1442]

Art. IV of the GPA does not refer to 'like products' as GATT Art. III. Instead, the GPA contains provisions for conditions for participation in Art. VIII, and technical specifications and tender documentation in Art. X of the GPA (2012). The provisions of the EU Directive referring to technical specifications, award criteria and suppliers' qualifications will therefore be examined under Art. VIII and X of the GPA (2012).

13.2.3 Locally-Established Suppliers

According to Art. IV:2 (a) of the GPA (2012), locally-established suppliers shall not be treated less favourably than another locally-established supplier on the basis of degree of foreign affiliation or ownership. Since the Massachusetts Burma Law treats majority-owned subsidiaries of persons doing business with Burma or persons having a majority-owned subsidiary in Burma worse than other locally-established suppliers, it violates Art. IV:2 (a) of the GPA.

Neither shall locally-established suppliers be discriminated against on the basis of the country of production of the good being supplied, Art. IV:2 (b) of the GPA. Since the Massachusetts Burma Law applies to persons who promote the sale of products that are largely traded by the government of Burma, it also violates Art. III:2 (b) of the GPA.

13.2.4 Conclusion

In conclusion, the Massachusetts Burma Law on government procurement discriminates *de iure* and *de facto* against foreign suppliers and violates Art. IV:1 (a) and (b) of the GPA (2012) as well as Art. IV:2 (a) and (b) since it discriminates also against locally-established suppliers on the basis of their foreign affiliation and the origin of the good being supplied.

The provisions in the EU Directive referring to technical specifications, award criteria and suppliers' qualifications will be examined under Art. VIII

1442 See the discussion under GATT Art. III pp. 181 et seqq.

and X of the GPA (2012) since these rules can be considered *lex specialis* rules for conditions of participation and product and service regulations.

13.3 *Art. VIII – Conditions for Participation*

The relevant provisions of Art. VIII of the GPA (2012) read:

> 1. A procuring entity shall limit any conditions for participation in a procurement to those that are essential to ensure a supplier has the legal and financial capacities and the commercial and technical abilities to undertake the relevant procurement.
>
> […]
>
> 3. In assessing whether a supplier satisfies the conditions for participation, a procuring entity:
>   (a) shall evaluate the financial capacity and the commercial and technical abilities of a supplier on the basis of that supplier's business activities both inside and outside the territory of the Party of the procuring entity; and
>   (b) shall base its evaluation on the conditions that the procuring entity has specified in advance in notices or tender documentation.
> 4. Where there is supporting evidence, a Party, including its procuring entities, may exclude a supplier on grounds such as:
>   (a) bankruptcy;
>   (b) false declarations;
>   (c) significant or persistent deficiencies in performance of any substantive requirement or obligation under a prior contract or contracts;
>   (d) final judgements in respect of serious crimes or other serious offences;
>   (e) professional misconduct or acts or omissions that adversely reflect on the commercial integrity of the supplier; or
>   (f) failure to pay taxes.

Art. VIII of the GPA (2012) provides that any conditions imposed on suppliers in the tendering process shall be essential to ensure the supplier's capacity to undertake the relevant procurement. This includes legal and financial capacities as well as commercial and technical abilities. Art. VIII (4) of the GPA (2012) contains a non-exhaustive list of exclusion grounds.

In its request to the DSB, the EU had asserted that the Massachusetts Burma Law violated Art. VIII (b) of the GPA (1994), the predecessor of the current rule on supplier qualifications, which contained similar obligations.[1443] Providing for origin-related conditions for suppliers, the Massachusetts Law does not relate to the legal, financial, technical and commercial capacities of suppliers. Origin-related conditions are not essential to ensure the firm's capability to fulfil the contract in question so that the Massachusetts Burma Law both violates Art. VIII (b) of the GPA (1994) and Art. VIII (1) of the GPA (2012).

Another question is whether governmental purchasing laws or administrative practices excluding suppliers that use child labour are prohibited under Art. VIII (1) of the GPA (2012). Art. 57 (4) lit. (a) of the EU Directive 2014/24/EU offers the opportunity for authorities to exclude operators that demonstrably violated EU social law or international labour law including the ILO Conventions on child labour. In addition, a conviction for the use of child labour is an explicitly mentioned exclusion ground, Art. 57 (1) lit. (f) of the EU Directive 2014/24/EU.

As mentioned above, Art. VIII (4) of the GPA contains a non-exhaustive list of exclusion grounds, enumerating grounds such as bankruptcy, final judgement in respect of serious crimes or offences and the failure to pay taxes. Given that Art. 9 of the ILO Convention No. 138 provides for the imposition of appropriate penalties in case of contravention of the minimum age legislation and that in many countries, child labour as defined by the ILO Convention 138 and 182 is prohibited and, in certain cases, may constitute a serious offence,[1444] a conviction for the use of child labour or a proven breach of EU or international child labour law should be seen as equally acceptable exclusion grounds. In the same vein, Steiner argues that to include the breach of the ILO Core Conventions in the list of exclusion grounds follows the rationale of Art. VIII (4) of the GPA (2012).[1445]

Already in the past, some legal authors had suggested that Art. VIII (b) of the GPA (1994) on supplier qualifications would allow for the imposition of qualifications based on human rights performance.[1446] Another author had argued that given that contract terms apparently may require successful tenders to meet specified social policy requirements in the performance of contracts, such qualification requirements could be 'essential to ensure the firm's capability to

1443 *United States – Measures Affecting Government Procurement*, Request for establishment of a panel by the European Communities, 9 September 1998, WT/DS88/3.

1444 Cf. for example § 5 (1) in conjunction with § 2 (1), § 58 (1), (5) Jugendarbeitsschutzgesetz of Germany; In the US, employers have to pay a civil penalty in case of employing minors under the age of 15, US Code, 29 CFR 57.3.

1445 Steiner (Die Berücksichtigung sozialer Aspekte), p. 39.

1446 Howse/Mutua, p. 16.

fulfil the contract in question' within the meaning of Art. VIII (b) of the GPA (1994).[1447] The suggested solution, i.e. to include the breach of the ILO Core Conventions on child labour in the list of possible exclusion grounds of Art. VIII (4) of the GPS (2012) seems to be an appropriate solution to accommodate human rights considerations when evaluating the qualification of suppliers. For example, based on this provision, the Massachusetts Law could have excluded suppliers proven to be involved with forced (child) labour from Myanmar.

13.4 *Art. X – Technical Specifications and Tender Documentation*

The term 'technical specification' is defined in Art. I (u) of the GPA (2012):

> (u) *technical specification* means a tendering requirement that:
> (i) lays down the characteristics of goods or services to be procured, including quality, performance, safety and dimensions, or the processes and methods for their production or provision; or
> (ii) addresses terminology, symbols, packaging, marking and labelling requirements as they apply to a good or service.

The term 'standard' is defined in Art. I (s) of the GPA and mirrors the definition contained in the TBT Agreement:

> (s) *standard* means a document approved by a recognized body, that provides, for common and repeated use, rules, guidelines or characteristics for products or related processes and production methods, with which compliance is not mandatory. It may also include or deal exclusively with terminology, symbols, packaging, marking or labelling requirements as they apply to a product, process or production method;

The relevant provisions of Art. X of the GPA (2012) read:

> *Technical Specifications*
> 1. A procurement entity shall not prepare, adopt or apply any technical specification or prescribe any conformity assessment procedure with the purpose or the effect of creating unnecessary obstacles to international trade.
> 2. In prescribing the technical specifications for the goods or services being procured, a procuring entity shall, where appropriate:

1447 McCrudden, p. 30.

(a) set out the technical specification in terms of performance and functional requirements, rather than design or descriptive characteristics; and
(b) base the technical specification on international standards, where such exist; otherwise, on national technical regulations, recognized international standards, or building codes.
[...]

6. For greater certainty, a Party, including its procuring entities, may, in accordance with this Article, prepare, adopt or apply technical specifications to promote the conversation of natural resources or protect the environment.

Tender Documentation

7. A procuring entity shall make available to suppliers tender documentation that includes all information necessary to permit suppliers to prepare and submit responsive tenders. Unless already provided in the notice of intended procurement, such documentation shall include a complete description of:
[...]
(c) all evaluation criteria the entity will apply in the awarding of the contract, and, except where price is the sole criterion, the relative importance of such criteria;

9. The evaluation criteria set out in the notice of intended procurement or tender documentation may include, among others, price and other cost factors, quality, technical merit, environmental characteristics and terms of delivery.

The following passage is also relevant for correctly construing the provisions on 'technical specifications' and 'evaluation criteria'.

Art. XXII Final Provisions
[...]

8. (a) The Committee shall undertake further work to facilitate the implementation of this Agreement and the negotiations provided for in paragraph 7, through the adoption of work programmes for the following items:
(iii) the treatment of sustainable procurement;

13.4.1 Technical Specifications and Evaluation Criteria

Art. X of the GPA (2012) contains product-and service-specific government procurement regulations including technical specifications and evaluation criteria. Technical specifications are defined in Art. I (u) of the GPA (2012). According to Art. X:1 and 2 of the GPA (2012), technical specifications entities shall not create unnecessary obstacles to international trade and be based on international standards. They may be adopted to promote the environment, Art. X:6 of the GPS (2012). According to Art. XII:2 (g) of the GPA, tender documentation shall contain all evaluation criteria for awarding the contract including environmental characteristics.

The question is whether the GPA (2012) allows technical specifications or award criteria to require specific social characteristics that do not have a physical impact on the product such as the non-use of child labour, i.e. non-product-related ppms. As some authors indicate, the definition of 'technical specifications' refers to process and production methods and therefore possibly goes beyond the product-process doctrine upheld by the *US–Tuna* cases.[1448] In contrast to the definition of a 'technical regulation' under the TBT Agreement, the wording does not contain any restricting terms such as 'their related' that might limit the coverage to requirements that are reflected in the final product.[1449] Such a reading would be of particular importance if national procurement measures allowed for npr-ppm-requirements in their technical specifications.

Annex VII to the EU Directive 2014/24/EU defines technical specifications as technical prescriptions that define characteristics of the required product or supply including environmental performance, marking and labelling, process and production methods and design such as accessibility for disabled persons. Having classified the use of child labour as a process and production method, it is conceivable that prescriptions regarding the use of child labour may be considered as technical specifications. However, the definition only refers to environmental characteristics. Social characteristics are mentioned only to the extent they concern the design of the product such as accessibility for disabled persons. Recital 99 confirms this approach limiting the use of social requirements mainly to the those that 'directly characterise the product or service in question'. Art. 42 of the EU Directive 2014/24/EU also does not refer to social criteria. Thus, the term 'technical specifications' as used by the EU Directive should be read as not to include social characteristics that are not reflected in the final product such as the use of child labour.[1450] In case of the EU Directive

1448 McCrudden, pp. 3, 36–42.

1449 See the discussion on the words 'their related' in relation to the TBT Agreement above pp. 257 et seqq.

1450 Such a reading of the EU Directive 2014/24/EU seems to be also the view of Steiner who holds the exclusion grounds of Art. 57 as the main entry points for the ILO Core Convention, cf. Steiner (Die Berücksichtigung sozialer Aspekte), p. 39.

2014/24/EU, the question of whether the scope of the term 'technical specifications' of the GPA (2012) includes non-product-related ppms does not arise.

Having said this, Art. 43 of the EU Directive sets forth that the contracting authorities may require in the technical specifications, award criteria or the contract performance conditions that the procurement shall carry a label as a proof for containing certain social characteristics, provided that certain conditions are fulfilled. The question arises whether like the approach under the TBT Agreement, labelling requirements may refer to social npr-ppm-measures such as the use of child labour. However, since the text relating to labelling requirements does not refer explicitly to process and production methods as in the TBT Agreement, one should be rather cautious and not extend the meaning of labelling requirements to social ppms not relating to physical characteristics.

The GPA (2012) seems to have the same approach: Art. X:6 only mentions the environment or natural resources when specifying the application of technical specifications. Art. I (u) (ii) of the GPA (2012) that defines 'technical specifications' mentions processes and productions methods' but does not refer to process and production methods when mentioning labelling requirements. It is therefore more convincing to follow an argument put forward by McCrudden who holds that the purpose of mentioning process and production methods and putting them under the discipline of the GPA (2012) may be to prevent the specification of processes by the purchaser which are available only to specific bidders and thus discriminatory.[1451] Thus, technical specifications so far cannot be interpreted so as to refer to social criteria not having a physical impact on the product.

Art. X:7 lit. c and 9 of the GPA (2012) are not so clear on the use of evaluation criteria in the tender documentation. Paragraph 9 explicitly mentions environmental characteristics as evaluation criteria but the list is not exclusive. Since the final provisions contained in Art. XXII refer to the adoption of a future work programme on sustainable procurement, it is conceivable to extend this list so as to include social characteristics. Steiner also seems to favour such an open approach to the GPA when referring to the 'constructive ambiguity' of the Agreement.[1452] As there is no indication in the text of the provisions that requirements relating to npr-ppms are excluded, it should be possible to qualify the non-use of child labour or respect for the ILO Core Conventions as evaluation criteria.

1451 McRudden, pp. 36–42.

1452 Presentation hold in Berne, 3rd of March 2015, on file with the author.

As regards contract award criteria and performance conditions, Art. 67 and 70 of the EU Directive 2014/24/EU do not contain any limitation for the use of social npr-ppms, if they relate to the subject-matter of the contract. Art. 67:2 (a) explicitly mentions social characteristics and Art. 67:3 (a) states that factors involved in the process of production shall be considered to the subject-matter of the contract. Since the non-use of child labour can be classified as such a factor in the production process, it should be possible to qualify it as an award criterion. Conditions of performance obviously may stipulate that child labour is forbidden during the implementation of the contract. Recital (97) seems to support such an approach: It states that award criteria or contract performance conditions may refer to the supply of Fairtrade products, i.e. the requirement that a minimum price and a price premium is paid to producers. Like labour standards, such a requirement also does not have a physical impact on the product.

13.4.2 Standards

The regime for technical specifications contained in Art. X of the GPA mirrors Art. 2.2 and 2.4 of the TBT Agreement and shall be interpreted accordingly, except where the different subject-matter calls for a different interpretation. While the former GPA (1994) referred to the definition of standards and technical regulations of the TBT Agreement through footnotes, the definition of 'standards' is now contained in the text of the revised GPA (2012).

Art. X:2 (b) of the GPA (2012) requires that technical specifications shall be based on international standards. Since the definition of 'standard' is the same as under the TBT Agreement referring to 'related process and production methods', the term 'standard' under the GPA (2012) should also be read so as to refer to non-binding documents that lay down product characteristics and production methods that are reflected in the final product, not including non-product-related ppm provisions. Thus, also under the GPA (2012), the term 'international standards' should not be read so as to refer to the relevant UN and ILO Conventions on child labour and in theory also not to the ISO 26 000 guidance.[1453] Equally, the existing private labelling regimes on child labour should not be classified as 'international standards' on child labour under the GPA (2012) for the time being.

Art. X:2 lit. b of the GPA (2012) also refers to national technical regulations, recognized national standards and building codes. National standards obviously include national non-binding rules prescribing certain product

1453 See the discussion on international standards above pp. 265 et seqq.

characteristics. Since there is no reason to interpret the term 'technical regulation' differently from the definition used in the TBT Agreement, also under the GPA (2012), it should be read so as to refer to binding rules on physical characteristics of the product. The same holds true for building codes. Instead of relating to existing private labelling schemes on child labour such as the GoodWeave label, building codes should be read to refer to labelling schemes on product characteristics.

Annex VII (2) of the EU Directive 2014/24/EU defines 'standard' as a technical specification adopted by a recognized standardization body for repeated application, with which compliance is not mandatory. International standards are those that have been adopted by international standardisation organizations. Thus, the ISO 26 000, which also refers to child labour, seems to come with the definition of an international standard. This is an indication that requirements relating to non-product-related social ppms are not totally excluded from the scope of the Directive, and that future revisions may also include them in the definition of technical specifications.

While the GPA (2012) so far does not include standards on child labour in its definitions of standards, the 'constructive ambiguity' of its provisions should make it possible to not stand in the way of legislation allowing for standards on social npr-ppm-prescriptions. It is for the future work of the Committee of Government Procurement to take such developments into account when designing its work programmes.

13.4.3 Unnecessary Obstacles to International Trade

Art. X:1 of the GPA (2012) requires that technical specifications shall not be applied with the purpose or the effect of creating unnecessary obstacles to international trade. By way of contextual interpretation, Art. X:1 of the GPA should follow the approach of Art. 2.2 of the TBT Agreement and be read as prohibiting only such obstacles that are not more trade-restrictive than necessary to fulfil a legitimate objective taking account of the risks non-fulfilment would create. Since it has been found that for the time being, technical specifications may not refer to the non-use of child labour in the production process, this provision will hardly be applied in the context of child labour.

13.4.4 Conclusion

For the time being, technical specifications do not refer to social npr-ppms such as the use of child labour. The provisions on evaluation criteria leave more room for interpretation and may allow for criteria such as the non-use of child labour in the production process.

With regard to technical specifications and evaluation criteria, the EU Directive 2014/24/EU is consistent with Art. X of the GPA (2012). However, its definition of international standards is broader as it also includes those standards by the ISO that refer to social npr-ppms such as child labour or other human rights and labour standards.

13.5 *Art. XV – Treatment of Tenders and Awarding of Contracts*

Art. XV:5 (a) and (b) of the GPA (2012) read:

> 5. Unless a procuring entity determines that it is not in the public interest to award a contract, the entity shall award the contract to the supplier that the entity has determined to be capable of fulfilling the terms of the contract and that, based solely on the evaluation criteria specified in the notices or tender documentation, has submitted:
>   (a) the most advantageous tender; or
>   (b) where price is the sole criterion, the lowest price.

This provision provides that the successful tender has to be either the lowest in price or the most advantageous according to the tender documentation including the evaluation criteria. This provision gives the procurement authorities considerable discretion, the only constraint being criteria set forth in the tender documentation.[1454] As examined above, evaluation criteria laid down in the tender documentation may be read to refer to social criteria such as the non-use of child labour. Thus, although procurement authorities may decide to choose the price as the sole criterion, they also may choose to make their decisions based on social and environmental criteria, even including non-product-related ppms. Some authors therefore conclude that the GPA (2012) is rather open to npr-ppms if compared to the GATT.[1455]

Art. 67 of the EU Directive 2014/24/EU is not as broad providing that the award is made to most *economically* advantageous tender on the basis of price or cost, using a cost-effectiveness approach, including criteria such as quality, environmental and/or social characteristics. Interestingly, the (non-exhaustive) list does now mention social characteristics explicitly in contrast to its predecessor, Directive 2004/18/EC. As examined above, such social characteristics may refer to social npr-ppms such as the non-use of child labour. The EU Directive 2014/24/EU therefore complies with the GPA (2012) as regards the award of contracts.

1454 Trepte, p. 1149.

1455 Steiner (Die Berücksichtigung sozialer Aspekte), p. 41.

In its request to the DSB, the EU rightly argued that the Massachusetts Burma Law was in contravention of Art. XIII:4 (b) of the GPA (1994), the former provision on the award of contracts, holding that by imposing a 10 per cent price increase on the basis of whether or not a company does business in or with Myanmar, the Massachusetts Law violated this provision.[1456] Since the current provision on the awarding of contracts provides for more or less the same conditions, the Massachusetts Law would also violate the GPA (2012). McCrudden has argued, a possible solution to this problem would have been to determine as a condition of the contract that those awarded the contract should not be able to operate in Myanmar during the duration of the contract.[1457] This proposal seems appealing, however, it also risks discriminating against Myanmar suppliers and violating Art. IV:1 (a) of the GPA (2012).

13.6 *Art. III – General Exceptions*

Art. III:2 of the GPA reads:

[...]

2. Subject to the requirement that such measures are not applied in a manner that would constitute a means of arbitrary or unjustifiable discrimination between Parties where the same conditions prevail or a disguised restriction on international trade, nothing in this Agreement shall be construed to prevent any Party from imposing or enforcing measures:
   (a) necessary to protect public morals, order or safety;
   (b) necessary to protect human, animal or plant life or health;
   (c) necessary to protect intellectual property; or
   (d) relating to goods or services of persons with disabilities, philanthropic institutions or prison labour.

The wording of Art. III is almost the same as that of GATT Art. XX. Reading the provision in its context, the same interpretation as of GATT Art. XX shall apply here. Accordingly, government procurement laws that contravene for example the non-discrimination obligation contained in Art. IV of the GPA (2012) can be justified if they have one of the goals explicitly mentioned, are proportionate to that objective and in their application neither unjustifiably nor arbitrarily discriminatory.[1458]

1456 *United States – Measures Affecting Government Procurement*, Request for establishment of a panel by the European Communities, 9 September 1998, WT/DS88/3.

1457 McCrudden, p. 30.

1458 See above pp. 199 et seqq.

The Massachusetts Burma Law may be justified under this provision. Since it responds also to forced child labour, it aims at implementing the legitimate objective of public morals. The next question in relation to public morals is whether it fulfils the necessity test, which includes a weighing and balancing of the different interests at stake.[1459] At first sight, as in the case of the US ban on any goods coming from Myanmar, it seems that the Massachusetts Law being a country-specific measure would not pass the necessity-test. Moreover, it was not explicitly adopted in response to the ILO recommendation under Art. 33 of the ILO Constitution to ILO members to review their relations, including economic ones, with Myanmar. This point can however not be decisive. Given that the ILO for the first time made such a recommendation and the resulting importance, all measures that are in accordance with such a recommendation should be regarded as necessary under the respective provisions of GATT Art. XX or Art. III:2 of the GPA (2012).[1460]

As to the conditions of arbitrary discrimination, there is nothing to suggest that the application of the Massachusetts Law resulted in arbitrary discrimination. Thus, the Massachusetts Law arguably could have been justified under the General Exceptions provision.[1461]

The EU Directive 2014/24/EU refers in Recital 41 of its Preamble to exceptions relating to public morality and security. This recital should be considered when determining exclusion grounds relating to child labour in accordance with Art. 57 of the Directive. In any event, allowing for exceptions on the grounds on public morals such as the use of child labour, the EU Directive 2012/24/EU is in accordance with the GPA (2012).

13.7 *Conclusion*

The GPA (2012) regulating government purchasing laws is in many aspects like the TBT Agreement. Its central pillars are the non-discrimination clause prohibiting *de iure* and *de facto* discrimination and discrimination against locally-established suppliers, supplier qualifications and the regime on technical specifications and evaluation criteria.

Whilst technical specifications may not be read to encompass social npr-ppms such as the non-use of child labour in the production process, evaluation criteria do. However, bidders may be excluded on grounds such as a conviction

1459 See above pp. 214 et seqq.

1460 See also the discussion on country-specific measures in relation to the necessity test under GATT Art. XX above p. 226.

1461 Cf. Howse/Mutua, p. 16.

for the use of child labour or a proven breach of EU or international child labour law.

Art. III:2 of the GPA (2012) provides for a public morals exception that shall be read in the same way as GATT Art. XX (a).

When awarding contracts, procuring entities have considerable discretion and may insert requirements providing for the non-use of child labour in their evaluation criteria or performance conditions.

The EU Directive 2014/24/EU is in accordance with the GPA (2012) and even goes further when referring to all international standards by the ISO including the ISO 26 000.

The Massachusetts Burma Law violates Art. IV:1 (a) and (b) and IV:2 (a) and (b) Art. III:2 (a) and (b), Art. VIII (1) of the GPA (2012), but may be justified under Art. III:2 of the GPA (2012).

Bearing in mind that according to Art. XXII:8 (a) (iii), the Committee on Government Procurement shall adopt a work programme on sustainable procurement, there is a certain 'constrictive ambiguity' as holds Steiner that also opens the room for eventually including social npr-ppms such as the use of child labour in the various provisions of the ppm. In the same vein, other authors hold that a "maturing of the GPA" with a view to improving it, is built into the text of the GPA (2012).[1462]

14 Non-WTO Norms as a Defence for Trade Measures on Child Labour

14.1 *Introduction*

As mentioned above, in case existing trade measures cannot be justified under substantive WTO law, the question arises whether ILO or UN Human Rights Conventions or recommendations of ILO or UN bodies constitute a valuable defence of countermeasures taken in response to child labour under WTO law. This problem concerns the issue of jurisdiction of WTO adjudicating bodies and the coherence of international law. These issues will be discussed in the following section, as well as the question whether WTO law precludes countermeasures in response to large scale violations of child labour under general public international law.

1462 Anderson/Arrowsmith, pp. 48 and 58.

14.2 *The Jurisdiction of WTO Panels*

The relevant provisions are Art. 3 (2), 7 (2), 19 (1) and 23 of the DSU. Art. 3 (2) reads:

> Recommendations and rulings of the DSB cannot add or diminish the rights and obligations provided in the covered agreements.

Art. 19 (1) provides:

> In their findings and recommendations, panels and the Appellate Body cannot add to or diminish the rights and obligations provided in the covered agreement.

Art. 7 (2) sets forth the terms of reference of panels referring to relevant provisions in any covered agreement cited by the parties to the dispute.

Art. 23 reads:

> (1) When members seek redress of a violation of obligations or other nullification or impairment of benefits under the covered agreements or an impediment to the attainment of any objective of the covered agreements, they shall have recourse to, and abide by, the rules and procedures of this Understanding.
>
> (2) Members shall: (a) not make a determination to the effect that a violation has occurred, that benefits have been nullified or impaired or that the attainment of any objective of the covered agreements has been impeded, except through recourse to dispute settlement in accordance with the rules and procedures of this Understanding, and shall make any such determination consistent with the findings contained in the panel or Appellate Body report adopted by the DSB or an arbitration award rendered under this Understanding.

An overall consensus exists that these provisions limit the jurisdiction of WTO panels and the Appellate Body to solve allegations of WTO violations by complaining parties.[1463] Thus, the usual starting point may only be a violation of the covered agreements, not a violation of a human rights treaty such as the CRC. In case of labour rights conditionality where the question is whether

1463 Pauwelyn (Conflict of Norms), p. 465; Marceau (WTO Dispute Settlement and Human Rights I), p. 762; Marceau (WTO Dispute Settlement and Human Rights II), p. 187 et seq.; Bartels (Applicable Law), p. 503.

human rights may be enforced through trade measures under WTO law, the limited jurisdiction of panels is usually not a problem.

However, Art. 23 of the DSU is considered to have exclusive jurisdiction, i.e. that where trade is affected, the WTO dispute mechanism is triggered, and no other dispute mechanism should deal with the case.[1464] The question is whether WTO members are only under an obligation to refrain from taking recourse to trade measures in response to violations of WTO law, not in response to non-WTO law. However, it is held that Art. 23 of the DSU was drafted to rule out the use of unilateral trade countermeasures other than in conformity with WTO law.[1465] Hence, trade measures in response to human rights violations would be subject to WTO dispute settlement.

For example, complaints on trade measures recommended by the International Labour Conference under the complaints procedure as in the case of Myanmar are under the exclusive jurisdiction of the WTO, which could find those trade measures in violation of WTO law and thus illegal. The possibility of having contradictory decisions of two international institutions can be termed as a conflict of law and unveils what has been called the 'global fragmentation of law'.[1466] A new ILO-WTO agreement on trade and child labour could attempt to resolve such an inter-institutional conflict.

14.3 *The Applicable Law*

Whilst it has been long-standing practice by the WTO adjudicating bodies to refer to the customary rules on treaty interpretation of Art. 31 and 32 of the VCLT and to rely on non-WTO rules to interpret GATT rules, most prominent examples being the interpretation of the term 'exhaustible natural resources' of GATT Art. XX (g) in *US–Shrimp* or the reliance on the good faith efforts of the United States in the conclusion of the Inter-American Convention in *US–Shrimp–Article* 21.5 as factual reference,[1467] legal scholars disagree on the applicable law before the WTO adjudicating bodies.[1468]

Pauwelyn is of the view that the main provisions on applicable law are Art. 7 (1) and (2) of the DSU.[1469] They read as requiring the examination of the

1464 Marceau (WTO Dispute Settlement and Human Rights I), p. 757 et seqq.

1465 Ibid., p. 760.

1466 See for example the various contributions in legal literature by Cottier/Delimatsis.

1467 *US–Shrimps–Article 21.5*, report of the Appellate Body, paras. 130 and 133; See also *EC–Biotech Products*, para. 7.90–7.94.

1468 For a thorough discussion of this debate, see also Cottier/Delimatsis/Gehne/Payosova, pp. 16–19.

1469 Pauwelyn (Conflict of Norms), p. 469.

panel request in the light of the provisions of the WTO covered agreements, not excluding other public international law.[1470] He argues that given that it is established that the WTO adjudicating bodies apply general international law such as procedural rules or rules of treaty interpretation or even rules such as Lomé Convention not being part of general international law, there is no reason not to apply non-WTO treaties.[1471] With regard to Art. 3 (2) of the DSU, he thinks that this provision sets forth the limits of interpretation, i.e. WTO adjudicating bodies may not create new rights and obligations.[1472] The provision does not however limit the extent to which other treaties that will be or have been concluded by WTO members apply.[1473] The applicability of other WTO law will instead be decided by the expression of state consent and conflict rules of international law.[1474] For example, it may be that in a human rights convention in which certain trade restrictions are imposed, and subsequently those trade restrictions are challenged before a WTO panel, the panel should apply those non-WTO treaties as a possible defence.[1475] Not applying WTO rules does not mean to diminish the rights of WTO members, rather the WTO member itself did that by concluding the other treaty including the conflict rule.[1476] However, WTO adjudicating bodies may not enforce judicially claims under other rules of international law.[1477] The merit of this approach is that a panel is precluded from finding a breach of WTO law.

Thus, while WTO members may not bring claims under human rights conventions, they may invoke for example the ILO recommendation of the Myanmar case providing for trade measures as a defence against the alleged violation of GATT Art. I or XI. Pauwelyn finds that the ILO recommendation as the latter and more specific norm should prevail over the WTO prohibition.[1478] However, he rightly does not contend that a WTO member may bring a complaint alleging that a countermeasure in response to human rights allegation under an economic cooperation agreement such as the Human Rights Clause in agreements of the EU was illegal.[1479] For this would include a prior finding

1470 Ibid.
1471 Ibid., p. 471.
1472 Pauwelyn (Human Rights in WTO Dispute Settlement), p. 215.
1473 Ibid.
1474 Ibid., p. 216.
1475 Pauwelyn (Conflict of Norms), p. 486.
1476 Ibid., p. 474.
1477 Ibid., p. 473.
1478 Pauwelyn (Human Rights in WTO Dispute Settlement), p. 219.
1479 Ibid.

of a violation of a non-WTO rule, which is more than examining claims of alleged WTO violations.[1480]

Bartels argues that the DSU does not place *a priori* a restriction on the sources of international applicable law.[1481] He regards Art. 3 (2) and 19 (2) of the DSU as conflict rules. He suggests that in the event of a conflict between the provisions of the covered agreements and any other applicable law, the covered agreements shall prevail.[1482] He however submits that in most cases, non-WTO law will be used in the interpretation or as evidence of a party's compliance with its obligations under these agreements.[1483]

Marceau argues that the WTO is a system of *lex specialis* that is intended to exclude more or less totally the application of the general legal consequences of wrongful acts, particular the application of countermeasures normally at the disposal of an injured party.[1484] She holds that the provisions on the limited jurisdiction of WTO panels mirror those on the applicable law, which prohibit the WTO adjudicating bodies to add or diminish the rights and obligations of WTO members under the covered agreements.[1485] WTO law cannot be overruled by situations and considerations belonging to another subsystem.[1486] If WTO panels could supersede and set aside a WTO provision and therefore giving legal effect to the non-WTO provision, they would add or diminish the WTO covered agreements.[1487] However, she is of the view that a good faith interpretation of the human rights and WTO obligations and rights of states should lead to their simultaneous consistent application.[1488] In the rare case of a conflict, a WTO panel would conclude that the panel does not have the competence to formally interpret and enforce other treaties and customs and that the panel is prohibited from reaching any conclusion that would add to or diminish the covered agreements.[1489] In case of conflict with *ius cogens*, she argues that the panel would probably adopt an interpretation of the relevant WTO provision that is in accordance with *ius cogens*.[1490] Another possibility

1480 Ibid., p. 223.
1481 Bartels (Applicable Law), p. 506.
1482 Ibid., p. 507.
1483 Bartels (Applicable Law), p. 519.
1484 Marceau (WTO Dispute Settlement and Human Rights I), p. 766.
1485 Marceau (WTO Dispute Settlement and Human Rights II), p. 189.
1486 Marceau (WTO Dispute Settlement and Human Rights I), p. 767.
1487 Marceau (WTO Dispute Settlement and Human Rights II), p. 195.
1488 Marceau (WTO Dispute Settlement and Human Rights I), p. 795.
1489 Ibid.
1490 Ibid., p. 802.

for the panel would be to let the WTO provision disappear and arrive at a *non-liquet* solution.[1491]

The main difference between the legal authors does therefore not relate to the enforcement of human rights through WTO panels but to the finding whether WTO law has been breached or not. This difference will however only be relevant if WTO law cannot be interpreted and applied in a way consistent with human rights treaties.

At this point, it must be recalled that most existing trade measures on child labour – in the view of this author – have the potential to be justified under WTO law. The Belgian Social Label Law complies already with the Code of Good Practice and could, in case of a violation of GATT Art. III:4, be justified under GATT Art. XX (a). The US ban on goods from Myanmar and bans under the Kimberley Process Certification Scheme violating GATT Art. XI and in the latter case also GATT Art. I could equally be justified under GATT Art. XX (a) or GATT Art. XXI. The EU GSP is justified under the Enabling Clause and possibly under GATT Art. XX (a).

Only the proposed EU Forced Labour Regulation, US ban on goods made with child labour and the US GSP cannot be justified neither under the Enabling Clause nor under GATT Art. XX (a). This could however easily be changed by add either flanking measures and securing a non-arbitrary implementation of the US GSP. Also, there is no human rights convention or a recommendation by the ILO or another human rights institution or an economic agreement that would allow for the mentioned trade measures on child labour. Thus, there is no need to apply human rights norms or recommendations directly in defence of the examined measures.

There is also no need to directly apply general public international law. As examined above, under certain circumstances, countermeasures in response to widespread use of child labour in the territory of one WTO member may legally be taken under GATT Art. XX (a), (b) and GATT Art. XXI. The dispute on applicable law does not have to be resolved at this point.

14.4 *Conclusion*

The jurisdiction of the WTO adjudicating bodies is limited to assessing violations of WTO law. In this sense, violations of non-WTO law such as human rights treaties cannot trigger the WTO dispute mechanism. A conflict may however arise if the ILO recommends trade measures that are in violation of WTO law. The WTO adjudicating bodies could find that those trade measures are

1491 Marceau (WTO Dispute Settlement and Human Rights II), p. 213.

illegal and must be disposed of. Such a conflict is an indication of the ongoing 'global fragmentation of international law'. A new cooperation agreement between the ILO and WTO could attempt to solve such conflicts.

A related but different issue is the question as to whether human rights treaties or ILO recommendations may be directly applied in WTO law and prevent WTO panels from finding a violation of WTO law. Since in the case of child labour, WTO obligations can be interpreted to be mainly consistent with international law on child labour, there is no need to directly apply ILO recommendations or for example the CRC. The same is true for the law on countermeasures since such measures in response to child labour consistent with public international law may be legally taken under WTO law.

Some final remarks should be made here. Firstly, the case of child labour demonstrates that, as contends Marceau, in most cases, human rights concerns can be taken account of by interpretation. Secondly, Pauwelyn and Marceau rightly do not consider Art. 3 (2) and 19 (2) as conflict rules.[1492] Their wording does not suggest a conflict. Thirdly, it might be different to apply general international law such as procedural law and rules of interpretation to fill in gaps and to place the WTO within the larger system of general international law than to apply other subsystems of international law such as human rights norms or environmental agreements.

15 Conclusion of Chapter 2

In conclusion, WTO law *de lege lata* offers considerable space to adopt unilateral trade measures on child labour. Existing trade measures on child labour comprise for example the US ban on goods produced with forced or indentured child labour, the proposed EU Forced Labour Regulation, the former 2003 US Burmese Freedom and Democracy Act banning all goods coming from Myanmar, the UFPLA, the US and EU GSPs, the Kimberley Certification Scheme and the Belgian Social Label law. Whereas the proposed EU Forced Labour Regulation, the US ban on goods produced with child labour and the Belgian Social Label Law are npr-ppm-measures focussing on prohibiting goods produced under certain process and production methods, the US and EU GSPs as well as the UFLPA, the US Burmese Freedom and Democracy Act and bans under the Kimberley Process Certification Scheme are country-specific

1492 Marceau (The WTO Dispute Settlement and Human Rights II), p. 195; Pauwelyn (Conflict of Norms), p. 352.

measures regulating the import of goods from certain destinations that require a different justification under WTO law.

The key legal findings relate to the issue of npr-ppm-measures under GATT law and the TBT Agreement, the question of whether to consider the regulatory purpose and trade effects of a trade measure under GATT Art. I and III, the implications of the *ius cogens* nature of the prohibition of child labour for its compatibility with WTO law and how to read GATT Art. XX and XXI.

While WTO-case law appears to be open but still indecisive on the general legality of npr-ppm-measures and their extraterritorial effect, this work argues that in case of trade measures on child labour, their extraterritoriality can be justified by referring in accordance with Art. 3 (2) DSU and Art. 31 (3) lit. c of the VCLT to general rules of public international law on countermeasures as stated in Art. 48 (1) lit. b and Art. 54 of the Articles on State Responsibility. That is, *argumentum a maiore ad minus*, origin-neutral measures such as the US ban on goods produced with forced or indentured child labour should be possible under to WTO law given that public international law allows for economic countermeasures in response to *ius cogens* human rights violations by a certain state. Hence, the major counterargument against npr-ppms can be rejected and the so-called product-process doctrine be dismissed.

Since the *EC–Asbestos* ruling of the Appellate Body, the regulatory intent of a measure can be considered under the criterion of consumers' interest when analysing whether products are 'like'. However, as of now, most people probably will still consider products made with child labour 'like' products not produced with child labour. This work also submits that the wording GATT Art. III 'so as to afford protection' provides a textual basis to consider the regulatory purpose under the equal treatment obligation when trade effects of a measure unclear. Decisions such as *Chile–Alcoholic Beverages* point into this direction. The case is however different with GATT Art. I where no such textual basis exists. Most trade measures on child labour will probably violate GATT Art. I or III.

By contrast, the Appellate Body ruling of *EC–Seal Products* provides quite some room for members to justify trade measures under GATT Art. XX (a) on public morals. Trade measures on child labour fall within the scope of this exception. GATT Art. XX (b) also applies. However, the WTO Appellate Body has not been conclusive on the issue of extraterritoriality so that this work suggests a legal argumentation referring to *ius cogens* and the law on countermeasures to defend trade measures on child labour, thereby increasing legal predictability and coherence with public international law. Another important issue regarding Art. XX (a) and (b) of the GATT is the broad proportionality test established by WTO jurisprudence including a 'weighing and balancing test' able to adequately consider non-economic values such as human rights. This trend towards proportionality rather than a strict necessity test has been called convincingly a modest constitutionalization of WTO case-law. The *US–Shrimp* case has been called the most important example where such a constitutional concept has been applied.[1493] However, blanket import bans on child labour without any flanking preventive or remedial measures will probably not pass the proportionality test. Finally, a new reading of the *chapeau* of GATT Art. XX has been discussed and found to be quite appealing but probably not making a big difference regarding the WTO compatibility of trade measures on child labour.

In accordance with the call for coherence in international law, GATT Art. XX (a) may also be read to allow for country-specific measures such as the US Burmese Freedom and Democracy Act.

GATT Art. XXI (b) (iii) has been found to be justiciable by *Russia–Traffic in Transit*.[1494] This work argues that an 'emergency in international relations' includes cases of grave and widespread child labour. Relating trade measures however have to make explicit how they protect the concerned members' essential security interest. In case of an existing UN Security Council Resolution, GATT Art. XXI (c) is available. The jurisdictional treatment of the security exceptions has been called a yardstick for the constitutionalization of world trade'.[1495]

While the term 'technical regulation' of the TBT Agreement applies to labelling rules on child labour, more policy-based measures such as import bans of products made with child labour should be analysed under GATT Art. III and XX, which are better suited to find the right balance between human rights and trade concerns. The GPA offers some space for governments to include social criteria relating to the non-use of child labour in their procurement laws.

There is some debate between legal scholars as to whether non-WTO norms may be directly applied by WTO panels and prevent them from finding a violation of WTO law. While such a proposal would certainly promote the importance of human rights conventions on child labour in WTO law, this issue will not be resolved here since most existing measures on child labour can be rescued under a human rights-friendly reading of WTO law.

There is thus a growing trend in WTO jurisprudence to take due account of non-economic values. WTO law is not considered to be a *domain reservé*, and

1493 Jackson (Sovereignty), p. 188.
1494 *Russia–Traffic in Transit*, report of the panel.
1495 Emerson, p. 153; Schloemann/Ohloff, p. 451.

general public international law and the concept of *ius cogens* may play an important role in interpretation.

However, despite such phenomena of constitutionalization in WTO law and a recent trend towards more integration of international law, it is questionable whether the current legal situation of having unilateral trade measures is the most adequate to help remedy the problem of child labour and trade.

Considering the analysis above, most of these measures will still violate the basic GATT non-discrimination obligations. Since governments are generally hesitant to adopt measures that violate main GATT rules, this represents a major obstacle for the adoption of unilateral trade measures to combat child labour.

Even under the public morals exception of GATT Art. XX (a), the proposed interpretation is still controversial. While the *EC–Seal Products* decision has opened the way for a broader reading of the term 'public morals', the issue of national measures with an extraterritorial effect has not been completely solved. It is also not sure whether labelling measures on child labour would be held to be consistent with the TBT Agreement. Thus, substantial coherence between trade and labour is possible but not always predictable.

CHAPTER 3

A Constitutionalist Approach to International Law

1 Introduction

Having found that there is space to consider unilateral measures on child labour under GATT rules *de lege lata*, the question is whether greater coherence and overcoming fragmentation in response to the issue of child labour is needed. Also, given that the case law of the WTO, especially on GATT Art. III and XX, and the TBT Agreement already has been influenced by constitutional thinking allowing for non-economic values and public international law to be taken into account in constitutional-like balancing exercises,[1] the traditional private law paradigm of international law does not seem to pose such a big hindrance in reconciling trade and child labour.

However, so far, the human rights regime and labour rights regime under the ILO operate in complete isolation from the trade regime under the WTO.[2] All attempts to formally integrate human or labour rights into the WTO have failed.[3] Apart from joint research projects, there is not much dialogue happening between the ILO and WTO.[4] These areas of international law are quite fragmented. However, in cases such as the Myanmar case where trade measures were recommended by the ILO, jurisdictions may overlap and inter-agency cooperation between the WTO and UN or ILO bodies would be recommendable and might even be required. It should be common practice that, as a minimum, the WTO adjudicating bodies consult the ILO and base their decision on relevant jurisprudence. At the moment, Art. 13 of the DSU allows to ask for a legal opinion of the other legal regime, but the Appellate Body in *US–Shrimp* has accorded panels a lot of discretion when assessing what weight they give to that advice.[5] The discretion of the panel includes for example the choice and evaluation of the source of the information or advice, and it may reject any advice, which it has recieved.[6] As carefully analysed by Foltea, so far the WTO panels have not showed sufficient institutional sensitivity to other

1 See Chapter 2, for example pp. 173 et seqq., p. 221 and pp. 270 et seqq.
2 Cf. Cottier (Implications of EC–Seal Products), pp. 70–74.
3 Cf. Choudhoury/Gehne/Heri/Humbert/Kaufmann/Nadakavukaren Schefer.
4 See for example WTO/ILO Jansen/Lee.
5 *US–Shrimp*, report of the Appellate Body, para. 104.
6 Ibid.

organizations and rather asked for factual information than for legal advice.[7] They rarely deferred to their legal opinion. According to Foltea, such problems are deeply rooted in the WTO system itself, meaning that 'trade should trump other societal values', but also in the governance of other international organizations.[8]

Another major shortcoming with regard to trade and child labour is that private actor complaints on behalf of children are not possible under the current dispute settlement system. Neither companies nor children adversely affected by trade measures do have standing under the WTO quasi-judicial system. In an era, where the global agricultural and food market is dominated by a few transnational corporations rather than states, one could also think of allowing for complaints against companies.[9] One could think of a right of children to bring complaints against the (foreign) company but also against their (own) government for failure to tackle child labour following the model of the NAALC.[10]

Finally, it is questionable whether unilateral measures such as blanket import bans without flanking measures are the most appropriate tool to remedy the problem of child labour. The analysis of social clauses on child labour in regional and bilateral trade agreements has shown that trade measures should be used as measures of last resort.[11] It also recommended the use of trade incentives as an important tool. Thus, the question arises whether a negotiated trade and labour agreement *de lege ferenda* would be recommendable. A new agreement could address the issue of cost and attempt to fairly distribute the financial burden eliminating child labour between states and other potential actors. For example, states complaining of child labour could be obliged to provide financial and technical resources for measures aimed at the eradication of child labour.

Thus, there could be some merit in devising a joint ILO-WTO regime *de lege ferenda*. Such a regime could serve as a model for linking trade and human and/or labour rights. However, the current legal order based on state consent and fragmentation of legal regimes does not seem to support such projects oriented towards more integration. The question therefore is whether new approaches to international law could promote the creation of such a regime.

Hence, this chapter will explore whether new approaches to international law are available to promote effective solutions such as a joint ILO-WTO

7 Foltea, p. 280.
8 Ibid., p. 16.
9 Oxfam/Heinrich-Boell-Stiftung.
10 Humbert (The Challenge of Child Labour), pp. 195–226.
11 Cf. Humbert (The Challenge of Child Labour), pp. 195–284.

regime. Put differently, submitting that the current theory underlying international law is ill-equipped to address pressing legal issues, new legal doctrine may be needed, being an essential tool to devise effective legal instruments.[12] Especially with regard to international organizations and the emergence of global governance, questions of sources, legal subjects, accountability and the applicability of international law arises.[13]

According to common positivist legal doctrine, which in contrast to the natural law theory developed by Grotius[14] perceived law as man-made, international law is perceived as the law *inter* nations, i.e. rules based on the behaviours of states.[15] In his theory of state sovereignty giving states supreme power, de Vattel tried to combine elements of naturalist and positivist elements.[16] It reflected the prevailing political order of a 'plurality of independent states' based on the European Peace of Westphalia of 1648 until more or less the post-war order of today.[17] In contrast to domestic law based on command and enforcement, international law is a horizontal system based on consensus, reciprocity and lacks central legislative and executive institutions with enforcement power.[18] In common positivist doctrine, its main legal sources are state consent and the principle of *pacta sunt servanda*. The traditional view is thus a contractualist or consensualist approach to international law.[19] With the establishment of the collective security system of the UN aimed at preserving peace and security after the Second World War, international law entered into a new phase of cooperation and developed new concepts such *ius cogens*, the international community and put more emphasis on the individual.[20] With regard to the relationship between domestic and international law, the monist school of Kelsen[21] deriving all law from the *Grundnorm* contrasts with the dualist school,[22] which differentiates between an international and domestic order.[23] As will be discussed below, the question is whether such an artificial

12 Cf. Klabbers, p. 993; von Bogdandy/Goldmann/Venzke, p. 125.
13 Cf. Klabbers.
14 For an excellent English version of the original work by Hugo Grotius, *De iure belli ac pacis libri tres, in quibus Jus Naturae et Gentium, item Juris Publici praecipua explicanter,* see Neff.
15 Cf. Malanczuk, p. 16.
16 Onuf.
17 Cassese (International Law in a Divided World), p. 37.
18 Cf. Malanczuk, p. 6.
19 Besson (Institutionalising global *demoi*-cracy), p. 59.
20 Ibid., pp. 30–31; see also Friedmann, pp. 3–19.
21 Kelsen, pp. 196–343.
22 Triepel.
23 Cf. Malanczuk, p. 63.

distinction between domestic, regional and global law is still adequate and a 'coherent framework of governance commensurate with the process of globalization and contemporary and future challenges' needed.[24] At the same time, as mentioned in the introduction to this book, there has been a vast proliferation of new legal topics along with new institutions such as the international law of the environment, of communications and human rights law, and law on climate change, leading to a specialization and fragmentation of international law.

Various new approaches to international law attempt to respond to the challenge of fragmentation of international law. Some attempt to establish coherence of international law relying on existing conflict rules of international law. Others question the legitimacy of the current international legal order based on state consent and look for additional sources rooted in a multi-level constitutionalism. The various approaches range from legal reasoning to applying concepts from constitutional, administrative, or international private law or even social theory to the international order. Critical voices point to the limits of international law or enquire into the concept of law as such as an adequate response to solve societal conflicts.

The following sections will first analyse the various approaches with a view as to whether they are apt to offer a basis for devising a new ILO-WTO enforcement regime on child labour, then discuss critiques and counter-arguments to the constitutional approach and conclude by presenting the theory of a new legal humanism in international law.

2 Different Approaches to International Law

2.1 *Legal Interpretation*

One prominent approach takes recourse to traditional methods of legal reasoning in order to respond to the challenge of fragmentation of international law.[25] The representatives of this approach perceive the emergence of new and special types of law such as human rights law, environmental law and trade law as well as so-called 'self-contained regimes' as a problem for the coherence and unity of international law.[26] The central question is how to deal with normative conflicts between rules or rules-systems. Representatives of this approach hold that conflict rules of international law constitute a coherent theory of

24 See below p. 332 and Cottier (Multilayered Governance), p. 675.
25 See for example UN (Fragmentation); Pauwelyn (Conflict of Norms); Neumann.
26 ILC (Fragmentation).

conflict of norms, holding that international law provides sufficient techniques to deal with challenges of fragmentation and coherence.[27] Such techniques are for example the *lex specialis* doctrine; the *lex posterior* doctrine, *ius cogens* and *erga omnes* concepts, systemic integration according to Art. 31 (3) lit. c of the VCLT and the principle of harmonization.[28] The eminent legal scholar Koskenniemi points in a similar direction when he holds that there is no reason to reconceive international law but instead a need to narrating regimes anew and to give voice to those not represented in the regime's institutions.[29]

This approach indeed offers valid solutions to the problem of child labour and trade. As examined above, recourse to the concepts of *ius cogens* and *erga omnes* as well as Art. 31 (3) lit. c of the VCLT makes substantial coherence between the human rights and trade regime possible.[30] However, the approach does not offer a conceptual framework for curing the legitimacy deficit of the WTO adjudicating bodies for example when dealing with non-trade issues such as child labour. It explicitly does not envisage change in institutional structures or inter-agency cooperation. It also does not deal with private actor participation in dispute settlement. More far-reaching concepts are needed to make international law work for finding new solutions for the problem of child labour.

2.2 *New Haven School*

The New Haven School follows a sociological approach and analyses international law *inter alia* with a view to the legal process of making of authoritative and controlling decisions.[31] Accordingly, 'the effective authority of any legal system depends in the long run upon the underlying common interest of the participants in the system and their recognition of such common interests, reflected in continuing predispositions to support the prescriptions and the procedures that comprise the system'.[32] In contrast to the positivist doctrine based on state consent, this school integrates also other actors than states including non-governmental organizations and the media into international legal decision-making.[33] This approach promotes interdisciplinary collaboration between lawyers and political scientists.[34] The main interest of adherents

27 Pauwelyn (Conflict of Norms), p. 490; ILC (Fragmentation), para. 20.
28 ILC (Fragmentation), para. 682.
29 (cited: Koskenniemi (The Fate of Public International Law)), p. 360.
30 See for example above pp. 96 et seqq. and pp. 203 et seqq.
31 See for example McDougal/Lasswell.
32 Ibid., p. 8.
33 Reisman.
34 See Koskenniemi (International Legal Theory and Doctrine), p. 979.

to the New Haven School was to understand past, present and future interactions between international and national law and eventually made them propose instead of following rules and hierarchies to focus on processes and functions operating within them, including making law at community levels.[35] Pursuing an anti-formalist approach, they put the complex social and power processes building world orders and the main factors influencing decisions at the centre of their work.[36] Most interesting for this work, assuming that law mainly serves policy, they stressed the importance of identifying the values policy makers and lawyers pursue when applying the law. Such values would be *inter alia* security, wealth, well-being and affection.[37] The goal of such value-oriented school was to establish either a minimum public order or an optimum public order, i.e. advancing human dignity through realizing the identified values.[38]

Such an analytical and value-oriented perception of international law constitutes a methodological approach potentially enriching any new approach to international law. However, the focus on politics and power contrasts with the search for a more coherent rules-based international legal framework reconciling trade with child labour. Other theories shall be looked at.

2.3 *Feminist Approaches to International Law*

Feminists for a long time have been asking for a radical shift in perspective in international law.[39] They criticize *inter alia* the absence of women in international legal institutions, the vocabulary of international law, which generally makes women invisible, the principles and rules of international law that operate differently for men and women and finally the gendered nature of basic concepts of international law such as 'states', 'security', 'order' and 'conflict'.[40] For example, the public/private distinction of international law has strongly been opposed.[41] Charlesworth has rightly stressed the discrimination against women by excluding acts by private actors from the definition of torture.[42] It is therefore to be welcomed that in 2008, the Committee against Torture in its General Comment No. 2 has clarified that in case government officials

35 See for a comprehensive analysis of this approach, García-Salmones Rovira, p. 209.
36 Ibid.
37 Ratner, p. 804.
38 Ibid.
39 Charlesworth, p. 393; Charlesworth/Chinkin.
40 Charlesworth (Feminist Methods), p. 381.
41 Ibid., p. 381.
42 Ibid.

fail to exercise due diligence to prevent or prosecute private actors of torture, the State bears responsibility and its officials should be considered as authors or otherwise responsible under the Convention.[43] And most importantly, the Committee has explicitly stated that it has applied this principle to States parties' failure to prevent and protect victims from gender-based violence, such as rape, domestic violence, female genital mutilation, and trafficking. However, in the view of feminist scholars, a lot remains to be done especially with regard to individual accountability for human rights abuses in internal conflicts, an area of law where a lot of definitions and concepts are based on stereotypes such as women as men's property or their role in childbearing.[44]

While the feminist method is a useful method to reveal the discriminatory structures and concepts of international law supporting the global domination of women by men, the feminist approach or method, while having the potential to highlight and give weight to the urgent need to abolish girls' labour, like the New Haven School, rather complements any new approach suggesting new bases for the global order than providing a stand-alone solution for problems of fragmentation or lack of accountability.

2.4 *Global Legal Pluralism and Conflicts-Law Approach*

Deploying insights from legal sociology and legal theory put forward by famous thinkers such as Luhmann or Polanyi,[45] the school of global legal pluralism seeks to capture the methodological challenge emerging from the evolving order of a denationalised world society that is not only fragmented into many different regulatory areas with a proliferation of global and national law-making but also confronted with the rise of non-state actors and increasing private law-making of non-statal regimes.[46] Its various adherents inquire into the nature of legal regulation of problems beyond the confines of jurisdiction, raise claims against legal unity, focus on 'regime-collisions' and submit that

43 Committee against Torture, General Comment No. 2, CAT/C/GC/2 24 January 2008.

44 Charlesworth (Feminist Methods), p. 386.

45 See in particular Joerges; Fischer-Lescano/Teubner, pp. 999 et seqq; for the adoption of the approach by Niklas Luhmann, see Fischer-Lescano.

46 For prominent representatives of the school of global legal pluralism, see for example Zumbansen; Teubner (Global Bukowina I); idem (Globale Bukowina II); idem (Globale Zivilverfassungen); Schiff Berman; Wai; Joerges; for an excellent account and analysis of the concept of global legal pluralism looking into its various meanings and history and background, partly coming from political theory, see Seinecke with further references, where he *inter alia* describes legal pluralism a way of looking at things, a nomological concept of law that aims to question supremacy and deconstruct legal paradigms. See also Viellechner (Transnationalisierung des Rechts).

'law can only, at the very best, offer a kind of damage limitation'.[47] They suggest procedural principles for managing hybridity,[48] show the way forward using conflict law and transnational private litigation for better global governance[49] and finally propose the concept of a 'responsive legal pluralism' that offers a new transnational conflict law that may amount to 'an adequate reconfiguration of the modern concept of constitutionalism'.[50]

2.4.1 From Global to Responsive Legal Pluralism

On a rather theoretical level, Zumbansen regards pluralism as an inherent trait of an evolving legal order and a way of questioning and reconstructing the project of law between places and spaces.[51]

Building on Luhmann's hypothesis that global law would experience a radical fragmentation not only on territorial but also on sectoral lines, Fischer-Lescano and Teubner in their excellent treatise on "regime-collisions" do away with any search for legal unity but instead put the emphasis on achieving normative compatibility of regimes.[52] They defend a multi-dimensional 'global legal pluralism' that also looks at the various emerging non-statal private legal regimes giving birth to a 'global law without a state'.[53] Using examples such as the so-called *lex mercatoria*, patent law or transnational copyright law, they propose what they call 'selective networking of colliding regimes' and hold that loose relationships between fragments of law should be created through on the one hand linking legal regimes with autonomous social sectors and on the other hand linking legal regimes with one another.[54] Regarding the latter, different principles of conflicts law should apply comprising new concepts such as the functional connection between the regime and the legal issue instead of choosing between nations.[55] More importantly, instead of focussing on collision rules, the new approach would develop substantive rules through the law of inter-regime-conflicts itself, requiring courts to create transnational substantive norms.[56] Also, conflict law would have as its main objective to

47 Fischer-Lescano/Teubner, pp. 1045 et seqq.

48 Schiff Berman.

49 Joerges; Wai.

50 Viellechner (Responsive legal pluralism), p. 314; see also idem (Berücksichtigungspflicht als Kollisionsregel).

51 Zumbansen.

52 Fischer-Lescano/Teubner (Regime Collisions) citing Niklas Luhmann, 'Die Weltgesellschaft', 57 Archiv für Rechts-und Sozialphilosophie 21 (1971).

53 Fischer-Lescano/Teubner, p. 1009.

54 Ibid., p. 1017.

55 Ibid., p. 1021.

56 Ibid., pp. 1022–1023.

establish compatibility between colliding rationality principles of global sectors, e. g. in the WTO case *Brazil–Measure Affecting Patent Protection.*[57] In the view of Fischer-Lescano and Teubner, with the Doha Declaration, this reconstruction of WTO law within the WTO legal system is not an external imposition of limits but the internal achievement of the WTO legal regime itself and reflects upon a process of mutual composition.[58] Instead of reconciling different normative commands, the authors envision the evolution of general incompatibility norms within the economic and health sector that protect for example certain health protection measures such as the Brazil AIDS programme from economic logic.[59]

Maintaining that the concept of *ius cogens* contained in Art. 53 of the VCLT cannot be applied to the various autonomous regimes where concepts such as an 'international *ordre public*', 'mandatory rules' and '*ordre public* transnational' prevail, Fischer-Lescano and Teubner hold that different regimes can establish their own standards for their version of a global *ius non dispositivum.*[60] Taking *lex constructionis* as an example, they hold that arbitration instances should develop their own intra-regime responsiveness to the immediate human and natural environment beyond contractual terms.[61] As regards the question how different international regime courts should take account of judgements by other courts, they propose instead of a *stare decisis* of superior courts the concept of 'default deference', it is the presumption that decisions of international regime courts do have the character of a precedent for one another, amount in fact to a form of judicial networking.[62]

In a similar vein, Schiff Berman pays due regard to this 'world of hybrid legal spaces'[63] and suggests 'procedural mechanisms for managing, without eliminating, hybridity':[64] if people cannot agree on norms, they may agree on procedural mechanisms to take hybridity seriously. He regards legal pluralism as a solution to sovereigntism and universalism and elaborates *inter alia* on mechanisms and principles such as dialectical interaction between courts, limited autonomy regimes with spaces for parallel civil and religious legal systems and

57 *Brazil–Patent Protection*, Request for Consultation by the United States.
58 Fischer-Lescano/Teubner, p. 1030.
59 Ibid., p. 1032.
60 Ibid, pp. 1032–1034.
61 Ibid., pp. 1034 et seqq.
62 Ibid., pp. 1039–1045.
63 Schiff Berman, p. 1158.
64 Ibid., p. 1164.

a pluralist approach to conflict of laws instead of the traditional approach of jurisdiction.[65]

Joerges and Wai conceive the conflicts-law approach as the adequate constitutional form of law-mediated democratic transnational governance in contrast to global governance.[66] They present for example the European standardisation process involving non-state actors and refraining from centralisation relying on national delegations as a dimension of conflict law and transnational governance. Putting this norm-generation process under public scrutiny will result in a model for the constitutionalization of private governance. Submitting that the WTO lacks the legitimate power to solve true conflicts, they suggest conceiving WTO law as (mere) conflicts law that exercises regulatory prudence – also presented as 'comity' – and accepts the need for legitimated judicial and administrative bodies when deciding matters of political sensitivity and far-reaching economic implications.[67] The approach emphasizes the contribution of international private law and transnational private litigation to social regulation through for example deciding on compensation of particular plaintiffs affected by transnational business activity.[68] Another example for its contribution to social regulation is the role of private law in constituting the terrain of transnational private ordering of e.g. contractual relations of retailers and their sub-contractors with regard to productions standards such as labour conditions.[69] According to this school of thought, international private law should be viewed as a tool for regulating society where traditional forms of state regulation are often ineffective.[70] That this is already the case is demonstrated by the fact that litigation is used in prominent campaigns by international NGOs such as the complaint against Shell's operation in Nigeria brought before a Dutch court or the court proceedings against the German textile discounter kik before a German civil court where victims of human rights violations claimed compensation for damage caused by a fire in a supplier factory in Pakistan under civil law.[71]

Approaching the field of constitutionalism, Viellechner suggests a 'responsive legal pluralism', i.e. a new kind of conflicts law that follows the model of

65 Schiff Berman, pp. 1197 et seqq.

66 Joerges, p. 415; Wai, p. 230.

67 Ibid., p. 445.

68 Wai, pp. 239–41.

69 Ibid., p. 243.

70 Ibid., p. 244.

71 See Friends of the Earth International (People v. Shell); ECCHR (Kik-Verfahren belegt: Deutschland muss Haftungsregeln von Unternehmen grundlegend reformieren).

international private law.[72] In an attempt to overcome outdated theories of monism and dualism that have re-appeared with different names such as a 'global constitutionalism', he seeks to remedy the deficiencies of radical legal pluralism and offers horizontal coordination among different legal orders.[73] Viellechner starts from conflicts law and the idea of 'reflexive law' developed by Teubner, and proposes, in a nutshell, 'responsivity [...] as a legally actionable principle of openness that may, under certain circumstances, even require the application of foreign public law as well as international and non-state law'.[74] Rejecting a common ground for different legal orders, responsivity combines the principles of complementary and subsidiarity and implies that different legal orders are both able and willing to consider each other on their own initiative. Equally, responsivity requires cooperation of courts. Due to its intellectual style as 'technique', it is apt to solve politicised conflicts.

In a similar way, Krisch argues for a postnational pluralism, calling into doubt the legalization of international politics with its potential for backlashes and destabilization.[75] Referring nevertheless to constitutional values such as democracy and the rule of law, he envisages postnational law not necessarily as binding but rather having a form of gradated authority resembling the common law's use of 'persuasive authority'.[76]

2.4.2 Implications for the Problem of Trade and Child Labour

At first sight, the various ideas of the school of legal pluralism and conflicts law seem to have the potential to open new ways for solving the problem of trade and child labour.

When revealing 'regime-collisions' and competing rationalities of for example economy and health, and proposing 'selective networking of competing regimes', the 'evolution of incompatibility norms' and judicial networking, Teubner/Fischer-Lescano rightly point to the limits of law and make useful but somewhat abstract suggestions how to deal with existing shortcomings of the global legal order.

The conflicts law approach offers new avenues for solving conflicts with regards to transnational corporate behaviour and its impacts on society. The merit of this approach is also that it attempts to adequately deal with paralegal

72 Viellechner (Responsive legal pluralism); idem (Berücksichtigungspflicht als Kollisionsregel).

73 Viellechner (Responsive legal pluralism), pp. 322 et seqq.

74 Ibid., pp. 322–326.

75 Krisch, p. 303.

76 Ibid.; p. 305.

regimes and put them under public scrutiny. Signalling a more plural approach than global governance, it does not have features of new hegemonic power or top-down control that is often associated with global governance.

Equally, to regard 'responsivity' as a legal actionable principle that may require the application of foreign public law or non-state law may be apt to open the way for devising a better integrated global legal order where trade and child labour are not separate regimes anymore. Finally, assigning postnational law a 'graded authority' suits the rather weak enforcement potential of international law and merits further attention. In a similar vein, Cottier and Hertig argue in favour of a 'graduated approach to constitutionalism'.[77]

However, the various approaches do not seem to answer pressing questions concerning the legitimacy of the international order and institutional structures. As Koskenniemi rightly holds, 'pluralism's main contribution lies in the awareness it brings of the biases of different legal vocabularies; but it cannot sustain a project in its own right'.[78] To perceive questions of transnational governance merely as conflicts between different (non-)regulatory systems appears to push aside the constitutional dimension of such governance questions. Moreover, global governance based on transnational networks of civil society, experts and other technocrats could also be a danger for democracy, leading to technical responses and a 'deformalisation'.[79] Critical voices have hold that the ambitious political vision for peace and justice cannot be achieved by regimes based on spontaneous private ordering.[80] As Petersmann convincingly argues with regard to international economic law, conflict-law principles 'cannot substitute the necessary review of the "constitutional coherence" of international economic law'.[81] Rather, as representatives of the conflicts-law approach themselves maintain, private international law including private litigation has an important complementary function for social regulation where such regulation is difficult in multilateral institutions or through national public regulations.[82]

With a view to the idea of an ILO-WTO enforcement regime for child labour, especially the conflict law approach would help to build on private multi-stakeholder-initiatives such as the Fair Wear Foundation on labour standards

77 See below, p. 322.
78 Koskenniemi (The Fate of Public International Law), p. 354.
79 Ibid., pp. 339–345.
80 von Bogdandy/Goldmann/Venzke (From Public International Law to International Public Law), p. 121.
81 Petersmann (Public Reason), p. 47.
82 See Wai, p. 241.

in the textile industry where representatives from industry, governments and non-governmental organizations attempt to improve labour conditions in global textile supply chains.[83] Equally, in some cases where child labour is found in global supply chains, the use of private transnational litigation may offer promising solutions.

The 'responsivity' principle would help to interpret WTO law in accordance with human rights and labour rights law or even to make human rights law override trade law. However, as mentioned above, it does not offer a framework for devising new institutional structures or push the participation of private actors as needed in the case of trade and child labour. Yet, it may be an important principle to help to develop a new thinking in international law. The 'graded authority' of law should be kept in mind when applying international law and potentially devising new regimes.

2.5 *Global Administrative Law*

The school of global administrative law seeks to respond to accountability deficits in the increasing exercise of transnational regulatory power emerged in the process of globalization in such fields as security, environmental protection and labour standards by creating a 'global administrative space' that is governed by global administrative law.[84] Such a global administrative space incorporates five main types of administration overcoming the classical dichotomy between inter-state relations governed by international law and the domestic regulatory space governed by national law: It comprises administration by formal international organizations; by transnational networks and coordination arrangements between national regulatory officials; by national regulators; hybrid intergovernmental-private administration and administration by private institutions.[85] Global administrative law comprises principles affecting the accountability of global administrative bodies such as transparency, participation, reasoned decision-making, legality, proportionality and effective review mechanisms.[86] Some adherents to this school argue for a set of different accountability mechanisms beyond the usual mechanisms of domestic administrative law.[87] In particular, they question that global accountability must conform to maximal principles of democratic participation. Rather,

83 See Fair Wear Foundation, https://www.fairwear.org/.
84 See for example Kingsbury/Krisch/Stewart; Grant/Keohane.
85 Kingsbury/Krisch/Stewart, p. 20.
86 Ibid., p. 17 and 37 et seqq.
87 Grant/Keohane.

effective accountability systems should contain elements from both delegation and participation models of accountability.[88]

This approach to international law contains many convincing elements. It is true that the current regime of transnational governance suffers from accountability deficits which could be mitigated by applying standards such as transparency, participation or effective review mechanisms. The differentiation between different accountability concepts based on participation and delegation is particularly useful. However, the approach does not answer the fundamental question on what basis such principles may be applied to the international order and what the normative basis of a global legal order should be.[89] Representatives of this school have also asked this question and proposed to base global administrative law on concepts such as individual rights and democracy, thereby arguing for a cosmopolitan conception of the international order.[90] To base the international order on concepts such as human rights and democracy means however to argue for an constitutional approach to international law since the protection of individual rights and democracy are fundamental elements of traditional constitutional law.[91] Thus, this approach should be regarded as complementing constitutional schools of thought rather than as a stand-alone theory. Implications of this approach for a joint ILO-WTO regime will be discussed under the constitutional approach.

2.6 *International Public Authority*

An approach close to global administrative law comes from German leading international scholars such as von Bogdandy and Wolfrum[92] who claim that in responding to demands from global society for legitimate and effective international institutions, a paradigm shift in public international law is needed.[93] Doing away with the private law paradigm of public international law and recognizing that international organizations increasingly pursue their own objectives without being held accountable for lack of standards, they advocate the notion of international public authority as the objective of their theory of international public law.[94] This theory consists of five elements: Firstly,

88 Ibid., p. 28.

89 See also von Bogdandy/Goldmann/Venzke, p. 131; O'Donoghue, p. 226.

90 Grant/Keohane, p. 51.

91 See also Kleinlein, pp. 92–93, who argues that also the school of administrative law discusses constitutional questions such as the legal basis for public power.

92 von Bogdandy/Goldmann/Venzke; Goldmann; see also Wolfrum, (Legitimacy of International Law).

93 von Bogdandy/Goldmann/Venzke, p. 115.

94 Ibid., pp. 124 et seqq.

international public law is inspired by domestic public law; secondly, common interests of the world society can exist and thus international public law may be the institutional framework for public policies; thirdly, international public law is limited to acts pursuing common interests, fourthly, freedom and human rights provide guidance for public law framework and fifthly, there is a focus on interpretation and doctrinal re-construction benefitting from practical uses of legal scholarship.[95] In particular, common interests are involved when the actor claims to act on behalf of a community interest and certainly in the case of such topics as poverty reduction, human rights advancement, environmental protection and economic stability.[96] Authority is defined as the acts based on international law that impact other actors' freedom; either collectively as states or individually as human beings.[97] Public authority affecting freedom may take a variety of different forms such as clever sanctions including trade counter measures, the award of damages enforceable in court in the context of the ICSID mechanism, the loss of reputation, legal reasoning in WTO decisions and authority through information of OECD or climate change reports. Scholarship then has the task of rendering a legal regime applicable to acts of international public authority. Or put differently, international public law needs to connect international public authority with the legitimizing potential of the domestic level.[98]

Similarly, the eminent scholar Wolfrum holds that international law has reached a different quality to amount to international governance requiring legitimacy.[99] Defining legitimacy as the justification of authority he points out that the traditional view of state consent and a chain of legitimacy may not be sufficient anymore to prove legitimacy. Emphasizing that the impact of international law on national law with quasi-judicial competences affecting citizens has changed, he stresses that certainly in human rights and economic law, citizens have become directly affected.[100] On the other hand, corporations are directly addressed and can pursue claims in investment disputes. Wolfrum questions for example whether the de-nationalization and de-parliamentarisation under the WTO regime where national policies have to be framed so as to not interfere with freedom of trade in goods may require application of democratic principles.[101] However also in investment

95 Ibid., p. 131 et seqq.
96 Ibid., p. 138.
97 Ibid., p. 139.
98 Goldmann, p. 467.
99 Wolfrum (Legitimacy of International Law), pp. 4–5.
100 Ibid., p. 12.
101 Ibid., p. 18.

law, the individual has more rights as NAFTA dispute settlement processes demonstrate.[102] Yet, enquiry into legitimacy should only be undertaken where international governance can be compared to national governance. Wolfrum considers various options for closing the legitimacy gap. One option would be to strengthen the influence of national parliaments on international relations through for example including legislature in decisions and the establishment of international organizations. Another option is to admit more NGOs in decision-making but also to strengthen judicial review of international decisions of international governance, especially at the international level. Finally, he stresses that legitimacy should be considered in context of international law and its values and not borrow from national constitutional law.[103]

Both approaches by von Bogdandy and Wolfrum focus on re-gaining legitimacy through better democratic participation including the legislature more into international process and strengthening judicial review but distinguish themselves from a constitutional approach to international law, especially rejecting the existence of a *pouvoir constituent* in world society.[104] However, if the aim is to bring more democracy and human rights protection to the international level, then, as Wolfrum rightly holds, a discussion of fundamental values is necessary. Thus, the constitutional approach to international law potentially based on constitutionalist values, merits a further look.

2.7 *Constitutional Approaches*

A variety of new approaches to international law draws on constitutional theory and multi-level governance. Being well aware of new challenges societies are facing arising from technological progress, climate change and new actors such as multinational corporations, they all have in common that they challenge the current bases of international law such as state consent and sovereignty and discuss the legitimacy of the global legal order.[105] Prior to discussing three prominent approaches to constitutionalism in international law, this chapter will briefly explain how the concepts of a 'constitution' and 'constitutionalism' evolved with regard to the modern state and discuss their applicability to other entities and legal orders.

---

102 Ibid., p. 19.

103 Ibid., p 24.

104 von Bogdandy/Goldmann/Venzke, p. 129.

105 See for example Kleinlein; Fassbender, p. 552; Petersmann (Public Reason); Cottier/Hertig; Peters (Compensatory Constitutionalism); Paulus (The International Legal System as a Constitution); Walker (Constitutionalism and pluralism); Kumm (The Cosmopolitan Turn in Constitutionalism).

2.7.1 Constitution, Constitutionalization, and Constitutionalism and the UN Charter as Constitution of the International Community

Central to the debate on the constitutionalization of the international order and constitutionalism in international law is the term 'constitution' in its normative sense as it evolved in relation to the modern nation state. To use the words of de Vattel from 1758, the term 'constitution' means 'Das Grundgesetz, das die Art und Weise der Ausübung der öffentlichen Gewalt bestimmt, bildet die Verfassung des Staates'.[106] Kleinlein traces comprehensively how the term 'constitution' in different eras and under distinct regimes from ancient Greece and the Roman empire to the French and American revolution and the German constitutional movement evolved.[107] Central to the concept of a constitution was the idea of the sovereignty of the people, the *demos*.[108] Art. XVI of the French Déclaration des droits de l'homme et du citoyen of 1789, which was made part of the constitution of 1791, enshrined the idea of certain citizens' rights and the separation of powers: 'Toute société, dans laquelle la garantie des droits n'est pas assurée ni la separation des pouvoirs déterminée, n'a point de constitution'.[109] In a similar vein, in the German constitutional movement, the term 'constitution' did not only refer to basic legal rules that limit and govern the exercise of all public authority but also to the question of democratic government or social justice.[110] This quest for a (written) constitution in several European nation states in the seventeenth and eighteenth century was historically referred to as "constitutionalism".[111] Based on this conception of a constitutionalism, 'global constitutionalism' is generally understood as the application of constitutional principles such as human rights protection, democracy and the rule of law to the international legal order.[112] 'Constitutionalization' on the other hand is the process whereby a legal order becomes a constitution or constitutional law'.[113]

When the debate on the constitution of the EU and the constitutionalization of the international order emerged with the advent of the 21st century, the crucial question among constitutional and international lawyers was whether the terms 'constitution' and 'constitutionalism' were intrinsically linked to

106 de Vattel, book I, chap. III, § 27.
107 Kleinlein, pp. 99–156.
108 Ibid, p. 115.
109 https://www.elysee.fr/la-presidence/la-declaration-des-droits-de-l-homme-et-du-citoyen.
110 Kleinlein, p. 118.
111 Peters (Compensatory Constitutionalism), p. 610.
112 Ibid., p. 583.
113 Ibid., p. 582.

states or whether constitutional thinking could also be established in international law.[114] Traditionally, there has been a dichotomy between the classical international law of co-existence[115] and the core precepts of constitutional law such as the rule of law, human rights and the principle of separation of powers, which were only applied with the nation state.[116]

Especially Swiss and German constitutional scholars tie the term 'constitution' in its normative sense to the existence of a nation state.[117] The traditional 'statist school' sees the state as a necessary precondition of a constitution, and the existence of a state necessarily linked to the notion of a nation that holds a relatively homogeneous identity.[118] The prominent '*no demos*' thesis of this school submits that the European Union lacks a constitutional subject, namely a nation.[119] This view is summarized by the famous sentence of Kirchhof: 'Where there is no state, there is no constitution, and where there is no people, there is no state'.[120] The German scholar Grimm pointed to the risk of diluting the term 'constitution'.[121] Grimm and Müller argued that by using constitutional language for international organizations, there would be the danger of legitimising political entities with a democratic deficit and a lack of respect for human rights.[122]

International lawyers in favour of modern constitutionalism convincingly dismantle the methodological approach of linking the legal concept of a nation state and a constitution to the existence of a homogenic nation.[123] They rightly hold that the homogeneity depends on the observer and does not serve

114 See for example the following authors who argue for a limitation of the use of the term 'constitution' to the traditional nation state: Grimm, pp. 7–10; Müller, p. 88; Möllers, p. 240. The following authors are among those arguing for a decoupling of the term constitution from the traditional nation state: Walker (The EU and WTO); Peters (Drei gute Gründe); Kumm, (The Cosmopolitan Turn in Constitutionalism); For an excellent and comprehensive discussion of the linkage between the term 'constitution' and the modern nation state with further references, see for example Kleinlein pp. 119–156 or Cottier/Hertig, pp. 275–298, who differentiate between the 'statist school' and the 'international school'.

115 See Allot, p. 35.

116 See Cottier/Hertig with further references, pp. 265–66. See also Fassbender, p. 555 et seq.

117 Grimm, p. 10; Isensee/Kirchhof, § 21 note 69.

118 Schmitt, pp. 12 et seqq., pp. 26 et seqq., pp. 38 et seqq.; BVerfGE 83, 37 (53 et seq.), decision by the Second Senate, 15 October 1990, 2 BvF 2, 6/89.

119 Böckenförde, pp. 96–106.

120 Kirchhof, pp. 57, 59; translation by the author, German original: „Wo kein Staat, da keine Verfassung, und wo kein Staatsvolk, da kein Staat."

121 Grimm, p. 10.

122 Ibid; Müller, p. 88.

123 Cottier/Hertig, pp. 290–293 with further references.

as benchmark. For example, Europe might seem to be homogenous from an Asian point of view but not from a French point of view. Most importantly, in times of rising migration and multi-ethnic societies, pointing to homogenous societies does not seem a promising approach. Also Germany is a country of emigrants and immigrants with migration waves back to the 19th century.[124] The homogenic nation is also not applicable to multinational states such as Canada and Belgium.[125] Similarly, federal states such as the US, Germany and the Swiss Confederation, where individual states kept their constitutions, do not fit in a clear-cut model of exclusively assigning constitutions to nation states.[126] Most significantly, Peters submits that only if legal terms and concepts adapt to the new trends in globalization, jurisprudence and international law will remain relevant.[127] With respect to the risk of diluting the term, she favours a broader constitutional concept that does not have a nation as it prerequisite and holds that a crucial element for following the constitutional paradigm is the participation of the individuum in political processes rather than the existence of a nation, in particular with regard to the EU.[128] Similarly, Cottier and Hertig convincingly point to a 'graduated approach to constitutionalism'.[129] Rather than stipulating minimum standards for a normative constitutional order, constitutions and constitutionalism should be conceived as a process where the legitimacy of a constitution may lag behind its formal authority.[130] Put differently, modern constitutionalism should be conceived as a necessary step to secure the values of constitutional ideas in an era of globalization, disciplining the power of non-state entities.[131] Drawing on Besson's theory on reasonable disagreement and the law, Cottier holds that disagreement on values is not only present at the international level but also the normal state of affairs in a domestic polity.[132] What differs, is a matter of degree, not of principle.[133]

The former judge of the ICJ, Mosler, in his seminal work on the *International Society as a Legal Community*, was one of the first scholars to infer from the

---

124 Plamper.
125 Cottier/Hertig, p. 291.
126 Cf. also Fassbender, p. 557.
127 Peters (Drei gute Gründe) p. 12.
128 Ibid., p. 23.
129 Peters (Drei gute Gründe) p. 22. Cottier/Hertig, pp. 293–298.
130 Weiler, p. 3; Cottier/Hertig, p. 294.
131 Cf: Cottier/Hertig, p. 298.
132 Cottier (Multilayered Governance), p. 670.
133 Ibid.

concept of *ius cogens* the existence of an international legal community with a public order consisting of rules and principles for its members:

> It [the uniformity of any legal community] may relate to legal rules which are binding within the community. The whole of the minimum can be called a common public order (ordre public international).[134]

Early theories on the notion of a constitution in international law and the special status of the UN Charter were developed by Verdross and Simma.[135] [136] Following the monist approach by Kelsen and his *Grundnorm* theory,[137] which claimed the unity of international and national law, they concluded that the constitutional law of the universal community was embedded in the UN Charter.[138] While other eminent scholars such as Georges Scelle[139] equally advocated an international constitutional law, the German and Polish immigrants Lassa Oppenheim and Hersch Lauterpacht with their famous opus of Oppenheim's International Law perceived international law rather as a common law type of system in the sense of a 'higher private law'.[140] The theme of an international constitution was *inter alia* elaborated by Tomuschat holding that '[T]he international community can indeed be conceived of as a legal entity, governed by a constitution'.[141] Drawing on Art. 53 of the VCLT and the former Art. 19 of Draft Articles on State Responsibility, which both refer to the international community as a guardian of fundamental interests to humanity, he conceives modern international law as having a constitution.[142] Both norms serve as evidence for the existence of common goods and interest of an international community as opposed to bilateral relations between states.[143] In particular, Art. 2 of the UN Charter prohibiting *inter alia* the use of force could be deemed to be a constitutional principle.[144] Instead of following the dualist or monist theories as to the impact of international law on domestic legal orders,

134 Mosler, p. 17.
135 Verdross/Simma (Universelles Völkerrecht I), pp. 5 and 80 et seqq.
136 For an excellent treatise on precursors of international constitutionalism, cf. Kleinlein, pp. 157–234.
137 Kelsen, pp. 196–343.
138 Verdross/Simma (Universelles Völkerrecht I), p. 5.
139 Scelle (Droit Constitutionel International).
140 Cf. Koskenniemi (The Fate of Public International Law), pp. 331–334.
141 Tomuschat (Obligations Arising for States), p. 216.
142 Tomuschat (Die internationale Gemeinschaft), p. 6–7.
143 Tomuschat (Die Internationale Gemeinschaft), p. 15; see also Hahn.
144 Ibid.

he considers international law as having a supplementary municipal constitutional function based on international human rights law.[145]

Drawing on the constitutional function of the UN Charter for the international community as proclaimed by Verdross and Simma, Fassbender goes a step further and has suggested conceiving the UN as the primary institutional representative of the international community and the UN Charter as its constitution.[146] Starting with the 'constitutional moment' of the drafting of the UN Charter in the San Francisco Conference after the Second World War, he thoroughly analyses the constitutional characteristics of the Charter such as its system of governance, its hierarchy of norms incorporated into its Art. 103 and its universality and inclusiveness, and concludes that indeed the UN Charter is *the* constitution of the international legal community, binding also on non-member states.[147]

While the view of Fassbender is certainly appealing, serious doubts arise with regard to constitutional character of the UN Charter as *the* constitution of the international community. Apart from the fact that it does not provide for judicial law enforcement by a constitutional court, its fragmentary character, its lack of a world parliament and government, its unclear relationship to *ius cogens* and to the constitution of member states and other international organizations put its constitutional character in question. Art. 103 of the UN Charter does not necessarily render opposing provisions of other treaties void in a constitutional manner.[148] So far, the UN Charter does not have such an 'omnipotence' as a national constitution would have.[149] It has also rightly been pointed that the 'reality of international relations does not quite fit into a view of the Charter as the comprehensive document of international legal relations'.[150] The UN Charter in fact does not function as an umbrella organization for its specialized regimes such as the WTO.[151]

Conceiving the constitutional approach generally as a plausible theory for current international law, different constitutional approaches will be discussed in the remaining sections.

145 Christina Tomuschat, 'International Law: Ensuring the Survival of Mankind on the Eve of a New Century, General Course on Public International Law', in 281 Recueil des Cours (1999), 10, 25, p. 237 quoted in von Bogdandy (Constitutionalism), p. 225.

146 Fassbender, pp. 567 et seq.

147 Ibid., pp. 573 et seqq.

148 Kleinlein, p. 711.

149 Cf. also Mosler, p. 16.

150 Paulus (The International Legal System as a Constitution), p. 78.

151 Ibid., p. 79.

2.7.2 'Citizen-Oriented Multi-level Constitutionalism'

Petersmann argued for a multi-level constitutionalism in order to overcome collective action problems in multi-level economic governance regarding the provision of international public goods such as international financial and energy security, the environment and international trade liberalization.[152] In his view, current national interest approaches to foreign policy impeded the collective supply of public goods.[153] From his perspective, citizen-oriented 'constitutional bottom-up approaches' to international economic law could protect constitutional rights most effectively and limit the 'collective action problems' in multi-level governance.[154] It was his normative premise that the less democratic procedures could control and guide multi-level governance in global institutions the more important were multi-level safeguards of substantive rights of citizens and of their judicial protection.[155] In his view, regular compliance by governments with most of the numerous rulings rendered by WTO dispute settlement bodies or investor-state arbitration proved the reality of multi-level constitutional, legal and judicial constraints on discretionary governance powers in international economic law.[156] In particular, drawing on EU law as a model, Petersmann promoted a human rights approach to trade that asks for a human rights interpretation of WTO obligations; for democratic functions of WTO rules that empowered citizens to invoke WTO guarantees of freedom and non-discrimination in domestic courts and for more democratic participation inside intergovernmental organization through consultative parliamentary bodies and consultation or participation of representative non-governmental organizations.[157] He opined that WTO law already has 'constitutional functions' protecting for example intellectual property rights in the TRIPS Agreement.[158] In his view, WTO law could and should be perceived as a multi-level 'constitutional framework' for limiting multi-level trade governance for the benefit of producers, traders, consumers and other citizens.[159] As a most effective strategy of constitutionalizing the WTO, he suggested that domestic, especially EU, judges should interpret international trade rules as a functional unity for the promotion and protection of the right of citizens.[160]

152 Petersmann (Public Reason).
153 Petersmann (Multi-levelMulti-level Trade Governance), p. 45.
154 Petersmann (Public Reason), p. 45.
155 Petersmann (Multi-level Trade Governance), p. 15.
156 Petersmann (Public Reason), p. 58.
157 Petersmann (Multi-level Trade Governance), pp. 19–28.
158 Ibid., p. 31.
159 Ibid. p. 33.
160 Ibid., pp. 38 and 54.

WTO Member States should negotiate reciprocal commitments to strengthen the domestic implementation of WTO rules in their domestic legislation, enabling domestic courts and citizens to enforce WTO guarantees against violations by domestic governments.

2.7.3 Constitutionalist Principles in International Law

> The democratic deficit of international law and global governance … is crucial because it de-legitimises international law and offers a reason for states not to apply and observe international law.[161]

Eminent scholars such as Peters, Kumm and Paulus, argue that traits of constitutional law are being and should be brought to the international sphere, or that at least, public international law should be reconceived in light of constitutional principles.[162]

2.7.3.1 *'Compensatory Constitutionalism'*

In an era of increasing interdependence of states and governance at the global level, the on-going de-constitutionalization at the national level in Peters' view should be compensated for by a constitutionalization at the international level in the sense of a 'compensatory constitutionalism'.[163] As governmental functions such as guaranteeing human security, freedom and equality are increasingly transferred to international levels and governance is exercised beyond national constitutional borders, only the various governance levels taken together can provide full constitutional protection.[164] Besson has called this concentration of international competences in the executive a 'deparlamentisation' of international matters at the national level.[165] A central argument is the observation that the international order is shifting from an order based on 'Westphalian sovereignty' to a "dualistic" world order based on state sovereignty and the autonomy of the individual.[166] Identifying different phenomena of a constitutionalization of international law such as the erosion of consent

161 Klabbers/Peters/Ulfstein, p. 263.

162 Peters/Klabbers/Ulfstein, p. 263; Paulus (The International Legal System as a Constitution), pp. 71, 85 et seqq; Kumm (The Cosmopolitan Turn in Constitutionalism), p. 271.

163 Peters (Compensatory Constitutionalism); Klabbers/Peters/Gulfstein (The Constitutionalization of International Law).

164 Peters (Compensatory Constitutionalism), p. 580.

165 Besson (Institutionalising global *demoi*-cracy), p. 62.

166 Peters (Compensatory Constitutionalism), pp. 586–587.

requirement, the existence of global community interests such as the common heritage of mankind, the marginalization of the principle of effectiveness and the emergence of standards of legitimacy for international recognition of statehood, the intertwinement of international and national constitutional law and finally the growing public-private linkage, Peters advocates the application of constitutional principles such as the rule of law, human rights protection, checks and balances and democracy at the international level in order to improve the effectiveness and fairness of the international legal order.[167] Such a global constitutionalism rejects the quest for a world state.[168] Discovering 'fragmentary constitutional law elements' at various levels of governance, she perceives a 'constitutional network' part of a 'constitutional order'.[169] Together with other prominent scholars, Peters has designed a global constitutional order with new roles for states, individuals and private actors, courts and international organizations.[170] In her view, the international community is the result or the precondition of the constitutionalization of the international legal order.[171] Most importantly, she holds in line with Georges Scelle[172] that natural persons are the ultimate unit of legal concern and thus the ultimate normative source – instead of state sovereignty.[173] In her view, natural persons have become legal subjects who participate in international law enforcement and contribute to law-making.[174] She discerns a trend towards empowerment of the individual in the international legal process which she perceives as a trend towards transnational 'citoyenneté'.[175] As regards states, she concludes that states are indispensable in a global constitutionalized order to protect the rights of individuals, but that such a constitutional order also needs to contain states.[176] As to international organizations, she identifies and advocates the application of constitutionalist principles to the law of international organizations.[177] With regard to the debate on the constitutionalization of the WTO, she argues for strengthening the legal relevance of non-trade issues such as the

167 Peters (Compensatory Constitutionalism), p. 583.
168 Peters (Compensatory Constitutionalism), p. 610; see also Paulus (The International Legal System as a Constitution), p. 85.
169 Peters (Compensatory Constitutionalism), pp. 601 and 605.
170 See Klabbers/Peters/Gulfstein (The Constitutionalization of International Law).
171 Ibid., p. 153.
172 Scelle (Le Milieu Intersocial), p. 42.
173 Klabbers/Peters/Gulfstein (The Constitutionalization of International Law), p. 155.
174 Ibid., pp. 157–179.
175 Ibid., p. 178.
176 Ibid., p. 201.
177 Ibid., p. 204.

environment and social concerns but opposes the idea that the WTO already has been constitutionalized since individuals are not yet sufficiently empowered vis-à-vis the organization.[178] Further, maintaining that NGO participation increases the constitutional legitimacy of the activity of international organizations, she is in favour of NGO involvement in international law-making and law-enforcement.[179] With regard to business actors, the central constitutional question is how to contain quasi-political power of non-state actors while leaving the ultimate responsibility with states.[180] Especially regarding private-public partnerships between industry, government and NGOs Peters insists that privatization must not undermine the rule of law and democracy.[181] Most importantly, with regard to privatized law enforcement such as the ICSID scheme, she holds that the adjudication should satisfy constitutional standards such as judicial review.[182] As to the often discussed privatization of WTO dispute settlement, she argues for upholding the inter-state system while increasing and formalizing the participatory opportunities of private actors.[183] With regard to the constitutional principle of democracy, Peters submits that global constitutionalism requires dual democratic mechanism, both at the national and at the global level.[184] At the global level, democratic relationships should be established between global citizens and international institutions through schemes of participation and representation such as referendums, parliamentary assemblies, NGO involvement and transparency.[185]

Finally, Peters argues that the constitutionalist reading may help to overcome the contention that international law is not 'real law' because of the lack of sanctions and the democratic deficit.[186] In the same vein Kumm suggests to understand constitutionalism as 'cognitive frame'.[187]

2.7.3.2 *A Constitutionalist Reading of International Law*

On a much more cautious note, Paulus has also argued for a constitutionalist reading of the constitutive instruments of the international organizations.[188]

---

178 Ibid., p. 215.
179 Ibid., p. 236.
180 Ibid., p. 246.
181 Ibid., pp. 246–248.
182 Ibid., p. 252.
183 Ibid., p. 254.
184 Ibid., pp. 263–341.
185 Ibid., pp. 296–333.
186 Ibid., p. 347.
187 Kumm (The Cosmopolitan Turn in Constitutionalism), p. 323.
188 Paulus (The International Legal System as a Constitution), p. 108.

Starting from an ever-increasing relevance of international governance for the individual human being, he asks whether domestic constitutional principles of democracy, the rule of law, separation of powers, federalism, human rights and solidarity can be fulfilled by the international legal order.[189] He arrives at mixed results. Hence, he argues by binding the exercise of international power of international institutions more to legal rules and strengthening deliberation and the inclusion of the individual stakeholders in international decision-making would make the way towards more checks and balances and human rights in the tradition of constitutionalism.[190] To use his words, 'constitutionalization is also a means for daring to think big [...]'.[191]

2.7.3.3 *'The Cosmopolitan Turn in Constitutionalism'*

Kumm defends a cosmopolitan paradigm asking the question of what else might 'make sense of the structure of human rights and constitutional rights practice across liberal democracies, with the principle of proportionality playing such a central role, and the increasingly intimate relationship between national and international rights practice?[192] His central claim is that a cosmopolitan paradigm is better able than a statist paradigm to explain contemporary public law practice.[193] His basic premise is that 'Cosmopolitan constitutionalism establishes an integrative basic conceptual framework for a general theory of public law that integrates national and international law'.[194] He rejects a statist paradigm of constitutionalism where all legality is defined by national constitutional standards.[195] In his view, the statist paradigm with its sharp distinction between international and national law tends to distort complex legal and political realities.[196] Kumm asserts that in international law, where no constitutional text exists, the cognitive frame is central to identify, structure und construe legal texts.[197] In his cosmopolitan constitutionalist model, based on public reason, Kumm starts from increased relevance of international governance and legitimacy issues in international law.[198] Similar

189 Ibid., p. 106.
190 Ibid., p. 108.
191 Ibid., p. 109.
192 Kumm (The Cosmopolitan Turn in Constitutionalism), p. 261.
193 Ibid., p. 262.
194 Ibid., p. 263.
195 Ibid., p. 275.
196 Ibid., p. 320.
197 Ibid., p. 266.
198 Kumm (The Cosmopolitan Turn in Constitutionalism), p. 268; Kumm (The Legitimacy of International Law).

to this study, where the separation of the trade and human rights regime is the starting point for the constitutionalist debate, he also mentions the pressures to link trade issues to human rights as new topics of international law and worth to address.[199] His core concern under the current legal structure is that the executive branch of states can easily sabotage effective collective action without effective legal remedies being provided by international law against such action.[200] He devises a constitutionalist framework based on four principles to be applied when assessing the legitimacy on international law. The first principle is the principle of international legality of international law, i.e. a presumption of the authority of international law that provides some degree of protection and security for the weak.[201] The other four principles are jurisdiction, procedure and outcomes, which together create the legitimacy standard of international law.[202] The principle of jurisdiction should be guided by subsidiarity, meaning that the community affected by issues and able to make effective decisions should decide, i.e. the global community on measures on carbon dioxide emissions because the whole community is affected by climate change.[203] By contrast, local communities should decide '*ambient* standards regarding air pollution'.[204] The specific test for a subsidiarity analysis would be whether there is a collective action problem that has to be decided at international level, and whether the reasons for deciding at that level weigh more than reasons for deciding at national level.[205] The third principle for assessing legitimacy on the international level is procedural legitimacy, i.e. adequate participation and accountability.[206] Submitting that electoral accountability in terms of direct elections are neither feasible nor necessary for procedural legitimacy, Kumm calls for sufficient transparency and participation to ensure that 'decision-makers are in fact responsive to constituents' concerns'.[207] He also mentions the principle of due process. The fourth principle refers to outcome legitimacy admitting.[208] Kumm stresses in particular two substantive principles, respect for human rights and reasonableness.[209] The essence of

199 Ibid, p. 913.
200 Kumm (The Cosmopolitan Turn in Constitutionalism), p. 273.
201 Kumm (The Legitimacy of International Law), pp. 917–921.
202 Ibid., p. 920.
203 Ibid., p. 923.
204 Ibid., p. 924.
205 Kumm (The Cosmopolitan Turn in Constitutionalism), p. 295.
206 Ibid., pp. 924–927.
207 Ibid., p. 926.
208 Ibid., p. 927.
209 Kumm (The Cosmopolitan Turn in Constitutionalism), p. 277.

Kumm's cosmopolitan constitutionalist model is that legitimacy-wise, international and national law have to be conceived together. In Kumm's words, 'citizens should regard themselves as constrained by international law and set up domestic political and legal institutions so as to ensure compliance with international law, to the extent that international law does not violate jurisdictional, procedural and outcome-related principles to such an extent that the presumption in favour of international law's authority is rebutted'.[210] Only if international law is taken seriously, collective action problems can be solved.

2.7.4 'Towards a Five Storey House'

> Countries, whether they like it or not, are exposed to, and part of, multi-layered or multi-level governance.[211]

Cottier's and Hertig's basic premise is that with governance expanding into international law, 21st century constitutionalism can no longer be limited to nation states.[212] Tracing the evolution from international law as a law of co-existence where states were juxtaposed and foreign policy a "constitution-free" and "morality-free"[213] zone to the 20th century law of cooperation, he discerns trends of internationalization of constitutional law and a constitutionalization of international law, arguing for a constitutionalism beyond the nation state.[214] In his view, to cope with globalization, states have entered into numerous bilateral and multilateral treaties and started to 'outsource' constitutional functions to international organizations.[215] At the same time, the increasing importance of private actors in the international sphere and the rudimentary mandatory hierarchical structure of the international system reflected in the concepts of *ius cogens*, obligations *erga omnes* and international crimes have contributed to a modest constitutionalization of international law.[216] Discussing increasing concerns as to the legitimacy of the WTO, he holds that the legitimacy of the WTO should not be assessed in isolation but as part of a broader framework of multi-layered governance. As Kumm, Cottier holds that the crucial point is to conceive domestic, regional and international levels together where one layer

210 Kumm (The Legitimacy of International Law), p. 928.
211 Cottier (Towards a Five Storey Howse), p. 496.
212 Cottier/Hertig, p. 299.
213 Allot, pp. 31 and 35.
214 Cottier/Hertig, p. 265 et seqq.
215 Cottier/Hertig, p. 269.
216 Cottier/Hertig, pp. 270 et seqq.

may compensate legitimacy problems of another layer.[217] Rejecting the idea that the concept of a constitution is confined to a nation state, he exposes the need for a constitutionalism beyond the nation state to respond effectively to the challenge of globalization and the increasing interdependence of states by securing constitutional values in the international sphere and disciplining the power of the emerging non-state polities and the de-nationalization of legal and political functions.[218] Responding to the main critique to the constitutional approach that common underlying values are missing that are necessary to build an international society with common legal structures, he submits that plurality and cultural diversity also exist within a nation state where a constitution is possible.[219] Drawing on Besson's idea of reasonable disagreement[220] being inherent in the law itself, and her concept of the rule of law as response to such reasonable disagreement, he argues convincingly that disagreement on values exists on all levels of governance.[221] In his view, between national and international systems of governance, there are differences in degree, not in principle so that a doctrine of multi-layered governance is possible.[222] There are not major differences between constitutional law and international law if one conceives a constitution rather in terms of an instrument of government.[223] In addition, he takes recourse to political philosophy relying on cosmopolitan schools of thought in order to defend the idea of common values.[224] As a conclusion, he puts forward the idea of a Five Storey House where all the different governance layers together, as a whole, constitute the constitutional system.[225] Ideally, in his view, such a house would assemble all the different schools of thought under one roof and make them work together.[226] Besides depicting existing realities, the idea of a house also stands for a normative concept. Drawing on established doctrines of federalism and following the model of the European Union constituting a legal system *sui generis*, the intention is to systematically include the different layers of governance, reaching from the level of communes to the regional levels such as the EU and the global level, which should be conceived in constitutional terms. Referring to

217 Cottier (The Legitimacy of WTO law), pp. 20–21.
218 Cottier/Hertig, pp. 297–298.
219 Cottier (Towards a Five Storey House), pp. 508–512.
220 Besson (The Morality of Conflict), p. 528 et seqq.
221 Cottier (Multilayered Governance), p. 671.
222 Ibid., p. 670.
223 Ibid., p. 671.
224 Cottier (Towards a Five Storey House), p. 512.
225 Cottier/Hertig, p. 301.
226 Cottier (Towards a Five Storey House), p. 498.

Jackson and his concept of 'sovereignty-modern', Cottier held that 'sovereignty is about allocating powers and asking whether an issue should be dealt with in Geneva, the headquarters of the WTO, the new World Trade Organization, or in Washington, or Brussels, and any other capital, or whether it should be left to sub-federal and local levels. Horizontally, the question is as to who should regulate: parliament, the executive branch or the judiciary? Sovereignty-modern thus stands for the proposition of vertical and horizontal separation of powers and checks and balances.[227] In a nutshell, the idea is to develop and find appropriate criteria for the allocation of regulatory powers to and within different layers of government including global, regional, domestic and local levels.[228] And this should be done using concepts from constitutional law: the protection of human rights and property rights, fairness, equal opportunities, distributive justice, democracy and accountable government, the rule of law, and checks and balances, both horizontal and vertical.[229] Cottier submits that a constitutional doctrine will work towards common institutions of dispute settlement and interaction of international institutions.[230] He holds that globalization and interdependence make a common framework necessary, which is able to deal with divergences and to develop governance towards common standards and mechanisms of discourse and dispute resolution among and within layers of governance.[231]

2.7.5 Implications for Measures on Trade and Child Labour

It is fairly obvious that the various constitutional approaches to international law offer an excellent framework and appropriate tools to devise new mechanisms and governance regimes to overcome the problem of trade and child labour. Given that the identified shortcomings for the solution of trade and child labour under the current legal order are *inter alia* the separation of the human rights and trade regime, the lack of an effective complaints mechanisms for private actors and questions of legitimacy of the WTO adjudicating and governance bodies, constitutional principles such as human rights and the judicial protection of individual rights, the rule of law, and democracy are evidently the right tools to remedy these gaps in the international order. As regards the issue of trade and child labour, in particular proposals regarding the linkage of the trade and human rights regime and a human rights approach

227 Cottier (John H. Jackson, Sovereignty-Modern), p. 324; See also Jackson (Sovereignty).
228 Cottier (Towards a Five Storey House), p. 506.
229 Ibid., p. 507.
230 Cottier (Trade and Human Rights), p. 130.
231 Cottier (Towards a Five Storey House), p. 532.

to trade, the empowerment of the individual, NGO involvement in law enforcement, the opening of the WTO dispute settlement for private actors, the integration of participatory elements in the structure of international institutions and multi-level governance are worth exploring. At the same time, the case of trade and child labour can serve as a model for how the interaction of different layers of governance could work and make proposals as to what issues should be solved at what layer including various avenues for dispute settlement. Thus, the constitutional approach seems to be a promising avenue to take. Most importantly, the fact that the International Law Commission has in its recently published report of October 2019 for the first time adopted in its Conclusion 23 a non-exhaustive list of peremptory norms of international law, i.e. *ius cogens* norms, and described them as norms reflecting protecting fundamental values of the international community makes such an approach even more feasible.[232]

2.7.6 Critique to the Constitutional Approach

Critique to the constitutional approach comes from various schools of thought. As already indicated above, global legal pluralists, supporters of national interest paradigms but also eminent legal scholars such as Koskenniemi and Howse raise substantive criticism. They question the existence of common universal values, ask what the use of the constitutional vocabulary may bring about or even point to the limits of international law.[233] In times of increasing trade wars,[234] terrorism and an emerging unilateralism putting multilateralism under threat,[235] such arguments should be taken seriously and thoroughly discussed.

2.7.6.1 *Global Subsidiarity*

2.7.6.1.1 Critique to Constitutionalism and the Concept of Subsidiarity

In an excellent political analysis Howse and Nicolaidis have traced how the conceptual foundation of 'embedded liberalism' underlying the post-war trading system under the 'insider network' ruling the GATT faced increased

---

232 ILO (Peremptory Norms of International Law), pp. 142, 208. For further details, see below, p. 364.

233 Goldsmith/Posner; Fischer-Lescano /Teubner/; Viellechner (Responsive legal pluralism); Koskenniemi (The Fate of Public International Law), pp. 345–350.

234 Cf. for example Süddeutsche Zeitung, 15 November 2018, ‚Katz und Maus'; idem, 14 May 2019, ‚Peking schlägt zurück'; idem 23 January 2020, ‚Handelsstreit auf offener Bühne, US-Präsident Trump droht der EU mit Zöllen, Kommissionschefin von der Leyen kündigt Abgaben für Klimasünder an'.

235 See for example Hamilton/Ohlberg.

challenges by economic pressures in the 1970s and 1980s and became prone to the ideology of free trade under the Washington Consensus.[236] In their view, the vision of trade liberalization embedded within interventionist welfare state policies, meaning that 'democracy happens inside states, bargains between national representatives',[237] was increasingly unable to answer pressing political questions such as how to deal with the newly industrializing developing countries competing successfully in labour-intensive industries such as textiles and how to protect intellectual property rights on the one hand, and how to judge domestic environmental policy measures as those challenged in the GATT *Tuna/Dolphin* cases on the other hand. Unable to explain why intellectual property rights should be within the trading system but environmental but labour standards kept out, the insider network of the GATT adopted the neoliberal view that links protection of property rights to growth and considers environmental and human rights as luxury goods that comes after the production of high real incomes.[238] As a result, the new trade agenda of the Uruguay Round agreements included new topics such as intellectual property rights but excluded labour standards and the environment.[239] The following legitimacy crises of the WTO evidenced by increasing protests from civil society, social movements and academia at WTO Ministerial Conferences in Seattle, Cancun and Doha was mitigated by the wise *Shrimps/Turtle* decision, where the Appellate Body reconciled trade and environmental values, linking the insider with the external world.[240]

As a response to the legitimacy crisis (which has nowadays turned into a threat of its existence), Howse and Nicolaidis suggest adapting the 'embedded liberalism' bargain and restructuring the trading regime. Strongly criticising the constitutionalist approach, they propose a model of 'global subsidiarity' that builds on ideas of comparative federalism.[241] With regard to constitutionalism, they reject the idea developed by Petersmann to perceive WTO obligations in terms of human rights including economic rights that traders and citizens can invoke directly under the WTO dispute settlement system.[242] They strongly criticize Petersmann and Cottier for transferring the EU model to the global level, mostly because of lack of an constitutional

236 Howse (From Politics to Technocracy); Howse/Nicolaidis.
237 Howse (From Politics to Technocracy–And Back again), p. 103.
238 Ibid., p. 104.
239 Howse (From Politics to Technocracy–And Back again), p. 103.
240 Cf. Howse/Nicolaidis, p. 320; Howse (From Politics to Technocracy–And Back again), p 110.
241 Howse/Nicolaidis, pp. 307–348.
242 Howse (From Politics to Technocracy–And Back again), p 105; Howse/Nicolaidis, p. 322.

telos.[243] In contrast to the WTO constitution, they argue, the federal idea was already implicit in the Treaty of Rome and the doctrine of direct effect the logical corollary and also supported by referrals from national courts on the basis on article 177 EC Treaty. A creation of a doctrine of direct effect under the WTO would undermine its legitimacy, partly because economic integration through direct effect also requires welfare-state and market-correcting policy necessary for co-opting and compensating potential losers. It is a social charter at WTO level that would be needed. Most importantly, constitutionalism would require constitutional sources of legitimacy, i.e. something like a world democratic state, which is not an option. To use their words, 'constitutionalization of non-constitutional structures cannot itself create the conditions of constitutional legitimacy, rather legitimate constitutionalism depends on those conditions'.[244] On the contrary, there would be a real risk that using the constitutional language would polarize the system's advocates and its critics. However, they admit that their model of global subsidiarity corresponds to what Cottier calls a 'modest constitutionalization' of the WTO.[245] In a nutshell, they propose more deference of WTO dispute settlement bodies to substantive domestic regulatory choices and to other international regimes including those on health, labour standards, the environment, human rights as well as being more politically inclusive. Their model of global subsidiarity is based on three principles, i.e. institutional sensitivity, political inclusiveness and top-down empowerment.

Institutional sensitivity refers to deference to states and institutional linkages between segmented regimes as well as for example *prima facie* recognition of the WTO of cases from more democratically legitimized institution.[246]

Political inclusiveness could mean that states have an obligation for domestic consultation regarding trade policies, giving global advocacy NGOs a voice in political negotiating and establishing transnational contact and enquiry points for domestic trade-relevant rule-making.[247]

And finally, top-down empowerment could mean that trade conditionality would include an agenda of empowerment for assisting countries with school training programmes and local democracy respected.[248] Interestingly, Howse

243 Howse/Nicolaidis, pp. 310 and 325 et seqq.
244 Ibid., p. 343.
245 Ibid., p. 311 and see above at p. 221.
246 Ibid., pp. 332 et seqq.
247 Ibid., pp. 336 et seqq.
248 Ibid., pp. 339 et seqq.

also asks for a support for developing countries: a joint WTO-World Bank-IMF-International Labour Organization commission.[249]

2.7.6.1.2 Discussion

As Howse and Nicolaidis admit, their model of global subsidiarity does not substantially differ from what Cottier identifies as the constitutional approach and has also much in common with what Petersmann and Peters suggest. The main ideas drawing on federalism including more deference to states and other global institutions, greater accountability and political inclusiveness are the same. Indeed, the only differences are the constitutionalist vocabulary and the rejection of the proposal by Petersmann to perceive WTO obligations as human rights including economic rights of citizens and traders with a direct right to action under the dispute settlement. Whether the latter is a recommendable and feasible proposal will be discussed in the next chapter when the chosen approach to international law will be tested against the case of trade and child labour. With regard to the use of constitutionalist vocabulary, Howse and Nicolaidis may have a point in times of populism with polarization and false accusations on the rise. However, it should be pointed out that the elements of the proposal of Howse and Nicolaidis such as deliberative democracy, federalism, human rights are constitutional principles. In conclusion, rather than being a critique, the model of Howse and Nicolaidis supplements the constitutionalist approach through enriching ideas.

2.7.6.2 *Trading Democracy*

Similarly to Howse and Nicolaidis, Cass in her excellent book on the constitutionalization of the WTO not totally dismissed the constitutional approach.[250] One of her main conclusions was that on the received account of constitutionalization in terms of a coherent system with some sort of foundation and a deliberative process, the WTO had not constitutionalized so far.[251] She held that what she called 'constitutional transformation theory', namely the constitutional approaches presented above by Cottier, Peters and others, were not satisfying because they ran the risk of not changing the agenda for free trade to the detriment of non-economic values such as health or the environment.[252] Instead, she proposed a concept called 'trading democracy'.[253] According to

249 Howse (From Politics to Technocracy–And Back again), p. 116.

250 Cass.

251 Ibid., p. 238.

252 Ibid., pp. 240 et seqq.

253 Ibid., p. 242.

this concept, 'trading democracy' and 'emphasizing development' should be at the focus of the WTO constitutionalization project.[254] She held that the claims of legitimacy, democracy and community should be taken more seriously by the international trade community.[255]

Her critique seems to be weak for two reasons: contrary to what she argues, non-economic values such as human rights, democracy and the rule of law are central to the constitutional approaches developed by Cottier, Petersmann and Peters.[256] What is however more concerning is the vagueness of her own idea: how should development and democracy be put at the centre of the WTO constitutionalization project? And to what extent is that different to existing proposals on constitutionalism? At least, she admitted herself that the way forward was subject to debate and proposed some steps as to a change of reading international law and better market access for developing countries.

2.7.6.3 *Global Legal Pluralism*

The core critique by legal pluralists is their rejection of the quest for legal unity or hierarchical systems. Teubner/Fischer-Lescano deny the existence of a 'cohesive glue' as stated by Tomuschat[257] or some 'overlapping consensus' in the Rawlsian sense and hold that 'processes of norm creation work each with their own vision of consensus, [...] and feign commensurability of the incommensurate through re-entry of external rationalities'.[258] They proclaim a deeply fragmented society that can be loosely connected through a 'network logic', 'compatibility norms' or a 'responsive legal pluralism'. Rejecting common ground for global values, they propagate functional solutions and transnational law-making processes involving civil society actors. By combining the principles of complementary and subsidiarity, 'responsivity' would offer horizontal coordination among different legal orders.

While at first sight the constitutional approach and the school of global legal pluralism seem to contradict each other, they have much in common. Indeed, adherents to both schools acknowledge the big achievement of the 20th century of having inserted a vertical dimension – in the form of *ius cogens* and *erga omnes* obligations created by the ICJ in the *Barcelona Traction* case[259]

254 Ibid., p. 243.
255 Ibid., p. 246.
256 See for example Cottier (Limits to International Trade), pp. 221–222.
257 Tomuschat (International Law as the Consitution of Mankind), pp. 37, 45.
258 Fischer-Lescano/Teubner, p. 1067.
259 ICJ *Barcelona Traction, Light and Power Company Ltd. (Belgium v. Spain)*, Judgement, Second Phase, ICJ Reports 1970, pp. 3–358, para. 33.

and incorporated into Art. 53 of the VCLT – and thus a form of hierarchy into the otherwise horizontal international law.[260] And yet, most importantly, legal scholars from both schools seem to be eager to stress that the special status of *ius cogens* may only be accorded to very few human rights and does not justify their characterization as constitutional norms.[261] Addressing the democratic deficit in the international regimes, they both recognize the important role of private actors such as NGOs in international law making and implementation. Both theories also rely on the interaction of courts in international law making. Remarkably, not only constitutionalists but also legal pluralists are well aware of the danger of moving from democracy to technocracy when focussing too much on functionality.[262] Yet they differ as to the key concept behind transnational governance, i.e. a global legal order based on interstate-consensus or rather functional regimes. The main difference lies in the firm denial by legal pluralists of common constitutional principles on which to base a monist-universalist legal order.[263] Stressing the difference in concepts of for instance liberty of trade and liberty in the ICCPR, global pluralists still seek to establish compatibility of norms.[264] The most explicit and probably practical proposal is the call for an actionable responsivity principle that should work as a conflict rule and contribute to horizontal coordination adding to the international conflict law approach by Neumann and Pauwelyn.[265]

Since also constitutionalists call for horizontal coordination and would probably not reject ideas how to best achieve it, the key issue to be resolved is the question of common values. A simple and obvious argument by the legal scholar Paulus seems not only to justify the need for common values but also to prove the existence of such values: Using the example of religious pluralism following the Westphalian Peace of 1648, he argues convincingly that any theory of legal pluralism itself must rely on the recognition of overarching values by the participants of the system.[266] In view of the fact that also other schools of thought such as the realist school question the existence of a value-based international legal order, this issue will be discussed after having presented the main ideas of these schools.

260 Cottier/Hertig, pp. 270 et seqq.; Fischer-Lescano/Teubner, p. 1059. However, Fischer-Lescano/Teubner at the same time hold that ius cogens cannot be applied to all autonomous regimes, see above, p. 312.
261 Fischer-Lescano/Teubner, p. 1064; Kleinlein, pp. 425–426.
262 Fischer-Lescano/Teubner, p. 1070.
263 Viellechner (Responsive legal pluralism), p. 323.
264 Fischer-Lescano/Teubner, p. 1067.
265 See above p. 308.
266 Paulus (Commentary to Fischer-Lescano/Teubner), p. 1050.

2.7.6.4 *The School of 'Critical Legal Studies'*

2.7.6.4.1 International Law as a 'Secular Faith'

This school analyses international law with a view to its language, its methodology and how it is made.[267] The eminent scholar Koskenniemi *inter alia* presents an analysis of international law with an excellent account of the origins of the project of modern international law.[268] He impressively traces how the 'cosmopolitan-minded lawyers' Oppenheim and Lauterpacht in the 1920s translated the diplomacy of states into a set of legal rules and institutions, enthusiastically pursuing their vision of a global rule of law based on the Kantian cosmopolitan idea.[269] But instead of leading to a cosmopolitan federation, international law became fragmented and deformalized, consisting of a 'mosaic of particular rules and institutions' dominated by technical experts with an increasing economic vocabulary rather than framed in legal terms of rights and obligations.[270] 'As our feet hit the ground, we found no Kantian federation but the naturalism of Pufendorf and Hobbes – powerful actors engaged in strategic games with their eye on the Pareto optimum', to use the words of Koskenniemi.[271]

Stressing the lack of common values, his conclusion is not to recast international law in constitutional terms. Common goods such as human rights, free trade or the environment would rather only be valid in their respective community. He infers: 'If deformalisation has set the house of international law on fire, to grasp at values is to throw gas on the flames'.[272]

Koskenniemi also rejects the legal strand of legal pluralism, very clearly articulating the danger of moving to functional regimes and perceiving 'legalisation' as a policy choice: 'Normative politics is replaced by what the new-speakers call "new global division of regulatory labour". When I hear this language, I recognise the blank stare in the eyes of my European colleagues – and share it'.[273]

Recognizing that the downside of the inter-war project of perceiving international law as rather apolitical, he explains the recent 'narrative in

267 de Schutter; D. Kennedy, A New Stream of International Law Scholarship, 7 Wisconsin ILJ (1988), pp. 6 et seq.; Koskenniemi (The Gentle Civilizer of Nations).

268 Koskenniemi (The Fate of Public International Law), pp. 331–333.

269 Ibid., p. 333.

270 Ibid., pp. 334–345.

271 Ibid., p. 345.

272 Ibid., p. 346.

273 Ibid., p. 354.

international relations science of law as a strategic game to realize self-interest' with an effort to bring back politics.[274]

In his view in accordance with the ILC Study Group[275] fragmentation can be responded by recognizing that 'international law is a legal system' with legal institutions that should be governed by public lawyers.[276] But hierarchy between legal regimes would be impossible. He also criticizes constitutionalism for being potentially hegemonic since in his opinion, if there was a common *pouvoir constituent*, the resulting constitution would be imperialist.

In his view, there is no need to reconceive international law, instead, it should be considered as a political project. This means for example politicising governance in MNCs, interest groups, banks, armies etc. He holds that international law as a sort of secular faith, a Kantian 'project of critical reason that measures today's state of affairs from the perspective of an ideal of universality'.[277]

2.7.6.4.2 Discussion

Whilst Koskenniemi convincingly depicts the evolution of modern international law and raises justified critique to the schools of constitutionalism and pluralism, he fails to see the merit of constitutionalism in its broader or more modest sense: To provide a legitimate basis and rationale for the global legal order beyond state consent. In times where globalization, international law and institutions are increasingly questioned and their existence threatened, it is necessary to search for justifications for states and citizens to constrain their sovereignty and empower international organizations. How such a constitutional approach will look like concretely and what does this mean for the allocation of power between legal subjects, legal systems, business and civil society of course has to be discussed in detail. In this context, it is noteworthy that Koskenniemi rejects the constitutionalist idea in the sense of one homogeneous order and a hierarchy of norms. Believing however in the Kantian idea of universality being the basis and the yardstick of international law against which states' behaviour is assessed, Koskenniemi does not seem to be that far away from the constitutionalist approaches presented above.

274 Ibid., p. 360, referring to Goldsmith/Posner.

275 ILC (Fragmentation).

276 Koskenniemi (The Fate of Public International Law), p. 348; Cf. also the legal interpretation approach to international law, p. 308.

277 Ibid., p. 361.

2.7.6.5 *The Concept of an International Constituency*

Similar to Koskenniemi, Aoife O'Donoghue appeals to the danger of imperialism inherent in international law.[278] In his view, cosmopolitanism aims at integrating international institutions and individuals, but the general conception of an international community focussing on states remains central. The statal view ignores the impact of de-colonisation and the role of the Global South and creates a hierarchy between those inside and outside the international community, the latter being for example states in conflict or transition.[279] Being critical of Klabbers' and Peters' approach to an international constitutionalism[280] and focussing on the theories of community that exemplify some of the more generally understood implications of its use, O'Donoghue in his study aims to analyse the international community's relationship with constituent and constituted power and to realise of what a ready-made solution, international community, would mean for global constitutionalisation.[281] The concept of an 'international community' should be replaced by the concept of an international constituency of states with a nexus between constituted and constituent power. In a nutshell, a constituency relates to actors affected by, and who affect, other actors within a global constitutionalising order.

This view seems to be even more ambitious than the constitutional approaches presented above. While a global order based on an international constituency is of course desirable, it will be subject to further discussion whether such a concept is feasible and not merely utopia.

2.7.6.6 *The National Interest Paradigm*

2.7.6.6.1 International Law as Politics

A core critique to any concept of a value-based cosmopolitan international legal order comes from recent strands in US international relations scholarship pointing to the limits of law, following the post-war realist school of *inter alia* Morgenthau, who put the concept of balance of power and the national interest at the centre of international relations and politics.[282] In their attempt to devise a new theory of international law, Goldsmith and Posner maintain that international law only comes into existence and is obeyed by if it is in the interest of states. That is that states do not comply because they have consented to it, or because international law has become part of their internal value set or

278 O'Donoghue.
279 Ibid., p. 8.
280 Ibid, p. 3.
281 Ibid., p. 10.
282 Goldsmith/Posner; Morgenthau; see also Ratner.

because they have a moral obligation in the sense of a cosmopolitan duty.[283] According to Goldsmith and Posner, international law has a limited role in advancing international cooperation.[284]

They elaborate their theory using *inter alia* trade law as an example: the success of the GATT can best be explained by coordination of state interests but it has not solved multilateral prisoners' dilemmas. In addition, in their view, legalism of GATT will cause problems if the underlying interest of states, i.e. their need to retain the flexibility to raise trade barriers when protectionist pressures emerge, are not observed: states will violate the rules or go to substitutes such as bilateral trade agreements,[285] an assumption that in the light of increasing bilateral trade agreements and the ongoing trade war between the US and China seems to be a real scenario.[286] Concerning WTO law, they observe that only the party that is concerned will take action and conclude that enforcement is bilateral.

Goldsmith and Posner hold that states rather choose a treaty than nonbinding agreements because legalized agreements reflect a greater commitment as a matter of convention than a nonlegalized agreement.[287] In their view, the reason why states prefer that legislative consent is given to agreements, i.e. treaties they adopt, is because it gives the other state more information about what the public thinks.

In terms of compliance, they hold that states comply because they fear retaliation or failure of cooperation if they do not and states want to obtain benefits of cooperation and coordination.[288]

Further, they hold that international law has no morality and no moral force because it is not based on democracy and no reliable institutions exist.[289] Instead, international law reflects what states do and not moral judgements or interest of its citizens. Thus, international law is politics of a special kind that follows the rational interest of states. To qualify international law as something different than politics needs an explanation of why states would follow

283 Goldsmith/Posner, pp. 13–15.

284 Ibid., p. 17.

285 Ibid., p. 162.

286 Süddeutsche Zeitung, Cerstin Gammelin, ‚Licht und Schatten, Die USA und China unterzeichnen ein erstes Abkommen zur Beilegung ihres Handelsstreits. Nutznießer könnte auch Deutschland sein, wo das Wachstum 2019 einbrach. Langfristig ist der Klimawandel das größte Konjunkturrisiko', 16. Januar 2020.

287 Goldsmith/Posner, p. 98.

288 Ibid., pp. 103–104.

289 Ibid., p. 199.

international law. And this would be moral reasons, i.e. because states think that this is the right thing to do.[290]

Finally, they reject a cosmopolitan duty of states to pursue global welfare because this contradicts the idea of liberal democracies with heterogenic interests of citizens and not one organizational interest as in case of for example Oxfam International.[291]

In conclusion, Goldsmith and Posner claim that international legal rhetoric masks behaviour driven by self-interest of states, that liberal democracies are unlikely to support a cosmopolitan foreign policy and that 'global problems may simply be unsolvable'.[292]

2.7.6.6.2 Discussion

In the light of recent developments such as an increasing nationalism and power-driven and autocratic policy style by political leaders such as Putin, Bolsonaro, Erdogan or Xi Jinping, and the new America-first paradigm established by US President Trump, putting the self-interest of states as main driver of politics and law seems to be appealing. To paraphrase Simma and Paulus, is it really far-fetched to regard the major state actors of the contemporary system as engaging in a permanent struggle for maximizing their own power and minimizing that of others?[293] As Koskenniemi puts it, it brings politics back to the elite circle of international experts and technocrats dominating international institutions. However, there are many fallacies in this approach.

To begin with, Goldsmith and Posner themselves admit that international law is a different discipline than politics when they acknowledge that states rather choose treaties than non-binding agreements because they want to convey a certain level of seriousness and sense of commitment, also based on legislative consent, and want to benefit from the rules of the VCLT, i.e. from the normative strength of law. In 1961, Lord McNair held in its treatise on the 'Law of Treaties' that

> No Government would decline to accept the principle *pacta sunt servanda*, and the very fact that Governments find it necessary to spend so much effort in explaining in a particular case that a *pactum* has ceased to exist, or that the act complained of is not a breach of it, either by reason

290 Ibid., p. 202.

291 Ibid., p. 211.

292 Ibid., pp. 226–227.

293 Simma/Paulus (The 'International Community'), p. 272.

> of an implied term or for some other reason, is the best acknowledgement of that principle.[294]

Further, as Koskenniemi also criticizes, 'state interest' is not a monolithic block but an 'object of struggle'.[295] Business, civil society and other public interest groups in a pluralist society all do lobby and advocacy work targeting their government, which in one case may lead to the ratification of the Uruguay legal agreements to promote free trade and in another case to stop negotiations of TTIP on environmental and social grounds.[296] Thus, states follow business interests but also seek to preserve common goods such as the environment and consumer interests. An indeed, international law may have become part of the 'internal value set' of a state. Interestingly, Goldsmith and Posner when discussing cosmopolitan duties of states also admit that 'state interest' in liberal democracies' is not homogenic but consists of different citizens' interest. Thus, the diffuse concept of 'state interest' is of limited value when trying to explain on what international law is based and why states observe rules of international law. The complex global legal order with its UN system including numerous human rights treaties with individual complaints procedures, the WTO with its dispute settlement system and multiple other international institutions and agreements may not be explained by pointing only to states pursuing their national interest.

2.7.6.7 *Conclusion*

While the various critiques to a constitutional approach either use merely different vocabulary or fail to offer feasible alternative models to explain current international law, they all raise one important question. They perhaps rightly question the existence of global values, which are needed to establish a legal unity and a constitutionalized legal order. Indeed, in light of the diversity of political systems, cultures and livelihoods worldwide, one may ask whether it is really the case that further than establishing an international community with the help of *ius cogens* and *erga omnes* obligations of states, the international order is constitutionalizing and increasingly based on common values or community interests? Can we relate to global values or ethical foundations beyond established principles of *pacta sunt servanda*, and self-determination? With regard to WTO-law, Bürgi Bonanomi has carefully analysed how the rule

294 Lord McNair, Law of Treaties (1963), p. 493 quoted in Henkin/Pugh/Schachter/Smit, p. 615.

295 Koskenniemi (The Fate of Public International Law), p. 348.

296 In 2016, protest by civil society led to a moratorium in the negotiation of TTIP because of fear of weakening environmental and consumer interests.

of law, the principle of good faith and the protection of legitimate expectations already govern the WTO framework and are part of the Agreement on Agriculture.[297] We should thus build on this and start our inquiry. If we come to find that we need and can build on a global value-based global order, we should then ask what are such values? Is it a tenable option to take recourse to domestic constitutional principles such as human rights, democracy and the rule of law and apply them to the international order? Where should one look for global values of a global order?

In order to answer these questions, it is necessary to take a step back and turn to the more general question of sources and whether the normative force of international law relies only on 'internal' factors as posited by legal positivism, or also on 'external' factors as maintained by natural law approaches.[298] Aren't many treaties already incorporating natural law principles and wasn't the claim of developing countries for a New International Economic Order to achieve a fairer distribution of wealth between rich and poor states based on equitable principles?[299] Is the global order really moving towards an order increasingly based on natural law and moral values? Is the way forward to elaborate on the 'Grotian tradition' in international law such as proposed for example by eminent legal scholars such as Lauterpacht[300] and Kokott[301]? Is 'a moral content in the law' needed as argued by Lauterpacht in order to adequately deal with pressing legal problems?[302] And if yes, what are these common values in a world with increasing religious, ethnic and cultural tensions, where inequality of wealth and power rises? Isn't the constitutional approach hegemonic and driven by Western values? To ask in the spirit of Simma and Paulus, is there a 'societal consensus' as a precondition for constitutional norms at the international level?[303]

297 Bürgi Bonanomi, pp. 224–228.
298 Cf. Koskenniemi (International Legal Theory and Doctrine), p. 980; Wolfrum (Sources), p. 300.
299 New International Economic Order, E/ESCWA/27/9/Report; for an excellent discussion of the NIEO, see Bürgi Bonanomi, pp. 12–13.
300 Lauterpacht.
301 Kokott.
302 Lauterpacht, p. 263.
303 Cf. Simma/Paulus (The 'International Community'), p. 268.

3 A New Legal Humanism

The following section will argue that taking recourse to principles of natural law beyond general principles of law already being a source of international law such as the principle of 'good faith' or 'estoppel' is needed and appropriate.[304] It will develop a new approach to international law based on constitutionalism and multi-level governance.

It will start by taking a closer look at the 'climax' of legal positivism,[305] the 'Pure Law Theory' by Kelsen and the concept of law by Hart, and ask whether it is still a valid theory to explain current international law. Identifying its limits, it will then discuss whether an approach based on natural law is appropriate. Concluding that a legitimate standard of current international law should contain natural law elements, i.e. global values, the following paragraphs will ask whether domestic constitutional principles such as human rights, democracy and the rule of law are recognized global values. Establishing that human rights and the rule of law are such values and even constitutional principles of the global legal order, the new approach to international law will be called a New Legal Humanism. Such an approach is in line with parallel trends in economic science calling for a 'human economy'.[306]

3.1 *Limits of Hart's Positivism and Kelsen's 'Pure Law Theory'*

3.1.1 The 'Grundnorm' Theory and Hart

According to the 'Pure Law Theory' by Kelsen, the 'Grundnorm' or the 'basic norm' is the source of any legal order, e.g. custom if legal norms evolve through custom, or constitutional law if norms evolve in accordance with the [written] constitution.[307] More concretely, in the latter case, the Grundnorm requires legal norms and subjects to comply with the will of the first historical constitutional assembly, the highest legal authority. At the same time, according to positivist legal theory, the 'Grundnorm' does not say anything on substance or moral values of the legal order, i.e. it does not say whether it should guarantee peace or pursue justice.[308] It also does not determine the validity of a legal order or norm. A legal norm or order is valid, if people by and large recognize and comply with it.[309] If a norm is not effective and never applied or complied

304 See Malanczuk, p. 49 for the principle of good faith and estoppel as being general principles of international law.

305 Shaw, p. 40.

306 Oxfam (Time to Care); Raworth.

307 Kelsen, pp. 196 et seqq.

308 Ibid., p. 204.

309 Ibid., p. 214.

with, it is not valid and ceases to exist.[310] Kelsen rightly argues that law is different to reality, because it addresses and assesses reality and this is only possible if it is not identical with reality. With regard to power, it he concludes that law cannot exist without power but it is a different category than power.[311]

According to Kelsen, the 'Grundnorm' of international law is custom, and one of the resulting norms is the principle of *pacta sunt servanda*, which constitutes the 'Grundnorm' of treaty law.[312] In essence, his 'Grundnorm' says that 'states, i.e. governments of states, ought to behave [...] how they customarily behaved'.[313] This 'Grundnorm' defines the source of international law, it does not justify it.[314] As already mentioned, having a monist view, Kelsen regarded international and national law as being part of one legal system. For in contrast to what dualists hold, no conflict between the two legal orders exists that is not solvable.[315] As in national law, where a norm not in accordance with the constitution continues to exist until a court declares it as not valid, a norm that contradicts a norm of international treaty law does not automatically cease to exist. Both national and international law derive from the same 'Grundnorm', either from the source of international law, i.e. custom or, or from national law, i.e. the first historic constitution. Both is possible.[316] In both cases, the principle of effectiveness of international law defines the scope of the national order, i.e. the beginning and end of its existence.[317] State sovereignty is restricted in accordance with international law. Discussing the Pure Law Theory, Kammerhofer distinguishes between the 'Rechtserzeugungs-(source of law creation) and Rechtserkenntnisquelle (source of law-cognition)' and holds with others that the 'Stufenbau' (hierarchy) theory is not prone to the 'sin of idealizing the law' but situates the law creation in the law itself, rather than in meta-legal concepts.[318]

In a similar sense, Hart as another prominent representative of legal positivism argues that there are no 'necessary connections between the content of law and morality', and that there are legal rights and duties which have no

310 Kelsen, p. 220.

311 Ibid., p. 221.

312 Ibid., pp. 222–223.

313 Ibid., p. 222; Cf. also Mosler, p. 16 where he refers to consensus as the constitutional element of law creation and holds that it is the members of the international society that develop together rules and principles, which makes them a legal community.

314 Kelsen, p. 223.

315 Ibid., p. 330.

316 Ibid., p. 339.

317 Ibid., p. 338.

318 Kammerhofer, p. 4

moral justification or force whatever'.[319] His system of law is based on the idea that the acknowledgement of a rule as authoritative depends on a secondary rule of recognition for conclusive identification of the primary rules of obligation.[320] Such recognition is expressed through the social pressure and may take the form of a written text, public monument or whatsoever.[321] However, isn't social pressure or any form of a rule of recognition based on morality? The following sections will come back to the question whether legal positivism as postulated by Hart and Kelsen is really sufficient to defend the validity of international law.

3.1.2 Discussion

The Pure Law Theory helps to better understand the meaning of central terms such as sources, validity and justification of international law, and provides good arguments for rejecting certain critiques of modern international law. Moreover, Kelsen's monist view supports the model of Cottier's Five Storey House and his multi-level constitutionalism: international and national law should be considered as one unit of one legal system, there is no reason why international law cannot constitute just another layer which in return impacts on the other layers of governance, regional, national and local.

Kelsen rightly distinguishes between the source and validity of international law. While custom and the principle of *pacta sunt servanda* may still explain to a large extent the origin and law-making process of international law, its validity depends on whether states by and large comply with it. Hence, single violations of international law normally do not question its validity as such. This means that even though states might often violate international law because compliance might not be in their national interest as Goldsmith and Posner submit, it is still real law and valid, and not policy. The fact that the majority of states including the US still refers to WTO and UN rules in case of trade conflicts or crises proves that the international legal order exists.[322] As the ICJ has stated in its Nicaragua judgement, the viability of a regime depends

319 Hart, p. 268.

320 Ibid., p. 95.

321 Ibid.

322 Cf. for example Süddeutsche Zeitung, Björn Finke, ,Trump freut sich über „hübschen Sieg", Nach dem Entscheid der Welthandelsorganisation verschärft sich der Streit zwischen EU und USA: Auf Flugzeuge und Waren im Wert von 7,5 Milliarden Dollar wird Washington nun Strafzölle erheben, 4 October 2019.

on whether its legal subjects justify their behaviour under its law.[323] And obviously, as Kelsen points out, law cannot be identical to policy because it assesses policy, which would not be possible in the first case.

However, Goldsmith and Posner put the right question when asking why states comply with international law, i.e. what makes the international order work, what is the reason for it. Having rejected their proposal of national interest being a convincing rationale, other explanations are needed. Neither Hart's 'rules of recognition' nor the 'Pure Law Theory' do provide an answer to this.[324] Kelsen explicitly states that his 'Grundnorm' does not justify a legal order, it only explains where it comes from.[325] This is why the concept of Kelsen's basic norm has been criticised for relying upon non-legal issues and being 'tautological: it merely repeats that states that obey rules ought to obey those rules'.[326] Others have criticised Kelsen as being circular because of his failure to identify his 'basic norm'.[327] One could of course argue that according to the 'Pure Law Theory' and its reliance on states' behaviour and the principle *pacta sunt servanda*, state consent would be the justification, i.e. states comply with international law because they have consented to it. Indeed, Verdross and Simma have argued that in terms of the 'Pure Law Theory', consensus is the historically first constitution and the original source of the law.[328] Yet, state consent fails when trying to find a rationale for the law of international governance organizations and the emergence of new legal subjects such as individual actors.[329] States are no longer the only law-making institutions. Governance has moved beyond traditional inter-state relations.[330] As the analysis of the problem of trade and child labour demonstrates, the principle of state consent reaches its limits when trying to explain why WTO-dispute settlement bodies should apply non-WTO law such as ILO norms or human rights or consult the ILO in cases where Art. 31 (3) para. c) of the VCLT does not help, as states in their view have only consented to the WTO covered agreements. Here, a constitutional approach making human rights binding on international organizations would help.

---

323 ICJ, Case Concerning Military and Paramilitary Activities in and against Nicaragua (*Nicaragua v. United States*), ICJ Reports 1986, https://www.icj-cij.org/decisions?type=1&from=1986&to=1986&sort_bef_combine=order_DESC, pp. 14–50, p. 98.

324 For a further discussion on whether morality is needed for the validity or legitimacy of law, see below p. 352.

325 Kelsen, p. 223.

326 Shaw, p. 41.

327 Lachenmann, p. 789.

328 Verdross/Simma (Universelles Völkerrecht II), p. 324.

329 Cf. Kumm (The Legitimacy of International Law), p. 907.

330 O'Donoghue, p. 244.

It is thus necessary to further enquire into sources and justification of international law beyond state consent approaches also based on natural law.

3.2 *Towards More Natural Law*

As Koskenniemi has rightly observed and criticised, the old debate on positivism versus naturalism and the question of the normative force international law has reappeared using new vocabulary from social rather than from legal science.[331] The next sections will thus firstly present which new sources or rationales for international law are currently being discussed under the heading of 'legitimacy', secondly turn to scholarship favouring the natural law approach and thirdly conclude by defending a value-oriented global legal order.

3.2.1 Legitimacy of International Law

According to the Concise Oxford English Dictionary, 'legitimacy means support for authority'.[332] Another definition of the Concise Oxford Dictionary of Politics & International Relations states that legitimacy is the 'property that a regime's procedures for making and enforcing laws are acceptable to its subjects'.[333] Recent legal scholarship has held that the discussion on justification of the law's claim to authority and its normative force is one on its legitimacy,[334] and has taken recourse to 'legitimacy' when looking for a rationale for international law. Boyle and Chinkin refer to the 'normative belief that a rule or institution ought to be obeyed' when discussing legitimacy.[335] Legitimacy gives international institutions the right to rule.[336] But when is this the case, when can international law claim authority? What is a 'compliance pull', to use the words of Franck?[337] Assessing the democracy-rule in the EU-context, Scharpf distinguishes between 'input-legitimacy', and 'output-legitimacy'.[338] While input-legitimacy focusses on procedural aspects such as participation, deliberation and fairness of decision-making, output-legitimacy refers to effectivity and solutions, i.e. the effect of policy and rules on society at large.[339] Transferring this to the global order, where democratic values may play less a role, it seems plausible to look for process-oriented criteria and solutions

---

331 Koskenniemi (International Legal Theory and Doctrine), pp. 981–984.
332 *Concise Oxford English Dictionary.*
333 *Concise Dictionary of Politics & International Relations.*
334 Besson (Theorizing the Sources), p. 175.
335 Boyle/Chinkin, p. 24.
336 Buchanan, p. 79.
337 Franck, p. 705.
338 Scharpf, pp. 16–28.
339 See also Cottier (The legitimacy of WTO law), pp. 16 et seqq.

for global society when defining the legitimacy standard of international law. Using the positivism/naturalism vocabulary, a standard of legitimacy of international law should be based on both the traditional sources of international law such as state practice accompanied by *opinio iuris*, i.e. positive law, and global values of the global society, i.e. natural law, thereby securing input- and output-legitimacy including the principles of fairness and effectivity. Indeed, in international legal doctrine, views reach from a 'service conception' promoting the effectivity of law to a legitimacy standard based on accountability and human rights. How to combine such approaches will be elaborated in turn.

Similar to Kelsen's 'Pure Law Theory', and in the tradition of the UK legal positivist Hart, Raz' service conception rejects morality and perceives law as purely instrumental, as a means to an end.[340] Accordingly, law enjoys legitimacy only when it serves those it addresses by improving their conformity to right reasons.[341] He argues that morality cannot be a condition for validity [here: legitimacy]. Citizens cannot first make a moral judgment which the law is meant to substitute. However, it is questionable whether there is *always* such necessity for citizens to make moral judgements before applying the law. It is also possible to conceive the relationship between law and the moral judgements of its subjects as mutually reinforcing in the sense that the law reflects and creates the moral values of society. GATT Art. XX (a) referring to public morals is an obvious case where morality has been positively imported into the law. Another example is the German 'Grundgesetz', the German constitution, which has shaped societal values but also incorporated new constitutional values such as animal welfare.[342] Hence, morality in the form of societal values may contribute to the legitimacy of international law.

Recent scholarship has referred both to the process of law-making and content or results of the law when defining legitimacy.[343] Franck defines legitimacy as a 'quality of a rule which derives from a perception on the part of those to whom it is addressed that it has come into being in accordance with right process'.[344] He holds that in the community of states, 'right process' includes the

340 Raz (The Authority of Law), p. 27; See Lefkovitz, p. 189.

341 Raz (Morality of Freedom); Raz (Revisiting the Service Conception), pp. 1003, 1012 et seqq.

342 Cf. Süddeutsche Zeitung, Kurt Kister, ‚70 Jahre Grundgesetz, Das bessere Deutschland – Erst ein Provisorium, dann fast schon eine weltliche Staatsreligion und stets Antithese zur finsteren Nazivergangenheit: über den erstaunlichen Erfolg des Grundgesetzes', 4./5. Mai 2019; See also the case of India, where the Indian constitution has also contributed to nation building, SZ Archiv December 2019.

343 See references in Wolfrum (Legitimacy), p. 809 et seq.

344 Franck, p. 706.

principles of coherence and adherence to hierarchy and community.[345] Based on rich evidence, Franck convincingly argues that a rule is legitimate and pulls compliance of states if applied equally to all and derived from a sense of general responsibility based on membership in a community, i.e. if distinctions in treatment are based on rationality and serve the underlying purpose of the community.

Equally emphasizing the need for right process, Besson opts for an approach in between legal positivism and morality. She argues for a strong factual relationship between law and morality and opposes the view that the validity of law flows from state consent.[346] In particular, she holds that 'in circumstances of pervasive and persistent disagreement about substantive moral issues and justice, the democratic nature of the law-making process is often regarded as the best justification for that claim [of authority]'.[347] In her view, 'developing international law in due process of equality of all those affected in that community is what international constitutionalism is about'.[348] She develops a model of global democracy based on a multitude of democratic subjects and deliberation and be deterritorialized, a *demoi*-cracy.[349] While her approach sounds convincing, it should be noted that a democratic process is of course also a value, and that it might be difficult to define and include all those affected.

Equally referring to democratic processes, Boyle and Chinkin criticize the non-democratic nature of the current customary international law process that undermines its legitimacy to marginalized groups such as women and indigenous people.[350]

The philosopher Buchanan convincingly argues that today, 'the legitimacy of international law is not just a concern of states, but also of non-state groups and individual citizens, who sometimes may reasonably question the legitimacy of international institutions even though they know that their own states have consented to them'.[351] As a result, an adequate standard of legitimacy should accommodate the fact that global governance institutions engage in rule-making and that private actors such as NGOs also contribute to law creation.[352] Buchanan together with Keohane therefore argue for more 'global

345 Ibid., p. 712.
346 Besson (Sources of International Law), p. 845–46.
347 Besson (Theorizing the Sources), p. 176; Besson (Institutionalising global *demoi*-cracy), p. 65.
348 Besson (Sources of International Law), p. 846.
349 Besson (Insitutionalising global *demoi*-cracy), p. 68.
350 Boyle/Chinkin, p. 29.
351 Buchanan, p. 87.
352 Ibid., p. 90.

democracy' but since they both find such a standard as too demanding in the end, they suggest instead a standard of 'Broad Accountability'.[353] In particular, they convincingly call for cooperation of international institutions with individual expert groups and transnational civil society organizations in transparent deliberative processes, thereby transferring democratic values.[354]

In this vein, Buchanan holds that beyond accountability, an international standard of legitimacy should also be based on human rights.[355] This seems logical. Obviously, if state consent alone is not sufficient and adequate anymore as the sole basis of international law because of a legitimacy crisis or gap[356] of the current global legal order, the individual is needed as a source and thus human rights.

In conclusion, in recent scholarship, the view that beyond states' will, a new standard of legitimacy for international law should also be based on values such as accountability, democratic processes – a new '*demoi*-cracy' – and human rights is gaining ground.

3.2.2 Taking Recourse to Natural Law

Earlier scholarship as the former ICJ judge Mosler has already in 1980 expressed the need for common values and goals for any legal community in quite simple terms:

> In any legal community there must be a minimum of uniformity which is indispensable in maintaining the community. This uniformity may relate to legal values which are considered to be the goal of the community or it may be found in legal principles which is the duty of all members to realise.[357]

Simma and Paulus have argued for an 'enlightened positivism' in international law that is open to reference to global values. However, still using the term 'positivism', they emphasize that they stay within the traditional regime of positive sources and in fact do not argue for a natural law influence.[358] They emphasize that according to the ICJ in the South Africa cases, 'courts can take account of moral principles only in so far as these are given a sufficient expression in

353 Buchanan/Keohane, pp. 25–62; Buchanan, p. 93.
354 Buchanan, p. 94.
355 Ibid., pp. 94–96.
356 Ibid., p. 66.
357 Mosler, p. 17.
358 Simma/Paulus (The Responsibility of Individuals), p. 303.

legal form'.[359] In fact, they argue that custom and general principles cannot be reduced to states' will but should be more open to common values.

Many legal writers think that general principles of law as stated in Art. 38 (1) lit. c of the Statute of the ICJ are already an affirmation of natural law.[360] For example, it has been held that general principles include a concept of natural justice that requires that positive norms should be applied respecting minimal standards of decency, fairness and reciprocity.[361]

The ICJ has in various cases referred to equity, i.e. a set of principles constituting the values of the system.[362] Rather than applying rules of abstract justice, equity has been derived from the applicable law.[363] However, in his dissenting opinion in the Second Phase of the *South West Africa* cases, judge Tanaka has argued for a wider interpretation and defined equity as a source of human rights.[364] In most cases, equity has been used to achieve equitable results but not to refer to natural law.[365]

Referring to case law such as the *Corfu Channel* case,[366] where 'elementary considerations of humanity' as general principles of law are being taken into account, or the *North Sea Continental Shelf* case,[367] where the court referred to a 'belief' as 'a subjective element' by states when establishing customary

359 Simma/Paulus, p. 316 quoting the ICJ South West Africa cases i.e. *Ethiopia v. South Africa, Liberia v. South Africa*, Judgement, Second Phase, July 18, ICJ Reports 1966, pp. 6–58, para. 49, https://www.icj-cij.org/decisions?type=1&from=1966&to=1966&sort_bef_combine=order_DESC.

360 Kokott, p. 12, See Shaw, p. 78 for further references.

361 Orakhelashvili, p. 532.

362 See Shaw, p. 83 and for example ICJ, case Concerning the Continental Shelf (*Tunisia/Libyian Arab Jamahiriya*), Judgement ICJ Reports 1982, pp. 18–94, p. 60, https://www.icj-cij.org/decisions?type=1&from=1982&to=1982&sort_bef_combine=order_DESC.

363 Shaw, p. 84.

364 See Shaw, p. 84 quoting ICJ South West Africa cases i.e. *Ethiopia v. South Africa; Liberia v. South Africa*, Judgement, Second Phase, July 18, ICJ Reports 1966, pp. 294–299, https://www.icj-cij.org/decisions?type=1&from=1966&to=1966&sort_bef_combine=order_DESC.

365 ICJ North Sea Continental Shelf case, (*Federal Republic of Germany v. Denmark; Federal Republic of Germany v. Netherlands*) Judgement of 20 February 1969, ICJ Reports 1969, pp. 3–56, pp. 49–50, https://www.icj-cij.org/decisions?type=1&from=1969&to=1969&sort_bef_combine=order_DESC.

366 ICJ Corfu Channel case (*United Kingdom of Great Britain and Northern Island v. Albania*), Judgement of 9th April 1949, Merits, ICJ Reports 1949, pp. 4–169, p. 22, https://www.icj-cij.org/decisions?type=1&from=1949&to=1949&sort_bef_combine=order_DESC.

367 ICJ North Sea Continental Shelf cases (*Federal Republic of Germany v. Denmark; Federal Republic of Germany v. Netherlands*), Judgement of 20 February of 1969, ICJ Reports 1969, pp. 3–56, para. 77, https://www.icj-cij.org/decisions?type=1&from=1969&to=1969&sort_bef_combine=order_DESC.

law, Lachenmann goes a step further and concludes that international law has become value-oriented, i.e. based on global values, and moved away from a purely positivist approach.[368] Indeed, in a similar vein, Cottier has stressed that equity directly relates to moral perceptions and imports them into the law in assessing justice. In particular, he has praised how the principle of equity has been used in the North Sea Continental Shelf case holding:

> It is here that equity experienced its renaissance and became one of the leading principles in allocating natural resources among nations. [...] Equity developed novel features in terms of legal methodology with a view to combining legal objectivity, fairness and the avoidance of unfettered subjectivity of decisions taken. [...] Finally, it raises the issue of extent to which the international law of the Society of States of the Westphalian system reaches beyond co-existence and is able to venture into domains of distributive justice among nations.[369]

Finally, taking the case of humanitarian intervention, Kokott has demonstrated convincingly the increasing natural law influences in current international law.[370] Quoting the Vice President of the Prussian Supreme Court von Kirchmann, she held that jurisprudence and 'whole libraries would become waste paper' if only state practice would be the main source of international law.[371]

Thus, it seems possible to conclude that international law also relies on global values, not just on states' will. Koskenniemi has stated that any plausible theory of international law should accommodate both an ethical and a factual perspective.[372] This sounds convincing, given that a useful theory of law needs to be flexible and able to respond to political developments and societal trends, and should not merely stick to existing rules and states' behaviour. It needs to be apt to respond to the challenges of globalization. Within certain limits, legal science should be able to transfer elements of an 'ought' into an 'is'.

3.3 *The Quest for Global Values*

Having established that a value-based global order is in principle possible, the question is now what such global values are and where to look for them. Recalling that the original question was whether principles from domestic constitutional law such as human rights, democracy and the rule of law can be

368 Lachenmann, p. 794.

369 Cottier (Equitable Principles), pp. 7–8.

370 Kokott.

371 Ibid., p. 7.

372 Koskenniemi (International Legal Theory and Doctrine), p. 984.

transferred to the international level, this study will concentrate on such constitutional values and look for appropriate sources. Since constitutional values go beyond equity and standards of decency, which can be said to be already part of the general principles of law, other sources will be considered.

Under a natural law approach, the source of origin of law is human nature, reason, the idea of justice, and some social necessity.[373] Natural law was the main legal doctrine in three periods of legal history and can be said to have three main characteristics: It derives from human nature and applies universally, it is based on reason and it replaces positive law if in contradiction.[374] The Greek and the Romans with Socrates and Cicero considered law as coming from human nature and reason.[375] Legal principles such as *suum cuique tribuere* stated in the *corpus iuris civilis* are proof of this thinking.[376] In the Early Modern Age, Grotius, 'the father of international law', equally considered that law was based on human nature, i.e. reason.[377]

Kant maintained however law that cannot be based on reason alone, it needs to be grounded in experience.[378] On the other hand, he was convinced that law cannot only come from positive laws either, he saw the need for natural law.[379] And this natural law would come from the moral human being behaving in accordance with his 'categorical imperative'. In its strongest version, the 'practical imperative' reads:

> Handle so, dass du die Menschheit, sowohl in Deiner Person als in der Person eines anderen, jederzeit zugleich als Zweck niemals bloß als Mittel brauchst (Act in such a way that you always treat human beings including your own person as well as other person as a purpose, not a means).[380]

Thus, the moral human being, the individual human being and its dignity should be the purpose of all law. Considerations of humanity and needs of the human being should be a basis of all law. Kant also held that without that moral disposition of human nature, hostile states would not observe the law.[381]

---

373 See Koskenniemi (Intenational Legal Theory and Doctrine), p. 980; Orakhekashvili, p. 523; Shaw p. 15; Kaufmann (Problemgeschichte der Rechtsphilosophie), p. 49.

374 Kaufmann (Problemgeschichte der Rechtsphilosophie), p. 30.

375 Ibid., p. 39.

376 Ibid.

377 Hugo Grotius, *De iure belli ac pacis* by Neff; Ibid., p. 49.

378 Cf. Kaufmann (Problemgeschichte der Rechtsphilosophie), p. 63.

379 Kant (Metaphysik der Sitten), pp. 61, 66 et seqq.

380 Ibid., p. 63.

381 Kant (Zum ewigen Frieden), p. 33.

It follows, that in the quest for societal and human values, one should look at human nature and take recourse to philosophy, the discipline that has the human being at its core. In order to prove whether such considerations on the morality of the human being reflect indeed societal needs, one should also look at public debate consisting of contributions by political and corporate decision makers, academics and NGOs and other authoritative representatives of community interests such as the Pope or artists.

Considering that the natural law approach can only complement existing positive law because positivism is, of course, a core element of law,[382] and the insight that law creates and reflects morality, one should also look at existing law embodying community interests. Thus, international conventions, custom and soft law instruments including international code of conducts are an important source. Especially international legal documents shared by the international community and supported by civil society should be looked at. Subsidiary sources such as judicial decisions and teachings of the most highly qualified publicists are also highly relevant under a natural law approach. Finally, since states are still the dominant actors of the international legal order, state practice needs to already reflect such values to a certain extent. This includes of course practice by international organizations.

Having established the sources of global values, the question is, are human rights such a global value?[383] Looking at the on-going massive human rights violations for example of the Uyghurs committed by the Chinese State or the lot of the Rohingya people in Myanmar or the economic and political crisis in Venezuela and the deprivation of the Venezuelan people of their basic economic and social rights, this is at least subject to question.

The existence and rise of illiberal democracies[384] and autocracies[385] around the world equally lets the question arise whether the idea of a global legal order based on democracy and the rule of law rather belongs to utopia. Some predict that times will change with an upcoming 'Chinese century' and that we are close to a 'Zeitenwende',[386] identifying a growing trend of 'Westlessness',[387]

---

382 Cf. Feuerbach quoted in Kaufmann S. 74.

383 Buchanan, p. 96.

384 Cf. Franke.

385 Leggewie.

386 Süddeutsche Zeitung, Kurt Kister, ‚Zeitenwende – Europa und die Welt', 31 December 2019; see also Süddeutsche Zeitung, SZ Spezial ‚Neue Weltordnung', 13th of February 2020, p. 11.

387 Süddeutsche Zeitung, Daniel Brössler, ‚Den Westen retten, Sicherheitskonferenz', 17th February 2020, p. 4.

i.e. the loss of dominance of the US and EU in global political affairs and the retreat of Western values.

3.3.1 Human Rights

Human rights are evidently based on human nature and should in theory be an obvious case for a fundamental value of our global legal order. At the domestic level, early documents in European and Anglo-American history assigning rights to individuals were the Magna Charta Libertatum of 1215 and the later Virginia Bill of Rights of 1776 as well as the French Declaration of the Rights of Man and the Citizen of 1789.[388] In international relations it was already in 1557, that Francisco de Vitoria thinking about what he conceived as international relations, i.e. relations between Spaniards and Native Americans, advocated the natural law idea that human beings have rights and claims simply because they were human beings, and that nobody was born as a slave.[389] However, the concept of human rights has been hotly debated ever since the commitment by states to promote respect for human rights has been incorporated into the UN Charter in San Francisco in 1945.[390] While there was a consensus among states after the human disaster of the Second World War that individuals have to be protected against their state,[391] there was no such unanimity as to whether and to what degree states and society may be held accountable for human rights violations, and as to whether and to what extent human rights were purely domestic affairs.[392] Similar to general international law, which has been subject to many debates with regard to its legal nature, human rights often have been regarded as being of a moral nature rather than legal rights.[393] Governments of East and West were strongly divided over whether human rights derive from the inherent dignity of humankind or are merely entitlements granted by governments – and thus rather political programmes and contingent on the political and cultural context.[394] The main arguments

388 Kälin/Künzli, p. 4.

389 Cf. Francisco de Vitoria, Relectiones Theologicae, De Indis (orig. 1532, publ. 1557), Sec. I, paragraph 24 in: The Classics of International Law, ed. Ernest Nys (Washington: Carnegie Institution 1917), p. 128 (engl. And 232 (lat.)) quoted in Anne Peters, *Beyond Human Rights*, pp. 11–12.

390 Cf. Alston (The UN's Human Rights Record).

391 Beitz, pp. 128–130.

392 Alston (The UN's Human Rights Record), p. 16.

393 See the critique of traditional human rights doctrine in Raz (Human Rights without Foundations).

394 Alston (The UN's Human Rights Record), p. 388; See also Dworkin, for example at p. xi arguing against legal positivism and in favour of the existence of individual rights prior to rights created by legislation. At p. 138 he describes the theory of political scepticism,

against the universality of human rights were that the concept of human rights is a Western concept and that no transcultural agreement on human goods exist.[395]

The question of sources of international human rights law and their universality have been subject of intense debates especially in the years preceding the Vienna World Conference on Human Rights in 1993 after break-down of the Soviet-Union and its communist regime.[396] While for example the US has mainly questioned the existence of economic, social and cultural rights and until today has not ratified the ICESCR,[397] China still strongly opposes any interference with domestic human rights matters and has not ratified the ICCPR.[398]

The starting point of the philosophical debate is the central statement of the Universal Declaration of Human Rights, that every human being is born equal in dignity and rights, and thus entitled to human rights simply by virtue of his and her humanity. This statement is obviously based of the philosophy of Kant who convincingly claimed that the individual and his morality should be the source and purpose of moral and legal thinking.[399] In this sense, his 'categorical imperative' is considered to be a philosophical foundation of the universality of human rights.[400] Even though such reasoning seems difficult to reject, cultural relativists – or liberal ironists as the philosopher Rorty calls himself – question that there is such a thing as a given human nature and doubt the existence of 'an order beyond time and change which both determines the point of human existence and establishes a hierarchy of responsibilities'.[401] Instead, they hold that culture, i.e. cultural and religious beliefs and practices, is the principal source of moral rights and rules, based on moral autonomy and communitarian self-determination.[402] What is true?

---

which holds that individuals only have the legal rights the Constitution grants them, being limited to the plain and uncontroversial violations of public morality.

395 See for example Perry, pp. 483 et seqq.; Leary (The Asian Region) p. 23; for an excellent overview of the debate over universalism versus relativism, see Kälin/Künzli, pp. 20–32.

396 Besson (Sources of International Human Rights Law), p. 840.

397 See status of ratifications and signatures to the ICESCR at https://indicators.ohchr.org/.

398 See the ratifications of the ICCPR, https://indicators.ohchr.org/; China's ruling party, the KP hardly tolerates critique on human rights violations and political leaders from the West do not dare to strongly criticize the government for their violation of freedom of speech, as the last visit of chancellor Merkel in China has shown. See www.zeit.de/politik/ausland/2019-09/china-angela-merkel-xi-jinping-hongkong-kommunistische-partei; See also Li, pp. 90–94.

399 See above p. 357.

400 Téson, p. 64.

401 Rorty (Contingency); Rorty (Kontingenz).

402 See Donnelly, p. 401.

Pope John Paul II wisely answered the question of the existence of 'objective norms of morality' as follows: '[T]he very progress of cultures demonstrates that there is something in man which transcends those cultures. This "something" is precisely human nature: This nature is itself the measure of culture and the condition ensuring that man does not become the prisoner of any of his cultures, but asserts his personal dignity by living in accordance with profound truth of his being'.[403] Thus, the answer is that yes, cultures determine human beings but not totally, there must be something such as an universal human nature that makes cultures change and is responsible for progress. To use the words of Donnelly, 'human nature", the realized nature of real human beings, is a social as well a "natural" product'.[404] This is what is at the core of Donnelly's account of a 'weak culturalism' of human rights and Perry has named pluralism about human good.[405] In more simple terms, 'Universalism about human good is correct: human beings are all alike in some respects such that some things good for some human beings are good for every human being and some things bad for some human beings are bad for every human being. But pluralism about human good is correct, too: there are many important respects in which human beings are not all alike; some things good for some human beings, including a concrete way of life, might not be good for every human being, and some things bad for some human beings might not be bad for every human being'.[406] And as Nussbaum has rightly stated with regard to local traditions, a conception of the human good can be regarded 'to be objective in the sense that it is justifiable by reference to reasons that do not derive merely from local traditions and practices, but rather from features of humanness that lie beneath all local traditions and are to be seen whether or not they are in fact recognized in local traditions'.[407]

By contrast, the view that 'human solidarity' – or human good inherent in human nature – should not be regarded as fact but rather 'as a goal to be achieved', does not seem plausible.[408] Rorty holds that solidarity rather than being discovered by reflection has to be created. But the outstanding question is how can solidarity be created if there is no such thing as a cross-cultural conviction among human beings that solidarity is a good thing? Admittedly, the extent to which solidarity among human beings should be realized changes

403 Pope John Paul II, *Veritatis Splendor*, 23 Origins 297, 314 (1993), quoted in Perry, p. 461.

404 Donnelly, p. 403.

405 Ibid., 401, Perry, p. 471.

406 Perry, pp. 472–473.

407 Nussbaum (Non-Relative Virtues), p. 243.

408 Rorty (Contingency), p. xvi.

overtime and is contingent on the cultural context. But such position is exactly what pluralism, or a weak culturalism is about.

Having accepted that there is a universal human nature and a transcultural consensus on the human good, the next question is what it is about? A significant transcultural consensus certainly exists as to the 'great evils of human experience, re-affirmed in every age and in every written history and in every tragedy and fiction: murder and destruction of life, imprisonment, enslavement, starvation, poverty, physical pain and torture, homelessness, friendliness'.[409] A more difficult question is whether certain cultural practices such as female circumcision or the subordinate position of women as a fundamental feature of Muslim practice should allow for deviation from this cross-cultural consensus and leave it to the particular culture and society how to deal with that practice. The answer is to have a productive moral discourse, which has to be conducted inter- as well as intra-culturally.[410] It is a wrong belief that cultures are monistic rather than being composed of subcultures.[411] Since in most societies, the power elite is composed of men and society male-dominated, it is for example often ignored what women would accept as part of their culture.[412] A prominent representative of such 'internal critique' is the famous Islamic human rights scholar An-Na'im who maintains that the cultural legitimacy of human rights standards with the 'major traditions has to be enhanced through internal dialogue and struggle to establish enlightened perceptions and interpretations of cultural values and norms'.[413] He suggest an '"enlightened construction" of fundamental Islamic sources in order to achieve complete legal equality for Muslim women and non-Muslims, thereby overcoming all human rights objections to the modern application of Islamic law'.[414] Having achieved an adequate level of legitimacy within each tradition, cross-cultural dialogue should follow.[415]

Having resolved the question of how to achieve a global or transcultural consensus on human good or values, the next question is how do they become human rights and why do we need rights? And is there a global consensus also on the concept of human rights as legal rights, Raz rightly asked 'why is

409 Stuart Hampshire, *Innocence and Experience* (1989), p. 90, quoted in Perry, p. 483; Donnelly, p. 404.
410 Cf. Perry, p. 490.
411 Kim, pp. 88–90.
412 Ibid. p. 90.
413 An-Na'im, (Towards a Cross-Cultural Approach), pp. 20–21.
414 An-Na'im (Islam, Islamic Law and the Dilemma of Cultural Legitimacy), p. 48.
415 An-Na'im (Towards a Cross-Cultural Approach), p. 21.

[it] that rights are of value to the right-holder and why do they involve duties on others? The explanation is that rights have a special role in our moral universe: they apply to cases where the value of something to a person is of a kind that warrants holding others duty-bound to respect or secure its enjoyment otherwise'.[416] Obviously rights help to protect human beings. A political account of human rights based on liberal justice theories advocated by the philosopher Rawls is as follows: 'Human Rights are a class of rights that play a special role in a reasonable Law of Peoples: they restrict the justifying reason for war and its conduct, and they specify limits to a regime's internal autonomy'.[417] It is however not true that human rights can be limited to 'rights which are morally valid against states in the international arena', as held by Raz.[418] A better definition is the one by Beitz, which says that 'human rights are requirements whose objects is to protect urgent individual interests against certain predictable dangers ("standards threats") to which they are vulnerable under typical circumstances of life in a modern world order composed of states'.[419] Buchanan has rightly added that it was not only the intention from drafters of the human rights regime to protect against state-inflicted harms but also to affirm equal status for all and to secure for all the conditions for a decent or minimally good human life, or ensuring that the state performs basic welfare state functions.[420] And Dworkin has defended his idea of individual rights as political trumps by holding that if government does not take rights seriously, then it does not take law seriously either. Without respect for rights, 'it neglects the one feature that distinguishes law from ordered brutality'.[421]

Against this convincing account of the international human rights theory, cultural relativists often state that tribes and indigenous communities have their own sophisticated mechanisms to protect human dignity.[422] While such indigenous communities may indeed exist and are capable of protecting the dignity of their members, most often in the Global South, modern nation states consist of dual societies including traditional cultures mixed with Westernized practices.[423] Repressive political leaders and urban elites use arguments of

---

416 Raz (Human Rights in the Emerging World Order), p. 222.

417 Raz (Human Rights without Foundation), p. 328 quoting Rawls, p. 79.

418 Raz (Human Rights without Foundations).

419 Beitz, p. 109; For a convincing presentation of 'a practical conception of human rights' developed by Rawls, Beitz and Lafont, see also Anne Peters, *Beyond Human Rights*, pp. 469–471.

420 Buchanan (Why International Legal Human Rights), p. 248.

421 Dworkin (Taking Rights Seriously), p. 204.

422 Cf. Donnelly, p. 410.

423 Ibid., p. 411.

moral imperialism or an inadequate Western concept of human rights while at the same time undermining traditional communities.[424] In such situations, recourse to international human rights is indispensable.

As a result, a convincing account of human rights principally accords the same human rights to every human being but allow for different interpretations and variations or even deviations due to cultural context. What this means exactly in individual cases has to be found via a legal and moral discourse. In this sense, Buchanan is right when he holds that to answer the question of universality of human rights and in order to make human rights a credible justification of the global legal order, international human rights and other institutions should engage in public deliberative processes thereby contributing to their own but also to the legitimacy of the international legal order.[425]

International human rights law confirms this result. The Vienna Declaration of the World Conference on Human Rights of 1993 reaffirms the commitment of all states to fulfil their obligations to promote universal respect for all human rights in accordance with international human rights documents and stresses their universal nature.[426] Since the end of the Second World War, there has been an impressive proliferation of human rights treaties. The most important international human rights instruments next to the UDHR, the ICCPR and the ICESCR, have been ratified by respectively by 173 states[427] and 170 states,[428] and the CRC by almost all except the US, i.e. 196 states.[429] There are several regional human rights regimes with the European Union with its European Court of Justice certainly being the most effective.[430] Also, since the adoption of the UN Charter, the international human rights implementation mechanisms has improved since individual human rights complaints procedures have increasingly been adopted and strengthened.[431]

The case of *ius cogens* confirms that the idea of human rights is of a universal nature and a fundamental value of the global legal order. Recently, the International Law Commission in its Conclusion 23 for the first time has adopted a non-exhaustive list of peremptory norms of general international

424 Ibid. pp. 412–413 with many examples; See also Kim, p. 89.

425 Ibid.

426 Paragraph 1 of the Vienna Declaration, UN A/CONF.157/22 of 6 July 1993; on this point, see also Kälin/Künzli, p. 35.

427 See the website of the OHCHR at https://indicators.ohchr.org/.

428 Ibid.

429 Ibid.

430 See Meron, pp. 440 et seqq.

431 See the Optional Protocols to the ICCPR, the ICESCR and the CRC in Humbert (The Challenge of Child Labour), pp. 130, 135 et seqq; See also Meron, pp. 339–344.

law including human rights norms such as the prohibition of genocide, crimes against humanity, racial discrimination and apartheid, slavery, torture and basic rules of international humanitarian law and the right of self-determination.[432] It is a major failure that exploitative child labour as a modern form of slavery has not been added to this list.[433] In its Conclusion 3, the ILC has confirmed that peremptory norms of general international law (*ius cogens*) reflect and protect fundamental values of the international community and are hierarchically superior to other rules of international law and universally applicable. It explained its Conclusion 3 referring *inter alia* to references in the ICJ's Advisory Opinion of 1951 on *Reservations to the Convention on the Prevention and Punishment of the Crime of Genocide* to 'the conscience of mankind' and 'moral law' and the famous *Kadi* judgement referring to *ius cogens* as a 'body of higher rules of public international law'.[434] Conclusion 3 clearly recognizes common values shared by the international community of states and confirms what Tomuschat concluded from Art. 53 of the VCLT and Art. 19 of the former ILC Draft on state responsibility about the existence of an international community.[435] The legal consequences of state responsibility are inserted into Conclusion 17 that stipulates that *ius cogens* norms give rise to obligations owed to the community as a whole, i.e. obligations *erga omnes*, in which all states have a legal interest, confirming the famous *Barcelona Traction* judgement by the ICJ[436] and numerous state practice.[437] Thus, while all internationally recognized human rights can be said to be universal by nature, some have acquired the status of *ius cogens*, which all states have to respect, and which all states can invoke. Reflecting community interests and collective interests of all

---

432 ILC (Peremptory Norms of International Law).

433 For an elaboration on the prohibition of exploitative child labour as a form of 'enslavement' and *ius cogens* prohibition, see Humbert (The Challenge of Child Labour), pp. 114–119. See also above, pp. 10 et seqq.

434 ICJ, *Reservations to the Convention on the Prevention and Punishment of the Crime of Genocide*, Advisory Opinion, ICJ. Reports 1951, pp. 15–69, p. 23, https://www.icj-cij.org/case/12; *Kadi v Council of the European Union and Commission of the European Communities*, Case No. T-315-01, Judgement of 21 September 2005, Second Chamber, Court of First Instance of the European Communities, [2005] ECR II-3649, para. 226.

435 See above p. 323.

436 ICJ Barcelona Traction, Light and Power Company, Limited Case (Belgium v. Spain), Judgement, 5th February 1970, ICJ Reports 1970, pp. 3–54, para. 33, https://www.icj-cij.org/decisions?type=1&from=1970&to=1970&sort_bef_combine=order_DESC.

437 See for example UN General Assembly, Sixth Committee, report of the International Law Commission, statement of the Czech Republic, UN Doc. A/C.6/49/SR.26, para. 19; Federal Court of Australia, Nulyarimma and Others v. Thompson, Appeal Decision of 1 September 1999, [1999] FCA 1192, 165, ALR 621, 96 FCR 153, ILDC 2773 (AU 1999), para. 81.

states subject to countermeasures, *ius cogens* human rights norms constitute certainly the core value of the global legal order.

Besson maintains that human rights are already 'objective law' as opposed to consent-based, and that the 'customization' of the Universal Bill of Human Rights including the UDHR and both of the Covenants has led to a 'generalization' of human rights treaties.[438] Recognizing that international law assumes that states have an objective interest in holding each other accountable for human rights violations as reflected in the possibility of inter-state complaints, Simma, quoting ICJ *Georgia v Russia*,[439] has commented that still today, inter-state obligations continue to 'govern the matter of human rights'.[440] While he admits that there is a collective interest behind human rights treaties allowing them to be invoked without material damage, he emphasizes that individuals only have a passive personality arguing that a genuine legal entitlement would entitle individuals a human right of procedure based in international law that entitles them to claim their rights at an international level.[441] It is of course true that the individual still has a weak procedural position in international law. However, Peters has rightly questioned whether individual international judicial procedures are a necessary condition to accord individuals international legal capacity.[442]

Whatever the exact status of the individual under international law may be, what is of central importance for now is the fact that both scholars adhere to the idea of universal human rights as central to the global legal order. Also Simma does not deny *per se* the objectivity of human rights law, or at least a collective interest, he just thinks that this not attainable under current international law without recourse to natural law and a constitutionalist view, i.e. the recognition and acceptance of common values.[443] At other occasions, he himself defends a global order with reference to 'Kantian' values such as the

438 Besson (Sources of International Human Rights Law), p. 867.

439 ICJ, Application of the International Convention on the Elimination of All Forms of Racial Discrimination (*Georgia v. Russian Federation*), Provisional Measures, Order of 15th of October 2008, ICJ Reports 2008, pp. 353–399, https://www.icj-cij.org/decisions?type=1&from=2008&to=2008&sort_bef_combine=order_DESC.

440 Simma (Sources of International Human Rights Law), p. 881. See also ICJ, Application of the Convention on Prevention and Punishment of the Crime of Genocide (*The Gambia v. Mynamar*), Request for the Indication of Provisional Measures, Order, 23 January 2020, General List No. 178, https://www.icj-cij.org/decisions?type=1&from=2020&to=2020&sort_bef_combine=order_DESC.

441 Simma (Sources of International Human Rights Law), pp. 872–873.

442 Peters (Beyond Human Rights), pp. 45 et seqq.

443 Simma (Sources of International Human Rights Law), p. 875.

UN system of universal human rights.[444] In sum, while it is subject to question as to whether all human rights have become customary law and qualify as objective law as yet, it seems possible to conclude that human rights are universal enough to provide a basis for an adequate standard of legitimacy for international law.

Meron even holds that human rights have influenced the evolution of international law to such an extent that there has been a 'humanization of international law'.[445] He analyses different areas of international law including humanitarian law and the law on state responsibility to conclude that there has been a shift in international law from a state-centred approach to and individual-centred approach.[446]

In light of the importance and central role of human rights in international law, the on-going human rights violations world-wide on their own do not suffice as an argument to reject human rights being a fundamental value of the global legal order. The fact that beyond most American, African, European states as well as Turkey and India, and in 2004 also China as a global power included human rights in their constitutions, demonstrates that human rights are also a value in domestic legal orders.[447]

Having established human rights as a fundamental global value, the question which needs to be answered is of course whether all human rights recorded in human rights documents form part of it, and what their respective scope is. An authoritative list of the core internationally recognized human rights is contained in the International Bill of Human Rights, comprising the UDHR and the two Covenants, the ICCPR including its Optional Protocols, and the ICESCR.[448] As stated in the commentaries to the UNGP, this list should be coupled with the ILO Core Conventions contained in the ILO Declaration on Fundamental Principles and Rights at Work of 1998.[449] Thus, a fundamental global value of human rights has to be based at least on these instruments.

The UN has also adopted a list of core human rights treaties in addition to the International Bill of Human Rights various conventions protecting particular human rights such as the International Convention on the Elimination of all Forms of Racial Discrimination, Convention against Torture and Other

---

444 Simma/Paulus (The International Community), p. 273.

445 Meron.

446 Ibid., p. 1.

447 Li, p. 92; Danish Institute for Human Rights, pp. 12 et seqq.

448 Kälin/Künzli, p. 42; Besson also refers to the International Bill of Human Rights, see above, p. 366.

449 Cf. Commentary to principle 12 of the UNGP, HRC, Res. 17/4 of 16 June 2011.

Cruel, Inhuman or Degrading Treatment or Punishment, the Convention on the Elimination of All Forms of Discrimination against Women, Convention on the Rights of the Child, International Convention on the Protection of the Rights of All Migrant Workers and Members of Their Families, International Convention on for the Protection of All Person from Enforced Disappearance, Convention on the Rights of Persons with Disabilities.[450] These conventions may be referred to depending on the individual case when applying and implementing human rights as a global value in the form of a constitutional principle as will be elaborated below.[451]

With regard to the content of the specific rights, the vast human rights jurisprudence of the treaty bodies and the General Comments give comprehensive guidance. As discussed above, the content may of course vary according to the national and cultural context.[452] The limit of such variations in interpretations is where the essence or the core of the relevant human right is affected in line with the German doctrine of the 'Wesensgehalt'.[453] The core is affected if the relevant human right does not offer any protection anymore and becomes useless.[454] This has to be determined on a case-by-case basis. The graver and the more intended the infringement, the more probable becomes such a violation of the core.[455] Regarding child labour this would be the case of prohibited child labour where a child's education and full development is impeded, in case of hazardous work and unconditional worst forms of child labour.[456]

3.3.2 Democracy and Cosmopolitanism

The more difficult question is whether the core constitutional principle of democracy can be said to be a global value and form the basis of a universal law. Is democracy also part of human nature and can be derived from the dignity of the human being and apply universally? Is democracy a human right?

On the one hand, it seems that democracy might be rather a form of government and more dependent on cultural context. On the other hand, human rights and democracy are obviously closely linked. According to the Vienna Human Rights Conference Declaration of 1993, '[d]emocracy, development

450 See UN OHCHR, The Core International Human Rights Instruments and their monitoring bodies, https://www.ohchr.org/EN/ProfessionalInterest/Pages/CoreInstruments.aspx.

451 See below p. 382.

452 See above, p. 364.

453 Cf. Pieroth/Schlink, pp. 76–78.

454 Ibid., p. 77.

455 Emmerich-Fritsche, p. 555.

456 See Humbert (The Challenge of Child Labour), p. 120.

and respect for human rights and fundamental freedoms are interdependent and mutually reinforcing'.[457] Democracy constitutes one of the foundations of human rights.[458] Accordingly, Art. 25 of the ICCPR protects the right to vote at elections and to take part in public affairs and Art. 18 and 19 of the ICCPR protect freedom of thought and expression as part of a number of civil liberties contained in the ICCPR. Without these rights, democracy as a form of government would not be possible. However, human rights and democracy are different concepts. While democracy cannot exist without human rights – at least not in the sense of a modern liberal democracy as opposed to a Kantian 'pure democracy' relating to a tyranny of the majority,[459] human rights can exist for a short time in a limited version in autocratic states. At least most economic, social and cultural rights are also compatible with other political systems as the former 'Soviet' approach to human rights proves.[460] Also, the Chinese delegation to the Vienna World Conference on Human Rights stressed that 'countries at different development stages or with different historical traditions and cultural backgrounds also have different understanding and practice of human rights', thus not denying per se the existence of human rights.[461] There is however also the 'substantive view' of democracy – in contrast to the 'procedural view' focussing on free and fair elections – holding that democracy and human rights are intertwined in a 'right of democratic governance'.[462] However, lacking a clear expression in international legal materials and given the ICJ's emphasis on the right of states to self-determination, so far a right to democracy' cannot be deemed to part of international law.[463]

The question is therefore whether the philosophy of cosmopolitanism may help to establish democracy as a global value.[464]

At the core of cosmopolitanism lies the concern for human beings as opposed to states.[465] The basic proposition is that each person is equally

457 Art. 8 of the Vienna Declaration and Programme of Action, World Conference on Human Rights of 14–15 June 1993, UN A/CONF. 157/23 of 12 July 1993.

458 Nowak, p. 22.

459 See for a comprehensive discussion of Kant's republican ideas Téson.

460 Shaw, p. 199.

461 Chinese Delegation to the Vienna World Conference on Human Rights quoted in Kälin/Künzli, p. 26, fn. 59.

462 For a comprehensive overview of a right to democracy see Fox, p. 19.

463 Fox, p. 17 quoting ICJ, Case Concerning Military and Paramilitary Activities in and against Nicaragua (*Nicaragua v. United States*), ICJ Reports 1986, pp. 14–50,https://www.icj-cij.org/decisions?type=1&from=1986&to=1986&sort_bef_combine=order_DESC.

464 See for example Held; Caney; Pogge.

465 Held, p. 12.

worthy of respect and that the dignity of reason and moral choice in every human being must be treated with respect, which implies that there are limits to the moral validity of particular communities, as shown especially by atrocities of the Holocaust committed under the Nazi-regime.[466] The roots of cosmopolitanism are to be found in the philosophy of the Stoics such as Seneca or Eptiket, who thought that humankind should live happily together in the *cosmos*, i.e. in the whole world, rather than in local communities.[467] The most famous thinker promoting cosmopolitan ideas is of course Kant with his notion of a '*Weltbürger*' (cosmopolitan citizen) and a '*Weltbürgerrecht*' (*ius cosmopoliticum*) as a necessary condition for perpetual peace.[468] According to Held, a 'cosmopolitan right' in the sense of Kant's right to hospitality is the capacity to present oneself and to be heard within and across political communities.[469] Cosmopolitans base their theory on Kant's thinking, according to which universal principles for society should be devised on the basis of public reason and impartial reasoning.[470] In the same vein, modern cosmopolitans have generated a set of principles for the global political order flowing from the meta-principle of autonomy and impartial reasoning.[471] The principles are about equal respect for human beings, about consent for deliberation and legitimate decision-making, about inclusiveness and subsidiarity for collective decision-making, prevention of harm and sustainability. Acknowledging the diversity of values and identities, cosmopolitans stress the need for democratic dialogue and acceptance of a plurality of value.[472] Cosmopolitan views reach from a 'strong' cosmopolitanism holding that all moral principles should apply universally in a Kantian sense[473] to a 'layered' cosmopolitanism meaning that only some moral principles are of a universal scope.[474] Especially the 'layered' or 'thin' cosmopolitanism requires ongoing dialogue to guarantee value pluralism and thus democratic public institutions.[475] Having the meta-principle

466 See Held with further references, pp. 12 et seqq.

467 Kaufmann (Problemgeschichte der Philosophie), p. 26.

468 Kant quoted in Held, p. 11; Kant (Zum ewigen Frieden, Ein philosophischer Entwurf) Chapter 2, p. 19, fn. 3.

469 Held, p. 11. Kant originally talks of a 'Hospitalitätsrecht' (right to hospitality), i.e. the right to attempt to get in contact and to tolerate each other, Kant (Zum ewigen Frieden), Dritter Definitivartikel zum ewigen Frieden.

470 See above p. 357.

471 Held, pp. 12 et seqq.

472 Ibid., p. 16.

473 Scheffler quoted in Held, p. 17.

474 Held, p. 18.

475 Ibid., p. 16.

of autonomy at its core, the basic concept of cosmopolitanism is a democratic society with principles of democratic life.[476] Responding to objections regarding a limited, Western-driven validity of cosmopolitan principles, cosmopolitan scholars, in the tradition of Kant's categorical imperative and using the 'meta-principle of impartial reasoning', hold that the test for the universal application of these principles is whether 'all parties would be equally prepared to accept the outcome as fair and reasonable irrespective of the social positions they might occupy now or in the future'.[477] Thus, people's equal interest in personal self-determination and autonomy and equal moral concern for each person lie at the heart of cosmopolitanism. Elaborating on Kant's law of humanity, cosmopolitan democratic law incorporates the cosmopolitan principles. States are just one space for policy making and legitimate power; individuals would also be citizens of political communities and regional and global networks.[478] Equally, Caney in his book 'Justice Beyond Borders: A Global Political Theory' defends a cosmopolitan democracy, holding that there are

> global norms of civil and political justice [...] and distributive justice [...]'. Drawing on these, it 'defends a non-statist political order, calling for accountable, global institutions.[479]

The theory of cosmopolitanism certainly sounds appealing being rooted in principles of humanity and egalitarian justice such as equal respect and concern for every human being in the tradition of Kantian philosophy. However, it has been widely criticised by so-called 'statists' such as Rawls and Miller[480] for being unsuitable in the international arena, which should be governed by principles based on respect for sovereignty of minimally just states and mutual assistance between them.[481] More recent critique argues that indeed, cosmopolitan principles are too ideal for being applied to the world as it is.[482] Being however well aware of increasing global interdependence and the shortcomings of a statist order, starting from a 'weak cosmopolitanism', Valentini offers her own approach to global justice suggesting that 'a just world order [...]

476 Ibid., p. 20.

477 Held, p. 22; Barry in Held, p. 22.

478 Held., p. 27.

479 Caney, p. 20.

480 Rawls (The Idea of Public Reason Revisited), pp. 175 et seqq.; Miller.

481 See for an excellent analysis of arguments provided by the school of 'cosmopolitanism' and 'statism', Valentini, pp. 1 et seqq.

482 Valentini, p. 14.

would contain a plurality of states and supranational institutions, the latter in charge of regulating global systemic coercion (especially of an economic nature) so as to make it compatible with everyone's right to freedom'.[483] The latter approach seems to be what Koskenniemi has called an 'institutional cosmopolitanism', i.e. an approach to international law that aims at legitimate international governance.[484]

Pointing already to solutions, Besson in her seminal work 'The Morality of Conflict: Reasonable Disagreement and the Law' has argue that any 'satisfactory political and legal theory should therefore provide a way of dealing with and accommodating moral disagreement and the fundamental problem of finding a legitimate and justifiable way of making collective binding decisions in the face of continuing moral conflict'.[485] In her view, the law's authority can be justified on grounds of coordination.[486] Supporting cosmopolitan schools of thought and referring to the important findings of Besson, Cottier develops his doctrine of a multi-layered governance on the premise that while there are common ethical foundations and shared beliefs, 'disagreement on values is present on all levels of governance', and it is for political processes and an effective dispute settlement to find appropriate solutions.[487]

While such an approach to global governance and international law is highly convincing and will be referred to below,[488] the question remains whether democracy already is such a common ethical foundation or a global shared value. It is at least subject to question whether cosmopolitan principles related to democracy are suited for a global justice theory applicable to the world at large. The universality of human rights based on human nature is much easier to defend than the universal applicability of cosmopolitan principles relating to a certain form of government. From a philosophical point of view, cosmopolitan principles stemming from the meta-principle of autonomy and impartial reasoning may be hard to reject. Kant put the requirement that states should be 'republican' in the First Definitive Article of his famous work 'Perpetual Peace'.[489] However, as mentioned above, an explanation why law is binding should not only rely on ethics and morality but also be rooted in

483 Ibid., p. 20.
484 Koskenniemi (International Theory and Doctrine), p. 979.
485 Besson (The Morality of Conflict), p. 528.
486 Ibid., p. 529.
487 Cottier (Multilayered Governance), p. 669.
488 See below, p. 389.
489 Kant (Zum ewigen Frieden) Erster Definitivartikel, p. 20.

positive law.[490] Thus, international legal materials and state practice have to be looked at.

Major UN documents such as the UN Charter in its Preamble 'We the peoples', and annual General Assembly resolutions since 1988 support the democracy as a core value of the UN.[491] The UN is firmly committed to promoting democracy.[492] Firstly, various UN documents suggest measures to strengthen democratic institutions and seek to establish a global consensus on democracy.[493] Secondly, electoral assistance has become an widely accepted part of UN practice.[494] And thirdly, the UN promoted democracy in its post-conflict-missions.[495]

In 2015, world leaders declared in the 2030 Agenda for Sustainable Development[496] democracy as essential for sustainable development confirming commitments made at the World Summit[497] in 2005 and in the Millennium Declaration.[498] Citing many more examples and referring to state practice, Peters has argued for an international legal requirement of domestic democracy establishing democracy as a global value.[499] However, as China as one of the global powers has not ratified the ICCPR, no global consensus exists on the central democratic right to vote enshrined in Art. 25 of the ICCPR. Most importantly, China as well as other East Asian states rather than incorporating core values of liberal democracy into their constitutions, have used constitutions for reform agendas regarding them 'as an inevitable part of modernization'.[500] Especially in China, the constitution and legislation are used as political tools for state-building and help to construct the political legitimacy of the Party leadership of the Communist Party of China (CPC) rather than protecting liberal values.[501] 'Maintaining the Party's leadership 'has been found as the most

---

490 Koskenniemi (International Legal Theory and Doctrine), p. 981.

491 See the UN and democracy athttps://www.un.org/en/global-issues/democracy.

492 Fox, pp. 21 et seqq.

493 See for example UN Secretary-General, 'An Agenda for Democratization', para. 56; UNGA Resolution 55/96 of 4th December 2000 'Promoting and Consolidating Democracy'.

494 Fox, p. 21.

495 See Fox, p. 21 for various examples.

496 UN (The Sustainable Development Agenda), https://www.un.org/sustainabledevelopment/development-agenda/.

497 UN, The World Summit 2005, High-Level Plenary Meeting of the 60th session of the General Assembly, Resolution A/RES/60/1.

498 United Nations Millenium Declaration, General Assembly resolution 55/2 of 8 September 2005.

499 Klabbers/Peters/Ulfstein, p. 273 et seqq.

500 Jiunn-Rong Yeh and Wen-Chen Chang, 'The emergence of East Asian constitutionalism: features in comparison' (2011) 59 AJIL (2011), pp. 805–840 quoted in Li, p. 74.

501 Li, p. 75.

fundamental principle of China's politics and the Chinese artist Ai Weiwei has called China a 'Mafiastaat' (Mafia state).[502] Instead of constitutionalism, China adheres to a socialist rule of law.[503] Considering that China is striving to gain global power without committing to democratic values, as has recently been held by two experts on Chinese policy,[504] it is difficult to recognize democracy as a universally recognized global value.

According to the organization Freedom House, democracy is in retreat.[505] Between 2005 and 2018, the share of 'Not Free' countries rose from 23 to 26 per-cent, while the share of 'Free' countries declined from 46 to 44 per cent.[506] By contrast, between 1988 until 2005, the share of 'Not Free' countries had dropped by 14 per cent. One reason for this trend is that newly erected democracies in the post-Soviet era have come under attack by nationalist leaders such as Victor Urban in Hungary.[507] At the same time, the change in the global balance of power with the BRICS, i.e. Brazil, India, China and South-Africa on the rise, made people in established democracies such as the US and EU Member States anxious of loss of wealth and let antiliberal populist movements from the far right arise.[508] Antiliberal movements and leaders spread around the world attacking democratic institutions, as the examples of the Brazilian President Jair Bolsonaro or the Russian President Putin demonstrate.[509] Liberal democracy following a Western or European model has not been established as global political model.[510] In view of these developments, it is not anymore possible to say that '"current international law" indicates a progressive and irreversible movement to a world community of democratic states', as it may have been in the beginning of the 21st century.[511]

The law of regional organizations points in the same direction. In contrast to America, Africa and Europe where the Organization of American States, the African Union and the EU have firm commitments to democracy, there

---

502 Süddeutsche Zeitung, Judith Wittwer, Christof Münger, Interview with Ai Weiwei, ‚Wenn ich könnte, ginge ich morgen zurück', 30 December 2019.

503 Li, p. 59.

504 Hamilton/Ohlberg.

505 Freedom House, *Democracy in Retreat*, Freedom in the World 2019,https://freedomhouse.org/report/freedom-world/2019/democracy-retreat.

506 Ibid., p. 1.

507 Ibid., p. 2.

508 Ibid., p. 2.

509 Ibid., p. 3. Süddeutsche Zeitung, Silke Bigalke, ‚Was zählt, sind seine Taten', 30. December 2020.

510 Cf. Süddeutsche Zeitung, Kurt Kister, ‚Konflikt der Zukunft', 4/5 June 2020.

511 Wheatley, Democracy, 2002, p. 234 quoted in Klabbers/Peters/Ulfstein, p. 276.

is no such norm in Asia. Only the preamble of the Charter of the Association of Southeast Asian Nations (ASEAN) of 2017 contains a commitment of the 'peoples of the member states' to adhere to democracy, the rule of law and human rights.[512] However, since only ten Southeast Asian nations are members not including China, this commitment is of limited scope. Equally, there is no organization of states in the Middle East promoting democracy. Also, at national level, no real democracies exist.

Most importantly, in contrast to the case of human rights, where there has been a proliferation of human rights treaties and human rights institutions with enforcement procedures, hardly any examples of democratic bodies exist at the international level. At regional level, there are parliamentary committees in EU regional trade agreements such as the CARIFORUM EU Economic Partnership Agreement or at the Council of Europe, the 'Parliamentary Assembly'.[513] It is however questionable whether the creation of such institutions would result in democratic decision-making at global level, since such committees only have been accorded consultative status, i.e. they do not have decision-making power.[514] Even the EU Parliament, which is certainly an exception in international governance, has only been accorded real decision-making power under the Treaty of Lisbon of 2012, Art. 289 TFEU. Its right to propose legislation is limited to special cases., Art. 289 (III) TFEU. Thus, even the most advanced model of supranational democracy shows only slow progress. And, most notably, as the crisis of the EU and Brexit demonstrates, there is also the danger that people lose faith in international institutions and turn to nationalist movements if they do not feel themselves represented at an international level.

Legal scholarship holds that making international law more democratic seems to be difficult to realise at the moment if not impossible.[515] Some voices such as Meron however argue for an entitlement to democracy based in the human rights instruments.[516] Most legal scholars looking for new approaches to international law presented in this work consider creating a world parliament as utopian and not desirable.[517] Even Besson advocating global democracy through her model of *demoi*-cracy is of the view that 'a world state has

512 Cf. The ASEAN Charter, 27th Reprint, November 2019, https://asean.org/.

513 For a short discussion of the CARIFORUM-EU EPA, see Humbert (The Callenge of Child Labour), p. 264.

514 Ibid., p. 265; Klabbers/Ulfstein,/Peters, p. 323.

515 Wolfrum (Legitimacy in International Law), p. 812.

516 Meron, p. 490.

517 See above for example pp. 326 et seqq.

long be regarded as neither feasible nor desirable given the resilience of the national state and its key role in the global law-making process'.[518] Instead, what most theories reviewed here propose is to give NGOs, i.e. interest groups of affected people or devoted to issues such as alleviation of poverty in case of Oxfam, a voice in international governance and dispute settlement, to strengthen the possibility of judicial review including direct effect of e.g. WTO law and to involve internationally recognized experts as in the case of human rights committees.[519] Hence, a more promising way than defining democracy as a global value is to infer a principle of participation and representation of interest groups from a constitutional principle of the rule of law.[520]

On a cautious note, Besson mentions vaguely the possibility of imitating the model of the EU Parliament and to establish a supranational forum where democratic representation of peoples besides that of states and citizens may be experimented.[521] However, she also stresses that direct participation in decision-making is not needed all levels.[522] More importantly, the 'proximity of national institutions to individuals makes them a primary forum of direct legitimation in the global law-making process' and this is why 'the focus of institutional measures should be on enhancing the democratic quality of representation at the *national level first*'.[523]

Also rejecting a Global Peoples' Assembly as unlikely to happen due to practical reasons and states' reluctance,[524] Peters makes however proposals of establishing parliamentary assemblies at the UN or WTO as part of her model of dual democracy at national and global level, referring to proposals made by the EU Parliament.[525] Admitting that such assemblies would possibly only have consultative status and thus 'not produce tangible democratic output', she argues that the added value would be of promoting public debate and deliberation, dialogue and mediation with national parliaments, constituting 'a modest building block of democratization of global governance'.[526] In the same vein, she as well as Besson, proposes to give foreign affected interests a voice in national democratic deliberations through for example exchanging

518 Besson (Institutionalising global *demoi*-cracy), p. 66.

519 See for example Klabers/Peters/Ulfstein, pp. 235–240; Wolfrum (Legitimacy, Some Introductory Considerations), p. 24.

520 See below p. 368.

521 Besson (Institutionalising global *demoi*-cracy), p. 80.

522 Ibid., p. 81.

523 Ibid., p. 78.

524 Klabbers/Peters/Ulfstein, pp. 322 et seqq., p. 320.

525 Ibid., pp. 322 et seqq., p. 324.

526 Ibid., p. 326.

parliamentarians among states in parliamentary sessions.[527] However, Peters also rejects accepting new models of 'participatory', 'deliberative' or 'contestatory' democracy as substitute for formal democracy.[528] She rightly holds that all three models rely on deliberation instead of voting, the core of democracy. Also, all three models refer to 'communities of interest' of affected people and 'functional constituencies' represented for example through NGOs. The delineation of such functional constituencies is however very difficult.[529] Also, NGOs cannot represent affected people because they are not elected. Most importantly, in many countries, there is an increasing lack of organized civil society because such organizing come increasingly under threat, which as referred to as 'shrinking spaces'.[530] In sum, these models are 'too weak to deserve the label democracy'.[531]

In conclusion, many legal scholars agree that democracy is difficult to establish at global level. Importantly, while nowadays democracy is one important field of activity of the UN, and one of its core values, it is not among its purposes enumerated in Art. 1 of the UN Charter as are peace, security and human rights. Considering state practice and the lacking commitment of the Asian and Middle East region to democracy, as well as the democratic deficit of international institutions at the international level, it is not yet possible to qualify democracy as a global value and appropriate basis for a global legal order. However, the principles inherent in democracy such as transparency and accountability can probably well be taken account of under the principle of the rule of law, examined in turn.[532]

3.3.3 The Rule of Law

The rule of law as a domestic constitutional principle refers to the domestic legal system and requires that acts of governments, its administration and private actors are bound by legal rules and are subject to judicial review.[533] It also refers to legal predictability, proportionality and access to judicial remedy.[534] In Anglo-American legal systems, the rule of law also relates to due process

527 Besson (Institutionalising global *demoi*-cracy), p. 78; Klabbers/Peters/Ulfstein, pp. 301–302.
528 Klabbers/Peters/Ulfstein, p. 270.
529 Ibid.
530 See for example, Oxfam (Space to be heard).
531 Klabbers/Peters/Ulfstein, p. 271.
532 See also pp. 386 et seqq.
533 Nowak, p. 59.
534 Degenhardt, paras. 214–367.

and humanity and fairness.[535] Judicial independence is central for the rule of law.[536]

In the German context, the rule of law is known as the 'Rechtsstaatsprinzip' referring to substantive and formal aspects and in France, the concept of the 'État de droit' equally implies notions of human rights and the supremacy of the law.[537] While Chinese Confucianism is rather hostile to the rule of law, there was also a legalist movement aiming at a 'rule by law'.[538] Also the Arab legal system with its Code *Hammurabi* knows the notion of supremacy of the law.[539] Taking all these different aspects into account, legal literature has defined the rule of law as comprising three core elements, i.e. a government of laws, the supremacy of laws and equality before the law.[540]

The UN have defined the rule of law as: 'a principle of governance in which all persons, institutions and entities, public and private, including the State itself, are accountable to laws that are publicly promulgated, equally enforced and independently adjudicated, and which are consistent with international human rights norms and standards. It requires, as well, measures to ensure adherence to the principles of supremacy of law, equality before the law, accountability to the law, fairness in the application of the law, separation of powers, participation in decision-making, legal certainty, avoidance of arbitrariness and procedural and legal transparency'.[541] This definition is a more substantive definition comprising human rights consistency.

Is the rule of law then a recognized global value of the international legal order?

The rule of law is a cornerstone especially of international human rights law. Cognisant of the atrocities of the Holocaust, the preamble of the UDHR proclaims that 'it is essential, if man is not to be compelled to have recourse, as a last resort, to rebellion against tyranny and oppression, that human rights should be protected by the rule of law'. Art. 2 (2) of the ICCPR obligates states to adopt legislative measures in order to implement the rights contained in the ICCPR. So does Art. 2 (1) of the ICESCR. Art. 2 (3) para. (b) of the ICCPR obliges states to guarantee the right to judicial remedy in case of human rights violations. Due process clauses are for example contained Art. 9, 10 and 14 of

535 Nowak, p. 59.
536 Meron, p. 164.
537 Chesterman, p. 1015.
538 Ibid., p. 1016.
539 Ibid.
540 Ibid., p. 1014.
541 UN (The rule of law).

the ICCPR, referring to a 'fair and public hearing' and procedural requirements for criminal prosecution.[542]

Acknowledging that the UDHR still is mainly soft law, the question is whether the rule of law as protected by human rights law has found its way into domestic constitutions? As stated above, all states have ratified the ICCPR except for China. However, China is obliged under Art. 2 (1) of the ICESCR to introduce legislation regarding economic, social and cultural rights. Thus, while judicial review as protected by the ICCPR is not yet binding on all states, all states can be said to be bound by human rights law through one of the core human rights covenants. In addition, in 2004, China has amended its constitution and obliged itself to respect human rights under Art. 33 and the rule of law contained in Art. 5 of the Chinese constitution.[543] Thus, it can thus be said that the rule of law is a value recognized by a majority of domestic legal orders.

As regards state practice however, the rule of law is still being systemically violated in most parts of the world. According to the WFP Rule of Law Index 2020, the rule of law can be said to be almost fully observed only in about 20 countries worldwide.[544] These are mostly Western-European countries plus for example Canada and New Zealand.

It should be noted however that the UN has undertaken numerous efforts to improve the rule of law at domestic level. Many peace operations such as in Guatemala, Liberia and Haiti had the establishment of the rule of law among their objectives.[545] The various post-conflict tribunals such as the International Criminal Tribunal for the Former Yugoslavia, the International Tribunal for Rwanda, the Special Court for Sierra Leone, the Extraordinary Chambers in the Courts of Cambodia an others also had the aim of restoring peace and justice and establish the (re)-rule of law.[546]

Looking at judicial review at the international level, it can be observed that after the Second World War, there has been a proliferation of international tribunals including the ICJ, the WTO dispute settlement, the International Tribunal for the Law of the Sea and international criminal courts such as the International Criminal Court. Also, there are more and more appellate bodies available such as Appellate Body reflecting the increasing effectiveness of quasi-judicial review and more due process requirements.[547] However, with

542 See also Klabbers/Peters/Ulfstein, p. 128.

543 Li, p. 73.

544 See World Justice Project, *Rule of Law Index 2023* and the interactive map: WJP Rule of Law Index https://worldjusticeproject.org/rule-of-law-index/global.

545 Chesterman, p. 1018.

546 Ibid.

547 See Klabbers/Peters/Ulfstein, p. 128.

the exception of the ICC, such courts only have jurisdiction if states have subjected themselves to them voluntarily and do not accord standing to private persons. There is currently no international court of human rights with compulsory jurisdiction, where individuals can file cases of human rights violations against governments or companies. There are only regional human rights courts such as the European Court of Human Rights and international human rights treaty bodies providing for quasi-judicial complaints procedures that are not binding on states.[548]

With regard to international organizations themselves, it is still subject to debate to what extend they are bound by international law.[549] Neither the UN nor the WTO as major international organizations are subject to judicial review by individuals or their member states.[550]

In sum, the rule of law is guaranteed only to some extent by international law and often violated in practice. What does this mean for the recognition of the rule of law as a global value?

First of all, it should be noted that the rule of law can also be traced back to the very foundation of international law principle of *pacta sunt servanda* meaning that states are obliged by law, i.e. the treaties that they have consented to. Taking the natural law influence seriously, the rule of law should be accepted as a core value of the international legal order. Being a cornerstone of human rights law and comprising principles of fairness and due process, the rule of law can be said to be based on universal values deriving from humanity and ideas of justice. In the same way as the ICJ has qualified 'equity as a legal concept [...] a direct emanation of the idea of justice',[551] the rule of law can be said to lie at the heart of the concept of law and global justice, and must not be absent in any legal order aiming at global justice. If the Radbruch'sche formula, 'law is there to serve justice', is to be followed, independent judicial review is a central value of any legal order.[552] And in line with Dworkin, who holds that any theory of law must include as topics legislation and adjudication, any legal order should address questions of judicial justice. Calling it 'law of integrity', Dworkin holds that ideas of justice, fairness and procedural due

548 See for example Humbert (The Challenge of Child Labour in International Law), pp. 153–154.

549 Klabbers; Reinisch; Klabbers/Peters/Ulfstein, pp. 212–214.

550 Klabbers/Peters/Ulfstein., p. 215; Chesterman, p. 1019.

551 ICJ, Case Concerning the Continental Shelf (*Tunisia/Libyian Arab Jamahiriya*), Judgement ICJ Reports 1982, pp. 18–94, p. 60, https://www.icj-cij.org/decisions?type=1&from=1982&to=1982&sort_bef_combine=order_DESC.

552 Lachenmann, p. 789.

process are an integral part of the law that a judge has to apply.[553] He submits that law consists of a coherent set of principles based on political and moral considerations leaving aside arbitrary decisions.[554] Locating 'integrity' in 'fraternity', i.e. in humanity and solidarity, Dworkin bases his approach on natural law influences without taking recourse to metaphysics.[555] Equally emanating from human nature and ideas of justice, the rule of law should be recognized as a global value inherent in the global legal order.

In a similar vein, Koskenniemi has rightly stated that any plausible theory of international law should be between 'is' and 'ought to be', i.e. consist of a factual perspective that takes well into account what actually happens in the world and not ignores power relations, but also contain a critical normative perspective on the use of international power, being able to limit freedoms of international actors.[556] Thus, a new theory of law not promoting the rule of law would just confirm the status quo and stick to the private law paradigm of international law or even go back to the 'national interest' mantra. It would not have any added value and its use could be questioned.

3.4 *Core Elements of a New Legal Humanism*

3.4.1 Putting Humanity at the Centre of Law

Having established that human rights and the rule of law are universal values reflected by state practice and as such an additional basis of the global legal order, the next question is of course what does this mean? How to make use of such values? What does this mean in legal terms, does this have consequences for law creation and application?

Recalling that the main critique against the constitutionalist approach was the lack of global values, does the existence of universal values of international law confirm the constitutionalist approach by Peters arguing for the application of principles derived from domestic constitutional law to the global level?[557] Or the more cautious idea by Cottier and Kumm of a 'Five Storey House' or a 'constitutionalist cosmopolitan paradigm' where all the different governance layers together, as a whole, constitute the constitutional system?[558]

Considering that democracy has not been found a universal value inherent in the global order as yet, a moderate approach to constitutionalism seems

553 Dworkin (Integrity), p. 142.

554 Ibid., p. 142.

555 Cf. Dworkin (Taking Rights Seriously), p. xi.

556 Koskenniemi (International Legal Theory and Doctrine), p. 984.

557 See above pp. 326 et seqq.

558 Cottier/Hertig, p. 301.

appropriate. The current international legal order based on states does not appear to be ready for a fully-fledged constitutional or cosmopolitan approach but rather to evolve more in the direction of a multi-storey house proposed by Cottier or what Valentini has called a 'weak constitutionalism' or a system of coercion subject to everyone's freedom with regard to supranational organizations.

The theory suggested in this study is a New Legal Humanism, i.e. a 'humanist approach' to international law, taking due account of the central importance of international human rights law and the individual human being as an additional source of international law. Put simply, such an approach highlights the natural law idea of putting humanity at the centre of international law. Recognizing that the existence of common values is proof of an international community and a growing constitutionalization, it builds upon the constitutionalist approach put forward by Peters, Cottier and other scholars while taking due account of current trend of retreat of democracy. Based on the thinking of 'humanists' of the Early Modern Age such as Gentili,[559] in contrast to pure legal positivism, it conveys a humanist idea where human beings are central. Legal humanists of the Early Modern Age analysed the Corpus civilius from Roman times and devised legal principles based on human values such as integrity, fairness and coherence, similar to what Dworkin has called its 'Law of Integrity'.[560] Also, a New Legal Humanism has the potential to reconcile Western legal philosophy with the Chinese political theory of communism and Marxism, the ‚real humanism', a categorical imperative to overthrow all systems where human beings are oppressed, and where the way is open to open to natural law and freedom of the human being.[561] The term Legal Humanism in contrast to 'constitutionalism' has the advantage to appeal to humanity rather than to Western political theory and is as such less contestable.

3.4.2 Legal Consequences of a New Legal Humanism

The question then is, what does this mean for international law, having qualified human rights and the rule of law as universal values? What does it mean in practice, taking recourse to global values? In order to have a positive impact on the global legal order, the existence of such global values should certainly influence law creation and application and be part of a new theory of law.[562]

559 In Preiser p. 891: De legationibus libri tres, (OUP New York, 1924).

560 Walters; pp. 352–375.

561 Kaufmann (Problemgeschichte der Rechtsphilosophie), p. 68.

562 Kokott, p. 8.

3.4.2.1 *New Constitutional Principles*

Lacking a global legislator who turns societal values into domestic municipal or even constitutional law, at the international level Art. 38 (1) ICJ Statute enumerating the sources of international law is the appropriate place to incorporate global values into the legal order. Although Art. 38 (1) ICJ Statute is in theory only of a declaratory nature since it is the states who have decided on the list of sources for the ICJ to be applied, it nevertheless is still the main provision containing a list of the formal sources of international law.[563]

Considering that global values have been derived from a manifold variety of different sources beyond existing positive law such as natural law, i.e. philosophical considerations on human nature and ideas of justice, contributions from society such as statements of political and corporate decision makers, the Pope as well as NGOs, state practice and soft law by the UN and other international organizations, domestic constitutions and legal literature, an appropriate way to accommodate such values under Art. 38 (1) of the Statute of the ICJ seems to create a new source of 'constitutional principles' under a new lit. e. Since legal principles in the sense of Art. 38 (1) lit. c ICJ Statute already are regarded as entry points for natural law, devising a new form of principle of fundamental importance is feasible. The universal nature of global values, not only reflected in state practice but also grounded in philosophy and reflecting views of individuals as well as international actors, justifies their qualification as constitutional principles of international law.

This approach is all the more viable given that leading scholars hold that general legal principles already may be induced not only from *foro domestico* but from a wider variety of sources such as international law or even legal logic.[564] Some scholars already have suggested looking for an '*opinio juris communis*' or a 'common legal conscience' when taking recourse to general principles of law.[565] Most relevant is the rather recently articulated 'principle of common concern of humankind' relating to issues such as climate change, distribution of technology, compliance in the field of human rights, combating marine pollution and income inequality and migration.[566] Similar to the genesis of customary law where evidence of an *opinio iuris* is needed, a normative statement needs to be shown to be part of the 'common legal conscience' in

563 Wolfrum (Sources), p. 301; See also Shaw, p. 55 maintaining that Art. 38 1) ICJ Statute expresses the universal perception as to the enumeration of sources of international law.

564 See for example with further references: Cassese (International Law), p. 192; Verdross/Simma, pp. 384–387; Voigt, pp. 153–157; Wolfrum (Sources), p. 300.

565 Cheng; Voigt, pp. 156–159; Bluntschli, p. 65.

566 Cottier (The Principle of Common Concern of Humankind), pp. 82–83.

order to become a general legal principle of international law. Such an *opinion iuris communis* depends not only on the recognition by states but on a global consensus supported by a wider spectrum of actors including international organizations such as the WTO, IMF, IBRD as well as international NGOs, communities, indigenous peoples etc.[567] In general, NGOs are increasingly attributed an important role in the law-making process.[568]

In a similar sense Kleinlein has argued for emerging constitutional norms in the form of general principles taken from the international sphere.[569] Following a discursive paradigm based on international relations theory, he submits that processes of argumentative self-entrapment and identity change are fundamental for normativity. Put simply, he holds that the creation of general principles of law requires a critical mass of verbal practice, including statements by government officials, judicial decisions of international courts and tribunals and blaming and shaming campaigns by NGOs, as well as a changed self-conception of an actor, i.e. an international organization. In contrast to the legal humanist approach, he does not only conceive human rights and the rule of law but also democracy already as possible general principles of international law. What is more convincing is that Kleinlein regards constitutional norms as principles in a double sense, both with regard to sources, i.e. as general principles of international law, and as principles in terms of legal theory.[570] Such general principles in his view should work as principles of collision between different regimes of fragmented public international law and optimization requirements.[571] Discussing the main legal theories from Raz to Dworkin, Esser, Alexy and other prominent scholars on the difference between rules and principles, Kleinlein focusses on the function of principles as optimization requirements in international law in cases of conflicts.[572]

This approach sounds convincing and is exactly what is needed in the case of trade and human rights. Thus, the new constitutional principles should be applied to establish coherence between trade and human rights law. However, the effect of the constitutional principles proposed here should even be more far reaching. Having human rights law as a constitutional principle means that all international actors are bound by international human rights – of

567 Voigt, pp. 158–159.
568 Wolfrum (Sources), p. 308.
569 Kleinlein.
570 Ibid., p. 714.
571 Ibid., pp. 619 et seqq.
572 Kleinlein, p. 665 with further references such as Dworkin (Taking Rights Seriously), pp. 24 et seqq.

course subject to restrictions inherent in human rights law such as the principle of proportionality[573] and the 'Wesengehaltstheorie'.[574] Accordingly, any rule of international law should reflect these constitutional values and be in accordance with human rights and subject to judicial review. In this sense, the international order is constitutionalizing and states and international organizations should not be free anymore to conclude treaties or behave otherwise contrary to human rights or the rule of law.[575] Thus, dispute settlement bodies of international organizations would have to apply human rights law regardless of the applicability of Art. 31 (3) lit. c of the VCLT to provisions such as GATT XX (a). The merit would be that the constraints of Art. 31 (3) lit. c) of the VLCT referring only to binding treaties between the parties, and Art. 31 (1) of the VLCT treating ILO and UN Conventions as facts lacking normative value, would be surmounted. In the long run, a contextual approach combing GATT Art. III and XX, relaxing the threshold for unilateral trade measures on human rights seems to be feasible.[576] In a similar vein, Kaufmann has argued for a new 'principle of multi-level consistency' within the meaning of Art. 38 (1) lit. c of Art. 38 ICJ Statute to help to solve the conflict of core labour standards and international economic law.[577] Also Cottier's model of a multi-layered constitutionalism refers to 'constitutionalist principles'.[578]

Having established the rule of law including judicial review as a constitutional principle also means to classify the principle of proportionality as a constitutional principle.[579] As analysed above, the principle of proportionality already is firmly entrenched in WTO case law, where the WTO adjudicating bodies have proven to be ready to conduct an elaborated proportionality test including a process of weighing and balancing of the interests and values in question. The principle of proportionality also forms part of other areas of international law such as the law of countermeasures, Art. 51 of the Articles on State Responsibility and is of course at the heart of human rights law, Art. 2 (2) of the ICCPR, Art. 4 of the ICESCR and even more so at regional level in the case of the ECHR where limitations of fundamental rights have to be 'necessary in a democratic society' according to Art. 8–11. The important function

573 See below, p. 385.
574 See above, p. 368.
575 See Schermers/Blokker, § 1579, who argue that international organizations are bound by customary law.
576 See above, p. 181.
577 Kaufmann (Globalization and Labour Rights), pp. 284–294.
578 Cottier/Delimatsis/Gehne/Payosova, p. 35.
579 See also, Cottier/Echandi/Liechti-McKee/Payosova/Sieber.

of the principle of proportionality is its ability to make different interests and values compatible, thereby contributing to overcome fragmentation of international law and achieve coherence. As discussed above, it has a constitutionalist function and can be said to have contributed to a modest constitutionalization of the WTO.[580] This important function has also been recognized by Peters who qualified the principle of proportionality as a global constitutional principle.[581] Referring to Mureinik, a constitutional lawyer from South Africa, she emphasizes the potential of the principle of proportionality to help establish a 'culture of justification' instead of a 'culture of authority' in international law.[582]

Giving full effect to the constitutional principle of the rule of law also means, in line with the rule of law definition of the UN, to ensure adherence to the principles of supremacy of law, equality before the law, accountability to the law, fairness in the application of the law, separation of powers, participation in decision-making, legal certainty, avoidance of arbitrariness and procedural and legal transparency also at the international level.[583] Thus, instead of asking for democratic processes at the international level, individual actors such as NGOs, community interest groups, trade unions and industry associations or corporations should be given a role in international decision-making through for example appropriate advisory boards, thereby achieving accountability and transparency in international decision-making. As required by Kumm, such procedural requirements in decision-making would ensure that decision-makers take due account of constituents' concerns.[584] Thus, the principle of transparency and accountability can be said also be said to be part of the set of global values and a 'New Legal Humanism'.

3.4.2.2 *New Legal Subjects and Judicial Review*

Taking the idea of having human rights and the rule of law as constitutional principles seriously means to devise a global law providing for new avenues for judicial review and new doctrines of international legal personality[585] and direct effect with the following consequences.

580 See above p. 221.
581 Peters (Proportionality).
582 Ibid., p. 262.
583 Cf. UN (The Rule of Law).
584 Cf. Kumm (The Legitimacy of International Law), p. 926.
585 For an extensive elaboration of the doctrine of the international legal personality of the human being see Peters (Beyond Human Rights), pp. 35–59.

Firstly, human beings should be accorded true international legal capacity, i.e. they should be recognized as genuine right-holders, independently of international treaty law, and be able to defend their rights before international courts or tribunals in the same way as corporations for example under NAFTA in investment disputes. The former judge of the ICJ Higgins already in 1997 observed a reformation in international law regarding the status of the individual.[586] Equally, eminent scholars such as Jennings and Watts have for a long time observed that international law recognizes individuals as legal subjects in limited circumstances. Jennings and Watts also held that states may confer upon individuals international rights, which citizens may enforce directly before international courts.[587] This approach has been elaborated on by many authors including Peters who has propagated a new doctrine of international legal personality of the human being.[588] With a view to the current lack of true international enforcement possibilities of individual rights, she rightly holds that the existence of an individual right is independent of the actual procedural ability of the rights-holder to enforce the right in court.[589] She submits that the international legal personality of human beings is rooted in Art. 16 of the ICCPR and forms a general principle of law.[590]

With a view to the problem of trade and child labour, according individuals and thus children international legal personality and devising an international procedure by reforming ILO complaints procedures and WTO dispute settlement so as to make children's rights actionable seems to be a possible was forward. For example, affected children by governments failing to tackle child labour could be offered access to judicial remedy before an international trade and labour court. NGOs protecting children's rights could also be accorded locus standi before such a court. The question here is whether exhaustion of local remedies is required and what the adequate legal remedies are.

Taking the rule of law and judicial review as new constitutional principles seriously also means that human rights should have direct effect in domestic law so as to make for example children's rights fully actionable in domestic courts. With regard to child labour, Art. 10 (3) of the ICESCR prohibiting the economic exploitation of child labour has been held to be suited to judicial

586 Higgins, pp. 213 et seqq.

587 Jennings/Watts, Oppenheim's International Law, pp. 846–847.

588 Peters (Beyond Human Rights).

589 Ibid., p. 46.

590 Ibid., p. 8.

determination.[591] The question is whether this also hold true for other human rights and ILO norms prohibiting child labour and what criteria should be used to define direct effect. Cottier suggests that a direct effect of international treaty norms should not only depend on whether they are considered sufficiently precise ('Bestimmtheit') but also on where courts in line of the separation of powers doctrine are able to resolve the case adequately, which should generally be the case because such interpretation is their core business.[592]

Other questions that need to be answered include: should General Comments and jurisprudence by human rights committees take precedence over national law and jurisprudence when defining human rights? And what is the consequence for human rights law and the jurisprudence of the treaty bodies in case of contradicting national court decisions? Is it feasible to establish an international court on human rights with the possibility to make binding rulings along the lines of the ECHR? What about the possibility to give preliminary rulings or even the capacity to set aside national court decisions or administrative measures? In Germany, courts have to 'take note of and consider the relevant case law of the international courts with jurisdiction for Germany'.[593] All these issues questions will be discussed further in the next chapter on legal implications of a New Legal Humanism.

3.4.2.3 *Human Rights Obligation for Companies?*

Another possibility to make children and human rights more effective is to impose human rights obligations on companies and to provide for an international procedure for example under the ILO under which victims of human rights violations could submit complaints.[594] The past of the UN Norms on the Responsibilities of Transnational Corporations and other Business Enterprises with regard to Human Rights made such proposal and provided for direct obligations for companies to respect human rights.[595] As to their enforcement, it has indeed been proposed the ILO could adopt individual complaints

591 Committee on Economic, Social and Cultural Rights, 'General Comment No. 3', in UN Compilation of General Comments and General Recommendations adopted by Human Rights Treaty Bodies, HRI/GEN/1/Rev. 7, 12 May 2004, p. 15, para. 10.

592 Cottier (Theory of Direct Effect). For a further discussion of direct effect of international law, see below p. 397.

593 BVerfG, Decision by the First Chamber of the Second Senate, 19 September 2006, -2 BvR 2115/01-, para. 43, http://www.bverfg.de/e/rk20060919_2bvr211501.html.

594 Humbert (The Challenge of Child Labour), pp. 218–226, pp. 337–339.

595 UN Sub-Commission on the Promotion and Protection of Human Rights, E/CN.4/Sub.2/2003/12/Rev.2.

procedures for enforcing human rights.[596] Taking due account of the increasing importance of transnational corporations and their impact on the daily life of the global population, it seems reasonable to oblige them directly by human rights treaties.[597] Whether this a feasible option will be discussed in the last chapter.

3.4.2.4 *Enforcement through Private Law*

A New Legal Humanism should also accommodate and support helpful ideas from legal pluralist or private law approaches to international law that suggest using conflict law and transnational private litigation for better global governance.[598] Put simply, the constitutional principle of human rights means that states have a legal duty to hold companies accountable for human rights violations abroad. Such a duty is already enshrined in principles 24 and 25 of the Maastricht Principles of 2011 and with regard to children's rights confirmed by Comment No. 16 of the Children's rights Committee.[599]

Thus, along the lines of the French *loi de vigilance*, domestic civil law could establish a corporate human rights due diligence duty and hold companies responsible for human rights violations committed abroad.[600] What elements such laws should have and how states should be obliged to implement such law will be discussed in the last chapter.

3.4.2.5 *Multi-level Governance*

Finally, the theory of a New Legal Humanism presupposes and supports the idea of a 'multi-storey house' or a 'cosmopolitan constitutionalist paradigm' by respectively Cottier and Kumm in the sense of a global integration law. The conclusion that the global legal order is based on constitutional principles suggests that this order constitutes one legal system that influences national law and cannot be separated from it. To give full effect to the constitutional principles of human rights and the rule of law including judicial review, national and international law have to complement each other and should be conceived as belonging to be one global order. As rightly held by Cottier,

596 Weissbrodt/Kruger, p. 917.

597 See for example Oxfam Germany/Heinrich Boell-Stiftung et al (Konzernatlas); Oxfam (Ripe for Change).

598 For a global legal pluralism see above pp. 310 et seqq.

599 Cf. de Schutter/Eide//Khalfan/Orellana/Salomon/ Seidermann; Committee on Children's Rights, General Comment No. 16 (2013), CRC/C/GC/16, Nr. 39–46, 53 and 62–65.

600 French *loi de viligilance*; for proposals under German law, see Klinger/Krajewski/Krebs/Hartmann and Initiative Lieferkettengesetz, Drillisch/Humbert/Leifker/Saage-Maaß.

a constitutional doctrine will and should work towards common institutions of dispute settlement and interaction of international institutions.[601] In his view, the dualist doctrine has had profound influence on current conceptions of direct effect and points to von Bogdandy who suggests that monism and dualism should cease to exist as doctrinal and theoretical notions for discussing the relationship between international and national law.[602] Also under a New Legal Humanism, human rights and especially the international prohibition of child labour as well as WTO law should in principle be accorded direct effect in domestic national orders. Other authors also argue in favour of overcoming dualism and establishing a form of judicial federalism where the national courts refer to international law.[603] Kumm, commenting on the *Görgülü* decision[604] by the German Constitutional Court and the resulting German constitutional duty to duly consider the ECHR and relevant jurisprudence, also rightly stated that 'within the cosmopolitan paradigm some form of cooperation between national and international courts is a natural corollary to a conception of rights that is universal and connected to public reason'.[605] Howse and Nicolaidis however strongly oppose such ideas of what they call a 'European "Federal Vision" alternative'.[606] They fear that a constitutionalization of the WTO driven by the judicial branch would necessarily lead to a libertarian bias in favour of trading rights.[607] However, under a New Legal Humanism, human rights would also have in principle direct effect and would be balanced against such trading rights. The issue of direct effect of human rights and trade law will be elaborated below when discussing more thoroughly the legal implications of a New Legal Humanism.[608]

Following the rather monist approach of a multi-storey house, the New Legal Humanism also offers help to overcome the lack of democratic processes at the international level. Since democracy cannot be conceived as constitutional principle of the global order, the submitted lack of democratic process should be compensated for with more transparency and participation at the domestic level in case of democratic regimes. For example, when international

601 Cottier (Trade and Human Rights), p. 130.

602 Cottier (The Impact of Justiciability), p. 308 and fn. 6.

603 Dupuy, p. 858.

604 BVerfGE 111, 307, para. 30, Decision of the Second Chamber of the Senate, 14 October 2004, 2 BvR 1481/04, https://www.bundesverfassungsgericht.de/SharedDocs/Entscheidungen/DE/2004/10/rs20041014_2bvr148104.html.

605 Kumm (The Cosmopolitan Turn in Constitutionalism), p. 310.

606 Howse/Nicolaidis, pp. 325–331; See also above, p. 336.

607 Ibid., p. 328.

608 See below p. 397.

trade agreements are drafted that impact on human rights and affect consumer interests, states should be more transparent and participatory by allowing open debate and parliamentary participation already when making treaties. And of course, the fact that for example new trade agreements must be in consistency with human rights provides another safeguard.[609]

Another example where democratic processes at national level can help to remedy the lack of democratic processes at the international level is standard setting within the meaning of Art. 2.4 of the TBT Agreement. When drafting standards within the meaning of Art. 2.4 of the TBT Agreement, WTO members should be subject to parliamentary approval and be transparent on the content of the standard. Otherwise, private standards negotiated by the ISO could become binding on WTO members through the back door, circumventing the legislative process and infringing democratic principles such as the separation of powers and the will of the people.

Conceiving international and national law as one integrated global legal order raises of course the question of what issue has to be decided at what level of such a 'multi-storey house'. An answer lies in one of the cornerstones of EU law, the principle of subsidiarity contained in Art. 5 (3) of the TEU, which Peters considers as a general principle of international law and which is central to the cosmopolitan constitutional paradigm elaborated by Kumm.[610] In a nutshell, the principle of subsidiarity means to carefully analyse whether there is a collective action problem that has to be decided at international level, and duly assess whether the reasons for deciding at the international level weigh more than reasons for deciding at national level.[611] It shall be held with Cottier and Jackson that

> Sovereignty-modern thus stands for the proposition of vertical and horizontal separation of powers and checks and balances.[612]

---

609 For further discussion, see Cottier (The Changing Structure of International Trade Law); Cottier (Front-loading), pp. 35–60; Cottier (Der Strukturwandel des Aussenwirtschaftsrechts).

610 Peters (Beyond Human Rights), p. 483; Kumm (The Cosmopolitan Turn in Constitutionalism), p. 295.

611 Kumm (The Cosmopolitan Turn in Constitutionalism), p. 295.

612 Cottier (John H. Jackson, Sovereignty-Modern), p. 324; See also Jackson (Sovereignty).

3.4.2.6 *Climate Change and Other Topics of Common Concern?*

The question is of course whether the New Legal Humanism is able to offer solutions for how to deal with other global problems such as climate change seriously threating humankind.[613] Since climate change affects nearly every aspect of human lives, with implications for a broad range of human rights — including but not limited to the rights to life, health, food, housing, and water – and, because of its long-term and irreversible impacts, it disproportionately affects the rights of children, young people, and future generations,[614] the constitutional principle of human rights is certainly able to help to remedy such concerns. For example, it may help to shape national and international measures to mitigate and adapt to climate change. Equally, other topics of common concern to humankind such as income inequality and marine pollution adversely impacting human rights may also be addressed by taking recourse to the constitutional principle of human rights. Equally, such topics could also be found to constitute a new (constitutional) principle in its own right. However, how this could look like and how exactly such constitutional principle relates to a future principle of common concern of humankind is beyond the scope of this work and will be left to future legal scholarship.

The humanist approach to international law and its concrete legal implications will be tested in the next chapter looking at the case of child labour and trade measures. The crucial question is whether this approach is able to offer help for the identified shortcomings under the current approach to international law and a feasible option for the future not belonging to utopia.

3.4.3 Potential Critique

One potential critique to a New Legal Humanism shall be briefly addressed here. As already mentioned above, human rights, the rule of law and democracy are intrinsically linked. The human right to vote is protected under Art. 25 of the ICCPR. Human rights can hardly be defended in an autocracy where the rule of law is suppressed. And democracy presupposes the existence of human rights. How can human rights and the rule of law then exist as a global constitutional principle if firstly, democracy is globally in retreat and secondly, true democratic processes in terms of electoral accountability are not feasible at global level? Two arguments can be raised. The first one is that many autocracies at least to some extent respect social and economic human rights, for example China. Hence, autocracies and human rights do not completely

613 Cf. Cottier (The Principle of Common Concern of Humankind).

614 German Institute for Human Rights/CIEL, p. 13.

exclude each other. The second one relates to the 'multi-storey house'-aspect of the New Legal Humanism. If national and international law are conceived as one legal system, electoral processes do not need to be established at all levels. On the global level, keeping the peace is of overriding interest and importance while direct participation dominates on the local and national levels. Democratic states should ensure at national level that civil servants representing democratically elected governments draft treaties that in turn must be ratified by the legislative. To ensure that the interests of people are duly considered when drafting treaties, the constitutional principle of the rule of law should make sure that the drafting process is sufficiently transparent and participatory at national and international level. Most importantly, subjecting international law adopted by international institutions to judicial review will help to protect citizens' human rights and compensate for a global legislator. Finally, participation of new individual legal subjects such as human beings and civil society in international decision-making will make sure that interests of affected people will be considered and contribute to reducing the lack of democratic processes.

CHAPTER 4

Implications of a New Legal Humanism for Trade and Child Labour

1 Introduction

This chapter explores how the constitutional principles of human rights and the rule of law emanating from a humanist approach to international law can help to remedy the identified shortcomings of the current legal order for the solution of the problem of trade and child labour. To recall, despite of possible compatibility of national trade measures on child labour with WTO law, this study concluded that under current international law, the lack of substantive coherence of the trade and human rights, the denial of access to justice for private actors and institutional questions such as the missing collaboration of the WTO and ILO have been found to be among the obstacles for an adequate protection of children from child labour and suggested to devise a joint ILO-WTO agreement.[1] Hence, this chapter starts by briefly summarizing how the constitutional principles of human rights and the rule of law can improve the coherence of WTO law with human rights. This will be followed by a discussion of the issue of direct effect of WTO-law and human rights, in particular the international prohibition of child labour. Drawing on existing recommendations for an ILO-WTO enforcement regime *de lege ferenda* by Humbert,[2] the remainder of the chapter will examine how a humanist approach to international law can help to devise such a regime. The question of whether companies should be direct duty-bearers of human rights under international law and possibly liable under transnational civil or criminal law will also be dealt with briefly. Most importantly, the chapter will examine how vertical and horizontal collaboration between the different actors should look like, i.e. on what principles multi-level governance under a New Legal Humanism will be based.

1 See above, pp. 304 et seqq.

2 Humbert (The Challenge of Child Labour), pp. 376–385.

2 Towards More Substantive Coherence of Trade and Human Rights Law

As discussed in Chapter 2 and 3, the new constitutional principles of human rights protection and of the rule of law should be applied to establish coherence between trade and human rights law. Having the effective protection of human rights law as a constitutional principle implies that all subjects of international law are bound by international human rights., i.e. including international organizations. In case of national measures on child labour, when applying GATT Art. XX (a), the WTO adjudicating bodies would have to refer to human rights law even if Art. 31 (3) lit. c of VCLT was found not to be fulfilled for example on the ground that the party to the dispute was not a party to the human rights convention referred to. Rather than treating ILO and UN human rights conventions as facts under the 'ordinary meaning' of Art. 31 (1) of the VCLT, the added value of having human rights as a constitutional principle is that human rights norms would be treated as normative rules. Art. 3.2 DSU on the jurisdiction of WTO adjudicating bodies would thus include human rights as a constitutional principle of the international order and could not be used as an argument to exclude the application of human rights treaties. Admittedly, in case of the right to protection from child labour as a norm of *ius cogens*, Art. 31 (1) of the VCLT, this would not pose such a problem because *ius cogens* norms apply *erga omnes*, and would to taken into account in any event. However, it is the merit of the New Legal Humanism that the doctrine of the sometimes-controversial issue of *ius cogens* is no longer needed because the core human rights are part of the new constitutional principle.[3] Also, in accordance with German doctrine of the 'Wesensgehalt', there is a core of every human right that must not be affected and thus of overriding interest.[4]

The constitutional principle of international human rights protection would also help to solve the question of extraterritoriality regarding GATT Art. XX (a) allowing for a reading in favour of trade measures aimed at improving human rights abroad. Referring to the Art. 48 (1) b) of the Articles on State Responsibility allowing for countermeasures in case of violations *erga omnes* 'owed to the community as a whole' it would be possible in case of violations of human rights recognised as a constitutional principle, that countermeasures apply to all states regardless of their status as customary law or norms of *ius cogens*. Of course, the elaborated necessity test developed by the WTO

3 See above p. 367 et seq. and also Cottier (Improving Compliance: *Jus Cogens* and International Law).

4 See above, p. 368.

adjudicating bodies in its rich case law would not be set aside. To the contrary, it would be reinforced by the constitutional principle of proportionality inherent in restrictions of human rights, reinforcing the modest constitutionalization in WTO case law when reconciling trade interests with societal values.[5] The new approach would however offer more legal predictability and coherent decision-making by obliging the WTO adjudicating bodies to refer to human rights law and the vast jurisprudence, including General Comments by human rights treaty and ILO bodies. In particular in all those cases, where no explicit entry point in the text of WTO law for human rights exists, and where WTO case law does not give clear instructions how to interpret a provision, the constitutional principle of human rights would make it clear that the relevant provision would have to be construed in such a way as to reconcile trade objectives and human rights. The constitutional principle of human rights would come in when trying to argue that the *bona fide* aim of human rights of a national measure should be taken into account under GATT Art. III when trade effects are unclear. In the long run, the constitutional reading could be used to apply the contextual approach in case of origin-neutral measures, whereby Art. III and GATT Art. XX are combined and a necessity and proportionality test is done when examining the discriminatory nature of the measure under GATT Art. III.[6] This would have the merit that the *bona fide* objective will be fully taken account of and have the same relevance as the trade-restrictiveness of the measure, being scrutinized both already under the equal treatment obligation. Members would not have to rely on exceptions to defend their trade measures but on their non-discriminatory nature, which would increase the political feasibility of trade measures with human rights or environmental objectives. Also, there would be no doubt anymore that human rights are one of the 'legitimate objectives' under 2.2 of the TBT Agreement when it comes to the justification of the measure. Equally, the GPA would also have to be read in the light of human rights norms even if entry points are missing. The Doha Decision of 2001 on the right to health and intellectual property is a precedent where trade rules were trumped by the human right to health.[7]

---

5 See above, p. 221.

6 See above, p. 181.

7 Doha WTO Ministerial 2001: TRIPS WT/MIN(01)/DEC/2, 20 November 2001, Declaration on the TRIPS agreement and public health, https://www.wto.org/english/thewto_e/minist_e/min01_e/mindecl_trips_e.htm.

3 Direct Effect of WTO-Law and Human Rights

3.1 *The Traditional Doctrine of Direct Effect*

Taking the rule of law and judicial review as new constitutional principles seriously also means that WTO-law and human rights, in particular the prohibition of child labour in accordance with Art. 32 of the CRC and the provisions of ILO Conventions No. 138 and 182, should be made fully actionable in domestic courts. Put differently, they should have direct effect or be self-executing so that a domestic body, a public authority or court, is authorized to apply the norm without further legislation.[8] The same should hold true for the trade provisions benefitting individuals contained in the proposed agreement. Only an effective enforcement through domestic courts can ensure the enjoyment of individual rights.[9] It is however subject to debate whether international law can stipulate direct effect.

According to the traditional view in domestic and international legal literature and practice, the question of direct effect is primarily a question of domestic law, unless settled by international agreement.[10] Although theories of dualism and monism rather concern the question whether an international treaty norm forms part of the domestic legal order,[11] the dualist doctrine has had profound influence on current conceptions of direct effect.[12] In Anglo-American law and EC law, only those rules of international law can be relied upon by individuals before domestic courts that were given direct effect or were self-executing in the sense that they benefit individuals or granted a cause of action and did not require implementation by domestic legislation in order to become domestically operational and effective.[13] Under EC case law for example, the well-established test for such a 'justiciability' of the norm is whether the norm is sufficiently precise for having direct effect, thereby focussing on the text and structure of the norms and their technical suitability.[14] The ECJ in *Fruchthandelsgesellschaft mbH Chemnitz v. Commission of the European Communities* has stated:

8 For an explanation of the different usages of the terms, see Engelberger, p. 151, fn. 590 with further references; Peters (Beyond Human Rights), p. 496.

9 Peters (Beyond Human Rights), p. 495.

10 Wüger, pp. 22–23; Peters (Beyond Human Rights), p. 497; Cottier (The Judge in International Economic Relations), pp. 109 et seqq.

11 Wüger, p. 5; Peters (Beyond Human Rights), pp. 500–501.

12 Cottier (The Impact of Justiciability), p. 308.

13 Cottier (The Impact of Justiciability), p. 308; Peters (Beyond Human Rights), p. 495.

14 Cottier (A Theory of Direct Effect), p. 105; Peters (Beyond Human Rights), p. 495.

> in order for a provision to have direct effect on a person other than the addressee, that provision must impose on the addressee an unconditional and sufficiently clear and precise obligation vis-à-vis the person concerned.[15]

However, in an era of increasing global integration and even more so under the proposed approach of a New Legal Humanism, direct effect of international law should be the rule. Especially in the case of human rights, it is of utmost importance that individuals across the globe have access to justice and can fully enjoy their rights under international law.

3.1.1 Child Labour and Human Rights

The question of direct effect of human rights meets with less resistance than for example WTO law. This is because one of the major counter-arguments stressed by the ECJ in *Portugal v. Council*,[16] the principle of reciprocity, is less affected. While it is certainly true that interstate obligations 'continue to govern the matter' of human rights,[17] such obligations arise *erga omnes*, which expresses the collective interest in their implementation. This is different to reciprocity and the reason why some scholars call human rights obligations 'integral'.[18] Country A would not be entitled to violate human rights of citizens of Country B because Country B has violated human rights of citizens Country A.[19] Accordingly, at least from an international law perspective, and because human rights are to be applied in *foro domestico*, it has been held that individuals should in principle be able to invoke them directly before the public organs of the concerned country including courts.[20] The debate here rather focusses on the question whether human rights are too vague or general in content to always have direct effect.[21] Tomuschat in his function of a being member of the HRC however has clearly stated with regard to the ICCPR that

15 European Court of Justice, T-254/97 [1999] ECR II-2743, para. 29, https://eur-lex.europa.eu/legal-content/HR/TXT/?uri=CELEX:61997TJ0254.

16 European Court of Justice, Case C-149/96, *Portugal v. Council*, [1999] ECR I-8395, paras. 43–46, https://eur-lex.europa.eu/legal-content/EN/TXT/HTML/?uri=ecli:ECLI:EU:C:1999:574.

17 Simma (Sources of International Human Rights Law), p. 881.

18 Dupuy, p. 854.

19 Ibid.

20 Dupuy, p. 854.

21 Ibid.; Wüger, p. 149.

> even in a country which has not made the Covenant part of its domestic law, individuals should have the right directly to invoke its provisions before domestic courts.[22]

As regards the ICESCR, its direct effect and justiciability has been questioned because of its obligation contained in Art. 2 (1) providing for the progressive realisation of the rights to the maximum of each party's available resources.[23] However, also here, the Committee on Economic, Social and Cultural Rights has clarified that a 'minimum threshold approach' has to be applied so that at least the core of the specific rights are subject to immediate implementation.[24] Most importantly for the purpose of this study, Art. 10 (3) of the ICESCR prohibiting the economic exploitation of children has been held to be suited to judicial determination.[25] The same goes for the fundamental ILO conventions including those on the prohibition of child labour No. 138 and 182.[26]

Moreover, norms of *ius cogens* because of their mandatory nature are held to have direct effect especially if they protect individuals as in the case of the prohibition of slavery.[27] Since the prohibition of child labour under international law can be said to be a modern form of slavery and as such part of *ius cogens*,[28] it should be accorded direct effect.

Finally, there is the argument of the local remedy rule. The international legal requirement of the exhaustion of local remedies before submitting individual complaints to the CESRC or the Committee of the Rights of the Child presupposes that local remedies are available.[29] This requirement makes perfect sense because national courts generally have the necessary local knowledge and can contribute with national experience and cultural conceptions.[30] With regard to direct effect, Peters rightly concludes that this requirement should also apply *vice versa*, i.e. to oblige states parties to make local remedies

22 Yearbook of the HRC (1977–78) para. 183 quoted in Tomuschat (Human Rights), p. 175.

23 Humbert (The Challenge of Child Labour), p. 65; Cf. also Wüger pp, 100–101, 415.

24 Committee on Economic, Social and Cultural Rights, 'General Comment No. 3', in UN Compilation of General Comments and General Recommendations adopted by Human Rights Treaty Bodies, HRI/GEN/1/Rev. 7, 12 May 2004, p. 15, para. 10; see also Emmerich-Fritsche, p. 555.

25 Committee on Economic, Social and Cultural Rights, 'General Comment No. 3', para 5.

26 Emmerich-Fritsche, p. 556. The fundamental ILO conventions are those contained in the ILO Declaration on Fundamental Principles and Rights at Work, see Humbert (The Challenge of Child Labour), p. 103.

27 Wüger, p. 91.

28 Humbert (The Challenge of Child Labour), pp. 114–119.

29 Nowak, p. 185.

30 Klabbers/Peters/Ulfstein (The Constitutionalization of International Law), p. 145.

available, otherwise the quasi-judicial procedures by these Committees would be meaningless. It follows that domestic courts have to be entitled to apply human rights law.

With regard to the domestic perspective, national courts such as the Swiss Federal Court already have applied the CRC in various cases.[31] In the *Görgülü* decision, the German Constitutional Court established a constitutional duty engage with ECHR.[32] Specifically, it held that domestic courts have to consider international norms according to the interpretation given by an international court, otherwise the relevant fundamental right under the Basic Law in conjunction with the rule of law would be violated.[33] Peters therefore rightly held that 'in a multi-level system, the domestic courts are the functional equivalent of international courts and arbitration bodies ("dédoublement fonctionnel")'.[34]

Court decisions such as *Milieudefensie v. Shell, Okpabi v. Royal Dutch Shell* and *Nevsun v. Araya*, 28 February 2020, confirm this trend to consider international human rights legislation in national jurisprudence. Specifically, the Dutch court in Shell held that:

> In its interpretation of the unwritten standard of care, the court follows the UN Guiding Principles (UNGP). The UNGP constitute an authoritative and internationally endorsed 'soft law' instrument, which set out the responsibilities of states and businesses in relation to human rights.[35]

In *Okpabi v. Shell Royal Dutch Shell*, the court's analysis highlights the growing importance of more active corporate governance, due diligence and internal controls for effectively managing significant human rights and environmental corporate risks.[36] In *Nevsun v. Araya*, the majority of the judges:

31 See Wüger for further references, pp. 398.

32 *Görgülü v. Germany (2004)*, BVerfGE 111, 307, 2 BvR 1481/04, Decision of the Second Chamber of the Senate, 14 October 2004, paras. 30, 62, https://www.bundesverfassungs gericht.de/SharedDocs/Entscheidungen/DE/2004/10/rs20041014_2bvr148104.html2.

33 Ibid., para. 63.

34 Peters (Beyound Human Rights), p. 487.

35 *Milieudefensie v. Royal Dutch Shell PLC*, The Hague (ECLI:NL:RBDHA:2021:5339), C/09/ 571932 / HA ZA 19–379, 26/05/2021, https://uitspraken.rechtspraak.nl/#!/details?id=ECLI: NL:RBDHA:2021:5339. para. 4.4.11.

36 White & Case, *Okpabi v Royal Dutch Shell Plc*: UK Supreme Court allows Nigerian citizens' environmental damage claim to proceed against UK parent company (2021), https: //www.whitecase.com/insight-alert/okpabi-v-royal-dutch-shell-plc-uk-supreme-court-all ows-nigerian-citizens.

> The majority recognized states as traditionally the main subjects of international law. Yet, in its view, international law has evolved from its purely sovereigntist origins such that it now extends, at least partially, to individuals and nonstate entities. Nonetheless, it acknowledged that "because some norms of international law are of a strictly interstate character, the trial judge will have to determine whether the specific norms relied on" are applicable to other nonstate entities (para. 113).[37]

To summarize, international law already legally requires that as a norm of *ius cogens,* the prohibition of child labour has to be applied by domestic courts and public authorities. Also, with regard to domestic law, domestic courts for instance in Germany and Switzerland already apply international human rights law and the CRC so that the assumption of direct effect of the prohibition of child labour should not meet with objections.

The humanist reading of international law confirms this approach and takes it a little bit further by establishing that all internationally recognized human rights contained in international conventions beyond *ius cogens* shall have direct effect and be invokable by domestic bodies. Some authors object to assigning direct effect to all human rights and prefer a division of labour between courts and legislature.[38] However, as has been said above, the international local remedy rule would not make sense if certain human rights could not be invoked before national courts. Most importantly, all human rights treaty organs have produced extensive jurisprudence and General Comments.[39] Even if some human rights are open-textured, courts are able to determine their content with the help of this rich case law. In accordance with the German 'Wesensgehaltstheorie', at least their core is justiciable.[40] Moreover, national legislation increasingly refers to 'human rights' without further explanation. One example is the French *loi de vigilance*,[41] another the Non-Financial Reporting Directive 2014/95/EU[42] and the German law implementing

37 Supreme Court of Canada (*Nevsun v. Araya*), 28 February 2020, 2020 SCC 5, Case No. 37919, para. 113; https://decisions.scc-csc.ca/scc-csc/scc-csc/en/item/18169/index.do.

38 Wüger, p. 101.

39 See for example Human Rights Treaty Bodies, General Comments https://www.ohchr.org/EN/HRBodies/Pages/TBGeneralComments.aspx.

40 See p. 368.

41 See above p. 9.

42 Directive 2014/95/EU of the European Parliament and of the Council of 22 October 2014 amending Directive 2013/34/EU as regards disclosure of non-financial and diversity information by certain large undertakings and groups L330/1.

it.[43] In that sense, the term 'human rights' does not differ from other legal terms that lawyers have to construe in line with existing jurisprudence. In an integrated global legal order, dialogue between courts and treaty bodies should be possible and part of routine.

The final question however is to what extent the rule of precedent applies and national courts can contradict existing international human rights case law, in other words in what way a hierarchy of courts should be established. Under the humanist approach, the protection of human rights against the misuse of power and the interest of the human being should be the central objective. Accordingly, national courts should in principle follow the case law and General Comments of the human rights treaty bodies along the lines of the German 'duty of engagement'. 'Views' of the human rights treaty bodies should be binding on national courts and public authorities. Only where international human rights treaty bodies evidently violate human rights, national courts should be authorized to decide otherwise.

3.1.2 WTO Law

Direct effect of WTO law meets with much more resistance. The US Congress has barred US courts from applying WTO law.[44] As stated above, referring to the principle of reciprocity, the ECJ has also denied in principle direct effect to WTO law.[45] Japan provides another example of the difficulty many WTO members have in accepting that international treaties take precedence over domestic laws when it comes to WTO law.[46] The question of whether WTO law should have direct effect is relevant for this study, because the proposed ILO-WTO Agreement will provide for the possibility of adopting incentive regimes along the lines of existing GSPs under the Enabling Clause taking into account the Appellate Body report *EC–Tariff Preferences*.[47] Thus, in this case, the question whether citizens and companies affected by the withdrawal of incentives should be entitled to invoke the violation of incentive rules before domestic courts is of some relevance. Can Petersmann's vision be realized and WTO law

---

43 Gesetz zur Stärkung der nichtfinanziellen Berichterstattung der Unternehmen in ihren Lage-und Konzernlageberichten (CSR-Richtlinie-Umsetzungsgesetz), 11. April 2017, BGBl.I/2017, S. 802.

44 See WTO Agreements 1994 Uruguay Round Agreements Act, 19 USCS § 3511, Pub. L No. 104–305 (1996), § 102 quoted in Cottier (A Theory of Direct Effect), p. 105, fn. 20.

45 European Court of Justice, Case C-149/96, *Portugal v. Council*, paras. 43–46, https://eur-lex.europa.eu/legal-content/EN/TXT/HTML/?uri=ecli:ECLI:EU:C:1999:574.

46 Matsushita/Schoenbaum/Mavroidis/Hahn, p. 46.

47 *EC–Tariff Preferences*, report of the Appellate Body.

be read to empower citizens to invoke WTO guarantees of freedom and non-discrimination in domestic courts?[48]

The arguments in favour of direct effect of WTO law are compelling. Legal scholars convincingly argue that direct effect is not only a question of the precise structure of a norm and its technical suitability but also a question of separation of powers, the rule of law and the principle of legality and democracy.[49] This is of course true if one compares human rights norms, which, as elaborated above, are already applied directly by national courts, and for example the principles of non-discrimination in Art. I and III of the GATT. Both norms have the same broad and open-textured language.[50] Especially with regard to the ECJ one can observe a dual standard under which the ECJ grants direct effect to the four freedoms of the internal market but not to WTO and GATT rules.[51] The real reason behind denying direct effect are about political economy and separation of powers, as the ECJ in *Portugal v. Council* has revealed.[52] It held that direct effect of WTO rules would

> deprive the legislative or executive organs of the Community of the scope of manoeuvre enjoyed by their counterparts in the Community's trading partners.[53]

This recourse to the principle of reciprocity, which would be violated if direct effect was granted in the EU but not the US, is however not a valid argument. Firstly, in cases other than WTO law, the ECJ allows individuals to invoke provisions of international agreements, even if this is not reciprocated by the other contracting party.[54] Secondly, already under current international law and even more so if one follows the New legal humanism and applies the constitutional principles of human rights and the rule of law, political reasons should not trump legal reasons. Such argument contradicts the principle of *pacta sunt servanda* by denying individuals relying on GATT provisions their rights

---

48 Petersmann (Multi-levelMulti-level Trade Governance), pp. 19–28.

49 Cottier (The Impact of Justiciability), p. 316; Cottier (A Theory of Direct Effect), pp. 103–123; Cottier (The Judge in International Economic Relations), pp. 99–122; Peters (Beyond Human Rights), pp. 495–525; Wüger.

50 Cottier (The Impact of Justiciability), p. 313.

51 Ibid.

52 Cf. Cottier (A Theory of Direct Effect), pp. 108 et seqq.; Peters (Beyond Human Rights), pp. 515–518.

53 European Court of Justice, Case C-149/96, *Portugal v. Council*, paras. 43–46, https://eur-lex.europa.eu/legal-content/EN/TXT/?uri=CELEX%3A61996CJ0149.

54 See references in Matsushita/Schoenbaum/Mavroidis/Hahn, p. 46.

granted by these provisions.[55] To give direct effect to GATT rules would do justice to the rationale of the GATT, which is to protect the economic wellbeing of individuals.[56] Thirdly, it is also not justifiable in an era of globalisation to treat international law differently from other branches of law and exclude it from judicial review.[57] The tradition of defining external relations as a matter of foreign policy beyond legal control gives the political branches too much discretion in shaping rights and obligations of economic operators.[58] It is therefore most welcome that the ECJ has changed its practice in relation to direct effect on GATS in a landmark ruling against Hungary, finding that EU members have to ensure compliance with Art. 1 (3) (a) of the GATS.[59]

It is suggested that the proper criteria to determine whether a norm should be given direct affect should be assessed in accordance with the constitutional principle of legality, meaning that only basic and essential policy decisions impacting on individual rights are to be taken by the legislator and are not left to courts or governments.[60] Thus, the rules of delegation of powers from the legislative to the executive branch should apply: a norm needs to define rights and obligations and be precise enough to be applicable by courts. The more it impinges on individual rights and liberty, the more precise a rule must be.[61] In addition, the question of direct effect should take account of the specific role of courts in protecting minorities in contrast to highly political issues with substantial budgetary implications and providing for complex regulatory systems.[62]

A similar view of direct effect holds that while the primary criteria concern the justiciability of a norm, i.e. whether it is *prima facie* specific enough and applies unconditionally, the direct effect of norms establishing individual rights should be the normal case.[63] Exceptions from this rule need to be justified.[64] The reason is that only then the international legal status of the individual will be fully realized.[65] International norms obliging individuals including

55 Cf. Cottier (A Theory of Direct Effect), pp. 108 et seqq.; Peters (Beyond Human Rights), pp. 515–518.
56 Peters (Beyond Human Rights), p. 518.
57 Cottier (The Judge in International Economic Relations), pp. 99–109.
58 Cottier (The Impact of Justiciability), p. 32.
59 European Court of Justice, Case C-66/18 Commission v. Hungary (ECLI:EU:C:2020:792), paras. 84–86; Cottier in Groeben Commentary on Art. 206/207 TFEU: Rdnr 19.
60 Cottier (A Theory of Direct Effect), p. 118.
61 Cottier (The Impact of Justiciability), p. 324.
62 Ibid., p. 325.
63 Peters (Beyond Human Rights), pp. 524–525.
64 Ibid.
65 Ibid., p. 519.

also some norms entitling individuals should have direct effect only in accordance with the principle of legality, especially with the requirement that legal obligations of the individual must be traceable back to a specific, accessible, and foreseeable legal foundation.[66]

While the latter approach seems to be slightly more far-reaching, in essence, both approaches are in favour of assuming direct effect of WTO, where the law is benefitting the individual. Primary criteria refer to the justiciability of the norm and can be refined with the help of the principle of legality. This approach is convincing all the more under a humanist reading of international law that explicitly seeks to strengthen the individual and the rule of law. In view of the fact that in German law, this concept has been worked well under the concept called the 'Wesentlichkeitstheorie'[67] meaning that essential issues limiting basic rights of individuals need to be regulated by the legislator, such an approach seems to be timely and urgently needed. Considering that international treaty norms all have been ratified by national parliaments, there is also no concern discernible that the will of the people is not sufficiently taken into account. By contrast, more judicial review and access to justice by individuals is a welcome means to mitigate the lack of democratic control in international governance.

Finally, the risk of creating an even more fragmented legal order by having diverting national case law on trade and child labour law can be mitigated by referring to the new constitutional principles of the rule of law and human rights establishing a duty of engagement of courts along the lines of the German Constitutional Court.[68] A national court having to decide on withdrawn trade concessions because of occurrence of child labour would have to follow case law of the WTO adjudicating bodies. As in human rights law, the rule of precedent should apply.

3.1.3 Interim Conclusion

In conclusion, the New Legal Humanism to international law stipulates that human rights and WTO law provisions benefitting individuals and being precise enough should have in principle direct effect.

A failure by states' parties to do so should be subject to dispute resolution under the proposed ILO-WTO Enforcement Regime. International procedures would thus strengthen local law enforcement of individual rights and contribute to effective multi-level governance.

66 Ibid, p. 525.
67 Degenhardt, pp. 112 et seqq.
68 See above p. 400.

4 Institutional Coherence: A New ILO-WTO Joint Implementation Mechanism on Child Labour

4.1 *Introduction*

The proposed agreement on trade measures and child labour would be based on existing ILO and WTO mechanisms.[69] While the UN implementation system provides for interstate and individual complaints procedures admitting cases of child labour under the ICESCR and the CRC, the ILO is more used to deal with cases involving employers. It has a better functioning collective complaints procedure and provides for the largest technical cooperation programme on child labour, IPEC.[70] Thus, it is well suited for a new enforcement mechanism on child labour. In addition, states have expressed their will in the Singapore Ministerial Declaration of 1996 that the ILO is the competent body to deal with the core labour standards including child labour.[71] The former Director-General of the ILO stated that while the ILO does not have a mandate for introducing a social clause into trade agreements, it is ready to cooperate in such an endeavour without prejudice to the impartiality and universality of its supervisory machinery.[72] He was convinced that especially the tripartite structure of the ILO can be a guarantee of a valid multilateral response to a challenge of such a clause.[73] Finally, Art. 33 of the ILO Constitution already allows ILO bodies to recommend trade measures as a possible sanction in response to child labour and made use of this possibility in the case of Myanmar.[74]

The following sections will first examine which forms of child labour should be subject to dispute resolution and possibly trade sanctions, then discuss the institutional structure and possible cooperative activities including a reporting mechanism and special incentive regimes, and finally elaborate on dispute resolution for states and individuals as well as enforcement through private law with companies as respondents.

---

69 See also Neumann, pp. 593–599, Blüthner, p. 417 et seqq., Reuß, pp. 186–198; Economic Strategy Institute/Morici/Schulz and Ehrenberg who discusses the possibility of an ILO/WTO cooperation agreement.

70 See Humbert (The Challenge of Child Labour), pp. 136, 178 et seqq.; International Programme on the Elimination of Child Labour, https://www.ilo.org/global/about-the-ilo/how-the-ilo-works/flagships/ipec-plus/lang--en/index.htm.

71 Singapore WTO Ministerial Declaration, WT/MIN(96)/DEC 18 December 1996, www.wto.org/english/thewto_e/minist_e/min96_e/wtodec_e.htm.

72 Hansenne, pp. 457–458.

73 Ibid.

74 See Humbert (The Challenge of Child Labour), pp. 183–192.

4.2 *Trade- and Country-Related Child Labour*

The relevant provisions on child labour should be taken from the ICCPR, ICESCR and its Optional Protocol, the CRC and its Optional Protocol on the Involvement of Children in Armed Conflicts, and ILO Conventions No. 138 and 182 on child labour. The preamble should also refer to all remaining UN and ILO Conventions relating to child labour and confirm that the protection from child labour forms part of *ius cogens* in order to highlight the high degree of acceptance worldwide of the prohibition of child labour. All types of child labour designated as exploitative by UNICEF and the ILO ranging from agriculture and plantation work to child soldiers would thus be prohibited by the new agreement.[75] In line with existing state obligations under the UN and ILO Conventions on child labour, states would have to implement child labour standards immediately, and not progressively.[76]

In accordance with the outcome of the discussion above, the treaty provisions on child labour should have direct effect, i.e. they should be actionable in domestic courts.

The crucial question is whether only trade-related child labour in the export sector or all types of child labour including child labour in the domestic and service sector should be subject to the new enforcement system including a complaints procedure allowing for trade measures as possible sanctions. As is the case with social clauses in regional or bilateral trade agreements,[77] the standards subject to dispute settlement should in principle be trade-related. The argument relating to the effectiveness of trade measures is only valid for the export sector.[78] Thus, in principle, only child labour in the export sector should be subject to the new enforcement system. This is all the more the case because domestic child labour such as tourism, prostitution or child labour in the domestic industry are subject to countermeasures, i.e. country-specific trade measures, which are more difficult to justify under GATT rules.

The proposed New Legal Humanism promoting multi-level governance and the principle of subsidiarity also favours a solution where child labour other than in the export sector would primarily be dealt with at the national level. It would only be subject to the new ILO-WTO dispute settlement followed by trade sanctions in case there had been ILO proceedings recommending trade measures. The collective action problem rather concerns trade relations and not the domestic industry.

75 Ibid., p. 18.
76 See for example ibid., p. 66.
77 Ibid., pp. 195–284.
78 Ibid., pp. 379–380.

While violating GATT Art. I and III, country-specific measures based on policy considerations referring to the general human rights application of a country can be justified under the general exceptions of GATT Art. XX or the security exception of GATT Art. XXI. In accordance with the legal analysis presented in Chapter 2, this will be the case if the ILO has recommended recurring to trade measures as in the case of Myanmar, or if there was a grave and widespread occurrence of child labour that would justify countermeasures under public international law. It has been argued that in the absence of effective international remedies for human rights atrocities, unilateral measures by states play an important role as part of a broader concerted, but decentralized global effort to encourage human rights compliance.[79] Hence, trade measures for other types of child labour than in the production of goods for export should be possible but carefully used and only as measures of last resort. Country-based child labour should be subject to a two-layered system: complaints concerning child labour in the domestic industry or in the services sector (so-called country-related child labour) should first pass through the ILO special procedures before a panel under the new agreement would decide on trade measures. This system will be elaborated on below.[80] In this context, it should be highlighted that political sanctions have to be carefully used because of their potential misuse and ineffectiveness.[81] Sanctions in many cases make matters worse for the most defenceless in the target state.[82] Often, the purpose of sanctions is to intensify opposition to the offending regime by aggravating the situation of the population. In such situations, human beings are used in a geo-political game. This in principle constitutes a violation of the Kantian injunction that persons should be treated as ends and not means, and contradicts the humanism approach.[83]

4.3 *Institutional Framework*

Under the new agreement, a Trade and Child Labour Council would be established to be the governing body, modelled on the Goods or Services Council. It would be open for trade and labour government officials of states parties. Based on the tripartite model of the ILO, each member shall also be represented by

---

79 Cleveland, p. 135 et seq.

80 A two-pronged ILO-WTO system has also been proposed by de Wet (The ILO and the social clause), pp. 60 et seqq.

81 Vázquez (Trade Sanctions and Human Rights), p. 837.

82 Cf. Shoyer/Soloy/Koff, p. 1349.

83 Vázquez (Trade Sanctions and Human Rights), p. 837.

delegates representing employers', workers' and non-governmental children's rights' organizations.

As concluded in the previous chapter, a New Legal Humanism requires increased participation of private actors in international decision-making in order to improve accountability and mitigate the lack of democracy. Including non-governmental children's rights' organization in a tripartite structure similar to the ILO would fulfil this ask. As has been elaborated by Van den Bossche, NGO involvement in WTO and other organizations activities does not only increase accountability but also bring about expertise and enrich political debates.[84] They can also compensate the lack of civil society participation at national level in some countries.

Art. 12 (3) of the ILO Constitution provides already for the possibility to consult NGOs. The International Organization of Employers and the World Trade Union Federation have for example general consultative status.[85] Also, the ILO has working relationships with NGOs included in a special list. Such NGOs have to share the objectives of the ILO and have an evident interest in working with the ILO.[86] For example, Amnesty International is currently included in this list. In accordance with Art. V:2 of the WTO Agreement, the General Council of the WTO also has issued 'Guidelines for Arrangements on Relations with Non-Governmental Organizations', which however limited the NGO involvement to specific symposia or fora and excluded them from consultative status in any WTO body.[87]

There are wide-spread concerns against an active and formal participation of NGOs in international organizations. Often, such objections are directed against international NGOs focussing on labour and the environment because such interests might be contrary to the states' parties' interests.[88] A major concern is the democratic deficit of NGOs, which are often not democratically elected and dependent on private donations.

Even trade unionists have objected to participation of non-workers organizations:

> Trade unions object to the formal representation of NGOs within the ILO, as they want to ensure that ILO workers' representatives are

84 Van den Bossche, p. 720.

85 See https://www.ilo.org/pardev/partnerships/civil-society/ngos/WCMS_201411/lang--en/index.htm.

86 See ILO Special List of NGOs, www.ilo.org/pardev/partnerships/civil-society/ngos/ilo-special-list-of-ngos/lang--en/index.htm.

87 See WT/L/162, 23 July 1996.

88 Cf. Van den Bossche, p. 721.

> democratically accountable to the workers themselves. Almost by definition, NGOs are not democratically accountable to workers. If they were, irrespective of legal status, they would be unions! Moreover, unions are suspicious of the increasing numbers of NGOs that are established, controlled, financed, or otherwise influenced by governments or employers, which – if represented within the ILO – would tilt the balance of power within the ILO further away from workers and their trade union representatives.[89]

Whilst this may hold true to some extent, in the age of globalization, workers' organizations neither represent adequately all workers' interests, excluding those working in the informal economy and those of women and children. Also, Krajewski rightly holds that NGOs represent societal concerns, thereby representing people on a functional rather than a territorial basis.[90] Hence, it is recommendable to allow NGO participation in international organizations under certain criteria. Such criteria may depend on the level of participation, as it is current practice under the ILO. With regard to the proposed ILO-WTO agreement, formal participation of children's organization is needed because of their special expertise and experience, which trade unions do not have. Their role in dispute resolution will be discussed below.

As said above, there should be safeguards against the democratic deficit of such NGOs and prevailing private interests. Along the lines of the criteria by the ECOSOC[91] and the ILO itself, such safeguards should include transparency requirements as to their structure and finances, their long-standing proven knowledge, achievements and experience in the relevant area, i.e. children's rights and child labour.

A so-called Child Labour and Trade Office staffed by experts on children's rights and child labour from both the WTO Secretariat and the International Labour Office would be established as the executive arm of the proposed Agreement.

The Council would also elect a roster of panellists in consultation with the WTO and ILO including both trade and labour law experts.[92] These panellists would sit on panels in case of disputes.

---

89 Interview with trade unionist Dave Spooner, IFWEA, 16 November 2006.

90 Krajewski (Democratic Legitimacy and Constitutional Perspectives of WTO Law), p. 185.

91 UN ECOSOC Consultative Relationship between the United Nations and Non-Governmental Organizations' (ECOSOC Resolution 1996/312), UN Document E/1996/312, 5 July 1996, para. 1.

92 See below, p. 416.

4.4 *Cooperative Activities*

The Council would function first of all as a forum for the exchange of information on trade and child labour policy of governments. It would promote cooperative activities based on the reports published by the ILO Committee of Experts and reports under the Trade Policy Review Mechanism (TPRM). To enhance coherence and cooperation, the Council would regularly invite the Director-General of the International Labour Office or its representative. Joint activities could for example consist of facilitating the implementation of new incentive regimes for the improvement of labour standards similar to the existing GSPs or other technical assistance and cooperation agreements.

4.4.1 Forum of Exchange

The Council would use the Concluding Observations made by the ILO Committees under the reporting procedure on implementation of ILO Conventions No. 138 and 182 by member states and the trade policy reviews of the TPRB. It would meet to discuss selected issues and situation of countries, and could adopt policy recommendations on how to address child labour or agree on other forms of collaboration.

4.4.2 Incentive Regimes

It has been found that GSPs with a positive conditionality approach can be consistent with the current GATT and may have a positive impact on the implementation of labour standards.[93]

The question however arises whether such GSPs are needed in case the proposed agreement on trade and child labour will be adopted. The proposed agreement is based on the assumption that member states, pushed by trade unions and NGOs, will complain about child labour in the export industry in other member states. Often the mere threat of trade measures should be enough to incite countries to act. On the other hand, states are reluctant to even mention the possibility of imposing trade measures for fear of disturbing their foreign trade relations. Thus, a more friendly incentive regime is additionally needed.

The Child Labour and Trade Division would thus devise model incentive regimes with regard to child labour based on the US-Cambodia FTA or existing GSPs.[94] The Appellate Body has established some legal criteria for the WTO-compatibility of GSPs.[95] In essence, it found that in line with the criteria of

93 Humbert (The Challenge of Child Labour), pp. 315 et seqq.

94 See Humbert (The Challenge of Child Labour), pp. 248 et seqq., pp. 284–318.

95 *EC–Tariff Preferences*, report of the Appellate Body.

the Enabling Clause, GSPs have to be 'generalized, non-reciprocal and non-discriminatory'. They should respond positively to the development and trade needs of developing countries. Such criteria should be refined by the Child Labour and Trade Division and WTO members' GSPs would have to follow these. As a result, the design of the GSP would be more multilateral, relieving GSPs of their colonial approach.[96]

The future criteria should correspond to the objective development need of the protection from economic exploitation of children. The threshold for graduation should not be too low. Withdrawal of trade preferences should be justified if a member state no longer implements ILO Convention No. 138 or 182 in law and in practice. Besides removing the beneficiary status of a country, it should also be possible to withdraw the special incentive arrangement only with respect to certain products. The national administrative decisions granting or withdrawing additional tariff preferences should explicitly be subjected to dispute resolution under the new ILO-WTO Agreement on child labour. The added value would be that labour experts are explicitly involved.

In line with what has been said above, the provisions stipulating the criteria for GSPs would have direct effect. Hence, companies could file suits before domestic courts where authorities deny certain tariff concessions contrary to GSPs. Or where states parties do not tackle child labour and tariff concessions are withdrawn. The direct effect should be explicitly prescribed by the proposed ILO-WTO Agreement as was the case with the GPA 1994.

4.4.3 Technical and Financial Cooperation

In accordance with the recommendations on social clauses in regional and bilateral trade agreements, the new agreement should provide for detailed clauses on technical and financial cooperation as well as capacity building especially in developing countries.[97]

Most importantly, developing countries struggling with child labour should have the possibility of initiating a TBP together with IPEC. These programmes are the most comprehensive approach to tackle the problem of child labour. Such a TBG rather is a national framework than a project, coordinated to develop and manage a series of interlinked policy and programme interventions at different policy levels which could be implemented separately by various development partners.[98]

---

96 Shaffer/Apea, p. 496.

97 Cf. Humbert (The Challenge of Child Labour), pp. 279–284.

98 See ILO/IPEC (Time-Bound-Programme Guidebook V-01); see also Humbert (The Challenge of Child Labour in International Law), pp. 180–182.

The international community should help to provide the necessary financial resources: Various UN and ILO Conventions provide for international cooperation and assistance in the implementation of economic rights, for example Art. 2 (1) of the ICESCR, Art. 4 of the CRC or Art. 8 of ILO Convention No. 182. While the prevailing view among scholars still holds that no legal obligation to cooperate or to assist exists,[99] a strong argument can be made to call for such an obligation under a new trade agreement on child labour.

4.5 *Dispute Settlement*

4.5.1 Interstate-Disputes

The consultation process and dispute settlement should be based on the principles underlying the DSU and the ILO special procedures. The distinct characteristics of the two approaches will be considered and drawn upon where appropriate.

4.5.1.1 *Consultations*

As under Art. 4 and 5 of the DSU, before entering into dispute resolution, any states' party to the agreement should have the right to request for consultations with another states' party on any specific matter regarding obligations under the trade and child labour agreement. The purpose of consultations under the DSU is to encourage parties to reach settlement in a less formalized environment before the dispute enters the more formal legal structure of the panel proceedings.[100]

As under GATT Art. XXII and XXIII and Art. 4 and 5 of the DSU, any member state to the new agreement may request consultations with another member state on any specific matter related to product-related child labour.

4.5.1.1.1 Third Parties

Interested third parties such as other member states may request for joining the consultations. In deviation to Art. 4.11 of the DSU, third parties do not need to proclaim a substantial interest since human rights obligations apply *erga omnes* in which all states have a collective interest.

Since under the humanist approach, (non-governmental) children's rights organizations are part of the formal delegation of member states, they should not only be allowed to participate in such consultations but also to initiate them.

99 Cf. for example Wolfrum (International Law of Cooperation), p. 1246.

100 Schuchhardt, p. 1217.

4.5.1.1.2 Timetable

An important aspect of the consultation procedure under the DSU is the duty of each member state to 'accord sympathetic consideration to and afford adequate opportunity regarding any representation made by another member', Art. 4.2 of the DSU. If the party to which the request was made fails to respond within 10 days, if it fails to enter into consultations within 30 days, or if the consultations fail to settle the dispute within 60 days, the complaining party may request the establishment of a panel by the DSB.[101]

The same should hold true for the new agreement. Equally, the parties would have the right to set the deadlines shorter, Art. 4.3 of the DSU. Developing countries however enjoy special and differential treatment, Art. 4.10 of the DSU. Their particular problems should be taken into account by allowing the parties to set a longer time-frame.[102]

4.5.1.1.3 ILO/IPEC Time-Bound-Programmes

Most importantly, developing countries should have the possibility of proposing a child labour eradication plan, in particular, of initiating a Time-Bound-programme (TBP) together with IPEC. If the country can demonstrate that it makes serious efforts to initiate a TBG including a specific project under IPEC, the dispute over the occurrence of child labour should for the time being be considered to be settled by way of satisfactory adjustment. After the country concerned has announced that it wants to initiate a TBG, the consultations will be suspended for five to seven months, depending on the scale of the problem.[103] If after that period, no or only insignificant progress has been made, the complainant party may request the establishment of a panel. In the subsequent proceedings, the panel will evaluate the situation in detail and determine whether measures taken by the country were insufficient to remedy the problem.

4.5.1.2 *Dispute Resolution*

4.5.1.2.1 Right to Request a Panel

If the consultations fail, either party may request the establishment of a panel by the Council, drawing on Art. 6.1 of the DSU. If a third party joined the consultations, it may also request the establishment of a panel. Private third parties such as international trade unions, employers' organizations or NGO on

101 Art. 4.3 and 4.7 of the DSU.

102 Zdouc, p. 1270.

103 For example, the planning process for the TBP in Ecuador was carried out over a period of five months, ILO/IPEC (Time-Bound-Programme Guidebook V-01), p. 10.

children's rights with formal status may also request a panel to be established. However, in the last case, the findings shall not be implemented via trade measures, as will be discussed below.

4.5.1.2.2 Standing

According to GATT Art. XXIII:1 and Art. 23 and 26 of the DSU, the jurisdiction of the WTO adjudicating bodies extends to violation or non-violation complaints, and situation complaints. Since the main objective of the proposed trade and child labour agreement is to induce countries to comply with their international child labour law obligations, complaints would be violation complaints. There is a controversy over standing under the DSU *de lege lata* relating to the nullification or impairment of benefits. It is argued that rather than inducing compliance, the aim of countermeasures under Art. 22.4 of the DSU is to maintain the balance of reciprocal trade concessions negotiated in the WTO Agreements.[104] Accordingly, adverse trade effects need be demonstrated. However, a good argument against such an additional requirement is Art. 3.8 of the DSU providing for a presumption to the effect that breach is considered *prima facie* to constitute a case of nullification and impairment.[105] In any event, since the agreement is *de lege ferenda*, the debate does not have to be resolved here. The necessary legal interest under the proposed agreement already follows from the prohibition of child labour as a constitutional principle.

4.5.1.2.3 Request for a Panel

Drawing on Art. 6.2 of the DSU, the legal request for the establishment of a panel should identify the specific violation – including whether it concerns insufficient national legislation or failure of law enforcement – and provide a brief summary of the legal basis of the complaint sufficient to present the problem clearly. This is in line with the DSU where legislation or the application of a regulation in a specific case may be challenged.[106] The violation should be attributable to another members' government.

4.5.1.2.4 Establishment and Mandate of a Panel

The Council will establish the panel by negative consensus, as under the DSU.[107] Panellists will be chosen by the parties to the dispute from a roster established by the Council similar to the indicative list required by Art. 8.4 of the DSU.

104 Shoyer/Soloy/Koff, p. 1350.
105 Zdouc, p. 1241.
106 Ibid., p. 1242.
107 Ibid., p. 1244.

Drawing on Art. 8.1 of the DSU, the roster shall be composed of an equal number of well-qualified governmental and non-governmental individuals in the field of trade and labour including persons who served on or presented a case to a panel or served under the ILO special procedures, served as a representative of a member to the ILO or WTO or taught or published in international trade and labour law or served as a senior trade policy official of a member. In line with Art. 8.4 of the DSU, members to the new Agreement can suggest individuals to the list, which would have to be approved by the Council. Drawing on Art. 8.6 of the DSU, the Child Labour and Trade Division should propose individuals for the panel to be established, who would have to be approved by the parties to the dispute. Under the DSU, there must be compelling reasons to reject proposed individuals. This has however not always been the case.[108] Citizens of member states that are parties to the dispute should not serve on the panel to be established, Art. 8.3 of the DSU.

Panellists would serve in their personal capacity. Similar to Art. 8.5 of the DSU, there should be three panellists, two having expertise in the field of labour and one trade expert. The reason is that the emphasis of the proceedings under the panel is on the finding concerning the labour rights violation; trade experts are rather required at a later stage.

Drawing on Art. 8.7 of the DSU, if there is no agreement within 20 days after the date of the establishment of a panel, at the request of either party, the chairman of the Council with the help of the Child Labour and Trade Division selects the panellists within 10 days. It has been argued that the current composition practice is often lengthy and problematic.[109] Proposals have been made that a standing body of panellist should be created and the right of parties to reject proposed individuals be abolished.[110] However, given the proven reluctance to transfer sovereignty in the field of labour rights to supranational bodies, these proposals should be saved for a more appropriate moment in the future.

Similar to Art. 7.1 of the DSU, the terms of reference of the panel will be based on the request. In particular, the terms of reference shall be:

> To examine, in the light of the relevant provisions of the Agreement in conjunction with the specific ILO or UN Convention, whether there has been a failure to adequately implement these provisions in law and

108 Ibid., p. 1250.

109 Zdouc, p. 1251.

110 Proposal of the European Communities referred to in Zdouc, p. 1251.

practice and to make such findings as will assist the Council in making the recommendations necessary to remedy the non-enforcement.

The panellists will decide in accordance with human and labour rights jurisprudence having due regard to the new constitutional principles as new sources of international law contained in Art. 38 (1) lit. e of the ICJ Statute. When construing the relevant provisions of the UN human rights treaty provisions, panellists shall be obliged to specifically follow the jurisprudence of the human rights treaty committees as well as the General Comments by the HRC, the Committee on Economic, Social and Cultural Rights and the Committee on the Rights of the Child as they – while not being binding *de lege lata* – already are considered to provide authoritative guidance.[111] Equally, the interpretations and recommendations delivered by the Committee of Experts on the Application of Conventions and Recommendations under the ILO (ILO Committee of Experts) with regard to the provisions of the ILO Conventions shall be considered as an authoritative source.[112] *De lege alta*, according to Art. 37 (and Art. 29) of the ILO Constitution, only the ICJ or a special tribunal appointed by the Governing Body may deliver authoritative interpretations. The ICJ has however only been asked once and there is no case where a special tribunal has been established.[113] Thus, this route has proven ineffective and should not be followed. By contrast, the recommendations by the ILO Committee of Experts – while not being binding in the formal sense under existing law – are well recognized and enjoy moral authority because of the independence and legal expertise and experience of the technical experts constituting the Committee. The incorporation of the ILO Committee's opinions and recommendations into national legislation, international instruments and court decisions is an obvious proof of such recognition among States parties.[114] Most importantly, in 2015, the ILO Committee of Experts stated that its chosen mandate of determining the legal scope, content and meaning of the provisions of the Conventions was welcomed by the Governing Body and had the support of the tripartite constituents, i.e. governments, workers' and employers' organizations.[115]

111 Cf. Humbert (The Challenge of Child Labour in International law), pp. 127, 133 et seq. and 138.

112 Ibid., p. 166.

113 See Humbert (The Challenge of Child Labour in International Law), p. 165.

114 With further references, see ILO (Monitoring Compliance), p. 25.

115 Ibid.

4.5.1.2.5 Panel Proceedings

The panel proceedings under the new agreement should mirror those provided for in Art. 12 of the DSU and Appendix 3. That is that panels should set precise deadlines for submissions and provide for public hearings. The timelines should be set up in consultation with the parties and be flexible enough to allow parties sufficient time to prepare their submissions. Considering that child labour is a delicate issue and often difficult to prove, time frames should be longer than those proposed in Appendix 3. There are no time limits for the submission of evidence to a panel.

In line with Art. 14 and 18 of the DSU, dispute settlement proceedings under the new agreement should be confidential.

4.5.1.2.6 Third Parties

As in the consultations stage and along the lines of Art. 10.2 of the DSU, any third party shall have an opportunity to join the proceedings and to be heard by the panel and to make written submissions. Since it has a legal interest qua the human rights obligation owed to it, the third party does not need to show a 'substantial interest'.

However, in contrast to Art. 10.4 of the DSU, a third party may not initiate a dispute settlement proceeding as a complainant in its own right, since this would obviously constitute a duplication of the same procedure. To compensate for this limitation, third parties shall be accorded full party status, i.e. the right to add to claims raised, to complain about additional failures by the government of the member concerned and the right to appeal the panels' finding.

Third parties should also include international trade unions, employers' organizations and NGOs on children's rights, as they are recognized members of the new agreement. They should be accorded full third-party status, i.e. the right to add claims raised and the right to appeal. The legal interest of NGOs already has been examined in the approval procedure and does not need to be shown here.[116] The proposed participation goes much further than the provision of mere '*amicus curiae*' briefs and is justified by the special knowledge and experience of these private parties, which may ensure better application of child labour law. Implementation of rulings via trade sanctions is however only possible if states parties are involved as claimants and respondents in the dispute.

116 See above, p. 410.

4.5.1.2.7 Right to Consult and Ask for Authoritative Interpretations

Art. 13 of the DSU contains the right to seek information. This includes the right to seek technical advice from any individual it deems appropriate, para. 1 of Art. 13 of the DSU, and to seek information from any relevant source and to consult experts to obtain their opinion on certain aspects of the matter, para. 2. In particular, Appendix 4 contains the right to request an advisory report from an Expert Review Group on a factual matter concerning a scientific or other technical matter raised by a party to the dispute. Expert Review Groups may deliver specific scientific advice as well as ascertain facts through interviews with national authorities or other sources such as academics, journalists, private witnesses or NGOs with competence in the labour rights field.

GATT Art. XXIII:2 provides for the right to consultation with any other intergovernmental organization.

The new ILO-WTO dispute settlement shall equally provide for a right to seek technical advice from relevant experts as well as the right to consult the ILO.

Since under the proposed ILO-WTO dispute settlement, panels shall be composed also of eminent labour rights experts and be obliged to consider and follow relevant human and labour rights jurisprudence as well as General Comments by human rights treaty bodies and findings and recommendations by the ILO Committee of Experts,[117] the right to seek advice and consult may at first sight play less a role than under the WTO DSU *de lege lata*. However, in case a new legal question arises where no recommendations or findings of the ILO Committee or jurisprudence of the human rights treaty bodies exist, and the panel deems it necessary to consult, the question is how such a right should be designed.

The crucial question *de lega lata* is whether the existing right to seek information is an adequate means to ask for legal advice. Foltea has convincingly shown that so far WTO panels have shown little institutional sensitivity to other organizations, not giving full normative relevance to the advice given and rarely asked for legal advice in accordance with Art. 13 of the DSU.[118] In case of the ILO, there has so far not even been any interaction apart from joint studies.

Thus, to make the right consult effective, the New Legal Humanism should be deployed to establish a general obligation for the panel under the new ILO-WTO joint mechanism to consult the ILO and defer to the legal advice given.[119]

---

117 See above, p. 417.

118 Foltea, pp. 185–279.

119 Cf. Neumann, p. 612 who derives an obligation to consult *inter alia* from the 'Störungsverbot', i.e. the prohibition to apply non-WTO without asking the relevant

As elaborated above, among the possible organs of the ILO delivering such an authoritative advice, the ILO Committee of Experts is most suited because it is one of the main supervisory bodies composed of independent experts disposing of the necessary legal expertise and experience. Thus, the new mechanism should provide that any interpretation and recommendation delivered by the Committee of Experts with regard to ILO Conventions and Recommendations shall be treated as an authoritative source as is the case with findings and assessments of the IMF in balance of payments disputes in accordance with Art. XV 2) of the GATT and Art. XII of GATS. In case the experts disagree, they have to decide by majority or follow the decision of a chair.

Such an obligation is feasible and viable with a view to Art. 23.10 para. 9 of CETA: According to this provision, the Panel of Experts should seek information from the ILO, including any pertinent available interpretative guidance, findings or decisions adopted by the ILO.[120]

The proposed right of the panel to seek technical advice under a new ILO-WTO dispute settlement procedure on child labour will be based on both the right to request an advisory report from an Expert Review Group and the existing possibility of conducting visits *in situ* of Commission of Inquiry under the ILO under Art. 26 of the Constitution. As will be recalled, in the Myanmar case, the Commission of Inquiry, during its country visits, carried out interviews with national authorities and any other witness it deemed useful.[121] Recommendations by the Commission of Inquiry become legally binding for the defaulting member if not referred to the ICJ.[122] The same should hold true for future recommendations by Commissions of Inquiry under the proposed ILO-WTO implementation mechanism. To make such legal advice really effective, States parties shall be under a duty to respond promptly and fully to requests made by such commissions or panels along the lines what Appellate Body has stated with regard to Art. 13.1 of the DSU.[123] Thus, it shall not be possible for a defendant state to refuse to answer or to cooperate as was

international organization in cases where it is probable that the proposed interpretation would interfere with the functioning of the other relevant international organization. See also Tietje (Global Governance and Inter-Agency Cooperation), p. 514 et seq. who infers a legal obligation to cooperate from the increasing phenomenon of overlapping jurisdiction of international organizations in international economic law and related areas.

120 Art. 23.10 para. 9 CETA, Council of Europe, Interinstitutional File: 2016/0206 (NLE), 14 September 2016, Comprehensive Agreement between Canada, on the one part, and the European Union and its Member States, of the other part.

121 See Humbert (The Challenge of Child Labour), p. 185.

122 Maupain, p. 99.

123 *Canada–Aircraft*, report of the Appellate Body, paras. 203–204.

the case with the Government of Myanmar with regard to questions of the ILO Commission of Inquiry.[124]

While the final report of the existing Expert Review Groups has a mere advisory function, under the proposed dispute settlement, the panel would have to follow the recommendations of the Commissions of Inquiry if the case has not been referred to the ICJ. If members of such commissions disagree, they have to decide by majority or follow a designated chair.

4.5.1.2.8 Standard of Review

The Appellate Body in *EC–Hormones* held that Art. 11 of the DSU was the provision dealing with standard of review.[125] Art. 11 of the DSU basically requires panels to take account of the evidence put before them and forbids them to wilfully disregard or distort such evidence. It is however in the discretion of the panel to decide which evidence it chooses to utilize in making findings.[126] The objective assessment of the facts goes to the very core of the integrity of the WTO dispute settlement.[127] The Appellate Body has defined the standard of review of panels with regard to facts as follows: panels must assess whether national authorities examined all relevant facts and assess whether an adequate explanation has been provided; they must however not conduct a *de novo* review.[128] Such doctrine should also apply under the new agreement in line with the principle of subsidiarity and effective multi-level governance.

With regard to the interpretation of WTO law, the WTO adjudicating bodies apply a *de novo* review.[129] This of course strengthens the effectiveness of international law. Likewise, the dispute settlement bodies under the new agreement should also engage in a *de novo review* when it comes to interpretation of ILO and UN provisions on the protection from child labour.

However, with regard to the application of international human rights law in the individual case in line with the principle of subsidiarity under the humanist approach, the adjudicating bodies should act with judicial restraint vis-à-vis local authorities and courts. In line with the doctrine of margin of appreciation developed by the European Court of Human Rights, domestic courts and authorities should also be accorded a certain latitude, when deciding

124 Cf. Humbert (The Challenge of Child Labour), pp. 184–185.

125 *EC–Hormones*, report of the Appellate Body, para. 116.

126 Zdouc, p. 1266.

127 Ibid., p. 1265.

128 *US–Cotton Yarn*, report of the Appellate Body, para. 74. For an excellent analysis of standards of review in WTO dispute resolution see Oesch (Standards of Review).

129 Oesch (Treatment of Domestic Law), p. 71.

whether domestic law and administrative decisions violate international children's rights so that local circumstances and culture can be adequately taken into account.[130] The limit of such discretion is however reached, when, as has been elaborated above, the essence or the core of the relevant human right is affected in line with the German doctrine of the 'Wesensgehalt'.[131] Such an approach serves the interest of the human being who is part of a certain culture and promotes an effective system of multi-level governance propagated by the humanist approach.

A similar approach can be observed under WTO law with regard to the interpretation of domestic law. Since the panel *US–Sections 301–310*, the WTO dispute settlement bodies have used a deferential approach and treated the interpretation of domestic legal norms as a question of fact.[132]

4.5.1.2.9 Interim Report

Similar to Art. 15 of the DSU, panels under the new agreement shall also adopt interim reports. These interim reports shall contain findings of facts, a determination according to the terms of reference, and, if necessary, recommendations and key points for an action plan sufficient to remedy the pattern of non-enforcement. This initial report should be issued 180 days after the establishment of the panel. This period is longer than that provided for in Art. 15.3 of the DSU, taking due account of the importance of the fact-finding process with the potential support of Expert Review Groups. Parties may submit written comments within a certain period determined by the panel. Most importantly, the defending party may indicate whether it agrees with the key points of the action plan.

4.5.1.2.10 Final Report

The panel drafts the final report containing its findings, reasoning and conclusions in written form. Regarding the new agreement that means that due account should be taken of the reasons for the occurrence of child labour in the territory of a developing country. In particular resource constraints should be considered when devising recommendations. According to Art. 19.1 of the DSU, the final panel report may suggest ways in which the member concerned could implement the recommendations. Although panels usually refrained

130 European Court of Human Rights, *Matthieu–Mohin and Clerfayt v Belgium*, Judgement of 2 March 1987, 2 March 1987, 9/1985/95/143, series A no.113, para. 54,; European Court of Human Rights, *Matthews v UK*, Judgement of 18 February 1999, 28 EHRR 361, para. 52.

131 See above p. 368 and cf. Pieroth/Schlink, pp. 76–78.

132 *US–Section 301 Trade Act*, para. 7.18; Oesch (Treatment of Domestic Law), p. 72.

from making use of this provision for being hesitant to interfere with the sovereign right of members, this provision shall be modified to the extent that panels should make specific recommendations, i.e. propose key points for an action plan to remedy the problem of child labour. These key points should, depending on each individual case, indicate whether, what and how much external financial and technical support from other members or the ILO/IPEC is advisable. Especially the trade expert should make recommendations based on the economic situation of the country. If the country concerned seeks to adopt a TBP under the ILO/IPEC, these key points should be followed.

The panel should issue the final report to all members of the Council. In deviation to Art. 12.9 of the DSU, the final report shall be submitted to the Council within 15 months after the panel has been established. In exceptional cases, the panel may suspend its work for the period not to exceed 12 months at the request of the complaining party, Art. 12.12 of the DSU.

The Council should adopt the report by negative consensus within 60 days after the submission, Art. 16.4 of the DSU. Once a report is put for adoption on a meeting of the Council, and the Council adopts the report, an appeal is not possible anymore. Otherwise any party to the dispute may appeal the decision within 60 days.

4.5.1.3 *Appellate Review*

In deviation to Art. 17 of the DSU, also third parties should have the right to appeal, but implementation of the findings via trade sanctions is not possible, as will be explained in the section on private actors' complaints.

The Appellate Body should be composed of seven persons, four labour and three trade persons who are appointed by the Council. Similar to Art. 17.3 of the DSU, persons shall be of recognized authority.

The remaining part of the Appellate Review procedure is the same as under Art. 17 of the DSU. In essence, that means that the proceedings shall not exceed 60 days from the date a party to the dispute formally notifies its decision to appeal to the date the Appellate Body circulates the report. According to Art. 17.6 of the DSU, an appeal shall be limited to issues of law covered in the panel report and legal interpretations covered by the panel. The Appellate Body may uphold, modify or reverse the legal findings and conclusions of the panel. The time frame for the adoption of the Appellate Body report by the Council shall not exceed 18 months after the establishment of a panel.

4.5.1.4 *Implementation and Enforcement of Dispute Settlement Decisions*

Similar to Art. 19.1 of the DSU, where a panel or an Appellate Body concludes that a government of a member has not adequately implemented the relevant child labour standards in law and practice, it should recommend that the member concerned brings its legislative and administrative practice into conformity with the standards contained in that Agreement. If the problem was the failure to adequately enforce child labour laws, the recommendations should include key points for an action plan developed with the support of the ILO/IPEC staff.

In line with Art. 21.3 of the DSU, the party concerned should state its intentions to implement the recommendations of the panel ruling at the Council meeting held within 30 days after the adoption of the report.

The enforcement procedure consists of a graded system of measures and penalties, including a TBG, monetary assessments and final suspension of trade benefits as a measure of last resort.

4.5.1.4.1 Implementation of a TBP and Cooperation with Private Sector Initiatives

If the complaint concerned the failure to adequately enforce child labour laws, the country concerned should announce its intentions to design and implement a TBP including specific measures to tackle the child labour problem in the export industry to the Council. The Council should then appoint two ILO/IPEC experts to assist the country and determine a period between seven and 12 months for the development of the national programme and the specific project.[133] The reason why a country should apply for a TBP in addition to a single project is the sustainability of such an approach. Sustained changes can only be achieved by empowering key agencies and institutions to mobilize financial and human resources and to implement interventions in an integrated and coordinated manner. Since child labour in the export industry will be the subject matter, the specific intervention will in most cases consist of direct actions such as industry-specific agreements, withdrawal of children from work, education and vocational programmes and income generating activities for parents.[134] ILO experts should also consult with governments on cooperating with public-private sector initiatives on reducing child labour such as the German Partnership for Sustainable Textiles.[135]

---

133 The planning of the TBP in Ecuador took five months, see above. Even in WTO proceedings, periods of time accorded to parties to implement recommendations also were as long as eight or seven months, Shoyer/Solovy/Koff, p. 1358.

134 ILO/IPEC (Time-Bound Programme, Guidebook V-04), p. 8.

135 Cf. https://www.ilo.org/berlin/presseinformationen/WCMS_314280/lang--de/index.htm.

4.5.1.4.2 Financial Assistance

Depending on the particular factors underlying the specific problem of child labour, IPEC may act as a facilitator and advocate with possible donors and execute its own initiatives.[136] As indicated above, international law provides for international cooperation and assistance to implement economic human rights.[137] In addition, provisions stipulating special and differential treatment of developing and least-developed countries such as Art. 21.8 and 24.1 of the DSU support such an approach. Thus, taking into account the causes of the specific child labour problem such as the reasons for non-compliance with international child labour law, IPEC experts should recommend the complainant country and third parties to provide a certain amount of financial assistance. However, the amount should not be as high as having the effect of reducing the incentive for the country concerned to act and mobilize domestic resources, thereby threatening country ownership of the project.

4.5.1.4.3 Inadequate Laws

In case that the subject matter of the complaint was inadequate legislation and not its application, the Council should determine a period no longer than 18 months during which the country should adopt and implement adequate legislation. In line with Art. 21.6 of the DSU, the Council should monitor the implementation of the recommendations.

4.5.1.4.4 Reconvention of a Panel and Monetary Assessment

If the country concerned does not make due efforts to design such a TBP and implement the specific intervention within the period determined by the Council, the complaining party may request to reconvene the panel, a procedure similar to the compliance review procedure contained in Art. 21.5 of the DSU. In case of failure to adopt adequate legislation, a panel may also be requested.

Drawing on the US-Chile FTA, the panel should draft its report within 90 days and impose an annual monetary assessment on the defending party in case it finds that the defending party had not made due efforts to implement its recommendations.[138] The financial amount would be determined primarily by trade experts and be based on the following criteria: the gravity of the problem, the trade effect – if any – of the non-enforcement of child labour standards, the reasons for non-enforcement such as lack of political will or potential

136 ILO/IPEC (Time-Bound-Programme Guidebook V-1), p. 18.

137 See above p. 413.

138 See Humbert (The Challenge of Child Labour), pp. 236–248.

resource constraints of the party, and the efforts made by the party to remedy the problem. Due account should be taken of the situation of least-developed countries, Art. 24.1 of the DSU. This reasoning is in accordance with the proportionality requirement of Art. 51 of the Articles on State Responsibility and the new constitutional principles of human rights and the rule of law under the new legal humanism.[139]

The trade expert of the panel should determine a fine taking into account the total volume of trade in goods between the parties. The fine to be paid should be high enough to have a deterrent effect. The fine should be paid into a fund established by the Council with the support of IPEC staff. It should be expended under the direction of a special committee established by the Council for the implementation of international child labour standards in the country. The merit of such a fine in comparison with the immediate imposition of trade measures is that the potential lack of political will of the government is targeted but trade relations are less affected.

4.5.1.4.5 Suspension of Trade Benefits

Similar to the implementation system under the US-Chile FTA, if the party complained against fails to pay the monetary assessment into the fund within 120 days, the complaining party may suspend trade benefits necessary to collect the assessment.[140] In line with Art. 22.2 and 22.6 of the DSU, the complaining party may request authorization from the Council to suspend the application of concessions or other obligations under the covered agreements including trade embargoes or punitive tariffs.

Art. 22.4 of the DSU stipulates that the level of suspension of benefits should be equivalent to the level of nullification or impairment. As held above, the level of nullification of trade benefits in case of violation of labour standards in other countries is difficult to establish. Therefore, it has been held that countermeasures are not possible in cases where illegally low labour standards do not lead to measurable trade effects.[141] While this argument may be valid *de lege lata*, it does not apply here. Firstly, it should be recalled that in case of child labour, this link to trade effects may be easier to establish than in case of violations of other labour standards since there is empirical evidence that child labour reduces manufacturing costs and may thus lead to a change in

139 ILC (Commentaries to the draft articles on Responsibility of States for Internationally Wrongful Acts), p. 134.

140 Ibid.

141 Blüthner, p. 427; Pearson, p. 186 also argues that punitive trade sanctions are a novel and potentially damaging GATT practice.

supply chains and domestic job losses.[142] Secondly, the rationale for countermeasures under the trade and child labour agreement *de lege ferenda* does not follow the reciprocity principle of trade law, it is to force governments to take appropriate measures for the abolition of child labour. Specifically, the suspension of trade benefits should be based on the following principles, drawing on Art. 22.3 of the DSU:

The complaining party should first seek to suspend concessions in the sector where the child labour occurred. If this is not effective, because for example child labourers move from the export garment industry to domestic work, the complaining party may seek to suspend benefits also in other sectors. In applying those principles, the complaining party should take into account the gravity of the problem, the importance of the sector for the country concerned and the consequences of such countermeasures. It should seek to suspend the smallest amounts of benefits possible in order to restrict the negative consequences for the children concerned. The worst case may be a trade embargo. In any event, the principle of proportionality should be observed. In addition, the complaining party should devise an emergency plan with support of IPEC in case employers start to dismiss children without providing for supportive educational measures.

4.5.1.4.6 Arbitration Procedure

In line with Art. 22.6 of the DSU, the Council may authorize the proposed suspension of benefits within 30 days, if no consensus exists to reject the request. The defending party may however request to reconvene the panel or to appoint a trade expert as an arbitrator to evaluate whether the requested suspension of trade benefits is manifestly excessive. In deviation to Art. 22.7 of the DSU, the guiding criteria for this decision should be whether the amount is high enough to induce compliance with child labour law while the principle of proportionality should be observed. The panel or the arbitrator should deliver its report within 60 days. The suspension of benefits should be temporary and should only be applied until the defending party has duly started to implement a TBP including the specific intervention devised together with ILO experts, or the determined monetary assessment has been paid into a fund.

4.5.1.5 *Procedure for Country-Related Child Labour*

As has been explored above, country-related child labour is not subject to dispute settlement under the new ILO-WTO implementation mechanism.

142 See Humbert (The Challenge of Child Labour), p. 29 with further references.

Instead, the existing ILO special procedures shall apply. In case the ILO Governing Body recommends trade measures in accordance with Art. 33 of the ILO Constitution as in the case of Myanmar,[143] the case shall be referred to the new Trade and Child Labour Council.

The Council would then appoint a panel consisting of two trade experts and one on labour rights to determine the level of suspension of trade benefits. Members may submit their views. The same principles as in case of trade-related child labour shall apply, i.e. the panel would consider the gravity of the problem, the importance of the sector considered for the suspension of trade benefits for the country concerned and the consequences of such countermeasures. The final report should be submitted to the Council no longer than after 90 days to the Council.

Since the complaints procedure under Art. 26 of the ILO Constitution gives the member failing to comply with international child labour law enough time to engage with IPEC on a possible TBP or to take other remedies, there shall not be a graded system of penalties.

4.5.2 Private Actors' Complaints Procedure

The New Legal Humanism' aims at strengthening rights of the individual. Drawing on Peters' doctrine of international legal personality of the human being,[144] also private actors with legal personality such as individuals including children and their representatives, trade unions and NGOs on children's rights but also industry associations should be given international legal personality. In consequence, they should not only be allowed to take part in consultations of states parties but also to file complaints and thus initiate panel proceedings in their own right. This is of major relevance since generally, private parties are much more willing than governments to bring complaints against foreign governments since they are less hesitant to interfere with national sovereignty or to disturb foreign relations.[145] The few amount of states complaints in regional trade agreements and the considerable number of publications under the NAALC is evidence of such reluctance.[146] Thus, despite the current limited right of NGOs to submit *amicus curiae* briefs under the current DSU,[147] and resistance by ILO constituents to formal NGO participation,[148] referring to

143 Humbert (The Challenge of Child Labour), pp. 183–192.

144 Peters (Beyond Human Rights).

145 Cf. van Liemt, p. 445.

146 Cf. Humbert (The Challenge of Child Labour), pp. 195–284.

147 Zdouc, p. 1240.

148 Hepple, p. 53.

the new constitutional principles as to human rights and more judicial review should make private actor complaints by NGOs possible. As has been discussed above, concerns as to private actors' democratic deficit can be remedied with transparency requirements and further admission criteria.

However, as mentioned above, in disputes initiated by NGOs or trade unions or industry associations, rulings are not subject to the enforcement system with regard to suspension of trade benefits. Significantly, in international law, as yet, there is no trade-related enforcement mechanism for human rights violations committed by state actors that may be initiated by private parties. Such a system is politically not feasible.

Since such private complaints are not followed by trade sanctions, they should be available also in case on non-trade-related child labour, i.e. complaints can be submitted in case of any substantiated violation of child labour as prohibited by the UN and ILO Conventions.

Thus, the rules for panel proceedings described above shall apply *mutatis mutandis* also in case of private actor complaints on behalf of affected children in case of child labour with the following deviations. As is the case with individual complaints before the human rights treaty bodies, domestic remedies have to be exhausted. The final panel report should state the violation of relevant child labour provisions by the State party concerned and order cessation. As suggested by Stoll/Gött/Abel in their proposal for a model labour chapter for EU trade agreements, the panel may also afford satisfaction to the injured party, i.e. the child represented by the NGO including a pecuniary damage, non-pecuniary damage and costs and expenses.[149] The findings and determinations shall be binding on the parties and be enforceable in domestic courts of any State party to the new agreement like domestic judgements as is the case with investment awards under ICSID.[150]

Besides possible compensation for the injury occurred to the child and its family, the merit of the proposed procedure for private actors under the new agreement is that it puts pressure on the respondent state by mobilizing shame such as does for example representations under Art. 24 of the ILO Constitution. Even the relatively weak public communication procedure under the NAALC on the enforcement of domestic labour law has brought about some concrete results.[151] In contrast to representations under the ILO system, the proposed procedure does allow for specific complaints by NGOs on children's rights and provides for a strict timetable, ensuring a stronger enforcement.

149 Stoll/Gött/Abel, p. 421.

150 Dolzer/Schreuer, p. 288.

151 Cf. Humbert (The Challenge of Child Labour in International Law), p. 224.

It is also recommendable to provide for a public communication procedure as suggested in 'The Challenge of Child Labour in international Law'[152] and as did Stoll/Gött/Abel. This would be complementary and a rather low-level procedure allowing interested parties to bring public complaints against governments and corporations acting in the territory of other States parties with domestic contact points. The procedure would be built on existing procedures under the National Contact Points of the OECD and the NAALC public communication procedure and end with action plans or in case of governments with ministerial consultations.

4.6 *Human Rights Obligations for Companies?*

4.6.1 Companies as Duty-Bearers

The question now is whether companies should be directly obliged by international human rights law and corresponding individual complaints procedures established. The traditional view is that in contrast to states, companies are not subjects of international law.[153] However, even the traditional view admits that investment treaties and state-investor arbitration rules often trump national law and give transnational companies such rights and power as to make them close to state actors and subjects of international law.[154]

Indeed, *ius cogens* norms because of their unconditionality have convincingly been argued to bind companies directly.[155] Also, it seems to be appealing to establish a rebuttable presumption of transnational companies being subjects of international law and thus obliged to respect human rights because of their sheer economic power and impact on society and political life.[156] Emmerich-Fritsche holds that only those human rights should be found to bind companies directly that at their core are sufficiently concrete and justiciable, and can be found to also aim at addressing enterprises.[157] Nowak distinguishes between the general applicability of human rights to private actors and their implementation and enforcement.[158] While human rights certainly protect and oblige private actors, their enforcement and implementation is done by states because according to traditional doctrine, international law has been conceived as a law inter nations. Peters is rather sceptical to establish

152 Ibid., pp. 382–383; Stoll/Gött/Abel, p. 405.
153 Verdross/Simma (Universelles Völkerecht II), p. 267; Shaw, p. 139.
154 Ibid., p. 270.
155 Nowrot, pp. 562–595.
156 Cf. Ibid., p. 696.
157 Emmerich-Fritsche, p. 554 et seqq.
158 Nowak, pp. 64–67.

a direct obligation of companies to respect human rights and supports such an obligation only in case of a regulatory gap in domestic law and introduced through a treaty, i.e. not by way of judicial or academic production of law.[159] She submits that as in case of direct effect, the principle of legality has to be observed and the obligation must be sufficiently foreseeability by the new addressee.[160] Most importantly, the state has the primary responsibility for implementing the common good.[161] These arguments seem to be convincing. In any event, in the case of the prohibition of child labour as a norm of *ius cogens,*[162] companies should be held to be directly obliged.

The crucial question is then how such an obligation should be enforced. It has been suggested to consider establishing a complaints procedure under the ILO.[163] However, as Peters herself admits, the existing human rights treaty bodies are possibly not suited for such cases between private actors. The same holds true for the ILO special complaints procedures. While the ILO has a tripartite structure allowing workers' and employers' associations to bring complaints, also representations under Art. 24 of the ILO Constitution address states parties. In line with the subsidiary principle and the local remedy rule, it should be primarily domestic courts that should decide in cases of human rights abuses of individuals by private actors. They have the necessary local knowledge and expertise to decide such cases between private actors. Also, enforcement is best be done at the local level. In case of states with weak law enforcement, transnational private litigation should come in. Home states of mother companies and international buyers should be obliged under international law to provide remedies for human rights victims. This seems to be a feasible route forward, as discussed in the next session.

4.6.2 Promoting a Private Law Approach for Liability of Transnational Companies

As indicated in the preceding chapter, in line with the conflicts-law-approach, international private law should be used as a tool for regulating society where traditional forms of state regulation are often ineffective.[164] Indeed, there is a proliferation of domestic legislation holding transnationally operating companies accountable for human rights abuses in their value chain.[165]

159 Peters (Beyond Human Rights), p. 108.
160 Ibid., p. 101.
161 Ibid., p. 108.
162 Cf. Humbert, pp. 114–119.
163 Peters (Beyond Human Rights), p. 109; Weissbrodt/Kruger, p. 917.
164 Ibid., p. 244.
165 See for an excellent overview Grabosch.

Prominent examples include the US California Transparency in Supply Chains Act of 2010 on slavery and human trafficking,[166] the French *loi de vigilance*,[167] the EU Directive on Non-Financial Reporting 2014/95/EU[168] and the Dutch *Wet Zorgplicht Kinderarbeid*.[169] In February 2022, the EU Commission has proposed a new Directive on Corporate Sustainability Due Diligence giving human rights victims a right to compensation.[170] The rationale of such laws is primarily to prevent companies and its business relationships doing harm abroad and to hold them legally accountable through public reporting obligations or civil and criminal liability. A related aim is to inform consumers and create market incentives for companies.[171] Legislative proposals by civil society primarily aim at providing individuals affected by human rights abuses adequate remedies and access to justice where local laws are inadequate and enforcement is weak.[172]

Such domestic legislation reflects a growing global trend towards regulation of corporate social responsibility, a topic formerly regarded as merely subject to voluntary measures.[173] A multitude of case studies by NGOs and media reports however have shown that human rights abuses in global supply chains are an still endemic part of global business activities and voluntary measures no adequate remedy.[174] Thus, there is a growing consensus also among the business community in favour of binding laws. In a recent survey of European companies done for a study commissioned by the European Commission, almost 70 per cent of companies responded that regulation requiring mandatory due diligence would have positive impacts on human rights.[175] The topic

166 California Code, Civil Code, CIV Sec. 1714.43, https://codes.findlaw.com/ca/civil-code/civ-sect-1714-43.html.

167 See above p. 9.

168 See above p. 9; for a critical assessment, see Humbert (CSR Directive and Its German Implementation).

169 *Wet Zorgplicht Kinderarbeid*, 7 February 2017, Kamerstukken 34506, nr. 1–3.

170 Proposal for a Directive of the European Parliament and of the Council on Corporate Sustainability Due Diligence and amending Directive (EU) 2019/1937, COM/2022/71 final.

171 Cf. Grabosch, p. 18 on the California Transparency Supply Chains Act.

172 Initiative Lieferkettengesetz, p. 8; ECCJ.; Konzernverantwortungsinitiative.

173 Cf. Humbert (Corporate Social Responsibility); EU Communication from the Commission to the European Parliament, the Council, The European Economic and Social Committee and the Committee of the Regions, 'A renewed EU strategy 2011–14 for Corporate Social Responsibility', 681, 25 October 2011.

174 See for example, Oxfam Germany (Sweet Fruit); ECCHR; Süddeutsche Zeitung, Caspar Dohmen, Christoph Gunn, Benedikt Peters, Nicolas Richter, 'Das Schlammgrab', 5th of June 2020.

175 EU Commission/British Institute for International and Comparative Law/Civic Consulting,/London School of Economics, p. 105.

of corporate environmental and human rights mandatory due diligence also has become more prominent in legal scholarship with a growing number of scholars writing in favour of such legislation.[176]

The principal elements of such legislation should be based on the UN Guiding Principles on Business and Human Rights (UNGP) adopted by the Human Rights Council in 2011.[177] The UNGP express the expectation that UN member states support measures providing an incentive for companies to fulfil their responsibilities voluntarily, where appropriate, with statutory regulation, in order to effectively safeguard human rights.[178] In accordance with existing proposals by civil society, such a statute regulating corporate supply chain human rights due diligence should provide that corporations are liable for human rights violations that arise as a result of their failure to comply with due diligence obligations.[179] Such due diligence obligations should draw on principle 17 of the UNGP including a human rights risk and impact assessments based on consultation of stakeholders and those affected, taking appropriate measures to prevent and mitigate such risks, communicating on such efforts and establishing a complaints mechanism for human rights victims. The due diligence obligations should apply to the entire field of a company's business operations, that is, to the entire value chain from the production of raw materials to waste disposal. They should include financial relationships such as investments.

The appropriateness of the measures depends on the company's size, its connection to and leverage on the supplier, the seriousness of the human rights violation and the foreseeability of the damage. The law should provide both for reporting obligations under public law including sanctions to prevent companies from doing harm and civil liability in order to provide an effective remedy for human rights victims. And most importantly, under EU law, in order to have jurisdiction in accordance with international private law, such domestic law in EU member states would have to be formulated as a mandatory overriding norm in accordance with Art. 16 Rome II Regulation.[180]

---

176 See for example pro legislation on mandatory due diligence Krajewski/Saage-Maasz; Schall; Mansel; Rühmkorf; Weller/Kaller/Schulz; Kaufmann (Konzerninitiative). For literature contra such proposals, see for example Spießhofer.

177 UN Human Rights Council Resolution 17/4 of 16 June 2011, https://www.ohchr.org/documents/publications/guidingprinciplesbusinesshr_en.pdf.

178 Commentary to Principle 3 of the UNGP, https://www.ohchr.org/documents/publications/guidingprinciplesbusinesshr_en.pdf.

179 Initiative Lieferkettengesetz; ECCJ (Model Legislation).

180 Cf. Regulation (EC) No 864/2007 of the European Parliament and of the Council of 11 July 2007 on the law applicable to non-contractual obligations (Rome II) L199/40.

At the international level, the humanist approach should help to support devising and adopting an UN Treaty on Business and Human Rights[181] that would synthesize national efforts on mandatory human rights due diligence legislation and obligate member states to take the necessary measures. The Human Rights Council in 2014 adopted a resolution to establish an intergovernmental working group to work on such convention.[182] In essence, the Third Draft provides in para. 7.1., that States Parties shall provide the court and State-based non-judicial mechanisms with necessary competences in accordance with this (Legally Binding Instrument) and to enable victims' access to adequate, timely and effective remedy and access to justice and to overcome specific obstacles which women and groups in vulnerable and marginalized face in accessing such mechanisms and redress.[183]

Considering that the primary obligation to promote, respect and fulfill human rights under international law lies with states, such national legislation with extraterritorial effects is preferable to establishing international procedures for holding transnational companies liable. The approach of a New Legal Humanism promotes such an approach, which complements the new dispute resolution under an ILO-WTO joint implementation mechanism on trade and child labour *de lege ferenda*.

While the EU initially opposed the process of devising such a treaty, it has now joined the negotiations.[184]

5 Conclusion

The humanist approach to international law may help to deliver feasible solutions for the problem of trade and child labour.

On the substantive level, the constitutional principle of human rights obliges states and international organizations to give due regard their human rights obligations when applying trade or other rules of international law. In principle, human rights and WTO law should be accorded direct effect and

181 Legally binding instrument to regulate, in international human rights law, the activities of transnational corporations and other business enterprises, OEIGWG CHAIRMANSHIP SECOND REVISED DRAFT 6 August 2020, https://www.ohchr.org/en/hrbodies/hrc/wgtranscorp/pages/igwgontnc.aspx.

182 UN Human Rights Council (UN Treaty).

183 OEIGW GCHAIRMANSHIP THIRD REVISED DRAFT 17/08/2021, Art. 7. 1, Access to remedy, (A/HRC/52/41/Add.1), https://www.business-humanrights.org/en/big-issues/binding-treaty/.

184 Treaty Alliance Deutschland, CorA-Netzwerk.

should be actionable before domestic courts. On the institutional level, the new approach supports more integration of trade and labour law and helps to devise an ILO-WTO enforcement regime for child labour.

The agreement should provide for child labour standards as defined in ILO Conventions No. 138 and 182 but also refer to the ICESCR and the CRC. Member states would have the obligation to adequately implement these Conventions in law and practice. In accordance with WTO law, the agreement will distinguish between product-related child labour standards and country-related child labour standards, each standard entailing different enforcement procedures.

There should be cooperative activities including consultations between member states on joint projects such as trade incentive regimes modelled on the US-Cambodia FTA. The institutional bodies of the agreement would consist of trade and labour experts from member states or ILO and WTO staff. Most importantly, following the tripartite model of the ILO, NGOs on children's rights should be accorded formal status and be allowed to participate in dispute resolution and initiative proceedings against member states.

The dispute resolution on issues regarding product-related child labour would be modelled on WTO and ILO procedures. The proposed New Legal Humanism would support an obligation to consult for WTO adjudicating bodies and to treat the information as authoritative legal advice. There would be a possibility for the country concerned of initiating a TBP. The international community should offer technical and financial assistance. The latter points are proof of the developmental approach of the system. Trade measures would be measures of last resort.

Finally, the New Legal Humanism can be relied upon when arguing for the adoption of a UN Treaty of Business and Human Rights that obligates member states to enact legislation on mandatory corporate human rights due diligence in the context of transnational business activities.

CHAPTER 5

Concluding Summary

1 Summary of Results

1.1 *Chapter 1*

Chapter 1 recalls child labour as a major challenge in today's globalization, which needs to be tackled by the international community. Revealing the international dimension of child labour, it demonstrates the limits of purely national solutions. It stresses the trade and child labour linkage, outlining the structure of the global economy where international value chains closely tie states together. Finally, it establishes the *ius cogens* nature of the right of children to be protected from child labour referring to Humbert.[1] The chapter concludes by emphasizing the need for global solutions including trade measures and national private law solutions holding companies accountable for human rights violations abroad.

1.2 *Chapter 2*

Chapter 2 analyses in detail the WTO law consistency of trade measures with child labour. Overall, WTO law *de lege lata* offers considerable space to accommodate child labour concerns. Prohibitions of child labour in trade measures may be used as long as such measures do not discriminate with respect to the origin of goods and take account of the interests of exporting countries, in particular of those of developing countries, and the children concerned. Under a human rights-based interpretation of the trade provisions most of the existing trade measures on child labour can be justified. A balance between trade and human rights concerns is possible.

Trade measures on child labour include for example the US ban on goods produced with forced or indentured child labour, the proposed EU Forced Labour Regulation, the UFPLA, the former 2003 US Burmese Freedom and Democracy Act banning all goods coming from Myanmar, the US and EU GSPs, the Kimberley Process Certification Scheme and the Belgian Social Label law. The US ban on goods produced with forced or indentured child labour, the proposed EU Forced Labour Regulation and the Belgian Social Label Law are npr-ppm-measures focussing on prohibiting goods produced under certain process

1 Humbert (The Challenge of Child Labour).

© FRANZISKA HUMBERT, 2024 | DOI:10.1163/9789004690905_007

and production methods in contrast to the US and EU GSPs, the UFLPA as well as the US Burmese Freedom and Democracy Act that are country-specific measures regulating the import of goods from certain destinations and require a different justification under WTO law.

The MFN treatment clause contained in GATT Art. I:1 is one of the central pillars of the WTO. It provides that WTO members shall not discriminate regarding imports. For example, withdrawal of trade concessions vis-à-vis Myanmar taken in response to the recommendations of the International Labour Conference under Art. 33 of the ILO Constitution would constitute *de iure* discrimination and violate GATT Art. I:1.

Regarding the 'like-product-issue', it has been established that the approach under GATT Art. I and III is similar. The same market-based criteria as established by the WTO jurisprudence under GATT Art. III should be used. PPM-measures are not *per se* prohibited under GATT Art. I.

In contrast to GATT Art. III, the regulatory purpose of the measure should not be considered. However, the 'asymmetric impact' requirement of potential trade effects also applies under GATT Art. I under the term 'any advantage'.

The term 'immediately and unconditionally' shall be understood to prohibit conditions that relate to the situation or conduct of specific countries. In addition, as under GATT Art. III, a 'supply substitutability' and 'inherence' test shall be conducted to consider producer concerns. This is recommendable from a developmental point of view as well as from a point of view of trade experts since both tests reflect a more real-world situation of trade.

Assuming there was no waiver, bans under the Kimberley Process Certification Scheme would constitute *de iure* violations of GATT Art. I:1, relating to the legal regime of other countries. The US ban on goods made with forced or indentured child labour, the proposed EU Forced Labour Regulation and the Belgian Social Label Law may constitute *de facto* violations of GATT Art. I:1 provided they have an asymmetric discriminatory impact that is not mitigated by supply substitutability.

According to WTO jurisprudence, the Enabling Clause is an exception to GATT Art. I:1 and allows for preferential tariff treatment accorded to developing countries if such treatment is generalized, non-reciprocal and non-discriminatory. The special incentive arrangements for sustainable development and good governance contained in the current EU GSP are consistent with the Enabling Clause. Since the labour clause of the US GSP grants the President too much discretion, it cannot be deemed to be non-discriminatory within the meaning of the Enabling Clause.

The national treatment clause contained in GATT Art. III is the second main pillar of WTO law. It requires the treatment of imported goods no worse than that of like domestic products. While WTO jurisprudence so far avoided to explicitly decide on the legality of npr-ppm-measures and their extraterritoriality, this work proposes to solve the matter regarding trade measures on child labour by referring to the international law of state responsibility and countermeasures in response to violations of *ius cogens*. Given that economic countermeasures in reaction to violations of *ius cogens* are possible under international law, origin-neutral trade measures on child labour as a norm of *ius cogens* should be permitted *a fortiori*. Whether npr-ppm-measures on child labour can also be justified because of their societal regulatory aim has been subject to much debate in jurisprudence and legal literature. The *EC–Asbestos* decision has clarified that the regulatory purpose may come in under the market-based criteria of consumer interests. That is, if market analysis demonstrates that imported products made with child labour are not 'like products' from domestic production not made with child labour, then trade measures on child labour will not violate GATT Art. III. So far however, this will not be the case in most countries.

This work submits that the wording GATT Art. III 'so as to afford protection' provides some textual basis to consider the regulatory purpose. This should be done under the equal treatment obligation but only in case trade effects of a measure are unclear. Decisions such as *Chile–Alcoholic Beverages* point into this direction. However, most measures on child labour will have a *bona fide* aim but an asymmetric discriminatory impact by treating most imported products worse than domestic products. This probably holds true for the Belgian Social Label Law and US ban on goods made with forced or indentured child labour. Thus, most of the measures on child labour are likely to contravene GATT Art. III.

The US ban on goods coming from Myanmar violates GATT Art. XI. In case national measures implemented under the Kimberley Process Certification Scheme ban diamonds coming from non-participants, they constitute an import prohibition and violate GATT Art. XI.

The Safeguard Clause contained in GATT Art. XIX does not provide an appropriate basis for justifying trade measures on child labour.

GATT Art. XX provides for general exceptions from substantive GATT obligations such as GATT Art. I, III and XI. The Appellate Body ruling of *EC–Seal Products* provides ample room for members to justify trade measures under GATT Art. XX (a) on public morals. Existing trade measures regarding child labour can be said to protect the public morals of the regulating state and the international community within the meaning of GATT Art. XX (a), in particular in the light of the fact that the international prohibition of child labour is part of *ius cogens* that applies *erga omnes* establishing a public order. To justify measures with an extraterritorial application under GATT Art. XX (a), public international law on extraterritorial effects of state acts as well the legal consequences of *ius cogens* regarding possible countermeasures may be referred to. GATT Art. XX (b) protecting health is also applicable to trade measures on child labour given that child labour often adversely impacts the mental and physical health of children.

The WTO adjudicating bodies have refined the earlier necessity test calling for a least trade-restrictive means test under GATT Art. XX (a) and (b) and made it evolve into a proportionality test that is able to take due account of non-economic values. This has been called a 'constitutionalization in a modest sense'. Under such a test, a blanket import ban on goods made with child labour without any flanking measures is likely to be contrary to GATT Art. XX (a). By contrast, preferential tariffs or labelling requirements implemented in a way that accommodates the interests of the exporting state and the children concerned would probably be found to be 'necessary'. Likewise, the EU GSP and the Belgian Social Label Law would probably pass the proportionality test.

In accordance with the general striving for more coherence in international law, the US ban on goods coming from Myanmar taken in response to the ILO recommendation, and measures implemented under the Kimberley Process Certification Scheme may be considered to be necessary in accordance with GATT Art. XX (a).

To date, it has been well established in WTO jurisprudence and legal literature that the *chapeau* is an expression of good faith and asks whether the application of a measure amounts to an *abus de droit*. This approach has been questioned by Bartels who argues against distinguishing between the content and the application of a measure. Instead, he suggests analysing the trade restrictiveness under the subparagraphs and the discriminatory elements of a measure under the *chapeau*, taking due account also of the passage 'where the same conditions prevail'. Such a straightforward approach makes sense for example where it is difficult to differentiate between content and application. It merits further consideration. However, it will probably not make much difference for measures on child labour. The Belgian Social Label Law or the US ban on goods coming from Myanmar would still pass the *chapeau* because in countries impacted by discriminatory trade effects, the same conditions would not prevail and the relevant measures would probably be justified.

GATT Art. XXI defends national security interests of WTO members and entitles them to take unilateral measures in response to non-economic action. According to the Appellate Body of *Russia–Traffic in Transit*, GATT Art. XXI (b) (iii) is justiciable. The term 'emergency in international relations' can be read to relate to wrongful acts of states including violations of *ius cogens*. Hence, in the case of Myanmar, where large scale *ius cogens* violations occurred, a wrongful act of a state can be assumed. However, to be able to rely on 'essential security interests', a member would have to specifically articulate the connection between the trade measure and its essential security interests. This is currently not the case with existing measures of child labour.

To the extent Security Council resolutions were adopted to ban trade in diamonds in certain territories, national measures implemented under the Kimberley Process Certification Scheme may be justified under GATT Art. XXI (c). The jurisdictional treatment of the security exceptions has been called a 'yardstick of the world order's constitutionalization'.[2]

The TBT Agreement contains disciplines for technical regulations that are mandatory and standards that are voluntary. The term 'technical regulation' should be read in a narrow way covering primarily technical rules involving or concerned with applied and industrial sciences with a rather strong product nexus. Trade measures on child labour with a looser product nexus should be assessed under GATT Art. III and XX.

The main substantive obligations refer to the principle of non-discrimination and the prohibition of trade restrictions constituting unnecessary obstacles to international trade. In contrast to GATT Art. III, a measure will only be discriminatory if the detrimental impact does not stem from a legitimate regulatory distinction rather than reflecting discrimination. The proportionality test of GATT Art. XX should be applied to achieve more balanced results. The provision on trade restrictions equally contains a proportionality test. Trade measures on child labour that fall within the scope of the TBT Agreement are the Belgian Social Label Law and the Kimberley Process Certification Scheme. They have both been found to be consistent with the principle of non-discrimination as well as with the obligation to refrain from creating unnecessary obstacle to international trade.

The central pillars of the GPA (2012) are the non-discrimination clause prohibiting *de iure* and *de facto* discrimination, supplier qualifications and the regime on technical specifications and evaluation criteria.

Whereas technical specifications may not be read to encompass social npr-ppms such as the non-use of child labour in the production process, evaluation criteria do.

There is some debate between legal scholars as to whether non-WTO norms such as the recommendation adopted by the International Labour Conference in the Myanmar case encompassing economic measures may be applied by

2 Emerson, p. 153; Schloemann/Ohloff, p. 451.

WTO panels and prevent them from finding a violation of WTO law. Since in case of trade measures on child labour, WTO obligations can be interpreted in accordance with human rights obligations, there is no need to apply human rights norms directly.

The chapter concludes by holding that most of the existing trade measures on child labour will be compatible with WTO law and that substantial coherence between trade and human rights and/or labour law is possible. It deplores however the fragmentation of international trade and child labour law and the insufficient institutional sensitivity of WTO panels to other international organizations. Also, children and private actors do not have effective access to dispute settlement and judicial review.

1.3 *Chapter 3*

Having in mind shortcomings of protection and fragmentation analysed in Chapter 2, Chapter 3 asks whether the common positivist doctrine underlying international law is sufficiently well-equipped to address pressing legal issues such as the challenge of child labour and trade including proposals for better collaboration of the ILO and the WTO including a joint implementation mechanism. The chapter thus turns to theorizing the foundations of international law and exploring in particular the prospects of constitutionalization and multi-layered governance.

Analysing manifold new approaches such as global legal pluralism, global administrative law and the variety of constitutionalist schools of thoughts that seek to respond to the phenomenon of fragmentation, the chapter finds that in principle, the constitutional approach seems to be a valid and well-suited to improve the basis for a more integrated legal order and an adequate institutional framework for trade and child labour. Discussing the different critiques, the study holds that at their core, they all criticise the lack of global values as a basis for a constitutional approach. Hence, the study continues by asking whether indeed current international law is only based on positivism or has evolved into a more value-based order. It finds that recourse to natural law is already happening and possible. Hence, what is needed is a test of whether the constitutional norms of human rights, democracy and the rule of law are global values enshrined in our global order.

Taking the natural law approach seriously, the quest for global values should take recourse to philosophy, the discipline that has the human being at its core. To prove whether moral considerations indeed reflect societal needs, public debate consisting of contributions by political and corporate decision makers, academics and NGOs and other authoritative representatives of community interests should be considered. Of course, existing positivist law already embodying community interests must also be included in the analysis. This includes international conventions, custom, general principles of international law and soft law instruments. Subsidiary sources of Art. 38 (1) of the ICJ such as judicial decisions, and teachings of the most highly qualified publicists constitute another important source under a natural law approach. Finally, global values must be reflected by state practice and acts of international organizations. The study concludes that while democracy cannot to be said a global value of the current global order, human rights and the rule of law can.

Based on these findings, the chapter suggests a New Legal Humanism approach to international law putting the individual human being at the centre. Recognizing that the existence of common values is proof of a growing constitutionalization of international law, it builds upon the constitutionalist approaches, while taking due account of current trend of retreat of democracy.

The added value of such a New Legal Humanism is to lay the foundation for devising answers to the fragmentation of trade and child labour such as the creation of new constitutional principles, an institutional framework, recognizing private actors as new subjects with enforceable rights as well as promoting direct effect of international norms.

1.4 *Chapter 4*

Chapter 4 elaborates the legal implications of such a new humanist approach to international law, in particular for trade and child labour.

Framing international law in terms of a New Legal Humanism means first of all to recognize the global values of human rights and the rule of law as new constitutional principles in terms of a new source of law within the meaning of Art. 38 (1) ICJ Statute. Thus, all international actors including international organizations are bound by human rights beyond *ius cogens* and the constraints of Art. 31 of the VCLT. Secondly, a New Legal Humanism would help to accept individuals as new subjects of international law with enforceable rights. Thirdly, such constitutional principles also help to argue in favour of direct effect of human, i.e. children's rights, and WTO-law. Fourthly, a New Legal Humanism would offer an adequate frame for a new ILO-WTO agreement to improve implementation of the human right to protection from child labour with substantive provisions on trade-related child labour following the model of social clauses including dispute resolution providing for trade sanctions. The constitutional principles of human rights and the rule of law also provide legal arguments when according civil society actors membership rights and the right to initiate dispute resolution. A New Legal Humanism would also support an obligation to consult for WTO adjudicating bodies and to treat the information as authoritative legal advice. Fifthly, it would support the application of the principle of proportionality and subsidiarity when building such systems of multi-level governance as the proposed ILO-WTO enforcement regime.

Sixthly and finally, a New Legal Humanism would also promote private law enforcement in business and human rights supporting rights human rights due diligence legislation as well as a UN Treaty on Business and Human Rights.

2 Epilogue

Realists object that the Hobbesian world is not ready for multi-level governance in times of raising nationalism. However, in the long-term, there is no other way out of current global political, ecological, economic and health crises, as problems are inherently interdependent and many public goods only can be properly produced on the global level and in close cooperation.

Although it seems utopian to make the claim for a new multilateral legal order under a Kantian approach when the Russian war against Ukraine puts the current world order under threat,[3] it is all the more needed given the importance and urgency of offering tools towards achieving a world order based on democracy, the rule of law and human rights.

The added value of a New Legal Humanism is to provide a cognitive frame to help shape the future in this direction. And given that the ILC has just begun to work on general principles of international law as a source of law, it seems timely to devise new constitutional principles.[4] The point is to know which direction we should take, step by step.

Having analysed the contemporary limitations of traditional constitutional values of democracy, the focus on human rights and the rule of law should, however, not be understood as limiting the new approach to these principles. While issues such as climate change seriously threatening the enjoyment of human rights can already be addressed under the new constitutional principle of human rights, a New Legal Humanism is also open to include more values and issues if found to be principles of global reach. This will potentially be the case with common concerns of humankind put forward by Cottier.[5] Gehne also has convincingly argued for conceiving sustainability as both a general principle of international law and a source of law. Gehne has qualified the

3 Cf. Carnegie Europe, Stefan Lehne, What kind of After Russia's War Against Ukraine: What Kind of World Order?, (2023), https://carnegieeurope.eu/2023/02/28/after-russia-s-war-against-ukraine-what-kind-of-world-order-pub-89130.

4 See, ILC, seventy-first session, Geneva, 29 April 7 June and 8 July, 9 August 2019.

5 Cottier (The Principle of Common Concern of Humankind).

concept of sustainable development as laid down in the Brundtland report[6] as a reconciliation and efficiency requirement that has the quality of a legal norm in accordance with legal sources theories developed by Kelsen, Alexey and Hart.[7] In her view, the concept of sustainable development may also serve as a constitutional principle that helps to create the constitution of a certain legal order.[8] More specifically, Gehne submits that this concept conveys a multi-level government approach that adds to transnational governance schemes on the international level.[9] Such a reading of the concept of sustainable development supports the approach suggested here, a New Legal Humanism that also calls for multi-level governance.

6 Brundtland Report.
7 Gehne, pp. 214, 255, 297 et seqq.
8 Ibid., pp. 266–268.
9 Ibid., p. 350.

Bibliography

UN and ILO documents are cited by their document number or by the name of the organization (the UN or ILO respectively) followed by the title of the document.

An-Na'im, Abdullahi Ahmed, 'Islam, Islamic Law and the Dilemma of Cultural Legitimacy for Universal Human Rights' in Claude E. Welch, Jr., Virginia A. Leary (ed.) *Asian Perspectives on Human Rights* (Boulder, San Francisco, Oxford: Westview Press, 1990), pp. 31–54 (cited: An-Na'im (Islam, Islamic and the Dilemma of Cultural Legitimacy)).

Anti-Slavery, ECCHR, The Greens/EFA, Progressing the proposed EU Regulation on prohibiting products made with forced labour: A Model Law, 2022, https://www.ecchr.eu/en/publication/progressing-the-proposed-eu-regulation-on-prohibiting-products-made-with-forced-labour-a-model-law/.

Ahmed An-Na'im, Abdullahi, 'Towards a Cross-Cultural Approach to Defining International Standards of Human Rights, The Meaning of Cruel, Inhuman, or Degrading Treatment or Punishment' in Abdullahi Ahmed An-Na'im (ed.) *Human Rights in Cross-Cultural Perspectives, A Quest for Consensus* (Philadelphia: University of Philadelphia Press, 1992), pp. 19–43 (cited: An-Na'im, (Towards a Cross-Cultural Approach)).

Allot, Philipp, 'The Concept of International Law', in EJIL 10 (1999), pp. 31–50.

Alston, Philip 'Art. 32 The Right to Protection from Economic Exploitation' in John Tobin (ed.), *The UN Convention on the Rights of the Child* (Cambridge University Press, 2019), pp. 1224–1272 (cited: Alston (The Right to Protection from Economic Exploitation)).

Alston, Philip, 'The UN's Human Rights Record: From San Francisco to Vienna and beyond', 16 HRQ (1994), pp. 375–390 (cited: Alston (The UN's Human Rights Record)).

American Law Institute, Restatement (Third) Foreign Relations Law of the United States, 2 (1987) (cited: Third Restatement of US Foreign Relations Law).

Anderson, Robert D., Arrowsmith, Sue, 'The WTO regime on government procurement: past, present, and the future' in Sue Arrowsmith and Robert D. Anderson (eds.), *The WTO Agreement on Government Procurement: Challenge and Reform* (New York, CUP 2011), pp. 3–58.

Appleton, Arthur E., 'Shrimp/Turtle: Untangling the Nets', in *Journal of International Economic Law* (1999), pp. 477–496.

Auger, Pat, Devinney, Timothey M., 'Do what Consumers say matter?', 2005, (on file with the author).

Auger, Pat, Burke, Paul, Devinney, Timothy M., Louviere, Jordan, J., 'What Will Consumers Pay for Social Product Features?', in *Journal of Business Ethics*, 42 (2003), pp. 281–304.

Bartels, Lorand, 'Applicable Law in WTO Dispute Settlement Proceedings', in *Journal of World Trade*, 35 (3) (2001), pp. 499–519 (cited: Bartels (Applicable Law)).

Bartels, Lorand, 'Article XX of GATT and the Problem of Extraterritorial Jurisdiction, The Case of Trade Measures for the Protection of Human Rights', in *Journal of World Trade*, 36 (2) (2002), pp. 353–403 (cited: Bartels (Extraterritorial Jurisdiction)).

Bartels, Lorand, 'The Chapeau of the General Exceptions in the WTO GATT and GATS Agreements: A reconstruction', 109 AJIL (2015), pp. 95–125 (cited: Bartels (The Chapeau)).

Bartels, Lorand, 'The WTO Enabling Clause and Positive Conditionality in the Community's GSP Program', in *Journal of International Economic Law*, 6 (2) (2003), pp. 502–532 (cited: Bartels (The WTO Enabling Clause)).

Beitz, Charles, *The Idea of Human Rights* (Oxford University Press, 2009).

Belk, Russell, W., Devinney, Timothey, Eckhardt, Giana, 'Consumer Ethics across Cultures', in *Consumption, Markets and Culture*, 8 (3) (2005), pp. 275–289.

Besson, Samantha, 'Institutionalising global *demoi*-cracy', in Lukas Meyer (ed.), *Legitimacy, Justice and Public International Law,* (Cambridge University Press 2009), pp. 58–91 (cited: Besson (Institutional global *demoi*-cracy)).

Besson, Samantha, 'Sources of International Human Rights Law, How general is general international law?' in Samantha Besson, Jean D'Aspremont, Séverine Kuchel (eds.) *The Oxford Handbook on the Sources of* International Law (Oxford University Press, 2017), pp. 837–870 (cited: Besson (Sources of International Human Rights Law)).

Besson, Samantha, The Morality of Conflict, Reasonable Disagreement and the Law (Oxford&Portand/Oregon:Hart Publishing, 2005) (cited: Besson (The Morality of Conflict)).

Besson, Samantha, Theorizing the Sources of International Law' in Samantha Besson, John Tsasioulas (eds.), *The Philosophy of International Law* (Oxford University Press: 2010), pp. 163–185 cited (Besson (Theorizing the Sources)).

Blüthner, Andreas, *Welthandel und Menschenrechte in der Arbeit, The Compatibility of Human Rights at Work with the WTO-System* (Frankfurt am Main: Peter Lang GmbH/ Europäischer Verlag der Wissenschaften, 2004).

Bluntschli, J. C., *Das moderne Völkerrecht der civilisierten Staaten: als Rechtsbuch dargestellt* (Nördlingen: Verlag der CH Beck'schen Buchhandlungen, 1878).

Böckenförde, Ernst, Wolfgang, *Staat, Verfassung, Demokratie* (Frankfurt am Main: Suhrkamp, 1991).

Boyle, Alan, Chinkin, Christin, *The Making of International Law* (Oxford University Press 2007).

Brigitte, 'Report on Child Soldiers', No. 23, November 2005.

Bronckers, Marco & McNelis, Natalie, 'Rethinking the "Like Product" Definition in WTO law: Antidumping and Environmental Protection', in Thomas Cottier and

Peter Mavroidis, (eds.), *Regulatory Barriers and The Principle of Non-Discrimination in World Trade Law* (Ann Arbor: University of Michigan Press, 2000), pp. 345–385.

Buchanan, Allan, 'The Legitimacy of International Law' in Samantha Besson, John Tsasioulas (eds.), *The Philosophy of International Law* (Oxford University Press, 2010), pp. 79–96 (cited: Buchanan (The Legitimacy of International Law)).

Buchanan, Allan, Keohane, Robert, 'The Legitimacy of Global Governance Institutions', in Rüdiger Wolfrum, Volker Röben (eds.), *Legitimacy in International Law*, Beiträge zum ausländischen öffentlichen Recht (Heidelberg: Springer 2008), pp. 25–62.

Buchanan, Allan, 'Why International Legal Human Rights?', in Rowen Cruft, Massimo Leno and Massimo Renzo (eds.), *Philosophical Foundations of Human Rights* (Oxford University Press, 2015), pp. 244–263 (cited: Buchanan (Why International Legal Human Rights?)).

Burda, Julien, *Travail des enfants et commerce international des marchandises: vers une prise en compte des droits humains à l'OMC?* (on file with the author).

Caney, Simon, *Justice Beyond Borders, A Global Political Theory* (Oxford University Press, 2005).

Casey, Christopher A., Congressional Research Service, 'Section 307 and Imports Produced by Forced Labor', 26 July 2022, https://crsreports.congress.gov.

Cass, Deborah, *The Constitutionalization of the World Trade Organization, Legitimacy, Democracy, and Community in the International Trading System* (Oxford University Press, 2005).

Cassese, Antonio, *International Law*, 2nd ed. (Oxford University Press, 2005).

Cassese, Antonio, *International Law in a Divided World* (Oxford: Clarendon Press, 1986) (cited: Cassese (International Law in a Divided World)).

Charlesworth, Hilary, ‚Feminist Methods in International Law', Symposium on Method, 93 AJIL (1999), pp. 378–394.

Charlesworth, Hilary, Chinkin, Christine and Wright, Shelley, 'Feminist Approaches to International Law', in *American Journal of International Law*, 85 (1991), pp. 616–645.

Charnovitz, Steve, 'The Moral Exception in Trade Policy', in *Virginia Journal of International Law*, 38 (1998), pp. 689–745 (cited: Charnovitz (The Moral Exception)).

Cheng, B., *General Principles of Law as applied by International Courts and Tribunals* (London: Stevens and Sons, 1953).

Chesterman, Simon, 'Rule of Law', in Rüdiger Wolfrum (ed.), Vol. VIII *Max Planck Encyclopaedia of Public International Law* (Oxford University Press, 2012), p. 1014–1022.

Choi, Won-Mog, *Towards a consistent GATT/WTO – 'Like Products' in International Law* (Oxford: Oxford University Press, 2003).

Choudhoury, Barnali, Gehne, Katja, Heri, Simone, Humbert, Franziska, Kaufmann, Christine and Nadakavukaren Schefer, Krista, 'A call for a WTO ministerial decision on trade and human rights', in Cottier, Thomas, Delimatsis, Panagiotis, (eds.) *The*

Prospects of International Trade Regulation (Cambridge University Press, 2011), pp. 323–358.

Cleveland, Sara H., 'Human Rights Sanctions and International Trade: A Theory of Compatibility', in *Journal of International Economic Law*, 5 (1) (2002), pp. 133–189.

Concise Oxford English Dictionary, 12th ed. (New York: Oxford University Press, 2011).

Concise Dictionary of Politics & International Relations, Garrett Brown, Ian McLeon, Alistair McMillan (eds.), 4th ed. (Oxford University Press, 2018).

Cone, Sydney M., 'The Appellate Body and Harrowsmith Country Life', in *Journal of World Trade Law*, 32 (2) (1998), pp. 103–117.

CorA-Netzwerk et al., *Anforderungen an wirkungsvolle Multi-Stakeholder-Initiativen zur Stärkung unternehmerischer Sorgfaltspflichten, Empfehlungen aus der Sicht der Zivilgesellschaft*, 17 July 2020, https://www.cora-netz.de/wp-content/uploads/2020/07/2020-07-17_MSI-Positionspapier_CorA-ForumMR-VENRO.pdf (cited: CorA-Netzwerk (Anforderungen an Multi-Stakeholder-Initiativen)).

Cottier, Thomas, 'A Theory of Direct Effect in Global Law', in Armin von Bogdandy / Petros C. Mavroidis / Yves Mény (eds.) *European Integration and International Coordination*, Studies in Transnational Economic Law in Honour of Claus-Dieter Ehlermann (The Hague/London/New York, 2002), pp. 99–123 (cited: Cottier (Theory of Direct Effect)).

Cottier, Thomas, 'Anti-Trust Rules in Domestic Jurisdiction' in Cottier, Thomas, Nadakavukaren Schefer, Krista (eds.) *Elgar Encyclopedia pf International Economic Law* (Cheltenham: Edward Elgar Publishing, 2017) (cited: Cottier (Anti-Trust Rules in Domestic Jurisdiction)).

Cottier, Thomas, ‚Der Strukturwandel des Aussenwirtschaftsrechts' in 29 Swiss Review of International and European Law (2019), pp. 203–230.

Cottier, Thomas, *Equitable Principles of Maritime Boundary Delimitation, The Quest for Distributive Justice in International Law* (Cambridge University Press, 2015).

Cottier, Thomas, 'From Progressive Liberalization to Progressive Regulation in WTO', in Vol. 9 (2) Journal of International Economic Law (2006), pp. 792–821 (cited: Cottier (From Progressive Liberalization to Progressive Regulation in WTO Law)).

Cottier, Thomas, 'Front-loading Trade Policy-Making in the European Union: Towards a Trade Act' in European Yearbook of International Economic Law (2017), pp. 35–60 (cited: Cottier (Front-loading)).

Cottier, Thomas, 'Improving Compliance: Jus Cogens and International Economic Law' in Maarten den Heijer, Harmen van der Wilt (eds.) *Jus Cogens: Quo Vadis?, Netherlands Yearbook of International Law* 46 (Leiden: Springer, 2015), pp. 329–356 (cited: Cottier (Improving Compliance: *Jus Cogens* and International Law)).

Cottier, Thomas, ‚International Trade Law: The Impact of Justiciability and Separations of Powers in EC Law', 5 *European Constitutional Law Review* (2009), pp. 307–326 (cited: (Cottier (The Impact of Justiciability)).

Cottier, Thomas, 'John H. Jackson, Sovereignty-Modern and the Constitutional Approach to International Law', 19 *JIEL* (2016), pp. 323–328 (cited: Cottier (John H. Jackson, Sovereignty-Modern)).

Cottier, Thomas, 'Limits to International Trade: The Constitutional Challenge', in: The American Society of International Law (ed.) *International Law in Ferment: A New Vision for Theory and Practice*. Proceedings of the 94th Annual Meeting, April 5–8, 2000, Washington, D.C. (2000), pp. 220–222 (cited: Cottier (Limits to International Trade)).

Cottier, Thomas, 'Multi-layered Governance, Pluralism and Moral Conflict, 16 *Indiana Journal of Global Legal Studies* (2009), pp. 647–679 (cited: Cottier (Multi-layered Governance)).

Cottier, Tomas, 'The Changing Structure of International Trade Law' in 21 Zeitschrift für europarechtliche Studien (2018), pp. 421–336 (cited: Cottier (The Changing Structure of International Law)).

Cottier, Thomas, 'The Implications of EC–Seal Products for the Protection of Core Labour Standards in WTO Law' in Henner Gött (ed.), *Labour Standards in International Economic Law* (Cham: Springer, 2018), pp. 69–92 (cited: Cottier (The Implications of EC–Seal Products)).

Cottier, Thomas, 'The Judge in International Economic Relations', in Mario Monti, Prinz Nikolaus von und zu Liechtenstein, Bo Westerdorf, Jay Westbrock, Luzins Wildhabrer (eds.), *Festschrift für Carl Baudenbacher, Economic Law and Justice in Times of Globalization* (Bern: Nomos, Stämpfli Verlag AG Bern, 2007) (cited: Cottier (The Judge in International Economic Relations)).

Cottier, Thomas, 'The legitimacy of WTO law' in Linda Yueh (ed.) *The Law and Economics of Globalization, New Challenges for a World in Flux* (Cheltenham: Edward Elgar, 2009), pp. 11–48 (cited: Cottier (The legitimacy of WTO law)).

Cottier, Thomas, 'The Principle of Common Concern of Humankind' in Thomas Cottier (ed.) *The Principles of Common Concern of Humankind in International Law* (Cambridge University Press, 2021) (cited: Cottier (The Principle of Common Concern of Humankind)).

Cottier, Thomas, ‚Towards a Five Storey Howse', in Christian Joerges and Ernst-Ulrich Petersmann (eds.), *Constitutionalism, Multi-level Trade Governance and International Economic Law* (Oxford, Portland, Oregon: Hart Publishing, 2011), pp. 495–532 (cited: Cottier (Towards a Five Storey House)).

Cottier, Thomas, 'Trade and Human Rights: A Relationship to Discover', in *Journal of International Economic Law*, 5 (1) (2000), pp. 111–132 (cited: Cottier (Trade and Human Rights)).

Cottier, Thomas, Caplazi, Alexandra, 'Labour Standards and World Trade Law: Interfacing Legitimate Concerns', in Thomas Geiser, Hans Schmid, Emil

Walter-Busch (eds.), *Arbeit in der Schweiz des 20. Jahrhunderts* (Bern at al.: Verlag Paul Haupt, 1998), pp. 469–507.

Cottier, Thomas, Delimatsis, Panagiotis, Gehne, Katja, Payosova, Tetyana, 'Introduction, Fragmentation and coherence in international trade regulation: analysis and conceptual foundation', in Thomas Cottier, Panagiotis Delimatsis, (eds.), *The Prospects of International Trade Regulation* (Cambridge University Press, 2011), pp. 1–65.

Cottier, Thomas, Echandi, Roberto, Liechti-McKee, Rachel, Payosova, Tetyana, Sieber, Charlotte, 'The Principle of Proportionality in International Law: Foundations and Variations', in 18 Journal of World Investment & Trade (2017), pp. 628–672.

Cottier Thomas, Hertig, Maya, 'The Prospects of 21st Century Constitutionalisation', 7 Max Planck Yearbook of United Nations Law (2003), pp. 261–328.

Cottier, Thomas, Oesch, Matthias, *International Trade Regulation, Law and Policy in the WTO, The European Union and Switzerland, Cases, Materials and Comments* (London/Berne: Cameron & May, Staempfli Publishers, 2005).

Cottier, Thomas, Pauwelyn Joost, Bürgi, Elisabeth, 'Linking Trade Regulation and Human Rights in International Law', in Thomas Cottier, Joost Pauwelyn, Elisabeth Bürgi (eds.), *Human Rights and International Trade* (Oxford: Oxford University Press, 2006), pp. 1–26 (cited: Cottier/Pauwelyn/Bürgi (Linking Trade Regulation and Human Rights in International Law)).

Crawford, James, *State Responsibility* (Cambridge University Press, 2013).

Danish Institute for Human Rights, *The Constitutional Protection of Human Rights*, (2014), https://www.humanrights.dk/sites/humanrights.dk/files/media/migrated/the_constitutional_protection_of_human_rights_en.pdf.

Davies, Arwel, ,National Treatment and Exceptions provisions' in Sue Arrowsmith and Robert D. Anderson (eds.), *The WTO Government Procurement: Challenge and Reform* (New York: Cambridge University Press, 2011), pp. 429–435.

Davey, William J. and Pauwelyn, Joost, 'MFN Unconditionality: A Legal Analysis of the Concept in View of its Evolution in the GATT/WTO Jurisprudence with Particular Reference to the Issue of "Like Product"', in Thomas Cottier, Petros C. Mavroidis, (eds.), *Regulatory Barriers and the Principle of Non-Discrimination in WTO Law: An Overview* (Ann Arbor: University of Michigan Press, 2000), pp. 13–50.

Degenhardt, Christoph, *Staatsrecht I*, 9th ed. (Heidelberg: C.F. Müller Juristischer Verlag, 1984).

De Janvry, Alain de, Finan, Frederico, Sadoulet, Elisabeth, University of California at Berkeley, Evaluating Brazil's Bolsa Escola Program: Impact on Schooling and Municipal Roles, June 2006, http://are.berkeley.edu/~esadoulet/papers/BolsaEscolaReport6-6.pdf.

Delimatsis, Panagiotis, 'Protecting Public Morals in a Digital Age: Revisiting the WTO Rulings on *US – Gambling* and *China – Publications and Audiovisual Products*', in Vol. 14 (2) JIEL (2011), pp. 257–293.

Demaret, Paul, Stewardson, Raoul, 'Border Tax Adjustments under GATT and EC Law and General Implications for Environmental Taxes', in *Journal of World Trade*, 28 (4), 1994, pp. 5–65.

De Schutter, Olivier, 'Les critical legal studies au pays du droit international public', 22 Droit et Société (1992), pp. 585–605.

De Schutter, Olivier, Eide, Ashborn, Khalfan, Ashfaq, Orellana, Marcos, Salomon, Margot, Seidermann, Ian, 'Commentary to the Maastricht Principles on Extraterritorial Obligations of States in the Area of Economic, Social and Cultural Rights' Vol. 34 (4), HRQ (2012), pp. 1084–1169.

Desmedt, Axel, 'Proportionality in WTO Law', in *Journal of International Economic Law*, (2001), pp. 441–480.

De Vattel, Emer, *Le Droit des Gens ou Principes de la Loi Naturelle, Appliqués à la Conduite et aux Affaires des Nations et des Souverains, Das Völkerrecht oder Grundsätze des Naturrechts, angewandt auf des Verhalten und die Angelegenheiten der Staaten und Staatsoberhäupter*1758, Deutsche Übersetzung von Dr. Wilhelm Euler, Schätzel, Walter (ed.) (Tübingen: J.C.B. Mohr, 1959).

De Wet, Erika, 'The ILO and the social clause: Stagnation or progress one step at a time?', in *Social and environmental standards in international trade agreements*, (Münster: Westfälisches Dampfboot, 1997), pp. 52–68 (cited: de Wet (The ILO and the social clause)).

DiMascio, Nicholas A., and Pauwelyn, Joost, 'Non-Discrimination in Trade and Investment Treaties: Worlds Apart or Two Sides of the Same Coin?', in *American Journal of International Law*, 102 (2008), pp. 48–89, https://ssrn.com/abstract=1669333 (cited: DiMascio/Pauwelyn (Non-Discrimination in Trade and Investment-Treaties)).

Dischendorfer, Martin, 'The Existence and Development of Multilateral Rules on Government Procurement under the Framework of the WTO', in *Public Procurement Law Review*, 1 (2000), pp. 1–38.

Dolzer, Rudolf, Schreuer, Christoph, *Principles of International Investment Law* (Oxford University Press, 2008).

Donnelly, Jack, 'Cultural Relativism and Universal Human Rights', 6 Human Rights Quarterly (1984), pp. 400–419.

Dupuy, Pierre-Marie, 'International and Domestic (Municipal) Law' in Rüdiger Wolfrum, (ed.), *Max Planck Encyclopaedia of Public International Law*, Vol. 5 (Oxford University Press, 2012), pp. 836–872.

Dworkin, Ronald, 'Integrity in the Law, Principles and Legal Interpretation', in Joel Feinberg, *Philosophy of Law*, pp. 134–150 (cited: Dworkin (Integrity)).

Dworkin, Ronald, *Taking Rights Seriously* (London: Duckworth, 1977) (cited: Dworkin (Taking Rights Seriously)).

Economic Strategy Institute, Morici, Peter and Evan Schulz, *Labour Standards in the Global Trading System* (Washington D.C.: Economic Strategy Institute, 2001).

Ehrenberg, Daniel, 'From Intention to Action, An ILO-GATT/WTO Enforcement Regime for International Labour Rights', in Lance A. Compa and Stephen F. Diamond (eds.), *Human rights, labour rights, and international trade* (Philadelphia: University of Pennsylvania Press, 1996), pp. 163–180.

Ehring, Lothar, '*De Facto* Discrimination in World Trade Law-National and Most-Favoured-Nation Treatment-or Equal Treatment?', in *Journal of World Trade*, 36 (5) (2002), pp. 921–978.

Emerson, Andrew, ‚Conceptualizing Security Exceptions: Legal Doctrine or Political Excuse? Vol. 11, No. 1 *JIEL* (2008), pp. 135–154.

Emmerich-Fritsche, Angelika, 'Zur Verbindlichkeit der Menschenrechte für transnationale Unternehmen', in Archiv des Völkerrechts (2007), pp. 541–565.

Engelberger, Lukas, *Die unmittelbare Anwendbarkeit des WTO-Rechts in der Schweiz, Grundlagen und Perspektiven im Kontext internationaler Rechtsentwicklungen,* Studien zum globalen Wirtschaftsrecht, Vol. 7, Thomas Cottier (ed.) (Bern: Peter Lang, 2004).

European Centre on Constitutional and Human Rights (ECCHR), Adjer, Corina, Saage-Maaß, Miriam, Vanpeperstrate, Ben, *Garment supply chains in intensive care, Human rights due diligence in times of (economic) crisis*, 16 April 2020, https://www.ecchr.eu/fileadmin/Publikationen/ECCHR_PP_SUPPLYCHAINS_COVID_EN.pdf (cited: ECCHR (Garment supply chains)).

European Centre for Constitutional and Human Rights (ECCHR), 'Fabrikbrand in Pakistan: Billige Textilproduktion, lebensgefährliche Arbeit', https://www.ecchr.eu/fileadmin/Fallbeschreibungen/Fallbeschreibung_KiK_Pakistan_August2019.pdf (cited: ECCHR (Fabrikbrand)).

European Centre on Constitutional and Human Rights, 'Kik-Verfahren belegt: Deutschland muss Haftungsregeln von Unternehmen grundlegend reformieren', 21 May 2019, https://www.ecchr.eu/nc/pressemitteilung/kik-verfahren-belegt-deutschland-muss-haftungspflichten-von-unternehmen-grundlegend-reformieren/ (cited: ECCHR (Kik-Verfahren belegt: Deutschland muss Haftungsregeln von Unternehmen grundlegend reformieren)).

European Coalition of Corporate Justice (ECCJ), *EU Model Legislation on Corporate Responsibility to Respect Human Rights and the Environment*, ECCJ Legal Brief, February 2020, https://corporatejustice.org/publications/eu-model-law-scg/ (cited: ECCJ (EU Model Legislation)).

EU Commission, 'EU-Canada Comprehensive Economic Trade Agreement, Standards and values in CETA, A progressive agreement for sustainable development', 2017, https://policy.trade.ec.europa.eu/eu-trade-relationships-country-and-region/countries-and-regions/canada/eu-canada-agreement_en (cited European Commission (EU-Canada Comprehensive Economic Trade Agreement)).

European Commission, 'Generalized System of Preferences', https://ec.europa.eu/trade/policy/countries-and-regions/development/generalised-scheme-of-preferences/index_en.htm (cited: European Commission (Generalized System of Preferences)).

European Commission, 'EU Trade policy and ACP Countries', https://ec.europa.eu/trade/policy/countries-and-regions/development/economic-partnerships/ (cited: European Commission (EU Trade policy and ACP Countries)).

EU Commission, British Institute for International and Comparative Law, Civic Consulting, London School of Economics, 'Study on due diligence requirements through the supply chain', commissioned by the European Commission, February 2020, https://op.europa.eu/de/publication-detail/-/publication/8ba0a8fd-4c83-11ea-b8b7-01aa75ed71a1/language-en.

Fassbender, Bardo, 'The United Nations Charter as a Constitution of the International Community', 38 Columbia Journal of Transnational Law (1998), pp. 529–619.

Evatt, Elizabeth, 'Ensuring Effective Supervisory Procedures: The Need for Resources', in Philip Alston and James Crawford (eds.), *The Future of Human Rights Treaty Monitoring* (Cambridge: Cambridge University Press, 2000), pp. 461–479.

Fauchald, Ole Kristian, 'Flexibility and Predictability under the World Trade Organization's Non-Discrimination Clauses', 37 (3) *Journal of World Trade* (2003) pp. 443–483.

Feddersen, Christoph T., *Der ordre public in der WTO, Auslegung und Bedeutung des Art. XX lit. a GATT im Rahmen der WTO-Streitbeilegung* (Berlin: Duncker & Humblot, 2002).

Fischer-Lescano, Andreas 'Die Emergenz von Globalverfassung', 63 ZaöRV (2003), pp. 717–760.

Fischer-Lescano, Andreas, Teubner, Gunther 'Regime Collisions: The Vain Search for Legal Unity in the Fragmentation of Global Law', 25 Michigan Journal of International Law (2004), pp. 999–1045.

Fitzgerald, Peter, L., 'Massachusetts, Burma, and the World Trade Organization: A Commentary on Blacklisting, Federalism, and Internet Advocacy in the Global Trading Era', in *Cornell International Law Journal*, 34 (2001), pp. 1–53.

Fitzmaurice, Sir, Gerald, 'The Law and Procedure of the International Court of Justice', in *British Yearbook of International Law*, 33 (1957), pp. 203–293.

Foltea, Marina *International Organizations in the WTO Dispute Settlement: How much institutional sensitivity?* (Cambridge University Press, 2012).

Fox, Gregory H., 'Democracy, Right to, International Protection', in Rüdiger Wolfrum, (ed.), Vol. III *Max Planck Encyclopaedia of Public International Law* (Oxford University Press, 2012), pp. 15–27.

Franck, Thomas, 'Legitimacy in the International System' in 82 AJIL 1998, pp. 704–759.

Franke, Siegfried, *Die gefährdete Demokratie: illiberale Demokratie, Populismus, Europaskepsis* (Baden-Baden: Nomos, 2017).

Friedmann, Wolfgang, *The Changing Structure of International Law* (London: Stevens, 1964).

Friends of the Earth International, People v. Shell, 4 April 2018, https://www.foei.org/news/climate_litigation_shell (cited: Friends of the Earth International (People v. Shell)).

Frowein, Jochen A., 'Obligations Erga Omnes', in Rudolf Bernhardt (ed.), *Encyclopedia of Public International Law*, Vol. III (Amsterdam: Elsevier Science B. V., 1997), pp. 757–759, (cited: Frowein (Obligations Erga Omnes)).

Frowein, Jochen A., 'Reactions by not Directly Affected States to Breaches of Public International Law', in *Recueil des Courts*, 248 (30) (1994), pp. 349–437 (cited: Frowein (Reactions)).

García-Salmones Mónica Rovira, 'Sources in the anti-formalist tradition', in Samantha Besson, Jean D'Aspremont, Séverine Kuchel (eds.) *The Oxford Handbook on the Sources of International* (Oxford University Press, 2017), pp. 203–224.

Gehne, Katja, *Nachhaltige Entwicklung als Rechtsprinzip* (Mohr Siebeck: Tübingen, 2011).

German Institute für Human Rights/CIEL, Nathaniel Elsen, Nina Eschke, *Climate Change and Human Rights* (2020), https://www.institut-fuer-menschenrechte.de/.

GATT, *Guide to GATT Law and Practice: Analytical Index of the GATT, Vol. 1* (Geneva: World Trade Organization, 1995) (cited: GATT Guide).

Goco, Jonell B., 'Non-Discrimination, "Likeness", and Market Definition in World Trade Organization Jurisprudence', in *Journal of World Trade*, 40(2) (2006), pp. 315–340.

Goldmann, Matthias, 'Sources in the Meta-Theory of International Law, Exploring the Hermeneutics, Authority, and Publicness of International Law' in Samantha Besson, Jean D'Aspremont, Séverine Kuchel (eds.) *The Oxford Handbook on the Sources of International* (Oxford University Press, 2017), pp. 447–468.

Goldsmith, Jack L., Posner, Eric A., *The Limits of International Law* (Oxford University Press, 2005).

Grabosch, Robert, *Companies and Human Rights, A Global Comparison of Legal Due Diligence Obligations*, (Berlin: Friedrich Ebert-Stiftung, 2020), http://library.fes.de/pdf-files/iez/16784.pdf.

Graf Vitzhum, Wolfgang, *Völkerrecht* (Berlin: De Gryuter, 3rd ed., 2004).

Grant, Ruth W., Keohane, Robert O. 'Accountability and Abuses of Power in World Politics', IILJ Working Paper 2004/7, Global Administrative Law Series.

Grimm, Dieter ‚Entwicklung und Funktion des Verfassungsbegriffs', in recht, Zeitschrift für juristische Ausbildung und Praxis, Sonderheft 2005, *Die Öffnung des Verfassungsrechts*, pp. 7–10.

Hahn, Michael J., *Die einseitige Aussetzung von GATT Verpflichtungen als Repressalie* (Berlin/Heidelberg: Springer Verlag, 1996).

Hart, H. L. A., *The Concept of Law*, 2nd ed. (Oxfaord: Clarendon Press, 1964).

Hailbronner, Kay, 'Sanctions and Third Parties and the Concept of International Public Order', in *Archiv des Völkerrechts*, 1992, pp. 2–15.

Hamilton, Clive, Ohlberg, Mareike, *Die lautlose Eroberung. Wie China westliche Demokratien unterwandert und die Welt neu ordnet* (München: DVA, 2020).

Hansenne, Michael, 'The Declaration of Philadelphia', *Labour Law Journal*, 45 (8) (1994), pp. 454–460.

Hanoitis, Tony, statement in 'Transcript of Roundtable Discussion', in Thomas Cottier, Petros C. Mavroidis (eds.), *Regulatory Barriers and the Principle of Non-Discrimination in WTO Law: An Overview* (Ann Arbor: University of Michigan Press, 2000), pp. 395–456.

Harrison, James, 'GSP Conditionality and Non-Discrimination', in *International Trade Law & Regulation*, 9 (6) (2003), pp. 159–166.

Heertje, Arnold, Wenzel, Heinz-Dieter, *Grundlagen der Volkswirtschaftslehre* (Berlin: Springer Verlag, 6th edn. 2002).

Held, David, 'Principles of cosmopolitan order' in Gillian Brock and Harry Brighthouse (eds.), *The Philosophy of Cosmopolitanism* (Cambridge University Press, 2005), pp. 10–27.

Henkin, Louis, Pugh Crawford, Richard, Schachter, Oscar, Smit, Hans, *International Law, Cases and Materials*, American Casebook Series (St. Paul, Minnesota: West Publishing Co., 1980).

Higgins, Rosalyn 'The Reformation in International Law' in Richard Rowlings (ed.), *Law, Society and Economy: centenary essays for the London School of Economics and Political Science 1885–1995* (Oxford: Clarendon Press, 1997), pp. 207–224.

Horn, Henrik, Mavroidis, Petros C., 'Still Hazy after All These Years: The Interpretation of National Treatment in the GATT/WTO Case-law on Tax Discrimination', in *European Journal of International Law*, 15 (2004), pp. 39–69.

Howse, Robert, 'Back to Court After Shrimp/Turtle? Almost But Not Quite Yet: India's Short Lived Challenge to Labour and Environmental Exceptions in the European Union's Generalized System of Preferences', in *American University International Law Review*, 18 (6) (2003), pp. 1333–1381 (cited: Howse (Shrimp/Turtle)).

Howse, Robert, 'From Politics to Technocracy – And Back Again: The Fate of the Multilateral Trading Regime' in 96 AJIL (2002), pp. 94–117 (cited: Howse (From Politics to Technocracy)).

Howse, Robert, 'India's WTO Challenge to Drug Enforcement Conditions in the European Community Generalized System of Preferences: A Little Known Case with Major Repercussions for "Political" Conditionality in US Trade Policy', in *Chicago Journal of International Law*, 4 (2003), pp. 385–405 (cited: Howse (India's WTO Challenge)).

Howse, Robert, Nicolaidis, Kalypso, 'Legitimacy through "Higher Law?" Why Constitutionalizing the WTO is a Step Too Far' in Thomas Cottier and Petros

C. Mavroidis (eds.) *The Role of the Judge in International Trade Regulation* (Michigan: The University of Michigan Press, Ann Arbor 2003).

Howse, Robert, Mutua, Makau, 'Protecting Human Rights in a Global Economy: Challenges for the World Trade Organization' (2000) in Hugo Stokke, Anne Tostensen, (eds.) Human Rights in Development Yearbook 1999/2000: The Millennium Edition ((2001), pp. 51–82, Buffalo Legal Studies Research Paper No. 2010–008, available at SSRN: https://ssrn.com/abstract=1533544.

Howse, Robert, Regan, Donald, 'The Product/Process Distinction – An Illusory Basis for Disciplining "Unilateralism" in Trade Policy', in *European Journal of International Law*, 11 (2000), pp. 249–289.

Howse, Robert and Trebilcock, M.J., 'The Fair Trade/Free Trade Debate: Trade, Labour, and the Environment', in *International Review of Law and Economics*, 16 (1996).

Howse, Robert and Türk, Elisabeth, 'The WTO Impact on Internal Regulations – A Case Study of the Canada – EC Asbestos Dispute', in Gráine de Búrca, Joanne Scott (eds.), *The EU and the WTO, Legal and Constitutional Issues* (Oxford et. al: Hart Publishing, 2001), pp. 284–328.

Hudec, Robert, *Essays on the Nature of International Trade Law* (London: Cameron & May, 1999) (cited: Hudec (Essays on the Nature of International Trade Law)).

Hudec, Robert E., 'GATT/WTO Constraints on National Regulation: Requiem for an "Aim and Effects" Test', in *The International Lawyer*, 32 (3) (1998), pp. 619–649 (cited: Hudec (Requiem for an Aim and Effects Test)).

Hudec, Robert E., '"Like Product": The Differences in Meaning in GATT Articles I and III', in Thomas Cottier, Petros C. Mavroidis (eds.), *Regulatory Barriers and the Principle of Non-Discrimination in WTO Law: An Overview* (Ann Arbor: University of Michigan Press, 2000), pp. 101–123, (cited: Hudec (Like Product)).

Hudec, Robert E., 'The Product-Process Distinction in GATT/WTO Jurisprudence', in Marco Bronckers and Reinhard Quick (eds.), *New Directions in International Economic Law, Essays in Honour of John H. Jackson*, (The Hague: Kluwer Law, 2000), pp. 187–217 (cited: Hudec (Product-Process Distinction)).

Humbert, Franziska, 'A Critical Assessment of the CSR Directive and Its German Implementation', in Schmalenbach Business Review, pp. 279–285 (cited (Humbert (CSR Directive and Its German Implementation)).

Humbert, Franziska, ‚Corporate Social Responsibility und die Frage nach staatlicher Regulierung: Eine rechtspolitische Einschätzung', 47, Heft 2–3, Zeitschrift für Unternehmens-und Gesellschaftsrecht (2018), pp. 295–333 (cited: Humbert (Corporate Social Responsibility)).

Humbert, Franziska, *The Challenge of Child Labour in International Law* (Cambridge University Press, 2009).

ILC, 'Draft articles on Responsibility of States for Internationally Wrongful Acts with commentaries', adopted by the International Law Commission at its fifty-third session (2001), A/56/10, Yearbook of the International Law Commission 2001, Vol. II, as corrected, UN (2008), https://legal.un.org/ilc/texts/instruments/english/commentaries/9_6_2001.pdf. (cited: ILC (Commentaries to the draft articles on Responsibility of States for Internationally Wrongful Acts)).

ILC, Draft Articles on the Law of Treaties with Commentaries, in Yearbook of the ILC, 1966, Vol. II, 1966 (cited: ILC (Draft Articles on the Law of Treaties with Commentaries, 1966)).

ILC, Report of the International Law Commission, 'Fragmentation of International Law: Difficulties Arising from the Diversification and Expansion of International Law', UN, General Assembly, Fifty-eighth session, 13 April 2006, A/CN.4/L.682, 2006 (cited: ILC (Fragmentation)).

ILC, 'Peremptory Norms of International Law (jus cogens)', Report of the International Law Commission, Chapter V, adopted by the Commission in its Seventy-first session (29 April–7 June and 8 July–9 August 2019), UN, Official Records of the General Assembly, A/74/10 (cited: ILC (Peremptory Norms of International Law)).

ILO, 'COVID-19 may push millions mor children into child labour – ILO and UNICEF', 12 June 2020, www.ilo.org/global/about-the-ilo/newsroom/news/WCMS_747583/lang--en/index.htm (ILO (COVID-19)).

ILO, *Global Estimates of Child Labour, Results and Trends, 2012–2016* (International Labour Office: Geneva, 2017) (cited: ILO (Global Estimates of Child Labour)).

ILO, 'ILO and WTO issue new joint study on 'Trade and employment: Challenges and policy research'; www.ilo.org/global/about-the-ilo/newsroom/news/WCMS_082146/lang--en/index.htm (cited: ILO (ILO and WTO)).

ILO, *Monitoring Compliance with International Labour Standards, The key role of the ILO Committee of Experts on the Application of Conventions and Recommendations* (Geneva: International Labour Office, 2019) (cited: ILO (Monitoring Compliance with International Labour Standards)).

ILO/IPEC, *IPEC Action against Child Labour: Highlights 2002* (Geneva: International Labour Office, 2002) (cited: ILO/IPEC (IPEC Action Against Child Labour: Highlights 2002)).

ILO/IPEC, *Time-Bound Programme, Manual for Action Planning Guidebook V*, https://www.ilo.org/ipec/Informationresources/WCMS_IPEC_PUB_3024/lang--en/index.htm (cited: ILO/IPEC (Time-Bound-Programme GuidebookV-01)).

ILO/IPEC, *Time-Bound Programme, Manual for Action Planning, Guidebook V-4*, https://www.ilo.org/ipec/Informationresources/WCMS_IPEC_PUB_3024/lang--en/index.htm (cited: ILO/IPEC (Time-Bound Programme, Guidebook V-04).

ILO/UNICEF, *Addressing Child Labour in the Bangladesh Garment Industry 1995–2001*, A synthesis of UNICEF and ILO evaluation studies of the Bangladesh garment sector projects (New York and Geneva: International Labour Office and UNICEF, 2004) (cited: ILO/UNICEF (Addressing Child Labour in the Bangladesh Garment Industry 1995–2001)).

ILO/UNICEF, *Child Labour, Global Estimates 2020, Trends and the Road Forward* (New York: ILO and UNICEF, 2021) (cited: ILO/UNICEF (Child Labour, Global Estimates, 2021)).

Initiative Lieferkettengesetz, Drillisch, Heike, Humbert, Franziska Leifker, Maren, Saage-Maaß, Miriam, *Rechtsgutachten zur Ausgestaltung eines Lieferkettengesetzes* (Berlin, 2020), https://lieferkettengesetz.de/.

International Cocoa Initiative, Marcella Vigneri, Marcella, Serra, Renata, Cardenas, Ana Lucia, 'Researching the Impact of Increased Cocoa Yields on the Labour Market and Child Labour Risk in Ghana and Côte d'Ivoire', 2016, https://www.cocoainitiative.org/

Internationale Gesellschaft für Politik, Nye, Joseph S. ‚Aus den Trümmern der Weltordnung, Trump demoliert die internationale Ordnung. Doch auch für Biden gäbe es in den Beziehungen zu China, Russland und dem Rest der Welt kein Zurück', 9 July 2020, https://www.ipg-journal.de/rubriken/aussen-und-sicherheitspolitik/artikel/aus-den-truemmern-der-weltordnung-4490/?utm_campaign=de_40_20200710&utm_medium=email&utm_source=newsletter.

Isensee, Josef, Kirchhof, Paul, *Handbuch des Staatsrechts der Bundesrepublik Deutschland,* Band II, *Verfassungsstaat*, 3rd ed. (Heidelberg: C.F. Müller Verlag, 2004).

ISO, *Guidance on Social Responsibility*, Working Draft 2, ISO TNB/WG SR N 80, 6/10/2006 (on file with the author) (cited: ISO (Guidance on Social Responsibility)).

Jackson, John H., 'Comments on Shrimp/Turtle and the Product/Process Distinction', in *European Journal of International Law*, 11 (2000), pp. 303–307 (cited: Jackson (Comments on Shrimp/Turtle)).

Jackson, John, *Sovereignty, the WTO and Changing Fundamentals in International Law*, (Cambridge University Press, 2006) (cited Jackson (Sovereignty)).

Jackson, John H., *The World Trading System, Law and Policy of International Economic Relations* 2nd ed. (Cambridge et al.: MIT Press, 1997) (cited: Jackson (The World Trading System)).

Jenks, Wilfried, 'Conflict of Law-Making Treaties', in *British Yearbook of International Law*, 30 (1953), pp. 401–453.

Jennings, Sir Robert and Watts, Sir Arthur, Vol. I *Oppenheim's International Law*, 9th ed., (Harlow: Longman Group ltd., 1992).

Joerges, Christian 'Three-Dimensional Conflicts Law as Constitutional Form', in C. Joerges and E.U. Petersmann (eds.), *Constitutionalism, Multi-level Trade Governance and International Economic Law* (Oxford: Hart Publishing, 2011) pp. 451–455.

Kälin, Walter, Künzli, Jörg, *Universeller Menschenrechtsschutz, Der Schutz des Individuums auf globaler und regionaler Ebene*, 3rd ed. (Basel: Helbing Lichtenhahn Verlag, 2013).

Kammerhofer, Jörg, Sources in Legal Positivist Theories: The Pure Theory's Structural Analysis of the Law' in Samantha Besson, Jean d'Aspremont (eds), *The Oxford Handbook of the Sources of International Law* (Oxford University Press, 2017), pp. 1–14, https://ssrn.com/abstract=2764238.

Kant, Immanuel, *Grundlegung zur Metaphysik der Sitten*, Valentiner, Theodor (ed.) (Ditzungen: Reclam, 1961) (cited: Kant (Metaphysik der Sitten)).

Kant, Immanuel, *Zum ewigen Frieden, Ein philosophischer Entwurf* Kant im Original, Band XVI, (Erlangen: Harald Fischer Verlag, 1984, Erstdruck Königsberg: Friedrich Nicolovius, 1795) (cited: Kant (Zum ewigen Frieden)).

Kaufmann, Arthur, Problemgeschichte der Philosophie in Arthur Kaufmann, Winfried Hassemer, Ulfrid Neumann (eds.), *Einführung in die Rechtsphilosophie und Rechtstheorie der Gegenwart* (Heidelberg: C.F. Müller, 20011), pp. 26–147 (cited: Kaufmann (Problemgeschichte der Philosophie)).

Kaufmann, Christine, *Globalisation and Labour Rights, The Conflict between Core Labour Rights and International Economic Law* (Oxford and Portland Oregon: Hart Publishing, 2007) (cited: (Kaufmann (Globalisation and Labour Rights)).

Kaufmann, Christine, ‚Konzernverantwortungsinitiative: Grenzenlose Verantwortlichkeit?', in ‚Schweizerische Zeitschrift für Wirtschafts-und Finanzmarktrecht' (2016), pp. 45–55 (cited: Kaufmann (Konzerninitiative)).

Kaufmann, Christine, Weber, Rolf, ‚Carbon-related border tax adjustment: mitigating climate change or restricting trade?' in 10:4, World Trade Review (2011), pp. 497–525.

Kelsen, Hans, *Reine Rechtslehre*, 2nd ed. (Wien, Franz Deuticke, 1960).

Kennedy, Kevin, 'GATT 1994', in Patrick F. J. Macrory, Arthur E. Appleton, Michael E. Plummer (eds.), *The World Trade Organization, Legal Economic and Political Analysis*, Vol. I (New York: Springer, 2005), pp. 89–186.

Kim, Nancy 'Toward a Feminist Theory of Human Rights: Straddling the Fence between Western Imperialism and Uncritical Absolutism', 25 Columbia Human Rights Law Review (1993), pp. 49–105.

Kingsbury, Ben, Krisch, Nico, Stewart, Richard B. 'The Emergence of Global Administrative Law' in 68 Law and Contemporary Problems, (2005), pp. 15–61.

Kirchhof, Paul, ‚Kompetenzaufteilung zwischen den Mitgliedstaaten und der EU', in Vertretung der Europäischen Kommission in der Bundesrepublik Deutschland (ed.), *Europäisches Forum: Die künftige Verfassungsordnung der Europäischen Union. Eine Dokumentation*, Reihe Europäische Gespräche 2/94, Bonn 1994, pp. 57–67.

Klabbers, Jan, Peters, Anne, Ulfstein, Geir, *The Constitutionalization of International Law* (Oxford University Press, 2009).

Kleinlein, Thomas, *Konstitutionalisierung im Völkerrecht, Konstruktion und Elemente einer idealistischen Völkerrechtslehre* (Heidelberg: Springer 2012).

Klinger, Remo, Krajewski, Markus, Krebs, David, Hartmann, Constantin, *Verankerung menschenrechtlicher Sorgfaltspflichten von Unternehmen im deutschen Recht*

(2016), Gutachten erstellt im Auftrag von Amnesty International, Brot für die Welt; Germanwatch; Oxfam Deutschland.

Kokott, Juliane, ‚Naturrecht und Positivismus im Völkerrecht', in Christian J. Meier-Schatz, Rainer J. Schweizer, *Recht und Internationalisierung*, Festgabe gewidmet dem Schweizerischen Juristenverein anlässlich des Juristentages 2000 in St. Gallen durch die Juristische Abteilung der Universität St. Gallen (Zürich: Schulthess, 2000), pp. 3–21.

Konzernverantwortungsinitiative, Initiativtext, https://konzern-initiative.ch/wp-content/uploads/2020/06/initiativtext-mit-erklarungen.pdf.

Koskenniemi, Martti 'International Legal Theory and Doctrine' in Rüdiger Wolfrum, (ed.), *Max Planck Encyclopaedia of Public International Law* Vol. 5 (Oxford University Press, 2012), pp. 976–986 (cited: Koskenniemi (International Theory and Doctrine)).

Koskenniemi, Martti, 'The Fate of Public International Law: Between Technique and Politics', in M. Koskenniemi (ed.), *The Politics of International Law* (Oxford, Portland, Oregon: Hart Publishing 2011), pp. 331–361 (cited: Koskenniemi (The Fate of Public International Law)).

Koskenniemi, Martti, *The Gentle Civilizer of Nations: The Rise and Fall of International Law 1870–1960* (Cambridge, 2002) (cited: Koskenniemie (The Gentle Civilizer of Nations)).

Krajewski, Markus, 'Democratic Legitimacy and Constitutional Perspectives of WTO Law', 35 (1) Journal of World Trade (2001), pp. 167–186 (cited: Krajewski (Democratic Legitimacy and Constitutional Perspectives of WTO Law)).

Krajewski, Markus, Saage-Maasz, Miriam, *Die Durchsetzung menschenrechtlicher Sorgfaltspflichten von Unternehmen-Zivilrechtliche Haftung und Berichterstattung als Steuerungsinstrumente* (Baden-Baden: Nomos, 2018).

Krisch, Nico *Beyond Consitutionalism: The Pluralist Structure of Postnational Law* (Oxford University Press: 2012).

Kumm, Matthias, 'The Cosmopolitan Turn in Constitutionalism: On the Relationship between Constitutionalism in an beyond the State', in Jeffroy L. Dunoff and Joel Trachtmann (eds.), *Ruling the World* (Cambridge University Press, 2009), pp. 258–324 (cited: Kumm (The Cosmopolitan Turn)).

Kumm, Matthias 'The Legitimacy of International Law: A Constitutionalist Framework of Analysis' 15 EJIL No. 5 (2004), pp. 907–931 (cited: Kumm (The Legitimacy of International Law)).

Lachenmann, Frauke, ‚Legal Positivism' in Rüdiger Wolfrum (ed.), Vol. 6, *Max Planck Encyclopaedia of Public International Law* (Oxford University Press, 2012), pp. 785–797.

Lauterpacht, Hersch 'The Grotian Tradition in International Law' in Andrea Bianchi (ed.) *Theory and Philosophy of International Law, Philosophical Enquiries and General Theoretical Concerns* Vol. 1, (Edward Elgar Publishing, 2017), pp. 212–264.

Leary, Virgina A., 'The Asian Region and the International Human Rights Movement' in Claude E. Welch, Jr., Virginia A. Leary (ed.) *Asian Perspectives on Human Rights* (Boulder, San Francisco, Oxford: Westview Press, 1990), p. 13–27 (cited: Leary (The Asian Region)).

Leary, Virginia A., 'Workers' Rights and International Trade: The Social Clause (GATT, ILO, NAFTA, US Laws)', in Jagdish N. Bhagwati and Rober. Hudec (eds.), *Fair Trade and Harmonization, Prerequisites for Free Trade?*, Vol. 2 (Legal Analysis) (Cambridge: MIT Press, 1996), pp. 177–229 (cited: Leary (Workers Rights and International Trade)).

Lee, Eddy, 'Globalization and labour standards: A review of issues', 136 (2) *International Labour Review*, (1997), pp. 173–189 (cited: Lee (Globalization and labour standards)).

Lefkovitz, David, ,The Sources of International Law: Some Philosophical Reflections' in Samantha Besson, John Tsasioulas (eds.), *The Philosophy of International Law* (Oxford University Press: 2010), pp. 187–203.

Leggewie, Claus, *Jetzt! – Opposition, Protest, Widerstand* (Frankfurt: Kiepenheuer & Witsch, 2020).

Li, Bin, 'China's Socialist Rule of Law and Global Constitutionalism', in Takao Suomi, Anne Peters, Dimitri Vanoverbeke, Matthias Kumm (eds.), *Global Constitutionalism from European and East Asian Perspectives* (Cambridge University Press 2018, www.cambridge.org/core), pp. 58–99.

Lopez-Hurtado, Carlos, 'Social Labelling and WTO Law', in *Journal of International Economic Law*, 5 (3) (2002), pp. 719–746.

Lowenfeld, A. F., 'Conflict, Balancing of Interest, and the Exercise of Jurisdiction to Prescribe: Reflections of the Insurance Antitrust Case', in *American Journal of International Law*, 89 (1995), pp. 42–53.

Malanczuk, Peter, *Akehurst's Modern Introduction to International Law* 7th ed. (London: Routledge, 1997).

Mansel, Heinz-Peter, ,Internationales Privatrecht de lege lata wie de lege ferenda und Menschenrechtsverantwortlichkeit deutscher Unternehmen', in Zeitschrift für Unternehmens-und Gesellschaftsrecht (2018), pp. 410–478.

Marceau, Gabrielle, 'Trade and Labour', in Daniel Bethlehem, Donald McRae, Rodney Neufeld, Isabelle van Damme, The Oxford Handbook of International Trade Law (Oxford University Press, 2009), pp. 539–569 (cited: Marceau (Trade and Labour)).

Marceau, Gabrielle, 'WTO Dispute Settlement and Human Rights', in *European Journal of International Law*, 13 (2000), pp. 753–814 (cited: Marceau (WTO Dispute Settlement and Human Rights I)).

Marceau, Gabrielle, 'The WTO Dispute Settlement and Human Rights', in Frederick Abbott, Christine Breining-Kaufmann, Thomas Cottier (eds.), *International Trade and Human Rights, Foundations and Conceptional Issues* (Ann Arbor: University Press of Michigan, 2006), pp. 181–258 (cited: Marceau (WTO Dispute Settlement and Human Rights II)).

Marceau, Gabrielle and Trachtmann, Joel P., 'The Technical Barriers to Trade Agreement, The Sanitary and Physosanitary Measures Agreement, and the General Agreement on Tariffs and Trade, A Map of the World Trade Organization Law of Domestic Regulation of Goods', in *Journal of World Trade Law*, 36 (5) (2002), pp. 811–881.

Matsushita, Mitsuo, Schoenbaum, Thomas J., Mavroidis, Peter, Hahn, Michael, *The World Trade Organization: Law, Practice and Policy*, 3rd ed. (Oxford University Press, 2015).

Mattoo, Aaditya, and Subramanian, Arvind, 'Regulatory Autonomy and Multilateral Disciplines: The Dilemma and a Possible Solution', in *Journal of International Economic Law*, 1 (1998), pp. 303–322.

Maupain, Francois, 'Is the ILO Effective in Upholding Workers' Rights?: Reflections on the Myanmar Experience', in Philipp Alston (ed.) *Labour Rights as Human Rights* (Oxford University Press, 2005), pp. 85–142.

Mavroidis, Petros C., '"Like Products": Some Thoughts at the Positions and Normative Level', in Thomas Cottier, Petros C. Mavroidis (eds.), *Regulatory Barriers and the Principle of Non-Discrimination in WTO Law: An Overview* (Ann Arbor: University of Michigan Press, 2000), pp. 125–135 (cited: Mavroidis (Like Products)).

McCrudden, Christopher, 'International Economic Law and the Pursuit of Human Rights: A Framework for Discussion of the Legality of 'Selective Purchasing' Laws under the WTO Government Procurement Agreement', in *Journal of International Economic Law*, 2 (1) (1999), pp. 3–48.

McDonald, Jan, 'Domestic regulation, international standards, and technical barriers to trade', in *World Trade Review*, 4 (2) (2005), pp. 249–271.

McDougal, Myres S., Lasswell, Harold D., 'The Identification and Appraisal of Diverse Systems of Public Order', in Myres S. McDougal et al. (eds.) *Studies in World Public Order*, (New Haven Press, 1987), pp. 3–41.

McRae, Donald, 'GATT Article XX and the WTO Appellate Body', in Marco Bronckers and Reinhard Quick (eds.), *New Directions in International Economic Law, Essays in Honour of John H. Jackson* (The Hague: Kluwer Law, 2000), pp. 219–236.

Meng, Werner, 'Extraterritorial Effects of Administrative, Judicial and Legislative Acts', in Rudolph Bernhardt (ed.), *Encyclopedia of Public International Law*, Vol. II (Amsterdam, London: Elsevier Science B.V., 1995), pp. 337–343.

Meron, Theodor, *Human Rights and Humanitarian Norms as Customary Law* (Oxford: Clarendon Press Oxford, 1989) (cited: Meron (Human Rights and Humanitarian Norms)).

Meron, Theodor, *The Humanization of International Law* (Leiden: MartinNijhoff Publishers, 2006) (Meron (The Humanization of International Law)).

Miller, David, *On Nationality* (Oxford: Clarendon Press 1995).

Möllers, Christoph, 'Verfassungsgebende Gewalt – Verfassung – Konstitutionalisierung', in von Bogdandy, Armin (ed.), *Europäisches Verfassungsrecht* (Berlin: Springer, 2009), pp. 227–278.

Morgenthau, Hans Joachim, *Politics among Nations, The Struggle for War and Peace*, 5th ed. (New York: Knopf, 1973).

Mosler, Hermann, *The International Society as a Legal Community* (Alphen aan den Rijn: Sijthoff & Nordhoff, 1980).

Müller, Jörg Paul, *Die demokratische Verfassung*, 2nd ed. (Zürich: Neue Züricher Zeitung, 2009).

Musselli, Irene, Solar, Jimena, Tribaldos, Theresa, Bürgi Bonanomi, Elisabeth, Centre for Development and Environment (CDE), University of Bern, 'Livestock Farming Act and WTO Compliance, Preferential Tariff Treatment Based on PPMs: A Case Study', Working Paper No. NRP73-WP05-2022, December 2022, pp. 1–51.

Myers, Antony, 'New report reveals child labour has increased in ten past years on West African cocoa farms', 7 May 2020, https://www.confectionerynews.com/Article/2020/05/07/New-report-reveals-child-labor-on-West-African-cocoa-farms-has-increased-in-past-10-years.

Nadakavukaren Schefer, Krista, 'Conflict Diamonds, Stopping Trade in Conflict Diamonds: Exploring the Trade and Human Rights Interface with the WTO Waiver for the Kimberley Process', in Thomas Cottier, Joost Pauwelyn, Elisabeth Bürgi (eds.), *Human Rights and International Trade* (Oxford: Oxford University Press, 2006), pp. 391–450.

Neff, Stephen, C. *Hugo Grotius on the Law of War and Peace* (Cambridge University Press, 2012).

Neumann, Jan, *Die Koordination des WTO-Rechts mit anderen völkerrechtlichen Ordnungen, Konflikte des materiellen Rechts und Konkurrenzen der Streitbeilegung* (Berlin: Duncker & Humblot, 2002).

Neumann, Jan, Türk, Elisabeth, ‚Necessity Revisited – Proportionality in World Trade Organization Law After *Korea–Beef*, *EC–Asbestos*, *EC–Sardines*, in 37 (1) Journal of World Trade (2003), pp. 199–233.

Neven, Damien J., 'How should "protection" be evaluated in Art. III GATT disputes?', in *European Journal of Political Economy*, 17 (2001), pp. 421–444.

Nowak, Manfred, *Einführung in das internationale Menschenrechtssystem* (Graz: Neuer Wissenschaftlicher Verlag, 2002).

Nowrot, Karsten, *Normative Ordnungsstruktur und private Wirkungsmacht: Konsequenzen der Beteiligung transnationaler Unternehmen an den Rechtssetzungsprozessen im internationalen Wirtschaftssystem* (Berlin: Berliner Wissenschaftsverlag 2006).

Nussbaum, Martha 'Non-Relative Virtues: An Aristotelian Approach', in Martha Nussbaum and Amartya Sen (eds.) *The Quality of Life* (Oxford University Press 1993), pp. 242–269.

O'Donoghue, Aoife, *Constitutionalism in Global Constitutionalization* (Cambridge University Press, 2014).

OECD, *Processes and Production Methods (PPMs): Conceptual Framework and Considerations on Use of PPM-Based Trade Measures*, OCDÉ/GD(97)137 (1997) (cited: OECD (PPMs)).

OECD, *Trade, Employment and Labour Standards: A Study of Core Workers' Rights and International Trade* (Paris: OECD, 1996) (cited: OECD (Trade, Employment and Labour Standards 1996)).

Oeschger, Andreas, Bürgi Bonanomi, Elisabeth, 'PPMs Are Back: The rise of new sustainability-oriented trade policies based on process and production methods', 4 April 2023, https://www.iisd.org/articles/policy-analysis/ppms-rise-new-sustainability-oriented-trade-policies-process-production-methods.

Oesch, Matthias, *Standards of Review in WTO Dispute Resolution* (Oxford: Oxford University Press, 2003) (cited: Oesch (Standards of Review)).

Oesch, Matthias, 'Standards of Review in WTO Dispute Resolution and the Treatment of Domestic Law' in Martin Nettesheim, ed. *WTO-Recht und Globalisierung* (Berlin: Duncker & Humblot, 2003), pp. 43–72 (cited: Oesch (Treatment of Domestic Law)).

Onuf, Nicholas Greenwood, 'Civitas Maxima Wolff, Vattel and the Fate of Republicanism', 88 AJIL (1994), pp. 280–303.

Orakhekashvili, Alexander, 'Natural Law and Justice' in Rüdiger Wolfrum (ed.) *Max Planck Encyclopedia of International Law*, Volume VII (2012), pp. 523–535.

Oxfam Germany, Humbert, Franziska, *Sweet Fruit, Bitter Truth*, (June 2018), www.oxfam.de/system/files/20160531-oxfam-sweet-fruit-bitter-truth-en.pdf (cited: Oxfam Germany (Sweet Fruit)).

Oxfam, *Ripe for Change*, (Oxford: Oxfam International, 2018) https://oi-files-d8-prod.s3.eu-west-2.amazonaws.com/s3fs-public/file_attachments/cr-ripe-for-change-supermarket-supply-chains-210618-en.pdf (cited: Oxfam (Ripe for Change)).

Oxfam, *Space to be heard, Mobilizing the power of people to reshape civic space*, 2018, https://www.oxfam.org/en/research/space-be-heard (cited: Oxfam (Space to be heard)).

Oxfam, *Trading Away Our Rights, Women Working in Global Suppply Chains* (Oxford: Oxfam International, 2004) (cited: Oxfam (Trading Away Our Rights)).

Oxfam, *Time to Care, Unpaid and Underpaid Care Work and the Global Economic Crisis*, Oxfam Briefing Paper January 2020, https://oxfamilibrary.openrepository.com/bitstream/handle/10546/620928/bp-time-to-care-inequality-200120-en.pdf (cited: Oxfam (Time to Care)).

Oxfam Germany, Heinrich Boell Stiftung et al., *Konzernatlas* (Paderborn: Bonifatius GmbH Druck 2017).

Partsch, Karl, ‚Reprisals', 1986, in Rudolf Bernhardt (ed.), Encyclopedia *in Public International Law*, Vol. IV (Amsterdam: Elsevier Science B. V., 1997), pp. 200–205.

Paulus, Andreas, 'Commentary to Andreas Fischer-Lescano & Gunther Teubner – The Legitimacy of International Law and the Role of the State', 25 Michigan Journal of International Law (2004), pp. 1047–1058 (cited: Paulus (Commentary to Fischer-Lescano/Teubner)).

Paulus, Andreas L. ‚The International Legal System as a Constitution', in Jeffrey L. Dunhoff, Joel P. Trachtmann (eds.), *Ruling the World, Constitutionalism, International Law, and Global Governance* (Cambridge University Press, 2012), pp. 69–110 (cited: Paulus (The International Legal System as a Constitution)).

Pauwelyn, Joost, *Conflict of Norms in Public International Law, How the WTO Law Relates to other Rules of International Law* (Cambridge: Cambridge University Press, 2003) (cited: Pauwelyn (Conflict of Norms)).

Pauwelyn, Joost, 'Human Rights in WTO Dispute Settlement', in Thomas Cottier, Joost Pauwelyn, Elisabeth Bürgi (eds.), *Human Rights and International Trade* (Oxford: Oxford University Press, 2006), pp. 205–231 (cited: Pauwelyn (Human Rights in WTO Dispute Settlement)).

Pauwelyn, Joost, 'The Nature of WTO Obligations', *Jean Monnet Working Paper*, 1 (2002) (New York: New York University School of Law, 2002) (cited: Pauwelyn (The Nature of WTO Obligations)).

Pearson, Charles, Labour Standards, in Patrick F. J. Marcory, Arthur E. Appleton, Michael G. Plummer (eds.), *The World Trade Organization, Legal, Economic and Political Analysis*, Vol. II (New York: Springer, 2005), pp. 171–188.

Peeters, Anne, 'The Belgian social label, A pilot project for involving governments in CSR', *European Review of Labour and Research*, 10 (3) (2004), pp. 393–400.

Perry, Michael, 'Are Human Rights Universal – The Relativist Challenge and Related Matters, 19 Human Rights Quarterly, pp. 461–509.

Peters, Anne, *Beyond Human Rights* (Cambridge University Press, www.cambridge.org /core, 2016) (cited: Peters (Beyond Human Rights)).

Peters, Anne 'Compensatory Constitutionalism: The Function and Potential of Fundamental International Norms and Structures' in 19 Leiden Journal of International Law (2006), pp. 579–610 cited (Peters (Compensatory Constitutionalism)).

Peters, Anne, ‚Drei gute Gründe für die Verfassungslesart der europäischen Verträge', in recht, Zeitschrift für juristische Ausbildung und Praxis, Sonderheft 2005, *Die Öffnung des Verfassungsrechts*, pp. 11–25 (cited: Peters (Drei gute Gründe)).

Peters, Anne, 'Proportionality as a global constitutional principle', in Anthony F. Lang, Antje Wiener (eds.), *Handbook on Global Constitutionalism* (Cheltenham: Edward Elgar Publishing, 2017), pp. 248–264 (cited: Peters (Proportionality)).

Petersmann, Ernst-Ulrich, 'Human Rights and the Law of the World Trade Organization', in *Journal of World Trade*, 37 (2) (2003), pp. 241–281.

Petersmann, Ernst-Ulrich, 'International Economic Law, 'Public Reason', and Multi-level Governance of Interdependent Public Goods', in Journal of International Economic Law, 14 (2011), pp. 23–76 (cited: Petersmann (Public Reason)).

Petersmann, Ernst-Ulrich, 'Multi-level Trade Governance in the WTO Requires Multi-level Constitutionalism', in Christian Joerges and Ernst-Ulrich Petersmann (eds.), *Constitutionalism, Multi-level Trade Governance and International Economic Law* (Oxford, Portland, Oregon: Hart Publishing, 2011), pp. 5–56 (cited: Petersmann (Multi-level Trade Governance)).

Pieroth, Bodo, Schlink, Bernhard, *Grundrechte, Staatsrecht II* (Heidelberg: C.F. Müller Juristischer Verlag, 9th edn. 1993).

Plamper, Jan, *Das neue Wir. Warum Migration dazugehört: Eine andere Geschichte der Deutschen* (Berlin: Fischer Verlag, 2019).

Pogge, Thomas, ‚A cosmopolitan perspective on the global economic order', in Gillian Brock, Brighthouse, Harry (eds.), *The Philosophy of Cosmopolitanism* (Cambridge University Press, 2005), pp. 93–109.

Quick, Reinhard and Lau, Christian, 'Environmentally Motivated Tax Distinctions and WTO Law, The European Commission's Green Paper on Integrated Product Policy in Light of the 'Like Product'-and 'PPM'-Debates', in *Journal of International Economic Law*, 6 (2) (2003), pp. 419–458.

Ratner, Steven R., 'Legal Realism School', in *Max Planck Encyclopaedia of International Law*, Volume Vol. 8 (2012), pp. 801–808.

Raworth, Kate, *Doughnut economics, seven ways to think like a 21st century economist* (White River Junction, Vermont: Chelsea Publishing, 2017).

Rawls, John, *The Law of Peoples* (Cambridge, MA: Harvard University Press, 1999).

Rawls, John, *The Law of Peoples with 'The idea of public reason revisited'* (Cambridge, Massachusetts: Harvard University Press, 2002) (cited: Rawls (The Idea of Public Reason Revisited)).

Raz, Joseph, 'Human Rights in the Emerging World Order, in *Philosophical Foundations of Human Rights* (Oxford University Press, 2015), pp. 217–243 (cited: Raz (Human Rights in the Emerging World Order)).

Raz, Joseph, 'Human Rights without Foundations' in Samantha Besson and John Tasioulias (eds.), *The Philosophy of International Law* (Oxford University Press, 2011) (cited: Raz (Human Rights without Foundations)).

Raz, Joseph, *The Morality of Freedom* (Oxford: Clarendon Press, 1986) (cited: Raz (Morality of Freedom)).

Raz, Joseph 'The Problem of Authority: Revisiting the Service Conception', in 90 Minnesota Law Review, (2006), pp. 1003–1044 (cited: Raz (Revisiting the Service Conception)).

Raz, Joseph, *The Authority of Law: Essays on Law and Morality* (Oxford: Clarendon Press, 1979) (cited: Raz (The Authority of Law)).

Regan, Donald H., 'Regulatory Purpose and "Like Products" in Art. III:4 of the GATT (With Additional Remarks on Article III:2)', in *Journal of World Trade*, 36 (3) (2002), pp. 443–478 (cited: Regan (Regulatory Purpose)).

Regan, Donald H., 'Further Thoughts on the Role of Regulatory Purpose Under Article III of the General Agreement on Tariffs and Trade', in *Journal of World Trade Law*, 37 (4) (2003), pp. 737–760 (cited: Regan (Further Thoughts)).

Reinisch, August, 'Sources of International Organization's Law, Why Custom and General Principles are Crucial in Samantha Besson, Jean D'Aspremont, Séverine Kuchel (eds.) *The Oxford Handbook on the Sources of International* (Oxford University Press, 2017), pp. 1007–1023.

Reisman, W. Michael, 'Unilateral Action and the Transformation of the World Constitutive Process: The Special Problem of Humanitarian Intervention', in 11 EJIL (2000), pp. 3–18.

Reuß, Matthias, *Menschenrechte durch Handelssanktionen: die Durchsetzung sozialer Standards im Rahmen der WTO* (Baden-Baden: Nomos Verlag, 1999).

Riedel, Eike, Will, Martin, 'Human Rights Clauses in External Agreements', in Philip Alston, Mara Bustelo, James Heenan (eds.), *The EU and Human Rights* (Oxford: Oxford University Press, 1999), pp. 723–754.

Roessler, Frieder, 'Beyond the Ostensible, A Tribute to Professor Robert Hudec's Insight on the Determination of the Likeness of Products Under the National Treatment Provisions of the General Agreement on Tariffs and Trade', in Journal of World Trad*e*, 37 (4) (2003), pp. 771–781 (cited: Roessler (Beyond the Ostensible)).

Roessler, Frieder, 'The Scope of Regulatory Autonomy of WTO Members under Article III:4 of the GATT: A Critical Appraisal of the Jurisprudence of the WTO Appellate Body', RSCAS Policy Paper 2015/04 (cited: Roessler (The Scope of Regulatory Autonomy)).

Rorty, Richard, *Contingency, Irony and Solidarity* (Cambridge University Press, 1989) (cited: Rorty (Contingency)).

Rorty, Richard, *Kontingenz, Ironie und Solidarität* (Frankfurt: Suhrkamp 1989) (cited: Rorty (Kontingenz)).

Rudolf, Peter, ‚Wen trifft's, Zu schnelle, zu harte Sanktionen gegen Iran könnten den Falschen schaden', in *Die Zeit*, No. 12, 16 March 2006.

Rühmkorf, Andreas, Corporate Social Responsibility in der Lieferkette: Governance und Verantwortlichkeiten, in Zeitschrift für Unternehmens-und Gesellschaftsrecht (2018), pp. 410–432.

Ruffert, Matthias, ‚Zuständigkeitsgrenzen internationaler Organisationen im institutionellen Rahmen der internationalen Gemeinschaft', in *Archiv des Völkerrechts*, 38 (2000), pp. 120–168.

Scelle, Georges, 'Précis de Droit des Gens, Proncipes et Systématique, Première Partie, Introduction, Le Milieu Intersocial', in '*Précis de Droit des Gens, Principes et*

Systématique I et II, Éditions du Centre Nationale de la Recherche Scientifique Paris 1984 (Sirey Paris 1932) (cited: Scelle (Le Milieu Intersocial)).

Scelle, Georges, 'Précis de Droits des Gens, Principes et Systématique, Deuxiéme Partie, Droit Constitutionnel International, Les Libertés Individuelles et Colllectives, L'Élaboration du Droit des Gens Positif', in *Précis de Droits des Gens, Principes et Systématique, I et II*, Éditions du Centre Nationale de la Recherche Scientifique Paris 1984 (Paris: Sirey, 1934) (cited: Scelle (Droit Constituell International)).

Schachter, Oscar, *International Law in Theory and Practice* (Dordrecht et al.: Martinus Nijhoff Publishers 1991).

Schall, Alexander, 'Die Mutter-Verantwortlichkeit für Menschenrechtsverletzungen ihrer Auslandstöchter', in Zeitschrift für Unternehmens-und Gesellschaftsrecht (2018), pp. 479–512.

Schall, Alexander, Theusinger, Ingo, Mansur Pour Rafsendjani (eds.), *Kommentar, Lieferkettensorgfaltspflichtengesetz* (Berlin: De Gruyter, 2023).

Scharpf, Fritz, *Regieren in Europa, Effektiv und demokratisch*? (Frankfurt: Campus-Verlag 1999).

Schermers, Henry G., Blokker, Niels M., *International Institutional Law*, 5th ed. (Dordrecht: Martinus Nijhoff 2011).

Schiff Berman, Paul, 'Global Legal Pluralism' in 80 Southern California Law Review, (2007), pp. 1155–1237.

Schlagenhof, Markus, 'Trade Measures Based on Environmental Process and Production Methods', in *Journal of World Trade*, 29 (6) (1995), pp. 123–155.

Schloemann Hannes L., Ohloff Stefan, '"Constitutionlization" and Dispute Settlement in the WTO: National Security as an Issue of Competence' I, 93 AJIL (1999), pp. 424–451.

Schmitt, Carl, *Der Begriff des Politischen* (Hanseatische Verlagsanstalt Hamburg, 1933).

Schuchhardt, Christiane, 'Consultations', in Patrick F. J. Marcory, Arthur E. Appleton, Michael G. Plummer, eds., *The World Trade Organization, Legal, Economic and Political Analysis*, Vol. I (New York: Springer, 2005), pp. 1198–1232.

Schröder, Meinhard, ‚Sanktionen', in Wolfgang Graf Vitzhum (ed.), *Völkerrecht*, (Berlin: De Gruyter, 3rd edn. 2004), pp. 582–588.

Seinecke, Ralf, *Das Recht des Rechtspluralismus* (Tübingen: Mohr Siebeck, 2015).

Shaffer, Gregory, Apea, Yvonne, 'GSP Programmes and their Historical-Political-Institutional Context', in Thomas Cottier, Joost Pauwelyn, Elisabeth Bürgi (eds.), *Human Rights and International Trade*, (Oxford: Oxford University Press, 2006), pp. 489–503.

Shaw, Malcolm, *International Law*, (Cambridge et al.: Cambridge University Press, 4th edn. 1997).

Sieghart, Paul, *The International Law of Human Rights* (Oxford: Clarendon Press Oxford, 1983).

Simma, Bruno, 'Sources of International Human Rights Law, Human Rights Treaties', in Samantha Besson, Jean D'Aspremont, Séverine Kuchel (eds.) *The Oxford Handbook on the Sources of International* (Oxford University Press, 2017), pp. 871–888 (cited: Simma (Sources of International Human Rights Law)).

Simma, Bruno and Alston, Philip, 'The Sources of Human Rights Law: Custom, Ius Cogens, and General Principles', in Philip Alston (ed.), *Human Rights Law* (Aldershot: Dartmouth Publishing Company Ltd., 1996), pp. 3–29.

Simma, Bruno, Andreas Paulus 'The Responsibility of Individuals for Human Rights Abuses in Internal Conflicts: A Positivist View', 93 AJIL (1999), pp. 302–316 (cited: Simma/Paulus (The Responsibility of Individuals)).

Simma, Bruno, Andreas Paulus, 'The 'International Community': Facing the Challenge of Globalization', 9 EJIL (1998), pp. 266–277 (cited: Simma/Paulus (The 'International Community')).

Slotboom, Marco M., 'Do Different Treaty Purposes Matter For Treaty Interpretation? The Elimination of Discriminatory Internal Taxes in EC and WTO Law', in *Journal of International Economic Law*, (2001), pp. 557–579.

Shoyer, Andrew W., Soloy, Eric M. and Koff, Alexander W., 'Implementation and Enforcement of Dispute Settlement Decisions', in Patrick F. J. Marcory, Arthur E. Appleton, Michael G. Plummer, *The World Trade Organization, Legal, Economic and Political Analysis*, Vol. I (New York: Springer, 2005), pp. 1341–1369.

Spießhofer, Birgit, ‚Was ist die „gesellschaftliche Verantwortung" von Unternehmen? Die Frage nach der Corporate Social Responsibility', in Zeitschrift für Internationales Wirtschaftsrecht (2019), pp. 65–72.

Steinberger, Helmut, 'Sovereignty', in Rudolph Bernhardt (ed.), *Encyclopedia of Public International Law*, Vol. IV (Amsterdam: Elsevier Science B.V., 2000), pp. 500–521.

Steiner, Marc, *Die Berücksichtigung sozialer Aspekte im Rahmen der öffentlichen Beschaffung, dritte Fassung*, Arbeitspapier erstellt im Auftrag der Interessengemeinschaft ökologische Beschaffung Schweiz (IGÖB) 2015, www.marc-steiner.ch/pdf/Sozialpapier_final_21_05_2015.pdf, (cited: Steiner (Die Berücksichtigung sozialer Aspekte)).

Steiner, Marc, ‚Nachhaltige öffentliche Beschaffung – ein Blick auf das Vergaberecht des Bundes und die Perspektiven' in: Zufferey/Stöckli (eds.), *Aktuelles Vergaberecht* (Zürich: 2014) (cited: Steiner (Nachhaltige öffentliche Beschaffung)).

Stoll, Peter, Gött, Henner, Abel, Patrick, ‚A Model Labour Chapter for Future EU Trade Agreements', in Henner Gött (ed.) *Labour Standards in International Economic Law* (Cham: Springer, 2018), pp. 381–420.

Tams, Christian J., 'All's Well that Ends Well, Comments on the ILC's Articles on State Responsibility', in *Zeitschrift für ausländisches öffentliches und Völkerrecht*, 62 (2002), pp. 759–796.

Téson, Fernando R., 'The Kantian Theory of International Law' in 92 Columbia Law Review (1992), pp. 53–102.

Teubner, Gunther 'Global Bukowina: Legal Pluralism in the World Society', in (ed. Gunter Teubner) *Global Law without a State*, pp. 3–28 (Teubner (Globale Bukowina II)).

Teubner, Gunther, ‚Globale Bukowina. Zur Emergenz eines transnationalen Rechtspluralismus' in 15 Rechtshistorisches Journal (1996), pp. 255–290 (cited: Teubner (Globale Bukowina I)).

Teubner, Gunther, Globale Zivilverfassungen: Alternativen zur staatszentrierten Verfassungstheorie', in 63 ZaöRV 63 (2003), pp. 1–28 (cited: Teubner (Globale Zivilverfassungen)).

Thaggert, Henry L., 'A Closer Look at the Tuna-Dolphin Case: "Like Products" and "Extrajurisdictionality" ', in James Cameron, Paul Demaret, Damien Geradin (eds.), *Trade and The Environment, The Search for Balance*, Vol. I (London: Cameron May, 1994), pp. 69–95.

Tietje, Christian, 'Global Governance and Inter-Agency Co-Operation in International Economic Law', in 36 (3) Journal of World Trade (2002), pp. 501–515 (cited: Tietje (Global Governance and Inter-Agency Cooperation)).

Tietje, Christian, 'Voluntary Eco-Labelling programmes and Questions of State Responsibility in the WTO/GATT Legal Systems', in *Journal of World Trade*, 29 (5) (1995), pp. 123–158 (Tietje (Voluntary Eco-Labelling)).

Tietje, Christian, Wolf, Sebastian, 'REACH Registration of Imported Substances – Compatibility with WTO Rules', in *Beiträge zum Transnationalen Wirtschaftsrecht*, Heft 42 (2005).

Tomuschat, Christian, ‚Die internationale Gemeinschaft', 33 AVR (1995), pp. 1–20.

Tomuschat, Christian, *Human Rights. Between Idealism and Realism* (Oxford University Press 2003) (cited: Tomuschat (Human Rights)).

Tomuschat, Christian, 'International Law as the Constitution of Mankind', in Tomuschat, Christian (ed.) *International Law on the Eve at the Twenty-First Century: Views from the International Law Commission*, A/CN.4(02)/IN5 (New York: UN, 1997) (cited: Tomuschat (International Law as the Constitution of Mankind)).

Tomuschat, Christian, 'Obligations Arising for States without or against their Will', in 241 Recueil des Cours 1993-IV (cited: Tomuschat (Obligations Arising for States)).

Treaty Alliance Deutschland, CorA-Netzwerk, Sarah Lincoln, Maren Leifker, Karolin Seitz, *Für eine menschenrechtliche Regulierung der globalen Wirtschaft, Positionspapier der Treaty Alliance Deutschland zum UN-Treaty-Prozess zu transnationalen Konzernen und anderen Unternehmen*, February 2019, https://www.medico.de/fileadmin/user_upload/media/un-treaty-alliance-positionspapier.pdf.

Trepte, Peter, 'The Agreement on Government Procurement', in Patrick F. J. Marcory, Arthur E. Appleton, Michael G. Plummer, *The World Trade Organization, Legal, Economic and Political Analysis*, Vol. II (New York: Springer, 2005), pp. 1123–1163.

Triepel, Heinrich, *Völkerrecht und Landesrecht* (Leipzig: Hirschfeldt, 1899).

UN, General Assembly, *Report of the World Commission on Environment and Development*, 11 December 1987, A/RES/42/187 (Brundtland Report).

UN, Human Rights Council, 'Elaboration of an international legally binding instrument on transnational corporations and other business enterprises with respect to human rights', 26th Session, 14th of July 2014, A/HRC/RES/26/9 (cited: UN Human Rights Council (UN Treaty)).

UN, Human Rights Council, 'Report of the Special Representative of the Secretary-General on the issue of human rights and transnational corporations and other business enterprises, John Ruggie, *Guiding Principles on Business and Human Rights: Implementing the United National "Protect, Respect and Remedy" Framework*', 21 March 2011, A/HRC/17/31 (cited: UN/Human Rights Council (UNGP)).

UN, Office of Legal Affairs, 'Materials on the Responsibility of States for Internationally Wrongful Acts', 2nd ed., February 2023 (cited: UN (Materials on the Responsibility of States for Internationally Wrongful Acts)).

UN, Security Council, Report of the Secretary-General, *The rule of law and transitional justice in conflict and post-conflict societies*, 23 August 2004, S/2004/616 (cited: UN (The Rule of Law)).

UN Sub-Commission on the Promotion and Protection of Human Rights, *Economic, Social and Cultural Rights, Norms on the responsibilities of transnational corporations and other business enterprises with regard to human rights*, 55th session, 26 August 2003, E/CN.4/Sub.2/2003/12/Rev.2.

UN Department of Economic and Social Affairs, *The 17 Goals*, https://sdgs.un.org/goals (cited: UN (The 17 Goals)).

UNICEF, Richards, Emily, Wilde, Luke, *Children's Rights in the Mining Sector* (Geneva: United Nations Childrens' Fund, 2015), https://www.unicef.org/csr/files/UNICEF_REPORT_ON_CHILD_RIGHTS_AND_THE_MINING_SECTOR_APRIL_27.pdf.

UNICEF, Fair Labour Association, *Mitigating Child Labour Risks in Cotton*, June 2017,https://www.fairlabor.org/projects/mitigating-child-labor-risks-in-cotton/.

UNICEF, *The State of the World's Children 1997*, Report of the Executive Director (Oxford University Press, 1997) (cited: UNICEF (The State of the World's Children 1997)).

Valentini, Laura, *Justice in a Globalized World* (Oxford University Press, 2011).

Van den Bossche, Peter, 'NGO Involvement in the WTO: A comparative perspective', in Vol. 11 (4) JIEL (2008), pp. 717–749 (cited as: Van den Bossche (NGO involvement)).

Van den Bossche, Peter, 'WTO law as a constraint on domestic environmental policy: an overview' Panagiotis Delimatstis, Leonie Reins (eds.) *Trade and Environmental Law* Volume XI (Cheltenham: Edward Elgar Publishing, 2021), pp. 25–43 (cited as: Van den Bossche (WTO law as a constraint)).

Van den Bossche, Peter, Zdouc, Werner, *The Law and Policy of the World Trade Organization, Text, Cases and Materials* (Cambridge University Press, 2022).

Van Liemt, Gijsbert, 'Minimum labour standards and international trade: Would a social clause work?, in *International Labour Review*, 128 (4) (1989), pp. 433–448.

Vázquez, Carlos Manuel, 'Trade Sanctions and Human Rights – Past, Present, and Future', in *Journal of International Economic Law*, 6 (4), pp. 797–839 (cited: Vázquez (Trade Sanctions and Human Rights)).

Verdross, Alfred, and Simma, Bruno, *Universelles Völkerrecht: Theorie und Praxis* (Berlin: Duncker & Humblot, 1976) (cited: Verdross/Simma (Universelles Völkerrecht I)).

Verdross, Alfred, and Simma, Bruno, *Universelles Völkerrecht, Theorie und Praxis* 3rd ed. (Berlin: Duncker & Humblot, 1984) (cited: Verdross/Simma (Universelles Völkerecht II)).

Verhoosel, Gaetan, *National Treatment and WTO Dispute Settlement, Adjudicating the Boundaries of Regulatory Autonomy*, (Oregon: Hart Publishing, 2002).

Viellechner, Lars, 'Berücksichtigungspflicht als Kollisionsregel, Zu den innerstaatlichen Wirkungen von völkerrechtlichen Verträgen und Entscheidungen internationaler Gerichte, insbesondere bei der Auslegung und Anwendung von Grundrechten' in Matz-Lück, Nele, Hong, Mathias (eds.) *Grundrechte und Grundfreiheiten im Mehrebenensystem – Konkurrenzen und Interferenzen*, Beiträge zum ausländischen öffentlichen Recht und Völkerrecht Armin von Bogdandy, Rüdiger Wolfrum (eds.), Band 229 (2011), pp. 109–159 (cited: Viellechner (Berücksichtigungspflicht als Kollisionsregel)).

Viellechner, Lars ‚Responsive legal pluralism: The emergence of transnational conflicts law', in 6:2 Transnational Legal Theory (2015,) pp. 312–322 (cited: Viellechner (Responsive legal pluralism)).

Viellechner, Lars, *Transnationalisierung des Rechts* (Weilerswist: Velbrück Wissenschaft, 2013) (cited: Viellechner (Transnationalisierung des Rechts)).

Voigt, Christina, *Sustainable Development as a Principle of International Law, Resolving Conflicts between Climate Measures and WTO Law* (Leiden: Martin Nijhoff Publishers, 2009).

von Bogdandy, Armin, 'Constitutionalism in International Law: Comment on a Proposal from Germany', in 47 Harvard International Law Journal (2006), pp. 223–242 (cited: von Bogdandy (Constitutionalism)).

von Bogdandy, Armin, Goldmann, Matthias, Venzke, Ingo ‚From Public International Law to International Public Law: Translating World Public Opinion into International Public Authority, 28 EJIL (2017), pp. 115–145 (cited: von Bogdandy/Goldmann/Venzke (From Public International Law to International Public Law)).

Vranes, Erich, 'Environmental taxes and border tax adjustments' in Panagiotis Delimatstis, Leonie Reins (eds.) *Trade and Environmental Law* Volume XI (Cheltenham: Edward Elgar Publishing, 2021).

Wai, Robert, 'Conflicts and Comity in Transnational Governance: Private International Law as Mechanism and Metaphor for Transnational Social Regulation through Plural Legal Regimes', in Christian Joerges and Ernst-Ulrich Petersmann (eds.), *Constitutionalism, Multi-level Trade Governance and International Economic Law* (Oxford: Hart Publishing, 2011), pp. 230–262.

Walker, Neil, Constitutionalism and pluralism' in Anthony F. Lang, Antje Wiener (ed.) *Handbook on global constitutionalism*, (Cheltenham: Edward Elgar Publishing, 2017), pp. 433–444 (cited: Walker (Constitutionalism and pluralism)).

Walker, Neil, 'The EU and WTO. Constitutionalism in a New Key', in G. de Búrca / J. Scott (eds.), *The EU and the WTO. Legal and Constitutional Issues*, pp. 31–57 (cited: Walker (The EU and WTO)).

Walters, Mark D., 'Legal Humanism and Law-As-Integrity', 67(2) Cambridge Law Journal (2008), pp. 352–375.

Weatherill, Stephen, Paul Beaumont, Paul, *EC Law, The Essential Guide to the Legal Workings of the European Community* (London: Penguin Books, 2nd edn. 1995).

Weiler, JH.H.H. ,Federalism and Constitutionalism: Europe's Sonderweg', The Harvard Jean Monnet Working Paper No. 10, 2000, https://jeanmonnetprogram.org/archive/papers/00/001001.html.

Weissbrodt, David, Kruger, Muria, 'Current Developments, Norms on the Responsibilities of Transnational Corporations and Other Business Enterprises with Regard to Human Rights', in 97 AJIL, (2003), pp. 901–922.

Weller, Marc-Philippe, Kaller, Luca, Schulz, Alix, ,Haftung deutscher Unternehmen für Menschenrechtsverletzungen im Ausland', in 216 AcP (2016), pp. 387–420.

Wells, Don, "Best Practice' in the Regulation of International Labour Standards: Lessons of the US-Cambodia Textile Agreement', in *Comparative Labour Law & Policy Journal*, 27 (2006), pp. 357–376.

Will, Ulrike, Climate Border Adjustments and WTO Law, Extending the EU Emissions Trading System to Imported Goods and Services (Leiden/Boston: Brill/Nijhoff, 2019).

Wolfrum, Rüdiger, 'International Law of Cooperation', in Rudolf Bernhardt (ed.), *Encyclopedia of Public International Law*, Vol. II (Amsterdam: Elsevier Scienec B. V., 1995), pp. 1242–1247 (cited: Wolfrum (International Law of Cooperation)).

Wolfrum, Rüdiger, 'Legitimacy in International Law' in Rüdiger Wolfrum (ed.), *Max Planck Encyclopaedia of Public International Law* Vol. 6 (Oxford University Press, 2012), pp. 808–814 (cited: Wolfrum (Legitimacy in International Law)).

Wolfrum, Rüdiger ,Legitimacy of International Law from a legal Perspective: Some Introductory Considerations' in Rüdiger Wolfrum, Volker Röben (eds.) *Legitimacy in International Law* (Berlin, Heidelberg: Springer, 2008), pp. 1–24 (cited: Wolfrum (Legitimacy of International Law)).

Wolfrum, Rüdiger, 'Sources of International Law' in Rüdiger Wolfrum (ed.) *Max Planck Encyclopaedia of International Law*, Vol. IX (Oxford University Press, 2012), pp. 299–312 (cited: Wolfrum (Sources)).

World Justice Project, *Rule of Law Index 2020*, https://worldjusticeproject.org/sites/default/files/documents/WJP-ROLI-2020-Online_0.pdf.

WTO, *WTO Analytical Index, Guide to WTO Law and Practice*, 1st edn. Vol. 2 (Geneva: WTO Publications, 2003) (cited: WTO Analytical Index).

WTO, 'The WTO and International Labour Organization', www.wto.org/english/thewto_e/coher_e/wto_ilo_e.htm (cited: WTO (The WTO and International Labour Organization)).

WTO/ILO, Jansen, Marion, Lee, Eddy, *Trade and Employment, Challenges for Policy Research*, 2007, http://www.wto.org/english/res_e/booksp_e/ilo_e.pdf.

Wüger, Daniel, Anwendbarkeit und Justiziabilität völkerrechtlicher Normen im schweizerischen Recht: Grundlagen, Methoden und Kriterien (Bern: Stämpfli Verlag AG Bern, 2005).

Zdouc, Wener, 'The Panel Process', in Patrick F. J. Marcory, Arthur E. Appleton, Michael G. Plummer (eds.) *The World Trade Organization, Legal, Economic and Political Analysis*, Vol. I (New York: Springer, 2005), pp. 1233–1276.

Zedalis, Rex J., 'Labeling of Genetically Modified Foods, The Limits of GATT Rules', in *Journal of World Trade*, 35 (2) (2001), pp. 301–347.

Zerk, Jennifer, 'Extraterritorial jurisdiction: lessons for the business and human rights sphere from six regulatory areas'. Corporate Social Responsibility Initiative Working Paper No. 59, (Cambridge, MA: John F. Kennedy School of Government, Harvard University, 2010), https://www.hks.harvard.edu/sites/default/files/centers/mrcbg/programs/cri/files/workingpaper_59_zerk.pdf.

Zhou, Weihuan, 'US–Clove Cigarettes and US–Tuna II (Mexico): Implications for the Role of Regulatory Purpose under Article III:4 of the GATT', Vol. 15, Issue 4, JIEL (December 2012), pp. 1075–1122.

Zumbansen, Peer, 'Transnational Legal Pluralism' in 1 (2) Transnational Legal Theory, pp. 141–189.

Table of WTO Reports

The reports are listed in order of their official dispute number (the oldest appear first). They are available under www.wto.org.

US–Gasoline: United States–Standards for Reformulated and Conventional Gasoline, WT/DS2/AB/R, report of the panel, 29 January 1996, and the Appellate Body, 20 May 1996.

Japan–Alcoholic Beverages: Japan–Taxes on Alcoholic Beverages, WT/DS8/AB/R, WT/DS10/AB/R, WT/DS11/AB/R, report of the panel, 11 July 1996, and the Appellate Body, 4 October 1996.

Australia–Salmon: Australia–Measures Affecting Importation of Salmon, WT/DS18/AB/R, report of the Appellate Body, 20 October 1998.

EC–Bananas III: European Communities–Regime for the Importation, Sale and Distribution of Bananas, WT/DS27/AB/R, report of the Appellate Body, 9 September 1997.

Canada–Periodicals: Canada–Certain Measures Concerning Periodicals, WT/DS31/AB/R, report of the panel, 14 March 1997, and the Appellate Body, 30 June 1997.

Indonesia–Automobile Industry: Indonesia–Certain Measures Affecting the Automobile Industry, WT/DS54/R, WT/DS55/R, WT/DS59/R, WT/DS64/R, report of the panel, 2 July 1998.

Argentina–Footwear: Argentina–Measures Affecting Imports of Footwear, Textiles, Apparel and Other Items, WT/DS56/AB/R and Corr.1, report of the Appellate Body, 27 March 1998.

US–Shrimp: United States–Import Prohibition of Certain Shrimps and Shrimp Products, WT/DS58/AB/R, report of the panel, 15 May 1998, and the Appellate Body, 12 October 1998.

US–Shrimp–Article 21.5: United States–Import Prohibition of Certain Shrimp and Shrimp Products – Recourse to Article 21.5 of the DSU by Malaysia, WT/DS58/AB/RW, report of the Appellate Body, 22 October 2001.

Canada–Aircraft: Canada–Measures Affecting the Export of Civilian Aircraft, WT/DS70/AB/R, report of the Appellate Body, 20 August 1999.

Korea–Alcoholic Beverages: Korea–Taxes on Alcoholic Beverages, WT/DS75/AB/R, WT/DS84/AB/R, report of the panel, 17 September 1998, and the Appellate Body Report, 18 January 1999.

Chile–Alcoholic Beverages: Chile–Taxes on Alcoholic Beverages, WT/DS87/AB/R, WT/DS110/AB/R, report of the panel, 15 June 1999, and the Appellate Body, 13 December 1999.

Argentina–Footwear: Argentina–Safeguard Measures on Imports of Footwear, WT/DS121/AB/R, report of the panel report of the panel, 25 June 1999, and the Appellate Body, 14 December 1999.

EC–Asbestos: European Communities–Measures Affecting Asbestos and Asbestos-Containing Products, WT/DS135/AB/R, report of the panel, 18 September 2000, and the Appellate Body, 12 March 2001.

Canada–Automotives: Canada–Certain Measures Affecting the Automotive Industry, WT/DS/139/AB/R, WT/DS142/AB/R, report of the panel, 11 February 2000, and report of the Appellate Body, 31 May 2000.

US–Section 301 Trade Act: United States–Sections 301–310 of The Trade Act of 1974, WT/DS152/R, report of the panel, 22 December 1999.

Argentina–Bovine Hides: Argentina–Measures Affecting the Export of Bovine Hides and the Import of Finished Leather, WT/DS155/R, report of the panel, 16 February 2001.

Korea–Beef: Korea–Measures Affecting Imports of Fresh, Chilled and Frozen Beef, WT/DS161/AB/R, report of the Appellate Body, 11 December 2000.

US–Cotton Yarn: United States–Transitional Safeguard Measure on Combed Cotton Yarn from Pakistan, WT/DS192/AB/R, report of the Appellate Body, 5 November 2001.

Brazil–Patent Protection: Brazil – Measure Affecting Patent Protection – Request for Consultation by the United States, WT/DS199/1, June 8, 2000.

US—Line Pipe: United States — Definitive Safeguard Measures on Imports of Circular Welded Carbon Quality Line Pipe from Korea, WT/DS202/AB/R, 15 February 2002.

EC–Sardines: European Communities – Trade Description of Sardines, WT/DS231/AB/R, report of the panel, 29 May 2002, and the Appellate Body, 26 September 2002.

EC–Tariff Preferences: European Communities–Conditions for the Granting of Tariff Preferences to Developing Countries, WT/DS246/AB/R, report of the panel, 1 December 2003 and the Appellate Body, 7 April 2004.

US–Gambling: United States–Measures Affecting the Cross-Border Supply of Gambling and Betting Services, WT/DS285/AB/R, report of the Appellate Body, 7 April 2005.

Mexico–Soft Drinks and Other Beverages: Mexico–Tax Measures on Soft Drinks and Other Beverages, WT/DS308/AB/R, report of the panel, 7 October 2005, and Appellate Body, 6 March 2006.

Brazil–Retreaded Tyres: Brazil–Measures Affecting Imports of Retreaded Tyres, WT/DS332/AB/R, report of the Appellate Body, 3 December 2007.

China–Publications and Audiovisuals Products: China–Measures Affecting Trading Rights and Distribution Services for Certain Publications and

Audiovisual Entertainment Products, WT/DS363/AB/R, report of the Appellate Body, 21 December 2009.

Thailand–Cigarettes (*Philippines*): Thailand–Customs and Fiscal Measures on Cigarettes from the Philippines, report of the Appellate Body, WT/DS371/AB/R, 7 June 2011.

Philippines–Distilled Spirits: Philippines–Taxes on Distilled Spirits, WT/DS396/AB/R, WT/DS403/AB/R, reports of the Appellate Body, 21 December 2011.

US–Clove Cigarettes: United States – Measures Affecting the Production and Sale of Clove Cigarettes, WT/DS406/AB/R, report of the Appellate Body, 4 April 2012.

US–Tuna II (*Mexico*): United States–Measures Concerning the Importation, Marketing and Sale of Tuna and Tuna Products, WT/DS381/AB/R, report of the Appellate Body, 16 May 2012.

US–Cool: United States–Certain Country of Origin Labelling (COOL) Requirements, WT/DS384/AB/R WT/DS386/AB/R, report of the Appellate Body, 29 June 2012.

EC–Seal Products: European Communities–Measures Prohibiting the Importation and Marketing of Seal Products, WT/DS400/R, WT/DS401/R, reports of the panel, 25 November 2013.

EC–Seal Products: European Communities–Measures Prohibiting the Importation and Marketing of Seal Products, WT/DS400/AB/R, WT/DS401/AB/R, reports of the Appellate Body, 22 May 2014.

Colombia–Textiles: Colombia – Measures Relating to the Importation of Textiles, Apparel and Footwear, WT/DS461/AB/R, report of the Appellate Body, 7 June 2016.

Indonesia–Import Licensing Regimes: Indonesia – Importation of Horticultural Products, Animals and Animal Products, WT/DS477/AB/R, WT/DS478/AB/R, reports of the Appellate Body, 9 November 2017.

Brazil–Taxation: Brazil – Measures Concerning Taxation and Charges, WT/DS472/R WT/DS497/R, reports of the Panel, 30 August 2017.

Brazil–Taxation: Brazil – Measures Concerning Taxation and Charges, WT/DS472/AB/R, WT/DS497/AB/R, reports of the Appellate Body, 13 December 2018.

Russia–Traffic in Transit: Russia – Measures Concerning Traffic in Transit, WT/DS512/R, report of the panel, 5 April 2019.

Saudi-Arabia–Protection of Intellectual Property Rights: Saudi-Arabia – Measures Concerning the Protection of Intellectual Property Rights, WT/DS567/R, 16 June 2020.

EU—Palm Oil (*Indonesia*): European Union – Certain Measures concerning Palm Oil and Oil Palm Crop-Based Biofuels, DS593, panel composed on 12 November 2020.

EU and Certain Member States—Palm Oil (*Malaysia*): European Union – Certain Measures concerning Palm Oil and Oil Palm Crop-Based Biofuels, DS600, panel composed on 29 July 2021.

Table of GATT 1947 Reports

The reports are listed in order of the date of adoption or, if unadopted, the date of publication (the oldest appear first). Reports will be cited by mentioning the name as indicated in italics.

Australia–Ammonium Sulfate: Australia–Subsidy on Ammonium Sulphate, Working Party report, adopted on 3 April 1950, BISD II/188 (1952).

Germany–Sardines: Germany – Tariff Treatment of Sardines, adopted on 31 October 1952, BISD 1S/53 (1953).

Belgian Family Allowances: Belgian Family Allowances, adopted on 7 November 1952, BISD 1S/59 (1953).

Italian Discrimination: Italian Discrimination Against Imported Agricultural Machinery, adopted on 23 October 1958, BISD 7S/60 (1959).

EC–Animal Fee Proteins: European Community – Measures on Animal Fee Proteins, adopted on 14 March 1978, BISD 25S/49 (1979).

Spain–Unroasted Coffee: Spain – Tariff Treatment of Unroasted Coffee, adopted on 11 June 1981, BISD 28S/102 (1982).

US–Nicaragua: United States – Trade Measures Affecting Nicaragua, not adopted, GATT Doc. L/6053, 13 October 1986.

US–Superfund: United States – Taxes on Petroleum and Certain Imported Substances, adopted on 17 June 1987, BISD 34S/136 (1988).

Japan–Imported Wines and Alcoholic Beverages: Japan – Customs Duties, Taxes and Labelling Practices on Imported Wines and Alcoholic Beverages, adopted on 10 November 1987, BISD 34S/38 (1988).

Japan–Dimension Lumber: Japan – Tariff Import of Spruce Pine Fir Dimension Lumber, adopted on 19 July 1989, BISD 36S/167 (1990).

US–Section 337: United-States – Section 337 of the Tariff Act of 1930, adopted on 7 November 1989, BISD 36S/345 (1990).

Thailand–Cigarettes: Thailand – Restrictions on Importation of and Internal Taxes on Cigarettes, adopted on 20 February 1990, BISD 37S/200 (1991).

EC–Parts and Components: European Economic Community – Regulation on Imports of Parts and Components, adopted on 16 May 1990, BISD 37S/132 (1991).

US–Tuna I: United States – Restrictions on Imports of Tuna, not adopted, BISD, 39S/155 (1993).

US–Tuna II: United States – Restrictions on Imports of Tuna, not adopted, 33 I.L.M. (1994), pp. 839–903.

US–Malt Beverages: United States – Measures Affecting Alcoholic and Malt Beverages, adopted on 19 June 1992, BISD 39S/206 (1993).

US–Taxes on Automobiles: United States – Taxes on Automobiles, not adopted, 33 I.L.M (1994), pp. 1397–1459.

Index

Footnotes are indicated with an *n*.